"Mary Guindon's first edition of *A Counseling Primer* was a gem that presented the basic information that beginning counseling students need to know through an engaging and careful balance of essential knowledge, skills, and self-reflection. In this second edition, the gem has become a rare diamond. This marriage of skills and self-growth encourages student readers to develop a professional identity as competent, compassionate, and self-compassionate counselors. Students will love this book and will find it difficult to put it down!"

—**Barbara Herlihy, PhD**, professor in practice, University of Texas at San Antonio; professor emerita, University of New Orleans; American Counseling Association Fellow

"This second edition, which includes a new section on counseling specialty areas written by expert contributors, is a basic but comprehensive text that is well organized, easily read, and up to the minute in theory and practice. It will help beginning students navigate the field and understand what the profession of counseling is, was, and will be, from its origins to the present day and beyond."

—**Lee J. Richmond, PhD**, professor emerita, Loyola University, Maryland; past ACA and NCDA President; senior partner, PsyCoun Consultants

"Counselors-in-training who read the second edition of this primer are in for a real treat! Mary Guindon's expertise as a counselor educator and commitment to the personal and professional development of counselor trainees come across clearly in this thoughtfully written text. She and her co-author, Jessica Lane, have made substantive revisions, resulting in a text that is even more comprehensive than the first edition. Their engaging writing style and the contents of this primer, which includes a new section on counseling specialty areas, make it a must read!"

—**Michelle Muratori, PhD**, senior counselor, Johns Hopkins Center for Talented Youth; faculty associate, Johns Hopkins School of Education

A Counseling Primer

A Counseling Primer, second edition, introduces students to the profession of counseling, reviews its training curriculum, discusses current professional standards, and presents basic counseling skills.

The text is designed to answer students' most commonly asked questions around the who, what, where, when, why, and how of counseling. Updated and aligned with the eight 2016 CACREP core areas, the second edition includes new chapters by experts from seven entry-level specialty areas, including school counseling, career counseling, and mental health counseling. The book also contains useful features to enhance the learning experience, including case examples, class handouts and activities, a sample syllabus, discussion questions, and more.

A variety of online resources including instructor's manual, PowerPoint slides, tests, class activities, and student supplements are also available for download.

In a comprehensive and accessible format, *A Counseling Primer*, second edition, provides students with a succinct, up-to-date picture of the counseling profession and the tools they need to make their contribution to the field.

Mary H. Guindon, PhD, is associate professor at Kansas State University and retired chair of the Department of Counseling and Human Services at Johns Hopkins University. She is a senior partner of PsyCoun Consultants.

Jessica J. Lane, PhD, is an assistant professor and counselor educator at Kansas State University. Dr. Lane was the 2018 Kansas Counselor of the Year.

A Counseling Primer

An Orientation to the Profession

Second Edition

Mary H. Guindon and Jessica J. Lane

Routledge
Taylor & Francis Group

NEW YORK AND LONDON

Second edition published 2020
by Routledge
52 Vanderbilt Avenue, New York, NY 10017

and by Routledge
2 Park Square, Milton Park, Abingdon, Oxon, OX14 4RN

Routledge is an imprint of the Taylor & Francis Group, an informa business

First published 2011 by Taylor & Francis

Library of Congress Cataloging-in-Publication Data
A catalog record for this title has been requested

ISBN: 978-1-138-33958-3 (hbk)
ISBN: 978-1-138-33961-3 (pbk)
ISBN: 978-0-429-43603-1 (ebk)

Typeset in Goudy
by Deanta Global Publishing Services

 Visit the eResources https://www.routledge.com/9781138339613

 Printed in the United Kingdom
by Henry Ling Limited

This book is dedicated to our children:

Jeffrey Richard Guindon
Jennifer Guindon Vellenga
George Norton Guindon
Luke Gregory Lane
Lauren Grace Lane

Brief Contents

Detailed Contents

Tables

Figures

Foreword

Textbooks adopted for use by graduate students new to the profession of counseling must be written in a way that captures the interest and encourages the professionalism of the beginning counselor. *A Counseling Primer: An Orientation to the Profession* can best be described as engaging, comprehensive, and motivating. Dr. Mary Guindon, a skilled writer and experienced counselor and counselor educator, has created a refreshingly captivating look at the profession of counseling grounded in the strength-based, developmental perspectives promoted by the American Counseling Association and its divisions and affiliates. Her co-author, Dr. Jessica Lane, brings additional perspective to this textbook.

A Counseling Primer presents an introduction to the counseling profession that provides students with a foundation for success and a comprehensive overview of the field, including the eight core Council for Accreditation of Counseling & Related Educational Programs (CACREP) training standards used for curriculum development in programs and departments of counselor education. The format of the book encourages self-reflection and introspection, so important for those entering the profession, and presents information about counselors and their clients, the meaning of counseling and its rich history, answers about the body of knowledge, settings, philosophical underpinnings of the role and world of the counselor, specialty areas contributed by leading experts, and basic and advanced counseling skills.

To create a therapeutic alliance that is effective, counselors must develop self-awareness of their own thoughts, feelings, and behaviors as well as those of their clients. In addition to the foundational content noted above, an extremely strong component of *A Counseling Primer* is its emphasis, in Part Three of the text, on counseling skills described in a way that promotes the self-awareness that is so pertinent to the development of professional and personal identity. The format of this part of the textbook is so expertly organized it could really be used as a guide for teaching a techniques course or a pre-practicum.

Without a doubt this textbook challenges readers using case studies, exercises, and vignettes that create a truly interactive, process-oriented experience. I recommend the book without hesitation or reservation and applaud the writer's ability to look into the minds and hearts of a reader in a way that invites, encourages, and affirms.

David Capuzzi, PhD, LPC, NCC
Past President
American Counseling Association
Senior Core Faculty, Clinical Mental Health
Counseling
Walden University

Preface

This book was born out of the wish to find an introductory counseling text that provides succinct, to-the-point, and user-friendly facts without sacrificing the basic knowledge beginning students need. A first course should cover information about the profession of counseling, review its training curriculum concisely, and introduce counseling skills briefly but thoroughly enough to provide understanding and contextual reference. It should also give students ample opportunity to gain the self-awareness needed to be effective professional helpers. A text for such a course should be broad and pragmatic yet suitable for a single semester. This basic counseling primer meets that need.

A primer is a book that covers the most basic principles of a particular discipline, the fundamental elements of which a profession's body of knowledge consists. This counseling primer is intended to provide just such an orientation. It introduces professional counseling, discusses its most basic counseling skills, and gives students a method to increase their own self-awareness as well as their awareness of others, knowledge essential to professional identity.

This primer offers a clear, understandable approach in a format that prepares students at the beginning of their programs of study for their future coursework. It helps them embark on a career path that asks no less of them than change and personal congruence. It deconstructs into manageable and understandable segments what can initially seem insurmountable. Although primarily intended for use as a text for beginning students in counselor education and counseling psychology introductory courses, this primer is appropriate for related human services and undergraduate courses for anyone interested in learning about professional counseling. Those entering graduate school in the helping professions may have an unclear idea about their career goals. Thus, this primer is also useful for people entering the many allied professions, in that it provides not only a basic orientation but explains the kinds of skills-building basic counseling activities common to all the helping professions.

The format is designed to answer students' most commonly asked questions. It is organized around the journalist's 5WH questions (who, what, where, when, why, and how). Part One introduces professional orientation topics under the chapter headings of Who? (counselors and clients), What? (definitions, history, trends, and the eight core body of knowledge standards), Where? (settings and surroundings), When? (processes, phases, and procedures), and Why (caring, social justice, advocacy). (Part Two is discussed below in the New to This Edition section.) Part Three – How? (skills and practices) – provides a brief explanation of helping process stages with discussions of essential attending and listening skills. It exposes students to the most basic counseling techniques at the earliest stage of their training. It presents information on basic responding, systematic inquiry, and responding to affect, cognition, and behavioral. Understanding these skills is an important ingredient in the formation of a professional identity. Additionally, beginning students are eager to learn about skills. Placing them at the start of their studies engages and energizes them. Together Parts One and Three are intended for use concurrently to teach essential knowledge about the core curriculum, fundamental attending skills, and self-awareness.

Post-modern constructionism and research in diverse populations have exploded in the academic literature over the last 25 years and new ways of doing counseling continue to proliferate and influence theory and practice. Placing basic skills in a first course frees up later theory and practice courses to concentrate on more recent and culturally relevant theories in the depth in which they need to be covered. It also sets the stage for basic skills-building practice across courses. Students are thus exposed to attending skills in a first orientation introductory course. They develop an early foundation and are able to continue practicing as they progress into other courses in the curriculum. It can also serve as a review of these skills for practicum, internship, and other experiential courses. It has the added advantage of being relevant to other helping professions. Those who work with clients or patients in other professional fields such as physical therapy, the law, and public health can find it useful to learn basic communication and relationship-building skills.

This second edition of the primer updates and aligns with the 2016 Council for Accreditation of Counseling and Related Educational Programs curriculum standards for professional orientation, specifically section 2F 1: Professional counseling orientation and ethical practice, and section 2F 5g, essential interviewing. It is intended to address professional identity and provide a basic overview of the eight CACREP common components.

Specifically, the primer provides information from the following Standards:

- history and philosophy of the counseling profession (Standard 2F1a)
- professional roles, functions, and relationships with human service and integrated behavioral health care systems, including interagency and interorganizational collaboration and consultation (Standard 2F1b)
- counselors' roles and responsibilities as members of interdisciplinary community outreach and emergency management response teams (Standard 2F1c)
- the role and process of the professional counselor advocating on behalf of the profession (2F1d) and advocacy processes needed to address institutional and social barriers that impede access, equity, and success for clients (2F1e)
- professional organizations, including membership benefits, activities, services to members and current issues (Standard 2F1f)
- professional credentialing, including certification, licensure, and accreditation practices and standards, and the effects of public policy on these issues (Standard 2F1g)
- ethical standards of professional counseling organizations and credentialing bodies, and applications of ethical and legal considerations in professional counseling (Standard 2F1i)
- strategies for personal and professional self-evaluation and implications for practice (Standard 2F1k)
- self-care strategies appropriate to the counselor role (Standard 2F1l)

It emphasizes some of the basic requirements for Counseling and Helping Relationships, in accordance with Standard 2F5:

- counselor characteristics and behaviors that influence helping processes (Standard 2F5f)
- an understanding of essential interviewing and counseling skills (Standard 2F5g)

The two body of knowledge chapters (Chapters 4 and 5) present overviews and summaries of core CACREP curricular standards from Section 2: Ethical Practice (Standard F1i,), Social and Cultural Diversity (Standard F2), Human Growth and Development (Standard F3), Career

Development (Standard F4), Counseling and Helping Relationships (Standard F5), Group Counseling and Group Work (Standard F6), Assessment and Testing (Standard F7), and Research and Program Evaluation (Standard F8). Each of these standards is covered in considerable depth and detail in other courses in the curriculum. Thus, this counseling primer orients students only to the most fundamental elements and concepts.

Self-reflection is an essential part of counselor training and identity, and an integral part of this book. Through the charts at the end of each chapter, students are given the opportunity to examine closely their own and others' thoughts, feelings, and actions within the context in which they take place. Context includes the personal, cultural, and societal factors that make up an individual's worldview. Students are encouraged to focus on the influence of their own and other's cultural meaning making. Students gain self-awareness and self-monitoring skills. They hone their ability to observe others' significant or noteworthy behaviors and come to conclusions about others' probable thoughts and possible feelings within their own unique contextual circumstances and in a broad framework of ideas and beliefs.

Individual chapters also include case studies with class discussion questions for further thought and exploration. The cases are intended to expose students to the kinds of issues that counselors may face. Questions are targeted toward each chapter's content, and thus, students need no specialized knowledge to grapple with them. Instructors can use these case studies as tools to help increase their students' critical thinking skills, to formulate varying responses, and to help them further understand the nature of unexamined assumptions and contextual issues.

Appendix A presents a personal journal in which students can write self-reflections every week. Students are encouraged to use the questions in each of the Thoughts, Feelings, Actions, and Context (TFAC) charts at the end of each chapter to organize their writings and consider new insights. Journaling will allow them to experience firsthand a commonly used counseling technique while they simultaneously process and absorb each chapter's materials. They should be encouraged to write without evaluating or interpreting. Instructors can then assign a cumulative experience paper at the end of the semester to give them the opportunity to apply and interpret the semester's learnings. Appendix B provides web resources for ethical codes and professional organizations, along with websites of organizations specializing in common issues presented to counselors.

The *Instructor Manual* and the *Student Supplement* augment the primer. Both are available on the publishers' website, www.routledge.com, which hosts downloadable versions available by searching on the author name or text's title. This will take you to the book's page and you'll be able to download the materials from there.

The instructor manual contains chapter notes with suggestions for activities to reinforce chapter content, including 10 training forms and personal journal instructions. It presents an example of an Introduction to Counseling syllabus for use with this text and a bank of test questions for each chapter for instructor use. Also included is a detailed outline of the text material in Microsoft Office PowerPoint format suitable for lectures and presentations.

The student supplement offers instructions for the journaling assignment that uses the TFAC tables. It also includes five training forms: My Personal Prescription, My Counselor Traits, the Counseling Skill Observation form, the Reflecting on My Discloser/Listener/Observer Role form, and the Group Presentation Evaluation form. The My Counselor Traits form applies the information presented in Chapter 2 on effective counselor characteristics. Students are given the opportunity to evaluate ways in which they relate to others. Based on their own evaluations, they can develop an ongoing plan and set goals toward individual growth. The Counseling Skill Observation form is a systematic tool for use with classroom exercises. It allows students to practice basic skills. After observing basic counseling skills simulations, students can practice how to give feedback that is helpful and constructive. They can reflect on the triad work of speaker (discloser), listener, and observer using the questions posed in the My Discloser/Listener/ Observer Role form. Also included in the supplement is a Group Presentation Evaluation form to be used with one of the sample syllabus's requirements.

New to This Edition

This entire text has been updated to reflect the 2016 CACREP Standards. Since the last edition of this text, social justice and advocacy have grown into full-fledged professional standards. To that end, Chapter 8 – Why? Answers about Caring and Social Justice – discusses both topics in greater depth.

In accordance with the 2016 CACREP Standard Section 5: Entry-Level Specialty areas, Part Two of this edition – What? Answers about Specialty Areas – presents basic information on the seven entry-level specialty areas: addictions counseling; career counseling; clinical mental health counseling; clinical rehabilitation counseling; college counseling and student affairs; marriage couple, and family counseling and therapy; and school counseling. Written by experts in each specialty, these chapters discuss foundations, including history and background of the specialty, relevant legislation, theories or models specific to the specialty, impact on the individual, family, and community, and counseling strategies and practices.

This edition includes an expanded list of useful websites and resources, found in Appendix B, and additional classroom exercises and activities, found in the instructor's manual. Also included in the instructor's manual are test questions specific to each of the specialty areas as well as additional outlines in Microsoft Office PowerPoint format.

Overall, the second edition of the *Counseling Primer* is more detailed and up to date. It should be useful for beginning students, their instructors, students at the field experience stage of their study, and graduates needing a refresher to sit for certification and licensure exams.

The Counseling Primer begins the process of vocationalization – socialization into this profession. Our sincere hope is that the chapters in this book provide students the opportunity for an "Ah-ha!" experience and prepare them to move on in their programs of study with enthusiasm and commitment.

About the Authors

Mary H. Guindon is former chair of and associate professor in the Department of Counseling and Human Services at Johns Hopkins University where she created programs in organizational counseling, counselor clinical supervision, and contemporary trauma response. She currently serves as a teaching associate professor for doctoral students and Kansas State University. She was formerly associate professor at Rider University and collegiate professor at University of Maryland University College – Europe. Her over 30 years of clinical practice, consulting, and teaching experience include counselor training and supervision, mental health and career development, adult transitions, grief and loss, and global counseling issues. She has published in the professional and popular press and has presented nationally and internationally at professional conferences and symposia. In addition to authoring the first edition of *A Counseling Primer: An Orientation to the Profession*, she has edited a book titled *Self-esteem across the Lifespan: Issues and Interventions*, also published by Routledge.

She previously served on the Maryland State Board of Professional Counselors and Therapists, the Maryland Work/Life Alliance Advisory Board, the publications committee of the American Counseling Association, the professional development committee of the National Career Development Association, and on the editorial board of the *Career Development Quarterly*. Formerly, she was president of the New Jersey Mental Health Counselors Association, president of New Jersey Association of Counselor Education and Supervision, and Mid-Atlantic district consultant for the American Mental Health Counselors Association. She has served as a consultant providing short-term, problem-solving counseling to U.S. military members in the United States and Europe. A licensed psychologist and Licensed Clinical Professional Counselor, Dr. Guindon provides executive, personal, and career coaching; consulting; and counselor supervision through senior partnership in PsyCoun Consultants (www.psycoun.com). She holds a PhD from the University of Virginia.

Jessica J. Lane is an assistant professor in counselor education and supervision at Kansas State University. Prior to serving as a counselor educator, she was an elementary teacher and school counselor in Kansas. She also served as faculty for nine years in preparing P-12 preservice teachers at Kansas State. Dr. Lane's research interests include: kindergarten transition; elementary school counseling; and collaboration between school counselors and administrators. An advocate for P-12 comprehensive school counseling programs, Dr. Lane has presented at international, national, regional, and state conferences. She is involved in school counselor advocacy at the state level through leadership roles, consultation, and professional presentations. She has served as president of the Kansas Association for Counselor Education and Supervision (KACES) and currently chairs an ad hoc committee for comprehensive school counseling efforts and a comprehensive school counseling bill for Kansas. She also serves as a program reviewer for the Kansas Department of Education. Dr. Lane was named the Kansas Counseling Association 2018 Counselor of the Year as well as the North Central Kansas Counseling Association Outstanding Counselor. She holds a PhD in Counselor Education and Supervision from Kansas State University.

About the Contributors

Täna Arnold, MS, PhD (ABD), has been an educator since 2009 when she graduated from Fort Hays State University with a Bachelor of Science Degree in Elementary Education. She taught for five years before completing a Master of Science in Counseling Degree, also from Fort Hays State University. She worked as a school counselor at Centennial Middle School in Montrose, Colorado for three years before moving to Manhattan, Kansas to pursue a PhD in Counselor Education and Supervision. Täna has also owned and operated a private counseling practice, ViewPoint Mental Health Counseling LLC, working primarily with the families of children and adolescents. As a Graduate Teaching Assistant, Täna teaches Educational Psychology to preservice teachers, works with master-level school counseling interns, and assists with research projects at local elementary schools.

Lyndsey Brown, MS, PhD (ABD), is a school counselor at Maize South High School in Wichita, Kansas. She is also in the PhD program for Counselor Education and Supervision at Kansas State University, where she supervises master-level school counseling interns. Lyndsey received her Master's degree in School Counseling and Bachelor's degree in Elementary Education from Kansas State University.

Doris W. Carroll, PhD, is associate professor at Kansas State University in Manhattan, Kansas. She teaches graduate courses and conducts applied research in counselor education, higher education administration, with emphasis in multicultural competence, counseling ethics, academic advising, online learning and curriculum development. She is recognized as an expert in multicultural competencies in graduate distance education and academic advising. Her current research interests involve racial and gendered microaggressions, especially within distance education communication. Dr. Carroll has published and presented in national and international venues, and she is a sought scholar on topics related to academic advising and student retention. She holds a PhD in Counseling Psychology from the University of Nebraska-Lincoln.

Samantha Holloway, MS, PhD (ABD), has been an educator since 2014 when she graduated from Kansas State University with a degree in Counselor Education and Supervision. Previously, Samantha earned a Bachelor's of Science degree in Biology from Washburn University. She has worked as a school counselor at Riley County, KS High School for the past five years. Currently, she is working on her doctorate in Counselor Education and Supervision from Kansas State University, where she supervises master-level school counseling interns.

Brandon Hunt, PhD, is a counselor education Professor at Georgia Southern University. Prior to that she was a faculty member at Pennsylvania State University for 22 years. She has years of clinical and supervision experience in counseling and numerous professional publications, grants and, presentations. Dr. Hunt served on the editorial board for the *Journal of Counseling*

& Development for 19 years. She is a Past Chair for the NBCC Board of Directors, and she also served on the CACREP Board of Directors. She was named a Fellow of the American Counseling Association in 2011. She holds a PhD from the University of Virginia.

Nathan C. D. Perron, PhD, is a core faculty member with Counseling@Northwestern, a Master of Arts in Counseling program through the Family Institute at Northwestern University in Evanston, Illinois. Nathan received his PhD in Counselor Education and Supervision from Northern Illinois University, and has been teaching counseling, psychology, and human services students since 2008. Nathan serves his local community in New Hampshire through private counseling practice, where he supports individuals, children and adolescents, couples, and families. Nathan practices, teaches, researches, and writes in areas of expertise including international counseling, child and adolescent counseling, crisis and trauma support, first responder support, and religion and faith in counseling. Nathan currently serves on the Executive Council for the International Association for Counselling in order to advance the counseling profession globally, and he is an active board member with Nationwide Chaplain Services in order to advance the support available for law enforcement and other first responders.

David M. Reile, PhD, is a licensed psychologist, executive coach, and Certified Career Counselor with over 25 years of education and experience in career planning, coaching, and psychological consultation. David's education includes a master's degree in counseling with a specialization in career development and a doctorate in counseling psychology with a specialization in psychological assessment. David's experience has been applied in organizational development and consultation as well as management of counselors and career development projects in a variety of settings, including health care, banking, international organizations, educational institutions, government, and private practice. He has been a faculty associate in various counseling master's programs at The University of Maryland, Johns Hopkins University, and Loyola University Maryland. David is a member of the Ethics Committee of the National Career Development Association, having served as its chair for many years. David is past president of the National Career Development Association (NCDA) where he served as a member of the Board from 2014 to 2018.

Stephen Southern, EdD, previously taught at Northwestern University, Texas A & M University–Corpus Christi, University of Southern Mississippi, University of North Texas, and Temple University. He is a licensed psychologist, marriage and family therapist, and professional counselor, as well as an AASECT Certified Sex Therapist, a Clinical Fellow in AAMFT, and an Approved Clinical Supervisor. Dr. Southern is Editor-in-Chief of *The Family Journal* and *Sexual Addiction & Compulsivity*. He is the past president of the International Association of Marriage and Family Counselors and received their Lifetime Achievement Award. Southern is a Fellow of the American Counseling Association and received the Legacy Award of the Association of Counselor Educators and Supervisors. Dr. Southern served on the boards of the International Association of Marriage and Family Counselors, the Mississippi Association of Marriage and Family Therapists, and the Society for Advancement of Sexual Health.

Barbara H. Suddarth, PhD, is the executive director of the Career Development Alliance (CDA) and a licensed psychologist with more than 20 years of professional experience in career counseling, executive coaching, and organizational consulting. Barbara earned a PhD in Counseling Psychology from the Pennsylvania State University and an MA in Community Counseling from the University of Maryland. She is a National Certified Counselor (NCC), National Certified Career Counselor (NCCC), and an active member of the American Psychological Association, as well as a Fellow of the National Career Development Association. In addition to her consulting and counseling work, Barbara is also active in providing nonprofit career services to underserved clients, nationally and internationally, through the R/S Foundation.

Mark S. Woodford, PhD, is a Professor in the Department of Counselor Education at The College of New Jersey. In addition to teaching courses on counseling boys and men, group counseling, and treating addiction and co-occurring courses, Dr. Woodford has worked in school- and community-based prevention programs, in home-based family counseling programs, and in a residential addictions treatment facility. Dr. Woodford's research interests are in gender-specific addiction and family counseling. He is the author of *Men, Addiction, and Intimacy: Strengthening Recovery by Fostering the Emotional Development of Boys and Men* (2012). He holds a PhD from the University of Virginia.

Acknowledgments

Mary H. Guindon: I am most indebted to every single student who ever took the first introductory counseling course with me. They challenged me, tested me, and inspired me to dedicate myself to their pursuit of excellence. The counseling profession is better off for their presence. I am grateful for the many former professors and supervisors, numerous colleagues and friends who had molded me into the professional I am today.

I am also indebted to the specialty areas contributors of this second edition. Each of them provided expertise that makes this section meaningful for beginning students' understanding, and the text more viable. Thank you, Mark Woodford; David Reile and Barbara Suddarth; Nathan Perron; Brandon Hunt; Doris Carroll, Stephen Southern; and Täna Arnold, Lyndsey Brown, and Samantha Kriley. Täna, Lyndsey, and Samantha contributed hours to update literature as part of their doctoral work. We are especially grateful to Täna for her additional work and support.

I am also grateful to the anonymous reviewers for their valuable input to previous iterations of this book. I thank Michelle Muratori who stepped forward to help me with the tests section of the instructor's manual in the first edition and the contributors for their input to the instructor's manual. Last, I am particularly indebted to Anna Moore for her shepherding of this project, to Ellie Duncan, Laurie Fuller, and all the staff at Routledge/Taylor & Francis for their dedication to its publication; and to Lisa Keating and the production team at Deanta Global.

Jessica J. Lane: I am indebted to the many students who have deepened my love of counseling and teaching. Every semester, each student brings his or her unique perspective to the classroom, which enriches my experience as a counselor educator. It has been a privilege to work with and learn alongside my many students turned colleagues; I can speak with great certainty that there are tremendous people in our schools and communities doing amazing work.

Just as I am indebted to my students, I am beyond thankful for my mentors. Without their passion, inspiration, and commitment to the profession, as well as their clear support of me, I would not be where I am today. Specifically, I want to thank Dr. Mary Guindon for her willingness to allow me to serve on this edition of the *Counseling Primer*. Dr. Guindon has a tremendous work ethic, a gift for writing and teaching, and above all, she models and exudes strength, compassion, and authenticity.

Last, I want to acknowledge my children, Luke and Lauren, who provide me with a sense of strength and purpose. Serving as a counselor educator and as a mother are two very demanding yet complementary roles. I strongly believe that being a counselor has made me a better mom, and in turn, being a mom has made me a better counselor.

Part One

Foundations

Orientation to the Profession

The chapters in the section present the basic body of knowledge of counseling as its own profession, including topics related to the identity of the professional counselor, and differentiates it from other helping professions. It covers its definitions, history, and the eight core Council for Accreditation of Counseling & Related Educational Programs (CACREP) standards. It also presents information on how counseling is practiced through describing settings in which counseling takes place, and describes the developmental nature of learning counseling skills. Each chapter includes case studies and this section ends with the importance of social justice and advocacy.

Chapter 1

Introduction

Mary H. Guindon

The eye never forgets what the heart has seen.

– Bantu proverb

POINTS TO PONDER

- What do counselors have in common?
- How do values influence our assumptions?
- What motivates people to become professional counselors?
- What can I expect in a counseling program?
- How do I begin?

What Students Ask

However it happened, you are now holding this book. You may have thumbed through the pages, looked over the table of contents, read a sentence here and there or been completely absorbed by one section. Maybe you ordered this book online as a course requirement or stopped by your college bookstore on your way to your first class. Or, perhaps you have just come from your first class meeting and just picked up this book. It could be you are not in a counseling program at all but are curious about counselors. However you came to this page, chances are you are much like my students: Something in this book energizes you. You may feel a stir of excitement.

When you enter a counseling-related program, you embark on a journey like no other. If you are anything at all like we were when we began, or like many students today, you have questions. Lots and lots of questions:

What do counselors really do?
Who are their clients?
What kinds of problems do clients have?
How does counseling help?
Why do people want to be counselors?
What does it take to be a professional counselor?
Where do counselors do their work?
Where are the jobs?

How do they know they've made a difference?

and…

Can I do this?
Is this where I belong?
To whom do I turn with my questions?

You may have many other questions as well. This book is designed to answer your questions and familiarize you with some basic counseling skills. Before you begin, you will want to put some thought into what has caused you to consider counseling as a profession. First, let's take a look at some of the students in a typical introductory counseling classroom.

Penny, age 22, came into class not really sure why she was there. She has just finished her bachelor's degree in English education at a small college where she excelled in her academics and in her extracurricular life. When she graduated she didn't know what she wanted to do with her degree. She has not seriously looked beyond the college days she loved. She just knows she wants to help people and would like to stay in a higher education setting.

Twenty-six-year-old Clarence, the holder of a bachelor's degree in psychology, has been working as a psychology aide in a psychiatric hospital for five years. A big man, he knows he wants to do more with his life than what has turned out to be not much more than using his physical strength to help the therapists restrain troubled patients.

Olivia, a 45-year-old stay-at-home mom of three, came into class sure that she would be the oldest and rustiest in her ability to do academic work. She has a degree in elementary education, taught for a few years, and has since done some part-time bookkeeping work while she reared her family. Now that her children are in college, she wants something different, something that allows her to express a side of her she hasn't been able to previously use.

Evan is a 37-year-old coach at a nearby secondary school. A wrestler in his youth, he has spent the last 10 years teaching math and coaching the varsity wrestling and track and field teams. He needs continuing education credits (CEUs) to keep his teaching certificate current. He figures counseling is a good way to earn them. He says he counsels his kids every day. He wants some concrete facts to go along with his experience.

Betsy is a bartender at a local tavern. At 29, she's never used her sociology degree. Like Evan, she also says she counsels people every day. She realizes that she wants to do so in some sort of mental health setting. She thinks she may want to work with addictions. She experienced counseling in her teens and has come into the class because she says she had a wonderful counselor who changed her life.

On the surface, these students seem to have little in common. They come from vastly different backgrounds. They are of different ages, races, ethnicities, genders, and sexual orientations. Yet they share important attributes. They are natural helpers. Whatever their personal stories, most of my students share one characteristic: They are empathetic. They feel what others feel. They have the ability to take another person's perspective, to walk in another's shoes.

They have other attributes in common: They observe. They notice what others may be thinking but not able to say. They see themselves as good at helping others solve their problems. They believe that they are sound advice givers. Moreover, they care deeply about the emotional wellbeing of their family and friends; even acquaintances or strangers stir their caring instincts. Although their motivations may not be identical, they come into the counseling profession to make a difference.

Does any of the foregoing describe you? If so, then you may be the person to whom others come with their problems. You may be the reliable one in your family. Or, perhaps you were the rebel, the one who drank too much or flirted with danger too often but somehow managed to come to this point in your life a little wiser with a lot to give to others. Either way, whether you came from a loving, supportive family or one that was emotionally difficult or absent altogether, you had and have an inclination to help others.

Give some serious thought to why helping through counseling interests you. Some students can pinpoint what brought them into a counseling program. For others, the decision-making process evolved over a period of time. For still others, this may be the first tentative step toward discovering if this is the field they want.

As you begin this program of study, you should consider if this is the profession for you. Counselor preparation will require you to spend a good amount of your time, your energy, and your financial resources. Now is the time for you to begin a journey of honest self-reflection. Before you can understand another, you need to understand yourself. This is an integral part of your professional identity. Start by taking a few minutes to read and consider this story:

Saga of Old Craggy

Once upon a time there was a woman named Jennie. She lived in the Rocky Mountains in Meadow Valley. She loved Dean who happened to be on the top of Old Craggy, a remote mountain in an inaccessible part of the Rockies. Jennie very much wanted to go to Dean but she had no means of getting to the top of the mountain. She went to Steve, a skilled professional helicopter pilot, and asked him to fly her to the top of Old Craggy. Steve said he would be glad to do so if she would consent to have sex with him before the flight. Jennie refused. She then sought out pot-smoking Carla to explain her plight but Carla just didn't want to get involved in the [1]situation. Jennie then felt she had no alternative but to accept Steve's offer. So she did. Steve fulfilled his promise to Jennie and flew her to the top of the mountain where Dean stood waiting. When she told Dean what she had to do in order to get to the top of the mountain, he was upset and told her he wanted nothing more to do with her. Heartsick and dejected, she turned to George who also lived on Craggy Mountain. She told him the whole story. George, feeling sympathy for Jennie and anger for the way Dean had treated her, sought out Dean and beat him up. When Jennie saw what had happened to Dean, she thought he had it coming and laughed at him.

How would you rate these characters? Who do you believe to be the *least* reprehensible person in the story? Who do you believe to be the *most* reprehensible? Which of these characters was justified in his or her actions? Which is totally abhorrent to you? Rank order them from the least to most offensive, intolerable, immoral, unpleasant, or whatever else comes to mind for you.

What brings you to that conclusion? If you had to be the counselor to one of these people, whom would you find hardest to help? Why? Whom would you want to help? Why? Can you articulate exactly how you feel about each one? What is about each of these characters that causes you to react the way you do? Could you defend your position for each character should you be asked to? Take a few minutes now to write your reaction before you proceed.

This is the kind of story that is guaranteed to punch your hot buttons. It touches right at the core of some basic values. It is a story that evokes feelings about love, sex, power, indifference, betrayal, violence, and ridicule.

The first author has used this exercise in the first class session of the introductory counseling course. Would it surprise you to know that different students rank these characters quite differently? What one student might find the most reprehensible another might find the least so. Some

1 Craggy Mountain is adapted from a well-known story, "Alligator River." No citation or attribution was found.

students have had intense, heated discussions about their choices while others are considerably less invested in them. The meaning and strength of students' values most likely account for this difference in their reactions.

Take another look at the story and your responses to it. What were your assumptions about the ages of these characters and their relationships to each other? How much would it matter to your answers if you knew the actual relationships of the characters? What if you were to discover that Dean was Jennie's 10-year-old son? What if he were only three? Would your rankings remain the same or change? What if Carla were Jennie's mother? Or, if she were a 13-year-old neighbor? Or, what if Steve were Jennie's female cousin? Or, George were Dean's father? What if you found out that Dean was African American and George was his white pastor? Or what if it were the other way around? You can see that knowing more about the context of the actions in the story might give you a different perspective and a different set of evaluations.

Every day, we make assumptions about the people with whom we interact. If you are to become an effective counselor, you will learn to check out your perceptions rather than making assumptions about others, even when things seem obvious.

Most of our assumptions are grounded in the values we hold. You must become aware of your assumptions and where they came from.

Assumptions and Values

Human beings hold many kinds of values. They are expressed in everything that they do. They are embedded in behavior, in language, in what humans manufacture and create, and in the institutions humans establish. Every thought, feeling, and action is connected to an internal image that is transformed through the use of language. Words link our inner subjective world and the outer world of concrete reality. Words are value laden. You cannot help another person with their values fulfillment if you have not done the work necessary to understand your own values.

More than three decades ago, Tjelveit (1986) offered suggestions for minimizing the possibility of counselors acting in ways that may be insensitive to their client's set of values. They stand today:

1. Become informed about the variety of values held in society.
2. Be aware of your own values.
3. Present value options to clients in an unbiased manner.
4. Be committed to client's freedom of choice.
5. Respect clients with values that differ from your own.
6. Consult with others when necessary.
7. Consider referring clients to another counselor when substantial moral, religious, or political value differences exist (pp. 515–537).

The American Counseling Association (ACA) *Code of Ethics* (2014) requires that counselors are aware of their own and their clients' values. In fact, counselors must also be aware of the assumptions they make about human nature itself. Their assumptions affect their understanding of client issues and influence their behaviors (Auger, 2004).

Personal values can influence what strategies and interventions the counselor selects. Counselors can communicate their values verbally and nonverbally. They can inadvertently influence client behaviors (Niles & Harris-Bowlsbey, 2017). You must ask yourself, "What are my core values? Do they fit with the values of this profession? Can I put my values aside in service to helping someone with a different set of values?"

Why a Career in Professional Counseling?

What has led to your interest in becoming a professional counselor? If someone asked you, could you tell them what counseling is? For now, there is no right or wrong answer to this question. There is only your answer. How you respond will give you an idea of what brought you here. Do you know the reason for considering a career in counseling? It is not enough to say you want to help others or that you are empathetic. What motivates you?

Motivators in themselves are neither good nor bad. Each motivator has the potential to be positive, of course. However, each can also have a deleterious effect. If counselors do not fully understand what motivates them, they have the potential of negatively affecting their clients' progress toward the resolution of their concerns. Without understanding their own issues, counselors' well-intentioned desire to help their clients may actually harm them. Self-awareness is the first step toward successfully coping with and solving one's own problems that otherwise might get in the way of helping others.

Let us take a look at some of the most common motivators that bring people into the counseling profession. As you consider each of these, give some thought to those that most closely fit you. Although it may be difficult to be fully honest – or aware – about your desire to help others, careful reflection will help you clarify your own motives and move you toward greater self-knowledge. Keep in mind that these motivators can be positive and need not be problematic.

1. *Some people want to make a difference in this world; they are altruistic.* Most people want to leave a mark on the world in one way or another. They want to do work that makes their lives worthwhile. Some counselors choose to make a difference through the changes they help their clients make. This is an honorable goal. Still, students can be unrealistic in their desire to see their efforts produce immediate changes. Client change is not often immediate or obvious. When change is not readily apparent, a student might feel frustrated and disappointed. These feelings have the potential of impeding the counseling process.

Some students are concerned about the inequities in the world; they want to address societal and political issues through their counseling skills. Students who come into counseling for this reason want to help the "casualties of the system: the discouraged, the disturbed, and the disturbing" (Peterson & Nisenholz, 1999, p. 2). This speaks to compassion and advocacy. It touches that part of us that desires to have purpose and meaning in life. Such altruism and idealism can bring great satisfaction. On the other hand, when change in the world is not forthcoming, the counselor can feel disillusioned and burned out. He may lose sight of the needs of his clients. If the counselor's goal is to change the world, she may feel that she has failed even when her clients are legitimately helped in profound ways.

Sometimes altruism is an expression of the counselors' spirituality or religious beliefs. Some have a deep need to express their religious convictions through a love for humanity. They want to do so one client at a time or one group at a time as a way of bettering society. This can be a positive, honorable motivator. However, when counseling is used as a vehicle to meet personal, religious agendas that may not fit the interests of the client, it can also be problematic, even harmful.

2. *Some people have a need to take care of others; they need to be needed.* Caring for others is a human trait and an admirable one. We are social animals who have concern for each other. However, in some cases, students who may have come from dysfunctional families took on the caregiver role to their parents and siblings at very young ages. These students may not know how to take care of their own legitimate needs. They may mistake taking care of others as a means to caring for self. One of the consequences of having been a caregiver to significant others is that no one may have attended to your needs and you may not have learned to ask for help when you needed it (Corey & Corey, 2016). Students who mistake advice-giving, gratuitous comforting, and the minimizing of other's pain for helping are, in fact, meeting their own needs rather than

the needs of others. They may become protective, possessive, or demanding of their clients. Not only does this damage the client's progress, it is a sure path to counselor burnout. Individuals with this motivator must learn to recognize their own needs and ask for help when they need it.

Ask yourself, "To what extent should anyone take responsibility for another fully functioning human being?" Many counselors-in-training struggle with a sense of obligation for resolving their clients' problems. On the other hand, many professionals subscribe to the belief that too much "helping" perpetuates dependency. The appropriate level of care and help varies according to contexts and circumstances. It can run the gamut from little ostensible help because it interferes with client self-sufficiency to comprehensive support for those in critical need. Effective counselors ask themselves if their need for love and attention is clouding the client's need for help. To discern the difference, self-work is a necessary component in training and throughout one's professional life.

3. *Some people see themselves as problem-solvers; they believe they are good listeners and advice givers.* The desire to help others solve their problems can be a potent positive influence on career choice. Students with this motivator have received positive feedback for their ability to listen, help, and solve problems. They are successful at giving advice; their abilities have become part of their persona. These individuals find fulfillment through the appreciation and adulation others give them for their efforts. They have the mistaken idea that advice giving equals helping. When they meet their needs in this way, they will inevitably be disappointed. Clients rarely show us this kind of appreciation. Some give us no positive feedback or recognition. Although there is a place for advice giving, its use is reserved for specific situations such as crisis intervention or assessment. Furthermore, problem solving is a collaborative process in which the counselor facilitates the client's desires and abilities.

Students who rely on the persona of the problem-solver to meet their own needs may fail to recognize and deal with their own problems. Moreover, although helping in the form of problem solving is undertaken with the best of intentions, it carries with it the connotation of inequality, even superiority. Although listening and helping are at the heart of counseling, giving advice and solving problems on the clients' behalf may not be helpful at all. It takes control away from clients and disempowers them. It can give the message that the counselor can fix the client, or even worse, that the client needs fixing and is too helpless to do the fixing himself. Effective counselors assume that most people, when given a choice and in an atmosphere of trust and encouragement, are competent and trustworthy and have the ability to set and attain goals that are in their own self-interest and in the interest of the greater good of society.

4. *Some people have made a career shift from another profession.* Some students see counseling as a natural progression and perhaps more satisfying alternative to their previous career. Many have been exposed to counselors operating in their workplaces. Professional counselors and other helping professionals have modeled good listening skills and effective problem-solving behaviors. Students admire their personal qualities and want to emulate them. Teachers, psychology aides, and others who work with counselors every day see them in action. They may be their friends and colleagues. They may have given these students a good idea about what is actually involved in being in the field and may have been instrumental in the student's decision-making process. These students often come into counseling programs with an understanding of the benefits and challenges of the profession. On the other hand, some students may have observed counselors in classroom settings or group activities without having any further knowledge of what they do. These students may have unrealistic notions of the profession.

Other students work in related helping professions; they see counseling as a way to enhance their present careers. Some of these students may have experience, education, or hands-on-training in other helping professions. Teachers, clergy, and athletic coaches as well as some nurses fall into this category. They see professional counseling as value added to their present career field. For example, teachers go up the pay scale with additional coursework and graduate degrees.

Many will finish their counseling programs with the intent of staying in their present professions, having acquired greater levels of knowledge and skill.

Still other students have made a career shift from a profession totally unrelated to the helping professions; they see counseling as a way to be truer to their present needs and interests. These students may have been in careers that suited them at earlier times in their lives, or their careers may never have allowed them to express who they really are. They yearn to be truer to their own natures and view counseling as a way to do this. They, too, may have an unrealistic understanding of the day-to-day work of the professional counselor.

5. *Some people have been in counseling themselves and want to become counselors as a result.* Some people enter the counseling profession as a result of having painful experiences. They have had the courage to seek counseling for them. Some of these students found the counseling experience life changing and rewarding; they want to have a similar positive impact on their own clients. Through hard work with a therapist who facilitated their growth and resolution of their painful experiences, they have come to terms with difficult issues. Other students have been the recipients of outstanding attention from their school counselors. Their encouragement and guidance may have made the difference between finishing school and dropping out or between attending college and going to work in a low-paying job. Their influence has not been forgotten. These professionals have modeled personal characteristics these students would like to have in their own careers. They want to give to others what has been given to them.

On the other hand, some students have been in counseling themselves and found the experience unsatisfying in important ways. They want to do better for their own clients. Unfortunately, some individuals who come into a counselor training program do so because they have had unhelpful, even damaging, experiences with their therapists or school counselors. They may have resolved their painful issues with a subsequent effective therapist, or they may have found the resolutions to their problems in other ways or may not have resolved them yet. They have not forgotten the negative effect a poor counselor had on them. They decide to enter the profession so that they can do better by their own clients. Students in this category need to be aware of their personal issues and do the difficult but essential work of addressing their own unfinished business. If they do not, they risk over-involvement with clients or may feel hostility toward those clients who recreate their own issues in counseling sessions.

6. *Some counselors want positions of status and influence; they have a need for power and control that they believe can be met in helping others.* The nature of the counseling relationship is an uneven one. Counselors are in a position of considerable power, control, and influence. However unintentionally, if a counselor attempts to solve problems *for* the client, she will likely breed negative feelings *in* the client. She runs the superiority risk; she will come across as being more competent, adept, or in some way better than the client. Furthermore, unless the counselor takes care to ensure an egalitarian relationship, she runs the risk of serving her own need for status rather than empowering her clients to find solutions to their own problems. The more she tries to control her clients, the more likely they will be to resist such control. Clearly, this is not a facilitative atmosphere for change.

Some students believe counseling is about being an expert. They come into a counseling program to fulfill the need of being the knower or the fixer who possesses the skill and knowledge to heal the broken client. A kind of arrogance is implicit in this belief. If you see yourself as full of wisdom just waiting to be dispensed to others or as the expert ready to share your expertise, you will be disappointed in the nature of the counseling process. Counselors' work and discipline is to assist others in finding their own wisdom and to recognize the expertise within themselves. Clients discover; counselors facilitate. They then move forward with their clients to help them set appropriate goals and attain them. Furthermore, counselors themselves very likely gain wisdom from every one of their clients. What clients bring to us in the ways they find to resolve their issues teach and train us to be more effective counselors and better human beings.

7. *Some people believe that they can make high-paying incomes.* Some counselors do develop their skills into high compensation levels. They are the exception. Some students have the mistaken idea that counselors (i.e., shrinks) are as the popular media depict them. Therapists are portrayed sitting in expensively decorated offices and doling out wisdom for which they are generously rewarded financially. This is not the reality for most counselors. Most are adequately compensated; some make very little. The realities are that those who most need our services often are those who are least able to afford them. Not all clients are insured; not all can pay out of pocket. They deserve our services no less than those who can pay high fees. In fact, the profession obliges us to advocate for those who cannot advocate for themselves. Compensation for many counselors comes in rewards other than financial.

8. *Some people have problems that they need addressed; they think they can resolve them by becoming therapists themselves.* Although this motivator may not be fully in their awareness, some students enter counseling programs because they need help with their own problems. They hope that counselor training will give them solutions. Some of these students did not receive the emotional attention they needed growing up; they want to give children the help they themselves never received in childhood or to give adults retrospectively the comfort they wish they could receive. In itself, this need not be problematic. Having experienced problems can make one more empathic to others. However, becoming a counselor to others is not a substitute for dealing with one's own issues. In fact, the counseling profession demands good mental health in those who enter it and remain in it.

You count on it: Your problems will find you. One day they will sit across from you in a counseling session. Thus, facing and resolving one's own issues so that they do not interfere with the client's work is a critical element of the profession. Counselors who do not resolve their own problems may impose on their clients those solutions and goals that they believe would have helped themselves but may not be effective or helpful to their clients. When counselors successfully resolve their problems, they can be moved to help those with similar problems. These "wounded healers" (Jung, 1969; Schneider & May, 1994) have great reserves of empathy and experiences from which to draw. Counseling skills help them to draw on their experiences appropriately and to use their empathy in therapeutically suitable ways.

How Well Do You Know Yourself?

These motivators are not mutually exclusive. Most people become counselors for a unique combination of reasons, many not on this list. You may identify with many of the motivators above or you may identify with none of them. Whatever your own motivators, you should work to be in touch with how they influence you as the person you are and the counselor you will become.

There is nothing inherently wrong with meeting many of one's needs through one's professional life. Corey and Corey (2016) point out that "in the ideal situation, your own needs are met at the same time that you are meeting your client's needs" (p. 7). However, you must take care that you are aware of your needs and attend to them in appropriate, enhancing ways that do not get in the way of the needs of your clients. You do not use your clients as the primary vehicle by which you meet your needs. They are not a substitute for healthy relationships outside the counseling office.

Your motivations can and do change over time. What has driven you to undertake the study of counseling may not be exactly the same as what will sustain you through your program of study, into your field experiences and internships, and ultimately into the role of a working counselor. Personal awareness and growth mean that you will not only learn, you will change. You cannot help but change. As you go through your course of studies, you will learn to become a more authentic individual. You may find this a challenging emotional experience.

At this point, some anxiety about entering this course of study is understandable and natural. Like many of my students, you may have self-doubts. Penny is not at all sure she is choosing the right program, wondering if she should become the English teacher she trained to become. Clarence wonders if he will be able to do the self-work necessary. Olivia wants to make a difference in the world but with her family obligations, she does not know if she wants this level of commitment as the means of doing so. Evan and Betsy are discovering that they were not doing counseling; they were dispensing advice. Both wonder if they can learn to keep their own needs and opinions out of the counseling process. Betsy is also concerned that she cannot be as effective at helping her future clients as her counselor was to her. Each does not want to share this information with their classmates or with their instructor. They do not yet know how much to disclose and how much to keep private. These are normal concerns.

You, too, may wonder whether you have what it takes to meet the demands that will be made of you. You may be concerned about the academic requirements or the necessity of looking at yourself honestly and openly or both. You may wonder if ultimately you will be able to help others by keeping yourself and your well-intentioned advice out of the way. This profession demands that its practitioners manage their own needs, wishes, and inclinations in service to their clients. Consequently, self-work is critical. You are about to embark on a career path that asks no less of you than change and personal congruence. To be a congruent human being means getting in touch with your own authentic thoughts, feelings, and actions and ensuring that they are in concert with each other. It is no easy task, but it is a rewarding one.

Thoughts, Feelings, Actions, and Context (TFAC)

You are embarking on a professional journey into a new area just as surely as if you were traveling to an unknown country. Much of what you will learn will come from your educational experiences, of course. Your academic training is the foundation but it is not all that is involved in becoming a professional counselor. You are about to begin a personal journey as well. This is the journey of self- knowledge. Much will be familiar to you and some will be quite new, even foreign. To be an effective counselor, you need to become what every good counselor is: a "reflective practitioner." You will learn to examine incidents in your life and your reactions to them. You will make a commitment to a deep level of personal awareness and growth. You do this when you complete the self-work required of you in many of your courses. You do this when you learn to accept feedback from your instructors and supervisors. You do this when you integrate what you learn into your behaviors, attitudes, and counseling skills.

Your Journal

To help you to understand your journey, you should begin recording your thoughts in a journal. Consider this journal the place where you note the points of interest along the way. Your journal can be a source of reflection and a place to revisit your motivations from time to time. You will find that writing in it on a regular basis whether daily or weekly can be insightful and rewarding. Appendix A, My Personal Journal, will assist you in formulating your reflections as you learn about counseling and about yourself.

Through readings, journal entries, class discussions, and participation in experiential activities, you will begin the process of assessing your own self-awareness. Your inner subjective experience is a traditional focus of professional counseling, distinguishing it from other related helping professions (Hansen, 2005; Hansen, Speciale, & Lemberger, 2014). You will examine closely your thoughts, feelings, and actions. You will also come to recognize and consider your own social, cultural, and personal background – the context from which you view the world. You will also have the opportunity to observe significant or meaningful behaviors of others in your life and in your classroom. You will consider their probable thoughts and possible feelings. You will learn how their particular context influences them in ways that may be quite different than yours.

Recognize that each of us constructs our own reality and we know our own and others' reality only through words – our internal and external dialog (Rudes & Gutterman, 2007; O'Reilly & Lester, 2017). Reflect on each of the questions in Table 1.1, the Thought, Feelings, Actions, and Context (TFAC) chart. Spend some time thinking about the TFAC categories for each question. For example, for the first question, consider what you a) *think* about entering a career in counseling, b) how you *feel* about it, and c) how your thoughts and feelings influence your *actions*. Then give some thought to d) your *context*. Are there any other factors, such as your current working situation or family dynamics, which might be influencing your TFA? What about your own particular demographics – your culture, gender, and so forth? Keep in mind that awareness is not static and fixed. Hansen (2009) suggests that conceptualizing self-awareness as self-storying is a more productive way to consider the self. He posits that "stories, by definition, are not final objective truths... storying implies an ongoing narrational process" (p. 191). Multiple storylines can be reflected on, expanded, or discarded.

Once you have considered your own point of view, work toward understanding what others might be experiencing by answering questions in the second part of the TFAC chart. You will find TFAC charts at the end of each chapter. For each of the questions, think through and respond to what might be others' probable thoughts. You cannot know for sure, of course, but counselors continually make educated evaluations about others' points of view. These are tentative thoughts based on observations that either may not be accurate but then again may be quite correct. They are the premises from which you initially proceed. You will learn to check out your observations but for now, hone your ability to make hunches grounded in your observations. Consider also what possible feelings others might be experiencing. What do you observe that might account for your assessment of probable thoughts and possible feelings? What can you discover about others' context – their cultural perspective, worldview, and so forth? Spend some time writing your responses in your journal. Is there anything else not already covered that might influence your observations of yourself and others? Specify these in the "Other?" category.

Write out your reflections for as many boxes on the chart as you can. Work toward checking off all the boxes. You will inevitably grow in self-awareness and increase your skill in fully observing others.

What Can You Expect?

As you progress through this particular course, this program of study, and beyond into your professional life, what lies ahead? If you are to be a successful counselor-in-training, you must ask questions. Don't underestimate the importance of asking questions of your instructors and of yourself. You also will learn to ask questions of your classmates, each of whom brings his and her unique expertise into the classroom. You are co-learners, not competitors, on a collaborative, skills-building, and caring professional journey. Your instructors and the professional counselors with whom you will be interacting are invested in your success. They want to know about and respond to your questions.

This primer is designed to answer the many questions you have as you enter this program and this profession. It is organized around the journalist's questions. Just as journalists want to know essential facts, the 5WH of a news story – the who, what, where, when, why, and how – you also need the facts, the 5WH of counseling. The first part of this book is organized around the 5W questions: Who (information about counselors and their clients); What (information about counseling's roots, its approaches, and practices); Where (information about settings and surroundings); When (information about sessions, stages, and processes); and Why (information about making a difference, caring, and social justice). The second part introduces counseling specialty areas, and the third part presents the practical question of How (information about the basic skills and practice of counseling).

Earlier in this chapter, we asked if you would be able to tell someone who inquired what counseling is. At that point, your answer was purely your own, based on your personal knowledge and experience. Are you beginning to have a clearer, more realistic understanding of the counseling profession? Counseling means different things in different settings and in various contexts and cultures. Some who go by the name "counselor" are not professional counselors, of course. We know of phone counselors, funeral counselors, camp counselors, financial counselors, and many others. None of these is what we mean by professional counselors. Professional counseling is far more complex.

The American Counseling Association (ACA) defines *counseling* as "a professional relationship that empowers diverse individuals, families, and groups to accomplish mental health, wellness, education, and career goals" (Kaplan, Tarvydas, & Gladding, 2014, p. 368). The course of study you are embarking on will train you in each of these elements and more. Training is multidisciplinary and draws not only on formal coursework but also on all our past experiences and knowledge. "Counseling inspires the student to be a knowledgeable generalist, a Renaissance scholar, a devourer of truth in any palatable form" (Kottler & Brown, 2000, p. 5).

Implicit to helping and counseling is its ethnic and cultural component. Humans represent multiple realities and diverse worldviews. Counselors in all disciplines are asked to assess and treat individuals from varying ethnic, racial, and cultural backgrounds. Although it may be true that many individuals prefer to receive counseling from a counselor of similar cultural background (Moore, 2000; Asnaani & Hofmann, 2012), a counselor who is culturally skilled can work with those of varying backgrounds. Without such skill, counseling techniques that are largely influenced by cultural forces specific to the European-American worldview may not be appropriate for those who are members of nondominant cultures (Jun, 2018; Lee, 2014; McAuliffe & Associates, 2013; Sue & Sue, 2016). Ethnocentric counselors (those who are not trained to be culturally skilled) may believe, however unintentionally, that one's own "cultural context may appear to be manifestations of all human behavior rather than manifestations of only one cultural possibility out of many possibilities" (Guindon & Sobhany, 2001, p. 271). Thus, students need to fully appreciate the implications of culture and its influence on all aspects of counseling. Much of the work you will do during your didactic and self-awareness training and throughout your counseling career will revisit these themes time and again. Furthermore, you will learn that social justice and advocacy are unique, integral aspects of the counseling profession.

Most counselors would agree that their lives were changed as a result of entering and successfully completing a counseling program. You have chosen a path that will involve the inner self-work necessary for personal growth. You quite simply cannot become a good counselor without it. Your program of study includes experiential courses or components of courses. In actuality, you may find that this is the most personally challenging program you could ever undertake. Counselor training is as much concerned with your ability to apply what you learn in simulated and real-life settings as with your ability to retain important concepts. In the experiential components, you will learn to draw from your academic course work, of course. But that's not all. Everything you are and everything you have done is there for you to remember, tap into, and use. Every life experience brings you closer to understanding human nature in its infinite variety. To do so well, you must genuinely understand yourself. You are the filter through which you will see your clients and their needs. Furthermore, you will find that you will apply what you learn to your own life. Kottler and Brown (2000) state, "Counseling trains people to be more passionate consumers of life" (p. 4). What other kind of training can make such a statement? I believe, as do most of my colleagues, that being a member of this profession is a privilege and an honor.

Are you ready to begin the journey?

Summary

The chapter began by presenting the many questions beginning students may ask. It discussed the importance of bringing assumptions and values into awareness so that they are not imposed on clients. It talked about what counselors have in common and delineated the various motivations of becoming professional counselors. It presented information on what students can expect in a counseling program and this primer and emphasized the importance of being open to diversity.

This was an excellent personal experience. The best I've ever had. I learned so much about myself.
– beginning student's first course evaluation comment

References

American Counseling Association. (2014). *2014 ACA code of ethics*. Alexandria, VA: Author.

Asnaani, A., & Hofmann, S. (2012). Collaboration in multicultural therapy: Establishing a strong therapeutic alliance across cultural lines. *Journal of Clinical Psychology, 68*, 187–197.

Auger, R. W. (2004). What we don't know CAN hurt us: Mental health counselors' implicit assumptions about human nature. *Journal of Mental Health Counseling, 26*, 13–24.

Corey, M. S., & Corey, G. (2016). *Becoming a helper*. Boston, MA: Cengage Learning.

Guindon, M. H., & Sobhany, M. S. (2001). Toward cultural competency in diagnosis. *International Journal for the Advancement of Counselling, 23*(4), 1–14.

Hansen, J. T. (2005). The devaluation of inner subjective experiences by the helping profession: A plea to reclaim the essence of the profession. *Journal of Counseling & Development, 83*, 406–415.

Hansen, J. T. (2009). Self-awareness revisited: Reconsidering a core value of the counseling profession. *Journal of Counseling & Development, 87*, 186–193.

Hansen, J. T., Speciale, M., & Lemberger, M. E. (2014). Humanism: The foundation and future of professional counseling. *Journal of Humanistic Counseling, 53*, 170–190.

Jun, H. (2018). *Social justice, multicultural counseling, and practice: Beyond a conventional approach*. Cham: Springer.

Jung, C. J. (1969). *The Psychology of the transference*. Princeton, NJ: Princeton University Press.

Kaplan, D. M., Tarvydas, V. M., & Gladding, S. T. (2014). 20/20: A vision for the future of counseling: The new consensus definition of counseling. *Journal of Counseling & Development, 92*, 366–372.

Kottler, J. A., & Brown, R. W. (2000). *Introduction to therapeutic counseling: Voices from the field*. Belmont, CA: Wadsworth/Brooks/Cole.

Lee, C. C. (2014). *Multicultural issues in counseling* (4th ed.). Alexandria, VA: American Counseling Association.

McAuliffe, G., & Associates (2013). *Culturally alert counseling: A comprehensive introduction* (2nd ed.). Thousand Oaks, CA: Sage Publications.

Moore, L. J. (2000). Psychiatric contribution to understanding racism. *Transcultural Psychiatry, 37*, 147–183.

Niles, S. G., & Harris-Bowlsbey, J. (2017). *Career development interventions*. Boston: Pearson.

O'Reilly, M., & Lester, J. N. (2017). *Examining mental health through cocial constructionism: The language of mental health*. Cham: Palgrave Macmillan.

Peterson, J. V., & Nisenholz, B. (1999). *Orientation to counseling* (4th ed.). Boston: Allyn & Bacon.

Rudes, J., & Gutterman, J. T. (2007). The value of social constructionism for the counseling profession: A reply to Hansen. *Journal of Counseling & Development, 85*, 387–392.

Schneider, K. J., & May, R. (1994). *The psychology of existence: An integrative, clinical perspective*. New York: McGraw-Hill.

Sue, D. W., & Sue, D. (2016). *Counseling the culturally diverse: theory and practice* (7th ed.). Hoboken, NJ: John Wiley & Sons.

Tjelveit, A. C. (1986). The ethics of value conversion in psychotherapy: Appropriate and inappropriate therapist influence on client values. *Clinical Psychology Review, 6*, 515–537.

Table 1.1 TFAC Chart – Thought, Feelings, Actions, and Context

Self	My Thoughts	My Feelings	My Actions	My Context	Other? (Specify)
Why am I considering a career in counseling?					
What are my own motivators?					
How prepared am I to undertake this journey?					
What are my concerns?					
What other questions do I have?					
How does my reality influence my reflections?					
Others	**Others' Probable Thoughts**	**Others' Possible Feelings**	**Others' Observable Actions**	**Others' Apparent Context**	**Other? (Specify)**
What have I learned about others in my class?					
What might be the point of view of my significant others as I undertake this journey?					
What might be the view of my instructor?					
What else might I ask others?					
How does my reality influence my observations?					

Note: T = Thoughts or Cognition F = Feelings or Affect A = Actions or Behavior C = Context (Factors that may further impact on TFAC, such as family, SES, ethnicity, current circumstances or unusual situations, etc.) Other = Anything else that might not be covered in TFAC, such as your hunches not yet grounded in facts or checked out with others.

Chapter 2

Who? Answers about Counselors and Clients

Mary H. Guindon

No one is useless in this world… who lightens the burden of it for anyone else.

– Charles Dickens

POINTS TO PONDER

- What are the similarities and differences in the many related helping professions?
- How is counseling distinguished from psychotherapy?
- What are the characteristics of the professional counselor?
- Who seeks counseling and what are their expectations?
- How do counselors determine their clients' needs?
- What is the counselor/client relationship like?
- What is cultural competency?

The Profession of Counseling

The words "professional" and "counseling" tend to be overused. Many kinds of people call themselves professionals when referring to their work, whether related to helping others or not. It seems that almost anyone who receives pay for any activity can claim he or she is a "professional." In addition, those who help others in almost any capacity tend to use the word "counseling" to describe at least some of what they do. However, the term "professional counseling" is used in this text to differentiate it from the kinds of activities that are either not directly related to this profession or are adjunctive to counseling but do not require advanced training. Other authors use terms such as therapeutic counseling or use the word counseling in combination with terms such as psychotherapy or guidance to differentiate it from nonprofessional fields. Others simply use the word counseling alone (Gladding, 2017). They are all talking about the same profession, the profession that includes school counselors, mental health counselors, career counselors, and others. In Chapter 3, we discuss these terms more fully and how they evolved historically. In this chapter, we are concerned with the contemporary identity of professional counselors: The Who of who we are.

To be considered a profession, five distinct characteristics must be present. A profession must have (a) a common body of knowledge acquired through specialized training; (b) a national or international organization that oversees its standards, competencies, and credentialing; (c) a prescribed and formalized code of ethical conduct; (d) sanctioned and legal recognition at the national and state level; and (e) a clear identity of its practitioners as members of the profession.

This book distinguishes the activity of counseling from the identity of the professional counselor. Several related professions practice counseling activities. Many of the basic skills described in Part Three of this book are common to the allied professions of psychiatry, psychology, social work, addictions work, and others. Professional counseling is similar to but distinct in both evident and subtle ways from other helping professions.

The Counseling-Related Professions

Categories of Helping

Individuals who offer services to those in emotional, mental health, or wellness need are best described as providing the service of helping. A basic tenet of this profession is counseling equals helping. Gladding (2018) in *The Counseling Dictionary* defines helping as "the informal or formal process of assisting individuals in their times of need" (p. 74). In general, helping in this context refers to a process that has clearly prescribed stages and activities and involves building a relationship to a lesser or greater extent with the recipient of the service, with the goal of assisting the recipient in resolving one or more problems. Many writers, most notably Corey and Corey (2015), refer to all the allied fields as the helping professions and mean all those who practice counseling. The clear categories, or levels, of helping are nonprofessionals, paraprofessionals, and professionals.

Nonprofessional helpers. Nonprofessional helpers are those who possess no specific or formalized training in counseling and are not members of an identifiable professional organization with a common body of knowledge, a code of ethics, or legal recognition. They possess tacit knowledge of human needs and differing kinds of wisdom gained through practical experience. Their skill varies widely. Some indigenous healers fall in this category as do many kinds of volunteers.

Paraprofessional helpers. Paraprofessionals are those individuals who are sometimes referred to as human services workers. In this category are those individuals who have received some formalized training in human services. Some have college degrees; others have been trained in specialized helping fields at the community college level; and still others have had on-the-job training or received instruction in particular workshops. Although they do not practice independently of professionals, they often provide first-line help to many people in need. This widely diverse category includes college resident hall workers, youth counselors, mental health technicians, psychology aides, career development facilitators, and some addictions counselors. Paraprofessionals do not meet the five criteria necessary to be considered members of a profession. However, they provide much-needed services and can have a positive influence on the mental health needs of their constituencies.

Professional helpers. Professionals are those individuals who belong to the allied helping or counseling professions that meet all five criteria. They possess training and advanced degrees beyond the bachelor's level and have had internship and work experience that includes supervision by more seasoned practitioners that ultimately leads to their ability to practice in a more professional capacity and in most cases independently. These individuals belong to the mental health fields of psychology, psychiatry, social work, marriage and family therapy, psychiatric nurse practitioner, professional counseling, some addictions counseling, and others. What further distinguishes them from the other categories is their ability to provide preventive and remedial services that are legally sanctioned through state certification or licensure. This sanctioning is based on national standards developed and maintained by professional organizations.

Psychotherapy and Counseling

Those in the related helping professions sometimes use the terms psychotherapy and psycho-therapist when referring to themselves and what they do. Nevertheless, no one profession goes by this name. *Psychotherapy* is a system of activities in which helping professionals provide mental health assistance to those who seek their services. The related helping professions engage in these activities as part of their services to clients. However, no distinct profession of psychotherapy as such exists nor meets the five criteria to be considered a profession in and of itself. The words counseling and psychotherapy are used synonymously and interchangeably by some authors and practitioners. Others distinguish between them by the level of assistance provided to the client. Counseling can involve psychotherapy but is not limited to it. Similarly, psychotherapy involves many of the same processes of counseling but does not encompass all counseling func-tions. *Counseling* refers to those activities that predominantly promote growth and wellness (i.e., mental health) but may also be involved with the remediation of mental distress and disorder. *Psychotherapy* refers to those activities that are predominantly involved with the amelioration and treatment of mental distress and disorder but may also be involved with promoting growth and wellness. It is generally – but not always – a question of emphasis and historical background. Professional counseling grew out of the guidance movement in the United States at the turn of the twentieth century; psychotherapy grew out of the psychoanalytic movement in Europe at about the same time. Chapter 3, "What? Answers about the Definition of Counseling, Its Past and Its Present," will help you to understand more fully these sometimes subtle differences.

The Allied Mental Health Professions

Although their philosophy of helping varies and thus their training is slightly different, in reality the allied professions often work in the same settings providing the same services. Each discipline has its own requirements for preparation and practice but much of their real-world work overlaps. Professional counselors will interact, consult, and collaborate with these other practitioners and should be informed about them.

According to the American Counseling Association (ACA, n.d.):

> the differences among counselors, psychologists, and psychiatrists can be summarized by differences in education and focus: Professional counselors have a graduate degree in coun-seling. A master's degree is the entry-level requirement. Counselors focus on client wellness, as opposed to psychopathology. Psychologists have a graduate degree in psychology, and licensed psychologists typically have a degree in clinical, counseling, or school psychol-ogy. Of all the mental health professions, psychologists are the best trained in conducting research. Psychiatrists are medical doctors who have usually completed a residency in psy-chiatry. Their niche is prescribing psychotropic drugs.

The various related professions are not particularly differentiated or understood by the general public. Nevertheless, they can be confusing to those who are looking at them from the outside and seeking to enter one of these professions. Unfortunately, some practitioners engage in what is known as "turf wars" in which one profession attempts to exclude members of another related profession from practicing in a particular setting, such as a community mental health center or a psychiatric hospital. Chapter 7, "When? Answers about Processes, Phases, and Procedures," will explain counseling credentialing in detail.

You need to have a clear idea of what is involved in each profession. Table 2.1 delineates most of the allied mental health disciplines, or the helping professions.

Approaches to Counseling

The Developmental Approach to Helping

Professional counselors work with their clients from a developmental perspective. They regard their clients as people who go through normal developmental stages across the lifespan and who may encounter troubles along the way. They see people as experiencing difficulties in making life transitions, or having problems in living. What may be developmentally appropriate at one stage of life may be inappropriate at another. They work in prevention and wellness as well as in remediation and intervention. The developmental/wellness approach to helping is the hallmark of the professional counselor. Relationship building and psychoeducation are key to the counseling process. This relationship is facilitated when the counselor and the client are both aware of the mental, physical, and social arenas of human life (Gladding, 2017).

Those who identify themselves as professional counselors work in many capacities. They are school, community, mental health, career, organizational, and rehabilitation counselors. They are also higher education student affairs counselors, and some are marriage and family counselors. What they have in common is the same basic training (a common body of knowledge) and a professional identity associated with their national professional organization, ACA, and one or more of its divisions. They may be affiliated with the state branches of ACA and its divisions. They also adhere to its Code of Ethics (https://www.counseling.org/docs/default-source/ethics/2014-code-of-ethics.pdf?sfvrsn=2d58522c_4). Each of the specializations within professional counseling is discussed in detail elsewhere in this text.

Counseling psychologists, whose professional organization is the American Psychological Association (APA), also work from the developmental approach, usually at the doctoral level. Some may be more closely aligned with the medical or psychopathological approach than are counselors whose affiliation is ACA. Nevertheless, counselors and counseling psychologists spring from the same root, historically and traditionally.

The Medical/Psychopathological Approach to Helping

The medical or psychopathological approach to helping is most associated with members of the allied medical professions such as psychiatrists, clinical nurse practitioners, and clinical psychologists. In this approach, recipients of services are patients who are diagnosed and treated for their mental health concerns in a way similar to and more closely aligned with their physical health. Diagnosis and treatment planning are necessary steps in working with some people such as those in psychiatric hospitals, mental health or community agencies, and other related settings. Providing a diagnosis is obligatory when insurance companies are involved. To receive reimbursement for services, clinicians must show that treatments are "medically necessitated." Helping professionals including community mental health counselors and addictions counselors and clinical social workers also can and do diagnose their clients and develop treatment plans for those with psychopathological disorders. However, not all professional counselors work with people that have diagnosable disorders. In addition, many of those who work solely within the framework of the medical approach may not work with their clients on the same developmental issues or problems in living, such as career-related or life transition issues, with which professional counselors work.

Psychiatrists are medical doctors and thus can prescribe medications. Professional counselors and others who work with mental disorders consult with psychiatrists who will diagnose, prescribe medications, and periodically evaluate treatment of their patients. Most psychiatrists themselves tend not to provide counseling services as frequently as other helping practitioners, but refer their patients out to credentialed psychotherapists for counseling and therapy.

Table 2.1 The Allied Mental Health Helping Professions

Discipline	Entry-Level Credential	Professional Organization	Common Settings
Professional Counselor: School Counselor	MS, MA, MEd	ACA, ASCA	Public and private schools
Professional Counselor: Community/Mental Health Counselor	MS, MA, MEd	ACA, AMHCA	Community agencies, mental health centers, psychiatric hospitals, private practice
Professional Counselor: Career/Organizational	MS, MA, MEd	ACA, NCDA, NECA	Colleges and universities, business and industry, government, career centers
Professional Counselor: Rehabilitation Counselor	MS, MA, MEd	ACA, ARCA	Rehabilitation centers, hospitals, governmental agencies
Professional Counselor: Higher Education Student Affairs Practice	MS, MA, MEd	ACA, ACPA, ACCA	Colleges and universities: advising, residence life; some counseling centers
Marriage, Couple, and Family Counselor (MFC)	MS, MA, MEd	AAMFT, IAMFC	Community agencies, mental centers, psychiatric hospitals, private practice
Play Therapist	MS, MA, MEd	APT	Community agencies, mental centers, psychiatric hospitals, private practice
Psychiatric Nurse Practitioner	MSN, RN	APNA	Psychiatric hospitals, medical centers, rehabilitation centers, private practice
Psychologist: Clinical	PhD, PsyD	APA(a), Div.12	Psychiatric hospitals, medical centers, private practice, community agencies, mental health centers, rehabilitation centers
Psychologist: Counseling	PhD, EdD	APA(a), Div. 17	Psychiatric hospitals, medical centers, private practice, community agencies, mental health centers
Psychologist: School	PhD, EdD	NASP, APA(a), Div 16	Schools, private practice
Social Worker: Clinical	MSW	NASW	Community agencies, mental health centers, psychiatric hospitals, private practice
Addictions Counselor; Professional Counselor: Addictions	AS, AA, or MS, MA	NAACT, ACA, IAAOC	Community agencies, mental health centers psychiatric hospitals, rehabilitation centers, addictions centers
Psychiatrist	MD	AMA, APA (b)	Psychiatric hospitals, medical centers, private practice, community agencies, mental health centers, rehabilitation centers

ACA = American Counseling Association. Divisions of ACA include:
IAAOC = International Association of Addictions and Offender Counselors
IAMFC = International Association of Marriage and Family Counselors
ACCA = American College Counseling Association
ARCA = American Rehabilitation Counselor Association
NCDA = National Career Development Association
NECA = National Employment Counseling Association
Associated with but independent of ACA:
AMHCA = American Mental Health Counseling Association
ASCA = American School Counseling Association
AMA = American Medical Association
APA (a) = American Psychological Association. Divisions in APA include:
    Div. 12 Clinical Psychology
    Div. 16 School Psychology
    Div. 17 Counseling Psychology
APA(b) = American Psychiatric Association
AAMFT = Association of Marriage and Family Therapists
APT = Association of Play Therapists
ACPA = American College Personnel Association
APNA = American Psychiatric Nurses Association
NAACT = National Association of Alcoholism Counselors and Trainers
NASP = National Association of School Psychologists
NASW = National Association of Social Workers

Although some mental health problems are ameliorated by the use of prescribed drugs alone, drugs in combination with counseling is the treatment of choice for many disorders. For other disorders, counseling and psychotherapy alone can be the choice.

The Social Systems/Case Management Approach to Helping

Marriage and family counselors and therapists and clinical social workers are likely to take a systems approach to counseling. In this approach, the client is seen as having problems living within his or her social and family system in addition to possibly having a diagnosable disorder. Rather than viewing clients as individuals in isolation, they view the client's concern as one factor among many others that may be impacting on mental health and emotional wellbeing. They are trained to consider their clients' social habitats and cultural environments. Social workers were historically trained to work with the underprivileged and with the social and family systems in which they exist. Today, social workers vary in what they do. Some provide case management services as well as counseling. To do clinical counseling, or psychotherapy, they seek additional training in clinical social work. Marriage and family counselors and therapists tend to work with couples and families in the resolution of issues that impact the entire family, although they may also see family members individually during the process of therapy. Today, professional counselors are trained to consider the context, or system, within which their clients live and work. Indeed, CACREP standards of training and ethical codes require it.

The Targeted Populations Approach to Helping

To work with some populations, helpers must have targeted and specialized knowledge and training. These helpers can come from different counseling-related professions. There are seven distinct specializations for which credentialing is offered by CACREP: Addictions Counseling; Career Counseling; Clinical Mental Health Counseling; Clinical Rehabilitation Counseling; College Counseling and Student Affairs; Marriage, Couple, and Family Therapy; and School Counseling. These specialties are discussed in Part Two of this text.

Some of these specialists are trained in other counseling-related professions. For example, addictions counselors and therapists come from across a spectrum of training programs. Also known as substance abuse counselors, they work from either the medical model/psychopathological approach or from the systems approach or both. Their training is highly specialized and tends to emphasize case management and patient compliance more heavily than psychotherapy and counseling strategies. They work generally within substance abuse settings in the community or in addictions units within larger organizations, such as hospitals or rehabilitation centers. Addictions counselors of the past received their training through workshops or at the community college level. They were thus considered to be paraprofessionals. More recently, addictions counselors have moved toward professionalism and many states now require graduate degrees and other credentialing activities of those who work with substance abusers. Many addictions counselors are now working on parity with other helping professionals and some professional counselors specialize in addictions through training in the ACA specialty area, Addictions Counseling (See Chapter 9).

Another example of a cross-disciplinary field, play therapy provides treatment through the use of play rather than traditional counseling skills. Play therapists may come from any one of the related helping professions but go on to specialize in the needs of children, particularly issues of trauma and loss. Young children do not have the verbal skills of adolescents and adults. Because they are unable to directly articulate their issues, play is used to elicit important therapeutic material and is the vehicle for providing treatment. Sand trays, dolls and puppets, games, art, and music are used in treatment. Play therapy can be effective with adults as well. Others who specialize in working with children are school psychologists and child psychologists. School psychologists provide services to children experiencing difficulties that impact learning including emotional difficulties and disorders. They work closely with school counselors. Child psychologists are clinical psychologists who specialize in working with issues and disorders that manifest in childhood. Although ACA does not have a specialty in play therapy, many professional counselors seek advanced training to become registered play therapists.

Personal and Professional Choice

Clearly, the helping professions overlap in scope of practice and setting. With the exception of psychiatrists, they are more alike than they are different. Nevertheless, they differ in their philosophical underpinnings, their areas of specialization, and the emphasis of their training programs. Any beginning counselor would do well to compare the programs of study for each of these professions and decide which best fits his own temperament, philosophy of life, and expectations of work. The level of work and specialization vary among the disciplines even when its members practice in related settings. Whichever related profession you choose, those who have gone before you will tell you that the process of reaching your goal is demanding. Your own developmental path will be personally rewarding, interpersonally satisfying, and intellectually stimulating. It is also guaranteed to be personally taxing, interpersonally exhausting, and intellectually challenging. The characteristics you possess and the ones you will develop through your training and beyond will influence how successful you can be. Let us turn now to those attributes, or personal characteristics, that make up effective counselors.

SIDEBAR 2.1

In Practice: What Would You Do?

Pam is a community mental health counselor with a large private agency assigned to offer services in the city's middle schools. She has several years' experience at her agency but this is her first month in the schools. The school counselor referred 13-year-old Lizzy because she was found in the school bathroom with marijuana, a felt tip marker hiding a drug pipe and a miniature spoon. Pam has just finished the first session.

> Lizzy says she's not involved with any drugs or alcohol. She insists she was holding these things for her 14-year-old boyfriend because he got in trouble and didn't want to be caught with them. I don't believe her. I know this boy and he's a troublemaker. She's begging me not to tell her parents. The parents came in as soon as the school counselor called them. They are waiting in my outer office. I know from Lizzy's records that her academic performance hasn't declined but she does cut some classes. I also know her parents don't put much emphasis on education. How do I gain Lizzy's trust and confidence when I also must let her parents know what's happened?

Class Discussion

1. What are some of the counselor characteristics that Pam is exhibiting?
2. What are some characteristics that she may be lacking?
3. What values might she hold?
4. If Lizzy were your client, what could you do to build a therapeutic environment and relationship with her?

Characteristics of the Professional Counselor

The quality of the therapeutic relationship has been shown over and over to be related to one's person, or one's personal style, regardless of the particular helping discipline or theoretical orientation. The introduction to this text described the attributes most commonly associated with counseling students. These basic attributes also describe professional counselors. Many writers have discussed what makes an effective counselor (Carkhuff, 2017; Corey & Corey, 2015; Neukrug, 2016; Nystul, 2015; Rogers, 1951). For more than 50 years, studies about the relationship between effective helping and personal characteristics consistently indicate that the quality of the counseling relationship is the major factor influencing successful outcome. Carl Rogers as early as 1942 stated that the personal characteristics of warmth and genuineness are crucial factors in building relationships. Regardless of exact discipline or theoretical orientation, it seems to be that the self of the individual – who the helper is as a person – and the ability to form and maintain a therapeutic bond are key ingredients necessary for a successful outcome. The therapeutic bond, then, depends upon the personal attributes of the counselor. In fact, the counselor's self may be the most important and significant part of counseling.

To be effective in helping others resolve whatever issues brought them into counseling, professional counselors have a number of important traits in common. Corey and Corey (2015) assert that there is an "Ideal Helper" with identifiable traits. No one counselor possesses every one of these traits at its ideal level; however, most counselors possess most of them. A note of caution: Don't expect to possess all of these traits at the outset of your training. Because they are ideal, professional counselors work to achieve, maintain, and improve upon them throughout their lives. If at this point in your career you compare yourself to all of these traits you may be setting yourself up for disappointment. What is important is that you are willing to assess your own strengths realistically and to recognize those attributes in yourself that need strengthening. The Thoughts, Feelings, Actions (TFAC) Chart at the end of this chapter will help you in making an honest assessment of yourself today and assist you in reaching toward becoming that Ideal Helper.

Effective Counselor Traits

Traits exhibited by effective counselors can be organized in many ways. Some texts list as few as four or five critical traits while others offer 25 or more. Together they cover about the same core attributes. A dozen essential traits contribute to effective counseling:

Empathy

Those who enter the counseling profession first and foremost are empathic toward others. They identify with other people and feel a connection and affinity for them. They have a special set of antennae that allows them to pick up what others may be feeling. They are able to take the point of view of another rather than seeing things only through their own point of view. They care about other human beings, particularly about their emotional wellbeing. Without empathy, we cannot begin the process of understanding our clients well enough to help them with whatever brought them to us in the first place. Empathy is the foundation of professional counseling. Upon it rests all other personal characteristics, the building blocks that make up the effective counselor.

Empathy alone, however, is not enough to help others make therapeutic changes. Empathy is simply a feeling. A person can have empathy for a character in a TV show. It is not necessary to act on that empathy or convey it to the individual on TV. The basis for therapeutic change begins when counselors not only feel empathy but use their skills to convey empathic understanding to their clients. Empathic understanding is how counselors communicate their perception of the others' feelings and thoughts. Most beginning counselors are naturally empathetic. However, empathic understanding is a set of skills that take training and practice.

Objectivity

The ability to be involved with another and at the same time stand back and see accurately what is happening with the other and in the relationship is an essential element of empathy. Developing this extra set of eyes and ears without being caught up in another's problems is a skill shared by all counselors. Objectivity allows them to respond without becoming swallowed up by another's pain or enmeshed in another's troubles. You need to understand the important difference between empathy and sympathy. An empathic person recognizes another's pain and suffering; a sympathetic person feels the pain as if it were her own. The empathic counselor has no personal need for the client who is emotionally suffering to recover right away. In fact, the empathic counselor recognizes the therapeutic importance of working through pain to reach wholeness. The sympathetic person, on the other hand, wants the sufferer to feel better so she will also feel better. In short, the empathic person does not confuse another person's pain, sorrow, anguish, or distress with her own. Sympathy does not lead to therapeutic change whereas empathy is a key condition in which it will take place. Objectivity allows the counselor to recognize the difference.

Sensitivity

Sensitivity is a part of empathy. Counselors have the ability and training to look past outer imperfections. Effective counselors understand that an individual's humanity is more important than whatever external factors, such as looks or social standing or behavior, make up that individual. Sensitivity implies that an individual feels empathy for fellow human beings regardless of their circumstances and offers back acceptance with kindness and warmth. Counselors exhibit sensitivity when they offer acceptance to others as they are, not as they "should" be. Counselors are "not ashamed of human nature, with its shortcomings, imperfections, and weaknesses" (Peterson & Nisenholz, 1999, p 6). At the same time, accepting the humanity of a person does not imply condoning specific behaviors that may be unacceptable or dangerous. Counselors offer compassion – a profound awareness of the pain of another human being coupled with a desire to help. Compassion allows counselors to respond to another's distress in appropriate ways. Without sensitivity, there is neither empathy nor compassion.

Observational Ability

Because counselors have a highly developed sense of empathy, they are natural observers of human life and the human condition. Observation of others is integral to the counseling process. However, effective counselors do more than passively watch. The role of the counselor is to help clients understand their own realities and to assist them in making appropriate and facilitative life choices. Counselors must make a tentative analysis of their client's thoughts, feelings, and actions without making assumptions about them. To do this, the counselor must be aware of the meaning of clients' behaviors, the probable feelings and thoughts underlying their behaviors, what motivates their actions, and the nature of the social context in which they live. Therefore, the counselor must have accurate perception; that is, an efficient perception of reality. Effective counselors are aware of their own environment and place in it. They are able to engage in abstract thinking about what they observe. They can generalize from all sources of personal and professional information without being biased by an undue distortion of reality.

Self-Awareness

Counselors are skilled in self-knowledge. They are willing to self-explore. Approximately 60 years ago, Tolbert (1959) stated that an understanding of oneself and insight into one's biases, attitudes, and values are necessary in helping others. Insight continues to be a significant component of counselor effectiveness today. Thus, a major source of counselor preparation involves training in awareness of the self and the development of this self into a fully functioning and effective person. Education cannot change basic personal attributes, but it can refine them. In fact, counselors have a personal responsibility to be committed to as great an awareness as they are capable of. They work on understanding their own life issues. Through healthy introspection and self-exploration, counselors show a willingness to continue to grow and change. Counselors are aware of their own needs. They are aware of their motivation for helping others. They pay attention to their feelings as well as their thoughts. They are mindful of how their behaviors might be impacting others. They grow in awareness of their personal strengths and continue to draw on them. They also grow in awareness of their own coping skills and their personal and professional limitations, and they take a serious look at any areas in which they can improve. Awareness of one's own issues and problems and the willingness to address unresolved personal conflicts in responsibly appropriate ways are part of ethical professional behavior.

Awareness and Acceptance of Diverse Worldviews

Counselors value, appreciate, and accept differences among and between people with regard to culture, ethnicity, age, ability, gender, race, religion, and sexual orientation. People live in two worlds, the world of their own cultural and racial-ethnic-gender heritage and the world of their present reality. These two worlds constitute their worldview. Just as effective counselors continually work to improve their own self-awareness, they also continually work to improve their awareness of the diversity of their fellow human beings. In other words, they are multiculturally aware. Awareness of one's own heritage and how it shapes one's worldview can contribute to effectiveness as a counselor. Lack of awareness can detract from it. Understanding the worldview of diverse others is essential in our multicultural society.

Yet understanding is not enough. Effective counselors possess a democratic character structure. They not only accept diversity and thus do not discriminate on the basis of class, education, culture, ethnicity, age, ability, gender, race, religion, and sexual orientation; they also do not attempt to change or control others' beliefs or actions embedded in their culture. They experience a sense of fellowship with humanity and respect for others (Brems, 2001). They believe diverse others to be capable, fully functioning beings (Kottler & Shepard, 2015). Counselors have high levels of tolerance of diverse thoughts, feelings, and actions; and when and where they can, they work to redress social injustice and oppression.

Open-Mindedness

Counselors realize that fixed and preconceived ideas can affect clients and counseling outcomes. Open-mindedness not only includes knowledge and acceptance of the world outside the counselor's world. It includes an understanding of one's own inner world and how internal standards, values, assumptions, and perceptions can be projected on the client if not attended to. Counselors are not only open and accepting of others; they are open-minded about themselves as well. They are involved and present in their interpersonal transactions. They operate in an open system in which exchanges of information with others such as supervisors, peers, and instructors are welcomed. Open-mindedness includes willingness to appropriately self-disclose and the ability to receive constructive feedback. Good counselors are able to receive feedback, consider it carefully, and integrate needed changes to their beliefs, attitudes, or behaviors. This kind of open-mindedness is the cornerstone of self-growth and awareness. Both are essential to the ability to be interpersonally honest, open, genuine, and without false pretense. Effective counselors are "self-revealing rather than self-concealing" (Kottler & Brown, 2000, p 16).

Integrity

Integrity involves personal values that guide ethical behavior. Integrity is not something we are; it is something we choose to do. It is based partly on one's own moral and ethical beliefs. Counselors are highly ethical. Those who are highly ethical draw on their professional Code of Ethics, of course, but highly ethical people also hold principles that guide them in their work and how they conduct their lives. One's ethical principles focus "on the objective, rational, and cognitive aspects of the decision-making process" (Ahia, 2003, p. 26).

Counselors strive to live by high standards of moral and ethical behavior. Morals must be differentiated from ethics. Morals involve one's understanding of what is right and what is wrong. Although not necessarily tied to religious beliefs, they are based on traditional and historical religious standards, such as do no harm or offer assistance to those in need. "Ethics usually involves a judgment of human decisions or behaviors against an accepted standard" (Ahia, 2003, p. 26). People make judgments and decisions about their own and others' moral or ethical behavior. Although counselors must evaluate their own behaviors, they do not judge the behaviors of their clients. Counselors hold a set of values that inform their ethics and thus their sense of integrity. Counselors make the choice to accept the innate humanity of their clients regardless of their behaviors. Values are integral to ethics and are a part of what it means to have integrity.

Integrity, moreover, involves more than ethics, morals, and values. It involves trustworthiness. Counselor trustworthiness includes reliability, responsibility, and predictability. To be reliable means that counselors are dependable and consistent in their actions. To be responsible means that counselors are accountable for their actions. To be predictable means that counselors will follow through on reasonable expectations. Trustworthiness can be summarized in one sentence: *Do not promise more than you can do, and be sure you do exactly as you have promised.* This is the essence of professionalism.

Problem-Solving Creativity

Counselors look at problems with fresh perspectives and find alternative possible solutions. They believe that people across the lifespan can achieve therapeutic change – in terms of cognition, behavior, affect, interpersonal relationships, and systems. Because they hold this belief, they see themselves as change agents with the ability to facilitate change through their problem-solving creativity.

Counselors are socially oriented in their problem solving. They do not meet their own needs for gratification through their actions to find solutions with others. Counselors are mission oriented and believe themselves to be part of a solution. They offer their help when it is sought but they do not impose their solutions on others from a mistaken belief that they know what is best for others. In other words, offering help does not mean telling others what to do. Counseling does not equal advice giving. Counselors, in fact, refrain from giving advice. They know that solutions that are meaningful must come from the client. Counselors' problem-solving ability comes in the form of facilitating choices for the client. They work with their clients to generate a range of solutions to their problems that are healthy and appropriate and that ultimately best meet their needs.

Good counselors have the ability to make new connections and create wholes out of elements that appear to be fragmented. Counselors offer fresh, innovative ways of doing or looking at things. They are original thinkers. They can redefine problems and rethink solutions. Thus, creativity is a characteristic of many counselors. Creativity comes in many forms. Some counselors are creative in the traditional sense of the word. They are artistic and may use various aspects of the arts such as music or drawing or poetry in their counseling approaches. Most, on the other hand, are creative in how they think and approach the world. "Creative thinking is the ability to think in novel and unusual ways and to come up with unique solutions to problems" (Santrock, 2015, p. 420).

Personal Energy

Counseling requires the ability to be fully present to another human being. It requires enormous attention to detail and copious amounts self-discipline. The profession is demanding, challenging, and never the same. It takes physical, emotional, and mental strength, and what Gladding (2009) calls a "capacity for self-denial – the ability to set aside personal needs to listen and take care of others' needs first" (p. 35).

Good health is a prerequisite of personal energy. Counselors recognize that if they are to set aside their own needs in service to their clients, the must take care of themselves first. Counselors strive for good self-care skills and healthy lifestyles. Good nutrition, physical activity, personal interests and recreational activities, and satisfying interpersonal relationships all contribute to personal energy. Counselors expend their energy in service to their clients. To fully focus on another human being is hard work. To be fully present to another's needs takes concentration of mind and body. Without personal energy, the counselor is less likely to be effective in totally attending to the needs of others. Stress and burnout are better withstood when the counselor's personal energy is high.

Competence

Counselors are highly proficient in their skills. They stay informed about the most effective practices in counseling, research, and program development and evaluation. Counselors deal with cognitive complexity well. Indeed, they are energized by it. They are divergent thinkers. Divergent thinking allows counselors to produce many different possibilities and solutions for the same issues and problems. In other words, through their training and continued education, they have a rich repertoire of strategies to draw on and can plan effectively for good solutions to problems. Their competence is metacognitive knowledge based. They routinely know how, when, and where to use counseling strategies. At the same time, they tolerate ambiguity and the unknown well and can examine unstructured situations and either find structure in them or create structure if and when needed.

From time to time, clients present issues that are not within the expertise of the counselor. Part of counselor competence is to know of those areas in which they are not sufficiently competent to counsel a particular client whose issues do not match their knowledge, training, and supervision. They are not naïve about their knowledge or level of expertise. Competent counselors recognize this and do not work in areas beyond their own training and experience. They are competent in knowing to whom to refer the client. They also are competent in seeking opportunities to expand their expertise and pursue training and supervision in new issues as they arise.

Counseling knowledge and training is not static; it is dynamic. Because of the constant need for upgrading and training, it is a never-ending career field!

Good Mental Health

Although counselors are not expected to be perfect or without problems, they can only be good helpers to others when they are psychologically intact and are not distracted by their own overwhelming troubles. Counselors are willing to undertake personal exploration and to experience the hard interpersonal work that leads to positive personal growth. They are real. This means they work at being authentic human beings, congruent in their thoughts, actions, and feelings. Good mental health includes the capacity for and tolerance of intimacy. Counselors can be emotionally close without experiencing personal discomfort. Those with good mental health are spontaneous. They have good levels of self-esteem and self-respect. They are autonomous individuals who can rely upon their own internal resources and potential but also form and maintain healthy relationships. As all humans do, they have basic needs for friendship, love, safety, respect, and belongingness. At the same time, they have good personal boundaries.

Those with good mental health are flexible. They do not fear the unknown, the new, or the unfamiliar. They are healthy risk takers. They tolerate ambiguity and not knowing about their lives and the world. They also have a strong sense of curiosity – a natural interest in people. They can experience and appreciate the world; they find pleasure and wonder in life. People with good mental health enjoy the humorous and can see the absurdities of life. Their humor, however, is not at the expense of others. It is a nonhostile and nonsarcastic humor.

Counselors may not be able to help others to a higher level of emotional and mental wellbeing than that which they themselves have attained. Unfortunately, some people do not recognize when their own psychological health is marginal. They may not have the ability to delay expression of their affect. They may not be able to judge their behaviors as problematic or their thoughts as illogical. Counselors who do not have good mental health cannot offer good service to their clients. They may even damage them. These impaired professionals need to seek help for themselves. We expect that clients are self-actualizing and we assist them in setting goals to reach their potentials. In the same way, we need to be working toward our highest level of potential as well.

Role of Values

Closely related to the characteristics of effective counselors are the values they hold. *Values* are the influences that motivate human beings and provide criteria for shaping their lives. Values are consciously or unconsciously held and mirror the worldview of an individual or an institution. They are socially constructed. That is, individuals and entire groups of individuals create their perceived social reality through language (O'Reilly & Lester, 2017; Rudes & Gutterman, 2007) and values are a part of quite subjective realities.

Counselors need to clearly understand their own values. Although they do not impose their values on their clients, in fact, no counseling or counselor is really value free or neutral. The institution of counseling is based on a specific set of values. Counseling theory and practice is traditionally grounded in the Western, dominant-culture worldview that values independence, materialism, and rationalism. This worldview values a reliance on individualism and autonomy, action-oriented problem solving, competitiveness and achievement, an orientation toward the future, and a work ethic in which hard work equals monetary and intrinsic reward. Thus, one value and, indeed, purpose of counseling is preparing clients to be competent in earning a living and in making a contribution to the world and society.

Another value is the expectation that individuals discuss their feelings. Notwithstanding, inherent in the Western, dominant-culture worldview is the preference for thoughts and actions over feelings. Many counseling strategies may attend to feelings but ultimately expect action. Others attend only to feelings or only to action. Yet some clients, either through their own personal values or through the values internalized from their own culture's worldview, value feelings over action or action without discussion of feelings.

Human beings hold personal, idiosyncratic values as well. These are internalized not only from their societal culture but also are a uniquely held set of values learned from family and institutions such as religion and social class. Values include beliefs about such things as the importance of work and money, abortion, same-sex marriage, sexual activity, alcohol, drugs, and many, many more. These values may vary from the dominant worldview or they may adhere to it.

Another value held by the counseling profession is that personal and dominant-culture values are not imposed on the client. Counselors do not deny the existence of their own values. The choice for the counselor is not between neutrality and some set of values. The choice for the counselor is between implicit and explicit values. By making values that are generally out of awareness explicit, counselors can evaluate them. They then work toward not imposing their own set of cultural and personal values on their clients.

One task of the counselor is to make values a conscious reality for their clients. Counselors strive to encourage the client to become aware of their own values, confront them if they are inappropriate with their own best interests and for their wellbeing, so that the client can internalize healthy values in keeping with his own culture. Another task is to create environments that help people to recognize their own appropriate values and fulfill them. You will be asked no less than to do the same in your program of study. You cannot help another person with their values fulfillment if you have not done the work necessary to understand your own values. You must ask yourself, "What are my core values? How well am I meeting them? Do they fit with the values of this profession?"

Who Are the Clients?

No one kind of person seeks counseling. Clients are all ages, races, ethnicities, sexual orientations, and ages; possessing varying levels of education, occupational and social status, monetary resources, and support of family and friends. Clients vary in their severity of symptoms, level of distress, and state of confusion. Some have good insight and self-awareness; others have little. Some have good social skills; others do not. Some have strong cognitive functioning skills; others have few. Some are emotionally healthy; others are not. Their time in counseling is voluntary or it is mandatory.

What they have in common is a need to change. Counseling equals change. Although some people are motivated to make the changes they need to lead satisfying lives, others are less motivated. Many people who come into counseling can be incongruent. Their thoughts, emotions, and behavior are out of sync. They feel stuck and see no way out of their current situation, dilemma, or circumstance. They may feel desperate, afraid, angry, ashamed, sad, or even indifferent.

Client Expectations and Experience

Many clients come into counseling to be fixed or to have the counselor fix someone else in their environment. They may be unsuccessfully coping with family discord, terminal illness, poor grades, job loss, sexual abuse, alcoholism, an ordinary life transition, or a myriad of other concerns. They see the counselor as someone who will listen, understand, and help them. Based on their past experiences, clients' perceptions about counseling vary. They may assign the counselor a preconceived role. They may have little or no experience with counseling. Cultural values will be part of their expectations. Many expect that the counselor will solve their problems, give them a magic answer, or take their pain away. They may come expecting to take a test that will tell them what to do with their lives. Many expect that they will be a passive recipient of the counselor's wisdom and expertise.

Counseling is not a simple matter of solving something. Instead, the counselor will assist the client in understanding that he is the only one who can do the solving, the only one who, in fact, is the expert in himself. The counselor's job is to help the client to understand the nature of counseling and the role of the counselor. Counseling can require not only understanding the issue initially brought to the counselor, but also how the issue fits within the general life pattern. The counselor will help the client recognize this and ultimately reach goals. Many clients find the professional counseling relationship to be a source of support that brings lifelong meaningful change. Many find it a place for reflection and a foundation for learning new information and practicing new behaviors.

Most people have tried every other means of solving their problems before they enter the counselor's door. They seek help with their problems because they want to think, feel, or behave differently. These individuals come to counseling voluntarily. Some people, however, do not seek counseling of their own volition. They may not believe that there is anything wrong with their thoughts, feelings, or behavior. They see no need to make changes. These people are forced to seek help by an authority outside of themselves. People in this category include adolescents who are referred to the school counselor for disruptive classroom behavior, those of all ages who have been mandated to seek help by the court systems for problems such as substance abuse or criminal behavior, for cognitive dysfunction, or for conditions of a divorce settlement and the like. They may not wish to be helped and they may be more difficult to help than those who want to make changes. Involuntary clients can be among the most challenging a counselor will encounter. They may feel they have been coerced and have little motivation to change. However, counselors learn skills that have the potential to be as effective with these clients as they are with those who come voluntarily.

Self-Disclosure and Risk Taking

People who come for counseling are courageous. A person who seeks help from a stranger puts herself in a position of vulnerability. The client knows that she may need to disclose information she might not want to disclose to even her closest family or friends. She is justifiably anxious or scared. The client takes a risk by exposing who she is to the counselor. She gives the counselor a part of her "being" in hopes that the counselor can make a difference. The client must be able to trust that she will not be hurt or abused in the process. This takes courage. Clients are less likely to disclose attitudes, feelings, and beliefs or to describe their actions unless they believe their counselor to be trustworthy. Throughout the counseling relationship the client will take risks in order to reach a successful outcome. The risk may be to relive painful experiences or discuss perceived faults and past failures. Or it may be trying new experiences and attempting new behaviors. The counselor's job is to create a therapeutic environment in which honest self-disclosure and healthy risk-taking can take place. The counselor must begin to build a trusting relationship, discover the nature of the problem, and develop a working plan to treat it. The counselor must understand psychopathology (mental disorder) and its assessment (diagnosis) as well as normal developmental issues and the cultural/contextual factors that affect the client. The counselor must engage in appraisal of the client.

Client Appraisal

Appraisal is central to treatment planning. Treatment begins the first minute of the first contact with a client. The counselor must gather enough specific and concrete information to make an accurate appraisal and develop a treatment plan that will help the client to function more successfully. Assessment, whether by observation, structured questioning, or testing, is essential.

Psychopathology

How do we distinguish between normal and abnormal? Between what is adaptive and maladaptive? Between functional and dysfunctional? Psychopathology, or a mental disorder, may be diagnosed when maladaptive, or dysfunctional behavior, thoughts, or feelings are (a) invasive, (b) enduring, (c) harmful, and (d) all-encompassing. When applied to mental disorders, the term abnormal (maladaptive or dysfunctional behavior or mental distress) implies a disruption in one or more levels of functioning in basic living skills, fundamental health and hygiene, work or school, and relationships. It can also imply some disruption in the understanding of reality. In order to determine the extent of abnormal functioning, a counselor performs some analysis of these factors through a process of diagnosis. Helping professionals use a common diagnostic system, *The Diagnostic and Statistical Manual of Mental Disorders-5* (DSM-5) (American Psychiatric Association, 2013), a method of classification that codifies mental disorders. Within the United States, it is the universally accepted and applied system that allows helping professionals to understand their clients. However, it is important to know that the DSM is not without substantial controversy. Many believe that its use results in labeling of clients that may dehumanize them. Labels can turn human beings into their disorders ("he's a bipolar;" "my next borderline is here"), rather than viewing them as distinct and unique individuals who happen to manifest symptoms that can be categorized. In addition, conceptualizations of mental disorders delineated in the DSM are themselves manifestations of an American/Eurocentric worldview to which many other cultures do not subscribe.

   Nevertheless, the DSM informs the discourse between and across related professions. It also allows for a system of uniform record keeping and accountability.

> DSM is intended to serve as a practical, functional, and flexible guide for organizing information that can aid in the accurate diagnosis and treatment of mental disorders... DSM has been used by clinicians and researchers from different orientations... all of whom strive for a common language to communicate the essential characteristics of mental disorders presented by their patients.
>
> (DSM-5, xli)

Developmental Issues

However, not all clients manifest psychopathology and not all counselors work with those with mental disorders. Clients may be experiencing difficulties in making life transitions, or having problems in living. Earlier in this chapter, professional counselors were described as working with their clients from a developmental perspective. Human development is defined as "the pattern of change that begins at conception and continues throughout the human life span... [and] involves growth, although it also includes decline brought on by aging and death" (Santrock, 2015, p. 4). Developmental issues, then, are life-span issues that are normal, and include predictable stages of growth and change as well as maintenance and regulation of one's capacities in later life (Baltes & Smith, 2003; Rowe & Kahn, 2015). Human beings progress through stages of development that "occur in a fixed sequence of maturation and are often related to age and maturity" (Gladding, 2018, p. 47). At each stage of development, humans accomplish developmental tasks unique to that stage of development, in order to grow and function normally. For example, at about the same general time, infants will smile, crawl and walk; young children will hop, skip, and run; older children will play games with rules; teenagers will increase in critical thinking skills and test the boundaries of their actions; younger adults will seek career identities, life partners and have children; and older adults will lose a spouse, leave the workforce, and so forth. Counselors are trained to understand and assess development stages.

Often transitions from one developmental stage to another involve adjustment, stress, or confusion. Emotional discomfort can accompany a particularly difficult transition. Change, although normal, can be stressful, even emotionally debilitating. Transition points often bring people into counseling. There are times when normal developmental tasks are not accomplished at the expected life stage, or not at all. There are times when people experience not only problems in living but actual trauma for which they need a counselor's assistance. Counselors work in prevention and wellness as well as in remediation and intervention and assess client functioning along a continuum of mental wellness to psychopathology. A discussion of appraisal continues in the section on "Assessment and Testing" in Chapter 5.

Counselor/Client Relationship

Therapeutic Alliance

If counseling is to be effective, the counselor and client form a therapeutic alliance, or a working relationship. This relationship is so essential that effective counseling is not likely to take place without it. The strength of the alliance between the client and the counselor or therapist can lead to a successful outcome, even more than the client problem, particular theory of counseling or therapy, or even the qualities of the counselor or therapist (Corey & Corey, 2015; Norcross, 2001; Ribeiro, Ribeiro, Gonçalves, Horvath, & Stiles, 2013). In order to create a therapeutic relationship the client must develop a strong level of trust in the counselor. The counselor, not the client, is responsible for building trust. This is accomplished through counselor actions that convey respect, acceptance, caring, and warmth. Counselors share their reactions – thoughts and feelings about the client's issues – with genuine concern and empathy. The counselors comport themselves in such a way that their personal characteristics are evident and congruent. In order to reach goals, the client enters into a collaborative association with the counselor. Counseling is a trusting journey taken by counselor and client. Counselors hold to the belief that people are capable of self-directed growth when involved in a collaborative, therapeutic relationship.

Optimal Core Conditions for Effective Counseling

The person-centered approach introduced by Rogers (1951) emphasizes the optimal core conditions necessary for building a therapeutic relationship in which effective counseling can take place. The core of the therapeutic relationship is respect for and belief in the clients' potential to cope with his life circumstances and to change what needs to be changed. The emphasis is on the person's innate striving for self-actualization. The counselor creates a permissive, growth-promoting environment that helps the client examine his thoughts, feelings, behaviors, and his personal and social environment; encourages self-disclosure; and facilitates motivation for change and problem solving. The counselor conveys to the client that the counseling space is psychologically safe and that what he says will be held in confidence. The counselor focuses on the quality of the therapeutic relationship. This means the counselor is authentic in the relationship. She openly expresses feelings and attitudes that are present in the relationship with the client. She learns along with the client. She is genuine, integrated, and authentic, thus serving as a model of a human being striving toward congruence.

Professional versus Social Relationship

The counseling relationship is just as real as any other relationship, yet it is distinctly different. A therapeutic alliance is not a personal friendship. Counseling is not an ordinary social exchange between two people. It can mimic friendship, but it is a professional helping relationship structured by the counselor. The relationship is one of distinct inequality. Status and power are inherent in the counselor's position. The counselor and the client abide by the counselor's rules. The counselor's job is to maintain boundaries and conduct himself ethically. The client's job is to work on her issues. The counseling relationship precludes the counselor from forming any other kind of relationship with the client. It also precludes counseling anyone with whom the counselor has a pre-existing personal relationship.

Diversity

Counselors recognize the importance of cultural competence. Any discussion of counselors and clients would be incomplete without grounding in the importance of diversity and issues of race, ethnicity, gender, sexual orientation, age, disability, religion, and socio-economic class. Counselors continually work toward understanding the worldview of diverse others. They are proactive in seeking to understand and interact with those who are unlike themselves along many dimensions. To do so, counselors continually work on a strong awareness of their own many dimensions. Their ethnicity, race, gender, age, class, status, and much more have shaped their worldview. Awareness of both their own and others' worldviews can contribute to counselor effectiveness. Lack of awareness can detract from it. To remain unaware is to risk inadvertently harming the client through ethnocentric judgments; that is, assuming that behaviors profoundly influenced by the European-American cultural context are expressions of all human behavior rather than expressions of only one cultural possibility (Jun, 2018; Lee, 2018; McAuliffe & Associates, 2013; Neukrug, 2016).

Counselors are multiculturally skilled and at the same time, do not make stereotypical assumptions about their clients because of their backgrounds. They do not view culture as a fixed set of unidimensional values and beliefs. "People are not stereotyped as possessing a set of static and generalized values, orientations, and ways of relating; they are not simply a manifestation of their nation, race, or ethnicity" (Guindon & Sobhany, 2001, p. 273). Human beings are fundamentally flexible and capable of an inherent ability to change.

Understandably many individuals prefer to receive help from a culturally similar counselor. Nevertheless, this is not always possible. Thus, counselors must be not only culturally sensitive but also culturally competent. They must translate their cultural understanding into skills that are discernable and helpful to the client. For example, clients differ in their levels of emotional openness, ways of communication, and expectations of counseling based on their own cultural experiences. The "reality of their problems (i.e., their experience of the problem) is a reflection of their cultural beliefs, education, occupation, religious affiliation, social class, and their past experience with mental health problems and treatment" (Guindon & Sobhany, 2001, p. 276). Cultural competency is a lifelong, skill-building process. Throughout their professional lives, counselors continue acquiring the skills necessary to identify and implement the techniques that are most effective with any client who seeks their help.

Thoughts, Feelings, Actions, and Context (TFAC)

The Introduction of this text presented the importance of congruence. Congruence in counselors means that they strive for an appropriate match between thoughts and feelings, between feelings and actions, and between actions and thoughts. They must also bring into awareness and understand the contextual factors that influence them across their thoughts, feelings, and actions. The chart in this chapter will assist you in monitoring yourself across the TFAC dimensions, as all effective counselors must. Continue to write in your journal about material in this chapter for each block in Table 2.2.

Energy spent on acting one way while feeling another, or thinking one thing and saying something opposed to that thinking, is stifling to healthy growth and mental wellbeing. Incongruence leads to stress, inauthenticity in life, and many times, unhappiness. In fact, incongruence will keep you from reaching your goals, including the goal of becoming a professional counselor.

There are times, of course, when people choose not to act on what they feel. They recognize a feeling and can bring into awareness. They consider why the feeling is present and then make a decision (think through) how they want to act. For example, you may be angry with a work colleague but it would not be appropriate to lash out either physically or verbally. That is not what congruence means. Congruence means that you can bring into awareness the fact that you are angry, recognize the source of the anger, and, if appropriate, discuss that source with the colleague in terms that will allow you and the colleague to reach a constructive result.

Summary

This chapter presented topics related to the identity of the professional counselor and differentiated it from other helping professions. It looked at the characteristics that those who wish to become counselors bring into the profession and described the additional characteristics that trainees will acquire as they progress through their programs of study and beyond. These are the traits of the ideal counselor. The role of values and personal awareness and congruence were emphasized. The chapter continued with a discussion of the kinds of clients that counselors are likely to encounter. It introduced the necessity of appraisal and the concepts of normal, abnormal, psychopathology, and diagnosis. It discussed the importance of viewing clients as having normal developmental issues or problems in living. The chapter presented a discussion of the client/counselor relationship and ended with a section on diversity.

Never take anything or anyone for granted and laugh a lot.

– a beginning counseling student

References

Ahia, C. E. (2003). *Legal and ethical dictionary for mental health professionals*. New York: University Press of America.

American Counseling Association. (n.d.). *10 Things to Know about Counselors and Counseling*. Retrieved from https://www.counseling.org/about-us/about-aca/aca-media-center

American Psychiatric Association. (2013). *Diagnostic and statistical manual of mental disorders* (5th ed.). Washington, DC: Author.

Baltes, P. B., & Smith, J. (2003). New frontiers in the future of aging: From successful aging of the young old to the dilemmas of the fourth age. *Gerontology, 49*, 123–135.

Brems, C. (2001). *Basic skills in psychotherapy and counseling*. Belmont, CA: Wadsworth, Brooks/Cole.

Carkhuff, R. (2017). *Toward effective counseling and psychotherapy*. New York: Routledge.

Corey, M. S., & Corey, G. (2015). *Becoming a helper* (7th ed.). Boston: Cengage.

Gladding, S. T. (2017). *Counseling: A comprehensive profession* (8th ed.). Upper Saddle River, NJ: Prentice Hall.

Gladding, S. T. (2018). *The counseling dictionary: Concise definitions of frequently used terms* (4th ed.). Alexandria, VA: The American Counseling Association.

Guindon, M. H., & Sobhany, M. S. (2001). Toward cultural competency in diagnosis. *International Journal for the Advancement of Counselling, 23*(4), 1–14.

Jun, H. (2018). *Social justice, multicultural counseling, and practice: Beyond a conventional approach.* Cham: Springer.

Kottler, J. A., & Brown, R. W. (2000). *Introduction to therapeutic counseling: Voices from the field.* Belmont, CA: Wadsworth/Brooks/Cole.

Kottler, J. A., & Shepard, D. S. (2015). *Introduction to counseling: Voices from the field* (8th ed.). Stamford, CT: Cengage.

Lee, C. C. (Ed.). (2018). *Multicultural issues in counseling: New approaches to diversity* (5th ed.). Alexandria, VA: American Counseling Association.

McAuliffe, G., & Associates (2013). *Culturally alert counseling: A comprehensive introduction* (2nd ed.). Thousands Oaks, CA: Sage Publications.

Neukrug, E. (2016). *The world of the counselor: An introduction to the counseling profession* (5th ed.). Boston: Cengage.

Norcross, J. C. (2001). Purposes, processes, and products of the task force on empirically supported therapy relationships. *Journal of the Division of Psychotherapy, 38*, 345–356.

Nystul, M. S. (2015). *Introduction to counseling: An art and science perspective.* Sage.

O'Reilly, M., & Lester, J. N. (2017). *Examining mental health through social constructionism: The language of mental health.* Palgrave Macmillan.

Peterson, J. V., & Nisenholz, B. (1999). *Orientation to counseling* (4th ed.). Boston: Allyn & Bacon.

Ribeiro, E., Ribeiro, A. P., Gonçalves, M. M., Horvath, A. O., & Stiles, W. B. (2013). How collaboration in therapy becomes therapeutic: The therapeutic collaboration coding system. *Psychology and Psychotherapy: Theory, Research and Practice, 86*, 294–314.

Rogers, C. (1951). *Client-centered therapy: Its current practice, implications, and theory.* Boston: Houghton Mifflin.

Rowe, J. W., & Kahn, R. L. (2015). Successful aging 2.0: Conceptual expansions for the 21st century. *The Journals of Gerontology: Series B, 70*, 593–596.

Rudes, J., & Gutterman, J. T. (2007). The value of social constructionism for the counseling profession: A reply to Hansen. *Journal of Counseling & Development, 85*, 387–392.

Santrock, J. W. (2015). *Life-span development* (15th ed.). New York: McGraw-Hill Education.

Segall, M. H., Dasen, P. R., Berry, J. W., & Poortinga, Y. H. (1990). *Human behavior in global perspective: An introduction to cross-cultural psychology.* New York: Pergamon Press.

Tolbert, E. L. (1959). *Introduction to counseling.* New York: McGraw-Hill.

Table 2.2 *TFAC Chart – Thought, Feelings, Actions, and Context Who Am I? Who Are Others?

Self	My Thoughts	My Feelings	My Actions	My Context	Other? (Specify)
My Effective Characteristics: What are my strengths?					
My Effective Characteristics: What are my areas for strengthening?					
My Effective Characteristics: What can I do to improve?					
What are my concerns?					
Others	**Others' Probable Thoughts**	**Others' Possible Feelings**	**Others' Observable Actions**	**Others Apparent Context**	**Other? (Specify)**
What characteristics do others in my class exhibit?					
What characteristics does my instructor exhibit?					
What else can others tell me?					

*For more information on TFAC, see Chapter 1.

Chapter 3

What? Answers about the Meaning of Counseling, Its Past, Its Present, and the Future

Mary H. Guindon and Jessica J. Lane

What is now proved was once only imagined.

– William Blake

POINTS TO PONDER

- What is a counselor?
- How did counseling develop into a distinct profession?
- Where does the body of knowledge for counseling come from?
- What are the major professional counseling organizations?
- What is the future of counseling?

What Is Counseling?

Everyone knows the word counselor, and most have a pretty good idea what it means. "Counselor" conjures up images of a person to whom others go for help with emotional, situational, psychological, or practical issues. From the beginning of human society, some members of every community have been such helpers. They attempted to heal emotional suffering and mental illness. They were empathic, caring, and trusted individuals to whom others turned with their problems. These helpers were the shamans, witchdoctors, mothers, aunts, fathers, uncles, and elders of their communities. Across the world, there is a widely held certainty that under the right conditions some members in every society are able to help others navigate their problems in living. It is a cross-cultural experience (Egan, 2019). The people to whom one goes for help are likely to be seen as more experienced or wiser than the one seeking help. When we have trouble figuring things out for ourselves we may seek others' good counsel; we want advice and guidance to help us cope with whatever life may throw at us. Those to whom we turn for such counseling are known to be skilled in helping others conquer life's challenges. Counselors who fit this definition continue to be with us. They might be a trusted friend, mentor, pastor, revered teacher, indigenous healer, or any number of others who offer (usually) sound support and direction. They generally have a pre-existing relationship with those that seek their assistance. In the broadest sense of the word, these were and continue to be counselors who offer support, guidance, and advice.

This is different from the socially sanctioned helpers that we know as professional counselors and the related helping professionals. An individual who practices the vocation of professional counseling has obtained a masters or doctorate in counseling and has passed competency tests. Professional counselors offer help and sometimes advice as people go through the normal stages and transitions of a lifetime. Counseling is a process that offers assistance and is mostly confined to persons in a place where a professional is listening intently, checking in to be sure that the client(s) is understood in both cultural and psychological sense, and moving toward some outcomes that enhance the client's wellbeing (Bernard & Hackney, 2017). They offer sound support and direction without usually being personally involved with the recipient of their counseling or having other kinds of relationships with them. Torrey (1986) suggests that a counselor is socially sanctioned, one whose specialty is offering help by talking and listening in order to stimulate people to change in their thoughts or actions or both so that difficulties in interpersonal relationship or problems with thoughts about the self are no longer experienced.

Kaplan, Tarvydas, and Gladding (2014) define *counseling* as "a professional relationship that empowers diverse individuals, families, and groups to accomplish mental health, wellness, education, and career goals" (p. 368). It is a collaborative effort between the counselor and the client. It is an interactive process that facilitates a greater understanding of the client and his environment; it involves clarifying values and establishing goals for future behavior. "Counseling is a professional relationship that empowers diverse individuals, families, and groups to accomplish mental health, wellness, education, and careers goals," (American Counseling Association, n.d.).

Clearly, counseling as a profession is more comprehensive, formalized, and structured than the counseling described in the first paragraph of this chapter. It has evolved from counseling as an activity practiced by many people across time and in all cultures to counseling as a profession. Professional counselors' roots are grounded in the history of human thought, philosophy, religion, psychology, sociology, anthropology, and education.

History

As far back as antiquity, counselors were teachers and religious leaders who guided and inspired. Moses, Jesus, Buddha, and Mohammed are examples of the religious leaders whose prudent counsel was sought. In the West, Greek philosophers Socrates, Plato, and Aristotle served as early teachers and mentors. In the Far East, Loa-Tzu and Confucius offered wise guidance. In the seventeenth century, European philosophers such as Descartes and Spinoza advanced the understanding of the general meaning of knowledge and experience, as well as the connections between mind and body. The inquiry into human experience continued with the work of John Locke, David Hume, John Stuart Mill, and many more. These philosophers influenced the emergence of psychology as a science (Kottler & Shepard, 2015).

Mental illness and attempts to address it have been with us since the earliest times. Examples include brain surgery of prehistoric peoples, the medical contributions of diagnosis and prognosis of Hippocrates, and the exorcisms of the Middle Ages and beyond. Only in the last two centuries have counseling and psychotherapy emerged as organized ways of helping. In fact, professional counseling today developed as a uniquely American system that drew heavily on the traditions of European and later American psychologists and adapted those traditions to the vocational and educational guidance needs of a fledgling country.

The Early Contributions of Psychology

Wilhelm Wundt influenced the field of psychology by founding the first experimental laboratory devoted to the human mind in Germany in 1879. Wundt asked his subjects to use self-reflection and verbalization as a means of understanding how the mind is structured. In the late nineteenth century Austrian Sigmund Freud, through work begun with his mentor and collaborator Joseph

Bruer, developed the "talking cure," a revolutionary system which first recognized the existence of the unconscious and then developed ways to help emotional suffering through catharsis, or the release of unconscious emotions. Although Freud was by no means the first or only person to address emotional illness, we can credit him with influencing a cadre of followers who at first adhered to his theories and practices and then branched out on their own to adapt, expand, and develop their own systems of talking as a means of helping. Psychologists such as Carl Jung (Analytic Psychology), Alfred Adler (Individual Psychology), Jacob Moreno (Group Psychotherapy and Psychodrama), and others began as Freudian psychoanalysts but developed their own theories and techniques that involved the use of talking to address emotional problems.

In the United States, the first person to be awarded a doctoral degree in psychology was G. Stanley Hall. He went on to found what was perhaps the first psychology laboratory at Johns Hopkins University in 1883. Hall was interested in the mental characteristics of children and later, at Clark University, used the scientific approach to study social problems. He founded one of the first psychology departments. Hall was the primary organizer of the American Psychological Association (APA), founded in 1892. His pioneering work garnered him the name "father of American psychology." Lightner Witmer, who was interested in applying the scientific findings of psychology in practical ways, founded the first psychology clinic in 1896 at the University of Pennsylvania. Witmer was also influential in the creation of school psychology. Behavioral psychologists made contributions as well. Expanding Pavlov's work on classical conditioning, John Watson conducted scientific experiments on human behavior and learning through reinforcement that influenced both psychology and education. William James was the first to use the title of professor of psychology at the end of the nineteenth century. James' (1913) work focused on the functions of the mind and the role of emotions, thoughts, reasoning, and behaviors. He and his colleagues investigated individuals' "free will" and conscious functioning.

Psychological and educational testing also began at the end of the nineteenth century. In France, Alfred Binet developed the first intelligence test, a unifactor construct. Its purpose was classroom placement of the mentally retarded. In the United States, Wechsler developed intelligence testing based on multifactor constructs (Anastasi & Urbina, 1997). Its purpose was to test various mental abilities rather than only one factor.

Clifford Beers also influenced the profession. He was hospitalized for bipolar depression and suicide attempts several times and found the conditions abhorrent. His book, A Mind That Found Itself (1908), advocated reform in the treatment of the mentally ill. He stated, "I hope to rob insanity of many of its terrors – at least those which do not rightly belong to it" (p. 4). His work led the way for the mental health movement. William James wrote the foreword to his book. Together, they provided the catalyst for the formation of the National Committee for Mental Hygiene and the National Mental Health Association. This was a major precursor of mental health counseling. Clifford Beers also was instrumental in developing the child guidance movement, and the Clifford W. Beers Guidance Clinic is still active today in treating children and their families.

Shortly after this period of time, existential and phenomenological psychology emerged out of the field of philosophy. Existentialists began to study the very existence of nature and to consider the meaning of reality as it related to the human mind. Its major American proponent, Rollo May (1996), challenged the idea that mental health means living without anxiety. He believed anxiety was essential to the therapeutic process and had the potential to lead to self-realization.

The Early Contributions of Vocational Guidance

At about the same time that psychology was developing and solidifying itself as a distinct profession during the nineteenth century, the social reform movement was underway in the

United States. Social workers worked with the poor, psychiatrists changed the way the mentally ill were treated, and educators instituted more humanistic methods in the classroom. All developed ideas and programs that led to the ideals that informed the practice of vocational guidance. This early period in the formation of the counseling profession primarily concentrated on guidance programs and activities.

With the burgeoning of the industrial age grew a parallel need for skilled workers in the North. The Civil War and its aftermath increased the need for a specialized workforce and led to an awareness of the need for vocational guidance. In 1881, Salmon Richards may have been the earliest person to advocate a guidance and counseling profession. He recommended that vocational assistance in every town be offered to those who may need it (Brown & Srebalus, 2003). He and other pioneers contributed to the growing awareness that individuals could develop more fully when they were directed or guided. In this time of major social reform, the United States bustled with new immigrants who would do the work required of a new industrial age. Workers needed training and skills in new technological fields. By the beginning of the twentieth century, the field of education spawned new programs to address the need, and vocational guidance was established. In 1908, Frank Parsons brought his interest in social reform to fruition first as director of the Breadwinner's Institute, a civic service program, and then when he organized the Vocational Bureau of Boston (Zunker, 2015). Parsons trained young men to be counselors and managers for YMCAs, schools, colleges, and businesses. In May of 1908, Parsons presented a report that described systematic guidance procedures. He died in September of that year. His landmark book, *Choosing a Vocation*, published in 1909, had an immediate impact and Parsons became known as the Father of Vocational Guidance. He believed that the best conditions for vocational success occur when career choices are based on matching personal traits with job factors. His procedures led the way to placing individuals in work settings that matched their skills and abilities, a revolutionary idea at the time.

His work spread quickly. Boston created the first counselor certification program. Harvard University adopted it, thus becoming the first college-based counselor education program (Schmidt, 2013). Boston's school superintendent designated over 100 elementary and secondary teachers to become vocational counselors. By 1910, 35 school systems across the country did the same. In the same year, the First National Conference on Vocational Guidance was held in Boston. Three years later, the first professional organization for counselors, National Vocational Guidance Association formed. This was a forerunner of what would become the American Counseling Association of today.

Parsons was not the only influence on the growth of the guidance movement. Jesse B. Davis is credited with creating the first known systematized school guidance program. In the Grand Rapid, Michigan school system in 1897 he began a program of vocational guidance and moral education. Ten years later in 1907 he encouraged English teachers to provide lessons in guidance to build character and prevent behavioral problems. His visionary work in guidance as a means of teaching students how to cope with life events and prevent possible problems was the precursor of what would one day become school counseling.

The federal government also had a role in the formation of the fledgling counseling field. For example, the Smith-Hughes Act of 1917 mandated funding for public schools to provide vocational education. World War I also contributed as the military began to test and place personnel to meet manpower needs. Counseling and guidance were important aspects of the placement process. The Army commissioned the development of several assessment instruments to measure aptitudes, abilities, and personality traits for screening purposes. At the end of the war, these instruments were used with civilians, particularly those transitioning to a peacetime country. Psychological testing grew more common and psychometrics became an integral area of psychology. Because the work of early counselors was testing oriented, vocational guidance became known as a more "scientific" endeavor than previously. This led to a legitimization of the fledgling profession and to a stronger professional identity. During the 1920s, guidance gained acceptance. However, because of its reliance on testing and the expert model, vocational guidance became known as the "test 'em and tell 'em" profession. Gains in acceptance were at the expense of incorporating developments from other behavioral sciences into guidance and counseling. As a result, those activities that created the guidance movement also led to its criticism. Its narrow focus began to be challenged and counselors wanted a broader role.

The Development of the Counseling Profession

The Trait and Factor Theory. E.G. Williamson and his colleagues at the University of Minnesota developed a trait and factor theory that led to Williamson's work, *How to Counsel Students* in 1939. This theory, also known as the Minnesota point of view, grew out of Frank Parson's work but was more comprehensive in the sense that it could be used with issues other than vocational decision making. It became the first formalized approach to counseling. The idea was that people possess *traits* (aptitudes, abilities, personalities, interests, and so forth) that can be combined in various ways to form *factors*, or constellations of characteristics. Counseling involved applying problem-solving procedures in a rational, scientific way that assisted clients to think or behave more productively and to become effective decision makers. Williamson's trait and factor theory was the predominant counseling approach, as distinct from Freud's psychoanalysis, throughout the next two decades.

Influences in the 1940s. Perhaps the greatest influence on the development of the counseling profession as distinct from either psychology or vocational guidance was the work of Carl Rogers. His first book *Counseling and Psychotherapy* (1942) challenged the trait and factor approach of Parsons and Williamson. He also challenged the assumptions and theories of psychoanalysis. He suggested that a nonjudgmental approach was the basis for effective treatment. Rogers believed that human beings are responsible for their own growth. He espoused the view that clients should be given respect and treated with what he termed "positive regard." In a climate of acceptance and genuineness, people are capable of making changes. He advocated for new techniques and methods that would honor the individual's ability to make healthy life choices. Rogers' work widely influenced the direction that vocational guidance, education, and psychotherapy would take. It infused a humanistic orientation to counseling and moved the profession from vocational guidance alone to a broader, more encompassing orientation.

A second important influence was World War II. Just as in World War I, the military needed improved methods of psychological testing. The war also created a need for civilian workers, and women entered the workforce in unprecedented numbers. With the change of women's roles came a lasting shift in perception of the work women could do. After World War II, the needs of returning disabled soldiers and others led to programs, particularly group counseling services, for veterans. The effects of World War II on soldiers and their loved ones and the work of the Veterans Administration (VA) also influenced the practice of family therapy. With these changes came a need for new ways of providing counseling services. The federal government funded training for counselors to institutions of higher education through the U.S. Office of Education. The VA funded financial aid to students in the form of stipends and grants for counselor training. It rewrote the standards for vocational counselors and created the term "counseling psychologist" (Gladding, 2012). These factors influenced graduate education programs to create and refine curricula for counselor education. For the first time, counseling was a profession distinct from vocational guidance, traditional psychoanalysis, and psychology.

Federal initiatives influenced mental health and community counseling as well. In 1946, the National Institute of Mental Health (NIMH) was established and the National Mental Health

Act authorized funds for research and training and for assistance to states for prevention, diagnosis, and treatment of people with mental disorders.

Influences of the 1950s. The decade of the 1950s is perhaps the most influential period of time in the advancement of professional counseling through the development of humanistic theories, federal legislation, and the establishment of professional organizations.

In 1951, Carl Rogers published his second and major work, *Client-Centered Therapy: Its Current Practice, Implications, and Theory.* Rogerian counseling – or nondirective, client-centered counseling – became the major focus of counselors' work. This was the dominant training of helping professionals throughout the 1960s and 1970s. Rogers believed that clients need a safe environment in which to address and resolve their problems. A therapeutic relationship between the counselor and the client is key. Rogers' techniques of acceptance, genuineness, and unconditional positive regard in an atmosphere of trust and nondirective communication became the hallmark of counseling and remain one of its major tenets today, particularly with regard to rapport and relationship building. Nevertheless, client-centered counseling was not without its limitations and critics. Although most counselors are trained in client-centered techniques, today many question its applicability to numerous diverse populations and various issues.

Other approaches and theories contributed and influenced the direction of professional counseling. In 1951, Fritz Perls and his colleagues published *Gestalt Therapy: Excitement and Growth in the Human Personality*, which outlined more directive yet humanistic ways of counseling. They focused on here-and-now awareness in contrast to the there-and-then focus of psychoanalysis. In 1953, B.F. Skinner first introduced behavioral therapy through research findings and greatly influenced education and counseling. The next year, Abraham Maslow helped to found humanistic psychology and went on to develop his now famous Hierarchy of Needs. In 1957, Albert Ellis introduced the methods of Rational Emotive Therapy (RET) and later expanded his work to its current form, Rational Emotive Behavior Therapy (REBT). These theories, discussed later in this book, are the early basis of the thoughts, feelings, actions (TFA) model used in this primer. (The concept of context did not enter the profession for many more years.)

Another significant theorist who began his work in the 1950s was Donald Super (1957). He was to become one of the most influential theorists of career development in the profession. From his career pattern study – a longitudinal study of 100 men from ninth grade through age 35 – he developed a theory of lifespan career development. He extended his research and refined his theory until his death in 1994.

The federal government influenced the direction of counseling through its legislation in this decade. Two major acts were to have far-reaching effects. In 1954, the Vocational Rehabilitation Act (VRA) mandated counseling services and authorized training funds for counselors to work with the disabled, including those with mental disabilities. The most significant legislation of the 1950s was the National Defense Education Act (NDEA) of 1958. In response to the Russian launching of Sputnik, funds were allocated for improving math and science performance in secondary schools and to promote the development of talented students in the United States. Title V of this act provided grants to provide counseling services in schools and to train school and career counselors in institutions of higher education. As a result, the number of counselors in schools increased dramatically and the 1960s became a boom era for school counselors and counselor educators.

The 1950s were years of active professional development. Two key organizations were established in 1952. Eliminating the word "guidance" from a previous division, the American Psychological Association (APA) chartered Division 17, the Division of Counseling Psychology. APA members, who wanted to work with clients with normal, development concerns rather than with the psychopathological patients treated by clinical psychologists, influenced its formation.

In the same year, the American Personnel and Guidance Association (APGA) was created to meet the needs of those interested in guidance, counseling, and personnel. It was formed from existing organizations: The American College Personnel Association, the National Association of Guidance Supervisors and Counselor Trainers, the National Vocational Guidance Association, and the Student Personnel Association for Teacher Education. The Counseling Association for Humanistic Education and Development (C-AHEAD) was also a founding association. The following year, the American School Counselors Association (ASCA) joined APGA and in 1958, the American Association of Rehabilitation Counselors (AARC), now the American Rehabilitation Counseling Association (ARCA), was chartered.

Other significant events occurred in the 1950s. The American Psychiatric Association published the first *Diagnostic and Statistical Manual of Mental Disorders* (DSM) in 1952. The DSM marked the start of the modern mental illness classification system. Antipsychotic medications were developed for use with the mentally ill, ushering in a new era in treatment through drugs. As a result, many psychiatric patients were released from inpatient mental hospitals and were allowed to receive treatment in outpatient centers. This decade also saw an influx of college counselors and the beginnings of college counseling centers.

Influences in the 1960s. The political unrest of the 1960s influenced the direction of professional counseling. The Civil Rights Movement, the Vietnam War, and toward the end of the decade, the Women's Movement, all played roles in changing the direction of professional counseling. Each underscored the need for theories that addressed the whole of society and the special needs of diverse groups. Up until this point, three major approaches to counseling existed: psychodynamic (i.e., psychoanalytic approach), directive (trait and factor), and client-centered (Rogerian). Although the work of Ellis, Perls, and Skinner had begun earlier, in the 1960s their approaches entered the repertoires of counselors with greater frequency.

Others joined them. Robert Carkhuff, who had studied with Rogers, researched and then operationalized Rogers' three core conditions for therapeutic change of empathy, congruence, and unconditional positive regard. He published the results in a landmark book, *Towards Effective Counseling and Psychotherapy* (Truax & Carkhuff, 1967). Aaron Beck published a psychological model proposing that thoughts play a significant role in the development and maintenance of depression. Bandura's behavioral work, Glasser's reality theory, the communication approach of transactional analysis, and existential approaches all had an influence on counselor activities. They are also discussed later in this book.

The government continued to play an important role. In 1962, The Manpower Development Training Act established counseling and guidance services to the disadvantaged and underemployed. The Community Mental Health Centers Act of 1963, one of the most sweeping and significant acts dealing with mental health needs of Americans, mandated the creation of mental health centers in over 2,000 locations and gave counselors opportunities to be employed outside of educational settings. These community centers offered direct counseling, outreach, and many other services in surrounding neighborhoods, or catchment areas. Community mental health centers also addressed alcoholism and drug abuse and offered substance abuse treatment.

The 1964 amendment to the NDEA Act of 1958 called for the addition of elementary school through junior college counselors. The Elementary and Secondary Education Act (ESEA) of 1965 further expanded the role of counselors and the services they could provide.

Professional organizations grew and began to become more specialized in the 1960s. In 1961, APGA published its first code of ethics and in 1964 recommended that the organization form branches in every state and foreign country. 1965 saw the chartering of the National Employment Counselors Association (NECA). In 1968, branches were given more authority through APGA's bylaws. Regional representatives were able to serve on the APGA board of directors for the first time.

Influences of the 1970s. The legislation of the 1960s opened the door for professional counselors to be employed in a variety of organizations such as mental health centers and clinical community settings by the 1970s. According to Kottler and Brown (2000), "At one time, 80 percent of all students enrolled in counseling programs were following a school-based employment track" (p. 33). The 1970s saw an influx of students who wanted to be trained to work outside of the school systems as community and mental health counselors. The term community counselor was introduced in the 1970s (Lewis, Lewis, Daniels, & D'Andrea, 2011) and came to describe those counselors who worked outside of education settings. Counselor education programs began to offer specialized training to accommodate this trend.

Thus, the established counseling profession that had previously focused mainly on educational settings experienced growth and expansion. New ways of doing counseling refined the work of Rogers and others. This was the period in which the terms helping skills and basic counseling skills began to be used to specify what counselors actually do. Approaches introduced by Egan (1970, 1975), Ivey (1971), and Carkhuff (1971) and his colleagues (Carkhuff & Anthony, 1979) outlined training in basic counseling skills that continue to be in use today and form the basis of the basic attending skills presented in the second part of this primer. The use of techniques associated with Gestalt and cognitive/behavioral theories and existential approaches increased.

Federal legislature again played a role. The Rehabilitation Act of 1973 mandated vocational services and employment counseling for those with severe physical and mental disabilities. In 1975, the U.S. Congress expanded the original Community Mental Health Centers Act to mandate a total of twelve services from the original five. These initiatives and others created a greater need for helping professionals of all kinds.

As the number of counselors in non-educational settings increased, so did a need for credentialing on parity with psychologists and social workers. Through the advocacy of APGA, licensure for counselors succeeded. Virginia was the first state to license professional counselors in 1976. Arkansas and Alabama followed shortly thereafter and the Licensed Professional Counselor (LPC) became a reality.

Professional organizations grew stronger and more active. Charters were granted to 56 branches and many local chapters. The Association of Counselor Educators and Supervisors (ACES) developed guidelines for counselor training at the master's and doctoral levels. The American Mental Health Counseling Association (AMHCA) was chartered by APGA and became one of its largest divisions. APGA also chartered the Association for Specialists in Group Work (ASGW) in the 1970s. Additional divisions were chartered to meet the specialized needs and interests of APGA members. The Association of Religious and Values Issues in Counseling later became the Association for Spiritual, Ethical, and Religious Values in Counseling (ASERVIC) of today (originally the National Catholic Guidance Conference). The Association for Non-White Concerns in Personnel and Guidance founded during this time is today the Association for Multicultural Counseling and Development (AMCD), and the Public Offender Counselor Association evolved into the present International Association of Addictions and Offender Counselors (IAAOC).

During the 1970s, APGA grew beyond its title. Professional counselors, although still part of schools and institutions of higher education, had moved into community agencies, mental health centers, substance abuse centers, hospitals, business and industry, and private practice. The words personnel and guidance no longer represented APGA's membership adequately, yet it was to be another decade before its name was changed.

Influences in the 1980s and 1990s. Before the 1980s, most counselors did not take an inclusive, diverse worldview of counseling processes or clientele. Theories were developed by and for the dominant, white culture, usually by males without an understanding of gender, race, ethnicity, sexual orientation, social economic class, and other issues of diversity that can affect how counselors offer services. Theories and their related techniques were assumed to be applicable to all peoples whatever problems brought them into counseling. When changes were not forth-coming, the client was blamed for her lack of progress. She was considered to be resistant or untreatable. As a result of the Civil Rights Movement and the Women's Movement, members of the helping professions recognized a need for change and a focus on multiculturalism in train-ing and services began. The Council for the Accreditation of Counseling and Related Helping Professions (CACREP) made changes by including in its standards the category of multicultural counseling. It required the infusion of multicultural competencies in curricula of graduate pro-grams. Since that time, research in diverse populations has exploded in the academic literature and new ways of doing counseling continue to proliferate and influence theory and practice.

These two decades saw the expansion and further professionalization of counseling. In 1981, CACREP was created with the purpose of setting up standards of training. Its task was to accredit schools that offer counselor education programs so that counselor training met a minimum stand-ard of knowledge and practice. Master's level standards for school, community, mental health counseling, and others are discussed below. In the same year, APGA established the National Board of Certified Counselors (NBCC), which administers the National Counselor Examination (NCE). This is the test that counselors take to become National Certified Counselors (NCCs) and is now used by a majority of the states as their state licensure exam. In 1997, 44 states and the District of Columbia had counselor licensure or certification. With the signing of legislation in California in 2009, professional counselors are now licensed in all 50 states and the District of Columbia. In 2009, there were approximately 45,000 NCCs worldwide.

Professional associations grew. In 1983, the APGA changed its name to the American Association for Counseling and Development (AACD) and changed again in 1992 to its present name, the American Counseling Association (ACA). Chi Sigma Iota, the counseling honorary society, founded in 1985 at Ohio University, spread quickly throughout the United States. Its mission is "to promote scholarship, research, professionalism, leadership, advocacy, and excel-lence in counseling, and to recognize high attainment in the pursuit of academic and clinical excellence in the profession of counseling" (Chi Sigma Iota, n.d.).

ACA chartered new associations to fit specialized needs in this time period. They included the Association for Counselors and Educators in Government (ACEG) in 1984, the Association of Adult Development and Aging (AADA) in 1986, the International Association of Marriage and Family Counselors (IAMFC) in 1989, and the American College Counseling Association (ACCA) in 1991). The latter was formed to give a professional home to college counselors within ACA when one of its founding members, the American College Personnel Association (ACPA) disaffiliated in 1992 to become an independent association. In 1996, a new division, the Association of Gay, Lesbian, and Bisexual Issues in Counseling (AGLBIC) was chartered.

The ACA actively pursued several professionalization initiatives during the 1990s. In 1995, the Governing Council created new identity, mission, and vision statements. It rewrote its mis-sion statement in 2005 to reflect the current status of its members today.

SIDEBAR 3.1

In Practice: What Would You Do?

Curt is a counselor at a career center of a community college in the Northwest. In addi-tion to working with the students in academic and career choices, his services are open to the members of the community in his county. In the course of his work, he often provides personal counseling when it impacts on career decisions.

David came in to see me hoping he could get back to school. He has finished three years of college in pre-med. Five years ago he was in a bad auto accident. He sustained a head injury. He says he's been through rehab and got a "clean bill of health" two years ago. The only permanent difficulty seems to be problems with memory. He says he has no problem memorizing facts and doesn't want any special accommodation in the classroom. Then he tells me he's sometimes "unsure of what he was supposed to do." When I tried to get more information, David got upset with me saying, "Things will never get better. The only thing that would help is to go back to before the accident! You can't help me."

Class Discussion

1. What, if anything, can Curt do to assure David that counseling is appropriate for him?
2. What might Curt set as counseling goals with David?
3. Given what you have learned about vocational guidance, what might help David?
4. Given what you have learned about counseling as a distinct profession, what approaches to counseling might help David?

Professional Counseling Today

Today ACA's mission has been refined to "promote the professional development of counselors, advocate for the profession, and ensure ethical, culturally-inclusive practices that protect those using counseling services," (American Counseling Association, n.d., mission and strategic plan, section 3). There are now over 100,000 credentialed professional mental health counselors and innumerable credentialed school counselors in the United States and 19 ACA-chartered divisions. Counselors for Social Justice (CSJ) was chartered in 2000 and the Association for Creativity in Counseling in 2004. Each division governs its activities independently and has representation on the national ACA governance board. Additionally, ACA Interest Networks are part of the ACA Connect Community and offer opportunities to connect, collaborate, and network with other counselors of similar interests and expertise. These networks include the ACA Ethics Interest Network, ACA Interest Network in Integrated Care, ACA Interest Network for Professional Counselors in Schools, ACA International Counseling Interest Network, Animal Assisted Therapy in Mental Health Interest Network, Distance Learning in Counseling Education, Forensic Counseling Interest Network, Grief and Bereavement Interest Network, Historical Issues in Counseling Network, Interest Network for Advances in Therapeutic Humor, Intimate Partner Violence Interest Network, Multiracial/Multiethnic Counseling Concerns Interest Network, Network for Jewish Interests, Neurocounseling Interest Network, Sexual Wellness in Counseling, Sports Counseling Interest Network, Traumatology Interest Network, Veteran's Interest Network, Wellness Interest Network, and Women's Interest Network.

At this writing, membership stands at 54,000. ACA has 56 chartered branches in the U.S., Europe, and Latin America that are divided into four regions. Each branch and region has its own governance as well. New areas of practice for counselors continue to develop and branches continue to grow. For example, in late 2018, Chi Sigma Iota, the counseling honorary society, had 5 regions, and 400 chapters with over 125,000 initiated members and continues to grow each year by approximately 7,000 members.

Political battles and turf wars previously meant the exclusion of professional counselors as providers of mental health services beyond educational settings. This has changed and continues to change as counselors' highly competent skill levels are more widely acknowledged. "The knowledge of what works and what does not and with whom is a huge factor in determining not only what to do, but also who should be doing it" (Guindon & Richmond, 2005, p. 93). The ACA continues to advocate for the inclusion of counselors in multiple organizations, including insurance providers, Health Maintenance Organizations (HMOs), and the federal government. Since 2006, after many years of advocacy by the ACA and AMHCA, mental health counselors are providers on parity with social workers at the Department of Veterans' Affairs (VA). The provision, included in S. 3421, the Veterans Benefits, Healthcare, and Information Act, opened up the VA health care system to mental health counselors, increasing access to care for veterans. Although rehabilitation counselors have been providing readjustment services for many years, mental health counselors were excluded until this act established Public Law 109-461, which provided explicit recognition for mental health counselors. In November 2009, The House of Representatives passed major health insurance reform legislation, H.R.3962, the Affordable Health Care for America Act. "The legislation includes a provision, in Section 1308 of the legislation, establishing Medicare coverage of medically-necessary outpatient mental health services provided by state-licensed professional counselors and state-licensed marriage and family therapists" (American Counseling Association, 2009, para. 1). Updates to the Affordable Care Act have allowed Medicare to cover care provided by psychiatrists, psychologists, mental health clinical nurse specialists, and clinical social workers. At the time of this writing, Medicare does yet include licensed professional counselors (LPCs) but ACA continues to advocate for their inclusion.

At the present time, H.R. 6157 was signed into law. This bill includes funding for important initiatives for school counseling and mental health. Funding for opioid response, child traumatic stress, national suicide prevention lifeline, and telehealth programs as well as funding to establish partnerships to train school counselors and mental health professionals for low-income communities are also part of this legislation. ACA members advocated for Senate and House approval for these efforts to benefit school counselors and other areas of mental health.

Types of Counseling Today

Today's professional counselors provide varying types of services. *The Occupational Outlook Handbook* (OOH) (U.S. Department of Labor, 2019) classifies counselors in several categories: (a) school and career counselors; (b) rehabilitation counselors; (c) substance abuse, behavioral disorder, and mental health counselors; and (d) marriage and family therapists. The OOH also presents information on gerontological, multicultural, genetic, and college student affairs counselors.

What do professional counselors who work in such diverse settings have in common? Of course, they are trained as counselors rather than in other related disciplines. The typical master's degree in counseling, regardless of specialization, is 48 credit hours, with some programs offering 60 credit master's degrees.

Professional counselors are first and foremost knowledgeable about the essential areas described by CACREP and NBCC and then go on to have specialized training beyond basic counseling courses. Basic courses are grouped into eight core areas: professional counseling orientation and ethical practice, social and cultural diversity, human growth and development, career development, counseling and helping relationships, group counseling and group work, assessment and testing, and research and program evaluation. This chapter oriented you to the history of the profession and its context today. Chapter 2 discussed the five essential characteristics of a profession. These are: (a) a common body of knowledge acquired through specialized training; (b) a national or international organization that oversees its standards, competencies, and credentialing; (c) a clear identity of its practitioners as members of the profession; (d) a prescribed and formalized code of ethical conduct; and (e) sanctioned and legal recognition at the national and state level. The following two chapters include information about the common body of knowledge for the counseling profession, those eight core areas that will be included in your program of study. CACREP and NBCC govern the common body of knowledge of professional counseling. These sister organizations of ACA oversee national standards, competencies, and credentialing. CACREP sets standards of training and the NBCC administers the NCE, which assesses these standards.

Professional counseling has established itself as a fully functioning member of the helping professions. In recent years, advocacy (for clients as well as the profession), social justice interventions to reduce institutional and social barriers for clients, issues of trauma, spirituality, and the continued growth of technology and tele-counseling have created new specializations. Most recently, the profession has begun addressing emergency preparedness by considering the "emerging roles of counselors during times of crises, disasters, and other trauma-causing events" (Beckett, 2008, p. 1).

Beyond the 2020s

A survey of private practice and community agency counselors conducted by Wesley J. Erwin of Minnesota State University Moorhead as reported in a *Counseling Today* article (Rollins, 2008) indicated the responses about future specialty areas chosen by 224 ACA members. They are Internet addiction, Internet sexual predators, working with racially/ethnically diverse clients, wars, and working with the elderly as the most significant emerging issues. A preponderance of ACA Division leaders interviewed for the same article pinpointed Internet addiction and pornography as important new issues. Other emerging issues indicated by this group of leaders included traumatic stress, natural disasters, concerns of military families, effects of technology, cyberbullying, changes in the nature of work, and job stress.

Beginning in 2005, the ACA spearheaded *20/20: A Vision for the Future of Counseling*. Approximately 30 counseling organizations met and collaborated on an initiative to further define the counseling profession and its direction (Kaplan et al., 2014; Kennedy, 2008). The group published *Principles for Unifying and Strengthening the Profession*, with 29 of the 30 counseling organizations endorsing seven principles that are critical to the future of the profession to provide one voice and collective vision.

These are:

- Sharing a common professional identity is critical for counselors.
- Presenting ourselves as a unified profession has multiple benefits.
- Working together to improve the public perception of counseling and to advocate for professional issues will strengthen the profession.
- Creating a portability system for licensure will benefit counselors and strengthen the counseling profession.
- Expanding and promoting our research base is essential to the efficacy of professional counselors and to the public perception of the profession.
- Focusing on students and prospective students is necessary to ensure the ongoing health of the counseling profession.
- Promoting client welfare and advocating for the populations we serve is a primary focus of the counseling profession (Kaplan & Gladding, 2011, p. 372).

Counseling as a distinct profession continues to grow around the world. New ways of accommodating diversity will increase internationally as well as in the United States. New, more culturally sensitive interventions in school settings will become more necessary and more commonplace as our immigrant populations grow. An emphasis on a positive rather than a deficit model of counseling will become more prominent. Increasing advocacy, support, and education of the benefits of counseling will be important, and providing a multicultural and social justice framed lens in working with all clients will be necessary. At the time of this writing, clients working through trauma, substance abuse, technology addiction and cyberbullying, adolescent suicide and suicidal ideations, or spirituality and gender identity issues are current concerns and will likely continue to be growing areas of need.

As society has become more mobile, people seek counseling for issues that they might have confided to a neighbor, friend, or family member in earlier generations. Counseling will expand in its recognition as the helping profession for everyday problems of living. In addition, professional school counseling is evolving into a model that will both fit the needs of the students in the rapidly changing society, and conform to the demands of school reform and accountability mandates, while working as leaders and advocates in schools to remove barriers to student success (Erford, 2018).

Professional Identity

You are in the process of developing a professional identity. This is not an easy endeavor. You must have self-awareness and self-confidence to be open to the cognitive, emotional, and behavioral changes you will make in order to be a successful counselor. Fully understanding how your own personal and professional identity can impact clients will make you a more effective practitioner. Specifically, the personal and the professional are intertwined facets that contribute to making counselors more confident and effective in serving the needs of their clients (Corey, 2013; Halbur & Halbur, 2015). Professional counselor identity includes a grounding in counseling history and philosophy; professional roles, functions, and relationships with other human service providers; professional credentialing; professional organizations; public and private policy processes and advocacy processes for the profession and clients; and ethical standards and legal considerations. Knowledge of these factors forms the basis of the counselor-in-training's initial vocationalization, or the individual's vocational socialization into a profession.

Summary

This chapter began by defining counseling in several ways, ending with the current ACA definition. Presented next was a history of counseling beginning with early healers and helpers. It discussed professional counseling as a uniquely American profession drawing on the contributions of psychology, particularly from Europe, and of the vocational guidance movement in the early part of the twentieth century in the United States. The influences of the succeeding decades and their contributions to the emergence of counseling as a distinct profession were presented. Included was an orientation to the American Counseling Association (ACA), its branches, divisions, functions, and types. This chapter ended with a discussion of professional counseling today and professional identity.

> *Until a few days ago, I had no idea how much counselors do. Now I have some idea what they do but no idea what I want to do!*
>
> – student's online comment to ACA website assignment

References

American Counseling Association. (2009). *ACA in the news: House passes major health care reform bill, including medicare coverage of counselors!* Retrieved from http://www.counseling.org/PressRoom/News Releases.aspx?AGuid=5357488a-894c-42d6-8fb2-0df167fed35b

American Counseling Association. (n.d.). *Our vision and mission: ACA's strategic plan.* Retrieved from https://www.counseling.org/about-us/about-aca/our-mission

Anastasi, A., & Urbina, S. (1997). *Psychological testing and assessment* (7th ed.). New York: Macmillan.

Beckett, C. (2008). CACREP's emergency preparedness efforts commended. *The CACREP connection*, Spring 2008. Alexandria, VA: Council for the Accreditation of Counseling and Related Educational Programs.

Beers, C. (1908). *A mind that found itself.* New York: Longman Green.

Bernard, M. J., & Hackney, L. H. (2017). *Professional counseling: A process guide to helping* (8th ed.). Boston, MA: Pearson Education (Merrill Counseling).

Brown, D., & Srebalus, D. J. (2003). *Introduction to the counseling profession* (3rd ed.). Boston: Allyn and Bacon.

Carkhuff, R. R. (1971). Training as a preferred mode of treatment. *Journal of Counseling Psychology, 18,* 123–131.

Carkhuff, R. R., & Anthony, W. A. (1979). *The skills of helping: An introduction to counseling.* Amherst, MA: Human Resource Development Press.

Chi Sigma Iota. (n.d.). Our mission. Retrieved https://www.csi-net.org/

Corey, G. (2013). *Theory and practice of counseling and psychotherapy* (9th ed.). Belmont, CA: Brooks/Cole.

Egan, G. (1970). *Encounter: Group processes for interpersonal growth.* Pacific Grove, CA: Brooks/Cole.

Egan, G. (1975). *The skilled helper: A problem management approach to helping.* Pacific Grove, CA: Brooks/Cole.

Egan, G. (2019). *The skilled helper: A problem-management and opportunity-development approach to helping* (11th ed.). Boston: Cengage.

Erford, T. B. (2018). *Orientation to the counseling profession: Advocacy, ethics, and essential professional foundations* (3rd ed.). Boston, MA: Pearson.

Gladding, S. T. (2012). *Counseling: A comprehensive profession* (7th ed.). New York: Pearson.

Guindon, M. H., & Richmond, L. J. (2005). Practice and research in career counseling and development--2004. *The Career Development Quarterly, 54,* 90–137.

Halbur, D. A., & Halbur, K. V. (2015). *Developing your theoretical orientation in counseling and psychotherapy* (3rd ed.). Hoboken, NJ: Pearson Education (Merrill Counseling).

Ivey, A. E. (1971). *Microcounseling: Innovations in interviewing training.* Springfield, IL: Thomas.

James, W. (1913). *The principles of psychology.* New York: Henry Holt & Co.

Kaplan, D. M., & Gladding, S. T. (2011). A vision for the future of counseling: The 20/20 principles for unifying and strengthening the profession. *Journal of Counseling & Development, 89,* 367–372.

Kaplan, D. M., Tarvydas, V. M., & Gladding, S. T. (2014). 20/20: A vision for the future of counseling: The new consensus definition of counseling. *Journal of Counseling & Development, 92,* 366–372.

Kennedy, A. (2008, November). Next step taken in shaping profession's future. *Counseling Today, 51,* 40–43.

Kottler, J. A., & Brown, R. W. (2000). *Introduction to therapeutic counseling: Voices from the field.* Belmont, CA: Wadsworth/Brooks/Cole.

Kottler, J. A., & Shepard, D. S. (2015). *Introduction to counseling: Voices from the field* (8th ed.). Stamford, CT: Cengage.

Lewis, J. A., Lewis, M. D., Daniels. J. A., & D'Andrea, M. J. (2011). *Community counseling: A multicultural-social justice perspective* (4th ed.). Belmont, CA: Brooks Cole, Cengage.

May, R. (1996). *Meaning of anxiety.* New York: W. W. Norton & Co.

Parsons, F. (1909). *Choosing a vocation.* Boston: Houghton Mifflin.

Perls, F. (1951). *Gestalt therapy: Excitement and growth in the human personality.* Oxford: Dell (originally published in 1951).

Rogers, C. (1942). *Counseling and psychotherapy.* Boston: Houghton Mifflin.

Rogers, C. (1951). *Client-centered therapy: Its current practice, implications, and theory.* Boston: Houghton Mifflin.

Rollins, J. (2008, July). Emerging client issues. *Counseling Today, 51*, 30–41.

Schmidt, J. J. (2013). *Counseling in schools: Comprehensive programs of responsive services for all students* (6th ed.). Boston: Pearson.

Super, D. E. (1957). *The psychology of careers.* New York: Harper.

Torrey, F. E. (1986). *The mind game: Witchdoctors and psychiatrists.* Lanham, MD: Rowman & Littlefield Publishers.

Truax, C. B., & Carkhuff, R. R. (1967). *Towards effective counseling and psychotherapy.* Chicago, IL: Aldine.

United States Department of Labor. (2019). *Occupational outlook handbook.* Retrieved from https://www.bls.gov/ooh/

Williamson, E. G. (1939). *How to counsel students: A manual for clinical counselors.* New York: McGraw-Hill.

Zunker, V. G. (2015). *Career counseling: A holistic approach* (9th ed.). Boston: Cengage.

Table 3.1 *TFAC Chart – Thought, Feelings, Actions, and Context

Self	My Thoughts	My Feelings	My Actions	My Context	Other? (Specify)
When I consider the history of counseling, what stands out for me the most?					
Which professional organizations attract me?					
What can I do now to get involved in state and national professional organizations?					
What are my concerns?					
Others	Others' Probable Thoughts	Others' Possible Feelings	Others' Observable Actions	Others' Apparent Context	Other? (Specify)
What might those in related helping professions know about counselors?					
What is the professional identity of my professors and instructors?					
What are professional counselors doing to advocate for counselors?					

*For more information on TFAC, see Chapter 1.

Chapter 4

What? Answers about the Body of Knowledge

Ethics, Social and Cultural Diversity, Human Growth and Development, and Career Development

Mary H. Guindon

> *To the small part of ignorance that we arrange and classify we give the name knowledge.*
> – Ambrose Bierce

POINTS TO PONDER

- How are ethics, morals, and the law distinguished?
- What must counselors do to ensure their ethical behavior?
- What is a dominant worldview?
- How does worldview develop and change?
- How does human behavior develop and change?
- What is the meaning of "career" in its broadest sense?
- What are the standards for career interventions at different developmental stages?

A professional counselor's identity is grounded in the standards of knowledge set by CACREP in Section 2 of the 2016 Standards: Professional Counseling Identity. You must demonstrate a good knowledge in each of these eight common core curricular experiences: 1) Professional Counseling Orientation and Ethical Practice, 2) Social and Cultural Diversity, 3) Human Growth and Development, 4) Career Development, 5) Counseling and Helping Relationships, 6) Group Counseling and Group Work, 7) Assessment and Testing, 8) Research and Program Evaluation. These areas comprise the basic course requirements in your counseling program of study. Part One of this primer is devoted to Standard 1, Professional Orientation and Ethical Practice. Part Two addresses the seven entry-level counseling specialty areas. Part Three addresses the basic parts of Standard 5, Helping Relationships, and presents the most basic essential interviewing and beginning skills you must master. Chapter 2 presented those parts of Standard 5 that address counselor characteristics and behaviors that influence helping processes. This chapter and the next present an overview of the common core curricular experiences that will be included in your professional counseling program of study. It reviews and summarizes the fundamental elements of each of these core areas. We will turn first to that part of Standard 1 that speaks to an important aspect of professional orientation, namely ethical principles and legal considerations.

Ethical Principles and Legal Considerations

(CACREP Standard, Section 2F-1i)

Ethics is an essential element in professional counseling and the related helping professions. Ethics in general develop from a need of a society and professions adopt codes of ethics to "ensure common standards... and guide professionals through the pitfalls of practice" (Ponton & Duba, 2009, p. 119). It is so important that it is included in each of the core areas of study. Ethical standards in general serve three purposes: To educate members about sound ethical conduct, to provide a mechanism for accountability, and to serve as a means for improving professional practice (Erford, 2018.) Each course within your counseling program will include ethical and legal issues.

Ethical behavior is one of the major tools with which counselors conduct their professional and, indeed, personal lives. State licensure laws require a specific course of study in ethical and legal issues. Every counselor is responsible for thoroughly knowing and understanding the ethical codes of his profession. This includes not only the codes of ACA and APA but also the codes of each specialty in which he practices (e.g., ASCA, NCDA, AMHCA). Websites to codes of ethics of various related helping professions are listed in Appendix B, "Internet Resources for Professional Counselors."

Few ethical dilemmas are black and white. Most are open to interpretation and judgment. Ethical codes provide guidelines for professional conduct but they do not necessarily provide definitive answers to the unique, complex circumstances that arise during the practice of counseling. Nevertheless, counselors are bound by their code of ethics. Although codes vary somewhat across disciplines, and individual work settings may have additional ethical guidelines, there are a number of common points. Many situations also have legal consequences. Before discussing ethical and legal issues specific to counseling, we must define some terms.

Morals, Ethics, and the Law

The meanings of morals and ethics vary. The meaning of law is clearer cut. Ahia (2003) differentiates these terms in the *Legal and Ethical Dictionary*:

Morality –Judgments as to whether a human act conforms to the accepted rules of righteousness or virtue, which implies the application of religious standards (p. 43)

Morals – Conduct or behavior related to one's belief structure regarding the nature of right or wrong. Morals, as with morality, imply a religious standard (p. 43).

Ethics – A branch of study of philosophy concerning how people ought to act toward each other, pronouncing judgments of values about those actions. A hierarchy of values that permits choices to be made based on distinguished levels of right or wrong. Ethics usually involves a judgment of human decisions or behaviors against an accepted standard primarily in non-religious context or situation (p. 26)

Ethical principles – Higher order norms within a society consistent with its moral principles and which constitute higher standards of moral behavior or attitude. The application of ethical rules and principles to determine what is the right moral decision when an ethical dilemma arises. It focuses on the objective, rational, and cognitive aspects of the decision-making process (p. 26).

Law – Basic rules of order as pronounced by a government. Statutory law refers to laws passed by legislatures and recorded in public documents. Case law or common law refers to the pronouncements of courts (p. 37).

Ahia differs from some authors about the inclusion of religion in the above definitions; other authors do not preclude the significance of spirituality in morals (Herlihy & Corey, 2015). Whatever your own moral stance and religious beliefs, you are expected to abide by your ethical code, even though you do so voluntarily. You must also abide by the law. Much of the time, morals, ethics, and the law will be in concert. They are based on the principle of helping rather than harming a client. Codes of ethics recognize the relationship between ethics and law. When morals, ethics, and the law are in conflict, the counselor must make a decision based on a set of values. Personal values influence how one views counseling and the manner in which we interact with clients, including the way we conduct client assessments, our views of the goals of counseling, the interventions we choose, the topics we select for discussion in counseling session, how we evaluate progress, and how we interpret client's life situations (Corey, 2013).

Gladding (2012) asserts, "Counselors who are not clear about their values, ethics, and legal responsibilities, as well as those of their clients, can cause harm despite their best intentions" (p. 58).

Ethical Decision Making

A code of ethics is intended to formalize statements that ensure the protection of clients' rights and set forth guidelines for professional conduct. Making ethical decisions can be difficult. In many instances, no one definitive answer is readily available. Counselors must analytically evaluate ethical standards and guidelines in applying principles in their practice (Herlihy & Corey, 2015). Ethical judgments can vary by setting and across cultures and are influenced by the tasks performed (e.g., career testing versus diagnosis of psychopathology). A set of ethical guidelines should be established by broad consensus through a set of values based on "universal truths": the principles of not killing, causing pain, or depriving freedom (Corey, Corey, & Callanan, 2015; Neukrug, Lovell, & Parker, 1996; Remley & Herlihy, 2007). Most people agree that ethical codes are designed to safeguard the public and guide professionals in their work so that they can provide the best service possible (Corey, Corey, & Callanan, 2015).

Professional ethical behavior is directed by these principles:

- *autonomy*, or fostering the right to control the direction of one's life;
- *non-maleficence*, or avoiding actions that cause harm;
- *beneficence*, or working for the good of the individual and society by promoting mental health and well-being;
- *justice*, or treating individuals equitably and fostering fairness and equality;
- *fidelity*, or honoring commitments and keeping promises, including fulfilling one's responsibilities of trust in professional relationships; and
- *veracity*, or dealing truthfully with individuals with whom counselors come into professional contact (American Counseling Association, 2014, p. 3).

Decision analysis helps counselors make the best possible decision in any given circumstance, clarify values, evaluate possible outcomes, and create rationality in what can be an intuitive process (see Cottone & Claus, 2000). Forester-Miller and Davis (2016) offer the following guidelines:

1. *Identify the problem.* Gather as much information as possible and be specific and objective.
2. *Apply Codes of Ethics.* Once the problem is clarified consult ACA and state codes of ethics for the appropriate action or solution. If the problem is not resolved, Forester-Miller and Davis point out that a complex dilemma exists and additional steps should be taken.
3. *Determine the nature and dimensions of the dilemma.* Steps to take include determining the ethical principles listed above take precedence and priority; consulting applicable professional literature; seeking out opinions of supervisors and more experienced counselors; and consulting with state and national professional organizations (e.g., ACA's Center for Counseling Practice, Policy, and Research). Professional judgment is necessary at this stage.
4. *Generate potential courses of action* by brainstorming solutions.

5. *Consider the potential consequences* of all options and determine a course of action.
6. *Evaluate the selected course of action.* At this step, Forester-Miller and Davis suggest applying Stadler's simple tests of justice, publicity, and universality (see Stadler, 1986). When satisfied that your solution to the complex dilemma passes all three tests, you then move to the last step:
7. *Implement the course of action.* This can be a difficult step, even when it is the right course of action.

Ethical Standards

You are held to ethical standards of ACA or APA or both from the day you become a counselor-in-training. The *2014 ACA Code of Ethics* (see https://www.counseling.org/docs/default-source/ethics/2014-code-of-ethics.pdf?sfvrsn=2d58522c_4) consists of nine standards:

- the counseling relationship;
- confidentiality and practice;
- professional responsibility;
- relationships with other professionals;
- evaluation, assessment, and interpretation;
- supervision, training, and teaching;
- research and publication;
- distance counseling, technology, and social media;
- resolving ethical issues.

The *Standards* define how you will conduct yourself as an ethical counselor in the ordinary course of your professional life. This is the place you will go for guidance when ethical dilemmas occur. You should learn these now and apply them throughout your educational experience. The ACA website has myriad resources available to assist counselors (see https://www.counseling.org/knowledge-center/ethics#ethicsresources). These include ethical decision making and ethical consultation services, and a podcast about the 2014 Code of Ethics. In addition, ACA's magazine, *Counseling Today*, offers a monthly column by leading experts on actual ethical or legal situations. Past columns are archived on the resources website.

Some of the major standards, among the many, to which you must adhere are introduced here.

Confidentiality, right to privacy, privileged communication, informed consent, and duty to warn. Clients share personal and private information with their counselors. Without assurance of *confidentiality*, clients would be unlikely to self-disclose the thoughts and feelings so essential to therapeutic change. Confidentiality protects the client from unwanted and unauthorized disclosures of facts about their personal lives. Trust and respect are essential ingredients of the counseling relationship. Trust allows the client to feel safe enough to self-disclose. Respect means the counselor understands that the client has a *right to privacy*, that nothing that is said in a counseling session will be revealed without his expressed consent. The client holds the right to privacy. It is guaranteed by the Fourth Amendment of the U.S. Constitution. Clients have the right to choose how, when, and if they will disclose or withhold information. Confidentiality is the counselor's professional responsibility. To breach confidentiality is an invasion of privacy.

Confidentiality and right to privacy should not be confused with *privileged communication*, another right guaranteed by the fourth amendment. By definition, the client's communication is legally protected from being disclosed in a court of law without his expressed consent. The client, not the counselor, also holds this privilege. The client is usually the only person who may waive this privilege. Communication is only privileged with counselors who are legally certified or licensed in their state of practice.

Because each state can vary in its interpretation of confidentiality and right to privileged communication, you need to find out the circumstances in your state. In most but not every state, laws about privileged communication are similar to the right afforded the legal and medical professions. As of 2018, the licensure board of 21 states and the District of Columbia have adopted the ACA Code of Ethics into their rules and regulations.

At the outset of the counseling interview, the counselor must explain counseling and its parameters through the process of *informed consent*. The counselor must inform the client about rights and responsibilities of the counselor and the client, including the limits to confidentiality, right to privacy, and privileged communication, as well as review the nature and process of counseling. Obtaining informed consent is the counselor's ethical and legal obligation. This is generally accomplished during the intake session or at the beginning of the first session through a written statement of disclosure. The statement also includes the counselor's professional qualifications, areas of expertise, billing information, office hours, course of action in case of emergency, and grievance procedures. In group work, additional information must be included. Clients have the right to know how group members are prescreened and how members will be protected in the group. If the counselor wants to share information about the client, she must obtain written consent. For example, the counselor may want to consult with another professional or transfer records to another helping professional. Before this happens, the client is informed and asked to sign a release form.

Exceptions to confidentiality must be explained at the outset of counseling. These include the possibility of danger to the self or another and abuse of a minor. In these cases, the counselor informs the client that she is taking action and does not need the client's consent to do so. Counselors have the obligation to protect their clients and are required to protect others from their clients when they have the knowledge to do so. In the latter case, the counselor has a legal *duty to warn*. This means if the counselor determines that what the client discloses indicates that he has the means and will to harm another and the counselor judges that the harm is imminent, she must break confidentiality in order to warn the person of the impending danger.

Multiple relationships. Multiple relationships occur when the counselor takes on more than one role with a client during treatment or at a later time. The counselor is obligated to protect the welfare of the client. The counseling relationship is one in which the counselor is privy to information he would not have had in any other circumstances. Relationships outside of the counseling relationship, therefore, can be problematic unless they can be shown to be potentially beneficial. Counselors who decide there is no potential for harm to clients or their family members may only enter into nonprofessional relationships when they can show that such interactions are beneficial to all involved, and only with the consent of the client. Circumstances of potential benefit include attending weddings and graduation parties, visiting hospitals, or exchanging goods or services. Counselors must document in their records the rationale, potential benefit, and anticipated positive consequences of a multiple relationship.

Professionals believe that nonprofessional relationships with clients, former clients, their significant others, and their family members should be avoided. Romantic or sexual relationships are prohibited for a period of at least five years following the last professional counseling contact (American Counseling Association, 2014), including both in-person and electronic interactions or relationships. The potential for harm and exploitation of the client must be seriously considered even beyond the five-year minimum.

Legal Considerations

The law also dictates professional counselors' behavior. A range of legal issues may impact on practice. These include the possibility of being sued for malpractice, testifying in court in cases of child abuse or divorce, having records subpoenaed, and meeting the requirements of certain laws or court rulings. Ethical codes provide for the suspension or expulsion of those who act unethically and irresponsibly. Although not common, perhaps the most common case involves sexual intimacy between therapist and client, a clear violation of ethical standards. Other common cases are failure to report child abuse and failure to warn the intended victim of harm by a client.

Counselors may be subject to malpractice or criminal liability complaints. Whenever a complainant believes ethical sanctions alone to be inadequate to redress a wrong, both civil and criminal suits can be brought against counselors. You need to be aware of potential legal implications of your work. You must thoroughly understand and adhere to laws having to do with child abuse, right to privacy, privileged communication, duty to report and protect, and duty to warn. This knowledge protects the public and also protects the counselor from spurious claims.

Social and Cultural Diversity

(CACREP Standard, Section 2F-2)

Professionals in today's world recognize the importance of a counselor's awareness, knowledge, and skills in working with clients who might be diverse with respect to race, ethnicity, SES, gender, sexual orientation, spiritual affiliation, disability, and age. Most of the theories and practices in the helping profession were developed with a Eurocentric worldview – by predominantly male, white Europeans or Americans of European descent for use with individuals like themselves. Their contributions are significant; they are the basis of professional counseling. Yet, traditional counseling may not be effective for a large segment of our population. Those from nondominant cultures and minority groups seek counseling less often or tend to terminate counseling sooner than their white, dominant culture counterparts. For these individuals, the Eurocentric nature of counseling continues to be problematic, especially in the current divisive climate and distrust.

Nevertheless, past practices inform present realities. Established techniques can lead to successful outcomes when suitably used in a culturally sensitive context (Sue & Sue, 2016). However, when counselors, knowingly or inadvertently, limit their knowledge of human behavior to individuals in a single society they are guilty of ethnocentric judgments. They may believe that behaviors influenced by factors specific to the cultural context of the United States may be expressions of all human behavior rather than expressions of only one cultural possibility out of many possibilities. We live in a global community; a preponderance of professional literature today concerns diverse populations rather than populations in general without attention to diversity. Hence, issues of diversity and cultural and social factors are integral to your ongoing training throughout your program of study and throughout your career. Both contextual research and practice integrate factors of social and cultural diversity into the knowledge base. Factors such as work, family, gender, community, race, ethnicity, social class, sexual orientation, and others must be considered in treatment and practice. As the population of the world becomes more diverse, the practice of psychotherapy must follow suit (Prochaska & Norcross, 2018).

Culture and Diverse Worldviews

Culture can be conceptualized in various ways. It can be defined as the shared values, beliefs, and practices associated with a given cultural group. It includes language and ways of behaving in the world. It also implies common life patterns and expectations of others. It encompasses an individual's worldview. When culture is defined mainly as values and beliefs, it can assume a static, frozen worldview and implies practices that cannot change. It makes little allowance for the adaptability and flexibility of human beings or for the active role they play in directing their unique worldviews as they grow and change throughout life.

Culture can also be defined as national affiliation, or race and ethnicity, or a system in change. Culture seen as simply national affiliation does not allow for other important factors such as poverty, lack of education, or deprived social status. The failure to distinguish such differences can lead the counselor to confuse reactions to poverty and discrimination with psychopathological problems. Some mistakenly believe race and ethnicity to be interchangeable terms. "Race is a socially constructed category that specifies identification of group members based on physical characteristics of genetic origins. Ethnicity is a sense of belongingness on the part of the individual to a common origin in terms of history, ancestry, nationality, language, and religion" (Guindon & Sobhany, 2001, p. 272).

Nevertheless, recent advances in genetics have changed the very meaning of race. Migration and Diaspora have led to new ideas of what it means to belong for many individuals. "They can change, add to, or reject cultural elements through social processes such as migrations and acculturation" (Guindon & Sobhany, 2001, p. 273). This is an important distinction for counselors to understand. Corey (2013) believes it is a good idea for counselors to ask clients to provide them with the information they need to work effectively. Specifically, this means incorporating culture into the therapeutic process (Corey, 2013). A culturally competent counselor has awareness, skills, and knowledge needed to address cultural issues and their intersections in the therapeutic process (Halbur & Halbur, 2015). There may be discrepancies between the counselor's and clients' perceptions that can affect intervention and treatment. For clients, the reality of their problems is embedded in culture. It echoes their cultural beliefs, education, occupation, religious affiliation, social class, and possibly their position within a subculture. Section III of the DSM-5 (American Psychiatric Association, 2013) presents diverse ways in which individuals in different cultural groups can experience and describe distress. In fact, it provides a Cultural Formulation Interview (pp. 750–757) to help counselors gather appropriate cultural information. It presents information on how to systematically assess cultural identity, evaluate cultural conceptualization of distress, understand culturally related psychosocial stressors, and consider cultural differences between the counselor and client, and cultural factors relevant to help seeking. The more culturally aware and sensitive you are, the better prepared and able you will be to effectively assist your clients.

Cultural Identity Development

People are unique, of course. Each of us develops our own identity from infancy, childhood, adolescence, and on throughout our lives. Cultural identity develops in the same way. To understand diverse others, we must realize that each person identifies and relates to others from several cultural frames of reference. Most minority individuals identify with more than one culture. Many see themselves as part of the dominant culture in which they live by virtue of their daily interactions in the mainstream culture. They also are part of the racial/ethnic subculture in which they most strongly identify. They may identify with more than one subculture. For example, an individual may be white, gay, and an immigrant; another may be black, a heterosexual female, and born in the South. Each has developed and acculturated in unique ways. Several models recognize stages of cultural identity development for various populations – minority, gender, white, gay and lesbian, and so forth. Most cultural identity models delineate stages that include an early conformity stage, an awareness or dissonance stage, and an integration or resolution stage. In the last stage, people are able to celebrate their own subculture at the same time as they recognize and appreciate positive aspects of other cultures, including the dominant culture.

Cultural Sensitivity and Cultural Competence

Counselors must ensure that they are culturally competent. The best-intentioned counselor may unknowingly have a mistaken understanding of culturally different clients. Counseling does not necessarily work well with a large segment of minority-culture clients for many reasons. According to Prochaska and Norcross (2018), the manifestation of psychopathology is often culturally determined. In particular, clients' complaints conforming to most diagnostic categories can be found throughout the world; the particular symptoms, course, and social response to such diagnoses are often heavily influenced by culture. Neukrug (2016) states that counselors may minimize the impact of social factors, misdiagnose their clients, or misconstrue cultural differences as psychopathology. A counselor may assume that the client fits in or should conform to dominant-culture values. A counselor may be ignorant of his own ethnocentrism, racism, prejudices, or position of cultural (white) privilege. Counselors may not understand cultural differences in the ways emotionally distressing symptoms are described. What may seem abnormal in the United States may be considered normal in another culture. Ways of assessing clients can be biased against minority cultures and thus lead to erroneous conclusions. Moreover, embedded in society is institutional racism, which means that materials used by counselors can also be biased, as can the very assumptions society makes about those who are marginalized by it.

According to Sue and Sue (2013), cultural competence is made up of three basic elements. The counselor must be aware of her own worldview, develop an understanding of the client's worldview, and develop culturally appropriate interventions. To be culturally competent, counselors must continuously update their knowledge about diverse populations of all types. Our civic, professional, and social responsibility obliges us to interact with and accept diverse groups of people. Understanding factors associated with race, ethnicity, social class, gender, age, sexual orientation, disability, immigrant populations, and others take time and a commitment to social justice in a changing world. To be culturally competent also means that one must be aware of the influences of one's own culture on one's cultural identity, and its concomitant prejudices and biases, and work toward broadening of one's worldview. Counselors are privileged to draw on many points of view and incorporate them into their own conceptual view of the world.

As you progress through your own vocationalization as a professional counselor you will also change your own ethnocentric worldview, whatever it may currently be. This profession demands it.

Human Growth and Development

(CACREP Standard, Section 2F-3)

Because professional counselors work with their clients from a developmental perspective at every stage of life, knowledge of the principles of human development is essential. At each stage of development, humans accomplish developmental tasks both unique and relatively predictable to that stage of development. Stages of growth, change, maintenance, and regulation of one's capacities occur throughout life (Santrock, 2015). Counselors must know theories of individual and family development and transition across the lifespan as well as theories of learning and personality development. They must understand a wide range of human behaviors. Although the philosophical underpinning of counseling is developmental, counselors must also gain knowledge of disability, psychopathology, situational and environmental factors, and "crisis, disasters, and trauma on diverse individuals across the lifespan" (Council for the Accreditation of Counseling and Related Educational Programs, 2015, p. 11) plus understand well addictions and addictive behaviors.

The study of human development is complex and holistic, and includes all aspects of growth and change. People are more than their thoughts, feelings, and actions. They are not simply made of discreet pieces of mind, body, behavior, and spirit. They are integrated wholes that include the systems in which they operate such as community, family, school, neighborhood, and nation. Developmental psychology addresses the areas of physical, sensorimotor, cognitive, intellectual, social, emotional, spiritual and moral development from before birth through death. Stages of life are generally categorized into infancy, early childhood, middle childhood, adolescence, young adulthood, middle adulthood, and late adulthood, or old age. As people live longer, researchers have recognized the need for a split in the last category between the young old (65–79) and the old old (over 80). Each of these stages has its own set of developmental tasks.

SIDEBAR 4.11

In Practice: What Would You Do?

Maureen is a high school counselor in an affluent suburb. As a new member of the staff, she spends much of her time consulting with professional staff, presenting school guidance curriculum to the administration, and doing classroom guidance work for tenth graders. She has little time for individual counseling, although she does run an after-school study skills group.

Seventeen-year-old Ruth came to see me in my office after I'd done a stress management lesson in her class. She said she felt she could talk to me. She told me that she has trouble getting her work done. Her records show her grades are dropping. Her family came here from Zimbabwe two years ago to escape "the turmoil." Although her parents are highly educated they now work two jobs each, with long hours in low-paying work. They are rarely home. Ruth is the primary caregiver for her sisters, ages 10 and 7. Two other siblings closer to her age had died before they immigrated. Her parents have also given her responsibility for running the household. Ruth seems tired and run down. She hasn't made any friends since she's been here but says she wouldn't have time for them anyway. She is considering leaving school even though she has just started her junior year, saying her life's work should be caring for her family. When I try to help, she tells me "You don't understand my family's ways." I'm not sure what to do. She's not an adult who should be given so much responsibility!

Class Discussion

1. What ethical concerns does Maureen face? How would you advise her to proceed?
2. What should Maureen do in order to be a culturally sensitive and competent counselor working with Ruth?
3. Considering her developmental life stage and her family background, do you think Ruth's behavior and circumstances are normal or abnormal? Why?
4. What do you think about Ruth's future career development? What kinds of career interventions, if any, might be appropriate for her?

Major Theories of Human Development

The study of human development is a field of its own. More theories of human development, behavior, and personality exist than can be briefly delineated in this text. Major theories that assist counselors in their work address different aspects of development and vary from each other in important ways. You will learn about the work of Piaget, Vygotsky, Erikson, Kohlberg, Gilligan, Levinson, Kegan, Bandura, and many others as you progress through your program of study. Some theorists like Piaget address only childhood development. Others like Levinson address only adulthood. Others offer lifespan developmental theories.

Jean Piaget (1896–1980) influenced research on child development perhaps more than any other individual. According to his cognitive-developmental theory, children adapt to their environments by actively constructing knowledge as they explore the world. As the brain develops and children gain more experiences, they develop significantly different ways of thinking. Piaget (1971) formulated four stages of cognitive development:

1. Sensorimotor (Birth–2 years). Infants think by acting on the environment with their eyes, ears, hands, and mouth.
2. Preoperational (2–7 years). Young children develop the use of symbols to make sense of their earlier sensorimotor discoveries. Thus, language and make-believe play develop but logical thinking has not yet emerged.
3. Concrete operational (7–11). Logical thinking develops as children are able to organize their environments and understand concepts of quantity and simpler math. They can categorize objects into hierarchies of classes and subclasses.
4. Formal operational (11+ years). Children are now able to think abstractly. They can logically use symbols to represent objects beyond their five senses. They are capable of higher math reasoning and can consider potential outcomes beyond those obvious at the concrete stage. Cognition through adolescence into adulthood involves more complex and abstract reasoning.

Erik Erikson (1902–1994), initially a follower of Freud, developed his own psychosocial theory. Erikson (1959/1980) formulated eight stages of development with corresponding psychosexual developmental tasks that must be accomplished. "A basic psychological conflict, which is resolved along a continuum from positive to negative, determines healthy or maladaptive outcomes at each stage" (Berk, 2004, p. 17). Erikson's eight stages of development are:

1. Basic trust versus mistrust (Birth–1 year). As they explore, infants gain confidence that the world is safe and good through warm, responsive caregivers. When infants are treated harshly or must wait too long for comfort, they develop mistrust.
2. Autonomy versus shame and doubt (1–3 years). Children master physical skills and sense of control. When unduly thwarted through overly shaming caretakers, shame and doubt develop.
3. Initiative versus guilt (3–6 years). Through make-believe, children experiment with their potential in the world and the kind of person they might become. Ambition and sense of responsibility develop in children with supportive caregivers whereas over controlling and demanding caregiving leads to guilt.
4. Industry versus diffusion (6–11 years). Children learn competence and develop the capacity for cooperation and work through school. Overly negative experiences from caregivers, teachers, and peers leads to sense of incompetence.
5. Identity versus identity confusion (adolescence). Children at adolescence attempt to answer Who am I? and What is my place in the world? They grapple with values and career goals. Positive experiences lead to positive identity and negative experiences lead to confusion about future adult roles.
6. Intimacy versus isolation (young adulthood). Young adults establish the capacity to form and sustain satisfying intimate relationships. Unsuccessful resolution of this stage results in the inability to form meaningful relationships and isolation.
7. Generativity versus stagnation (middle adulthood). Generativity is defined as the desire to give back to and support the next generation. It can be accomplished in myriad ways. Those

who are not successful in negotiating this stage feels a lack of accomplishment or meaning in life.

8. Ego integrity versus despair (old age). Integrity means the capacity to reflect back on life as worthwhile and the kind of person one became. Satisfaction, wisdom, and reconciliation with death result. If feelings of life satisfaction do not develop, people feel despair and fear dying.

In the years since the Piaget and Erikson developed their theories, much more research has refined, added on to, or even refuted their work. Nevertheless, they are useful guidelines even today. Human development takes place across all dimensions: Biological, physical, behavioral, cognitive, and emotional. It is "complex and nonlinear and cannot be separated from context. Dramatic differences exist in how individuals develop and change throughout life" (Guindon, 2010, p. 45). Nevertheless, in general, development (a) is continuous throughout life; (b) is a combination of genetics and learning (nature/nurture); (c) is unique but sequential and systematic; (d) involves stages of stability and change while the core self remains the same; (e) can be painful in transition from one stage to the next; and (f) is growth-enhancing and positive. At all stages, every individual must negotiate specific developmental tasks. Change is inevitable whether in the more predictable stages of early life or in the less predictable later adult life stages. Individuals do not necessarily progress at the same rates of change through each of the areas of development. For example, at the age of 14, a child might be young for her age in sensorimotor tasks, mature in cognitive functioning, and at average age in social emotional development. How and when individuals manage their developmental changes is influenced by situational and environmental factors. Counselors assist people in managing change successfully or assist those who have not been able to successfully negotiate changes in the past. Thus, a thorough understanding of human development is essential.

Life Transitions

Many clients first seek help at developmental transition points across the lifespan. Individuals can expect many transitions to occur over a lifetime even though the nature or sequence of those occurrences cannot always be predicted. People either manage transitions well or they do not, and counselors can be of enormous benefit to clients at critical life points. A *transition* is any event or time passage that results in a change in how an individual perceives herself, the world around her, or her relationship with others (Schlossberg, Waters, & Goodman, 1995). A transition can be either anticipated or unanticipated. It is either welcome or it is unwelcome. It can occur in any setting: at work, at home, or within oneself. It can be meaningful and profound or unimportant and inconsequential. It is easy to deal with or difficult. A transition is an inevitable part of life. How people deal with transitions depends upon their perceptions of the transition, their personal characteristics, and their support systems.

What Is Normal? What Is Abnormal?

In order to understand the wide range of possible human behaviors including disability, addiction, and psychopathology, we must first understand what is considered normal human behavior and what is considered abnormal.

What is your definition of abnormal behavior? Who is abnormal? Who is normal? A person can look "normal" but act "abnormal." Or look "abnormal" and be "normal." What is weird, bizarre, or strange behavior? It's fair to say we know it when we see it. Or do we?

Abnormal can mean socially unacceptable. Yet what is socially unacceptable? To whom? Most cultural relativists espouse the abnormal-as-socially-unacceptable view. This means that what is normal in one culture may not be normal in another. Most agree that there is no such thing as a "sick" society or culture. An individual or group of individuals within any culture may be "sick" or "abnormal" but not all members of that society are. On the other hand, abnormal might mean special, unique, or even creative. Where there is only a narrow socially acceptable view of normalcy there is little room for individuality or creativity. Abnormal can mean maladaptive or dysfunctional. This is the approach we use when we study, assess, and diagnose mental disorders. Still, mental distress is not by itself abnormal or maladaptive or dysfunctional. Human beings exhibit a wide array of thoughts, behaviors, and feelings that are well within the normal range. Being knowledgeable about human development helps us to discern the parameters of normal and abnormal behavior.

Career Development

(CACREP Standard, Section 2F-4)

Career development is a specialized part of human development. Many beginning counseling students have the mistaken idea that the course they must take in career development is only about academic or employment concerns. Although professional counseling's roots are in the vocational guidance movement of the early twentieth century, today career development involves career and life planning across the lifespan. It acknowledges the pervasiveness of work in everyone's life. Career counseling addresses no less than the client's sense of identity in the world beyond home and relationship, whether the client is a student, employed or self-employed worker, volunteer, or stay-at-home-spouse. It includes discovery of a purposeful life pattern across the lifespan. The National Career Development Association (NCDA) states that people want to achieve. Work "represents the need to do, to achieve, and to know that one is needed by others and is important" (National Career Development Association, 2011, p. 1). "Work is a major way for individuals to recognize and understand both who they are and why they exist in terms of making contributions to society that bring personal meaning and satisfaction to them" (National Career Development Association, 2011, p. 2). Career development encompasses an array of activities and is appropriate for people at all stages of life. "These stages are: (a) pre-school age youth; (b) K-6 school grades; (c) 7–9 school grades; (d) 10–12 school grades; (e) adults (ages 18–65), and (f) retired persons" (National Career Development Association, 2011, p. 1).

Major Career Theories

Career development and life planning has its own set of theories and techniques. Beginning with the publication of *Choosing a Vocation* (Parsons, 1909) through the postmodern, constructionist approaches of our present time, career researchers have presented theories of career behavior that guide interventions.

The trait and factor approach, introduced in Chapter 3 is still in use today. It is perhaps the most well-known of career counseling activities. Parsons proposed a three-step process to help people choose a vocation. The counselor assists clients to 1) gain knowledge of the self through discovery of their interests, aptitudes, and values; 2) gain knowledge of the world of work and specific occupations including the requirements, advantages, disadvantages, and opportunities; and 3) make a match between the self and the world through the process of what Parson termed "true reasoning." Today counselors still use this basic model by providing clients with assessments and activities that provide information about skills, interests, values, goals, and resources about the world of work. Counselors help clients to make the match by looking at many career alternatives either through published materials, the Internet, or in person. The counselor facilitates the client's choice through offering the same kinds of counseling services that take place in other kinds of counseling.

Career counselors draw on many other theories in their work. For example, John Holland's personality theory of occupational choice (Holland, 1973; Holland & Gottfredson, 1976) expanded the trait and factor approach to include the idea that people express their personalities in the work environment. It posited that genetic and environmental influences lead people to preferred methods of dealing with environmental tasks. Holland identified six personality types. Occupations are identified by the same type names. In the broad categories of working with things, ideas, data, and people, those who are *Realistic* are those who prefer to handle *things*. *Investigative* people prefer to deal with *things and ideas*. *Artistic* people prefer to deal with *ideas and people*. *Those who are Social* prefer to deal with *people*. Those who are *Enterprising* prefer to deal with *data and people*., and those who are Conventional prefer to deal with *data and things*. People and jobs are assigned a three-letter Holland code based on an assessment inventory. The first letter indicates the highest score, the second the next highest and so on. For example, many counselors have the Holland code of *Social, Artistic, Enterprising* (SAE) or *Artistic, Social, Enterprising* (ASE). Holland codes are used to classify jobs in many occupational resource documents, particularly by the U.S. government. The SAE occupational code includes the counseling profession. Holland's work is highly researched and is consistently shown to have a high level of validity.

One of the most influential career theories is Super's Lifespan Developmental Approach to Career Counseling (Super, 1980). Donald Super began work on his theory in the 1950s and continued to research and refine his theory for over 40 years. Super believed that career development is a complex, lifelong process of developing and implementing an occupational self-concept and that work is a method of realizing the self-concept (Super, 1980). Super presented stages of career development through which people move over a lifetime. The stages are birth, growth (up to age 14), exploration (14–24), establishment (24–44), maintenance (44–64), decline (64 and on), and death. Each stage has several substages and at each stage there are developmental career tasks that an individual must accomplish to move successfully to the next stage. In addition to this major lifetime five-stage cycle, people recycle through these five mini-stages each time they make a change in life or career. For Super, career consists of all life roles, and at any given time the importance, or salience, of each role may differ. Life roles include child, student, leisurite, citizen, worker, spouse, parent, homemaker, and pensioner. When Super developed his theory, people tended to enter one career and stay in it for a long period of time, even life. Today, careers tend to follow a less predictable pattern. Nevertheless, his theory continues to have utility.

These are three of many career development theories that you will study. Some others you will study include social learning theory, social cognitive career, the theory of circumspection and compromise, career construction approach, and many more.

Career Interventions

Career counselors engage in an array of intervention strategies to assist their clients in making good career and life-planning decisions. Activities vary at different ages and life stages. "Career development is a continuous life process through which individuals explore activities, make decisions, and assume a variety of roles" (National Career Development Association, 2011, p. 5). National Career Development Guidelines (NCDG) Framework delineates three main domains that are organized around broad competencies at each developmental level. The three domains are Personal Social Development (PS), Educational Achievement and Lifelong Learning (ED), and Career Management (CM). Each of these domains specifies goals for career development competency (see https://ncda.org/aws/NCDA/asset_manager/get_file/3384?ver=16587).

Today's career counselors work with issues across the lifespan. They address concerns of identity and how it is implemented in paid and unpaid work. Career is a lifelong continuous process in which each person evaluates and integrates the self and the perception of the world to meet personal and career goals. The counselor assists the client in making decisions and setting goals to meet those decisions through formal and informal assessment, counseling, and coaching.

Much of the work done by career counseling involves technology and is known as Computer Assisted Career Guidance (CACG). It takes advantage of the power of the Internet. One of the most utilized Internet systems is O*Net (https://www.onetonline.org/), the Federal website that provides a tool for career exploration and job analysis, and has detailed descriptions of the world of work. Career Counseling is one of the areas in which counselors can specialize. Chapter 10 discusses this specialty in more depth.

Summary

This chapter is the first of two that provides an orientation to the common components of all professional counseling programs presenting four of the eight core CACREP areas. A section on the importance of ethics in counseling discussed key ethical and legal concepts. It presented the basics of the essential area of diversity and multiculturalism, discussing the phenomenon of cultural identity development and the significance of cultural sensitivity in counseling. It continued with an orientation to the common components of human development and life stages. The chapter ended with the area of career development, and included information on some major career theories and career/life interventions.

> *How can I decide what to do when I don't even know who I really am? The more I learn to look at myself, the less I know!*
>
> – student to instructor during practicum supervision session

References

Ahia, C. E. (2003). *Legal and ethical dictionary for mental health professionals.* New York: University Press of America.

American Counseling Association. (2014). *2014 ACA code of ethics.* Alexandria, VA: Author.

American Psychiatric Association. (2013). *Diagnostic and statistical manual of mental disorders* (5th ed.). Washington, DC: Author.

Berk, L. E. (2004). *Development through the lifespan* (3rd ed.). New York: Allyn & Bacon.

Corey, G. (2013). *Theory and practice of counseling and psychotherapy* (9th ed.). Belmont, CA: Brooks/Cole.

Corey, G., Corey, M. S., & Callanan, P. (2015). *Issues and ethics in the helping professions* (9th ed.). Boston: Cengage.

Cottone, R. R., & Claus, R. E. (2000). Ethical decision-making models: A review of the literature. *Journal of Counseling & Development, 78,* 275–283.

Erford, T. B. (2018). *Orientation to the counseling profession: Advocacy, ethics, and essential professional foundations* (3rd ed.). Boston, MA: Pearson.

Erikson, E. H. (1959/1980). *Identity and the life cycle.* New York: Norton.

Forester-Miller, H., & Davis, T. E. (2016). *Practitioner's guide to ethical decision making* (Rev. ed.). Retrieved from http://www.counseling.org/docs/default-source/ ethics/practioner's-guide-toethical-decision-making.pdf

Gladding, S. T. (2012). *Counseling: A comprehensive profession* (7th ed.). New York: Pearson.

Guindon, M. H. (Ed.). (2010). *Self-esteem across the lifespan: Issues and interventions.* New York: Routledge/ Taylor & Francis Group.

Guindon, M. H., & Sobhany, M. S. (2001). Toward cultural competency in diagnosis. *International Journal for the Advancement of Counselling, 23*(4), 1–14.

Halbur, D. A., & Halbur, K. V. (2015). *Developing your theoretical orientation in counseling and psychotherapy* (3rd ed.). Hoboken, NJ: Pearson Education.

Herlihy, B., & Corey, G. (2015). *ACA ethical standards casebook* (7th ed.). Alexandria, VA: American Counseling Association.

Holland, J. L. (1973). *Making vocational choices: A theory of career.* Englewood Cliffs, NJ: Prentice Hall.

Holland, J. L., & Gottfredson, G. D. (1976). Using a typology of persons and environments to explain careers: Some extensions and clarifications. *Counseling Psychologist, 6,* 20–29.

National Career Development Association. (2011). *Career development: A policy statement of the National Career Development Association Board of Directors* (Adopted March 16, 1993; revised 2011). Retrieved from https://ncda.org/aws/NCDA/pt/sp/guidelines.

Neukrug, E. (2016). *The world of the counselor: An introduction to the counseling profession* (5th ed.). Boston: Cengage.

Neukrug, E., Lovell, C., & Parker, R. J. (1996). Employing ethical codes and decision-making models: A development process. *Counseling and Values, 40,* 98–106.

Parsons, F. (1909). *Choosing a vocation.* Boston: Houghton Mifflin.

Piaget, J. (1971). *Biology and knowledge.* Chicago, IL: University of Chicago Press.

Ponton, R. F., & Duba, J. D. (2009). *The ACA Code of Ethics:* Articulating counseling's professional covenant. *Journal of Counseling & Development, 87,* 117–121.

Prochaska, J.O., & Norcross, J. C. (2018). *Systems of psychotherapy: A transtheoretical analysis.* (9th ed.). New York: Oxford University Press.

Remley, T. P., & Herlihy, B. (2007). *Ethical, legal, and professional issues in counseling, updated* (2nd ed.). Upper Saddle River, NJ: Pearson Merrill/Prentice Hall.

Santrock, J. W. (2015). *Life-span development* (15th ed.). New York: McGraw-Hill Education.

Schlossberg, N. K., Waters, E. B., & Goodman, J. (1995). *Counseling adults in transition: Linking practice with theory* (2nd ed.). New York: Springer.

Stadler, H. A. (1986). Making hard choices: Clarifying controversial ethical issues. *Counseling & Human Development, 19,* 1–10.

Sue, D. W., & Sue, D. (2016). *Counseling the culturally diverse: Theory and practice* (7th ed.). Hoboken, NJ: John Wiley & Sons.

Super, D. E. (1980). A life-span, life-space approach to career development. *Journal of Vocational Behavior, 16,* 282–298.

Table 4.1 *TFAC Chart – Thought, Feelings, Actions, and Context

Self	My Thoughts	My Feelings	My Actions	My Context	Other? (Specify)
What ethical issues most concern me?					
How closely aligned are my own moral beliefs with my professional code of ethics?					
What is my belief about multiple relationships?					
What is my own worldview? How has it changed over the years?					
How culturally competent at this stage of my development as a counselor?					
Where do I see myself in my own cultural identity development?					
Where am I in my own development? How have I negotiated past developmental stages?					
How do I see the information on career development affecting my own career/ educational decision?					
How might I develop my own career/life plan?					
What are my concerns?					
Others	**Others' Probable Thoughts**	**Others' Possible Feelings**	**Others' Observable Actions**	**Others' Apparent Context**	**Other? (Specify)**
What are the most essential ethics standards?					
What are some of the important legal requirements in my state?					
What is the worldview of my family of origin?					
How culturally competent are others in my life?					
What can my family members tell me about their developmental stages? about mine?					
How have career stages influenced my classmates', students', instructors', and family members' choices?					
Other?					

*For more information on TFAC, see Chapter 1.

Chapter 5

What? Answers about the Body of Knowledge
Helping Relationships, Group Work, Assessment, and Research and Program Development

Mary H. Guindon

An investment in knowledge pays the best dividend.

– Benjamin Franklin

POINTS TO PONDER

- What are the major theories of counseling and psychotherapy?
- What is group counseling and how does it work?
- What is the role of assessment in counseling and what are the types of appraisal?
- How and why do counselors use assessment and appraisal?
- What must counselors know about research and program development?

Counseling Helping Relationships

(CACREP Standard, Section 2F-5)

Essential Interviewing and Counseling Skills

Throughout this primer and in your program of study, you are given opportunities to grow in self-awareness, a skill critical to a therapeutic counselor-client relationship and to maintaining appropriate professional boundaries. In Part Three, you will begin learning the essential interviewing skills of basic and advanced active listening and questioning, and the use of affective, cognitive and behavioral interventions. These basic skills and the more advanced skills you will learn later are based on theories and practices developed over more than a century. Counseling is a profession in which many styles and techniques make up the work of a client session.

Importance of Theory

How do you know what you are doing works? The simple answer is that we rarely ever really know. The more accurate answer is that each of us is obligated to develop and apply counseling methods using the research of theoreticians of over a century of work and wisdom of seasoned practitioners. When practice is based on research and the practitioner proceeds from some kind of theoretical base, she is more likely to successfully answer this question. At the same time, we do not want to lose sight of the client as a unique individual who cannot be neatly pigeonholed into any one theory.

Effective counseling strategies are grounded in theory. However, theory is not fact. A theory can never be proven. It never becomes a fact, but theories are supported by facts. A theory is a generally accepted explanation of a concept. A concept is made up of a number of facts that seem to point to a conclusion about a phenomenon, but we can never reach a final conclusion. In the sciences, including behavioral science, theory must be supported and based on facts. A theory must be consistent and it must describe reality. Theories are important because they allow us to understand reality and to predict future occurrences of a phenomenon, including human behavior and personality. Sometimes a counselor is tempted to use a technique because she likes it or has a hunch it can be successful, and a client is willing to cooperate. Ethical and effective professional counselors understand many theories and can apply techniques that fit the client's needs and are grounded in sound research.

Using their knowledge, experience, and observations, counselors choose from among many theories and their related techniques to bring the best possible service to meet individual client needs. Not all theories or techniques are equally effective – or even appropriate – for any one client. No one theory can possibly fit all circumstances or be effective for all clients even when they present with similar issues and concerns. The counselor's job in formulating practices to suit clients is to investigate and examine many theories to determine what set of treatment goals is most likely to assist each client. Therefore, counselors must be well educated in many theories and practices. They must also take into consideration their own styles and personalities.

Neophyte counselors sometimes think of themselves as "eclectic," by which they mean that they believe themselves able to pick and choose whatever practices attract them regardless of theoretical orientation. This approach is fraught with problems. A more responsible approach takes the position that counselors can and should certainly use more than one theoretical orientation to inform their practice, but that what they do and how they do it is grounded in a thorough knowledge of what is most likely to work with each client. You are encouraged to develop your own theory of counseling and practice that draws on an in-depth understanding of existing theories and continues to evolve as you gain experience throughout your career and as the profession itself evolves.

Major Counseling Theories

Theories can address affective, cognitive, behavioral, or systemic interventions, or a combination of these. Not all theories are equally comprehensive. Some theories target awareness and perception, some target behaviors and action, and some are more integrative or systemic in approach. Kottler and Shepard (2015) divide the first two categories into insight-oriented and action-oriented approaches. To be insightful means to be self-aware. Self-awareness is the ability to understand aspects of one's self and to find solutions to one's problems. Action-oriented approaches are those that believe solutions to one's problems will be found in changes of behavior. The theories targeting insight and self-awareness include psychoanalytic/psychodynamic, Adlerian, existential, client-centered, and Gestalt. Theories targeting behavior and action include behavioral, cognitive/behavioral, reality, strategic, and brief psychotherapy. Integrative approaches use interventions from different counseling approaches based upon conceptual principles and practice that goes beyond simply combining different counseling approaches. Those that are integrative include family systems, feminist, and narrative.

Psychoanalytic/psychodynamic. Sigmund Freud (1856–1939) formulated the first *psychoanalytic theory*. His great and enduring contribution is the identification of the unconscious mind. Freud believed that maladjustment results from material repressed into the unconscious. People's behavior is influenced by experiences that are not in conscious awareness. The goal of therapy is to make the contents of the unconscious conscious. By doing so, the client will understand the reasons for her behavior and thus change it. There are three layers of the mind – the conscious, consisting of events currently in awareness; the preconscious, consisting of events not presently in but easily brought into awareness; and the unconscious, consisting of those psychic events that are not in awareness and can be made to be in awareness only through considerable effort and anxiety. Personality consists of the Id, Ego, and Superego. The Id is the source of psychic energy and the instincts of sex and aggression. The pleasure principle states that the purpose of the Id is to reduce tension, avoid pain, and gain pleasure. The Id only desires and acts. It does not think. The Ego is the intermediary between the Id and the external world. It controls and governs the Id and Superego. The reality principle states that the purpose of the Ego is to think realistically and logically and formulate plans of action for satisfying the Id's needs. The Superego is the social, moral, and judicial portion of personality and strives for perfection. It represents the ideals and values of behavior and the dictates of society. An individual is born with only Id and develops Ego and Superego during the stages of psychosexual development beginning in infancy. The material in the Id is so threatening to the individual that defense mechanisms are created by the Ego to reduce anxiety through distorting reality. This is an unconscious process and serves to protect the individual from psychic harm. The major defense mechanism is *repression*, the process by which the Ego keeps threatening material from breaking into awareness. Some of the more common defense mechanism are *denial* (the inability to accept reality or fact, not recognizing that a painful event, thought or feeling exists), *rationalization* (logically justifying one's unacceptable perceptions, feelings, or behaviors in a rational or logical manner, thus avoiding the true, more painful explanation), *regression* (reverting to an earlier stage of development to protect oneself from unacceptable impulses or thoughts), *reaction formation* (converting unwanted or dangerous impulses, thoughts, or feelings impulses into their opposites, such as acting overly caring when hostile and angry), *projection* (incorrectly attributing one's undesirable impulses, thoughts, or feelings to another person who does not have those same thoughts, feelings, or impulses), and *displacement* (redirecting impulses, thoughts, or feelings from one person or object to another person or object). *Transference* is the projection or displacement of affect from a forgotten childhood memory to someone in the present. Inappropriate feelings toward another are rooted in previous, early experiences. For example, a person may begin acting toward a boss based on feelings she had about her mother. The purpose of psychoanalytic therapy is to work with the client's transference in the session so that unconscious repressed material can be brought into consciousness and resolved. Therapists use the techniques of free association, dream analysis, and resistance to resolve early conflicts.

For Freud, these conflicts concerned early sexual fantasies and aggression. His theory is deterministic and pessimistic. Other psychoanalytic theorists – those who work with making unconscious material conscious – differed from Freud in the nature of this material. Carl Jung (1875–1961), originally a member of Freud's inner circle, developed *Analytic Psychology*, a healthier, more optimistic view of personality. Jung's theory includes the concept of a personal unconscious consisting of an individual's personal experiences that are accessible to the conscious mind and the collective unconscious consisting of primal experiences common to human beings from antiquity. The collective unconscious consists of archetypes, those positive but also negative, frightening images that represent these common experiences. The purpose of Jungian therapy is to bring archetypes from the collected unconscious into awareness. Jungian analysis uses free association, dream analysis, and imagination and sees the material as symbolic of the archetypes. Jungians use these symbols to explain hidden archetypal needs and work with clients to understand and integrate their needs into self-acceptance. Other well-known psychoanalytic/psychodynamic theorists include Anna Freud, Otto Rank, and Erik Erikson.

Generally, the term *psychoanalysis* refers to those techniques used by therapists who use Freudian concepts and treatments. Today's psychoanalysts help clients "examine... assumptions, understand their origins in their lives, modify them if necessary, and make better choices for themselves [and utilize] the concept of the unconscious determinants of behavior and the influence of the past on the present" (American Psychoanalytic Association, n.d.). *Psychodynamic* refers to techniques used by those who work predominantly with unconscious material and use various practices to bring it into consciousness but is considered to be less intensive than psychoanalysis.

Adlerian. Alfred Adler (1870–1937), like Jung, was initially one of Freud's inner circle. However, he did not accept Freud's original theories of the unconscious as the repository of sexual energy and aggression. For example, he opposed the belief that dreams were sexual wish fulfillment and did not believe in the compartmentalization of the Id, Ego, and Superego. He developed "*individual psychology*," a term which refers to the indivisibility of the personality in its psychological structure. He maintained that difficulties are rooted in a feeling of inferiority – the *inferiority complex*, a psychological sense of inferiority that is wholly or partly unconscious. Many dysfunctional symptoms can be traced to overcompensation for this feeling. The inferiority complex derives from restrictions on the individual's need for self-assertion. Inferiority, or feelings of lack of worth, becomes maladjustment or pathological when the individual is overwhelmed by a sense of inadequacy and is thus incapable of normal development. Adler believed such individuals to be discouraged rather than "sick."

Adler's (1963) theory emphasizes that all people strive to reach goals so that they will feel superior, strong, and complete. Thus, individuals strive toward superiority. Adler used the term *superiority complex* to indicate the state that develops when an individual tries to overcome their inferiority by suppressing their existing feelings. He stated that people have an image about what their perfect self should be. He named this image the *fictional finalism*. Although the image may be altered, the common direction throughout one's life stays the same. Adler believed the conscious and unconscious worked in union with one another toward the realization of a perfect self. Fictional finalism applies clearer direction to decisions that are to be made concerning oneself. The fictional goal is the imagined central goal that guides an individual's behavior. It is the motivating force behind behavior. An individual's *style of life* is the overall pattern that influences her feeling, thinking, and behaving.

An important Adlerian concept is *social interest*. He believed that human beings innately know that they have a duty to other fellow human beings. Each of us possesses an unconscious sense of social unity and that our life tasks – our friendships, love, work, spirituality, and self-acceptance – are aimed at developing a feeling of belonging and responsibility to society. Social feeling is so fundamental that even those who have not developed this ability to consider others fully still make efforts to appear as if they had done so. Another important concept is that of *birth order*. Adler believed that each child is born into a unique family circumstance as the first, middle, or youngest child. This position in the family, or the family constellation, influences one's Style of Life, such as Avoiding or Ruling/Dominant, or Socially Useful.

The goal of Adlerian counseling is to restore confidence in the self to overcome feelings of inferiority. Counseling processes consist of four phases: (a) establishing the relationship; (b) assessment and analysis, which includes exploring the clients lifestyle, early recollections, family constellation and birth order, dreams, and life tasks; (c) insight and interpretation, to uncover the client's private logic about their beliefs, attitudes and perceptions; and (d) reorientation, in which the counselor offers alternative ideas about the private logic. If this changes, behavior will follow.

Some Adlerian techniques are *paradoxical intention*, in which the client exaggerates debilitating thoughts and behaviors; *acting as if*, in which the client is instructed to act out a role as if she could do it; *spitting in the soup*, in which the counselor ascertains and brings to the client's attention the payoff of behavior and then reduces its usefulness; and *pushing the button*, in which the counselor assists the client in alternate experiences and feelings so the client becomes aware that she controls emotions.

Behavioral. Behavioral theories developed out of academic research on the nature of learning. The basic premise is that behavior is learned and thus can be unlearned or relearned. Behaviorism is not concerned with the unconscious. Observable symptoms not underlying causal factors are the focus of treatment. Feelings and thoughts do not play a significant role in counseling. The history and practice of behavioral approaches to counseling and therapy can be divided into classical conditioning, operant conditioning, and cognitive behavioral. The latter has evolved into an approach of its own and will be discussed in the following section.

In *classical conditioning*, a neutral stimulus is repeatedly paired with another stimulus that evokes a natural or unconditioned response, so that the previously neutral stimulus creates a conditioned response. This results in learning. *Reinforcement* is the process by which a stimulus, or reinforcer, increases the probability of a response. Positive reinforcement is the introduction of a desirable stimulus to increase a target behavior. For example, a child might be given a special, desirable treat (the desirable stimulus) when she makes her bed every day for a week (the target behavior). Negative reinforcement is the removal of an aversive stimulus to increase a target behavior. In the same case, a child might be excused from doing the dishes on weekdays (the aversive stimulus) if she does her homework (the target behavior) each day instead. *Punishment* is the introduction of an aversive stimulus to reduce the frequency of a target behavior, that is, the introduction of something unpleasant following a behavior. An example would be if the same child were spanked (aversive stimulus) for not making her bed (target behavior), or yelled at for not doing dishes. *Extinction* is the elimination of a behavior; the behavior disappears because no consequences are presented.

Operant conditioning is a kind of learning in which the acquisition of a desirable response (or elimination of a maladaptive response) is a function of its consequences, or its rewards and punishments. How people operate depends upon the result of their behaviors.

B. F. Skinner (1904–1990) developed behavior modification, the major use of operant conditioning principles. The use of reinforcers to control behaviors and manage a client's environment was a common theme in counseling. The social environment was the target area and schools particularly embraced behavior modification as a way to help students and control the learning environment. *Modeling* is a kind of learning found in a social environment in which an individual observes others performing a perceived desirable behavior and then imitates it. The principle of modeling is based on the *social learning* work of Albert Bandura (1925–present) and generally involves learning complex behaviors in a short amount of time.

Maladaptive behavior is learned as a way to either increase positive reinforcement or to decrease an aversive stimulus. It is situation specific to one's culture, social class, and time. Behavioral techniques can assist individuals to unlearn undesirable behaviors and learn more adaptive behaviors. Because all behavior can be learned, unlearned, and relearned, insight is not a major focus. The counseling process concerns itself with changing behaviors by helping clients extinguish maladaptive behaviors and learning more adaptive ones through establishing and maintaining appropriate goals. The basic treatment is concrete and structured and includes behavioral homework assignments between sessions. Clients are actively involved in their own treatment through working with the counselor to (a) analyze and define behavior; (b) choose a target goal that is concrete and time limited; (c) select practices based on behavioral principles; (d) monitor, evaluate, and modify progress; and (e) generalize new learned behaviors. Some common techniques include *behavioral contracting*, in which clients enter into a formalized agreement to perform specific tasks or behaviors; *role playing*, in which clients practice alternative behaviors; *token economies*, in which a valued object or token is given immediately as a tangible reinforcer for appropriate behavior; *relaxation training and systematic desensitization*, a process in which the client's anxiety is reduced through pairing it with muscular or mental relaxation; and *self-management* in which clients are taught to manage their own problems in structured ways. *Time-out* is an effective and popular strategy in which a child is isolated from the reinforcement activity in order to extinguish an undesirable behavior. Less common and controversial techniques are *aversion therapy*, which uses procedures such as unpleasant or disgusting images or electric shock to inhibit dysfunctional behaviors; and *satiation*, which uses an excessive amount of reinforcement of a maladaptive behavior to make this undesired reinforcer lose its effectiveness.

Arnold Lazarus (1932–present) developed *Multimodal Therapy*, a more encompassing variation of the behavioral approach. He combined attributes of several approaches into a comprehensive and flexible system. His system considers seven areas, or modalities of personality, using the acronym BASIC ID. His approach gathers information about and develops treatment plans on Behavior, Affect, Sensory/physical factors, Imagery, Cognitions, Interpersonal/Environmental Factors, and Drugs/biochemical/neurophysiological reactions (Lazarus, 1989).

Cognitive and cognitive behavioral. While behavioral techniques are effective in changing observable behaviors, some theorists believe that thoughts that cannot be observed can influence feelings, be the source of distress, and affect behavior. Cognitive approaches focus on the meaning an individual gives to a situation. Psychological problems are believed to result from the way people think. The hallmark is the process of cognitive restructuring.

The major proponent of the cognitive approach is Aaron Beck (1921–present). Beck's (1995) *Cognitive Therapy* posits that dysfunctional thinking is common to all psychological disturbances. The fundamental elements of this approach are (a) cognition affects behavior, (b) cognition can be monitored and altered, and (c) change in behavior can result from change in cognition. A realistic evaluation results in a modification of thinking that produces an improvement in affect and behavior. Levels of cognitions are automatic thoughts – streams of cognitions constantly in the mind; intermediate beliefs – those extreme and absolute rules and attitudes that shape automatic thoughts; core beliefs – those central ideas about the self that underlie automatic thoughts and are reflected in intermediate beliefs; and schemas – those specific rules that control information processing and behavior. The goal of counseling is to assist clients in recognizing cognitive errors by bringing them into awareness, identifying these errors through their own information-processing systems, and then correcting them through changes in cognition at each level. This is accomplished through a case conceptualization method. The client first, lists the problem; second, hypothesizes the underlying belief systems affecting the problem; third, looks at the relationship between the belief system and the current problem; fourth, considers the precipitants of the current problem; and last, comes to an understanding about the development of the core, faulty belief. Counseling is structured, time-limited, and involves questionnaires, inventories, and homework (Beck & Weishear, 2014).

The cognitive behavioral approach addresses a hybrid of behavioral and cognitive processes. Its major proponent is Albert Ellis (1913–2007), who was the first to systematically show how beliefs determine the way people feel and behave. His approach emphasized the idea that psychological problems arise from misperceptions and mistaken cognitions. Ellis (1962) posited that maladaptive behavior is a habitual, dysfunctional pattern that results from "emotional" reactions that are mainly caused by conscious and unconscious evaluations and beliefs. Emotional reactions are not caused by events but by people's beliefs about those events. He developed the *ABCDEF Theory* in which A is the activating event, B is the often irrational belief about the event, and C is the emotional consequence. Anxiety and fear are irrational consequences of irrational beliefs which cannot be validated or disproved and prevent individuals from going back to the activating event to resolve it. For example, (A) a student may receive a grade of C– on one assignment in a course. This is the activating event. (B) The student feels that the instructor should appreciate her hard work and is a jerk for not giving her a better grade. It is awful that the student made such a conscientious effort and she was not valued the way she should be. This is the belief. (C) The student experiences deep shame and anger, and is anxious about flunking out of the program. This is the emotional consequence of the belief. Counselors (D) help clients to bring beliefs into awareness so that they can be disputed and (E) a new, more rational and healthy effect is realized, resulting in more appropriate feelings (F). In our example, the counselor (D) would dispute the client's belief and assist the student in examining the logic of her belief, asking if it is truly terrible that she got a less than average grade or just undesirable. The counselor would point out that the student is "awfulizing" and "catastrophizing" the event into failing out of the program. The student would then (E) be able to engage in more realistic and rational self-talk with a healthier effect, saying that although she is disappointed in her grade, it is not the end of the world or her academic career. She would see that she can take steps to talk with the instructor about her work and obtain a more positive grade the next time. She would then (F) have a more rational feeling that she may be disappointed about the grade, but she is no longer devastated and anxious.

Ellis's Rational Emotive Behavioral Therapy (REBT) works toward what he termed a philosophic reorientation of a people's life outlook (Ellis & Dryden, 1997). It makes use of psychological homework in which the client is taught to recognize self-defeating beliefs and through a process of cognitive restructuring, change them to rational beliefs based in reality rather than in faulty perception. Irrational beliefs come from unconditional "shoulds," "oughts," and "musts" that people attribute to events. The goal of counseling is to minimize the client's hostility and anxiety; decrease the client's self-defeating viewpoint; gain a more realistic, tolerant philosophy of life; and teach the client to observe irrational beliefs in order to dispute and change them (Ellis, 2014; Ellis & Dryden, 1997). REBT counselors do not believe that warm relationships with clients are sufficient or necessary for effective change. In fact, the process is confrontive, active, and based on the method of scientific questioning, debating, and challenging.

Existential/Humanistic and Client Centered. Often termed the "Third Force," existential/humanistic counseling developed out of dissatisfaction with the psychoanalytic and behavioral approaches. The field of philosophy, particularly the existential writings of Kierkegaard, Nietzsche, Heidegger, Sartre, and others greatly influenced Rollo May (1950) and Victor Frankl (1963), who set the direction of counseling and psychotherapy in the middle of the twentieth century. *Existentialism* is a point of view that reflects on the human condition. It espouses the belief that no one has the right to impose one's values on another and each person is responsible for his own behavior. The concepts of awareness, being, authenticity, and responsibility are the hallmarks of *existential counseling*. Central to existential counseling is *anxiety*, a condition that is universal and intrinsic to being alive. The sources of anxiety are isolation, meaningless, death, and freedom (Yalom, 1980). The premise is that the awareness of death is transformative and that anxiety is a normal, desirable state in which to make lasting changes. Through becoming aware of one's death and the finiteness of life, people learn that they are responsible for making meaning of their existence.

Humanistic, existential counselors work by entering the client's reality and staying in the here and now. The therapeutic alliance is sufficient for change. Few specific techniques are directly associated with existential counseling. Rather, the goal is to assist clients in discovering meaning in life. Therapeutic goals are phenomenological in nature and counselors are fully present and authentic themselves. They assist their clients in confronting their anxieties so that they can increase authenticity, accept responsibility, and live purposefully. Counselors help clients become aware of their unconscious fears such as fear of death, lack of purpose in life, avoidance of responsibility, and their ultimate aloneness and isolation. Facing anxiety is a necessary step toward authenticity. When clients are in touch with their anxieties, they can make choices that lead to more adaptive and fulfilling lives. They discover their own freedom in the world and the ways they choose to act.

Grounded in existentialism, *humanistic approaches* developed new ways of working with clients. The process of therapy is the vehicle for positive change. The predominant figure associated with existential humanistic counseling is Carl Rogers (1902–1987), perhaps the most influential figure in counseling and psychotherapy. He introduced *person-centered (i.e., client-centered) counseling*, also termed Rogerian or *nondirective counseling*. Before Carl Rogers' (1942, 1951) groundbreaking, seminal works, counseling in the United States consisted mainly of either psychoanalytic or guidance work, both using the position of the helper as expert. Both processes were directive and authoritative. Advice giving and interpretation were the norm. With the appearance of Carl Rogers, both disciplines changed irrevocably. Clients were more respected for their own decision-making abilities and expected to take more responsibility for the direction of their own treatment and its results.

Rogers (1957) believed that the therapeutic relationship under the ideal conditions of caring and compassion was necessary and sufficient for change to occur. His self-theory stressed the self-actualizing tendency of all people. He believed individuals naturally develop into fully functioning, fully aware selves if they are in nurturing, healthy environments. He believed that people have a strong need to be well regarded. They experience a natural growth process that too often can be thwarted through restrictive conditions of worth placed on them by others. In order to meet others' conditions of regard and worth, individuals can develop a distorted sense of self and act in unnatural, unhealthy ways. Maladaptive behavior results from a psychological vulnerability.

For Rogers, therapy in an environment of safety and mutual respect creates freedom for the counselor and client to be themselves. The counselor is authentic, genuine, and transparent. Such an environment gives the client the chance to develop a congruent, authentic sense of self, or what Rogers termed the ideal self. The counselor offers warmth, congruence, unconditional positive regard, acceptance, and empathic understanding. The latter allows the counselor to enter the clients' point of reference and communicate this understanding to the client. When these conditions are achieved in a therapeutic relationship, change will occur because the client opens up to the counselor and comes to understand and resolve issues that resulted from and were based on past conditional relationships. Techniques in client-centered counseling include being psychologically present, congruent in verbal and nonverbal messages, and listening empathetically. Although not exclusively based on the person-centered approached, many of the attending and listening skills discussed in Part Two are based on Rogers' philosophy.

Gestalt. Fritz Perls' (1893–1970) work came out of the existential, phenomenological movement. He developed some of the same basic concepts as the client-centered approach, but his techniques were dramatically different. For Perls (Perls, Hefferline, & Goodman, 1965), the individual's world is defined by the subjective reality of perceptions. He contended that the individual is constantly attempting to maintain emotional and psychological equilibrium, or balance, which is continually disturbed by needs and is regained through the gratification of those needs. Opposite, internal conflicts – or polarities – exist among thoughts, values, traits, and actions. *Gestalt theory* posits that the individual herself determines the essence of her existence through contact with the environment. Maladjustment and psychic distress result from disturbances that inhibit contact with the environment. *Introjection* is the phenomenon of believing whole concepts rather than discriminating parts of concepts. Introjectors have difficulty knowing what it is they actually believe. *Projection* is the phenomenon of making someone other than oneself responsible for what originates in the self. Projectors do not accept their feelings and thus attach them to someone else. *Retroflection* involves doing to oneself what one would like to do to others. Retroflectors redirect feelings inwardly. *Confluence* is the absence of a psychic boundary between oneself and the environment. Confluentors have difficulty recognizing their own thoughts and speaking for themselves. *Deflection* uses the process of distraction, making difficult to maintain sustained contact with others. Deflectors try to diffuse contact by the overuse of questions, humor, or abstract generalizations.

Perceptions are ordered into an experience called *figure-ground*, known as *the Gestalt*. The figure is immediately perceived and in awareness. The ground is what is further from perception or not in awareness. Individuals seek closure and tend to see figure as complete rather than as only a part of what is available to perception. *Unfinished business* is that material that is forced into the background and thus is out of awareness but nevertheless continues to influence present behavior. The hallmark of Gestalt is the *here and now orientation*, which focuses on concrete present behavior such as posture, mannerisms, facial expressions, voice, breathing, and the like as indicators of maladjustments. Gestalt theory considers awareness itself to be curative and thus therapy is experiential, or phenomenological in nature.

In the Gestalt approach, the counselor facilitates the client's awareness of the self by assisting the client to bring into awareness all the feelings, behaviors, experiences, and unfinished situations that are part of the self. Gestalt counseling addresses what is currently happening within the individual rather than past experiences. Techniques include *enactment*, in which the client is instructed to put feelings or thoughts into action using the *empty chair* or *top dog/underdog strategy*; *exaggeration*, in which the client is asked to exaggerate a feeling, movement, or thought; *integrating and loosening*, in which the client is invited to imagine the opposite of whatever is believed to be fact; *stay with it*, in which the client is encouraged to stay with the feeling being expressed. Other techniques are dream work, guided fantasy, and body awareness work. These techniques assist the client in bringing unfinished business from the past into present awareness so it can be resolved.

Reality. *Reality Therapy* was initially developed by William Glasser (1925–2013) and emphasizes personal choice, responsibility, and transformation. It encourages success, personal planning, and action. It addresses a behavior as the best attempt an individual can make at a particular time to satisfy one or more basic needs. Such behavior is part of genetic structure. Most problems concern the inability to connect with others and to form and maintain successful relationships. Many individuals have the mistaken belief that others have control of them. Maladjustment results when individuals lose effective control of their perceptions about their own needs. This leads to loss of control in their lives. Reality Theory and its related *Choice Theory* (Glasser, 1998) posit that individuals choose to be miserable. In other words, reactions such as depression, anxiety, and guilt are chosen responses. Keeping anger submerged, attempting to gain control over others, forcing others to help us, and excusing one's own ineffectualness are chosen behaviors. They result from an attempt to gain control over our own lives. Glasser's Choice Theory suggests that individuals are responsible for what they do.

Reality Therapy concentrates on total behavior but also focuses on the parts the client chooses to change through examining current acting and thinking. Responsible behavior is the goal of counseling. The hallmark question in Reality Therapy is to ask, "What are you doing to get what you want?" The counselor assists the client in establishing and reestablishing satisfying relationships by first being in a satisfying relationship with the counselor in session. Techniques used include *positiveness*, in which the client is encouraged to break negative patterns and focus on constructive aspects in the here and how; *controlling perceptions* that teach the client meditations to gain control over life; *confrontation* about the client's explanations, excuses, and rationalizations; *plans*, in which the counselors encourage the client to make a written plan with specific action steps toward success; and *pinning down*, in which the counselor helps the client make a commitment to take positive action to attain a goal.

Wubbolding (1991), Glasser's colleague, expanded Reality Therapy. He states that all humans have the basic needs of survival, belonging, power, freedom, and fun. People act to meet these needs, often ineffectively, whether or not in their awareness. Wubbolding's *WDEP system* is a process of therapy in which clients are asked to define and clarify their **W**ants; to examine clients' total behaviors, feelings, self-talk, and actions and what **D**irection they want to take; to **E**valuate themselves through continually searching even when it is uncomfortable; and having done so, to formulate specific and attainable positive **P**lans and the commitment to accomplish them.

Brief, Strategic, and Solution-Focused. Several brief models have developed over the last 40 years. Whereas most of the approaches discussed thus far are intended to be implemented over several weeks, months, or longer, a group of theories responded to the need for shorter interventions that are effective in assisting people in making changes. Much of the acceptance of brief approaches has come in response to the limited number of sessions managed care (insurance) companies will pay for. Counselors who are reliant on insurance reimbursement for their livelihood no longer can offer treatment over the course of months or years. School counselors rarely see their students for more than a few sessions. Therefore, counselors must learn intervention methods that honor the needs of the client and at the same time provide effective services over a small number of sessions. The brief and solution-focused therapies emerged as the treatment of choice for many counselors. *Brief counseling* is considered to be between one and 20 sessions. *Solution-focused* approaches take the position that individuals already have strengths, internal and external resources, and problem-solving skills that can be discovered and drawn upon to solve their problems. The process is collaborative. The philosophy is that small changes can lead to big results. As the name suggests, it stresses solutions to rather than causes of problems.

Grounded in the work of Milton Erickson (1901–1980), one brief approach, *Strategic Therapy* (Haley, 1973), recognizes that a client's attempts to solve problems generally result in solutions that actually perpetuate the problem in a circular repetitive, vicious cycle of behaviors. For example, if a child does not pick up his clothes when the parent asks, the parent will raise her voice. When this does not work, the parent will raise her voice even more, ending in the same result of not picking up the clothes. This is termed *"more of the same"* attempts at solutions (Watzlawick, Weakland, & Fisch, 1974). Counselors emphasize that clients have problem-solving capability but that the process they use does not work. Counselors work with clients to break the cycle so that new behaviors can be learned through the use of metaphor, hypnotic suggestions, paradoxical intent, and prescribing the symptom.

Another brief approach, *Solution-Focused Brief Therapy* (de Shazer, 1985; Berg, 1994), focuses on the future rather than the problem. The belief is that focusing on the problem itself may hinder finding a solution. Thus, counselors work with clients to envision what their world would be like if the problem did not exist. The approach uses the technique of questioning. The *"miracle question"* asks the client to respond by describing the world as if a miracle happened and the problem was gone. The counselor then helps the client make the "miracle" a reality. The *scaling technique* asks the client to rank order problems or symptoms on a scale of one to ten. The counselor asks a series of questions to assist the client in changing the scale to a more adaptive or satisfying future. The *exceptions question* asks the client to identify a time when the problem was absent or less severe. The counselor helps the client identify what was different to make it so. *Coping questions* help clients to see that they have resources to solve their problems and engineer a more positive future.

Systems/Family. In more recent years, counseling has evolved to include more than individual determinants of behavior, thoughts, and feelings. Human beings are not creatures in a vacuum. The environment plays a dominant role in how people adapt. Maladaptive behavior is not only internally created but may also be a direct result of adaptive behaviors to various systems in which an individual lives. Family, school, church, work, society, and other sociological systems all have a major impact on development. A systems perspective involves understanding systems theories and major models of interventions.

One important and predominant approach is *family systems*. This approach is not one theory but a set of theories, each with its own distinct set of tenets and associated techniques. Together they recognize the significance of treating the whole family. Families are unique systems within broader societal systems (Carter & McGoldrick, 2005). In general systems theory, each system has a boundary, or a limited area, that allows it to maintain its structure while it interacts with other systems around it. Families can be healthy or dysfunctional. Healthy families are open about their concerns, share feelings, and have a comprehensible understanding of each family member's role within the system. Parents take an appropriate parental role; create structure and reasonable, healthy rules. Children understand their role within the structure and follow the rules. Boundaries between family members are known but not overly restrictive. Although there is constancy in boundaries and rules, as family members grow and change, the boundaries and family rules change with them. When boundaries between and among family members are either too rigid or too loose, dysfunction results. The major contributors to family systems are *Conjoint Family Therapy* (Satir, 1967), *Strategic Family Therapy* (Haley, (1973), *Structural Family Therapy* (Minuchin, 1974), *Multigenerational or Bowenian Family Therapy* (Bowen, 1978), and *Internal Family Systems Therapy* (Schwartz, 1995). Although each approach has its distinct features, each recognizes that families have their own distinct ways of interacting with mechanisms that can be positive and negative. The therapist enters the family system in order to better understand its roles and procedures and to break dysfunctional systems. The therapist then works with family members to change maladaptive behaviors so that healthier patterns can be learned and practiced.

Family counseling and therapy is effective in treating marital and sexual problems and difficult or aggressive children and adolescents. By the 1990s treatment for addictions, depression, and family discord as well more serious psychotic disorders were found to be effective as well.

Marriage, Couple, and Family Counseling and Therapy is a CACREP entry-level specialty area. To learn more, see Chapter 14.

Feminist. Grounded in the multicultural movement of the 1960s, feminism is another important systems approach. It asserts that external forces in the world rather than an individual's internal shortcomings may be the source of many disorders and psychological distress. The groundbreaking work of Jean Baker Miller (1986), Carol Gilligan (1982) and their colleagues at the Stone Center at Wellesley led the way in transforming the way therapy can be conducted with women as distinct from men. The Stone Center theorists developed Relational-Cultural Theory to emphasize the importance of relationship in women's lives.

Feminist theory acknowledges that being female in a male-dominant culture can be problematic. Violence – physical, emotional, psychological – is a common consequence of being a woman in this culture and often goes unrecognized and untreated. It is the only approach that recognizes the central importance of reproductive and biological issues as part of a woman's reality. First menses, sexuality, childbearing, and menopause play a role in women's wellbeing throughout life. Additionally, in a world where independence and self-sufficiency are seen as the healthy norm, the feminine attributes of connection and caring are often considered inherent weakness and unhealthy dependency. In feminist counseling they are seen as strengths to draw on.

Thus, women need information and education about these and other issues and the therapist's role is to provide it. A feminist therapist may use any of these techniques:

1. **Raising consciousness.** The counselor strives to help women realize the effects of living unfulfilling lives based on prescribed gender roles that limit potential and result in anger,

resentment, and frustration. This can manifest in self-destructive behaviors and harmful relationships.

2. **Validating experiences.** The counselor shares herself and her own experiences of being a woman and helps the client understand that her reactions may be normal responses to abnormal circumstances.

3. **Making appropriate choices.** The counselor will help the client realize that she has choices regardless of her present circumstances. The counselor will give support to make the choices she needs to make based on what she authentically wants.

4. **Enhancing self-esteem.** The therapist will assist the client in learning how to value herself and to recognize her strengths and talents.

5. Providing opportunities for **group work.** She will facilitate her client's growth in the company of other women. Many women feel isolated in many aspects of their lives and having support from other women can be healing.

6. **Giving information.** The counselor will direct the client to community resources when they are needed. She may refer the client to a career counselor or recommend an abuse shelter. She will recommend books to educate and train the client. She will disclose to the client her own experiences as a woman when they provide significant information to the client.

7. **Using expressive approaches.** Some feminist counselors may use one or more of the expressive arts such as music, art, dance, or guided imagery to help the client heal and grow.

Narrative. The narrative approach arose out of the *constructivist view*, a major tenet of the postmodernist movement. It posits that there are no objective truths; there are many truths, or multiple possible interpretations of any event. In other words, the world can never be known directly. Each individual mentally constructs the world and its meaning through cognitive processes. Thus, each person's world is uniquely constructed within his own social, cultural, and political context. Meaning for each person is revealed through interlinking life stories, and every person's story is as valid – or true – as anyone else's. The individual's stories are comprised of events occurring over time that are linked by a theme. Like any story, there is a plot that emerges as certain events are either retained or discarded based on their importance or validity to the individual. As the story and the plot unfold, the individual selects certain events and ignores others so that a consistent life story can be told.

The life story shapes a person's life and affects her perceptions of events so that they conform to her understanding of the world and her own inner reality. Stories can be inspiring or oppressive. Maladaptive behavior results from *problem-saturated stories* (Monk, Winslade, & Crocket, 1997) that become the individual's driving, major identity. Examples are seeing oneself as a victim with no hope, or identifying oneself as a failure in life. Such stories are a dominant negative influence in the way people see their capabilities and live their lives.

Narrative counseling uses several strategies that allow the client to tell her story and restructure it in a meaningful way, or reconstruct her internal reality. The client learns to first deconstruct and then reconstruct her dominant story through the process of *restorying*. Behavioral, cognitive, or emotional stories can be the focus of work. The premise is that when clients are able to construct and understand the theme and plot of their unique life story, they will be able to reauthor their stories in healthier, more adaptive ways.

The counselor first and foremost listens to the story, thus honoring the client's reality. The counselor explores with the client the influential moments and turning points of his life, his significant memories, and important relationships. The counselor helps the client discover and concentrate on the intentions, worth, goals, and dreams that have guided life, even when difficulties and obstacles were encountered. Together they process and identify past, forgotten stories that help the client understand that he has within him healthy, adaptive, even heroic ways of being in the world. Strengths are identified and incorporated into new narratives for the future.

Additional Approaches. More ways of doing counseling exist than can be delineated in any one introductory text. These are only a few examples.

Crisis counseling uses specific strategies to assist clients in effectively negotiate their way through unexpected traumatic events. It is "directive in nature and... focuses on helping a client find ways to respond productively and constructively in the midst of a chaotically urgent or acute emotionally disturbing situation" (Gladding, 2018, p. 41). It is action-oriented so that clients will find the resources to deal with internal and/or external crises. Rather than a theory, it is a set of prescribed techniques for events that are usually time limited, and generally lasting only up to a few weeks. It is important to bear in mind that not only are there many different kinds of crises (normal developmental events such as retirement; and unexpected, traumatic circumstances such as natural disasters, acts of terrorism, accidents, even job loss), but that individual reactions to crises vary greatly. There are several models of crisis counseling. Assessing the circumstances of the crisis – including the client's perception of the event – is always the first step, followed by offering support – including safety needs if need be – providing education, and helping the client use or develop various coping skills.

The *expressive arts approaches* contribute a variety of methods. The use of art, music, drama, and dance recognize that nonverbal methods can address therapeutic material that "talk therapy" cannot. They can circumvent resistance, defenses, and anxieties more quickly than cognitive and action-oriented processes. *Play therapy* is particularly effective with children who do not have sufficient cognitive development or verbal facility for other approaches and is growing in usage, especially among school counselors. Psychopharmacology and biofeedback can be helpful.

A major trend in the profession is toward the integration of various modalities of treatment for the betterment of the client. As a counselor-in-training, you should be knowledgeable and well versed in the more traditional approaches and learn about many newer theories. You will continue to upgrade your knowledge and skills of existing and emerging theories and techniques throughout your professional career.

Group Work

(CACREP Standard, Section 2F- 6)

Many of the approaches discussed in the previous section are used not only with individual clients but with groups of clients as well. Group counseling, however, has features that are distinct from individual counseling. The history of its evolution over the course of the last century show that group work has increased in use for many problems and can be as effective as or more effective than individual counseling (Corey, 2016).

The History of Group Counseling and Therapy

Historically, the development of group approaches parallels the history of psychotherapy and counseling. The same factors influenced the growth and refinement of both. Before 1900, group work mainly involved assisting individuals at the margins of society with increasing personal and social skills such as cleanliness and nutrition. Early in the twentieth century, members of the medical profession began to recognize the therapeutic value of bringing patients together to discuss their concerns. Dr. Joseph Pratt is credited with being the first to practice group treatment in 1905. His tuberculosis patients came together to hear him speak and to then discuss their own stories and offer encouragement to each other. Researchers began studying the nature of group dynamics and processes. Studies in human behavior indicated that people acted differently as individuals and as members of a collective. Freud (1975) first published *Group Psychology and the Analysis of the Ego* in the 1920s. It became the standard for early group work. His definition of a *psychodynamic group* is one in which there is a leader with whom members identify and form attachments, and identify and form attachments with each other.

As the century progressed, other theorists and therapists contributed their own perspective and changed the nature of early group work into the entity we call group counseling and psychotherapy today. Jacob Moreno founded the American Society for Group Psychotherapy and Psychodrama in 1942. Moreno developed an action-oriented approach to group work using what he termed psychodrama in which members act out their problems, hopes, and desires much like in improvisational theater. Goal setting for resolution of issues so that members can live more productive, creative lives is the hallmark of this method. The American Group Therapy Association formed in 1943 and became the American Group Psychotherapy Association (AGPA) in 1952. These associations today are interdisciplinary, made up of many related helping professionals.

The Second World War created a need for group work with returning veterans and spawned a variety of research into group therapy, resulting in its use as a major treatment method. *T-groups* (*training groups*) and *psychoeducational groups* emerged during this period. Social changes in the 1960s and 1970s presented new conceptualizations of group work, including the entry of *encounter groups* and *self-help groups*. Although less popular today, T-groups developed by Kurt Lewin were originally concerned with task performance and problem solving in a work setting and evolved to an emphasis on interpersonal relationships. The major focus is on learning how each group members' behavior influences other members and the group's work. *Psychoeducational groups*, as the name implies, emphasize teaching group members one or more sets of didactic information that address psychological issues. The groups are structured into a prescribed number of predetermined sessions. They "deal with imparting, discussing, and integrating factual information" (Corey, Corey, & Corey, 2014, p. 8). Some examples are career transitions, stress management, assertiveness training, self-esteem, anger management, and substance use and abuse. Encounter groups emphasize growth and change of individual group members with a focus on expression of feelings and internal processes in response to what is occurring within the group in the here and now.

One of the most influential contributions in group work was the publication of *The Theory and Practice of Group Psychotherapy* (Yalom, 1970). Yalom believed that the interpersonal characteristics of group members are the main factor in group work and contribute to its methods and goals. The hallmark of the interpersonal group approach is the ability of members to develop positive relationships with other group members so that improved relationships outside of the group will result. Members address how they experience each other in the here and now. Group work targets the process of the group itself rather than the direct resolution of problems.

In the last 30 years, group counseling has responded to the need for understanding cultural differences in the ways people relate and interact with each other. The effects of the environment, family, and socioeconomic class, as well as race, gender, ethnicity, and the various ways in which humans differ from each other can be effectively addressed through group work. Corey, Corey, and Corey (2014) advocate for an awareness of one's own worldview and the impact of culture when working with diverse group members. They discuss "a conceptual framework that organizes diversity competence into three areas: beliefs and attitudes, knowledge, and skills (p. 15).

Types of Group Work

Group counseling and psychotherapy is not one approach but a different set of approaches that can be used in different circumstances. Some distinguish between group counseling and group psychotherapy in much the same way that individual counseling and psychotherapy are distinguished. Namely, group psychotherapy is longer and more likely to deal with more severe psychological problems, whereas group counseling tends to focus on developmental problems amenable to shorter-term treatment. Ideally, both would have approximately eight to twelve members and one or two facilitators who interact closely with members. Today, common types of groups are psychoeducational, guidance, work or task, counseling, psychotherapeutic, and self-help and support. Psychoeducational and guidance groups generally involve information giving and skills building. They target a larger number of participants with less direct interaction with facilitators. School classroom and college career activities are examples. The work or task group involves a common goal of improving performance. It is typically found in workplace settings with normally functioning individuals. Counseling groups assist normally functioning participants to

> address personal and interpersonal problems of living and promote personal and interpersonal growth and development among people who may be experiencing transitory maladjustment, who are at risk for the development of personal or interpersonal problems, or who seek enhancement of personal qualities and abilities.
>
> (Association for Specialists in Group Work, 2002, p. 4)

Psychotherapy groups "address personal and interpersonal problems of living, remediate perceptual and cognitive distortions or repetitive patterns of dysfunctional behavior, and promote personal and interpersonal growth and development among people who may be experiencing severe and/or chronic maladjustment" (Association for Specialists in Group Work, 2002, p. 4). Self-help and support groups are characterized by the absence of a professional facilitator. Members are generally self-selected to address a common issue. Alcoholics Anonymous is an example.

Group Process

In group work, typical stages unfold as the group works together. The process by which this occurs seems to be a universal phenomenon. People come together as a collection of strangers and ultimately become a cohesive unit. *Group process* is thought to be all the "interactions of group members and how their relations influence the group as it develops" (Gladding, 2018, p. 71); and usually their interactions with the group facilitator. In the first stage, members are cautious of each other, fearing rejection by fellow group members or by the facilitator. In the second stage, members make attempts to address issues and often experience conflict with each other and toward the facilitator. The third stage is characterized by cohesion. The group comes together to form an identity of its own beyond that of its individual members and is thus ready for the last stage in which they begin to work together toward common goals.

Counselor's Role as Facilitator

The group leader, or facilitator, has a distinct, prescribed role within the group to assist members in reaching their goals. The facilitator first and foremost models healthy, appropriate communications and behaviors. She is the single most important factor in the success of the group. In addition to the traits necessary for successful individual counseling, group counselors must have courage to be vulnerable, open, and real in front of others and to be nondefensive in the face of criticism. Group leaders must be highly self-aware and comfortable with self-disclosing their perceptions and experiences of the group as it progresses. The facilitator's job is to let the group process unfold and to help group members authentically encounter and communicate with each other. Necessary skills include basic active listening, reflecting content and feeling, clarifying, summarizing, empathizing, questioning, interpreting for group members, confronting, making connections, and supporting (Corey, Corey & Corey, 2014). The facilitator must be able to evaluate the dynamics of the group and assess behavior and symptoms. When necessary, the facilitator will protect group members by blocking counterproductive or dysfunctional behaviors expressed by other members.

Group work often involves more than one facilitator. In fact, some prefer working in pairs and see it as the more productive method for group work. Coleaders can work together to prevent burnout, take on different levels of involvement such as facilitator or observer, and gain different perspectives on clients' issues and group process.

You will have opportunities to be a member of a group and to lead and co-lead groups in your program of study. Some students find this to be initially challenging, even daunting. It may not be easy to learn about your authentic self and to have the courage to self-disclose how you experience your fellow classmates. It is, however, necessary if you are to become a professional counselor. Most students come to value their experiences in group work as among the most significant of their training.

SIDEBAR 5.1

In Practice: What Would You Do?

Elaine has been licensed for a year and is now in private practice. She has been seeing 34-year-old Gayle weekly for three months concerning her "nervousness" about speaking up. She says her job requires her to give regular presentations, which she hates. She also doesn't like interacting with her colleagues when they don't agree with her.

> Gayle seems to have quite a level of sophistication regarding counseling. She's been in counseling many times ever since she was a teenager. I think she's a therapy junkie. She constantly uses jargon, especially terms from self-help groups like "feeding my inner child" and "toxic people." She says she's had extensive assertiveness training, and she's done considerable dream work and journaling. She also meditates regularly, is in a yoga group, and joins every support group she can find. As far as I can tell, she doesn't have friends. I think she's using these groups as her only social outlet. How can I help her when she seems to know more than I do?

Class Discussion

1. Which of the counseling theories presented in this chapter might have the most meaning in working with Gayle? Which would you consider before continuing with her?
2. How might Gayle's "sophistication" change (or not change) the counseling techniques Elaine chose or will choose in working with her?
3. Is Gayle a good candidate for group counseling? If so, what types of group work might be most beneficial? If not, why not?
4. Should Elaine consider testing Gayle? If so, for what purpose? If not, why not?
5. Elaine is considering conducting a study on "therapy junkies." If Gayle agreed to participate in the research study, what kind of study might be useful to learning about this population?

Assessment and Testing

(CACREP Standard, Section 2F-7)

Appraisal is any method that measures, assesses, or sets a value on one or more characteristics of individuals, groups, programs, or systems. It is a method by which information may be collected so that counselors gain information to understand and respond to their clients' needs. Appraisal is a necessary skill and includes a broad range of activities. It plays an important role in counseling and is a significant aspect of counselors' work (Whiston, 2017).

Types of Appraisal

Although the word appraisal may bring "testing" to mind, in fact, appraisal is an encompassing word that includes several activities. To understand these activities we must be clear on terminology. When using the word, measurement, counselors mean the activity of assigning numeric or categorical value to human characteristics using to a set of predetermined rules (Aiken & Groth-Marnat, 2005). Not all appraisals include measurement, however. Gladding (2018) defines the following activities appraisal in *The Counseling Dictionary*:

Assessment: Collecting data, such as those found administering tests or inventories, and evaluating the data and/or utilizing behavioral observations to gain information and make decisions about the diagnosis, treatment, and possible outcome of a counseling situation (p. 13).

Diagnosis: An interpretation, derived from the use of assessment information, about a person's condition (e.g., his or her level of functioning) (p. 47).

Evaluation: The process of collecting, analyzing, and judging data in order to make a decision. (p. 58).

Inventory: A list of questions, statements, or words to which an individual responds (e.g., agrees or disagrees). Inventories are designed to measure a dimension or personality, interest, aptitude, or other behavioral characteristic (p. 85).

Test:... an objective or projective instrument that measures behavior(s) or reported behaviors and characteristics (p. 157).

Assessment and evaluation may or may not involve tests or inventories. Tests are objective measures while inventories are subjective. Both have qualities that indicate how usable they are. These qualities are validity, reliability, and standardization. *Validity* is the level to which a test actually measures what it claims to measure. *Reliability* is its consistency and repeatability. *Standardization* refers to the conditions of uniformity under which an assessment is administered and scored. Standardized tests and inventories are developed on norms of a representative sample of people who have previously taken the assessment, or on criteria which are developed according to a predetermined level of achievement. Standardized measures make it possible to compare results for different individuals or the same individual across time.

Counselors use appraisal so that their decisions are sound and their interventions fit the needs of their clients (Hood & Johnson, 2007; Hays, 2017). There are five appraisal functions. These are (a) to identify counseling goals and their achievement; (b) to assist clients in making personal, academic, and career decisions for their optimal development; (c) to make decisions about placement and/or classification; (d) for program evaluation and accountability; and (e) to diagnose behaviors, conditions, and disorders.

Counselors use objective and subjective methods of appraisal to develop counseling plans, set goals, teach decision-making skills, and assist their clients in identifying problems, areas of strength, or discovering effective problem-solving strategies. Most people are likely most familiar with assessments that assist them with making academic and career decisions. School and college counselors can offer various assessment instruments of interests, skills, abilities, personality traits, and values to help students realistically understand themselves and their potential development. Appraisal methods are useful in documenting baselines and recording progress on such factors as career knowledge and maturity or coping strategies. Certainly students are most familiar with assessments used for placement and classification decisions. Student placements result from data gathering that can be used to evaluate students' academic potential. Students may be grouped according to their aptitude and/or achievement levels. This function continues to be under considerable scrutiny and criticism because diverse factors of race, gender, ethnicity, language, disability, culture, and others may not be taken into consideration. The appraisal industry has responded with more culturally unbiased instruments.

Appraisal can also provide vital information to enhance student developmental stages and growth and assist students in making personal, academic, and career decisions. Assessment instruments can measure students' levels of development across all grades. Such areas as career maturity, coping strategies, and cognition can be assessed in order to document baselines and to record progress.

Another important function of appraisal is to evaluate programs. Counselors in all settings need to be accountable for the quality and effectiveness of their services (Astramovich & Coker, 2007; Egan, 2013; Whiston, 2017). Many of the same assessment instruments used for individual appraisal are used in program evaluation. Used in this way, assessment results can give counselors feedback on their services and provide direction for new or additional services and improve practices. Program evaluation allows policy makers good information about the effectiveness of programs so they can make informed choices (Fitzpatrick, Sanders, & Worthen, 2017).

The last function of appraisal is to diagnose behaviors, conditions, and disorders. An accurate and reliable diagnosis leads to appropriate treatment. The use of diagnosis affects the quality of care, the outcome of client issues, the client's experience of counseling, and even the cost of health care.

Diagnostic Assessment

The major goals of diagnosis are to identify mental health problems, recognize factors contributing to and maintaining identified problems, select goals and implement interventions, and revise strategies when needed. Diagnosis is central to professional communication and treatment planning. Various assessment instruments and other appraisal methods allow counselors to gather information on the client's presenting concern and contributing factors associated with the problem. They can identify those factors that may hinder developmental growth as well as individual strengths and weaknesses. Appraisal of interpersonal and academic skill deficiencies can help identify the need for treatment, remedial training, or skills development, or it can discover factors inherent in the client's family, community, or society that may be maladaptive or dysfunctional.

As discussed in Chapter 2, in the section on Client Appraisal, the major source of formalized diagnosis of psychopathology in the United States is the *Diagnostic and Statistical Manual of Mental Disorders* (DSM; American Psychiatric Association, 2013). The system used in the DSM is discussed in Chapter 7, "When? Answers about Processes, Phases, and Procedures," and in Chapter 11, "Clinical Mental Health Counseling."

Research and Program Evaluation

(CACREP Standard, Section 2F-8)

Although each individual is unique, many people come into counseling and psychotherapy with clusters of issues and problems that are similar. The majority of these issues are highly researched.

Whether or not you will do original research in your career as a counselor, you will need to be an intelligent, knowledgeable consumer of research. Consequently, you will learn how to read and understand others' research findings and discriminate good research from spurious research. You will be trained in understanding research methods, statistical analysis, and needs assessment, and as well as program evaluation. You very likely will be in a position to perform the latter or use its findings to improve your practice many times in your career. In the past, behavioral sciences and education have been accused of using processes too loosely based on conjecture and past practice rather than on well-researched outcomes. Today, professional organizations and training programs strongly encouraged those in the helping profession to engage in *evidence-based practice* (EBP) to justify the use of specific interventions. EBP is a process by which evidence of effectiveness outcomes are collected, cataloged, interpreted, and integrated through systematic research, examination of client reports and practitioner observations, and analysis (Melnyk & Fineout-Overholt, 2011; Zyromski & Mariani, 2016).

Research is science and scientists search for knowledge through research. Scientific research is simply the process of asking and answering questions about phenomena that interest us and inform our practices. In searching for answers, researchers must be prepared to tolerate uncertainty. Some questions are not easily answered. Research methods are a way of thinking, or a process of inquiry, in order to find answers.

Research Methods

Social scientists have many research methods available to them. The type of method chosen is driven by the questions asked, and often the number of resources and amount of time available. *Quantitative research* relies on numbers, is objective, and uses deductive reasoning. It is broadly broken down into descriptive research and experimental methods. *Descriptive methods*, as the word suggests, attempt to describe a phenomenon as it exists by gathering data in the form of surveys such as questionnaires and case studies. *Experimental methods* use controlled conditions to describe and analyze data by manipulating one or more variables and controlling others. The purpose is to discover causes and effects. Bridging descriptive and experimental methods is the *comparative study method*. Called *correlational studies*, they attempt to discover similarities and differences between and among variables but they do not make any statements about cause and effect. They simply compare measures and their direction (positive or negative) and degree.

Qualitative methods are a non-numerical way to collect data in order to explain the attributes of a phenomenon or source of data. It is subjective and uses inductive reasoning. It attempts to understand phenomena as they occur without preconceived ideas about them. The main emphasis is to the unique phenomenological world or viewpoint of others. It is suited to complex social, psychological, or educational issues for which numbers would tell an inadequate story or miss data altogether. Thus, in-depth interviews and field research are two methods that can garner such data.

Quantitative methods. Whichever quantitative method is chosen, researchers use a scientific inquiry method to reach conclusions about the questions they ask. Existing information is stated and logical rules are followed. The process generally includes a major premise, or a tentative answer to a question; a minor premise, derived from the major premise; and the conclusion. Many research designs exist. Most involve quantitative methods that involve five phases. In the idea-generating phase, inspiration can come from many places – the research and theories of others or the researcher's own interests. In this phase, researchers conduct a review of existing literature to see what others have discovered about an idea. Once an informal question is generated, the researcher moves to the second, problem definition, phase, in which the ideas are formalized into testable research questions. Drawing upon relevant content acquired in findings in professional literature, the researcher's goal is to justify the necessity, or desirability, of undertaking a systematic study of the issue addressed. This phase is characterized by thinking through and developing answers to these questions: How does my idea compare to existing theory and research? Does my idea make sense? Is it logical? What answer does my idea predict?

When these questions are satisfactorily answered the researcher enters the procedures-design phase. Content in this phase varies depending upon the type of research undertaken. In quantitative research, the research idea is translated into a testable hypothesis. The researcher must plan each step in the research design. It may include descriptions of those who will participate or be studied, definitions of variables involved, data gathering instrument(s), research/evaluation design, and data analysis plans. Ethical issues must be considered. All these early phases are included in planning the research study. Researchers often cannot include in their studies an entire population when they gather information. They use statistics, or methods, that will allow them to study a representative sample and generalize their results to the entire population.

The observation phase is the central activity during which actual data is gathered. This is the phase most familiar to everyone when they think of research and is best understood as the "doing the research" phase. The data gathered during this phase will begin to answer the question or questions raised earlier but the answers will not be properly understood until the results are later evaluated and interpreted in the next phase. In the data-analysis phase, the researcher generally uses statistical procedures which were previously determined in the research-design phase. Many types of statistics are available, depending on the nature of the questions asked and the characteristics of the data. Once the data are analyzed the researcher attempts to make sense of the study's results in the interpretation phase. First, the statistical findings are interpreted. The researcher attempts to discover how the findings relate to the research question asked and if there might be other interpretations of the data. The researcher will then discuss the findings. A final written report will include all the steps undertaken in the study and the extent to which a researcher can generalize the findings to populations other than those who participated in the study involved. A statement on limitations is usually included and can refer to the subject group(s) used in the study and to tests, rating scales, and questionnaires used.

Once the researcher has drawn conclusions and written a research paper describing all of the above steps, he enters the final, or public announcement, phase. Researchers make their work public through publishing their papers in academic journals or books and presenting their findings at professional conferences. In doing so, they allow others to judge, challenge, or build on their work.

This describes the basic, traditional scientific inquiry research process. However, in the behavioral sciences including in counseling, other research processes are also used. Researching human behavior requires a complex set of approaches. Methodological diversity is important (Heppner, Wampold, Owen, Thompson, & Wang, 2016).

Qualitative methods. Qualitative research does not involve statistical analysis because it does not use numbers. Qualitative researchers do not begin with a hypothesis that must be tested. Rather, they allow the data to emerge from the phenomenon they want to know about, and then categorize data into patterns that seem to indicate the nature of the phenomenon and generate a resulting hypothesis or theory, known as *grounded theory*. They make no statements about the generalizability of the data to any circumstance other than the one they study in reporting their results (Lincoln & Guba, 1985). Borrowed from anthropological and sociological disciplines, qualitative research in counseling allows researchers to discover truths that may not have been evident by the use the traditional scientific inquiry methods of quantitative research. Qualitative researchers collect data through participant and nonparticipant observation, ethnography, interviews and storytelling, and many other non-numerical methods. They analyze the data by looking for patterns and a "thick description" of the data, including direct quotes from interviewees and detailed notes from field study observations.

Program Evaluation

Program evaluation is the kind of research many counselors are most likely to perform because they are responsible for the outcomes of their work. "a program is an ongoing, planned intervention that seeks to achieve some particular outcome(s) in response to some perceived educational, social, or commercial problem" (Fitzpatrick, Sanders, & Worthen, 2011, p. 8). Program evaluations are undertaken to ascertain the effectiveness of counseling programs. The result will ultimately be used to make program decisions. Although program evaluation uses the same basic procedures as any research model and the same research skills are necessary, there are some major differences. The fundamental question in this kind of research will depend upon whom or what group has commissioned the study. Program evaluation is generally purposive, or undertaken to find a certain set of facts. It may involve a needs assessment and a conclusion about services, or the outcome. The program evaluator must consider the context and the process of the study. She must weigh the existing goals and priorities of her research to see if they are attuned to the needs of those to be served. The evaluator will receive input from sources that may or may not have been originally in her design. She may be doing a needs assessment, studying day-to-day operations of an organization or its processes, measuring results or outcomes. The researcher may consider the impact of the assessment or the extent to which a program causes changes in the desired direction. Policies may depend upon the results. The researcher may be interested in measuring efficiency, quantifying the outcomes, and discovering the time or monetary costs. Researchers can be commissioned to perform cost-benefit analyses wherein desired outcomes are compared against actual costs. Often the results are presented in a report to those who commissioned the research rather than in professional journals and books or at conferences.

Action research is a specialized example of qualitative research used in schools. It is "a systematic inquiry into the teaching and learning environment… [that] gathers information about how schools perform, the impact of instruction, and how students are learning." It is "a process of cyclical inquiry resulting in ongoing and continuous improvement" (Dahir & Stone, 2009).

Summary

This chapter continued the introduction of core CACREP areas of study. The importance of theory and its role in counseling was reviewed, along with the general categories into which theories fall followed by examples of kinds of interventions, strategies, and techniques associated with each. The chapter continued with a discussion of group work and process, its history and types, and the role of the facilitator. It provided an orientation to the use of assessment and testing and research and program evaluation, both important elements of the counselor's work.

> *I didn't want to take the career course and I certainly didn't see why I had to take research or testing to be a mental health counselor. Okay, I admit it. I actually enjoyed them. And I get it now. I know I can't be a good counselor without these courses.*
>
> – student to her advisor

References

Adler, A. (1963). *The practice and theory of individual psychology.* Patterson, NJ: Littlefield, Adams.

Aiken, L. R., Jr., & Groth-Marnat, G. (2005). *Psychological testing and assessment* (12th ed.). Boston: Allyn & Bacon.

American Psychiatric Association. (2013). *Diagnostic and statistical manual of mental disorders* (5th ed.). Washington, DC: Author.

American Psychoanalytic Association. (n.d.) *Why psychoanalysis?* Retrieved from http://www.apsa.org/About_Psychoanalysis/Why_Psychoanalysis_.aspx

Association for Specialists in Group Work. (2002). *Professional standards for the training of group workers.* Retrieved from http://www.asgw.org/PDF/training_standards.pdf

Astramovich, R. L., & Coker, J. K. (2007). Program evaluation: The accountability bridge model for counselors. *Journal of Counseling & Development, 85,* 162–172.

Beck, A. T., & Weishear, M. (2014). Cognitive therapy. In D. Wedding & R. J. Corsini (Eds.), *Current psychotherapies* (10th ed., pp. 231–264). Belmont, CA: Brooks/Cole, Cengage.

Beck, J. S. (1995). *Cognitive therapy: Basics and beyond.* New York: Guilford.

Berg, I. K. (1994). *Family based services: A solution-focused approach.* New York: Norton.

Bowen, M. (1978). *Family therapy in clinical practice.* New York: Jason Aronson.

Carter, B., & McGoldrick, M. (Eds.). (2005). *The expanded family life cycle: Individual, family, and social perspectives* (3rd ed.). Boston: Allyn & Bacon.

Corey, G. (2016). *Theory and practice of group counseling* (9th ed.). Boston: Cengage Learning.

Corey, M. S., Corey, G., & Corey, C. (2014). *Groups: Process and practice* (9th ed.) Belmont, CA: Brooks/Cole Cengage Learning.

Dahir, C. A., & Stone, C. B. (2009). School counselor accountability: The path to social justice and systemic change. *Journal of Counseling & Development, 87,* 12–20.

de Shazer, S. (1985). *Keys to solutions in brief therapy.* New York: W. W. Norton.

Egan, G. (2013). *The skilled helper: A problem-management and opportunity-development approach to helping.* Belmont, CA: Brooks/Cole, Cengage Learning.

Ellis, A. E. (1962). *Reason and emotion in psychotherapy.* New York: Lyle Stuart.

Ellis, A. E. (2014). Rational-emotive behavioral therapy. In D. Wedding & R. J. Corsini (Eds.), *Current psychotherapies* (10th ed., pp. 151–191). Belmont, CA: Brooks/Cole, Cengage Learning.

Ellis, A. E., & Dryden, W. (1997). *The practice of rational emotive behavior therapy* (2nd ed.). New York: Springer.

Fitzpatrick, J. L., Sanders, J. R., & Worthen, B. R. (2011). *Program evaluation: Alternative approaches and practical guidelines* (3rd ed.). Pearson.

Fitzpatrick, J. L., Sanders, J. R., & Worthen, B. R. (2017). *Program evaluation: Alternative approaches and practical guidelines* (4th ed.). Upper Saddle River, NJ: Pearson.

Frankl, V. (1963). *Man's search for meaning.* Boston: Beacon.

Freud, S. (1975). *Group psychology and the analysis of the ego* (J. Strachey, trans.). New York: Norton (Original work published in 1922).

Gilligan, C. (1982). *In a different voice.* Cambridge, MA: Harvard University Press.

Gladding, S. T. (2018). *The counseling dictionary* (4th ed.). Alexandria, VA: American Counseling Association.

Glasser, W. (1998). *Choice theory.* New York: Harper Collins.

Haley, J. (1973). *Uncommon therapy: The psychiatric techniques of milton H. Erickson, M. D.* New York: Norton.

Hays, D. G. (2017). *Assessment in counseling: Procedures and practices.* Alexandria, VA: John Wiley & Sons.

Heppner, P. P., Wampold, B. E., Owen, J., Thompson, M. N., & Wang, K. T. (2016). *Research design in counseling* (4th ed.). Boston: Cengage Learning.

Hood, A. B., & Johnson, R. W. (2007). *Assessment in counseling* (4th ed.). Alexandria, VA: American Counseling Association.

Kottler, J. A., & Shepard, D. S. (2015). *Introduction to counseling: Voices from the field* (8th ed.). Stamford, CT: Cengage Learning.

Lazarus, A. A. (1989). *The practice of multimodal therapy: Systematic, comprehensive, and effective psychotherapy.* Baltimore, MD: Johns Hopkins University Press.

Lincoln, Y., & Guba, E. G. (1985). *Naturalist inquiry.* Newbury Park, CA: Sage Publications.

May, R. (1950). *The meaning of anxiety.* New York: Ronald Press.

Melnyk, B. M., & Fineout-Overholt, E. (2011). *Evidence-based practice in nursing and healthcare: A guide to best practice.* Philadelphia, PA: Lippincott Williams & Wilkins.

Miller, J. B. (1986). *Toward a new psychology of women.* Boston, MA: Beacon.

Minuchin, S. (1974). *Families and family therapy*. Cambridge, MA: Harvard University Press.

Monk, G., Winslade, J., & Crocket, K. (Eds.). (1997). *Narrative therapy in practice: The archaeology of hope*. San Francisco, CA: Jossey-Bass.

Perls, F., Hefferline, R. F., & Goodman, P. (1965). *Gestalt therapy*. Oxford: Dell.

Rogers, C. (1942). *Counseling and psychotherapy*. Boston: Houghton Mifflin.

Rogers, C. (1951). *Client-centered therapy: Its current practice, implications, and theory*. Boston: Houghton Mifflin.

Rogers, C. R. (1957). The necessary and sufficient conditions of therapeutic personality change. *Journal of Counseling Psychology, 2*, 95–103.

Satir, V. (1967). *Conjoint family therapy*. Palo Alto, CA: Science and Behavior Books.

Schwartz, R. (1995). *Internal family systems therapy*. New York: Guilford.

Watzlawick, P., Weakland, J. H., & Fisch, R. (1974). *Change: Principles of problem formulation and problem resolution*. New York: Norton.

Whiston, S. C. (2017). *Principles and applications of assessment in counseling* (5th ed.). Boston: Cengage Learning.

Wubbolding, R. E. (1991). *Understanding reality therapy*. New York: Harper Collins.

Yalom, I. (1970). *The theory and practice of group psychotherapy*. New York: Basic Books.

Yalom, I. (1980). *Existential psychotherapy*. New York: Basic Books.

Zyromski, B., & Mariani, M. A. (2016). *Facilitating evidence-based, data-driven school counseling: A manual for practice*. Thousand Oaks, CA: Corwin/Sage.

Table 5.1 *TFAC Chart – Thought, Feelings, Actions, and Context

Self	My Thoughts	My Feelings	My Actions	My Context	Other? (Specify)
Which counseling theories appeal to me most right now and why?					
Which techniques attract me the most and why?					
What do I anticipate it will be like to be part of a group? To facilitate a group?					
What is my past experience with testing and assessment?					
What is my stance on the need for research and program evaluation?					
What concerns do I have?					
Others	**Others' Probable Thoughts**	**Others' Possible Feelings**	**Others' Observable Actions**	**Others' Apparent Context**	**Other? (Specify)**
What theories and techniques do my instructors favor?					
What theories and techniques are counselors in my area of interest using?					
What are the group experiences of my classmates and instructors?					
How do instructors and counselors use assessment in their work?					
How do instructors and counselors use research and/or program evaluation?					
Other?					

*For more information on TFAC, see Chapter 1.

Chapter 6

Where? Answers about Settings and Surroundings

Mary H. Guindon

Do what you can, with what you have, where you are.

– Theodore Roosevelt

POINTS TO PONDER

- What are the differences and similarities in the work settings of various kinds of counselors?
- Where do counselors with different specialties work?
- What is private practice?
- How do counselors provide services on the Internet?
- What do counseling offices look like?
- How do I pick a field placement setting?
- What are some new and emerging settings for practice?

Settings Where Counseling Takes Place

The last two chapters presented the core areas that make counseling a unique profession. All professional counselors are trained in these areas. The basic core counseling master's degree is sufficient for some settings; for others, counselors must meet additional course work in specialty areas. The Council for Accreditation in Counseling and Related Educational Programs (CACREP) Standards (2015) recognizes seven specialties at the master's level: addictions counseling; career counseling; clinical mental health counseling; clinical rehabilitation counseling; college counseling and student affairs; marriage, couple, and family therapy; and school counseling. At the doctoral level, CACREP provides accreditation in the area of Counselor Education and Supervision.

Each of these specialties has its own set of learning domains in addition to the eight core areas that constitute the counseling profession common knowledge base. Part Two of this text discusses each of these specialty areas. In this chapter, we discuss how counselors with these different specializations may be found working in diverse settings performing a variety of functions, and how some may be found in the same settings working in different specializations. The most common settings in which counseling takes place are briefly discussed here.

Schools

With its roots in the school guidance movement of the early twentieth century, school counseling today is perhaps the most common career field for counselors. School counselors work in elementary, middle, and secondary schools. Some clinical mental health counselors or family therapists who specialize in counseling children and their families can also be found within school walls.

Counseling and guidance services. School may be what most people associate with the term counselor. Few of us have not come across our school counselor in middle and secondary school. Usually, the school counselor is the first and perhaps only professional counselor many people encounter. Today's school counselor bears only a passing resemblance to the vocational guidance worker upon which the foundation of our profession is built. Today, 32 states have adopted comprehensive school counseling programs in public elementary and secondary schools (American School Counselor Association, 2018). The school's mission, of course, is to educate. Student achievement is the primary focus of the school and a concern to the community. School counselors support the school mission by implementing various services that target academic, career, and socio-emotional needs of students. Developmental counseling and guidance, program management, consultation and leadership, advocacy, and personal counseling make up the counselor's typical workday. Professional school counselors are "uniquely qualified to address all students' academic, career and social/emotional development needs by designing, implementing, evaluating and enhancing a comprehensive school counseling program that promotes and enhances student success" (American School Counselor Association, n.d.).

School counselors at each academic level implement programs. They promote the academic, career, social, and emotional development and wellbeing of students. They also engage in administrative and program management duties. Comprehensive school counseling programs address developmental needs so that students are academically successful. Effective programs are integrated into the overall educational practices of the school, and are distinct entities within the school with their own specific goals and an organized curriculum that includes age-appropriate, sequential activities. According to ASCA (n.d.), to be effective school counselors, counselors need sources of information about academic achievement, accountability, advocacy, career counseling, comprehensive school counseling programs, conflict resolution and bullying, group counseling, health, and violence prevention/safe schools.

Today counselors offer comprehensive direct and indirect services. Direct services include individual counseling, group counseling, classroom guidance, and psychoeducational activities. Individual and group counseling may address school performance or personal issues. Study skills, career or college planning, peer relationships, conflicts at home, family issues such as divorce or death of a family member, substance abuse, issues of sexuality, and crisis are just some of the issues brought into counseling. School counseling is generally short term. When counselors encounter more serious issues or those that cannot be resolved in a few sessions, they refer out to other helping professionals. Classroom guidance is a direct service that addresses study skills and career planning and other age-appropriate, developmental concerns and can be effective in cases of school violence, disaster, or the death of a teacher or student.

Indirect services include consultation and coordination activities. Consultation is a skill by which counselors offer their problem-solving and communication expertise to teachers, administrators, or family members. The focus is on an identified student's academic progress or wellbeing. Often the counselor advocates on the student's behalf if she also provides direct counseling to the student. Consultation can occur in the broader context of the community. Thus, school counselors must be informed on legal issues, suicide or violence, disaster and crisis, good public relations, and myriad other topics. The school counselor is one of several experts who collaborate for the betterment of the student or a group of students. Collaborative consultation is a comprehensive, usually preventive service. School counselors often serve on various school teams and offer their expertise in the many core areas in which they are trained and knowledgeable such as human development, group process, communication skills, and conflict resolution. Counselors at all levels create and implement the school guidance curriculum. At the elementary level, counselors assist children successfully negotiate developmental tasks and help them deal with problems at school and at home. The mission is to assist young children in healthy self-concept development and appropriate independence. Elementary school counseling is the newest school discipline. Primary prevention is a key concern as society has increasingly recognized that problems experienced early in life can have long-standing consequences. Elementary school counselors function to prevent more serious problems by intervening for such issues as peer relationships, diversity, learning difficulties, divorce, and abuse. They also work in growth-enhancing areas of career identity, self-esteem, social skills, and myriad other topics. Elementary school counselors work with students, families, teachers, and at times, members of the community. Creating and managing school programs is an integral part of the elementary school counselor's work.

At the middle school level, counselors add issues around the developmental changes occurring to children in later childhood and early adolescence. The mission is to assist students in gaining greater self-awareness and understanding their developing values. Children experience dramatic physical and emotional changes during these years and the middle school counselor's job can be a challenging one. Sexuality, romantic relationships, changing relationships with parents, career concerns, academic performance, and classroom behavior are some of the issues that are addressed. Although not part of the assigned role, counselors may also be involved in academic testing and placement coordination duties as well as advising and scheduling. Group counseling and classroom guidance activities are common. Referrals for serious issues are part of the counselor's job and a network of community resources is essential.

In secondary school, counselors spend much of their time on career and college concerns. Activities include reviewing transcripts, writing letters of recommendation for college admissions, and other tasks. Depending upon the enlightenment of the administration, high school counselors' tasks vary on the amount of time spent on the administrative areas of class scheduling and educational planning. The counselor's mission is to assist students in mastering interpersonal success, clarifying vocational identity, and encouraging social interest. Secondary school counselors provide individual counseling on a wide range of personal issues and may provide group counseling for issues of sexuality, pregnancy, racial tensions, substance abuse prevention, college aspirations, career concerns, and many more. They make referrals to other helping professionals as serious issues of psychopathology, addictions, eating disorders, and suicidal ideation become more common or begin to manifest in later adolescence or young adulthood.

Today's realities have outgrown traditional individual counseling models. School counselors have shifted their focus from traditional functions to comprehensive developmental school counseling programs that target systemic change. They have the potential to overcome institutional K-12 school barriers, particularly for urban students and families. Whereas individual and group counseling were mainstays of school counselors of the past, now they are seen as instances for collaborative work in advocacy to assist in closing achievement and opportunity gaps. Nevertheless, although individual and group counseling cannot meet the needs of all students in K-12 urban schools, they remain an important part of a school's comprehensive program (Gysbers & Henderson, 2012).

School-based agencies. A trend in recent years has been to place community agency representatives directly into schools, particularly at the secondary level. Depending upon resources, social workers, psychologists, clinical mental health counselors, and family counselors who are employed by local community or mental health agencies may be on site in schools every day, a part of every day, or one day a week. School counselors work closely with their agency counter-parts to provide services to students who need more in-depth counseling than they are able to provide, either because of time constraints or lack of specialized training. Students with the more serious issues discussed earlier can receive counseling without having to take off time to travel to an agency. Time for counseling is scheduled into their school day.

Preventive and early intervention services are also offered in some schools. For example, in Montgomery County, Maryland, Linkages to Learning is a collaboration of the county schools, the county health and human services department, and local non-profit community agencies. Linkages to Learning provides health, mental health, social services, and educational support to at-risk children and their families in school settings. The aim is to enhance school, home, and community adjustment and performance.

Higher Education Settings

At the post-secondary level, professional counselors work in universities, four-year colleges, community colleges, and vocational-technical schools. Counselors fall into two categories: those who provide personal and career counseling and those who provide student personnel services. Each is a distinct discipline.

SIDEBAR 6.1

In Practice: What Would You Do?

Donna is an intern in a rural county in the Midwest. She is in her last semester before graduating. Her office is a storage room consisting of two chairs, several large boxes of sup-plies, and no outside window. There is a two-way mirror with a camera on one wall. Donna always explains to her clients that her supervisor will review the tapes with her but that no one else will see them. Until now, she believes she has done very good work with her clients. She has seen Jim, 27, for six sessions. He is a mail clerk at the local public water service office.

> Jim is extremely shy and says it's always been that way. It took him a while to open up to me and when he did, he confided that he longs for a friend he can talk to and dreams of having a girlfriend. He says he stuttered when he was in school and sometimes people make fun of him and have for as long as he can remember. It's hard for him to interact with people. He's not sure what to do or say. He says he usually goes along with whatever anyone wants. We've role-played some conversations he might have at social gatherings but so far he hasn't followed through. I think we are moving at a snail's pace but I'm wondering, too, if I'm pushing him too hard.

Class Discussion

1. What counseling setting(s) and specialty(ies) might Donna be training for?
2. How conducive is Donna's counseling space to her client's self-disclosure?
3. Given her restrictions, what might Donna do to her office?
4. Considering what you have learned so far in previous chapters, how do you think Donna should proceed with Jim?

Counseling centers. Most institutions of higher education have student counseling centers that provide personal, academic, and career counseling to students and alumni. Centers may make services available to faculty and staff and the broader community. Centers vary in the services they offer. Larger universities provide comprehensive services and smaller institutions only specific targeted services.

Counseling centers assist students in acquiring the skills, dispositions, and resources needed to succeed in college, and pursue productive, fulfilling lives; and help students cope with personal and academic difficulties. The mission of a full-service counseling center is to be responsive to the counseling and psychiatric needs of its students by providing individual and group counseling, crisis management, and consultation, and to provide psychoeducational outreach services to the campus and the broader community. Counselors are licensed practitioners with mental health expertise and work alongside licensed clinical or counseling psychologists or licensed clinical social workers. Treatment modalities cover a range of approaches but brief techniques are typically used because the number of sessions is limited, usually six to twelve, depending upon the policy of the center. The goal of individual counseling is to stabilize and assist students so that they can return to their normal day-to-day functioning. Group counseling is often preventive and the treatment of choice for many students. Talking with other students who have similar experiences in a supportive group environment helps provide perspective and is therapeutic in itself. Examples of college groups are stress management programs; study skills training; anxiety or depression support; understanding the self; eating disorders, bipolar disorder support, divorce support; peer relationships, including exclusion from peer groups such as fraternities and sororities; and various groups for diverse or minority populations, athletes, international students, older returning students, or first-generation college students.

Outreach brings mental health-related information to the campus community for educational and preventive purposes. Activities include workshops and psychoeducational presentations to students and residence life staff, and meetings with student affairs professional staff throughout the campus community. Examples are prevention of drug and alcohol misuse, suicide prevention and intervention, and crisis intervention or disaster mental health response. Other services provided in counseling centers are 24-hour emergency response, walk-in services, testing services, and learning disabilities evaluation.

Career and placement centers. A major emphasis in higher education is career services that assist students and alumni in their exploration of academic majors and professional opportunities. Community colleges commonly have full-service career centers available to students and the communities they serve. Colleges and universities may house career services in their counseling centers or they may be freestanding centers in their own right. Each school within a major university may have its own career center. Vocational-technical colleges may have full-service career centers or target only employment counseling and job search. Activities found in career centers include career counseling; career workshops on interests, skills, or values clarification; testing and assessment; career resource libraries, including access to computer-generated programs and the Internet; interviewing and job search workshops; résumé and letter-writing skills; career fairs; on-campus recruiting program; or facilitating professional experience programs such as work-study or summer internships.

Student affairs. Professional counselors who work in student personnel services in higher education share careers with those trained in student affairs and higher education administration, a distinct and separate career field. Both have their roots in the early years of the vocational guidance movement of the early twentieth century. The American College Personnel Association (ACPA) was one of the four founding organization of the American Personnel and Guidance Association (ACPG), now ACA. In 1992, ACPA became an independent association. To takes its place under the ACA umbrella was the American College Counseling Association

(ACCA). Other professional associations for this career field are the National Association of Student Personnel Administration (NASPA) and the National Association of Women Deans, Administrators, and Counselors (NAWDAC). Many additional associations target specific functions within higher education such as advising, registration and admissions, campus activities, and the like. An example is the National Academic Advising Association (NACADA), which promotes and supports quality academic advising in institutions of higher education (see http://www.nacada.ksu.edu). Variously called college student personnel, student affairs administration, and now student affairs in higher education, the mission is to create and manage educational settings by addressing the needs of diverse and changing student populations and by facilitating healthy developmental changes for individuals and groups. Practitioners receive training at the post-baccalaureate level in understanding higher education systems, and student affairs roles, responsibilities, and systems in the broader educational environment. Graduates are experts in individual, group, organizational, and leadership theories and their relevance to student affairs practice. They are knowledgeable in student and personal development and learning theory. Depending upon their graduate programs of study, practitioners may or may not have expertise and skill in counseling. They may advise student groups and organizations, implement and evaluate educational and student service-based programs, or perform administration services in various student affairs functions. Examples are residence life and student housing; campus community outreach, volunteer and civic opportunities; recruitment and minority affairs; alumni relations; admissions and academic advising; student activities, including Greek advisors; campus recreation; academic support, peer mentoring, and tutoring; cultural programs; diversity and equal opportunity education; and many more.

Community and Mental Health Settings

Historically, clinical mental health counseling has its roots in community counseling. In 2009, community and mental health counselors were merged into one specialty, Clinical Mental Health Counseling. However, community and mental health settings are not exactly the same and a review of community mental health history is necessary.

The term *community counseling* was originally used to indicate counseling activities that were carried out in settings other than schools and higher education institutions. Counselors began expanding their services beyond the educational settings in the 1960s as a result of federal legislation. The Community Mental Health Centers Act of 1963 mandated the creation of mental health centers in over 2,000 locations. The profession responded by offering training to meet the need, and the community counseling specialty was born. Over the years, additional federal legislation created much of what exists today in community mental health settings. States were divided into catchment areas that provide comprehensive services to approximately 200,000 residents. In each catchment area, the community center provides services in inpatient care, outpatient counseling, partial day care, crisis intervention, and consultation and education. Funding for full services, however, has decreased over the years and all areas are not equally served.

Today, community counseling is much broader and more comprehensive than described in its original mission. Community counseling is defined as "comprehensive helping framework that is grounded in multicultural competence and oriented toward social justice" (Lewis, Lewis, Daniels, & D'Andrea, 2011, p. 9). Community counselors perform many roles and purposes in an assortment of settings, and how they work with clients differs from one population to another.

Direct and indirect services to help community members live more effectively and to prevent the problems most frequently faced by those who use the services. Counselors in non-school settings offer individual, group, and family counseling; long-term, short-term, or crisis counseling;

psychoeducational workshops; consultation; and advocacy services. A counselor may work in a community-based agency, in an affiliated psychiatric hospital, in a private mental health center, in a vocational rehabilitation center, in a substance abuse facility, in prisons, with the federal government or military, independently in a sole proprietorship or group practice, as a consultant in a nonprofit mental health clinic, or in an employee assistance program as either a consultant or service provider. Community counselors may also work in public employment agencies or state and local career centers or practice independently with those seeking assistance on academic, career, and job search issues. Each of these specialties provides different opportunities. The setting may be the same or quite different for each of these services. Community and mental health facilities vary from state to state in how their services are organized. One facility may divide clients by age or gender, another by severity of disorder, still another may separate mental health concerns from substance abuse and addictions.

Mental health settings. *Mental health counselors* are those who identify themselves as distinctly affiliated with professional counseling and whose "theoretical basis is counseling and not psychiatry, psychology, or social work" (Palmo, Weikel, & Borsos, 2006, p. 52). Initially professional counselors were not among those included in the mental health professions. The National Institute of Mental Health (NIMH) added mental health counselors to psychiatrists, psychologists, social workers, and psychiatric nurses in 1986. The term mental health counseling is used by any of the allied helping professions that offer mental health services.

The counseling profession, with its emphasis on serving those who fall into the "normal" category, traditionally had a slightly different role in mental health practice but since has come to offer the same services as other professions through its upgrading in training and through the advocacy efforts of the American Mental Health Counselors Association (AMHCA). Mental health counselors must possess skills that are generalizable across a wide variety of concerns. They are trained in psychopathology, diagnosis and treatment planning, addictions, and many other topics critical to providing services to those with psychopathological disorders. They also provide primary, secondary, and tertiary care.

> Primary prevention means that, through promoting healthy behaviors, many disorders may be prevented altogether before problems reach a critical point and before they exact a psychological toll. Secondary prevention means that disorders can be minimized by early identification and treatment. Tertiary treatment means providing interventions for fully developed disorders so that their effects and symptoms can be managed.
>
> (Guindon, Giordano, & Wright, 2019, p. 364)

Although clinical mental health counselors can be found in a variety of settings, including psychiatric hospitals, many work in outpatient community agencies or private practice. They may be assigned to clients with needs ranging from those with developmental issues of life transition or adjustment to those with lifelong mental health problems. Depending upon the focus of the agency, clients may be young children, adolescents, adults of all ages and life stages, or those who are at the end of life. Counselors are well skilled in assessment, interviewing, and diversity. They are excellent at establishing rapport and building relationships. Clinical mental health counselors may need to decide quickly, often as a member of a treatment team, whether a distressed client is in crisis or of dangerous to the self or others. Sometimes clients will need to be hospitalized, especially when they need acute care; other times, outpatient care may be more appropriate. In still other cases, when a deteriorating chronic disorder is present, partial-hospitalization day treatment may be the best course of action. The setting will be determined by the diagnosis and the best course of treatment. In addition to the level of care, the type of care – individual, group, or family – will determine the setting.

Marriage and family counselors specialize in the same general issues as mental health counselors, but their emphasis is holistic. The family unit is the client, not just one individual within the family. They concentrate on "problems, needs and changing patterns of couples and family relationships" (Reevy, Ozer, & Ito, 2010, p. 55). "Marriage and Family Counselors practice in a variety of settings, including independent practice, community mental health agencies, managed care organizations, hospitals, employee assistance programs, and houses of worship" (Dunham, 2017, p. 888). Several professional organizations support the training and credentialing of marriage and family therapists, including the International Association of Marriage and Family Counselors (IAMFC), the American Association for Marriage and Family Therapy (AAMFT), and the Commission on Accreditation for Marriage and Family Therapy (CAMFT).

Substance abuse settings. *Substance abuse counselors* work in various settings in which addiction is the treatment goal. Although addictions counseling is its own area of specialization, substance abuse is so common that a client may present with issues related to abuse in any setting. People can abuse not only drugs and alcohol but many other substances, including food. Counselors must be trained in recognizing substance abuse even if only to know when and where to refer. Alcohol and other drugs (AOD) are a serious physical and mental health risk and addiction problems manifest in nearly every counseling setting. Those with AOD problems may present in counseling settings at any point along a continuum of abuse. They may need a variety of services along a prevention/intervention continuum. They can be found in rehabilitation centers, psychiatric hospitals, outpatient facilities, and private practice settings to name a few. A substance abuse problem is present when "a client's use of alcohol or another mood-altering drug has undesired effects on his or her life or on the lives of others" (Lewis, Dana & Blevins, 2015, p. 4), whereas addiction is a present only when physical symptoms of withdrawal or tolerance to the substance are present (Lewis, Dana, & Blevins, 2015). The Center for Substance Abuse Treatment (U. S. Substance Abuse and Mental Health Services Administration n.d.) seeks to expand and improve access, while reducing barriers for those needing treatment in any substance-use and abuse area. They also recommend individuals can be identified and assessed directly or through appropriate prevention services such as mental health centers, school counseling, suicide helplines, or private practice.

Substance abuse counselors may treat others affected by a client's addiction, such as their children or adult children of alcoholics (ACOAs). Substance abuse counselors can also work with those who have been convicted of driving under the influence (DUI) or with inmates in prison settings who have alcohol or drug-related problems. The International Association of Addiction and Offender Counselors (IAAOC) (who also work in forensics and criminal justice) and the National Association of Alcohol and Drug Abuse Counselors (NAADAC) oversee the professional activities of substance abuse counselors.

Rehabilitation settings. *Rehabilitation counselors* specialize in helping those with disabilities of all kinds overcome their skill deficits and societal barriers to become as fully functioning as feasible. According to The American Rehabilitation Counseling Association (ARCA),

> Rehabilitation counseling is a systematic process which assists persons with physical, mental, developmental, cognitive, and emotional disabilities to achieve their personal, career, and independent living goals in the most integrated settings possible through the application of the counseling process. The counseling process involves communication, goal setting, and beneficial growth or change through self-advocacy, psychological, vocational, social, and behavioral interventions.

> (n.d., Scope of Practice Statement)

ARCA, along with the Commission on Rehabilitation Certification (CCRC), oversees the work of rehabilitation counselors. These counselors work with those with physical disabilities such as blindness or head injuries, the mentally ill released from psychiatric hospitals, prisoners after release from prison, substance abusers upon their release from inpatient facilities, those who are developmental disabilities, and in some cases, those who are involuntarily unemployed. Each area is a specialty of its own.

Rehabilitation counselors are found in state, federal, and private agencies that specialize in specific disorders. They are also found in Veterans Administration hospitals, assisting veterans and their families with managing a disability or with issues of grief and family relationships.

The Americans with Disabilities Act (ADA) strives to eliminate societal and employment barriers so that fuller, more productive lives are possible for those with disabilities. Under ADA, employment discrimination is prohibited against qualified individuals with disabilities. Individuals are considered to have a qualified disability if they meet the legitimate skill, experience, education, or other requirements of an employment position that they hold or seek, and who can perform the "essential functions" of the position with or without reasonable accommodation. The ADA prohibits discrimination in all employment practices, including job application procedures, hiring, firing, advancement, compensation, and training. This applies to all employment-related activities. Hence, career and employment counselors also may work in rehabilitation settings.

Business, Industry and Governmental Settings

As the counseling professional has matured over the last 25 years, opportunities in business, industry, and governmental agencies have become available. Corporate America now recognizes that the most important capital of any company is its human capital and consequently attends to retaining valued employees. They invest considerable time and money in quality of life, or work/life programs. Training programs are extensive and can rival educational opportunities in higher educational institutions. Professional counselors offer counseling and consulting services that maximize the potential of working adults in corporate settings. Counselors have a unique set of skills in interpersonal communication and relationship building, leadership training, facilitation of human development, transition management, career development, diversity and cross-cultural understanding, stress, burnout and violence, and other mental health and wellness concerns. This growing specialty of organizational counseling can be found as part of corporate human resource department, under the broad title of human resource development, or in employee relations, or in any number of other parts of organizations. Counselors can be found in career development centers of large corporations or in training and education departments of smaller companies. Some may work as organizational development specialists along with those OD specialists trained in Schools of Business at major universities.

Many offer direct services through employee assistance programs (EAPs) either in-house or as consultants. Generally, EAP counselors are contracted by corporations to assist employees who have personal or emotional issues that interfere with their job performance and productivity. Originally, the purpose of EAPs was to address substance abuse problems in the workplace. They have expanded to include most other mental health issues such as family turmoil, depression, stress reactions, and money problems. In recent years, EAP counselors have begun to work on prevention of disorders as well as intervention.

Governmental agencies at the local, state, and federal levels have employed counselors in limited roles since the beginning of the profession, particularly manpower workers and employment counselors in the federal government, and community counselors in public state and county agencies. In more recent times, the factors that have led to the increased employment of counselors in business and industry have also influenced governmental needs. In early 2007, Congress voted into law a provision for Licensed Professional Counselors to be included as mental health providers to those qualifying for services through the Veterans Administration. Mental health counselors are needed to staff statewide networks to improve services for children and adolescents with serious emotional disturbances and for their family members. In addition, according to the Bureau of Labor Statistics, "there will be a continued need for counselors to work with military veterans to provide them the appropriate mental health or substance abuse counseling care" (Job Outlook, para. 3, U. S. Department of Labor, 2018a.).

In fact, there are many counseling services available to military members and their families. Many are civil servants employed directly by the U.S Military Command. For those who hold licenses in any of the related helping professional, another option is to contract with private providers to offer counseling services as Military and Family Life Counselors (MFLCs). This "program supports service members, their families and survivors with non-medical counseling worldwide. Trained to work with the military community, [they] deliver valuable face-to-face counseling services, briefings and presentations to the military community both on and off the installation" (Military One Source, n.d.).

The Military and Government Counseling Association (MGCA), a division of ACA, encourages and delivers "meaningful guidance, counseling, and educational programs to all members of the Armed Services, their family members, and civilian employees of Local, State and Federal Governmental Agencies" (Military and Government Counseling Association, n.d.). Part of their mission is to foster communications with the nonmilitary community and to also work with State and Federal agencies.

Private Practice Settings

For some counselors, private practice may be the setting of choice. Practitioners who deal with mental health issues must be licensed to practice regardless of their setting. Licensure requirements are discussed in the next chapter. Counselors in private practice may specialize in any of the areas of practice discussed previously. They are well versed in common presenting concerns such as depression, anxiety, grief and loss, and many more. They may specialize in one or more particular disorder or population or way of providing treatment. Some see only children or families. Others see only couples or women, or adults in transition, or the elderly.

For many who practice on their own, insurance reimbursement is a necessary part of their work world. Insurance realities are a part of any setting but for the private practitioner the reality is immediate and affects day-to-day practice and revenue. Most clients cannot or will not pay out of pocket and expect to be reimbursed at least partially for their expenses. Although some mental health counselors practice without the need to take insurance, most must work with the managed care industry and abide by its guidelines. Managed care organizations are medical care programs that finance and deliver health care intended to reduce unnecessary costs through various techniques and mechanisms. The nature of therapy may be dictated by managed care personnel rather than by the expertise of the counselor and the needs of the client. Managed care workers determine how many sessions and for what disorders their company will pay. Often they will approve no more than three to five sessions without further validation, making it difficult for practitioners to effectively write longer-term treatment plans. Brief treatment approaches have gained in popularity because of the current climate.

Most managed care companies require the allied helping professionals share notes and histories in order to approve treatment. Consequently, mental health counselors cannot guarantee that what clients tell them will be kept confidential. The purpose of treatment and the therapeutic relationship itself can be undermined. Many counselors in private practice are justifiably concerned about losing control of the services they offer and in the quality of the counseling they provide. They are concerned about who sees their clients' records, what happens to them in computer databases, and how they are transmitted over the Internet. If counselors are not compliant with the dictates of managed care companies, they can lose revenue or be excluded altogether from their referral systems.

The Health Insurance Portability and Accountability Act (HIPAA) standards apply to counseling in a variety of ways. HIPAA was enacted in 1996. This new set of guidelines put in place standards to address the privacy of patient information. Identifiable health information, or PHI, can be items such as dates of service, treatment plans, and data. It is necessary for counselors to be aware of the implications of using technology for such information keeping. The HITECH Act of 2009 supplements HIPAA and provides additional guidelines for counselors using technology for information keeping (Wilkinson & Reinhardt, 2015).

Clinical mental health counselors, of course, are not the only professional counselors in private practice. Academic and career counselors may also have private practices. They offer the same kinds of services that are offered in educational and community settings. Most deal with clients that do not expect to pursue insurance reimbursement. Academic counselors in private practice may assist students in finding the right college fit or learning better study skills, or handling relationship issues. Some school counselors, with their breadth of knowledge and experience, go into private practice and may offer either direct or consultation services to one or more sectors of the community. Career counselors in private practice offer the same kinds of services that those in educational settings offer but their clientele are usually those who are not affiliated with higher education. Their issues generally involve life transitions and career planning. Other counselors work as consultants to organizations in offering executive or career coaching to employees. Generally, a counselor who specializes in increasing professional and personal effectiveness offers performance improvement counseling, or executive coaching. The service can be initiated by the company or sought by the individual.

Some counselors in private practice are well versed in academic or career issues as well as mental health issues. Table 6.1 delineates some of the typical presenting concerns of clients in mental health and/or private practice settings that also may have career and life planning issues.

Table 6.1 Typical Presenting Concerns of Clients in Mental Health and/or Private Practice Settings and Suitability of Career and Life Planning

Presenting Concern	Level of Career Intervention		
	Primary	Secondary	Tertiary
Mental Illness concerns of Those with SMD*		X	X
Personality Disorders		X	X
Depressive disorders	X	X	X
Anxiety Disorders	X	X	X
Substance-Related Disorders		X	X
Job Loss Issues	X	X	
Occupational Stress Reactions	X	X	

Primary: Career and lifestyle planning may prevent threats to mental health.
Secondary: Career and lifestyle planning may moderate effects of existing mental health disorders and/or minimize severity of disorder through early identification and treatment of work-life issues.
Tertiary: Career and lifestyle planning techniques may be possible and/or suitable in concert with mental health counseling for full developed disorder.
*SMD Severe Mental Disorders
Reprinted from Guindon, M.H., Giordano, F.G., & Wright, K.S. (2019). The Convergence of Career and Mental Health Approaches to Counseling. In D. Capuzzi and M. Stauffer (Eds.) *Career Counseling: Foundations, Perspectives, and Applications* (3rd ed., p. 365). New York: Routledge.

Social Media

Today service delivery can involve the telephone, teleconferencing, or the Internet through emails, synchronous chat, and web conferencing. The Internet has been a boon to those who do not ordinarily have access to mental health services such as rural populations or the homebound. Technology in counseling, however, is not new. Computer-assisted guidance programs have been available for decades, as have computerized assessment and career resources. The majority of Americans possess and use cell phones that may affect their interactions and relationships, especially with significant others. Many young people in particular build and maintain primary relationships at a distance, through Instagram, Snapchat, Twitter, and the like. The instantaneous, global, public nature of social media as a household necessity has also changed the way some counselors provide services and conduct business. Most counselors, especially those in private practice, typically develop a website that provides information about their services, areas of practice, and other essential information. Counseling takes place through a combination of emails, chat rooms, instant messaging, and telephone sessions. At the end of 2009, a search of the term "Internet therapy" produced over 35 million sites and "online counseling" over 31 million sites. In 2018, "Internet therapy" yielded 152 million results and "online counseling" produced 222 million results. The quick burgeoning of online counseling has meant a need for regulation.

With such an explosion over recent years came the need for related ethical codes. ACA, APA, NCDA, and AMHCA to name a few professional organizations now have codes of ethics and standards for counseling on the Internet. The Internet is fraught with unqualified and unethical people who claim to do E-therapy, E-counseling, or E-coaching. The National Board for Certified Counselors (NBCC) has a clear policy regarding distance professional counseling services (2016).

Professional counselors must take responsibility to ensure the competence of their work and to protect their clients from harm. Special issues include management of confidentiality, duty to warn, electronic transfer of client information, counselor and client identification concerns, prescreening and appropriateness for online counseling, boundaries of competence, and legal considerations such as licensure across state lines, and referral resources. Professional counselors who practice through social media must ensure the quality and scope of their services.

Trends across Settings

The future for counseling is bright. The *Occupational Outlook Handbook* (U. S. Department of Labor, 2018a) reports that employment is expected to grow faster than average for school and career counselors from 2016 to 2026. Higher student enrollments in elementary, middle, and high schools are expected to increase demand for school counselors. School counselors' responsibilities are growing as society changes. School counselors include in their work crisis intervention, prevention counseling, substance abuse, and suicide. Job prospects in rural and urban, inner-city areas are strong. Career counselors are projected to increase in universities as more campuses open onsite career centers and needs of those career changers, laid-off workers, and military personnel transition into the civilian job market.

Demand for substance abuse, behavioral disorder, and mental health counselors and marriage and family therapists is projected to grow by 23 percent from 2016 to 2026, much faster than the average for all occupations (U. S. Department of Labor, 2018b). Growth is expected due to the increasing use of integrated care. More workplaces are offering employee assistance programs, and executive and career coaching as specialties within counseling are growing. Nevertheless, it must be noted that the state of the economy may influence future funding availability.

Diversity is an integral competency area in all the allied helping professions. For many years, ACA (2015) has developed multicultural and social justice ideals and competencies. These can be accessed under Resources on the ACA website (www.counseling.org). CACREP (n.d.) has further emphasized the importance of multicultural awareness and diversity issues throughout the core curriculum. Each specialty area addresses training requirements in Diversity and Advocacy.

New areas of practice continue to grow. Some counselors working in any of the settings discussed here also may have expertise in the creative arts such as music, dance, drama, or art therapy. The use of play therapy has increased as its effectiveness in reducing challenging behaviors associated with social, emotional, behavioral, and learning difficulties in children and adolescents has been recognized. At the other end of the lifespan, as the population continues to gray, counselors are working with issues of aging, death, dying, and grief in many traditional settings and have increased their presence in retirement facilities and independent and assisted-living facilities as the Baby Boomers continue to age.

Interest in spirituality across all settings has grown in recent years with the recognition that people are more than their thoughts, feelings, actions, and systems. Many people need to have purpose, meaning, and transcendence in life addressed whether they have religious convictions or not. Most counselors address these existential concerns in some of their clients. Pastoral counseling is a specialty area that directly addresses religious issues, as does Christian counseling, a sub-discipline of community/mental health counseling. Recognizing that counselors need to address the whole person, the Association for Spiritual, Ethical, and Religious Values in Counseling (ASERVIC) offers Competencies for Addressing Spiritual and Religious Issues in counseling available on its website (www.aservic.org).

In the contemporary world, people need counseling services more than ever before. Adults and children no longer feel as safe as they once did; many have experienced trauma either first hand or vicariously. Some individuals face the reality of war, terrorism, and disaster in their lives or in the lives of loved ones. School shootings continue to increase. A range of psychosocial factors affects long-term mental health and adjustment. CACREP first infused emergency preparedness language into some of the eight core curricular requirements in 2009. The requirements are in response to the need for counseling professionals to be on call as responders in times of natural disasters and national emergencies. Since then, counselors have been integral members of disaster response teams. Counseling in all settings can assist individuals and family members in learning to manage their emotional environment and come to terms with their traumatic experiences. Bullying as a prevention and intervention area of interest has emerged. Forensic counseling is of interest and a growing specialty. Large-scale crises or disasters, war, terrorism, mass shootings, and school and community violence are demanding new responses from counselors across settings. Interventions extending the scope of crisis intervention services have been developed and implemented to meet the challenge. Critical incident stress management response teams have formed in schools, universities, and business settings. Counselors can offer training and consultation services providing immediate assistance in times of such events and in post-disaster support groups and debriefings as means of preventing or moderating the development of pathological post-trauma reactions.

The needs of those affected by war and worldwide conflicts are an emerging and critical area of care. Mental health counselors in government, private, and non-profit agencies are seeing an influx of military and non-military returnees and their family members. All counselors must be knowledgeable about the effects of trauma on the survivors and their family members. School counselors must address the considerable emotional needs of children whose parents are either deployed or have returned from combat areas. Some of these parents never return and others return severely wounded. Children of immigrants are also a concern. A change in the growing population of students from various countries has increased the need for a range of psychosocial services. Issues of personal trauma may need to be adequately addressed. Some adults and children have been witness to violence, war, and human atrocities. Many have come from horrific living conditions. Many are subjected to racial labeling. Among other reactions, these individuals have a diminished sense of security due to inadequate social support networks; frequent moves; and attachment, separation, and loss needs, as well as traumatic stress disorders. The same can be said about children in American schools.

As the world becomes more connected, international concerns have come to the forefront. The globalization of counseling means that counselors are finding new settings worldwide in which to work. Models of helping from other parts of the world are no longer being marginalized or ignored.

> The growth counseling around the world is one of the major and most exciting emerging trends in the counseling profession.... Most advocate the development of their own theories/techniques and programs to meet their unique needs or at least significantly tailoring existing U.S. practices to their own cultures.
>
> (Hohenshil, 2010)

> As our world becomes increasingly connected economically, politically, technologically, and culturally, counseling is transforming from a Western-based practice to a global phenomenon. The globalization of counseling has placed the field on the cusp of growth and innovation. Such changes involve not only a willingness to adapt and perhaps redefine current counseling theories, but to hold our most basic assumptions regarding the nature of human change so loosely that we are willing to let counseling develop and evolve indigenously in international communities.
>
> (Lorelle, Byrd & Crockett, 2012, p. 115)

The counseling profession, therefore, has much to give to but also much to learn from the rest of the world.

Technology continues to offer new opportunities. Virtual reality simulation allows practitioners to assist clients with many issues. Phobia, PTSD, and pain management are just a few of the issues in which this cutting-edge technology is growing in usage. Internet use and addiction, Internet addiction predators, and gaming addiction have also been identified as significant emerging concerns regarding technology (Hagedorn & Young, 2011). ACA and NBCC and most other helping professions have developed web counseling guidelines and practitioners are increasingly encouraged to adhere to their guidelines. Counselors should evaluate the use of online counseling for specific concerns and seek additional specialized training.

Physical Surroundings

The environment in which counseling takes place matters – to you and to your clients. Regardless of the specialty, most counseling settings typically have common characteristics. Counselors must have a place to go where they can meet their clients in privacy. Unless they are doing outreach, visiting classrooms, or doing home visits, that place will be the office. The space must be comfortable, inviting, quiet, and safe. The waiting room or outer office should be secluded so that clients do not run into each other. Some counselors have two doors to the office, one for arrivals and one for departures. How the office is decorated depends upon personal taste but the more neutral the surroundings the less likely a client will be to be distracted from the business at hand. Pleasant, warm decorations that elicit calmness can be effective. Austere, rundown, or overly cluttered environments are not. Some counselors make use of therapeutic props in the décor. These are items that may be used during counseling sessions and add to the ambience when they are not. Such items as stuffed animals, soft balls, magic wands, floor cushions, throw pillows, polished stones, and the like can liven up an office and make the clients feel at home. A box of tissue is a must. Personal mementos such as family photos, on the other hand, do not belong in a counseling office. They can be distancing to the client. Offices should be free from other distractions. Confidentiality should be considered above all else. The office itself should be soundproofed. Client records should be out of sight; telephones should not ring or go to audible voicemail. The session itself is a time when others who work in the setting should not knock on the door or disturb the session.

Room arrangement is important. The room should be softly lit but not dark. The view from the window should be pleasant, or if that is not possible, the windowsills or window coverings should compensate for the lack of view. There are many ways to arrange an office, but furniture arrangement matters. It speaks volumes about approachability or possible intrusiveness. Many counselors subscribe to the belief that there should be no barriers between the counselor and the client. Often this is the case; however, cultural issues and personal space needs must be considered. Talking across a desk is formal and off-putting. It portrays a strong corporate message that the counselor is the expert, not one in whom a client would confide or be in relationship with. Most counselors place the desk against a wall to preclude this possibility. More conducive to relationship building is two comfortable chairs or a chair and a loveseat across from each other, slightly angled, or at right angles. Sometimes counseling takes place across the edge of a desk with the client at one end and the counselor situated at the desk's corner, especially when papers – exercises, forms, and assessments, for example – are used. For some clients, especially in the earliest stage of counseling, this can feel less threatening than sitting directly across from the counselor. A well-thought-out office space is a kind of nonverbal communication and conducive to positive relationship building.

Those who use social media (phone, email, instant messaging, Twitter, and the like) must ensure that their settings meet the same confidentiality, privacy, and HIPAA regulations as their face-to-face counseling. Again, training needs to stay current to keep up with the fast-paced changes of the plugged-in world

In the Field

Toward the end of your program of study, you will begin to counsel actual clients under controlled and supervised conditions. "These experiences will provide opportunities for students to counsel clients who represent the ethnic and demographic diversity of their community" (Council for the Accreditation of Counseling and Related Educational Programs, 2016, p. 15). Where you choose to complete your internship will likely determine where you enter the profession. School counselors will choose their settings according to the age of the students they are most interested in; depending upon state requirements, they might work with all levels. Higher education counselors have several settings from which to choose. Community and mental health counselors have a greater array of possible choices, as do counselors in choosing one of the specialty areas.

The Practicum

Most programs require their students to complete coursework in a highly controlled environment. Many have training labs within their own programs but some will require students to go out in the field for this experience. In either case, students develop their basic counseling skills under close supervision of an instructor. The training consists of 100 total clock hours over a minimum of 10 weeks and 40 hours of direct work with clients in individual counseling and group work. In a campus training lab, students generally see clients from the community who incur no cost or pay greatly reduced fees. You will be expected to see individual clients as well as run at least one group. You will likely conduct intake sessions and you will have at least one client that you will follow through several sessions. Your facility may have counseling rooms with one-way mirrors that will allow your supervisor and your fellow students to observe your sessions. You will be required to record your sessions, depending upon the facility and always with the formalized permission of the client. Some counseling labs have state-of-the-art computer feeds that allow observation from remote locations, such as your classroom or your supervisor's office. Some counseling programs have no labs at all but will assign you an office space. You will still be required to record your session with your client's permission. The purpose of recording is for you to be able to hear and often transcribe your sessions, and to share them with your instructor for a detailed review. Counseling skills are developed not in the didactic part of your program but in the doing.

The Internship

The internship is intended to create the kinds of comprehensive work practices professional counselors experience that are appropriate to the designated program area. Internships vary considerably, not just by type of counseling but by level and quality of training, access to clients, and expertise of the supervisor. Before you choose a site, or agree to a site chosen for you, you should inform yourself as much as possible about the site's mission, counseling philosophy, and the clientele they serve (DeSole, 2006). Make at least one visit, check out the website, talk to past interns, seek the counsel of trusted instructors or internship coordinators. The on-site supervisor is your best link to the real world of counseling. A good supervisor will share with you not only the formalized expectations of the setting but the fine distinctions and unwritten expectations that are a necessary part of being an effective counselor.

The internship is a major time commitment. It will require you to complete 600 total clock hours and 240 hours of direct service with clients appropriate to your program of study. You will participate in supervision from both your course instructor and the site supervisor on an individual or triadic basis for one hour per week, and group basis for one and a half hours per week.

In addition to direct service, there should be opportunities to become familiar with a variety of professional activities such as record keeping, assessment, information and referral processes, and staff meetings. You want to ensure that you experience first-hand the real-life tasks that define the counselor's role in the setting that will best prepare you for the professional counseling specialty in which you have invested years of time, work, and money. You will come to understand what it means to be a counseling professional by acting in ways consistent with the identity that your texts, instructors, and classroom activities can only help you approximate.

Summary

This chapter began with a discussion of the environments in which counseling takes place. It was organized around the broad specialty areas of school, higher education, community, and the Internet. Key knowledge and skills possessed by counselors in various specialty areas were discussed. The future of counseling and trends across settings were noted with special attention to play therapy, gerontological counseling, spirituality, and counseling for large-scale trauma and disaster. The chapter continued with explanations of physical surroundings, the setup of counseling centers and rooms, and included a discussion of the issues of privacy and confidentiality. A section about practicum and internships settings ended the chapter

Now what?
— student to his instructor upon completing all coursework except the internship

References

American Counseling Association. (2015). *Multicultural and social justice counseling competencies*. Retrieved from https://www.counseling.org/docs/default-source/competencies/multicultural-and-social-justice-co unseling-competencies.pdf?sfvrsn=8573422c_20

American Rehabilitation Counseling Association (ARCA). (n.d.) *Scope of practice statement*. Retrieved February 6, 2019, from: https://www.crccertification.com/scope-of-practice

American School Counselor Association. (n.d.). *The role of the school counselor*. Retrieved January 15, 2019, from: https://www.schoolcounselor.org/asca/media/asca/Careers-Roles/RoleStatement.pdf

American School Counselor Association. (2018). *State school counseling mandates and legislation*. Retrieved January 15, 2019, from: https://www.schoolcounselor.org/school-counselors-members/careers-roles/sta te-school-counseling-mandates-and-legislation

Association for Spiritual, Ethical, and Religious Values in Counseling. (n.d.). *Competencies for addressing spiritual and religious issues in counseling*. Retrieved from http://www.aservic.org/resources/spiritual-co mpetencies/

Council for the Accreditation of Counseling and Related Educational Programs (CACREP). (2009). *2009 CACREP standards*. Retrieved from http://www.cacrep.org/wp-content/ uploads/2017/07/2009-Standards.pdf

Council for the Accreditation in Counseling and Related Educational Programs (CACREP). (2015). *2016 CACREP standards*. Retrieve from https://www.cacrep.org/for-programs/2016-cacrep-standards/

DeSole, L. M. (2006). *Making contact: The therapist's guide to conducting a successful first interview*. Boston: Pearson/Allyn & Bacon.

Dunham, S. M. (2017). International Association of Marriage and Family Counselors. In J. Carlson & S. B. Dermer (Eds.), *The SAGE encyclopedia of marriage, family, and couples counseling* (pp. 888–889) Thousand Oaks, CA: SAGE Publications.

Guindon, M. H., Giordano, F. G., & Wright, K. S. (2019). The convergence of career and mental health approaches to counseling. In D. Capuzzi & M. D. Stauffer (Eds.), *Career counseling: Foundations, perspectives, and applications* (3rd ed., pp. 347–373). New York: Routledge.

Gysbers, N. C., & Henderson, P. (2012). *Developing & managing: Your school guidance & counseling program*. Alexandria, VA: American Counseling Association.

Hagedorn, W. B., & Young, T. (2011). Identifying and intervening with students exhibiting signs of gaming addiction and other addictive behaviors: Implications for professional school counselors. *Professional School Counseling, 14*(4), 250–260.

Hohenshil, T. H. (2010). International counseling introduction. *Journal of Counseling & Development, 88*(1), 3.

Lewis, J. A., Lewis, M. D., Daniels, J. A., & D'Andrea, M. J. (2011). *Community counseling: A multicultural-social justice perspective* (4th ed.). Belmont, CA: Brooks/Cole.

Lewis, J. A., Dana, R. Q., & Blevins, G. A. (2015). *Substance abuse counseling* (5th ed.). Stamford, CT: Cengage Learning.

Lorelle, S., Byrd, R., & Crockett, S. (2012). Globalization and counseling: Professional issues for counselors. *The Professional Counselor, 2*(2), 115–123.

Military One Source. (n.d.). *Military and family life counseling – The essentials*. Retrieved from https://www w.militaryonesource.mil/confidential-help/non-medical-counseling/military-and-family-life-counseling /military-and-family-life-counseling-the-essentials

Military and Government Counseling Association. (n.d.). *Serving those who serve*. Retrieved from http://acegonline.org.

National Academic Advising Association (NACADA). *The global community for academic advising*. Retrieved from http://www.nacada.ksu.edu

National Board for Certified Counselors. (2016, February). *Policy regarding the provision of distance professional services*. Retrieved from http://www.nbcc.org/Assets/Ethics/NBCCPolicyRegardingPracticeofDistanceCounselingBoard.pdf

Palmo, A. J., Weikel, W. J., & Borsos, D. P. (2006). *Foundations of mental health counseling* (3rd ed.). Springfield, IL: Charles C. Thomas.

Reevy, G., Ozer, Y. M., & Ito, Y. (2010). *Encyclopedia of emotion* (1st ed.). Santa Barbara, CA: Greenwood.

U. S. Department of Labor, Bureau of Labor Statistics. (2018a). *Occupational outlook handbook*. Retrieved from https://www.bls.gov/ooh/community-and-social-service/school-and-career-counselors.html

U. S. Department of Labor, Bureau of Labor Statistics. (2018b). *Occupational outlook handbook*. Retrieved from https://www.bls.gov/ooh/community-and-social-service/substance-abuse-behavioral-disorder-and-mental-health-counselors.htm?view:full

U. S. Substance Abuse and Mental Health Services Administration, Center for Substance Abuse Treatment. (n.d.). Retrieved from https://www.samhsa.gov/about-us/who-we-are/offices-centers/csat

Wilkinson, T., & Reinhardt, R. (2015). Technology in counselor education: HIPAA and HITECH as best practice. *The Professional Counselor, 5*(3), 407–418.

Table 6.2 *TFAC Chart – Thought, Feelings, Actions, and Context

Self	My Thoughts	My Feelings	My Actions	My Context	Other? (Specify)
Which counseling specialty fits me best?					
What settings appeal to me?					
How do I view private practice?					
What is my stance on Internet counseling?					
Where would I like to be trained for my field work (practicum/ internship)?					
How do I see myself working with other counseling specialties and other helping professions?					
What concerns do I have?					
Others Choose two counselors from different specialties and interview them:	Others' Probable Thoughts	Others' Possible Feelings	Others' Observable Actions	Others' Apparent Context	Other? (Specify)
What services do they provide?					
What can working counselors tell me about their environments?					
What do counselors say about Internet counseling?					
What do they see as the emerging settings for practice?					
What are their views on physical settings for practice?					
What else can they tell you?					

*For more information on TFAC, see Chapter 1.

Chapter 7

When? Answers about Processes, Phases, and Procedures

Mary H. Guindon

> *By persevering the egg walks on legs.*
>
> – Ethiopian proverb

POINTS TO PONDER

- What are the stages of counseling?
- How do counselors structure ongoing sessions?
- When will I have the credentials I must have to practice?
- When should I seek supervision?
- What is consultation?
- When should I seek continuing education opportunities?
- How and when will I recognize burnout and what should I do about it?

The Counseling Process

The Developmental Approach

In Chapter 2 you first learned about the developmental approach to counseling that considers the client's life stage and developmental level and encourages movement within and between levels (Ivey, Ivey, & Zalaquett, 2014). Individuals progress through developmental levels, or stages, in relatively similar or predictable sequences. In order to grow and function effectively at each stage of development, people accomplish developmental tasks unique to that stage. Just as people move through the lifespan in relatively predictable ways, so, too, do professional counselors and their clients move through stages of counseling, accomplishing important tasks in the process.

Many models of helping delineate the developmental counseling process in a varying number of stages. Two well-known models, Egan's (2009) three-stage model, first published in 1975, and Carkhuff's (2009) seven-stage model, originally developed in 1969, are discussed in the next section. Both models are the basis for other subsequent models. Both have undergone changes over the years, especially in moving the models from solely process focused to more client focused.

At the minimum, counseling involves a beginning, or intake stage; a middle, or working stage; and an end, or termination stage. Within each of these can be many other sub-stages or phases. These stages provide structure for both the counselor and the client. You will learn how to communicate and build a relationship with your clients. Without some level of structure, you run the risk of engaging in an interesting conversation with no appreciable result. The purpose of counseling is to empower the client, whatever age, to cope with life, to make effective decisions, and to participate in growth-enhancing activities. Change must occur. That takes structure. Counselors, through the structure they use, teach their clients at least indirectly a process for handling their concerns as well as directly helping them find ways to manage problems and develop their resources and opportunities.

Counseling Stages

Counseling is neither a random activity where the practitioner is there simply to befriend or to offer sympathy nor a product that you can touch or feel. It is a process. It has a certain rhythm and flow. When you do effective work, you and your client are in the flow together. Put another way, flow is a productive, interactive process distinguished by a one-of-a-kind, special relationship between counselor and client. Process in counseling means the procedures the counselor uses and goals that the counselor wants to accomplish in order to help the client make changes to reach a desired outcome. Process can be described in terms of counselor activities or as the effects those activities have on the client experiences. The second part of this primer is devoted to specific process skills. For now, we look at the stages that allow process to unfold.

In Egan's (2009) three-stage model, Stage I is the current scenario, Stage II is the preferred scenario, and Stage III is action strategies and plans. Each stage has specific counseling and client developmental tasks. In Stage I, the key issues that need changing are discovered. The client tells her story and the counselor identifies and clarifies problems as well as opportunities that will lead to change. In Stage II, the counselor helps the client find solutions to problems by setting goals. The client looks at possibilities for a better future and the counselor helps the client in setting goals for change and encourages commitment to them. In Stage III, the counselor and client identify the work that needs to be done to accomplish her goals. Egan calls these "problem managing accomplishments." Once the client and counselor generate the best choice of action from a range of possible actions, they formulate a plan that leads to action and outcomes.

Carkhuff's (2009) seven-stage helping model involves three phases of learning: exploring, understanding, and acting. This road map targets a combination of helper skills and helpee goals. The counselor (a) attends and (b) responds by entering the client's world and communicating understanding of the client's perspective. This results in (c) exploration by the client, which leads to (d) "personalizing" by the counselor, or responding from the counselor's perspective. This leads to in (e) client understanding which in turn leads to (f) the counselor initiating possible plans to reach goals, and ends in (g) the client's action.

Many other authors have discussed similar stages in the counseling process. For example, Corey and Corey's (2015) five-stage approach consists of (a) establishing a working relationship, (b) identifying clients' problems, (c) helping clients create goals, (d) encouraging client exploration and taking action, and (e) termination. Patterson and Welfel (1994) delineate a three-stage process in which both client work and counselor work is explained. Work means "the experience of exploring with an effort toward understanding more deeply, clarifying what is vague, discovering new insights that relate to one's concerns, and developing action plans" (p. 34). Their three stages are initial disclosure, in-depth exploration, and commitment to action.

None of these models is meant to be linear. As the concerns of the client and the goals of the counselor change, stages may be cycled through again. The counselor's job is to create safety so the client can explore issues that may not have been present or even in the client's awareness at the beginning of the process. The counselor creates enough influence for the client to trust him and to want to make changes.

Perhaps two of the most common and at the same time difficult concepts for beginning counselors to understand are that structure is necessary and that process takes time. You have spent a lifetime building relationships in random, unstructured ways. In our day-to-day lives and in social situations we don't expect much structure and don't often take time to clarify what is vague. We tend to accept what people tell us at face value. We may offer solutions based on surface understanding. It can feel unnatural to structure communication and intrusive to ask for clarification. In today's world, we are accustomed to instant solutions and offer ours readily. That is quite simply not how counseling works. Counseling is effective because it develops in stages. It begins with the first initial interview and usually ends when a goal has been met or there is no longer a need. Egan (2014, as cited in Corey & Corey, 2015, p. 164) sums up the work of the counseling process in four basic client questions:

What is going on?
What does a better future look like?
What do I have to do to get what I need or want?
How do I make it all happen?

Counseling Procedures

First Sessions

The counseling process begins from the first contact. The first interview usually accomplishes two primary purposes. It collects necessary information and establishes the beginning of the counseling relationship (Corey & Corey, 2015; Cormier & Hackney, 2012; Gladding, 2018; Ivey, Packard, & Ivey, 2017). This involves a complex set of tasks (Ivey, Packard, & Ivey, 2017). At the beginning of the initial interview the counselor will not know why the client is seeking help. Counselors are trained to consider each client a unique individual. They want to know who this person really is. What are the issues? What drives him? Does he have support from family and friends? Is he able to work toward solutions with you? Is he psychologically impaired? The counselor must listen carefully and try hard to understand the client's point of view.

Although there is no one formula for beginning a first session, most counselors would agree that they do not start with asking about the problem in the first sentence. Rather, they might engage in a few introductory words as they would in any setting. Parking, the weather, or the adequacy of directions to the site are often good openers and are likely to put the client at ease. They would then move to inquiring about how they can help or what causes the client to seek out the counselor.

You can be assured that the client is likely to be at least somewhat anxious. Coming to counseling is a big step into the unknown. Recognize, too, that some counselors can be anxious as well. They do not know what the client will be like, what the issues are, or how to proceed. Other unknowns can be of concern. The first meeting is an important one because in this meeting the client will decide whether you can help and whether he wants to return for a second session. Early on it is best to exchange information about the reason for the visit and the purpose of counseling. You will let the client know what to expect from you as the counselor. Unless there has been a previous intake session with another helping professional, you will need to gather information in a formalized way. You gather this information through an assessment process. Information is two-way. The client will tell you why she is there. The client's presenting concern is that problem that initially brought her into counseling. This is called the presenting concern because it may or may not be the critical issue. You will provide information to educate the client about counseling, your qualifications, and how you work. You will also explain limits of confidentiality, duty to warn, length of sessions, fees if you charge them, and other information. You will give a clear-cut definition of counseling, introduce the idea of process, begin structure, and lay out ground rules. You must fully inform your client of what she is to expect and you will ask her to sign an informed consent document. Because so much information must be provided, some counselors underscore what they say by providing their clients with a fact sheet that they can take home to review at their own time and pace. This helps alleviate some of the anxiety and makes people feel less vulnerable.

Beginning counseling sessions include a discussion of the client's expectations. The counselor may ask "What brings you here today?" or "What do you hope to accomplish?" as ways of determining the purpose of the visit. The counselor ascertains the client's past experience with counseling, if any, and how the client views the experiences. Were issues resolved? Was the counseling relationship positive and helpful? Questions such as these not only garner important information; they are the basis of early relationship building.

Commonly, the client may initiate the first contact. Sometimes, however, the counselor initiates the contact. A school counselor, for example, might call a student into his office either to get acquainted at the beginning of the school year or as a referral from a teacher. In this case, the counselor is more likely to begin with the purpose for the meeting rather than in engaging in small talk. Court-mandated clients will come because they must and the counselor will know the reason for the interview. In these cases, the counselor might begin with a sentence or two of small talk and then state the purpose of the meeting.

The Intake

Formalized initial information gathering is called the *intake*. In some agencies, the person who will be assigned to the client does not necessarily conduct the intake. In other cases, the assigned counselor conducts the intake interview as part of the first session. The client will fill out a form either before they arrive in your office or at the beginning of the intake session. This is a way to collect basic demographic information. You will collect detailed information about the client's presenting concern, his emotional state or psychological level of functioning, precipitating events and much more. When counselors conduct assessments, they present themselves in such a way that a positive human connection is possible for the client. Although counselors gather as much information as possible, they know that they are dealing with unique individuals. Their humanity comes first. Establishing a relationship is paramount. You must set up the fundamental conditions that create a trusting environment in which the client feels safe to disclose and explore. Listen and offer support first, and gather information to fill in gaps as the session progresses rather than overwhelming your client with questions written on a form.

Case Conceptualization

Assessment, whether by observation, structured questioning, or testing, is essential. The counselor must gather enough specific and concrete information to make an accurate appraisal and develop a treatment plan that will help the client to function more successfully. Counselors thoroughly and comprehensively describe their clients' concerns so that goals can be set and treatment leading to effective resolution of their clients' presenting concerns can be planned. This can happen in the initial intake but it can also occur over the first few sessions.

Counselors engage in various ways of conceptualizing their clients' concerns. Regardless of theoretical orientation, counselors include these factors in *case conceptualizations*: general demographic information; the presenting concern; behavioral descriptions; feelings and emotions experienced; cognitive patterns and beliefs about the self, others, the presenting problem, and life events; interpersonal and relational patterns and ways of coping; family issues; and any other environmental factors that may be impacting on the presenting concern. At intake and throughout counseling, counselors appraise their clients in order to assist them in identifying problems, areas of strength, or discovering effective problem-solving strategies.

Client Appraisal and Diagnosis

Appraisal is a specific set of skills. Refer back to "Assessment and Testing" in Chapter 5 for more general information. Helping professionals must first and foremost identify mental health issues. Although not all clients have diagnosable disorders, all do have presenting concerns that the counselor must document. They can then select appropriate treatment goals and implement interventions that are most likely to be effective. When the counselor sets goals it is often called treatment planning, or action planning.

Human beings are not static. One issue may resolve and another may be presented to the counselor. Therefore, appraisal of the client's progress and current state is on ongoing activity and strategies are revised when needed.

Some counselors, such as clinical mental health or addictions counselors, predominantly focus on clients with mental disorders. Others, such as school counselors or career counselors, focus on problems of adjustment and emotional wellbeing and refer out more serious concerns. In either case, counselors must recognize mental conditions. In the United States, the *Diagnostic and Statistical Manual of Mental Disorders* (American Psychiatric Association, 2013) is the categorical classification system used to make a diagnosis and identify different psychopathological disorders. This 5th edition of the *DSM* "is a classification of mental disorders with associated criteria designed to facilitate more reliable diagnoses of these disorders" (American Psychiatric Association, 2013, p. xli). It recognizes "that mental disorders do not always fit completely within the boundaries of a single disorder" (p. xli). Cross-cutting symptom measures draw attention to symptoms that are important across diagnoses. Because of the possibility of mental disorder, counselors are trained in the use of the DSM even when their responsibility does not formally include diagnosis. Counselors must be able to identify disorders and recognize factors contributing to and maintaining problems. They must know when to refer to other mental health professionals if they are not qualified to diagnose or treat a disorder.

The *DSM-5* is organized on developmental and lifespan considerations and recognizes that diagnoses must also consider cultural issues. "Cultural meanings, habits, and traditions can also contribute to either stigma or support in the social and familial response to mental illness" (APA, 2013, p. 14). Nevertheless, the DSM is not without controversy. Counselors must reconcile the difference in the philosophical stance of professional counseling with a need for assessment and diagnosis.

Client Self-Exploration and Awareness

Assessment is more than diagnosis. Over time, the counselor will come to know the whole self of the client. This includes more than the client's thoughts, feelings, actions, and systems. It includes the client's life roles such as worker, spouse, parent, child, and others. It includes the spiritual, physical, and social self as well as the client's unique life history and experiences. The counselor must check out physical symptoms, changes in behavior, sleeping patterns, use of humor, current emotional state, language skills, ability to deal with the abstract, level of functioning, and much more.

Understanding the client is not the counselor's exclusive domain. On the contrary, the entire assessment process involves the client's in-depth self-exploration that leads to their own self-understanding. Through the core conditions of respect and genuine acceptance, the counselor helps the client explore who he is and what he wants. The emotional release of sharing the story along with its pain often is enough for the client in the early part of counseling. Clarity of what may be keeping the client stuck or frustrated or resistant to change allows the client to consider options for the future. With insight, fears diminish and resistance to possible change lessens. The client wants to move forward, to do what it takes to solve the problem and change patterns of thoughts and behaviors. At this point, the counseling shifts from information gathering and rapport building to the next stage of action planning. The counselor and client are ready to form a working alliance.

Timing

Timing of stage transitions. How does the counselor know "that the timing is right for a transition from diagnosis and in-depth exploration to goal setting and commitment to action?" (Patterson & Welfel, 1994, p. 116). The simple answer is when the assessment and early exploration stage are no longer generating new information for the counselor or new insights for the client. If the sessions seem to be going over the same information, it is time to move on. The counselor will pick up on cues in the statements the client makes. They indicate restlessness and a need for change. The initial relief of being able to bring problems out in the open will be replaced by a need for action even when emotional or psychic pain is involved. The client has grown in the willingness to take risk. The counselor will then be ready to lead the way toward the transition into goal setting, action planning, and commitment to change.

The transition can happen in the first session, the second, the tenth, or the twentieth. No timetable can determine when it is time for the working alliance. Sometimes, action planning is a practical event dictated by the number of total sessions allotted. Sometimes, the counselor structures sessions so that the action stage follows quickly after information gathering. Other times, the structure is more fluid and the transition will occur at no preset time. As you learn the skills you need to be an effective counselor, you will gain experience in recognizing the shift from information gathering to goal setting.

Length of sessions. Counseling sessions vary in length depending upon the setting and purpose of counseling, the client's needs, and the counselors' preset structure. Intake sessions may last up to an hour and a half and sometimes more. School counselors may have only 15 to 20 minutes to devote to individual counseling. Community and mental health counselors generally see their clients for 45 to 50 minutes. Family counselors may see the family members together for longer periods of time. Group counseling sessions vary. Sessions can last anywhere from 45 minutes to one hour to all day but often one and half hours to two is common practice. In cases of crisis or suicide risk, counselors work with their clients as long as is necessary.

The Working Alliance

Once the counselor has gathered sufficient information, the presenting concern has been identified, a tentative appraisal or diagnosis is made, the counselor conceptualizes the client and her issues, and the client understands what needs to be changed, the *working alliance stage* begins. Goal setting takes place. The client, with the help of the counselor, sets goals for making decisions between or among alternatives, or making changes, or a combination of the two. The process is conceptualized in this way:

Making Decisions. Decision making is not simple. It is based on what is valued. A decision can be lifestyle related.

- Where do I want to work or live?
- What do I want to do?
- How important is my avocation?
- Who do I want to spend my time or my life with?

Making Change. Change is difficult. It takes energy and commitment. Change could be about acquiring new habits.

- How do I cope with authority figures?
- How do I change my life's work?
- Should I stay with my spouse?
- What can I do to feel better? To be less angry? To get along better?

Lessening Uncertainty. Deciding among alternatives and making changes can be filled with uncertainty and the counselor assists in reducing the uncertainty. This involves looking at feelings about issues brought into counseling. Lessening of uncertainty involves content issues and evaluating needs and wants.

- How do I decide between alternatives?
- Why do I feel so stuck?
- How do I make a decision or a change?

It may not seem that some issues are about decision making or change. For example, a client may come to counseling because he has experienced the loss of a loved one and is feeling grief. Where is the decision or change in that? The counselor offers a supportive environment in which the client works through the natural process of grieving. Problems occur when grieving is not allowed to proceed naturally. Grieving is a process of separating the self from the loss so that one can survive and come back to wholeness. The client learns to accept the loss. Pain diminishes. Identity without the loved one means change. Change involves decisions. It results in growth. Successful grieving creates growth.

Not all individuals are ready to make changes. The *Stages of Change* model (Prochaska & DiClemente, 1992), initially developed in the field of addictions, explains how some people work through various stages of readiness. The stages of change are:

1. Precontemplation – Not yet acknowledging that a problem behavior needs changing
2. Contemplation – Acknowledging a problem but not yet ready to make a change
3. Preparation/Determination – Getting ready to change
4. Action/Willpower – Process of changing behavior
5. Maintenance – Maintaining the change
6. Relapse – abandoning the new changes and returning to problematic behavior

Once the individual is firmly in stage 2, the process of articulating goals ensures that the client and the counselor understand each other and choose appropriate intervention or prevention strategies. What the goals are and how they will be carried out will depend upon the counselor's theoretical orientation, the nature of the issue to be resolved, and the characteristics of the client. You need to be comfortable with techniques across a range of theoretical orientations in order to meet the needs of your client. No single theory or approach is suitable for every client or every concern.

In setting goals, many counselors encourage clients to commit to action-based contracts. These are explicit verbal or written agreements that certain actions will take place in the immediate future, often before the next counseling session. The client commits to performing an action or set of actions by a specified date. Contracts are concrete and can be measured in terms of completion. Contracts put the client in control of her own behavior. The counselor may give homework assignments to help the client reach goals. Assignments are as varied as issues themselves.

Examples are journal writing, practicing small behavioral changes, disputing irrational thoughts, and many more.

Whether or not formal contracts are used, counseling involves a commitment to a plan of action. Good plans not only address problems directly but also attempt to anticipate issues that may come up during the process of meeting goals. The counselor and client process what happens from session to session and adjust actions to meet circumstances as they arise. The working alliance stage involves client performance and counselor support and feedback. The most effective working alliances draw on client strengths rather than focus on deficits. Counselors help clients see and draw on their own considerable resources. Action plans allow clients to manage their concerns with as much responsibility as possible. This is the essence of empowerment. The amount of responsibility that a client can handle will depend upon age, level of functioning, as well as internal and external resources.

The working alliance is a mutual partnership. Goals are prioritized so that the client can first gain relief from the most pressing concerns and also experience some success. Success in small goals leads to the confidence to take on more challenging goals. In each session, one issue may be resolved only to be replaced by a new one. Both the beginning of each session and the presentation of a new issue means the counselor must return to the early relationship-building stage. Each new issue is a new mini-intake. You will once again build up trust, uncover issues through some kind of appraisal, and move on to goal setting and action planning. Each stage and substage of counseling takes considerable expertise and skill.

Termination and Follow-up

How do you know when counseling is done? Ideally, when the outcome has satisfactorily resolved the client's concerns and goals have been met. At this point, the client and counselor move to the termination stage. Either party can initiate termination. Sometimes clients will terminate prematurely, even suddenly. Sometimes they run out of resources and cannot continue. They may not have resolved issues at all but have decided not to return. Obviously, this is not an ideal situation. Counselors attempt to bring these clients to some kind of closure or make arrangements for them to get other kinds of support or to see other helping professionals.

Generally, both parties agree upon the time for the end of counseling. They give each other cues and verbal indications that it is time to end, that what needed to be achieved has taken place. Counselor or client or both recognize that necessary growth has occurred and that issues have been satisfactorily resolved. Of course, the overall length of counseling relationships varies. However, counselors plan for the eventuality of termination from the beginning. This is part of structure. Counselors and clients both need time to prepare for the end of a relationship. Generally, termination does not occur in just one, last session. It occurs over a period of time. A rule of thumb states that termination should take about one-third as many sessions as have come before. So that if the client has come to nine sessions, termination should take approximately three more. Some suggest one-sixth is the optimal number, one or two in this case. Cormier and Hackney (2012) state that more than three months of counseling requires three to four weeks of termination activities. Regardless of how many sessions are spent on termination issues, counselors help clients understand the consequences of termination. They talk about the meaning of the counseling experience, how they will continue to apply new behaviors and insights, and often discuss the significance of the counseling relationship itself. Feelings of loss and sadness are not uncommon. They discuss preparations for support beyond counseling. Counselor and client review what occurred over the course of the counseling experience and examine how problems have been reduced or changed and in what ways the client will cope with similar issues or life's exigencies in the future.

Some clients resist termination even when there are no significant problems to resolve. The counseling relationship is powerful. Some people do not want it to end. They will ask for more appointments or raise new issues. The counselor must determine if the issue raised is legitimate or a matter of client resistance to ending. In some instances, the counselor may be resistant to termination. The relationship is significant for the counselor, too, and it can be hard to say goodbye. Supervision or consultation with counseling peers helps the counselor work through the resistance in service to the need for ending. When no growth-enhancing work is needed, she accepts the fact that it is time to terminate.

In many cases, counselors make arrangements for a follow-up visit at some point in the future. This is likened to a checkup with the doctor or a car's routine tune-up. Clients are invited to return to process what has gone on with respect to the client's issues. It shows clients that they are valued and that the counselor cares about their progress. Follow-ups can be short-term, within three to six months, or long-term, at least six months later (Cormier & Hackney, 2012). Occasionally, clients will return to a follow-up session with a new presenting concern. In these cases, the counselor will treat it as a new intake and make decisions about appropriateness for treatment just as he would with a new client.

SIDEBAR 7.1

In Practice: What Would You Do?

Leon is leading a group in an outpatient facility at the Veterans Administration. A Navy retiree himself, he just completed his master's degree and is under supervision of the facility's psychiatrist. He feels overwhelmed with his individual client caseload and prefers group work. He thinks he can help more people and finds it an efficient way to work. He is expected to keep an eye out for patients who need individual counseling. He is discussing with his VA colleague Jackie, 41, a mother of two and a staff sergeant in the Reserves, who was recalled to active duty and served in Iraq on two 15-month rotations before she was released halfway through the second rotation for "medical reasons."

Jackie spent several months in a rehab center before she returned home to her family. During group sessions, she is sullen, tearful, and frequently scans the doors and windows of the group room. Neighbors and family members report that Jackie was always angry and suspicious. They say her behavior post-Iraq is nothing new. She frequently complained to the school principal that other kids disliked her kids. She won't open up in group because she says most people aren't trustworthy and that you must constantly be on guard to prevent being taken advantage of. I checked it out. Her record doesn't say anything about PTSD. I don't think group is helping her but that's on her treatment plan. I sure don't have time to see her individually. She reminds me too much of some of the sailors I used to know!

Class Discussion

1. Should Leon continue to see her in group, individually, or both, or refer her to someone else? Support your answer.
2. What should he be ready to discuss with his supervisor?
3. What should his supervisor know about Leon's past training and expertise?
4. If you were Leon's colleague, what would you want to discuss with him?

Credentialing

Becoming a professional counselor takes more than academic training. In order to practice you must be credentialed and credentialing varies according to discipline, state, and national requirements. When you started on this path toward a career as a professional counselor, you may not have known how much credentialing plays a significant role in your future. Earlier you learned that each profession has a common body of knowledge and that national organizations determine its content. National organizations oversee credentialing as well. In addition, state laws and statutes regulate the ability to practice counseling in a particular state. Although in many states, requirements are similar to national professional association requirements, differences do exist. Furthermore, state credentials are not portable from one state to another. To practice in one state does not give you the right to practice in another. The National Board of Certified Counselors along with the American Association of State Counseling Boards (AASCB), the Association for Counselor Education and Supervision (ACES), and the American Mental Health Counselors Association (AMHCA) are working together to forge a reasonable process for licensed counselors for a uniform licensure endorsement (Portability Task Force, 2017).

State Credentials

Many students initially have difficulty understanding the differences in licensure and certification. The term licensure generally refers to a state credential and a legal process with legal sanctions. The term certification may refer to either a state or national credential. Both have similar processes. The individual seeking credentialing must meet prescribed education and field practice requirements. Certification recognizes competence at a standard level and allows practitioners to use the title counselor. The best-known state-level certification recognition is that of school counselor (American School Counselor Association, n.d.), although a few states refer to this credential as licensure. As a rule, students who graduate with a master's degree in school counseling need not take additional training in the state in which they received their degree. To practice as a clinical mental health counselor, however, individuals must continue on to pursue additional coursework, supervision of their professional experiences, and, in most cases, they must also sit for an examination. As of 2009, all 50 states plus the District of Columbia, Guam, and Puerto Rico have credentialing laws that allow counselors to practice. Most states refer to this credential as the Licensed Professional Counselor (LPC). Some states use the term Licensed Clinical Professional Counselor (LCPC), others use Licensed Mental Health Counselor (LMHC), and a few states use the term Certified Professional Counselor (CPC). Most states also have provisional licenses that allow beginning counselors to practice under supervision while they acquire the necessary coursework and hours to practice independently. Requirements vary from state to state. Certification or licensure consists of a master's degree in counseling or a closely related field, anywhere from 30 to 60 graduate credits, 1000 to 3000 hours of supervised experience beyond the master's degree, and the passing of an examination. The American Counseling Association provides links to individual state professional licensure board websites (https://www.schoolcounselor.org/school-counselors-members/careers-roles/state-certification-requirements).

National Credentials

Although credentialing varies across states, national standards ensure that counselors have a coherent identity and meet the same criteria. The American Counseling Association has been and continues to be active in setting national standards and advocating for state credentialing.

The ACA was instrumental in creating the National Board of Certified Counselors (NBCC) which oversees national standards. It administers the National Counselor Examination (NCE) that counselors must take to become National Certified Counselors (NCCs). To sit for the exam, counselors must hold a minimum of a master's degree in counseling or a closely related field that includes the eight core areas discussed in Chapters 4 and 5, and have at least two years of supervised counseling experience. A majority of the states use the NCE as their state licensure exam. Information on specific state requirements is found on the NBCC website (http://nbcc. org/stateexamination).

NBCC also oversees credentialing in the specialty areas of National Certified School Counselor (NCSC), Certified Clinical Mental Health Counselor (CCMHC), and Master Addictions Counselor (MAC). A related NBCC credentialing organization, the Center for Credentialing and Education (CCE), oversees certification for Approved Clinical Supervisor (ACS); Board Certified Coach (BCC); Global Career Development Facilitator (GCDF); and Board Certified-TeleMental Health Provider (BC-TMH); Distance Credentialed Counseling (DCC), which sets standards for technology-assisted counselors who conduct counseling by phone and the internet; Distance Credentialed Facilitator (DCF); and Human Services – Board Certified Practitioner (HS-BCP). (Requirement information can be found at http://www.nbcc.org.)

NBCC also promotes standards and certification around the world through NBCC International (http://www.nbccinternational.org).

Accreditation

Higher education institutions must first meet accreditation standards set by one of six regional commissions such as the Middle States Association of Colleges and Schools, or by national organizations such as the National Council for Accreditation of Teacher Education. Specialized accreditation applies to specific preparation programs within institutions. CACREP sets minimum standards of training for professional counselors. CACREP accreditation is a voluntary credential. CACREP delineates the requirements that institutions of higher education must meet. The process involves two essential elements. Programs must write a self-study in which they present detailed information about the curriculum, faculty resources, clinical experiences, supervisor qualifications, and program evaluation processes. The second step involves an on-site visit during which a team of evaluators visits the campus to validate the information provided in the self-study.

Supervision

During your program of study, the time will come when you will be supervised. This occurs during several courses. You will receive feedback in every experiential course that provides you with opportunities to practice counseling. At first, you will practice with your classmates. Later you will counsel real clients in practicum and internship courses. These are closely supervised experiences during which seasoned on-site counselors and course instructors will watch you counsel in person through one-way mirrors or by video streaming. Depending upon the resources in your institution, you may be provided with feedback to recorded sessions instead. If you are not going on for further credentialing, you will no longer be required to seek supervision after earning the master's degree. If you want to become a licensed counselor, you will be required to be under further supervision by a licensed professional generally for around two years of full-time professional employment. In either case, once you can practice independently you will no longer need to be supervised. However, you will want to consider supervision throughout your professional career.

How will you decide when you might want to seek supervision? The answer lies in the purposes of supervision itself. Although many models of supervision exist, three main purposes are common to all. Supervision provides (a) feedback on counseling and psychotherapy skill development; (b) training on issues or methods of providing services as they arise in practice; and (c) a forum to process one's own issues that may be triggered by client's problems. You should seek supervision from an experienced and licensed colleague whenever any of these three purposes exists.

Ethics dictate that you not practice beyond your area of competence. Therefore, if a client has a concern in which you are not well versed you must either refer to someone who is or seek training. If you choose the latter course of action, you must stay under supervision with someone who is an expert in the area of concern until she is satisfied that you can address the concern independently. For example, if you are a school counselor, you may have a student with an eating disorder. If you have little or no experience with this disorder, of course, you will refer out to someone who does for further treatment. However, you may very well need to see the student about other issues as part of your student caseload assignment. Consequently, you must seek supervision about eating disorders. Even if you have been trained but have no experience in a particular disorder and method of treatment, you will seek supervision when an individual with the disorder becomes your client. For example, you may have learned about anxiety disorders in your program of study but if a client has been diagnosed at intake with a form of anxiety, Post-traumatic Stress Disorder (PTSD), then you must seek supervision or refer the client out elsewhere.

If you find that you are not comfortable with a client's problem, it may be that it brings up feelings with a similar issue you have experienced in the past. Countertransference may account for this. *Countertransference* has to do with the feelings that a counselor may unconsciously attribute (or transfer) to the client that originate in the counselor's past. You must seek individual supervision to deal with your past unresolved issue. Otherwise, you may not be effective with your client. Although you may not intend to, you could influence the direction of therapeutic change to resolve your own issues rather than those of your client. At times, you may not recognize that a client's concerns are recreating issues for you. Consequently, many counselors check in with peer supervisors on a regular basis. Some counselors belong to peer-supervision groups and routinely meet to discuss their concerns with each other. This is a good way to address the third supervision purpose of processing your own issues as they arise in your clients.

Consultation

At times, counselors act as consultants to other professionals. A *consultant* is a counselor who offers expertise to a constituency that wants to solve a problem. A counseling consultant helps first to define the problem or potential problem and then resolve it. "Consultant relationships are described as triadic (i.e., client, consultant, problem) and are content based, goal directed and process oriented" (Gladding, 2018, p. 37). Consultation is one of the primary functions of school counselors because they provide their expertise to teachers, administrators, parents, and the community. Many other professional counselors also provide consultation services to many constituencies. This is an important part of clinical mental health counselors' work in community mental health settings. Career, rehabilitation, and addictions counselors offer their specialized expertise as consultants in such organizations and in corporate settings.

When are counselors qualified to be consultants? It depends upon the need and purpose of consultation. A counselor might become a consultant early in her career on core issues such as communication skills or developmental concerns, or much later as expertise changes and grows or becomes targeted in a specialty area. School counselors use consultation skills in the daily practice of their profession from the beginning of their careers. Other counselors may or may not be so well versed. As you progress through your career you will continue to retrain and upgrade your skills. If you are not trained in consultation, you may want to seek opportunities to learn these specialized skills in order to add consulting services to your repertoire of activities.

Continuing Education

The master's degree is an entry-level degree. You will have ample opportunities to further hone your skills and become competent in areas of special interest. As long as you are in this profession you will learn and grow personally and professionally. To maintain your national or state credentials you will be required to seek some form of continuing education. You may wish to attend workshops at professional conferences, or take courses online or through educational reading materials. You must ensure that credentialing organizations such as NBCC approve the learning experiences. Training and education opportunities are excellent ways to gain the knowledge you need to develop specialized areas of expertise. Remember to formally keep track of all approved learning experiences. You may decide to take additional graduate courses or perhaps go on for a doctoral degree. The possibilities for your future are many and exciting.

Stress and Burnout

Over time, every counselor has the potential to experience burnout. Counselors are human and have the same difficulties and problems as all other human beings. They deal with their own issues of death, loss, illness, job stress, and the other vicissitudes of life. Because counselors listen to others' stories and attend to the many troubles that plague humankind, they must be especially careful to attend to their stress levels. They must be aware of burnout when it occurs and take steps to ensure that they remain effective in their work. You learned in Chapter 2 that an essential characteristic of counselors is high energy and the ability to take care of their own physical and emotional needs. Good nutrition, physical activity, personal interests, and recreational activities, and satisfying interpersonal relationships all contribute to personal energy. Stress and burnout reduce that energy.

Stress is a state of tension that arouses autonomic responses that impair optimal functioning. Stressors are those events that have the potential to produce stress. Stress occurs when there is an imbalance between external demands and a person's ability to adequately respond. Stress may result from objective demands in the environment but the subjective experience of stressors varies with the individual's perceptions. The individual may be unable to muster the internal and personal resources necessary to counteract stress effectively. Results include symptoms such as headaches, sleep disorders, anxiety and depression, hypertension, substance abuse, family disruption, and domestic abuse. If a counselor experiences high levels of stress, she may not be effective in helping others. Ultimately, stress levels that are not adequately attended to will result in burnout.

Burnout is the depletion of energy to the point that the individual is no longer healthily engaged in an activity or with others. It is emotional exhaustion arising from excessive demands imposed by others. For counselors, it is a response to the chronic strain of dealing with others' problems. Burnout is a unique kind of stress that results from the social interaction inherent in a counseling relationship. Burnout is accompanied by an overload of stressors. It negatively influences the counselor's motivation, behaviors, and attitudes. A normally committed counselor disengages from professional obligations, at least emotionally and often literally. Anger, resentment, guilt, indifference, fatigue, cynicism, a sense of failure, and negativity are some common emotional responses. Colds and flu, excessive use of drugs and alcohol, marital discord, high absenteeism, inability to listen to clients or concentrate on their concerns, isolation, and withdrawal from social contact are a few other responses. Clearly, stress and burnout will have negative effects on clients.

Self-Care

You are at the beginning of your training. Many academic, experiential, and personal demands will be made on you. Now is the time to attend to your own levels of stress. Self-care is not a luxury or self-indulgence. It is a professional obligation. Learn now how to minimize your reactions to stress. Learn how to recognize the symptoms of burnout and what to do about it.

Listen to the wisdom of your body. Stress can surface in your thoughts, feelings, and actions. It will manifest in some people physically, others emotionally, and still others mentally. Learn how you react in stressful situations. Not all activities targeted at reducing stress and burnout work equally well in all people. Learn your triggers and your solutions. The self-awareness work you do throughout your program of study should help you get more in touch with your own needs and your own solutions.

Here are ten suggestions:

- Don't be a loner. Avoid isolation. Develop and nurture relationships with family, other students, and friends. Support is essential to managing stress.
- Take care of yourself physically. Eat properly, get enough sleep, go for checkups regularly and don't ignore physical symptoms.
- Reduce demands and intensity. Try not to procrastinate. Allow time to complete projects without putting time pressure on yourself.
- Live life in moderation. Learn to pace yourself. Prioritize and balance your life roles and activities. Intense concentration in one area at the expense of others leads to stress and burnout.
- Learn to say "no" to demands if they are not truly essential. Counselors are natural helpers and tend to overextend whenever they are asked for help. Refuse additional demands on your time, resources, and emotions. Take control of what you can control.
- Learn to delegate. Allow others in your life to help themselves. You don't need to do it all at work or at home.
- Reevaluate your values. As you grow and change so will those things that are meaningful to you. Begin separating the essential from the nonessential. You will have more energy more time, and begin to feel more authentic and centered.
- Along with reevaluating, try to spend more time taking care of your real needs and pursuing your own interests instead of worrying about things you cannot change.
- Make time for fun. Eliminate guilt from leisure time. Enjoy the moments of your life and keep a sense of humor.
- See a counselor! If you want to be a counselor, you believe that everyone has the right to lead balanced, fulfilling lives. That applies to you, too.

Summary

This chapter began with the developmental nature of acquiring counseling skills and likened it to the developmental nature of counseling itself. Several models of helping and the stages of the counseling process were presented. Students learned about the necessity of structure and about counseling procedures for the first session, assessment and diagnosis, case conceptualization, treatment planning and goal setting, the working alliance and action planning, and termination and follow-up. This was followed by a discussion of the client's need for self-exploration and understanding. The timing within and between sessions followed. Next, a section on credentialing included national and state standards and requirements for certification and licensure. Students learned about the purpose and need for supervision, the concept of consultation, and the responsibility for continuing education. The chapter ended with a discussion of stress and burnout and suggestions for reducing them.

> *This class has taught me to look at all angles when possible… I think I am finally figuring some things out.*
> – mid-life student transitioning from science into counseling

References

American School Counselor Association. (n.d.). *State certification requirements.* Retrieved from: https://www.schoolcounselor.org/school-counselors-members/careers-roles/state-certification-requirements

American Psychiatric Association. (2013). *Diagnostic and statistical manual of mental disorders* (5th ed.). Washington, DC: Author.

Carkhuff, R. R. (2009). *The art of helping* (9th ed.). Amherst, MA: Human Resource Development Press.

Corey, M. S., & Corey, G. (2015). *Becoming a helper* (7th ed.) Boston, MA: Cengage Learning.

Cormier, L. S., & Hackney, H. (2012). *Counseling strategies and interventions.* Upper Saddle River, NJ: Pearson.

Egan, G. (2009). *The Skilled Helper: A problem-management and opportunity-development approach to helping.* Pacific Grove, CA: Thomson Brooks/Cole.

Gladding, S.T. (2018). *Counseling: A comprehensive profession* (8th ed.) New York: Pearson Education.

Ivey, A. E., Ivey, M. B., & Zalaquett, C. P. (2014). *Intentional interviewing and counseling: Facilitating client development in a multicultural society.* Belmont, CA: Brooks/Cole – Cengage Learning.

Ivey, A. E., Packard, N. G., & Ivey, M. B. (2017). *Basic attending skills* (6th ed.). Hanover, MA: Microtraining Associates, Inc.

Patterson, L. E., & Welfel, E. R. (1994). *The counseling process* (4th ed.). Pacific Grove, CA: Brooks/Cole.

Portability Task Force. (2017). *Joint statement on a National Counselor Licensure Endorsement process.* Retrieved from https://www.nbcc.org/Assets/Portability/Portability-Statement-Endorsement-Process.pdf

Prochaska, J. O., & DiClemente, C. C. (1992). *Stages of change in the modification of problem behaviors.* Newbury Park, CA: Sage.

Table 7.1 *TFAC Chart – Thought, Feelings, Actions, and Context

Self	My Thoughts	My Feelings	My Actions	My Context	Other? (Specify)
How do I respond to structure?					
What is my stance on diagnosis?					
How do I handle endings and loss?					
What is my attitude about the need for credentials to practice?					
How do I respond to corrective feedback?					
Where do I see myself five years after completing my program of study? How will I get there?					
How do I respond to stress? How will I prevent burnout?					
What concerns do I have?					
Others	**Others' Probable Thoughts**	**Others' Possible Feelings**	**Others' Observable Actions**	**Others' Apparent Context**	**Other? (Specify)**
What can your instructors tell you about counseling stages?					
How do they structure intake sessions or the first session?					
What can they tell you about counseling stages?					
How do instructors and working professionals appraise their clients?					
What is their experience with credentialing?					
What is their experience as a supervisee and supervisor?					
How do they handle stress and burnout?					
What else can you learn from them about timing issues?					

*For more information on TFAC, see Chapter 1.

Chapter 8

Why? Answers about Caring and Social Justice

Mary H. Guindon and Jessica J. Lane

> *When helping others, do not look for a reward; if you are looking for rewards, don't help others.*
> – Chinese proverb

Points to Ponder

- Why do counselors choose to work in the profession?
- Why are counselors involved in social justice issues?
- What is advocacy and how do counselors advocate for their clients?

The Heart of Counseling

Why do we do what we do? In Chapter 1 you met some beginning students and learned what brought them into a counseling program. Other students in their first class came for different reasons:

Tamika states that never a day goes by that people don't tell her their personal problems. She has a degree in psychology and went on for training as a credentialed masseuse. Now 32, she believes a counseling credential will legitimatize what she has been doing for the last few years. Her neighbor, Jan, a divorced grandmother who never worked outside the home, has come into the class because she says she had a wonderful counselor who changed her life. She wants to do the same for other women. She is not entirely sure she can be a counselor but she would like to try. Forty-five-year-old Carlos is a Sergeant Major in the U.S. Army about to retire after 25 years' service. He knows the toll war takes on soldiers and their families. He wants to spend the next phase of his life helping other members of the military transition into civilian life and careers just as he is about to do.

Clearly, these students care. Compassion is an ingredient in any helper's motivation. Compassion is defined as "deep awareness of the suffering of another coupled with the wish to relieve it" (Houghton Mifflin, 2002, p. 292). The definition of compassionate is "Feeling or showing compassion; sympathetic." To be a professional counselor, however, is to check sympathy at the door of the counseling office and replace it with empathy while not losing compassion. You learned in Chapter 2 the importance of objectivity and the difference between empathy and sympathy. Empathy recognizes pain and suffering and wants to make a difference; sympathy feels the pain personally and wants to fix it. The empathic person does not confuse another person's troubles with her own. Think of counseling as compassionate caring, a term often used in the medical professions. It assumes a trained approach to alleviating problems. You will be trained to take your compassionate yearnings and translate them into creating an atmosphere of empathy necessary for healing and change.

In Chapter 1 you also learned about some other basic motivations for entering the profession. What motivates us to be professional counselors is as varied as the reasons for seeking training itself. Each is legitimate. Our motivators, however, do not alone answer the why of the actual reality of the work.

What is it that keeps counselors going when the rewards are often more intrinsic than extrinsic? The hours can be long, the compensation inadequate, the investment in lifelong training high, and the consequences of hearing painful life stories difficult. Few clients will thank you for your services. You may never know if you made a difference.

As you recall, the term transference comes originally from Freudian psychoanalysis in which the client unconsciously transfers repressed and unresolved feelings, perceptions, and beliefs onto the counselor as if he was a person from the past, particularly a parent. Even when you find yourself liking your clients and feeling a special connection with them, you must constantly be alert to the possibility of countertransference. You must guard against the possibility of countertransference when you dislike your client or even wish he would go away. Neither is an appropriate response. As you learned in the last chapter you must spend your time, effort, and at times your own money to seek supervision to deal with your issues when you find them sitting across from you. The life of a counselor is demanding. Yet most professional counselors find the work fulfilling. What makes those who do this kind of work a contented lot? Every counselor has her own reasons, yet each has the same reason.

We believe being a counselor is one of life's rare privileges. To be trusted by strangers, to care deeply, to know you might make a difference to someone in a time of need is noble work indeed. To enter into another's world and to witness extraordinary courage, bravery in the face of adversity, and commitment to life-altering change is reward enough. We have learned more from my clients than we have taught; we have gained more than we have given.

The various helping professions' codes of ethics discourage bartering for services by accepting services or goods, including gifts. Nevertheless, we know our clients have given us many gifts. They are not tangible, of course, but they have enriched our lives in immeasurable ways. We learn life lessons from our clients (and students) even as we assist them in coming to terms with their own issues. This is the "why" of our professional lives. Here are four examples. We hope they inspire you in some small way as they profoundly inspired us.

SIDEBAR 8.1

In Practice: What Would You Do?

Keith is in his second year as a middle-school counselor in a predominantly African American and Latino/a urban neighborhood riddled with crime and poverty. The teaching staff is 45% African American, 25% Latino/a, 20% White, and 10% Asian. As one of four counselors, Keith, who is White, is responsible for seventh grade academic advising, career counseling, and guidance classroom lessons. He wants to run an assertiveness training group for biracial children after school hours because he has observed some of his biracial kids being bullied for being "too White." He spread the word to the teaching staff but so far, no one has signed up for the group. He then sent out letters to all the seventh grade parents.

This seems like a no brainer to me. So far, no response from the parents either. I can't seem to get either the teachers or the students interested. A couple of the African American teachers approached me and told me that targeting these kids was a bad idea. What else can I do to help these kids? We've done quite a few activities on bullying in the classroom and for the teachers. That hasn't seemed to help these kids. I can't stand to just sit by and watch them being bullied like that. It's just wrong!

Class Discussion

1. Why do you think the teachers believe this group to be a bad idea?
2. What can Keith do to be a social advocate for these biracial students? For all his students?
3. What external factors might be influencing the parents and students?
4. How might you advise Keith about ACA's stance on social change?

Case Studies

The Gift of Courage (Mary Guindon)

Emmaline came to me as a referral from her husband's friend. The friend – my former client – stated that her husband "didn't know what to do with her, that she was out of control." When we first met, she reported symptoms consistent with panic attacks bordering on agoraphobia, a disorder that prevents its sufferers from interacting outside of perceived safe places. People with full-blown agoraphobia confine themselves to their homes.

Emmaline was a 44-year-old woman with a strict, traditional Italian American upbringing in which the father was the unquestioned patriarch and daughters were reared to make good marriages and homes for their husbands. She was a small woman, neat, sweet of face, well dressed, and pleasant. She had been married for almost 20 years to a conservative, successful Italian American businessman. The only child of difficult, somewhat cold but nevertheless loving parents, Emmaline reported that she was bright in school and considered herself artistic. Her mother contracted cancer when she was 14. She was the major caregiver throughout high school and college until her mother's death when Emmaline was 19. She reported that it was a nurse who told her that her mother had died. No one else was there at the time. She went to the funeral and this loss was never discussed again in her home. She quit college to work as a part-time secretary and be the homemaker for her father. She left her father's home when she married four years later. Emmaline worked part time as a corporate secretary while her husband built his business. She became a full-time homemaker at 30 when her first child, a son, was born. At 39, she lost a hydrocephalic daughter at birth. She reported that this loss was never discussed either. She never quite recovered from that loss.

Her family now consisted of a demanding, verbally abusive husband, a good-natured but rebellious adolescent son, and an angry, abusive, and demanding father who still lived in his home. In her marriage, she was responsible for not only all the domestic duties of a traditional wife but also most of the traditional male roles, such as mowing the lawn and house repairs. Her husband devoted himself entirely to his business and participated in no household chores or child-rearing duties. He expected a clean, orderly house; dinner on time; an obedient child; and a cheerful wife. Emmaline had one friend among the other stay-at-home moms in her neighborhood and felt close to a female cousin and her 10-year-old niece, although she spent little time with them. She was active in her church community and volunteered at her son's school.

A few months before she came to see me, her father had a stroke. He now needed care but refused to leave his home. Emmaline split her time between being a caretaker to her father, a homemaker, a mother, the demands of her husband, dealing with her son's emerging adolescent rebellion, and her obligations at church and her son's school. She was overwhelmed with care-taking responsibilities with neither enough time nor emotional support in her long days. She reported this was the beginning of her feelings of anxiety and panic.

As we worked together, Emmaline came to understand that she had no control in her life, had abandoned her own desires from her the time her mother became ill, and was overwhelmed with the needs of her family. She did not believe she had choices in her life. She was desperately unhappy but knew no way out of her situation. In addition, with the care of her father came the realization that she had never been allowed to grieve the death of either her mother or her daughter. She continually felt crushing sadness, emptiness, and a yearning for female compan-ionship. Because she had known only verbal abuse from the men in her life, she was terrified of making changes. She felt trapped and guilty when she wanted to take time to rest or to do any-thing other than take care of her family obligations.

Emmaline set self-care goals with me as we worked on her anxiety attacks. What might seem easy steps to others were monumentally frightening for her. Her family's negative reactions felt like abandonment to her. She had lost her mother at an early age and did not want to risk losing, emotionally or in reality, the family she deeply loved. She showed considerable courage as she learned to set limits on her own time with her family members. As frightening as it was to face a barrage of verbal abuse, Emmaline told her family that she was taking some time for herself. She insisted on nursing care help for her father and twice-monthly household help in her own home. Her son began taking on household chores for the first time. Changes for her were arduous. She faced resistance and anger at home each step of the way. Her family refused to participate in counseling and ridiculed her for going. Yet she never missed a session. She practiced making reasonable requests of her family even though it felt to her selfish and unwarranted. She made small changes week after week, despite her feelings of anxiety and fear. She slowly began to have some sense of control. She came to understand that she could be a person in her own right and that meeting her own needs along with those of her family was possible.

Emmaline reached out to her cousin and her young niece. They began having "girl days" that energized and renewed her. She nurtured her friendship with her neighbor and in time they became confidantes to each other. Each step she initiated terrified her, yet she faced her fears and made changes in her life. In time, her husband agreed to go to couples counseling with one of my colleagues. Together they learned to share household responsibilities and to communicate with each other. Her son, too, attended counseling. They grew together into a healthier family.

As I watched her make changes despite her anxieties, I wondered if I could have been as courageous in the face of so much criticism, ridicule, and early socialization. I will never forget Emmaline. She taught me what courage means and about the human spirit. One day, a few years after our last session, she wrote me about the time we had spent in counseling: *Layer by layer my spirit was awakened.*

The Gift of Visibility (Jessica J. Lane)

Sheena, a third-grade student, was quickly referred to me at the start of the school year by the worried principal, classroom teacher, and support staff. Sheena's family had already moved 10 times by the time Sheena came to our school during her last month of second grade. During that time the seasoned classroom teacher and principal could not keep Sheena in the classroom a full day due to her many social-emotional outbursts and tantrums. It was evident they were at a loss with how to support her social-emotional needs and minimize her outbursts, and wanted to start the school year on a very different trajectory.

As an eager new school counselor, I wanted to make a connection with this student right away and aid the situation. I knew it wouldn't be easy, but I was anxious to prove myself and help Sheena stay in the classroom as much as possible. Upon my initial meeting with Sheena, she seemed bubbly, ornery, funny, and full of life. However, Sheena seemed to lack very basic social skills and understanding of social norms, which likely impacted her ability to make friends and participate in group activities in the classroom.

It was clear that Sheena was very bright, but academically behind. This was not surprising, and likely a consequence of her transient, hit-and-miss education. Most notably she seemed to crave attention of any sort; she thrived on one-on-one conversations and desperately wanted to be heard and noticed. Finding healthy and appropriate ways for her to get attention would be important.

Sheena's mom had multiple crippling health issues, including seizures that limited her ability to drive and her mobility at home. As a result, Sheena's grandma came in and out of the home serving as a caregiver, with the primary focus being on mom, and then to assist and help where and as she could with the four children. Sheena's stepdad worked two jobs to pay for the mounting medical bills, and admitted that he was rarely home. Upon meeting dad for a parent consult, which was rescheduled multiple times because of his many work and home requirements, dad seemed exhausted, and overwhelmed. He offered in our meeting, very matter of fact, "Sheena is the youngest of the four children in our blended family. She is the *only* one who does not have medical issues or mental health concerns, and as a result, she is often placed on the back burner, because she doesn't have an immediate need. I simply don't have time to help with her homework. The best I can do is talk to her like an adult in hopes that she will learn some of the vocabulary to help her reading. If you could give her more attention at school that would really help."

What I saw before me that day was a man who was doing his best to hold it all together, but didn't have the time, money, or resources to make it all happen. I was empathetic to the many demands placed on him, serving as the breadwinner and caregiver for his wife and four children. Through our conversation I also received a clearer picture of a little girl who was not getting the attention she needed to be successful and was crying out in any way possible to be seen.

I worked with Sheena throughout the school year. I made sure that Sheena was discussed and supported at education intervention meetings, and that her behaviors and academics were closely monitored. I encouraged the staff to acknowledge and compliment her vocabulary whenever she used words beyond the average third grader. This boosted her self-esteem and encouraged her work in both reading and spelling. She thrived off of the praise and positive individual attention.

Sheena and I developed a strong relationship. She looked forward to seeing me for classroom lessons, and she and I had individual counseling sessions where we worked on social skills and self-regulation. The individual attention and psychoeducational sessions carried over into healthier classroom interactions and social situations. She worked hard to learn to be patient and to build relationships with her peers. Sheena had made amazing gains throughout the school year, jumping an unheard of four grade levels in her reading – from below grade level to above. Sheena was staying in the classroom all day; she was making friends. Things seemed to be going rather well.

However, during the first two weeks of May, Sheena's behavior changed and reverted backward. She became more disruptive in the classroom, in the lunchroom, and on the bus. One morning before the school day began, I received a call from the school secretary, "Sheena had a bad morning on the bus, she is being removed from breakfast because of her behavior. She is coming to see you, because we don't know what to do with her."

I was worried: it wasn't even 8 a.m., the start of our traditional school day, and Sheena had already been in trouble multiple times. I went to greet her in the hallway, and as she came down the hall, she was cussing and crying with every step. At a loss, I helped her find a seat and squatted down to calmly talk to her on her level. I shared, almost as a review for myself, how things had been going so well, how she had been in the classroom all day, how she was doing so well in her schoolwork, and how something had changed. Perhaps she could help me to understand. Through the sobs, she caught her breath and said, "It's almost my birthday, and everyone has forgotten my birthday for the last three years. Everybody always forgets about me. Summer is almost here and what will I do without school?"

It was clear that while Sheena was making gains, she was still fearful of old patterns. Her change in behavior came from a fear of being forgotten or "invisible," the fear of future inconsistency and lack of routine, or soon not having the same supports that school had provided for her that year. I did my best to reassure Sheena that morning and said I would talk to grandma or mom so they knew her concerns. Once I had calmed Sheena down and got her off to class, I then immediately called and spoke with Sheena's mom and offered some community resources for clothes, food, and summer activities to help over the summer. Recognizing that pride can often be a deterrent for families to accept help, I was delicate in how I approached the topic, but she was extremely appreciative. I also offered to pack a "care kit" for her to give Sheena on her birthday, comprised of clothes, books, and a journal. My hope was that they would be able to offer Sheena some basic "gifts" to make her feel visible and special. Over the last few months Sheena had grown quite a bit and her clothes were beginning to not fit her. I also felt that offering some books would positively occupy Sheena during the summer and support her new love of reading and academics. Both mom and grandma couldn't have been more appreciative to be connected to the resources and to be able to offer something special to Sheena on her birthday.

The morning of Sheena's birthday I was sure to greet her as the day began to gauge how things might go, and to put in any necessary safeguards. Sheena was beaming that morning with a proud smile from ear-to-ear that I will never forget. She came right up to me, tapped me on the shoulder, and whispered, "My grandma and momma say that you have angel's wings, you just don't like to show them. You know just how to make everyone feel special." I will never forget how proud I felt that morning, and how much I learned about the importance of making sure that as counselors we do our best to offer the basic tenets of being heard, seen, and valued to each of our clients. Sheena had a great day and a calm rest of the school year without any other problems because she felt visible. I helped to offer Sheena the gift of visibility, but she offered me so much more.

The Gift of Advocacy (Jessica J. Lane)

Clay, a fourth-grader, was the youngest of three kids; a dark-haired, quiet boy, who was naturally shy around his parents, his two boisterous older sisters, and his many friends. Clay was referred to me by his parents. Clay's parents were very involved in Clay's schooling. They worked tirelessly with him each night on reading and homework. They were concerned about Clay's grades and how he was falling further and further behind, as well as how he was becoming even *more* quiet and reserved at home. Upon consultation, they could not pinpoint any specific change, and were seeking additional support. From reading Clay's grades and cumulative folder, Clay seemed to be a lower student academically, and school was very difficult for him; he was reading two grade levels below his peers, and was one grade level lower in math.

I decided on some individual sessions with Clay to build rapport and to see what kind of supports he might need. In our individual sessions, I observed just as I had during classroom counseling lessons a cheerful but reserved boy, who had a willingness to please, work hard, and engage. During our sessions Clay shared how school was getting harder and harder and he didn't know why. I brought the parents' concerns to the student intervention team to gather some collective feedback. During the meeting, the classroom teacher mentioned how Clay was low in all subjects. The music and gym teachers expressed how worried they were regarding Clay's inattentiveness. They also mentioned how Clay would seem to look off into space, seeming distracted or unengaged. The gym and music teachers wanted me to discuss the potential signs and symptoms of Attention Deficit Disorder (ADD) with the parents and asked to have him screened. They felt his behavior was impeding his learning in traditional subjects and his learning within their respective classrooms.

I had a different perception of Clay. While we were aware he was functioning lower than his peers academically, I also saw him listening attentively, trying his hardest, staying on task, and always coming with a cheerful, upbeat attitude. Clearly there was a disconnect and I suspected the issue was not an attention issue. I also did some classroom observation and did not see those symptoms.

I met with the parents and professionally presented the various concerns from among the teachers, as well as my observations and experiences with Clay, and elicited the parents' thoughts and feelings. Clay's mom was a nurse and shared how she had seen and worked with many children who were diagnosed with Attention Deficit Disorder and she felt her son did not display those same characteristics. She was adamant her child did not have this disorder and took a very defensive posture. I expressed to his parents how lucky Clay was to have them be so invested in him and his education. I shared with Clay's mom and dad how much I valued their opinion and their willingness to work with us to determine the best way to support Clay and recommended that we start with him receiving a physical with their family physician to rule out anything medical as it seemed something was missing. My counselor training always said to start there.

Within two weeks, Clay's mom called me crying, stating what they had learned from the physical. Clay had suffered hearing loss in his right ear at some point. It became clear how the positioning of where the teacher stood, either on Clay's right or left side, would have a dramatic impact on his ability to hear, listen, be attentive, and follow directions. In turn, it would also have a dramatic impact on his learning. From that meeting, the parents were able to then get a follow-up appointment and get Clay a hearing aid. Immediately upon receiving his hearing aid, Clay's grades improved across the board, and his reading ability took off, particularly in his ability to read aloud. Now he could hear the words, consistently hear the directions, and become more confident in his abilities. I continued to work with Clay in an individual capacity as he adjusted to having a hearing aid, as he was feeling "different, but improved" as he said. It was transformative to see Clay become a more confident and outgoing boy who again interacted with his peers. With a little counselor advocacy and collaboration with all parties involved, the student was able to get the appropriate help and support. This translated into improved grades, academic growth, and heightened confidence. What could have been a deteriorating school experience or a horrible misdiagnosis for this young child turned out to be a game changer. Years later I still have the handwritten letter I received on the last day of school from Clay's father thanking me for the work that I do as a school counselor, and the tremendous impact it had on his son. I also have the hand-drawn picture from Clay thanking me for changing his life.

The Gift of Hope (Mary Guindon)

I first met Larry in a partial-day treatment program at a community mental health center in the South. He was a member of a social skills group I co-led during my first semester as an intern. It combined the chronically mentally ill with those from a nearby addictions halfway house. A recovering alcoholic, he was 38 but looked over 50. He had deep wrinkles, few teeth, clean but worn clothing, and stooped slightly. Years of addiction that deteriorated into homelessness had taken its toll. He had been in and out of the mental health system for much of his adult life. During social events structured for the patients, I found Larry to be full of life and kind to others, yet he interacted little during group.

In the second semester, I was assigned to the alcoholism unit in another part of the facility. As I waited to talk with my supervisor about my caseload, I overheard the director talking. He said, "Give Larry to her, he's so fried she can't do anything to help him but she can't hurt him either." I was shocked that he would speak so of another human being and offended to know he believed I couldn't do anything to help. I received his file with little comment from my supervisor. I looked at the four-inch-high document and felt some distress. I read through the case notes, wondering if the director was right. What could I, a mere beginner, do to help someone that experienced therapists had not already attempted over the years?

Full of my own inadequacy, I returned the next day to meet with Larry for our scheduled session. I did not know what I should do. I began by providing him with the introductory kinds of comments I had been trained to provide. He looked at me as he must have looked at every helper before. He was polite but with a weary, "I've heard it all before" look in his eye. Toward the end of our first session, I helped Larry set a goal for the next session as I had been told to do. When we met again, he had not done the agreed-upon task. Out of my own desperation and feeling of incompetence, I placed his bulky folder on the table next to us. I disclosed to him exactly how I was feeling. I told him that I did not know what I could do to help him that others had not already done. He lowered his head and nodded politely but made no comment. I wanted so badly to make a difference with this man but knew that it was not likely. I took a chance. I said, "It seems to me that everyone has been working harder for you than you have. Everyone seems to be dancing around for your benefit but you sit the dance out." He sat up and looked at me with a puzzled expression. Slowly, a different look came over him. He straightened himself from his stooped position. He said, "Before the drink got to me, I used to dance every chance I got." I wasn't sure he understood the metaphor. I asked him if he was good at dancing. When he said yes I asked him what else he was good at. That seemed to open up a flood of positive memories for him.

I met with him every week for the rest of the semester. I do not now remember what, exactly, we accomplished or how we terminated. I know that I did not think Larry made a change or discovery during our time together. I began to understand the devastating effect chronic alcoholism can have and was saddened by Larry's apparent lack of progress and my ineffectiveness, even though my supervisor and my instructor had assured me that nothing of significance could have been done. They told me that there was not much hope for this particular population.

My family and I moved away from that area. I encountered many other clients who were tagged with the label of hopelessness. I did what I could for them. I guarded against burnout. I worried in my heart that I was not making any sort of difference in the long run, even when short-term gains were visible. I received little positive feedback.

Several years later, my husband attended a conference back in that town where I had done my internship. When he returned, he told me about a strange encounter. He had worn a nametag on his lapel when he and some colleagues went out to lunch at a local restaurant. A well-dressed stranger came up to him and said, "Excuse me, sir, are you Mary's husband?" When he indicated that he was, the man said, "Tell her she changed my life that day. I'm sober six years, got my GED, went back to school, and now I'm a middle school teacher. Tell her please for me that I love the dance!"

Not often do we receive feedback that we have made this kind of difference. The gift I received from Larry will stay with me forever. I share it with my students: Although you may never receive this gift, remember that you do make a difference. No matter how damaged a child, how lost an adolescent, or – yes – how hopeless an adult, do what you do for the exception to all the statistics that tell you it will not matter. You may not know who that exception is, so *do it for them all.*

Social Justice and Advocacy

Professional counselors work with an array of people from all walks of life. Since its inception, members of the profession have been in a position to witness the disenfranchisement and marginalization of many of their clients. They have come to understand that no matter how skilled, experienced, knowledgeable, well meaning, and caring they are, they cannot help clients make changes that are not within their power to make. By merely focusing on providing counseling support to the individual, and neglecting or assuming value neutrality of the environmental factors of the client, the counseling profession runs the risk of perpetuating and minimizing the societal risks. People do not live in a vacuum and counselors must not practice in one regardless of their settings.

Perhaps the most significant Why is not about the individual, group, or family counseling counselors actually do, as important as that is. Counselors are concerned with social justice. Social justice, broadly defined, includes a vision where equitable resources are distributed, and all members are psychologically and physically safe (Lee, 2018). Further, it entails "scholarship and professional action designed to change societal values, structures, policies, and practices such that disadvantaged or marginalized groups gain increased access to... tools of self-determination" (Goodman et al., 2004, p. 795) such as "adequate food, sleep, wages, education, safety, opportunity, institutional support, health care, child care, and loving relationships" (Smith, 2003, p. 167, as quoted in Goodman et al., 2004, p. 795). Social justice is an integral part of counseling practices. Labeled a "fifth force" alongside psychodynamic, cognitive behavioral, existential-humanistic, and multicultural forces in counseling (Lee, 2018; Ratts, D'Andrea, & Arredondo, 2004), social justice is the next logical step in multicultural counseling – moving from understanding marginalized and oppressed groups, to advocating for social action and change for social equity for all (Lee, 2018). Counselors for Social Justice, a division of ACA, defines social justice counseling as representing

> a multifaceted approach to counseling in which practitioners strive to simultaneously promote human development and the common good through addressing challenges related to both individual and distributive justice. Social justice counseling includes empowerment of the individual as well as active confrontation of injustice and inequality in society as they impact clientele as well as those in their systemic contexts. In doing so, social justice counselors direct attention to the promotion of four critical principles that guide their work; equity, access, participation, and harmony. This work is done with a focus on the cultural, contextual, and individual needs of those served.
>
> (n.d.)

Counselors believe it important to right societal wrongs when they are made aware of them and if they reasonably can do so. American Counseling Association (ACA) "members help advocate for equity and fair treatment for all people and groups in order to end oppression and injustice affecting clients, students, families, communities, schools, workplaces, governments, and other social and institutional systems" (n.d.).

> Oppression is forcing something which is undesirable or harmful upon a person or group; and/or depriving a person or group of something that is needed, wanted, and/or helpful. In order to be oppressive, it must also threaten or ruin a person's mental or physical health, well-being, or coping ability.
>
> (Hanna, Talley, & Guindon, 2000, p. 432)

Therefore, oppression can be related in some way or another to many problems presented to counselors.

White Eurocentric ways of thinking still dominate American culture, but they often do not match the many diverse, cultural experiences of the United States. Unfortunately, members of nondominant cultures make up a disproportionate number of our clientele. Many live in environments of oppression even when it is unintentional. Consequently, oppression has important implications for mental health (David & Derthick, 2018; Lord & Dufort, 1996). However well intentioned, many White Americans do not truly understand the set of advantages they have by virtue of their Whiteness. This *White privilege* means that they benefit from an economic, social, or political world created for them and essentially closed to people of color simply by virtue of *their* color. Just as socioeconomic status, gender, sex, race, religion, and language can be a hindrance, it can also be a privilege or birthright. Just because one is born into privilege does not necessarily mean an individual is racist or prejudiced but it does mean that one may be unaware of having many advantages regardless of their own socio-economic status.

The multicultural counseling movement led the way in bringing the need for social justice to the forefront of the counseling profession. The ways in which counseling students are trained has been revolutionized as a result (D'Andrea & Heckman, 2008). Under the leadership of Lewis, Arnold, House, and Toporek (2002), the American Counseling Association Governing Council endorsed a set of advocacy competencies that all professional counselors should have. "When counselors become aware of external factors that act as barriers to an individual's development, they may choose to respond through advocacy. The client/student advocate role is especially significant when individuals or vulnerable groups lack access to needed services." (Lewis et al., 2002, p. 1).

> An advocacy orientation involves not only systems change interventions but also the implementation of empowerment strategies in direct counseling. Advocacy-oriented counselors recognize the impact of social, political, economic, and cultural factors on human development. They also help their clients and students understand their own lives in context. This lays the groundwork for self-advocacy.... In direct interventions, the counselor is able to:
>
> 1. Identify strengths and resources of clients and students.
> 2. Identify the social, political, economic, and cultural factors that affect the client/student.
> 3. Recognize the signs indicating that an individual's behaviors and concerns reflect responses to systemic or internalized oppression.
> 4. At an appropriate development level, help the individual identify the external barriers that affect his or her development.
> 5. Train students and clients in self-advocacy skills.
> 6. Help students and clients develop self-advocacy action plan.
>
> (Lewis et al., 2002, p. 1)

Counselors address social injustices by advocating for their clients. Social justice seeks to "challenge inherent inequities in social systems... and to promote access and equity within the context of personal and professional awareness," (Lee, 2018, p. 11). Three levels of awareness help to promote social justice: awareness of self, interpersonal awareness, and systems awareness (Lee, 2018). By having a strong awareness of these three areas, and advocating for all three levels, counselors can work to improve the circumstances and barriers for their clients.

The ACA Advocacy Competencies (Ratts, Toporek, & Lewis, 2010) suggest that counselors operate in two areas of concern: school/community collaboration and systems advocacy. Thus, counselors advocate through taking initiatives at the environmental level. They disseminate information to the public about the profession and about the barriers that disempowered people experience. They act as change agents whenever they can. They influence public policy as part of their work and engage in social/political action. In these ways, counselors not only make a difference for individuals and groups but can assist in changing systems for the betterment of society. Roysircar (2009) recommends that counselor-advocates must learn about sociopolitical realities in order to inspire collective action. This includes "discussions and redefinitions of the injustice or immorality of specific social conditions, an external attribution of blame for them, a corresponding sense of internal responsibility for corrective action, and some kind of action agenda for solving them" (Roysircar, 2009, p. 291).

The social advocacy movement, however, is not without its critics. Smith, Reynolds, and Rovnak (2009) suggested that it "lacks sufficient moderation and sometimes attempts to promote various agendas (e.g., personal, political) under the guise of 'social action'" (p. 483), and even redefining the role of counseling itself. Although they endorse the intentions of the movement, they recommend that, as admirable as it is, the counseling profession should "proceed with caution and begin a systematic effort to firmly establish this trend in counseling theory and practice and further investigate the impact of this movement…" (p. 490).

Regardless, of one's stance, the counseling profession cannot become complacent, and must strive to improve the lives and circumstances of the clients they serve. Counselors must work to be tireless advocates and change agents for those with whom they serve, helping to eradicate the "isms" that negatively impact the mental health of those they counsel by way of sexism, ageism, racism, heterosexism, ableism, classism, and anti-Semitism (Ratts, Toporek, & Lewis, 2010). As a helping profession, counselors must serve as advocates to eliminate the various forms of disenfranchisement that individuals, groups of people, and systems currently experience. Counseling is not just the "intervention *into* the lives of clients, but as an action both *with* and *for* in social, political, and economic arenas" (Lee, 2018, p. 4). There are many ways to engage in social advocacy. Gladding (2018) suggests making others aware of the needs of those with no adequate voice of their own. This can be accomplished through presentations, writing editorials, volunteering, and influencing the political process at multiple levels. Counselors can stay informed and work for the passage of important and critical laws.

Professional counselors also are involved in advocating for the advancement of the profession as well. Counselors stay informed about the needs of their own profession. They work for the passage of important and critical laws. ACA maintains an Office of Public Policy that can be found at its website (https://www.counseling.org/government-affairs/public-policy) (American Counseling Association, 2019). Here you will find legislative updates, information on current issues, resources and publications, and much more.

Summary

This chapter discussed the reasons counselors choose to work in the profession. It reviewed the meaning of compassion and the differences between empathy and sympathy. Four case studies from the author's experiences highlighted the intrinsic rewards of a counselor. The chapter ended with a discussion about the importance of social justice as a response to societal inequities and oppression. It presented information on advocacy.

> *Are you an angel?*
>
> – Emmaline

References

American Counseling Association. (n.d.). *Liberty and justice for all* (Position Statement). Alexandria, VA: Author. Retrieved from https://www.counseling.org/about-us/social-justice/liberty-and-justice-for-all

American Counseling Association. (2019). *Government affairs: Latest news & updates*. Retrieved from https://www.counseling.org/government-affairs/public-policy

Counselors for Social Justice. (n.d.). *What is social justice in counseling?* Retrieved from https://counseling-csj.org/

D'Andrea, M., & Heckman, E. F. (2008). Contributing to the ongoing evolution of the multicultural counseling movement: An introduction to the special issue. *Journal of Counseling & Development, 86,* 259–260.

David, E. J. R., & Derthick, A. (2018). *The psychology of oppression.* New York: Springer.

Gladding, S. T. (2018). *Counseling: A comprehensive profession* (8th ed.). New York: Pearson.

Goodman, L. A., Liang, B., Helms, J. E., Latta, R. E., Sparks, E., & Weintraub, S. R. (2004). Training counseling psychologists as social justice agents: Feminist and multicultural principles in action. *The Counseling Psychologist, 32,* 793–837.

Hanna, F. J., Talley, W. B., & Guindon, M. H. (2000). The power of perception: Toward a model of cultural oppression and liberation. *Journal of Counseling & Development, 78,* 430–441.

Houghton Mifflin. (2002). *The American heritage college dictionary* (4th ed.). Boston: Author.

Lee, C. C. (2018). *Counseling for social justice.* Alexandria, VA: American Counseling Association.

Lewis, J. A., Arnold, M. S., House, R., & Toporek, R. L. (2002). *Advocacy competencies.* Retrieved July 1, 2009, from http://www.counseling.org/Publications/

Lord, J., & Dufort, F. (1996). Power and oppression in mental health. *Canadian Journal of Community Mental Health, 15*(2), 5–11.

Ratts, M., D'Andrea, M., & Arrendondo, P. (2004). Social justice counseling: "Fifth force" in field. *Counseling Today, 47,* 28–30.

Ratts, M. J., Toporek, R., & Lewis, J. A. (2010). *ACA advocacy competencies: A social justice framework for counselors.* Alexandria, VA: American Counseling Association.

Roysircar, G. (2009). A big picture of advocacy: Counselor, heal society and thyself. *Journal of Counseling & Development, 87,* 288–294.

Smith, J. M. (2003). *A potent spell: Mother love and the power of fear.* Boston: Houghton Mifflin.

Smith, S. D., Reynolds, C. A., & Rovnak, A. (2009). A critical analysis of the social advocacy movement in counseling. *Journal of Counseling & Development, 87,* 483–491.

Table 8.1 *TFAC Chart – Thought, Feelings, Actions, and Context

Self	My Thoughts	My Feelings	My Actions	My Context	Other? (Specify)
How do I react when I feel compassion?					
How does another's sympathy toward me affect me?					
How do I recognize empathy in myself and from others toward me?					
What is my position on the effect of the dominant culture on my life?					
What do I understand about White privilege?					
How do I believe about unintentional oppression?					
What do I do to right wrongs that I see?					
What am I willing to do to advocate for others?					
What other concerns do I have?					
Others	**Others' Probable Thoughts**	**Others' Possible Feelings**	**Others' Observable Actions**	**Other's Apparent Context**	**Other? (Specify)**
How do others express their compassion?					
When you show sympathy how do others react?					
How do others describe instances of empathic understanding?					
What are some of the reasons others are professional helpers?					
What can they tell you about social inequities?					
How do they advocate?					
What else can they tell you?					

*For more information on TFAC, see Chapter 1.

Part Two

What? Answers about Specialty Areas

Each of the chapters in this section presents basic information on CACREP Standard Section 5: Entry-level Specialty areas – Addictions counseling; career counseling; clinical mental health counseling; clinical rehabilitation counseling; college counseling and student affairs; marriage, couple, and family counseling and therapy; and school counseling.

Each chapter discusses foundations, contextual dimensions, and practice. Especially:

History and background of the specialty (include any relevant legislation)
Theories/models specific to the specialty
Impact on the individual, family, and community
Counseling strategies/practices/treatment

As you read each of these chapters, give thought to which of these specialty areas you find especially appealing. Can you see yourself being a counselor in one of these? More than one?

Use the TFAC chart for each specialty that you are considering for your future career (Table P2.1).

Table P2.1 *TFAC Chart – Thought, Feelings, Actions, and Context

Self	My Thoughts	My Feelings	My Actions	My Context	Other? (Specify)
What appeals to me about this specialty?					
What does not appeal to me about this specialty?					
What do I need to find out about this specialty?					
What are my concerns?					
Others	**Others' Probable Thoughts**	**Others' Possible Feelings**	**Others' Observable Actions**	**Others Apparent Context**	**Other? (Specify)**
What does my instructor share about this specialty?					
What else can others tell me about this specialty?					

*For more information on TFAC, see Chapter 1.

Chapter 9

Addictions Counseling

Mark S. Woodford

Things do not change; we change.

– Henry David Thoreau

POINTS TO PONDER

- What is your mental image of someone who is suffering from addiction? Is it different from your image of an "addict"?
- What do you think causes addiction? Is it primarily a biological, psychological, social, or spiritual disorder?
- How do you engage a client in counseling who is ambivalent about changing their behaviors?
- How do you engage a client if they have been mandated for addiction counseling by the court system, their employer, or their loved ones to get help?

"What were they thinking?" How often have we heard this question asked of someone who behaves in a seemingly mindless and compulsive way that causes harm to themselves and others? Founders of Alcoholics Anonymous describe this process related to problematic alcohol use as "cunning, baffling, powerful" (Alcoholics Anonymous, 2001, pp. 58–59). Often addiction counselors are in the precarious position of having to explain to family members "what on earth could have caused" a loved one's behavior when they were in the active throes of suffering the consequences of addiction. Although there is a complexity and nuance that is difficult to describe to the layperson, our understanding of addictive processes in the twenty-first century is laying the foundation for treatments that are effective in establishing long-term recovery for those suffering from addiction and co-occurring disorders. Models that may explain the behaviors of someone who is acting "out of character" and "out of their mind" in active addiction range from biological (genetic, neurological, and physiological) to psychological (cognitive-behavioral, personality, and intrapsychic) to social and environmental (coping and social learning) (DiClemente, 2018; Miller, Forcehimes, & Zweben, 2011). The history of addiction counseling reflects efforts at using a variety of treatment and recovery models that either emphasize or downplay the biological, psychological, social, and spiritual aspects of this substantial challenge to the health and wellbeing of individuals, families, and society. Current state-of-the-art addiction counseling interventions use a combination of these aspects in an integrative biopsychosocial framework.

The American Society of Addiction Medicine (ASAM) defines addiction as "a primary, chronic disease of brain reward, motivation, memory and related circuitry. Dysfunction in these circuits leads to characteristic biological, psychological, social, and spiritual manifestations" (American Society of Addiction Medicine, 2011). Importantly, ASAM views addiction research as a "medical-scientific-clinical discipline" that is a "specialized area of great importance and high prevalence that cuts across organ systems and health professional disciplines" (Saitz, 2017, p. 429). Even though the word "addiction" is omitted from the fifth edition of the *Diagnostic and Statistical Manual of Mental Disorders* (DSM-V) (American Psychiatric Association, 2013) "because of its uncertain definition and its potentially negative connotation" (p. 485), it remains a favored term by journalists and clinicians (Saitz, 2017). Additionally, it is widely used to refer to the specialty areas within counseling (e.g., the International Association of Addictions and Offender Counseling [IAAOC], a division of the American Counseling Association) and medicine (e.g., the American Society of Addiction Medicine [ASAM]).

SIDEBAR 9.1

Self-Awareness

Try to visualize someone (fictional or real) who might represent or characterize your conceptualization of a person who suffers from addiction. What words would you use to describe them? What "typical" behaviors would they exhibit? What might they be thinking and feeling about their condition? How would they describe themselves?

Although the word "addiction" is not found in the DSM-V, "Substance Use Disorders" (SUDS) and "Addictive (Non-Substance Related) Disorders" (ADS) are included, with "Gambling Disorder" being the only non-substance-related addictive disorder listed in the fifth edition (American Psychiatric Association, 2013). The criteria for the SUDS and ADS are primarily behavioral and dependent on self-report and collateral information from others. They include behaviors such as taking larger amounts than intended, having a desire to cut down or control use without success, clinically significant consequences related to social and work roles, and the development of tolerance and withdrawal symptoms. Readers are referred to the DSM-V for a full list of disorders, criteria, and specifiers (e.g., mild, moderate, or severe), which indicate the number of symptomatic criteria that are met and provide clarity about the severity of impairment and the stage of remission of the individual seeking help. Without specifiers, one loses clinical information that can hinder treatment planning and making accurate prognostic predictions (Kelly, Saitz, & Wakeman, 2016).

In regard to the one "Addictive (Non-Substance Related) Disorder" found in the DSM-V, Gambling Disorder, criteria follow similar problematic behavioral patterns as the SUDS, which result in clinically significant impairment and the need for professional assistance. With the increased availability of gambling in society (Shaffer, Martin, Kleschinsky, & Neporent, 2012; Shaffer & LaPlante, 2013), including the normalization of the lottery, casinos, and gambling through mobile applications and the Internet, there is concern that the early onset of gambling behaviors in youth will increase the severity of gambling problems later in life (Peters et al., 2015). Additionally, a positive correlation exists among adolescent gambling, substance use, unsafe sex, and delinquency (Peters et al., 2015) that may involve neurodevelopment. For example, with intense drives for novelty, and an immature inhibitory control system, adolescents are predisposed to risky behaviors that are often associated with co-occurring psychiatric disorders and addictive behaviors (Chambers, Taylor, & Potenza, 2003). Relatedly, the DSM-V does not include other "behavioral addictions," even though various groups of researchers and clinicians have lobbied for their inclusion. Examples would include sexual addiction (Grubbs, Hook, Griffin, Penberthy, & Kraus, 2018) and Internet addiction, with potential subtypes such as Internet gaming disorder and Internet pornography addiction (Hajela & Love, 2017). Additionally, other problematic behaviors may carry the label as potential addictions without inclusion in the DSM, such as food addiction (Vella & Pai, 2017) and work and shopping addictions (Porter, 2015).

As recommended by several sources in the literature (Saitz, 2017; Kelly et al., 2016), we will avoid using the terms "substance abuser" and "addict" or "alcoholic" to describe a person with a substance use disorder, and "dirty" or "clean" to refer to the results from a urine toxicology screen, opting instead for either "positive" or "negative" drug screens. We have come a long way from the language of the first professional treatment providers of the 1870s who founded the "American Association for the Cure of Inebriates" (Whitley, 2010, p. 348). Our changes in language help to reduce stigma and cognitive bias associated with terms like "addict" and "dirty urine screens" (Kelly et al., 2016). Importantly, reducing the use of potentially stigmatizing language, and instead using "person-first" terminology (e.g., "person with an alcohol use disorder"), may improve clinical outcomes and treatment engagement from individuals avoiding stigmatizing labels (i.e., stigma has been negatively associated with self-efficacy, drink refusal self-efficacy, and seeking social support); relatedly, non-stigmatizing language and patient care models may reduce institutional stigma (Robinson, 2017).

SIDEBAR 9.2

In Practice; What Would You Do?

The words that we use to describe social issues and health conditions reflect our biases, values, and personal beliefs. There is scientific evidence that certain commonly used terms in the addiction field may actually induce biases against individuals suffering from addiction.

Class Discussion

1. What if your client was involved in a 12-Step program and wanted to be called an "alcoholic" or an "addict," instead of a "person with a substance use disorder"?
2. What would be the costs and benefits of that choice?
3. What are your thoughts and feelings about the terms "addict" and "alcoholic"?

Depending on whether you are in the counseling and/or medical fields, the terms for describing with whom we are working may vary from "consumers," to "patients," to "students," to "clients." Based on the guidance of a national curriculum committee composed of a multidisciplinary panel of experts in the addiction field who helped to create a technical assistance publication (TAP 21), *Addiction Counseling Competencies: The Knowledge, Skills, and Attitudes of Professional Practice* (CSAT, 2006), the term *client* will be used in this chapter to refer to individuals seeking professional help. Furthermore, in terms of therapeutic practice, we will defer to TAP 21 and in most cases use the term *counseling* (rather than "treatment," "psychotherapy," "remediation," or "therapeutic interventions") to describe the "collaborative process that facilitates the client's progress toward mutually determined treatment goals and objectives" (CSAT, 2006, p. 101).

Lastly, the term "recovery" may mean different things to different people. Does it mean in *remission* and actively making changes in one's life or simply remaining *abstinent* (Laudet, 2007; White, 2007)? In this chapter, unless otherwise specified, recovery means, "a voluntarily maintained lifestyle characterized by sobriety, personal health, and citizenship" (The Betty Ford

Institute Consensus Panel, 2007, p. 222). The term *sobriety* in this definition "refers to abstinence from alcohol and all other non-prescribed drugs," *personal health* refers to "improved quality of personal life," and *citizenship* to "living with regard and respect for those around you" (p. 222).

History of Addiction Counseling

Although the practice of addiction counseling in the twenty-first century is a *professional* endeavor with training standards, licensure/certification regulations, and professional associations, throughout its history the field has been sustained and uplifted by individuals and groups of people who have had a significant *personal* investment in its success relative to other health care professions. For example, particularly in the 1960s and 1970s, frontline addiction counselors were often individuals in recovery from substance use disorders themselves who had limited formal academic training, but who had substantial experience in applying knowledge that they had acquired in their own recovery to help those "still suffering" from addiction (Keller & Dermatis, 1999). As such, applying principles of *Alcoholics Anonymous* (AA) and *Narcotics Anonymous* (NA), specifically 12-Step work with clients, became a significant piece of the approach of early workers in this field in the mid- to late twentieth century. We see the outgrowth of this approach in one of several addiction counseling "tools in the toolbox" still used today, called "twelve-step facilitation" (Kingree, 2013; Pilkey, Steinberg, & Martino, 2015) (included in the models section below), that can be part of an integrative counseling approach to increase social support networks in recovery.

There is a long history, thoroughly documented by William White in *Slaying the Dragon: The History of Addiction Treatment and Recovery in America* (2nd edition; 2014), of addiction treatment movements involving some combination of medical professionals and recovering individuals working as healing agents of addiction in society. White aptly describes the roots of the mutual aid groups of the 1800s in the United States juxtaposed to the "inebriate homes" and alcohol treatment asylums of that period. A history of lay therapy movements after the turn of the twentieth century and the founding of Alcoholics Anonymous in 1935 contributed to the staffing of "outpatient alcoholism clinics" and inpatient programs based on the "Minnesota Model," which included a multidisciplinary team of medical professionals and recovering individuals (White, 2014, pp. 211). *Narcotics Anonymous*, founded in the early 1950s, supported individuals recovering from substance use disorders other than alcohol, e.g., opioid and stimulant use disorders, and by the 1960s, therapeutic communities (TCs) often staffed by recovering individuals introduced clients to recovery through intense communal living (White, 2014). However, these early TCs were not without their critics, who saw this milieu as having harsh, unorthodox counseling practices and fostering dependence by failing to help clients establish connections to a broader community life that could support long-term recovery outside the TC. Alterations to the TC model have made it a viable option for individuals who cannot remain in the context of their home community in order to initiate recovery (Yates, Burns, & McCabe, 2017).

Since the 1970s, the federal government has for the most part developed drug policy that has treated addiction from a legal versus a public health standpoint, which has had implications for funding related to prevention and treatment versus law enforcement. Examples include the 1970 Controlled Substance Act that scheduled drugs according to their potential for addiction, making some drugs illegal and others legal for medical purposes, and created laws and prison terms for violations, which shifted the conversation from addiction treatment to criminal acts. The 1980s brought "zero tolerance" policies for drug use, the 1984 Crime Control Act that mandated penalties for drug possession, and the 1986 Anti-Drug Abuse Act that placed two-thirds of funding toward law enforcement and one-third for prevention and treatment. In summary, the 1970s and 1980s brought policies and practices that collectively represent "the war on drugs" in the United States (White, 2005, 2014).

On the prevention and treatment side, public perception was shifting in the 1970s as the National Council on Alcoholism promoted the concept of alcoholism as a public health issue and as prominent people (e.g., First Lady Betty Ford) announced their recovery status at press conferences. The National Institute on Alcoholism and Alcohol Abuse (NIAAA) and the National Institute on Drug Abuse (NIDA), established in the National Institutes of Health (NIH), promoted addiction research, and training at the state levels helped to bring a deeper level of education and professionalization to the addiction-counseling field. The National Association of Alcoholism Counselors and Trainers (known today as NAADAC: The Association of Addiction Professionals) was established in 1972 and state counselor associations and certification systems, as well as national accreditation and state licensure standards for treatment programs, ushered in the modern era of addiction treatment in the 1980s (White, 2014). This was a time of accelerated growth and turbulence in the profession. For-profit franchises and hospitals providing inpatient and residential treatment proliferated as insurance companies began to pay for addiction treatment. Yet there were disconnections between treatment providers who saw alcohol use disorders treatment separate from other drug treatment, and addiction and mental health issues as largely distinct treatment arenas. The rising cost to insurance companies and unethical and aggressive marketing strategies brought about managed behavioral health care practices, resulting in many for-profit program closures. Consequently, addiction treatment services moved into other areas, such as child welfare and criminal justice systems, employee assistance and public health programs, and government (local, state, and federal)-funded agencies (White, 2005). Today, addiction counseling happens in these and other designated alcohol and other drug treatment programs, including prevention organizations, private practice, recovery residences, recovery community organizations, recovery high schools, collegiate recovery programs, spiritual programs and organizations, and mutual-aid support groups (Ashford & Brown, 2017). In the twenty-first century, the addiction treatment profession is comprised of a combination of professionals, paraprofessionals, and lay members who face the "medicalization of addiction," "demands for addiction-specific training, treatment-protocol changes, advanced professional training, and an emphasis on evidenced-based practice" and an expanding definition of recovery (Ashford & Brown, 2017, p. 327) that may include controlled use and harm reduction models. These changes will challenge how we approach the stigma of addiction and how we have a dialogue about our ideologies and knowledge gaps that define our beliefs and practices as counselors (Doukas & Cullen, 2011; Ashford & Brown, 2017). For example, we will need to prepare for the organizational challenges that we will face as we continue to implement evidence-based practices (EBP). This requires attending to staff attitudes about the level of difficulty of the EBP and their experience with implementing other EBPs, as well as the professional experiences and influence of key stakeholders in the process (clinical staff, directors, grant-writing staff, etc.) (Kelly, Hegarty, Barry, Dyer, & Horgan, 2017; Lundgren, Amodeo, Chassler, Krull, & Sullivan, 2013).

Working with individuals and their families who are suffering from addiction is not for the faint of heart. However, one of the major payoffs is seeing the dramatic physical, mental, emotional, and spiritual turnarounds that happen in people's lives and the ripple effect that these changes have on loved ones and their extended families and communities. Even as the profession has changed since the 1980s, this one aspect remains the same: It is rewarding work.

Theories and Models of Addiction Counseling

Bio-Psycho-Social Theory

The U.S. Congress designated the 1990s to be the "Decade of the Brain" and President George H. W. Bush proclaimed that:

The human brain, a 3-pound mass of interwoven nerve cells that controls our activity, is one of the most magnificent – and mysterious – wonders of creation. The seat of human intelligence, interpreter of senses, and controller of movement, this incredible organ continues to intrigue scientists and layman alike.

(Project on the Decade of the Brain, 1990)

Since 1990, there have been thousands of articles published on the neuroscience of the brain. Neuroimaging techniques provide a clearer picture of the structures and functions of the brain at different levels: at the molecular level for genes, proteins and synapses; at the cellular level with neurons and neuronal microcircuits; and at the brain-systems level involving neural pathways and behavior patterns (Prieto et al., 2016). Consequently, modern theories of addiction have pulled heavily from the *biological* sciences (genetic, neurological, and physiological), specifically neuroscience research related to: cellular synaptic plasticity; executive functioning (prefrontal cortex); processes of relapse (related to the functioning of the amygdala and the prefrontal cortex); reward/stress systems (mesolimbic and hypothalamus-pituitary-adrenal); and the dopamine/reward (mesolimbic) system (Koob & Le Moal, 2006; Erickson, 2018).

However, the brain does not create the mind in isolation. What we refer to as the "mind" is much more than the three-pound organ inside our skull. Through the brain stem, and the vagal nerve system that travels down around the heart and into the gut (Porges, 2011), the brain connects to the larger central nervous system to monitor our internal and external environments, to help regulate our vital functions, and to act as one embodied mind to monitor, modulate, and modify behaviors (Siegel, 2010). Every experience – *psychological* (cognitive, behavioral, emotional, and intrapsychic processes) and *social* (environmental, coping and social learning processes) – shapes the maturation of the nervous system to function as a whole in concert with other bodily systems, e.g., the cardiovascular, endocrine, respiratory, and musculoskeletal systems that we need to engage in life and to face the challenges of addiction recovery. Imagine the havoc that addiction plays on these intricately interconnected *biopsychosocial* systems in the body, as well as on the social and emotional lives of our clients' loved ones.

Optimal conditions for maturity of our "3-pound mass," and for recovery within all of the bodily systems affected by addiction, include *healthy food, positive relationships, abundant sleep, new experiences, and physical and mental exercise*. These factors – which should be a part of each individual's unique integrated biopsychosocial treatment plan for addiction – change the structure and function of our brain through a process called "neuroplasticity" (Siegel, 2007). The "plastic" nature of our brain means that it adapts to internal and external conditions and molds and models itself accordingly. Imagine a sculpture (the mind) that sculpts itself (the brain) as it interacts with its environment – a remarkable process.

Current neuroscience research offers the scientific underpinning for state-of-the-art addiction counseling models that are available to use in various combinations in an individualized, integrative biopsychosocial treatment plan. The models summarized below are evidence-based and appear in TAP 21, *Addiction Counseling Competencies: The Knowledge, Skills, and Attitudes of Professional Practice* (CSAT, 2006; revised in 2017), and the Substance Abuse and Mental Health Services Administrations' "Evidence-Based Practices Resource Center" (https://www.sa mhsa.gov/ebp-resource-center).

Models of Addiction Counseling

Stages of Change (SOC) and Motivational Interviewing (MI). (Connors, DiClemente, Velasquez, & Donovan, 2013; CSAT, 2017; Miller & Rollnick, 2013.) Very few people come into counseling with little to no ambivalence about changing their behaviors. The stages of change (SOC) model developed by Prochaska and DiClemente (1984) recognizes this process as being *normal*. Part of your clients will want to change, while part of them will not. This ambivalence is a fundamental concept to grasp before working with individuals who are suffering from addiction. Using motivational interviewing (Miller & Rollnick, 2013), we can attend to a client's stages of change to help them resolve their ambivalence, which manifests as inner conflicts (thoughts and feelings) about changing their behavior at this time in their life. The stages of change are *precontemplation* (never considered changing), *contemplation* (ambivalent about changing), *preparation* (preparing to change), *action* (actively making changes), and *maintenance* (maintaining change over time) (Prochaska & DiClemente, 1984). If we do not recognize the ambivalence of the contemplation stage (where most people enter counseling), then we may unintentionally evoke feelings of resistance by moving too quickly into action planning when clients are not at that stage of change.

The SOC and MI models provide a framework for recognizing where clients are in their change process. Perhaps they have not thought about changing their behavior (precontemplation stage) until someone confronted them (e.g., through a medical exam or poor work performance evaluation). Once challenged, they start to sense their own ambivalence about changing. For example, on the one hand, they may think, "I don't have a problem… I don't drink more than my friends do." On the other, they may be saying, "I *have* been feeling kind of shaky lately in the morning, but it's probably lack of sleep or stress or something like that." This pendulum swing, between reasons for not changing and acknowledging that perhaps something has to change, is indicative of the ambivalence of the contemplation stage of change. Anyone confronted, labeled, and/or blamed for problematic behaviors at this stage of change will likely push back in a defensive manner. This is where motivational interviewing strategies, such as using a Decisional Balance tool (described in the counseling practice section below), are effective at providing a mirror for the client to see their own ambivalence outside of themselves. This awareness and recognition open the door of opportunity for clients to work toward resolving their ambivalence about changing.

MI is a client-centered approach that directly addresses the ambivalence of the contemplation stage of change with active listening, empathy, and support. Clients can then explore both sides of their ambivalence and resolve the inner conflict that comes from the discrepancy between their current behaviors and what they want to do with their life (goals). MI is essential to minimizing defensiveness, avoiding argumentation, and supporting a client's hope and sense of self-efficacy that intentional behavior change is possible at this point of their life. Importantly, MI respects clients' autonomy, freedom of choice, and their readiness to change.

If MI is addressing the ambivalence accurately, the client is moving into preparing for action (preparation stage) and begins to engage in "change talk" (e.g., "I've got to do something about this"), which can be further reinforced by evoking (giving voice to) the client's own *intrinsic* (internal) motivation for change. Contrast this process with the external "motivation" that may have come from loved ones and other concerned significant others (e.g., bosses) with confrontations of arguing, begging, pleading, and nagging, and you can see how intrinsic motivation is more likely to carry over into following through with action plans. In the action stage, MI works with clients to plan and to formulate immediate steps to take, and to increase commitment to engaging in new behaviors related to starting the addiction recovery process.

Lastly, MI recognizes what the SOC model calls the "maintenance stage" of change, in that recovery is a long-term process whereby intentional behavior change in the short term (action stage) when consistently applied leads to maintaining change over time, a key challenge of long-term recovery from addiction. Together, SOC and MI engage clients "where they are" in counseling and offer a foundation for other addiction counseling models.

Cognitive-Behavioral Therapy and Relapse Prevention. (Larimer, Palmer, & Marlatt, 1999.) In early recovery, clients are generally in a vulnerable state of mind and are at-risk for lapsing into addictive behaviors. As clients move into the action stage of change, cognitive behavioral therapy (CBT), and specifically relapse prevention (RP) models based on CBT, have been used to aid with maintaining abstinence (or controlled use if that is the goal) in early recovery. RP models work to help clients identify high-risk situations that may contribute to a brief lapse or a full relapse into old behaviors. In this model, factors that may lead to relapse separate into two categories: immediate determinants and covert antecedents.

Immediate determinants divide into intrapersonal (internal) and interpersonal (external) high-risk situations. Internal emotional states, whether positive or negative, are immediate determinants of a relapse episode. For example, being bored, frustrated, angry, sad, or anxious may be as risky as celebrations or seeing advertisements for one's favorite bar or drink specials. These internal states trigger thoughts of use, including two particular types that are specific to RP: positive outcome expectancies and the abstinence violation effect. The former is a thought pattern of having high expectations for positive effects from engaging in the addictive behavior, while discounting or ignoring what happened in the past related to negatives consequences; the latter is a response to an initial lapse where one thinks, "Well, I've done it now… all is lost."

Among the most immediate and powerful external determinants of relapse are *other people*, and specifically situations that involve interpersonal conflict with significant others, social pressure (whether verbal or nonverbal) to engage in addictive behaviors, and a lack of copies strategies to deal with both. RP seeks to identify "people, places, and things" (which is a saying from self-help and mutual-help support groups) that will trigger the covert antecedents of relapse, e.g., urges and cravings. RP defines an urge as being an impulse to engage in addictive behavior that comes on suddenly in unexpected ways, while a craving is a desire to re-experience the effects of the addictive behavior. In addition to immediate high-risk situations, RP examines broader *lifestyle factors* that can contribute to relapse, like chronic stress, which includes elements of negative emotional states and potential high expectancies for a return to addictive behaviors as a way to cope with stress, e.g., "It would be great to unwind with a drink" (or other addictive process; "I owe it to myself for all of the stress that I've been under lately." RP makes these thought patterns and subjective desires more visible to the client during high-risk times in their life so that they can make healthier behavioral choices in recovery.

Contingency Management (CM) and Community Reinforcement Approach (CRA). (Higgins, Silverman, & Heil, 2008; Meyers, Villaneuva & Smith, 2005.) CM and CRA base their interventions on principles related to operant conditioning and behavior modification. Specifically, they use positive reinforcement for healthy behaviors and negative reinforcement to discourage addictive behaviors. CM provides specific incentives that are of value to the client that will compete with the pleasurable "reward" of the addictive behaviors. Both CM and CRA have specific protocols for analyzing a client's behavior. CM focuses on clearly defining targeted behaviors for developing incentives for change, and then offers immediate rewards for achieving positive behavioral goals. CRA uses a functional analysis of addictive behaviors in context and then devises treatment plans for specific behavioral changes that function as immediate rewards for healthy behaviors (or as natural consequences for unhealthy ones) in the context of the client's life.

Both CM and CRA lean heavily on environmental contingencies for change, i.e., reinforcers in the client's immediate environment (e.g., family, friends, work, and community). For example, CRA, and its variants for adolescents (A-CRA) and concerned family members (Community Reinforcement and Family Training, or CRAFT) focus on rearranging environmental contingencies to support healthy behaviors and discourage unhealthy activities. They provide relationship counseling, behavioral skills training to facilitate communication and problem solving in interpersonal contexts, and job-related skills to broaden the intervention spectrum to include multiple social contexts and systems in which clients live and work.

Twelve-Step Facilitation and Mutual-Help Groups. (Beck et al., 2017; Fenner & Gifford, 2012; Kingree, 2013; Nowinski, 2012.) Social support is crucial to initiate and sustain recovery from addiction. Twelve-Step Facilitation (TSF) is one counseling approach that seeks to engage clients in a process of recovery that includes social support and may continue long after formal treatment processes have concluded. Applying principles from such programs as *Alcoholics Anonymous* (AA), *Narcotics Anonymous* (NA), and *Gamblers Anonymous* (GA), counselors introduce clients to 12-Step work and concepts related to: acceptance of the addiction and surrender to the recovery process and to a "higher power" (meaning something greater than one's self, e.g., "God as we understand Him"), changing "people, places, and things" (meaning routines that are associated with old behavior patterns), identifying and bonding with supportive people in recovery (e.g., a "sponsor" and a "home group"), and becoming actively involved in the recovering community. Counselors-in-training are encouraged to attend an open self-help meeting in their communities in order to learn more about the 12-Step recovery process. Table 9.1 offers guidelines for visiting an "open" 12-Step meeting, which accommodates visitors. "Closed" meetings are only for individuals who are in recovery. Table 9.1 also includes links for alternatives to 12-Step groups, such SMART and WFS discussed below.

In addition to 12-Step approaches, counselors may introduce clients to mutual help groups like the Self-Management and Recovery Training (SMART Recovery) program or Women for Sobriety (WFS). These groups offer alternatives to the 12-Step concept of giving up control to a "higher power," which may not match with a client's needs, personal beliefs, or preferences. The SMART Recovery program is a non-profit organization that offers mutual support in face-to-face group and online formats (Horvath & Yeterian, 2012). MI and CBT approaches blend in SMART Recovery to encourage self-empowerment for building a sense of self-efficacy with a range of addictive behaviors. Individuals participating in the SMART process determine what "recovery" will look like for themselves, which may include controlled use or abstinence. Similarly, WFS is a secular, abstinence-based mutual help group approach for women that offers a "New Life" program with "13 affirmations," called the "Statements of Acceptance," which emphasize positive thinking and taking personal responsibility for one's personal growth in recovery (Fenner & Gifford, 2012). In contrast with accepting powerlessness over alcohol in AA, WFS uses a cognitive-behavioral approach to empower women to gain inner strength by changing their thinking patterns and habits, to deal with underlying issues from the past that may be affecting current behavior, and to establish a secure, confident self in recovery.

Table 9.1 Guidelines for Visiting Self-Help/Mutual-Help Groups

1. Search for a meeting near you at https://www.aa.org/ (Alcoholics Anonymous) or https:// na.org/ (Narcotics Anonymous), https://www.smartrecovery.org/ (SMART Recovery), or https:// womenforsobriety.org/ (Women for Sobriety).
2. Attend meetings designated as "Open" meetings. Open meetings accommodate visitors, whereas "Closed" meetings are designated only for individuals who are in recovery (e.g., in the case of AA, for those who "have a desire to stop drinking.") When you arrive at the meeting, it is a good idea to ask, "Is this meeting an open or closed meeting?"
3. In general, the chair of the meetings will ask if there are any visitors (or "newcomers") to the meeting. You may wish to say, "Hello, my name is _____ (first name only), and I am a visitor." If you wish to say that you are a student hoping to learn more about addiction, or that you are a "counselor-in-training," feel free to do so. Group members are very likely to approach you to introduce themselves and to greet you. In most cases, they are "reaching out" to help others (e.g., they are reaching out to those "still suffering.").
4. Please do not take notes during the meeting.
5. Most importantly – remember to respect the anonymity of the participants. You may see someone you know. To paraphrase what you may hear at these meetings: "Who you see there, and what you hear there, let it stay there."

SIDEBAR 9.3

Self-Help or Mutual-Help Groups

One way to strengthen your education about addiction and understand the power of a supportive recovery network is to attend an "open" self-help or mutual-help group.

See Table 9.1 above for guidelines for visiting an open meeting.

As counselors (and human beings), our reactions to things that we see and hear (and read) are influenced by our value systems, which in turn, are colored by our family of origin issues, our age, gender, race/ethnicity, sexual orientation, social class, and our view of spirituality and religion. Taking these various factors into consideration, consider your personal reactions to the meeting(s) and their respective recovery models. What are your gut and intellectual level reactions to what happened at the meeting? What are your biases around recovery support groups? How might your value-based reactions affect your decision to refer clients to these groups? Would you refer a client to the particular meeting you attended?

Transdiagnostic Approaches for Addiction and Co-Occurring Disorders. Transdiagnostic interventions are receiving increasing attention by clinicians and researchers as a way to capitalize on the common factors across evidence-based practices that have been proven effective for multiple disorders (McEvoy, Nathan, & Norton, 2009; Murray et al., 2014). Examples of current transdiagnostic approaches that address a broad spectrum of behavioral and mental health challenges include: Acceptance and Commitment Therapy (Hayes & Levin, 2012; Hayes, Strosahl, & Wilson, 2012), Dialectical Behavior Therapy (Dimeff & Koerner, 2007; Lungu & Linehan, 2016), mindfulness-based approaches (Baer, 2006; Bentley, Nock, Sauer-Zavala, Gorman, & Barlow, 2017; Bowen, Chawla, & Marlatt, 2011; Craske, 2012), and motivational enhancement and motivational interviewing approaches (Boswell, Bentley, & Barlow, 2015; Mistler, Sheidow, & Davis, 2016).

One objective of these approaches is to increase the psychological flexibility of clients to face adverse challenges in recovery. Psychological flexibility, an underlying theory of Acceptance and Commitment Therapy (referred to as ACT and pronounced as the word "act") (Hayes & Levin, 2012; Hayes, Strosahl, & Wilson, 2012; Villatte et al., 2016), is an empirically supported process defined as contacting the present moment fully as a conscious human being, and based on what the situation affords, changing or persisting in behavior in the service of chosen values. It expands upon traditional relapse prevention cognitive-behavioral strategies (Marlatt & Gordon, 1985; Larimer, Palmer, & Marlatt, 1999) by using mindfulness- and acceptance-based approaches (Bowen, Chawla, & Marlatt, 2011; Turner, Welches, & Conti, 2013; Li, Howard, Garland, McGovern, & Lazar, 2017).

These expanded models of relapse prevention, referred to as the third wave of CBT, are empirically supported cognitive-behavioral therapy approaches (Vieten, Astin, Buscemi, & Galloway, 2010). Like ACT, Dialectical Behavior Therapy (Dimeff & Koerner, 2007; Lungu & Linehan, 2016) and other mindfulness-based treatment approaches (Baer, 2006; Bentley et al., 2017; Bowen, Chawla, & Marlatt, 2011; Craske, 2012) employ overlapping concepts, such as: experiential avoidance, acceptance, cognitive defusion, mindfulness, relationship enhancement, values, emotional deepening, initiating contact with the present moment, empathic joining, interpersonal deepening, dialectics, and building flexible behavioral repertoires. These "third wave" models are "transdiagnostic" (Craske, 2012; McEvoy, Nathan, & Norton, 2009) because they apply the same underlying treatment principles across mental disorders without tailoring the protocol to specific diagnoses. Specifically, transdiagnostic approaches: (a) emphasize functional links between components of the transdiagnostic formulation (e.g., thoughts, behaviors, physiology, and emotions), which is then individualized during therapy, and (b) increase the flexibility for clients to identify and challenge a variety of problematic cognitions and behaviors that may contribute to the same emotional response (e.g., anxiety) in relation to different cues (e.g., interoceptive cues, social interactions), as well as to different emotional responses (e.g., depression, anxiety, anger) (Murray et al., 2014). The breadth of problems addressed is one of the main scientific requirements of a model that claims to be "transdiagnostic." As an example, there are controlled ACT studies on: substance use disorders, work stress, pain, smoking, anxiety, depression, diabetes management, stigma toward substance users in recovery, adjustment to cancer, epilepsy, coping with psychosis, borderline personality disorder, trichotillomania, obsessive-compulsive disorder, weight-management and self-stigma, post-traumatic stress disorder and trauma-related symptoms (to name a few) (Hayes, Strosahl & Wilson, 2012).

Family Systems Approaches. Addiction has an impact on family members in multiple ways, as you will see in the relevant section below. Loved ones often approach addiction counselors at three different phases of engagement in the treatment process, (a) pre-treatment, (b) during treatment, and (c) post-treatment, with each phase having its own set of challenges.

In the pre-treatment phase, family members are often looking for professional help to intervene with their loved one who is suffering from addiction. The media has portrayed family interventions as being confrontational and "a last stand" against the enabling of the addictive behaviors. This portrayal is based on practices used by interventionists in the early days of the treatment boom of the 1980s. Today, models such as the Community Reinforcement and Family Training (CRAFT) approach (an outgrowth of the CRA model discussed above) offer behavioral treatments that teach family members how to interact differently with their loved ones, such that the person suffering from addiction reduces their substance use and seeks help. CRAFT is non-confrontational and includes a focus on the well-being of the loved one as a priority of counseling (in addition to helping the individual with addiction get the help they need). Like CRA, family members are taught a variety of skills that include goal setting, positive communication, problem solving, the rewarding of clean/sober behavior, and the withdrawal of rewards for using behavior (Meyers, Villaneuva & Smith, 2005).

During treatment, family-involved counseling includes attempts to educate families about the relationship patterns that typically contribute to the formation and continuation of addiction. This occurs in a variety of ways, including but not limited to: (a) family groups that are primarily psycho-educational, (b) conjoint family sessions that include the individual in treatment and their family members, (c) multi-family groups that involve the same families in a group counseling process over time, (d) couples counseling (e.g., Behavioral Couples Therapy; McCrady et al., 2016), and (e) children of addicted individuals (COA) treatment groups. Post-treatment interventions involve traditional marriage and family therapy work that may focus on communication skills, problem-solving skills, structural family interventions, etc., as well as themes related to self-care in the family context, regulation and expression of emotions/affect, relationship patterns (e.g., enmeshed versus disengaged), family rules (e.g., "don't talk, don't trust, don't feel"), and rigidly prescribed roles in response to the addictive behaviors in the family. Additionally, several empirically grounded, family-based approaches have been developed primarily as systemic treatment models for adolescents and their families: Functional Family Therapy (FFT) (Hartnett, Carr, Hamilton, & O'Reilly, 2017), Multidimensional Family Therapy (MDFT) (Liddle, 2016), and Multisystemic Therapy (Henggeler & Schaeffer, 2016). With these models, family members look for positive solutions to problems in the family system, work for effective behavior change, and adjust parenting strategies accordingly. Each approach offers individual, family, and systemic-level interventions for the adolescents and their families.

Impact on the Individual, Family, and Community

Why would anyone set out in life to develop an addictive disorder with all of the potentially negative consequences to oneself or others that go along with that process? Obviously, no one expects or intends to end up with an addiction. DiClemente (2018) emphasizes the importance of *context* in the initiation of substance use, particularly in relation to individual, parental/family, peers/friends, and social/environmental risk and protective factors. A conceptual framework borrowed from neuroclinical research, the Addictions Neuroclinical Assessment (ANA) (Kwako, Momenan, Litten, Koob, & Goldman, 2016), will help to organize how this process has an impact on the individual, who in turn behaves in a way that takes a toll on each of these larger systems in which that person lives and works.

Starting with the context of individual brain development, the ANA organizes three functional domain areas heuristically to show how individuals progress through stages involved in developing impulsivity, compulsivity, and dysfunctional behaviors associated with addiction; they are the executive functioning, incentive-salience, and negative emotionality domain areas. The *executive functioning* domain is involved with "top-down" (prefrontal cortex) processes (highlighted in italics below). Individuals addicted to various substances exhibit impairment in neural networks in this domain area. For example, research shows that *attention* is impaired by alcohol, cocaine, and nicotine, *planning* by nicotine and opioids, and *working memory* by alcohol, cocaine, and cannabis, while *response inhibition* is affected by heroin, methamphetamine, and gambling, *behavioral flexibility* by cocaine and amphetamines, and the *valuation of future events* by alcohol and nicotine (Kwako et al., 2016). These executive functioning processes help to organize our behaviors over time. Consequently, individuals with SUDS and addictive disorders are at an increased risk for detrimental consequences, e.g., "aggressive and/or risk-taking behaviors such as unsafe sex, acts of violence, motor accidents, and injuries that can lead to legal problems," which in turn link to a range of other physical, psychological, social, and economically adverse outcomes (Mahmoud, Finnell, Savage, Puskar, & Mitchell, 2017, p. 537).

The *incentive salience* domain is "defined as a psychological process that transforms the perception of stimuli, imbuing them with salience, and making them attractive" (Kwako et al., 2016, p. 182). Individuals who are developing substance use and addictive disorders engage in binge-intoxication cycles that result in increased craving in response to cues in the environment, attentional bias, and conditioned responses (reactivity) that lead to habit formation. As the cycle continues, the individual begins to have increases in negative emotional responses to various stimuli that ordinarily would not create a feeling of dysphoria (and increased craving). This is the domain area called *negative emotionality*. Importantly, individuals suffering from substance use disorders have increased activity in brain stress systems (e.g., hypothalamic-pituitary-adrenal axis and cortisol) and decreased activity in brain anti-stress systems (e.g., endorphins and oxytocin) (Kwako et al., 2016, p. 182); a condition indicated by the two-fold blow of having fight or flight systems heightened, while naturally calming systems are dampened.

At this stage, the individual exhibits repeated and regular use of substances and/or addictive behaviors, as manifested by an increase in quantity and frequency, and a narrowing of behavioral and environmental repertoires. Natural negative social consequences happen in the environment, yet the individual's attitudes, expectancies, and beliefs shift to favor substance use and addictive behaviors. Ordinary coping mechanisms are replaced by more substance use (which then reinforces the value of the continued substance use). These processes happen in the *context* of one's individual personality and co-occurring challenges (plus a layer of added intermittent dysphoria), family and ethnocultural influences, interpersonal relationships, social support for substance use and addictive behaviors, and societal factors (DiClemente, 2018).

Additional individual consequences range from cognitive impairment and criminal behavior to cancers and other chronic diseases (e.g., diabetes), organ damage, and overdose, to injury (e.g., resulting from impaired driving), "hospitalization, intensive care, increased mortality, and premature death" (Mahmoud et al., 2017, p. 537). The impact on families ranges from feelings of isolation, worry, anger, guilt, and shame to relational, financial, and emotional strain, to physical health problems, such as stress, migraines, and ulcers (Townsend, Biegel, Ishler, Wieder, & Rini, 2006). Costs to society are exorbitant, with an estimated 20.3 million adults and 1.3 million adolescents with substance use disorders in the United States (SAMHSA, 2013). In addition to 70,000 deaths annually, the annual costs related to lost work productivity, emergency room visits and health care, and crime are more than $700 billion dollars (Volkow, Koob, & McLellan, 2016).

SIDEBAR 9.4

Self-Awareness: Impact of Addiction on Individuals and Families

Where have you seen the impact of addiction in your lifetime? How has it affected individuals and families in your life? Given the complexity inherent in understanding addiction, how would you explain addiction to the significant others who have been impacted by someone suffering from a substance use disorder?

Addiction Counseling Practices

Engaging Clients in Counseling

The practice of addiction counseling involves a number of tasks and responsibilities, as seen in Table 9.2. Importantly, even as we try to orient clients to the counseling setting and gather information in an intake and clinical evaluation using setting-specific screening and assessment tools, we need to focus intentionally on the process of building rapport and engaging clients in the counseling process. This lays the foundation for effective treatment planning, counseling, and client and family education that follows.

As the SOC and MI approaches emphasized, we need to meet clients "where they are," which includes thoughts and feelings of ambivalence about changing. Table 9.3 gives examples from MI of open-ended questions to meet clients where they are and to elicit change talk in the process. These questions ask clients to ponder their desire, ability, reasons, needs, and commitment to change at this time in their life (Miller, Forcehimes, & Zweben, 2011).

In the rapport building stage, we can explore what brought them in for counseling at this point in their life, looking for the meaning of specific events that precipitated treatment (as well as any previous treatment episodes). We are looking for their perceptions about their addictive behaviors and being curious about the pros and cons of their current behavioral patterns in light of what significant other's in their life might think, as well as what they value and want in their own life. Tools such as the Decisional Balance exercise can help clients sort out the cost and benefits for changing *and* not changing at this time; using scaling questions can help to ascertain their desire and urgency to address their behaviors in counseling (CSAT, 2017). For example, "On a scale from 1 to 10, 1 being not important at all, and 10 being extremely important, how would you rate your *desire* to change at this time?" You can substitute *ability, commitment,* etc. in this type of question as well. It is imperative that addiction counselors consider how a client's

Table 9.2 Basic Tasks and Responsibilities of an Addiction Counselor

A. Clinical Evaluation

Screening
Assessment
Intake
Orientation

B. Treatment Planning
C. Referral
D. Service Coordination (Case Management)

Implementing the Treatment Plan
Consulting
Continuing Assessment and Treatment Planning

E. Counseling

Individual Counseling
Group Counseling
Counseling for Families, Couples, and Significant Others

F. Client, Family, and Community Education
G. Documentation (Report and Record Keeping)
H. Crisis Intervention
I. Professional and Ethical Responsibilities

Basic tasks and responsibilities taken directly from the Technical Assistance Publication (TAP 21, CSAT, 2006) entitled "Addiction Counseling Competencies: Knowledge, Skills, and Attitudes"

Table 9.3 Motivational Interviewing Sample Questions to Elicit Change Talk

Ask open questions that *evoke the client's own motivation* for change:

"How might you *like* for things to be differently?" (Desire)
"If you did decide to quit, how *could* you do it?" (Ability)
"What *reasons* might there be for you to make a change?" (Reasons)
"How *important* is it for you to do something about your _____ (substance use)?" (Need)
"What do you think you'll *do?*" (Commitment)
Listen for *change talk* and reflect, affirm, and summarize.

ethnocultural background plays a part in the expression of their values, beliefs, and attitudes surrounding the addictive behaviors or co-occurring challenges that are being discussed in the engagement phase of counseling. For example, what roles have gender, cultural beliefs, socioeconomic status, and privilege and oppression played in a client's behavioral choices surrounding the use of alcohol and other drugs? Consider contextual factors underlying a client's attitudes and reactions to having to seek help for addiction from a professional.

Strengthening Coping Skills

As clients move into the action stage of change, relapse prevention strategies help clients to manage urges, cravings, and thoughts of engaging in addictive behaviors. Addiction counseling practices include helping clients to be aware of emotional states and identify high-risk situations that may shift their affect in different contexts. Ethnocultural considerations include asking about the ways that clients eat, work, play, and relax, and other patterns related to managing emotions and thoughts about family rituals, specifically celebrations and/or difficult times, such as coping with illness and death. Additionally, culture and family may affect one's access to substances and addictive behaviors and be intertwined with one's ethnic identity. How will family members and friends react to a client seeking help and/or having a relapse after having been in recovery?

Other addiction counseling practices that build coping skills include enhancing self-efficacy by discussing how to move through these high-risk situations and managing a lapse if one occurs. For example, discussing the abstinence violation effect, talking about the placebo effect of alcohol and other drug expectancies, and imagining "relapse road maps" before heading down that path in real life. In CBT language, these practices are focused on cognitive restructuring and global lifestyle and self-control strategies (Larimer, Palmer, & Marlatt, 1999).

Reinforcing Behavioral Change

If a client experiences a "slip," "lapse," or "relapse," then practices focused on how to cope with the immediate consequences and deciding what to do next are paramount. With a recurrence of the addictive behavior, the client is encouraged to reenter the preparation and action stages of change. Counselors can applaud clients for having the willingness to return to counseling and to explore the meaning of the relapse with the goal of finding coping strategies that can be alternatives to the addictive behaviors in the future.

Using the CRA and CM approaches, addiction counselors can do a functional analysis of the using behavior and explore the possibility of alternative activities to using and finding motivational incentives for engaging in healthy behaviors. Career and employment counseling can assist in setting long-term, values-based goals. Interpersonal relationships play a role in the addictive process, and therefore, practicing sobriety skills, e.g., drink or drug use refusal and assertiveness skills, can reinforce behavior change. Additionally, if clients are receiving medication-assisted therapy to help manage cravings, then monitoring medication use may be a key to sustaining recovery.

Many of these addiction-counseling practices will require a treatment team approach involving culturally competent professionals specifically trained to deal with family and interpersonal conflicts and to manage co-existing psychiatric problems. Seeking additional training in family systems and transdiagnostic models can help with involving family and significant others in treatment and helping clients to achieve balanced living in recovery. Helping clients to assess whether they need to shore up social supports will mean that counselors have skills in facilitating connections with mutual-help and self-help programs (e.g., TSF, SMART Recovery, and WFS) in order to help clients build a recovery support system that will last well into the maintenance stage of change and into long-term recovery.

Summary

We began with the question, "What were they thinking?" The theories and models of addiction counseling presented in this chapter offer a complex understanding of the biological, psychological, and social forces that lead to addiction. However, the short answer in terms of addressing a loved one's question about this baffling process is, "They weren't thinking." In fact, there was likely minimal executive brain function or conscious awareness of feeling involved. The fact that we can explain this process in a concrete way to individuals, families, and society makes the twenty-first century an exciting time to enter into the addiction-counseling field. Treatment models today integrate science-based interventions in a biopsychosocial framework and offer multiple ways for individuals to find their way into a strong, sustained recovery from addiction.

I was shocked at how normal people in recovery looked when I went to a self-help meeting. It was nothing like I had expected. I don't know what I expected, but my heart was overwhelmed with joy by the sense of community in that room. It was inspiring. Recovery from addiction is possible.

– recovering client

References

Alcoholics Anonymous. (2001). *Alcoholics anonymous: The story of how many thousands of men and women have recovered from alcoholism* (4th ed.). New York City: Alcoholics Anonymous World Services, Inc.

American Psychiatric Association. (2013). *Diagnostic and statistical manual of mental disorders* (5th ed.). Arlington, VA: American Psychiatric Publishing.

American Society of Addiction Medicine. (2011, April 12). Retrieved from: http://www.asam.org/for-the-public/definition-of-addiction

Ashford, R. D., & Brown, A. (2017). Bridging the gaps: Intergenerational findings from the substance use disorder and recovery field. *Journal of Intergenerational Relationships, 15*, 326–351.

Baer, R. A. (2006). *Mindfulness-based treatment approaches: Clinician's guide to evidence base and applications.* San Diego, CA: Elsevier Academic Press.

Beck, A. K., Forbes, E., Baker, A. L., Kelly, P. J., Deane, F. P., Shakeshaft, A., Hunt, D., & Kelly, J. F. (2017). Systematic review of SMART recovery: Outcomes, process variables, and implications for research. *Psychology of Addictive Behaviors, 31*, 1–20.

Bentley, K. H., Nock, M. K., Sauer-Zavala, S., Gorman, B. S., & Barlow, D. H. (2017). A functional analysis of two transdiagnostic, emotion-focused interventions on nonsuicidal self-injury. *Journal of Consulting and Clinical Psychology, 85*, 632–646.

Boswell, J. F., Bentley, K. H., & Barlow, D. H. (2015). Motivation facilitation in the unified protocol for transdiagnostic treatment of emotional disorder. In H. Arkowitz, W. R. Miller, S. Rollnick, H. Arkowitz, W. R. Miller, & S. Rollnick (Eds.), *Motivational interviewing in the treatment of psychological problems* (pp. 33–57). New York: Guilford Press.

Bowen, S., Chawla, N., & Marlatt, G. A. (2011). *Mindfulness-based relapse prevention for addictive behaviors: A clinician's guide.* New York: Guilford Press.

Center for Substance Abuse Treatment. (2006). *Addiction counseling competencies: The knowledge, skills, and attitudes of professional practice.* Technical Assistance Publication (TAP) Series 21. DHHS Publication No. (SMA) 15-4171. Rockville, MD: Substance Abuse and Mental Health Services Administration, 2006 (revised in 2017).

Center for Substance Abuse Treatment. (2017). *Enhancing motivation for change in substance abuse treatment: Treatment Improvement Protocol (TIP) series 35.* DHHS Publication No. SMA 13-4212. Rockville, MD: Substance Abuse and Mental Health Services Administration.

Chambers, R. A., Taylor, J. R, & Potenza, M. N. (2003). Developmental neurocircuitry of motivation in adolescence: A critical period of addiction vulnerability. *American Journal of Psychiatry, 160*, 1041–1052.

Connors, G. J., DiClemente, C. C., Velasquez, M. M., & Donovan, D. M. (2013). *Substance abuse treatment and the stages of change: Selecting and planning interventions* (2nd ed.). New York: Guilford Press.

Craske, M. G. (2012). Transdiagnostic treatment for anxiety and depression. *Depression and Anxiety, 29*, 749–753.

DiClemente, C. C. (2018). *Addiction and change: How addictions develop and addicted people recover* (2nd ed.). New York: The Guilford Press.

Dimeff, L. A., & Koerner, K. (2007). *Dialectical behavior therapy in clinical practice: Applications across disorders and settings.* New York: Guilford Press.

Doukas, N., & Cullen, J. (2011). Addiction counselors in recovery: Perceived barriers in the workplace. *Journal of Addiction Research & Therapy, 2*(3), 1–7.

Erickson, C. K. (2018). *The science of addiction: From neurobiology to treatment* (2nd ed.). New York: Norton.

Fenner, R. M., & Gifford, M. H. (2012). Women for sobriety: 35 years of challenges, changes, and continuity. *Journal of Groups in Addiction & Recovery, 7*(2–4), 142–170.

Grubbs, J. B., Hook, J. N., Griffin, B. J., Penberthy, J. K., & Kraus, S. W. (2018). Clinical assessment and diagnosis of sexual addiction. In T. Birchard & J. Benfield (Eds.), *The Routledge international handbook of sexual addiction* (pp. 167–180). New York: Routledge/Taylor & Francis Group.

Hajela, R., & Love, T. (2017). Addiction beyond substances – What's up with the DSM? *Sexual Addiction & Compulsivity, 24*(1–2), 11–22.

Hartnett, D., Carr, A., Hamilton, E., & O'Reilly, G. (2017). The effectiveness of functional family therapy for adolescent behavioral and substance misuse problems: A meta-analysis. *Family Process, 56*, 607–619.

Hayes, S. C., & Levin, M. E. (2012). *Mindfulness and acceptance for addictive behaviors: Applying contextual CBT to substance abuse & behavioral addictions.* Oakland, CA: New Harbinger Publications, Inc.

Hayes, S. C., Strosahl, K. D., & Wilson, K. G. (2012). *Acceptance and commitment therapy: The process and practice of mindful change* (2nd ed.). New York: Guilford Press.

Henggeler, S. W., & Schaeffer, C. M. (2016). Multisystemic therapy®: Clinical overview, outcomes, and implementation research. *Family Process, 55*, 514–528.

Higgins, S. T., Silverman, K., & Heil, S. H. (2008). *Contingency management in substance abuse treatment* (S. T. Higgins, K. Silverman, & S. H. Heil, Eds.). New York: Guilford Press.

Horvath, A., & Yeterian, J. (2012). SMART recovery: Self-empowering, science-based addiction recovery support. *Journal of Groups in Addiction & Recovery, 7*(2–4), 102–117.

Keller, D. S., & Dermatis, H. (1999). Current status of professional training in the addictions. *Substance Abuse, 20*, 123–140.

Kelly, J. F., Saitz, R., & Wakeman, S. (2016). Language, substance use disorders, and policy: The need to reach consensus on an "addiction-ary." *Alcoholism Treatment Quarterly, 34*, 116–123.

Kelly, P., Hegarty, J., Barry, J., Dyer, K. R., & Horgan, A. (2017). A systematic review of the relationship between staff perceptions of organizational readiness to change and the process of innovation adoption in substance misuse treatment programs. *Journal of Substance Abuse Treatment, 80*, 6–25.

Kingree, J. B. (2013). Twelve-step facilitation therapy. In P. M. Miller, S. A. Ball, M. E. Bates, A. W. Blume, K. M. Kampman, D. J. Kavanagh … & P. De Witte (Eds.), *Comprehensive addictive behaviors and disorders, Vol. 3: Interventions for addiction* (pp. 137–146). San Diego, CA: Elsevier Academic Press.

Koob, G. F., & Le Moal, M. (2006). *Neurobiology of addiction.* London: Elsevier.

Kwako, L. E., Momenan, R., Litten, R. Z., Koob, G. F., & Goldman, D. (2016). Addictions neuroclinical assessment: A neuroscience-based framework for addictive disorders. *Biological Psychiatry, 80*, 179–189.

Larimer, M. E., Palmer, R. S., & Marlatt, G. A. (1999). Relapse prevention: An overview of Marlatt's cognitive-behavioral model. *Alcohol Research & Health, 23*, 151–160.

Laudet, A. B. (2007). What does recovery mean to you? Lessons from the recovery experience for research and practice. *Journal of Substance Abuse Treatment, 33*, 243–256.

Li, W., Howard, M. O., Garland, E. L., McGovern, P., & Lazar, M. (2017). Mindfulness treatment for substance misuse: A systematic review and meta-analysis. *Journal of Substance Abuse Treatment, 75*, 62–96.

Liddle, H. A. (2016). Multidimensional family therapy: Evidence base for transdiagnostic treatment outcomes, change mechanisms, and implementation in community settings. *Family Process, 55*, 558–576.

Lundgren, L., Amodeo, M., Chassler, D., Krull, I., & Sullivan, L. (2013). Organizational readiness for change in community-based addiction treatment programs and adherence in implementing evidence-based practices: A national study. *Journal of Substance Abuse Treatment, 45*, 457–465.

Lungu, A., & Linehan, M. M. (2016). Dialectical behavior therapy: A comprehensive multi- and transdiagnostic intervention. In C. M. Nezu, A. M. Nezu, C. M. Nezu, & A. M. Nezu (Eds.), *The Oxford handbook of cognitive and behavioral therapies* (pp. 200–214). New York: Oxford University Press.

Mahmoud, K. F., Finnell, D., Savage, C. L., Puskar, K. R., & Mitchell, A. M. (2017). A concept analysis of substance misuse to inform contemporary terminology. *Archives of Psychiatric Nursing, 31*, 532–540.

Marlatt, G. A., & Gordon, J. R. (Eds.). (1985). *Relapse prevention: Maintenance strategies in the treatment of addictive disorders.* New York: Guilford Press.

McCrady, B. S., Wilson, A. D., Muñoz, R. E., Fink, B. C., Fokas, K., & Borders, A. (2016). Alcohol-focused behavioral couple therapy. *Family Process, 55*, 443–459.

McEvoy, P. M., Nathan, P., & Norton, P. J. (2009). Efficacy of transdiagnostic treatments: A review of published outcome studies and future research directions. *Journal of Cognitive Psychotherapy, 23*(1), 20–33.

Meyers, R. J., Villanueva, M., & Smith, J. E. (2005). The community reinforcement approach: History and new directions. *Journal of Cognitive Psychotherapy, 19*, 247–260.

Miller, W. R., Forcehimes, A., & Zweben, A. (2011). *Treating addictions: A guide for professionals*. New York: The Guildford Press.

Miller, W. R., & Rollnick, S. (2013). *Motivational interviewing: Helping people change* (3rd ed.). New York: Guilford Press.

Mistler, L. A., Sheidow, A. J., & Davis, M. (2016). Transdiagnostic motivational enhancement therapy to reduce treatment attrition: Use in emerging adults. *Cognitive and Behavioral Practice, 23*, 368–384.

Murray, L. K., Dorsey, S., Haroz, E., Lee, C., Alsiary, M. M., Haydary, A., Weiss, W., & Bolton, P. (2014). A common elements treatment approach for adult mental health problems in low- and middle-income countries. *Cognitive and Behavioral Practice, 21*, 111–123.

Nowinski, J. (2012). Facilitating 12-step recovery from substance abuse. In S. T. Walters & F. Rotgers (Eds.), *Treating substance abuse: Theory and technique* (3rd ed., pp. 191–223). New York: Guilford Press.

Peters, E. N., Nordeck, C., Zanetti, G., O'Grady, K. E., Serpelloni, G., Rimondo, C., Blanco, c., Welsh, C., & Schwartz, R. P. (2015). Relationship of gambling with tobacco, alcohol, and illicit drug use among adolescents in the USA: Review of the literature 2000–2014. *The American Journal on Addictions, 24*, 206–216.

Pilkey, D., Steinberg, H., & Martino, S. (2015). Evidence-based treatments for substance use disorders. In A. D. Kaye, N. Vadivelu, & R. D. Urman (Eds.), *Substance abuse: Inpatient and outpatient management for every clinician* (pp. 209–227). New York: Springer Science + Business Media.

Porges, S. W. (2011). *The Polyvagal theory: Neurophysiological foundations of emotions, attachment, communication, and self-regulation*. New York: W. W. Norton & Co.

Porter, G. (2015). Is work addiction a proper label for high work investment habits? In I. Harpaz & R. Snir (Eds.), *Heavy work investment: Its nature, sources, outcomes, and future directions* (pp. 303–321). New York: Routledge/Taylor & Francis Group.

Prieto, A., Prieto, B., Ortigosa, E. M., Ros, E., Pelayo, F., Ortega, J., & Rojas, I. (2016). Neural networks: An overview of early research, current frameworks and new challenges. *Neurocomputing: An International Journal, 214*, 242–268.

Prochaska, J. O., & DiClemente, C. C. (1984). *The transtheoretical approach: Crossing the traditional boundaries of therapy*. Malabar, FL: Krieger.

Project on the Decade of the Brain [Presidential Proclamation 6158]. (1990, July 17). Retrieved from https://www.loc.gov/loc/brain/proclaim.html

Robinson, S. M. (2017). "Alcoholic" or "Person with alcohol use disorder"? Applying person-first diagnostic terminology in the clinical domain. *Substance Abuse, 38*(1), 9–14.

Saitz, R. (2017). Valid, reproducible, clinically useful, nonstigmatizing terminology for the disease and its treatment: Addiction, substance use disorder, and medication. *Journal of Addiction Medicine, 11*, 246–247.

Shaffer, H., Martin, R., Kleschinsky, J., & Neporent, L. (2012). *Change your gambling, Change your life: Strategies for managing your gambling and improving your finances, relationships, and health*. San Francisco, CA: Jossey-Bass.

Shaffer, H. J., & LaPlante, D. A. (2013). Considering a critique of pathological gambling prevalence research. *Addiction Research & Theory, 21*(1), 12–14.

Siegel, D. J. (2007). *The mindful brain: Reflection and attunement in the cultivation of well-being*. New York: Norton.

Siegel, D. J. (2010). *Mindsight: The new science of personal transformation*. New York: Random House.

Substance Abuse and Mental Health Services Administration. (2013). *2013 National survey on drug use and health*. Washington, DC: U.S. Department of Health and Human Services.

The Betty Ford Institute Consensus Panel. (2007). What is recovery? A working definition from the Betty Ford Institute. *Journal of Substance Abuse Treatment, 33*, 221–228.

Townsend, A. L., Biegel, D. E., Ishler, K. J., Wieder, B., & Rini, A. (2006). Families of persons with substance use and mental disorders: A literature review and conceptual framework. *Family Relations: An Interdisciplinary Journal of Applied Family Studies, 55*, 473–486.

Turner, N., Welches, P., & Conti, S. (2013). *Mindfulness-based sobriety: A clinician's treatment guide for addiction recovery using relapse prevention therapy, acceptance and commitment therapy, and motivational interviewing.* Oakland, CA: New Harbinger Publications.

Vieten, C., Astin, J. A., Buscemi, R., & Galloway, G. P. (2010). Development of an acceptance-based coping intervention for alcohol dependence relapse prevention. *Substance Abuse, 31*, 108–116.

Vella, S.-L., & Pai, N. (2017). What is in a name? Is food addiction a misnomer? *Asian Journal of Psychiatry, 25*, 123–126.

Villatte, J. L., Vilardaga, R., Villatte, M., Vilardaga, J. P., Atkins, D. C., & Hayes, S. C. (2016). Acceptance and commitment therapy modules: Differential impact on treatment processes and outcomes. *Behaviour Research and Therapy, 77*, 52–61.

Volkow, N. D., Koob, G. F., & McLellan, A. T. (2016). Neurobiologic advances from the brain disease model of addiction. *The New England Journal of Medicine, 374*, 363–371.

White, W. L. (2005). History of drug policy, treatment, and recovery. In R. H. Coombs (Ed.), *Addiction counseling review: Preparing for comprehensive, certification and licensing examinations* (pp. 81–102). Mahwah, NJ: Lawrence Erlbaum Associates Publishers.

White, W. L. (2007). Addiction recovery: Its definitions and conceptual boundaries. *Journal of Substance Abuse Treatment, 33*, 229–241.

White, W. L. (2014). *Slaying the dragon: The history of addiction treatment and recovery in America* (2nd ed.). Bloomington, IL: Chestnut Health Systems/Lighthouse Institute.

Whitley, C. E. M. (2010). Social work clinical supervision in the addictions: Importance of understanding professional cultures. *Journal of Social Work Practice in the Addictions, 10*, 343–362.

Yates, R., Burns, J., & McCabe, L. (2017). Integration: Too much of a bad thing? *Journal of Groups in Addiction & Recovery, 12*(2–3), 196–206.

Chapter 10

Career Counseling

David M. Reile and Barbara H. Suddarth

Whatever you are, be a good one.

– Abraham Lincoln

POINTS TO PONDER

- How did you choose your career?
- What have been the influences on your career choice?
- Have you ever wanted to know if there is one perfect career for you?
- What are the major career development theories?

This chapter provides an overview of the process and practice of career counseling and career development. As you will discover in the theory section of this chapter, there are a number of different models used to define and describe the process and stages of career planning and development. In the broadest sense, however, they typically share the same deep structural themes. In nearly every model, an individual reaches a point in which there is a perceived need for assistance brought on either by a new stage of development/maturation, a crisis, or a desire for change. The role of the career counselor is to help clients better understand themselves and the world of work, and to make an informed and satisfying career decision. It is important that career counselors understand the unique perspective and background of each client (in terms of gender, race, ethnicity, etc.), but career counselors also recognize that anyone who is interested in working may benefit from career counseling. The premier organization dedicated to the work of career counselors, the National Career Development Association (NCDA), has a long history of supporting individuals regardless of background and opposing discrimination against anyone on any personal characteristic that is unrelated to job performance (National Career Development Association, 2016).

History and Background

The profession of counseling owes much to the field of vocational (career) guidance. The field of career counseling is as old as the profession of counseling itself. In fact, the National Career Development Association (NCDA), the organization which represents and serves career development professionals in the United States and has many members globally as well, is a founding member of the American Counseling Association (ACA). When ACA was formed in 1952,

NCDA, through its predecessor organization (the National Vocational Guidance Association), was already 39 years old, having formed in 1913 (Herr, 2013). Even the founder of modern psychology, Sigmund Freud, acknowledged the important role of an occupation when he commented on the importance of love and work and its influence on our humanity (Freud, 1930). Such a statement would seem to imply that career and work share equal importance with relationships in our lives.

Career counselors are first and foremost counselors. They are generally trained as mental health providers and frequently complete internships in mental health counseling settings. However, they also receive additional specialized training, experience, and supervision in the practice of career counseling. Career counselors may explore the entirety of their clients' lives, including relationships. In recent years, career counseling has been portrayed as nothing more than advising students on which major to choose or helping job seekers with their resumes. And while career counselors may assist with resumes, job interviews, or choosing an academic major, they also support clients in exploring their thoughts and feelings related to work, the impact of a career change on the family, anxiety or depression that may arise out of a job loss, the stress of sexual harassment or bullying on the job, and a myriad of other work and interpersonal issues. In fact, in many ways, career counseling is the most complete form of counseling as it addresses the total person, as Freud posited, in work and in love.

Terminology

Work, job, employment, occupation, profession, and career are often used interchangeably. In certain ways they can be synonymous while in other ways they are unique. For the purposes of this chapter, we will focus on two primary definitions:

1. *Career:* Career may be defined as a series of jobs held over a period of time requiring a set of particular skills or knowledge. *Career* may also be used to define a specific employment objective or change in employment status/objective. When referring to a person's employment history, *career* may be used as a term by itself. When referring to a person's specific occupation, one may say that a person has a *career in "X"*. Part of the use of the term career is a subjective one and may be based on the individual's opinion or that of an external party.
2. *Career Development:* One of the most classic definitions describes career development as "the lifelong behavioral processes and the influences upon them which lead to one's work values, choice of occupation(s), creation of a career pattern, decision-making style, role integration, self and career identity, educational literacy and related phenomena" (Herr & Cramer, 1996, p. 32).

Another definition also acknowledges the lifelong aspect of one's career, the impact of our changing life roles, and the interplay of the totality of our lives within the society where we live and work (Hutchison & Niles, 2016).

SIDEBAR 10.1

What do you think?

How are the terms *work, job, employment, occupation, profession,* and *career* similar and how are they different? Why might it matter?

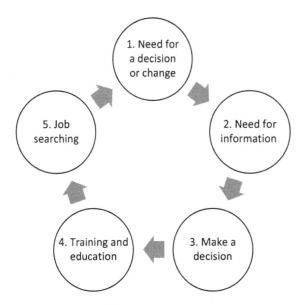

Figure 10.1 Steps Involved in the Career Planning and Development Process.

Career Planning and Development Process

In order to fully understand the field of career counseling, a counselor needs to be aware of the steps involved in the career planning and development process (see Figure 10.1). These steps are typically viewed in a circular rather than a linear fashion. As such, after obtaining a job, an individual will likely return at some point to a need for a new career-related decision or change and the cycle will repeat.

Step 1: A need for a decision or change – This step is characterized by an individual realizing that a career decision or a change in direction or job is needed.

Step 2: A need for information – This step represents a period in which an individual gathers information about her/himself through assessment of interests, values, skills, etc. In addition, an individual gathers information about the world of work, including career options as well as education and training.

Step 3: Make a decision – This step involves making a decision about education and training and/or moving into a job directly.

Step 4: Training and education – Following on from the information-gathering and decision-making steps, an individual determines if training or education is required; if so, what area(s) to explore; how to pay for it; and how, when and where to obtain it.

Step 5: Job searching – This step then focuses on the specific tasks related to obtaining a job.

Job Search Process

Just as there are a variety of stages in the overall career planning and development process, there are distinct elements and actions involved in the job search process. Career counselors may find themselves assisting individual clients as they take these steps. A well-executed job search frequently entails *networking, informational interviews, locating and understanding vacancy announcements, resume and/or job application reviews and edits, job interview preparation, salary negotiation,* and then *on-the-job growth and development*. Each of these areas could be described in extensive detail while acknowledging that best practices continue to evolve. For the purpose of this chapter, it is enough to recognize that career counselors are often called upon to provide guidance to job seekers in any or all of these areas.

Theories

Classic Theories

Career development theories have their roots in many of the major theoretical orientations familiar to psychology and counseling students. From psychodynamic to learning theory, corresponding career development theories exist. However, certain theories have predominated the field throughout most of the twentieth century (Hutchison & Niles, 2016).

Trait and Factor. Frank Parsons is known as the father of vocational guidance (career development), and for good reason (Crites, 1973). His classic book, *Choosing a Vocation*, was published in 1909. In this work he advocated a formalized process for helping people choose a career path. This process has been termed the *Trait and Factor Approach*. Parsons stated that there are three elements to providing career service to a client. First, the career counselor must understand the client's traits. *Traits* are measurable, personal qualities. Through a variety of means (including formal and informal assessments), a career counselor helps clients gain knowledge of themselves along with their aptitudes, abilities, interests, ambitions, and resources. Additionally, a career counselor helps clients assess any limitations that might exist as well as the causes of these limitations.

As the career counselor is helping clients assess their traits, the career counselor must understand a host of work environment factors. *Factors* involve the knowledge and understanding of the requirements and conditions of success, advantages and disadvantages inherent in the labor market, compensation which someone might expect in a given field, how wide or narrow opportunities may be and various prospects that may or may not exist in different lines of work (Parsons, 1909).

In its most basic form, the trait and factor approach requires the career counselor to have a thorough understanding of the client and the world of work in general and, specifically, the area(s) of interest to the client. But once this information is obtained and understood, Parsons indicated that the career counselor applies *true reasoning* on the relationship between these traits and factors to assist the client in arriving at a satisfactory career choice. This matching process (or true reasoning) places the career counselor solidly in the role of expert and means that clients are dependent upon the career counselor's ability to adequately and accurately assess the salient factors in clients' lives pertaining to particular career options. Further, the career counselor must have expertise in a wide variety of career areas and the world of work in general to be able to help match clients to a particular career.

While this process has gradually been replaced by other theoretical perspectives, its influence can be seen in the other three classic theoretical perspectives. While each of these remaining classic theories has added significant elements to the process of choosing a career, they also incorporate a trait-and-factor matching component.

SIDEBAR 10.2

What do *you* think?

Does Parsons' theory resonate with you? What traits do you see most clearly in yourself? What factors in the workplace are most attractive to you? How would you describe your "true reasoning" ability up to this point in your career? Which elements of Parsons' theory do you agree with and which elements might not seem relevant today? How would you imagine using Parsons' theory with clients today?

Person-Environment Fit. One of the best-known and most widely used theories of career development was developed by John Holland (Holland, 1997). His theory has been referred to by many names. It was certainly influenced by Parsons' approach and has thus been referred to as a trait and factor theory. As it involves the matching of interests to career fields and it has also been called a "matching" theory. With Holland's approach to assessing interests, it has been called an "interest" theory. Finally, because of the emphasis on connecting personal preferences with work environments, it is often known as a "person-environment fit" theory.

The essence of Holland's theory is that people's interests can be categorized into one or more primary themes. Work environments can also be grouped according to these same themes. Helping clients understand their interests and the work environments that correspond to these interests, Holland believed, will lead to a satisfying career choice. The axiom "Birds of a feather flock together" is an apt description of this approach. Holland believed that our choice of a career (or vocation) is actually the way in which we express our identity and our personality (Holland, 1997). It is believed that if a person has enough interest in a particular area s/he will develop the skills needed to be successful in a career within that field. Additionally, a high degree of skill in a particular area often influences an individual to express liking of that field and view it as a potentially attractive career option. While there is not a direct one-to-one correlation between interest and skill, there is enough connection to warrant exploration.

Holland developed six principal interest categories: *Realistic, Investigative, Artistic, Social, Enterprising,* and *Conventional* (Gottfredson & Holland, 1996). Briefly, the six interest themes can be described as follows:

Realistic – A preference for working outdoors and with tools and equipment; more likely to be action oriented than to use verbal or written expression; typical careers include police officer, carpenter, and mechanic.

Investigative – A preference for research and understanding how things work and why they are the way they are; scientifically minded with interests in areas like chemistry, mathematics, and computers; typical careers include engineering, forensic chemistry, and detective.

Artistic – A preference for creativity and unconventional activities; an interest and appreciation for music, drama, literature, and art; typical careers include musician, photographer, and writer.

Social – A preference for working with and in service to others; interested in helping people, caring for others, and teaching/training; typical careers include elementary school teacher, social worker, and nurse.

Enterprising – A preference for leading and directing the work of others; interests include finance, politics, and risk taking; typical careers include business executive, salesperson, and manager.

Conventional – A preference for order and structure; interested in data management and setting up systems; typical careers include accounting, software development, and administrative assistant.

Taking the first letter of these six themes results in the acronym RIASEC. Holland postulated that these six themes could be arranged on a hexagon (see Figure 10.2).

By convention, the Realistic interest theme is typically placed in the upper left-hand corner with the interest categories arranged in a clockwise fashion in the order RIASEC. While the interest types are mutually exclusive, Holland advanced the notion that the closer in proximity the interests themes were on the hexagon, the more *congruence* existed between the areas of interest. This concept of congruence is significant in Holland's theory. Holland theorized that people generally had two or three primary areas of interest and that the closer these areas

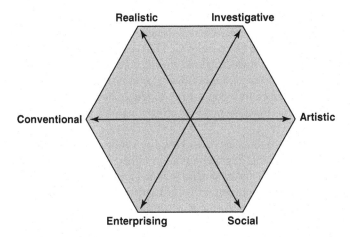

Figure 10.2 Holland's Hexagon.
Adapted and reproduced by special permission of the Publisher, Psychological Assessment Resources, Inc., 16204 North Florida Avenue, Lutz, Florida 33549, from the Self-Directed Search Form R 4th Edition: You and Your Career Booklet by John L. Holland, Ph.D., Copyright 1977, 1985, 1991, 1994 by PAR. Further reproduction is prohibited without permission from PAR, Inc.

of interest were on the hexagon, the greater likelihood of finding a career that matched those interests and the greater degree of satisfaction one would have in that career.

Holland's theory has influenced the field of career counseling enormously. Numerous well-known assessments use the RIASEC interest themes, not the least of which is Holland's own *Self-Directed Search (SDS)*. Others include, but are not limited to, the *Strong Interest Inventory*, the *Kuder Career Planning System*, the *Find Your Interests* portion of the *ASVAB Career Exploration Program*, and the O*NET (*Occupational Information Network*) *Interest Profiler* (National Center for O*NET Development, 1999).

Despite the volume of supportive research and the wide utilization of Holland's theory, most career counselors today view interest assessment and this theory as representing just one facet of how a person develops, chooses, plans, and grows in a career. Still, Holland's person-environment fit theory remains a major force and influence within career counseling.

SIDEBAR 10.3

What do *you* think?

Does Holland's theory resonate with you? Can you see yourself in one or more of the interest themes (RIASEC)? Which elements of Holland's theory do you agree with and which elements might not seem relevant today? How would you imagine using Holland's theory with clients today?

Developmental. Donald Super contributed the concept that career development is a lifelong process and is seen as the leading proponent of a developmental theory of career counseling (Super, 1980). Super believed that career development is the process of developing and implementing a self-concept (Super, 1988). Self-concept, in essence, is the totality of who we are and involves how we see ourselves in a variety of life stages throughout our life span.

Essentially, Super stated that career development occurs throughout a person's life and involves specific developmental tasks that need to be completed. This is referred to as the *Life Span* portion of his theory. The developmental stages include *growth* (ages 0–15), *exploration* (ages 15–25), *establishment* (ages 25–45), *maintenance* (ages 45–65), and *disengagement* (65+). The ages associated with these stages differ from individual to individual, and may shift with broader changes in society. For example, disengagement at or around age 65 is certainly no longer true for many.

Super also believed that career is a lifestyle concept involving the totality of life roles in which one is engaged. This is referred to as the *Life Space* component of his theory. These roles include *child, student, worker, spouse/partner, homemaker, parent, leisurite, and citizen*. While not everyone engages in every one of these roles (i.e., spouse/partner or homemaker), generally people find themselves engaged in most of these roles at various times in their lives and may move in and out of roles depending on life circumstances (i.e., being a student in elementary school through college and then again later in life). Note that Super saw the life role of homemaker not as gender specific, but rather a role that men and women engage in through a variety of tasks that go into the establishment and care of one's home life.

Super represented this part of his theory in what is referred to as the *Career Life Rainbow*. This rainbow, or semi-circle, is divided into 5-year increments from birth to age 80+. In the center and moving upward/outward are the life roles arranged in order from child to citizen.

Another of Super's major contributions to the field of career counseling was the inclusion of values as a source of influence in career development. He postulated that values differ in importance across cultures but that people do endeavor to achieve satisfaction of their values through work (Super & Sverko, 1995). In other words, Super viewed values as aspects of work that related to job satisfaction. Super's original *Work Values Inventory* examined 15 work values: altruism, esthetics, creativity, intellectual stimulation, independence, achievement, prestige, management, economic returns, security, surroundings, supervisory relations, associates, variety, and way of life (Zytowski, 1994).

SIDEBAR 10.4

What do *you* think?

Does Super's theory resonate with you? Which elements of Super's theory do you agree with and which elements might not seem relevant today? If you were to explore your own life roles today and compare them with where you were 10 years ago or where you think you might be 10 years from now, what changes could you envision? How would you imagine using Super's theory with clients today?

Learning theory. John Krumboltz (Krumboltz, Mitchell, & Jones, 1976) was an early proponent of and adapted the concepts of social learning theory to career development. Krumboltz's theory, *Social Learning Theory of Career Decision Making* (SLTCDM), reinforced the idea that career choice is the result of learning; specifically, through instrumental and associative learning. *Instrumental learning* occurs when a person is positively reinforced for a given behavior. *Associative learning* occurs when a person models behavior after observing another perform the same or similar behavior. Associative learning may also be termed *observational learning* (Sharf,

2006). In adapting these concepts to career development, Krumboltz postulated that a child who performs well in math class, for instance, and is rewarded through good grades is likely to continue doing well in math. As the reinforcement and rewards continue, the same child is likely to increase in skill and will later choose a career where mathematical abilities are critical. By the same token, a child who sees a parent and/or older sibling work on cars and receive praise for this will be more likely to engage in similar behavior and will express a liking for mechanical work. The expression of interest coupled with positive reinforcement will lead the same child to develop skills in auto mechanics.

Krumboltz also incorporated the influences of genetic endowments and special abilities, environmental conditions and events, and the concepts of self-observation generalizations, and task approach skills into the field of career development (Brown & Associates, 2002). With regard to *genetic endowments* and *special abilities*, Krumboltz indicated that people are born with certain innate or natural tendencies. For example, a child may show a propensity in music, art, or athletics at a young age. Next, *environmental conditions* help to reinforce these traits. Family and community support, academic or other learning opportunities, and later employment prospects help to enhance and refine an individual's inherited traits. Individuals then begin to evaluate their performance in relationship to their own and other's expectations and they tend to generalize successes or failures to other settings and situations. Krumboltz describes this process as *self-observation generalizations*. Finally, *task approach skills* include work habits, emotional responses, and problem-solving skills. All of these elements interact together and ultimately influence an individual's career decisions.

Krumboltz later distanced himself somewhat from this theory. He came to believe that career development is more a matter of chance experiences and encounters. This is briefly described in the section below.

SIDEBAR 10.5

What do *you* think?

Does Krumboltz's Social Learning theory resonate with you? Which elements of this theory do you agree with and which elements might not seem relevant today? How have your innate abilities and life experiences shaped your career choices? How would you imagine using Krumboltz's theory with clients today?

Transition. Nancy Schlossberg's perspective and approach grew out of her research and work with mid-to late career workers who found themselves out of a job after corporate layoffs and who were unable to find similar employment (at least in terms of pay and status). The resulting job loss and career/job change had a profound impact on the career and personal identities of these individuals. Much of Schlossberg's theory was based on analyses of the factors that described individuals who were better able to cope with life and work transitions (Charner & Schlossberg, 1986).

Schlossberg stated that a *transition* is an *event* (something that occurs) or a *non-event* (something that was expected to happen but didn't) that results in a change in a person's life. The changes that occur as a result of the transition impact a person's life roles, relationships, routines, and assumptions about self. Transitions come in all shapes and sizes, including social milestones (a wedding or the birth of a child), ones we choose (moving to a new city), a surprise (an unexpected job loss), or a combination of transitions that come at the same time (getting married, moving, and starting a new job) (Schlossberg, 1989).

Schlossberg believed that the ease or severity of a transition was determined by four factors (called the 4 S model). These included the *Situation* (the timing of the transition, its impact, and the degree of control the person may have); the *Self* (a person's coping skills, experience with similar transitions, and overall outlook on life); the *Supports* (how much individual, financial, family, and/or community support is available); and the *Strategies* for dealing with the transition. Schlossberg identified a number of strategies for coping that included one's ability to change the meaning of a transition from negative to positive (e.g., losing a job one didn't like enabled the person to find a better, more enjoyable job); examining options (seeing a variety of available choices and opportunities for coping with the transition); and even selective denial (briefly ignoring a negative transition while gathering resources to cope) (Schlossberg, 1989).

Schlossberg's transition theory may be viewed not so much as a career development theory but as a life change theory with career and job implications. At the same time, Schlossberg's theory has contributed greatly to career counselors' ability to help clients cope with job loss and other significant life transitions. For example, the classic theories can be used to help clients understand their interests or help them with making a career choice. Schlossberg's theory helps a counselor aid a client in understanding and making meaning out of the loss of a job or the experience of another kind of transition (such as moving or graduation) and learning how to cope with the impact of the transition while determining a new direction. Finally, Schlossberg's introduction of the concept of non-events (things that we expect to happen that don't) has contributed to counselors' understanding of the significant impact things such as not getting a promotion or not being offered a job can have in people's lives.

SIDEBAR 10.6

What do *you* think?

Does Schlossberg's Transition theory resonate with you? Which elements of this theory do you agree with and which elements might not seem relevant today? How have events and non-events shaped your life and career decisions? How would you imagine using Schlossberg's theory with clients today?

Integrative Life Planning (IPL). Sunny Hansen believed that the theories of career development and counseling were too focused on a Western concept of life and work and tended to be male dominated. While not ignoring the constructs of how career concepts are developed in individuals, she concentrated instead on the practical aspects of integrating career into life. She postulated that there are seven major elements to connecting work and life and that these are areas to which each person must attend (Hansen, 1997). She used the metaphor of a quilt to indicate how our lives (and career) are part of a whole.

A) *Finding work that needs doing in changing global contexts* – The world of work is changing constantly. Adapting to the change means looking for new areas of employment that can help people stay engaged and employed.
B) *Weaving our lives into a meaningful whole* – While work is an important part of people's lives, it is only one part. They need to recognize and attend to the other significant components.
C) *Connecting family and work* – Continuing on with the previous concept, people need to connect their family life to their work life. Achieving balance is critical.

D) *Valuing pluralism and inclusivity* – Recognize that there is more than one right way to do something. Value the ideas, perspectives, and worth of all those around us.

E) *Managing personal transitions and organizational change* – Change is constant. How people cope with personal and organizational change will determine how happy and successful they can be in work and life.

F) *Exploring spirituality, meaning, and life purpose* – Work needs to be more than just a means to an end and life needs to be about more than just acquisition. People should connect with the spiritual side of themselves and determine what life and work mean to them.

G) *Attending to personal, emotional, and physical health* – At all ages and stages, but particularly as individuals age, it is important to pay attention to and guard their health. Note: This element was added in a later revision (Hansen & Suddarth, 2008).

Hansen advocated for career counselors to incorporate these discussion areas in their work with clients. She believed it is among the many duties of career counselors to help adult clients understand these areas, to help them see the interrelatedness of the various tasks, and to help them prioritize the tasks according to their needs and the needs of society (Hansen, 2000).

Hansen saw her theory as one way to help clients reflect and act on their life career choices and decisions in some different ways. She viewed *Integrative Life Planning* as offering a holistic lens through which to examine the contexts of people's lives and determine ways to assist them with emerging career and life planning issues. In working with clients, a career counselor might ask how each of these tasks is being attended to in their lives with the goal being a more integrated work, family, and community individual (Hansen, 2000).

SIDEBAR 10.7

What do *you* think?

Does Hansen's Integrative Life Planning theory resonate with you? Which elements of this theory do you agree with and which elements might not seem relevant today? Are you attending to any or all of these areas in your life? How would you imagine using Hansen's theory with clients today?

Happenstance. Later in his career, John Krumboltz began to rethink the SLTCDM. Out of his consideration emerged what he termed a *happenstance theory* (Krumboltz & Levin, 2004). In essence, Krumboltz postulated that a career is not so much planned as it emerges as a result of chance encounters. To illustrate, a child happens to meet a classmate who teaches her/him a game or a sport. This child then practices that new skill and develops into an athlete who obtains a scholarship to college. In college, the coach of the team on which the young adult plays recommends an academic major to the student. The student signs up for that major and develops a career as a result. At any point along the path, a different chance encounter could alter the course and result in a different career choice and life for the individual.

Krumboltz believed that not only does happenstance, or chance, play a critical role but that the individual must be prepared to make use of the new learning, experience or encounter. As a result, life offers a multitude of possibilities that involve random encounters intersecting with a person's preparation for dealing with new information.

SIDEBAR 10.8

What do _you_ think?

Does Krumboltz's Happenstance theory resonate with you? Which elements of this theory do you agree with and which elements might not seem relevant today? Does this seem like a new theory or an addendum to Krumboltz's SLTCDM? How have chance experiences or happenstance impacted your career decisions? How would you imagine using Happenstance theory with clients today?

Career Construction. Mark Savickas (1989) has developed a model for helping clients understand their lives and the influences on their career direction. He sees career counseling, in part, as helping clients tell their stories. He has also postulated that we must actively master what we have passively suffered. In other words, whatever difficulties we encountered in our early lives continue to influence our lives and careers. Savickas has developed a _career construction interview_ that he makes available free of charge on his website (Vocopher.com), along with his _Life-Design Counseling Manual_ (Savickas, 2015).

The career construction interview is set up so that a counselor asks a client to share stories about major life influences, including favorite books, television shows, and/or magazines; favorite motto; most admired person(s); and earliest recollections. A client's answers to these questions, Savickas believes, will help the counselor understand the client's preoccupations, self-conceptualizations, the environment in which a client would like to live and work, and the script the client is working from, as well as the formula for achieving success in life and work and, finally, the advice the client is giving to her/himself (Savickas, 2015). Because of the personal and sensitive nature of the material that can emerge from the career construction interview, beginning counselors who are interested in using Savickas' theory should work under the supervision of an experienced counselor.

SIDEBAR 10.9

What do _you_ think?

Does Savickas' Career Construction theory resonate with you? Which elements of this theory do you agree with and which elements might not seem relevant today? Do you agree or disagree with the notion that we must "actively master what we have passively suffered?" Why or why not? How would you imagine using this theory with clients today?

Career Assessments

Career counselors use a variety of tools and assessments to help inform their work with clients. Some of these tools require advanced graduate-level coursework in psychometrics and statistics while others are available after completing specialized training on the particular assessment. A variety of tools that require no specialized training can still provide valuable information to career counselors and their clients. Formal assessment instruments, including those used in career counseling, are divided into three categories – A, B, and C. There are no specific qualifications for purchasing, administering, and interpreting A-level assessments. These types of assessments include certain card sorts and basic checklists (e.g., place a check mark next to the type of work environments you prefer). Qualifications for purchasing, administering, and interpreting B-level assessments typically include a master's degree in counseling or a closely related field with specific training in clinical and counseling assessment instruments and/or specialized training in the use and interpretation of a specific assessment tool (e.g., the *Myers-Briggs Type Indicator*). Qualifications for purchasing, administering, and interpreting C-level assessments typically include a doctorate in psychology or a closely related field with formal training in the use of clinical and counseling assessment instruments. A license to practice in the profession may also be a requirement.

Interests

Often the most widely assessed characteristics by career counselor are interests – the things we like to do. Interest assessments generally compare a person's responses to a variety of questions with the responses of a large representative sample of those who report being happy and successful in various careers fields. Holland's person-environment fit theory underlies most of these assessments and his RIASEC model is employed by the most widely used interest assessments.

Holland's own assessment, the *SDS*, is available online to the general public from PAR, Inc. The SDS also comes in a paper version with accompanying booklets (*Occupations Finder* and *Educational Opportunities Finder*) that allow one to compare interest codes to careers and educational options as well as a career-oriented workbook (*You and Your Career*). The online version is highly interactive and includes a Holland interest code summary (typically the individual's two or three highest RIASEC interests); a personalized list of occupations and educational programs, information about income, connections to career clusters, and links to related job listings.

The **Strong Interest Inventory (SII)** is published by CPP Inc. and is available through an online portal. The SII utilizes Holland's RIASEC model as the basis for its General Occupational Themes. Results are presented first as an individual's top two or three highest RIASEC interests. Next, an individual's top five (out of 30) Basic Interest Scale results are shown. The 30 Basic Interest Scales represent potential work and leisure activities as well as fields of study. Next, clients are presented with graphics illustrating the degree of similarity and difference between their own interest patterns and large samples of people working in 130 occupations. This section includes a summary of the top 10 careers that are most similar to the client's interests. Finally, a client's preferences are depicted on five Personal Style scales focused on work style (working alone versus with people), learning environment (practical versus academic), leadership style (preference for being in charge or not), risk taking (liking for risk or not), and team orientation (independent versus team work). Results can be presented to clients online (with a variety of links for more information) or in an eight-page paper handout.

Skills

There are a variety of ways in which career counselors help clients to assess their skills. These include card sorts, checklists, and formal assessments, including aptitude batteries. Two assessments that are used frequently are *SkillScan* and the *Armed Services Vocational Aptitude Battery* (ASVAB). Counselors often combine skills and interest assessments to help clients get a broader picture of what they like to do (interests) and what they can do (skills). For some, interest assessments may be challenging (i.e., a client who hasn't been exposed to a broad number careers or interest areas might not have enough information to adequately assess interests). However, skills assessments, particularly those that are simply self-report, can be problematic as well. Individuals may over- or underestimate their proficiency in a particular skill. Also, exposure and experience is an issue. If you haven't worked on a computer or acted in a play before, how will you know if you have skills in these areas? This doesn't mean that skills assessments have no place in the work of career counselors. In order to more accurately assess client skills, however, career counselors need to help clients compare their results with other factors grounded in real-world performance, such as their grades, any work experiences, and feedback from employers, coworkers, friends, and family members.

Skillscan (SkillScan.com) comes in two forms – a card sort and an online version. The online version includes a variety of links and activities but both versions use a similar self-report and sorting technique. Clients are presented with 60 transferable skills that cover six major skill areas (*Relationship, Communication, Management/Leadership, Physical/Technical, Creative*, and *Analytical*). Clients are asked to rate their ability into two categories (Competent and Minimal or No Ability). Skills rated as "Competent" are then divided into four areas based on a client's interest in using these skills at work (Major Role, Secondary Role, Minor Role, or Unwilling to Use). Finally, skills rated as "Minimal or No Ability" can be categorized in terms of a desire for future development. Counselors can assist clients in determining which skills might be explored for future employment and/or development. The results from SkillScan can also be used in crafting a resume, in examining transferrable job skills (those skills in one job that might be useful in another), and even in exploring activities the client might pursue for leisure or retirement. The types of clients who might most benefit from SkillScan are those who have enough education, work experience, and exposure to the world of work to be able to accurately assess their skills.

The Armed Services Vocational Aptitude Battery (ASVAB) is widely known as the assessment used to determine individuals' qualifications for a range of military occupational specialties (Official-ASVAB.com, 2018). The ASVAB is administered free of charge at more than 14,000 high schools throughout the United States. Scores in four critical areas (*Arithmetic Reasoning, Work Knowledge, Paragraph Comprehension*, and *Mathematics Knowledge*) count toward an Armed Forces Qualifying Test (AFQT) score. This score is used to determine candidates' qualifications for enlisting in the U.S. military. There are five other subtests that are administered on the ASVAB – General Science, Electronics Information, Auto Information, Shop Information, Mechanical Comprehension, and Assembling Objects. When the ASVAB assessment is combined with the ASVAB Career Exploration Program (ASVABProgram.com), individuals are able to research a variety of careers and educational options related to their aptitudes and interests as well as learning more about careers in the military. The ASVAB and the CEP are typically used by high school students in the tenth to twelfth grades.

Values

Donald Super (Zytowski, 1994) is among the first career development theorists to include values assessment as a central part of career counseling. Super postulated that generalized expressions of job satisfaction tended to relate to expressions of satisfaction with specific aspects of work. Super termed these "*work values*" (Zytowski, 1994). Values can also be viewed as elements that provide motivation and meaning in our lives and they certainly impact career choice as well as on-the-job satisfaction. Many people express dissatisfaction with their career and/or job when that job is significantly out of sync with their personal and career values. There are a variety of work values assessments, including Super's own *Work Values Inventory* (WVI). The WVI assesses 15 values, including achievement, prestige, and economic returns.

Other work values assessments include card sorts, checklists, and various web-based assessments. For example, the *O*Net*, developed under the sponsorship of the U.S. Department of Labor offers a values assessment (*Work Importance Locator*) available for free. This can be downloaded as a paper/pencil assessment and as a card sort. Once completed, a user can browse jobs based on one or a combination of five work values – *Achievement, Independence, Recognition, Relationships, Support,* and *Working Conditions.* This can also be accessed for free online.

Clients who express dissatisfaction with their jobs or who indicate that they want more meaning and purpose in their life and work might benefit from exploring their values, perhaps before any other kind of assessment. The career counselor may then help the client assess education, training, career, and/or job options on the basis of the client's values.

Personality and Strengths

Many career counselors use personality assessments or strengths-based assessments. The most common personality assessment used in career counseling is the *Myers-Briggs Type Indicator* (MBTI). The MBTI is published by CPP Inc. There are also a number of free and for fee assessments online that purport to use the same 16 personality types as the MBTI. A quick search online will reveal many such assessments. However, the MBTI is considered the premier tool with more than 70 years of validity and reliability research behind it (CPP. com, 2018).

The MBTI is useful for helping clients to understand themselves and others. It explores personality based on four dimensions that look at where we get our energy (Extravert-Introvert or E/I); how we take in information (Sensing-Intuition or S/N); how we make decisions (Thinking-Feeling or T/F); and how we tend to live our lives (Judging-Perceiving or J/P). As a result, clients can also see what kinds of work environments might mesh better with their personality. When interpreted skillfully, the results of the MBTI can offer clients useful insights into their personalities within a positive, ego-syntonic frame of reference. However, when interpreted hurriedly or with less care or skill, the MBTI can be used to pigeon-hole clients (e.g., You're an ENTJ so you should be an X; or You would like that because you are an INFJ). This overly simplistic approach can have a lasting negative impact on clients' understanding of their options, as well as their view of counseling in general and career counseling in particular.

Strengths-based assessment has become increasingly popular in recent years. One of the best known of these tools is the *Clifton StrengthsFinder 2.0.* This assessment was developed in the late 1990s by a team at Gallup under the leadership of Don Clifton, known as the Father of Strengths Psychology (Rath, 2007). The *StrengthsFinder* was originally released in 2001 with the 2.0 version available in 2007. The assessment looks at 34 themes (areas of strength), also referred to as "categories of talents" (Asplund et. al., 2014). These themes include areas such as *Achiever, Communication, Developer, Empathy, Learner,* and *Self-Assurance* (Rath, 2007). The *StrengthsFinder 2.0* can be used to help individuals and teams understand their strengths in work and academic settings (Asplund et. al., 2014). With its focus on strengths versus deficits, career counselors can use this assessment to help clients understand areas of work that may capitalize on their talents.

Another strengths-based assessment is the *VIA Survey* (viacharacter.org). A team of 55 social scientists, led by Christopher Peterson and Martin Seligman, developed the *Via Survey.* This free online assessment examines 24 "Character Strengths" and six "Virtues." The 24 character strengths are divided across the six virtues of *Wisdom, Courage, Humanity, Justice, Temperance,* and *Transcendence.* The VIA Survey purports to examine all life spheres, not just the work domain, and endeavors to focus on character strengths and virtues that are more universal in nature rather than a Western work setting (Valley Industry Institute, 2018). The *VIA Survey* helps individuals understand "What is best about who you are," concentrating on core character strengths (Neimiec, 2013).

Using Career Assessments Responsibly with Clients

As previously stated, career counselors are first and foremost counselors. As such they follow the same guidelines and ethical standards as other counselors. This includes the administration and interpretation of assessments with clients. Career counselors do not misuse assessment results and interpretations and they respect clients' rights to know the results of any assessments and to understand the interpretations of the same (American Counseling Association, 2014; National Career Development Association, 2015). Further, career counselors use only assessments for which they have been trained and they take care to explain to clients the nature and purposes of any assessment (American Counseling Association, 2014; National Career Development Association, 2015).

What follows is a brief outline that career counselors may consider when preparing for and using assessments with clients, presuming that the counselor is well trained and qualified to administer and interpret career assessments.

1) *Benefit of assessment* – A career counselor first determines if a client may benefit from the results of a particular assessment. Often clients come to career counselors requesting to "take the test that will tell me what I should do for my career." A career counselor recognizes that an assessment might not be in the best interest of a client or might not always be the right place to start.

2) *Prepare the client for assessment* – A career counselor ensures that clients fully understand the purpose of the assessment (i.e., interest, skills, values, strengths, personality, etc.) and what the results will and won't provide for the client.

3) *Selection of the assessment* – Career counselors recognize that not all assessments are right for every client. As a result, the career counselor will choose an assessment that is considered reliable and valid for a particular client based on the client's age, educational level, demographic background, and financial ability. If any concerns exist for a particular assessment (i.e., it wasn't normed for the client's gender or race), the career counselor fully informs the client and explains if and why s/he believes the assessment may still be of benefit to the client and in what context.

4) *Review the results* – Before sharing any assessment results with a client, a career counselor reviews the results and fully understands their meaning. Should any issues be present which the counselor believes might impact the reliability or validity of the results, the career counselor will make certain the client is aware of these concerns.

5) *Provide a thorough interpretation* – When interpreting career assessment results, the career counselor ensures that the client fully understands the results. The career counselor will ask the client at various intervals if the results make sense and if there are any questions. Once the results are interpreted, the career counselor works with the client to determine next steps and to assist the client in making use of the results.

For more information on career assessments, the reader is referred to *A Counselor's Guide to Career Assessment Instruments* (6th ed.) (Wood & Hays, 2013).

Summary

Career counseling may be viewed as providing a one-time service. For example, a client who needs assistance in making a career choice or help with a resume or job interviewing may seek help from a career counselor. However, career counseling is more typically viewed as a life-long process. This is especially true when seen through a developmental lens. As individuals are living and working longer, career counselors are being asked to help people determine not only career options and job search assistance during the traditional 40+ years of work life (ages 25 – 65), but for post-high school training and education and/or work options as well as post-retirement career and life planning. As such, career counselors need to be aware of a wide range of career and lifestyle issues that impact an individual's career and life goals.

> *I was really lost until I met with a career counselor. She helped me to think about my life in a very broad way and I'm now more confident about my career direction.*
>
> – career counseling client

References

American Counseling Association. (2014). *ACA code of ethics*. Alexandria, VA: Author. Retrieved from https://www.counseling.org/knowledge-center/ethics

Asplund, A., Agrawal, S., Hodges, T., Harter, J., & Lopez, S. J. (2014). *The Clifton StrengthsFinder 2.0 technical report: Development and validation*. Retrieved from https://www.gallup.com/services/176321/clifton-strengthsfinder-technical-report-development-validation.aspx

Brown, D. , & Associates (2002). *Career choice and development* (4th ed.). San Francisco, CA: Jossey-Bass.

Charner, I., & Schlossberg, N. K. (1986). Variations by theme: The life transitions of clerical workers. *Vocational Guidance Quarterly, 34*, 212–224.

CPP. (2018). *The Myers-Briggs type indicator*. Retrieved from https://www.cpp.com/en-US/Products-and-Services/Myers-Briggs

Crites, J. O. (1973). Career maturity. *NCME Measurement in Education, 4*(2), 1–8.

Freud, S. (1930). *Civilization and its discontents*. Oxford: Hogarth.

Gottfredson, G. D., & Holland, J. L. (1996). *Dictionary of Holland occupational codes* (3rd ed.). Odessa, FL: Psychological Assessment Resources.

Hansen, L. S. (1997). *Integrative life planning: Critical tasks for career development and changing life patterns*. San Francisco, CA: Jossey-Bass.

Hansen, S., & Suddarth, B. (2008). What is integrative life planning? *Career Developments, 24*(4), 6–9.

Herr, E. L. (2013), Trends in the history of vocational guidance. *Career Development Quarterly, 61*, 277–282.

Herr, E. L., & Cramer, S. H. (1996). *Career guidance and counseling through the life span* (5th ed.). New York: Harper Collins.

Holland, J. L. (1997). *Making vocational choices: A theory of vocational personalities and work environments* (3rd ed.). Odessa, FL: Psychological Assessment Resources.

Hutchison, B., & Niles, S. G. (2016). Career development theories. In I. Marini & M. A. In Stebnicki (Eds.), *The professional counselor's desk reference* (pp. 285–289). New York: Springer Publishing Co.

Krumboltz, J., Mitchell, A., & Jones, G. (1976). A social learning theory of career selection. *The counseling psychologist, 6*(1), 71–81.

Krumboltz, J. D., & Levin A. S. (2004). *Luck is no accident: Making the most of happenstance in your life and career*. Manassas Park, VA: Impact Publishers.

National Career Development Association. (2015). *National career development association code of ethics*. Retrieved from https://www.ncda.org/aws/NCDA/pt/sp/guidelines

National Career Development Association. (2016). *Non-discrimination statement of the Board of the National Career Development Association*. Retrieved from https://www.ncda.org/aws/NCDA/pt/sp/about

National Center for O*NET Development. (1999). *O*NET interest profiler*. Raleigh, NC: Author.

Neimiec, R. (2013). *VIA survey or StrengthsFinder: Comparing the two most dominant strengths tests in the world*. Retrieved from https://www.psychologytoday.com/us/blog/what-matters-most/201312/survey-or-strengthsfinder

Official-ASVAB.com. (2018). Retrieved from http://www.official-asvab.com

Parsons, F. (1909). *Choosing a vocation*. Boston, MA: Houghton Mifflin.

Rath, T. (2007). *StrengthsFinder 2.0*. New York: Gallup Press.

Savickas, M. L. (1989). Career-style assessment. In T. Sweeney (Ed.), *Adlerian counseling: A practical approach for a new decade* (3rd ed., pp. 289–320). Muncie, IN: Accelerated Development.

Savickas, M. L. (2015). *Life-design counseling manual*. Author.

Schlossberg, N. K. (1989). *Overwhelmed: Coping with life's ups and downs*. Lexington, KY: Lexington Press.

Sharf, R. S. (2006). *Applying career development theory to counseling*. Boston, MA: Thomson, Brooks/Cole.

Super, D. E. (1980). A life-span, life-space approach to career development. *Journal of Vocational Behavior, 16*, 282–298.

Super, D. E. (1988). Vocational adjustment: Implementing a self-concept. *Career Development Quarterly, 36*, 351–357.

Super, D. E., & Sverko, B. (Eds.). (1995). *Life roles, values, and careers: International findings of the work importance study*. San Francisco, CA: Jossey-Bass.

Valley Industry Institute. (2018). VIA FAQs. Retrieved from http://www.viacharacter.org/www/About-Institute/FAQs

Wood, C., & Hays, D. G. (2013). *A counselor's guide to career assessment instruments* (6th ed.). Broken Arrow, OK: NCDA.

Zytowski, D. G. (1994). A Super contribution to vocational theory: Work values. *Career Development Quarterly, 43*, 25–31.

Chapter 11

Clinical Mental Health Counseling

Nathan C. D. Perron

> *What do we live for, if it is not to make life less difficult for each other?*
>
> – George Eliot

POINTS TO PONDER

- How did Clinical Mental Health Counseling develop into a viable profession?
- How is Clinical Mental Health Counseling distinct from the other helping professions?
- What priorities become evident for Clinical Mental Health Counselors when applying theoretical approaches to the work of supporting people?
- In what settings might Clinical Mental Health Counselors serve?
- What skills are necessary to develop in order to become an effective Clinical Mental Health Counselor?

Clinical Mental Health Counseling (CMHC) is a relatively young profession among the helping services, and one that continues to experience rapid growth. The need for increased focus on mental health and wellness remains highly important to Clinical Mental Health Counselors (CMHCs), because the prevalence of mental illness remains high (National Institute of Mental Health [NIMH], 2018; World Health Organization [WHO], 2017).

The early influences on CMHC are evident from a variety of places, and the profession has been exercised in a variety of different ways from many different settings. The origin of the CMHC profession comes more directly from education and indirectly from psychology (Spruill, 1999), but there are additional influences ranging from vocational guidance, to social work and psychiatry.

In an effort to unify and strengthen the profession, the American Counseling Association (ACA) promoted a study to identify a clear description of what Clinical Mental Health Counseling sets out to accomplish (Kaplan, Tarvydas, & Gladding, 2014). The conclusive results indicated that counselors overwhelmingly identified with the definition: "Counseling is a professional relationship that empowers diverse individuals, families, and groups to accomplish mental health, wellness, education, and career goals" (Kaplan et al., 2014, p. 92). How one will accomplish these noteworthy goals is another matter entirely, because diversity is another hallmark that reflects the approaches and the people serving within the CMHC profession. Understanding the history of the profession will help clarify what hurdles have been crossed to bring effective care to people, it will cast light on what procedures to know for offering service now, and it will demonstrate how the profession might advance even further in the future.

History and Background of Clinical Mental Health Counseling

The field of clinical mental health counseling offers a unique yet collaborative history. While many of the helping professions share elements of training and focus for serving the public, CMHCs enjoy a distinct history that followed a history of changes and developments that contributed to the strong profession it is today. Counselors may be compared with the teachers, religious leaders, and philosophers of ancient history, including Jesus, Buddha, Socrates, Plato, Confucius, Hippocrates, and many others.

Pre-1900s

Roots of mental health have been traced as far back as 1793, when Philippe Pinel, who directed a mental hospital in Paris, advocated for the moral treatment of patients, and emphasized the value of liberty and equality among those receiving services (Brooks & Weikel, 1986; Smith & Robinson, 1995). Pinel began introducing revolutionary concepts like banning the use of corporal punishment, chained containment, and heightened restrictiveness. Smith and Robinson (1995) identified a number of other reformers that were beginning to emphasize the humane treatment of mental hospital patients also in England and the United States.

Wilhelm Wundt of Germany was one of the first to begin conducting experiments with the human mind based on self-reflection and verbalization. This soon led to Sigmund Freud's work in the late 19th century, as he further explored the notion of a 'talking cure,' where a strong emphasis on the unconscious and influences of emotions became an area of greater focus. These historical points of exploration were the catalyst influencing the development of counseling theory as it is known today (Guindon, 2011).

At the same time psychology was developing, social reform was emerging in the United States. Vocational guidance and counseling began to influence the development of social workers supporting the poor, psychiatrists advocating for the needs exhibited with mental illness, and the need for humanistic approaches in the educational system. Previous chapters also detail the development of vocational guidance, pioneered by the initiation of vocational guidance counseling in 1881 by Salmon Richards, and the establishment of the first guidance counseling school in 1897 by Jesse B. Davis. The emergence of psychology, social reform, and education throughout the 19th century provided the ideal context for mental health counseling to meet the needs that became more evident within society.

1900–1930s

Clinical Mental Health Counseling remains highly influenced from the early development of vocational guidance. Frank Parsons established the Vocational Bureau of Boston in 1908 and published his book *Choosing a Vocation* in 1909. These influences soon led to Harvard University establishing the first college-based counselor education program where select school teachers began receiving training to become vocational counselors. This step officially merged vocational guidance with the educational system. This advanced further to the point that the Smith-Hughes Act of 1917 required funding for public schools to provide vocational education. It was also during this time that Frank Parsons coined the term 'counselors' prior to World War II to distinguish his work between his roles as an attorney (legal counselor) and his work in vocational guidance (Field, 2017).

Soon counseling and guidance also became an important factor with placing new recruits to the U.S. military during World War I, when assessment instruments began evaluating personality traits, abilities, and aptitudes. The use of these instruments transitioned nicely into civilian life after the war, and they continued to provide input into employment procedures. The Trait and Factor Theory of E.G. Williamson grew out of this vocational placement process, and it led to the influential publication of Williamson's (1939) *How to Counsel Students* in 1939.

1940s

The 1940s ushered a new era of humanistic approaches led by Carl Rogers. Rogers deviated from both the labeling and factoring process of vocational guidance, as well as the analyzing and diagnosing procedures of psychoanalysis. Rogers focused on person-centered interactions and supported people through empathy, authenticity, and unconditional positive regard. No doubt these humanistic approaches began influencing the approach of social services to the public. In 1946, the National Institute of Mental Health (NIMH) was established and federal funds were released to explore further ways to support those experiencing mental illness through the National Mental Health Act. (Guindon, 2011).

1950s

In 1952, the first counseling association was established and named the American Personnel and Guidance Association (APGA), and it was instituted with several founding divisions: the National Vocational Guidance Association (NVGA, currently identified as the National Career Development Association [NCDA]), the National Association of Guidance and Counselor Trainers (NAGCT), the Student Personnel Association for Teacher Education (SPATE), and the American College Personnel Association (American Counseling Association, 2018b; Field, 2017). The APGA would later change the title to the American Association for Counseling and Development (AACD) in 1983, and finally to the title American Counseling Association in 1992, as it currently remains (American Counseling Association, 2018a; Field, 2017).

Recognizing the cultural need developing, the American Psychological Association (APA) modified their own Division 17 to be known as the Division of Counseling Psychology in 1952. This change was implemented because "APA members who wanted to work with clients with normal, development concerns rather than with the psychopathological patients treated by clinical psychologists, influenced its formation" (Guindon, 2011, p. 41). Also in 1952, the American Psychiatric Association (APA, 2013) published the first *Diagnostic and Statistical Manual of Mental Disorders* (*DSM*). This marked the origin of the mental health classification system that remains in use more than 65 years later.

Governmental policies continued to reflect the growing acceptance of mental health services in U.S. society. In 1954, The Vocational Rehabilitation Act (VRA) provided funding for training and services for the disabled to receive necessary mental health support. The National Defense Education Act (NDEA) of 1958 then became possibly one of the most significant pieces of legislation of the 1950s. Under NDEA, Title V of the legislation provided increased funding for counseling services in schools and higher education. This quickly led to a boom in school counselor and counselor education programs in the 1960s (Spruill, 1999), and now mental health counseling draws significant origins from this education and school guidance movement.

1960s

By the 1960s, behavioral approaches to counseling joined the previous three psychological theories already widely practiced: psychodynamic (psychoanalysis), directive (trait and factor), and client-centered (Rogerian). In many ways, the approaches to counseling continued to resonate closely with the sister field of psychology regarding theoretical approaches.

Counseling legislation continued to make advancements during this era; the Manpower Development Training Act of 1962 was passed, and counseling and guidance services were established for the disadvantaged and underemployed. This was followed quickly by the Community Mental Health Centers Act of 1963, which proved to be one of the most significant acts that mandated the opening at least 2000 mental health centers to serve people outside educational settings (Guindon, 2011). The Community Mental Health Centers Act in 1963 instituted a wave of new community mental health centers that arose. This provided new job opportunities for NDEA counselors who previously centered around educational settings (Spruill, 1999).

Legislation continued opening the doors for counseling services and in 1964, the NDEA of 1958 was expanded to include counseling services for elementary school students and junior college students. The Secondary Education Act of 1965 redirected a substantial portion of the funding for mental health services to veterans returning from Vietnam, and those with graduate degrees from counselor education programs discovered an increase in job opportunities (Smith & Robinson, 1995). This means that within two years, CMHCs found a tremendous increase in job opportunities both inside and outside schools, and with military veterans.

1970s

Rapid growth and development of the counseling profession led to the sharp increase of CMHCs in the 1970s. During this time, counseling practitioners began using terms like *helping skills* and *basic counseling skills* to fully describe what actually happened under the care of CMHCs (Guindon, 2011). Professional organizations also became more organized and influential in the 1970s, developing branches and organizing systems of service delivery. Such organizations included the Association for Multicultural Counseling and Development (AMCD) in 1972 (previously The Association for Non-White Concerns in Personnel and Guidance), the Association for Specialists in Group Work (ASGW) in 1973, the Association of Spiritual, Ethical, and Religious Values in Counseling (ASERVIC) in 1974 (previously the Association of Religious and Values Issues in Counseling, and originally the National Catholic Guidance Conference) to name a few (ACA, 2018b).

Possibly one of the most notable associations to emerge was the American Mental Health Counselors Association (AMHCA) in 1976, which was established as a non-profit agency with a goal of securing federal funds for counselors working in mental health agencies or a variety of other clinical settings (ACA, 2018b; Field, 2017). AMHCA was first developed in May 1976 when Jim Messina and Nancy Spisso reflected on the lack of professional and organizational representation for CMHCs. This resulted in an article submitted to the *APGA Guidepost* calling for representation for non-school counselors that identified with APGA (Weikel, 1985). Initial efforts to organize as a division of ACA were halted because of some logistical complications. When those complications were resolved, AMHCA began the process of merging under the auspices of ACA, which was finally approved in 1978 (American Counseling Association, 2018b; Field, 2017).

Smith and Robinson (1995) described how the convergence of AMHCA and ACA was met with some challenges over the years. While AMHCA remained focused on pointed agendas with professional standards, professional acknowledgment, moving appropriate legislation, and reimbursement by third-party providers, the ACA agenda was sometimes more broadly focused. AMHCA has continued to exist with mutual respect and collaboration with other divisions, which is likely related to the fact that many members often are affiliated also with other divisions.

Advances in the profession continued to occur, with Virginia becoming the first state to license CMHCs as Licensed Professional Counselors in 1976, followed shortly by Arkansas and Alabama (Guindon, 2011). The APGA empowered a licensure committee to work closely with a state licensure committee, which resulted in this successful Virginia license approval. It is noteworthy that California's Marriage, Family, and Child Counseling licensure law of 1964 was authorized as a ground-breaking achievement prior to the existence of the APGA, and they later became the last state to license CMHCs in the same manner (Bloom et al., 1990).

AMHCA leadership continued working to advance their identity as a counseling profession (Kline, 1999), and they collaborated with the Association for Counselor Education and Supervision (ACES) to form a Joint Committee on Education and Training for Mental Health Counselors in 1978. This quickly led to the formation of the National Academy of Certified Clinical Mental Health Counselors (NACCMHC) in 1979, in order to develop a competency-based system that identified semester hours and requirements. This move quickly led to the publication of the *Ideal Training Standards for Mental Health Counselors* by Messina and Seiler (1981; Smith and Robinson 1995). Due to financial challenges, the NACCMHC would later be subsumed under the National Board for Certified Counselors (NBCC) in 1993 (Field, 2017).

1980s

Professional development and multicultural inclusion continued to expand throughout the 1980s. In 1981, the APGA formed the National Board of Certified Counselors (NBCC), which began administering the National Counselor Examination (NCE) as a competency standard for assessing CMHCs. NBCC also began administering the National Mental Health Counseling Exam (NMHCE) as another form of competency assessment. The Council for Accreditation of Counseling and Related Educational Programs (CACREP, 2016) was also established in 1981 with a purpose of accrediting counseling programs under a set of standards that would distinguish the profession. These standards were developed and established by the ACES (Field, 2017).

Due to the rapid changes in professional development, the APGA changed its name to the American Association for Counseling and Development (AACD) in 1983. In 1985, Chi Sigma Iota (CSI) became the counseling honor society in higher education. Then in 1986, the National Institute of Mental Health (NIMH) added CMHCs to their list of professionals, alongside psychiatrists, psychologists, social workers, and psychiatric nurses. The desired standards for counselor educators to prepare students for mental health counseling also was established formally by CACREP in 1988 (Smith & Robinson, 1995).

1990s

The 1990s introduced a time of greater development, with many new divisions becoming established and reflecting the deepening expanse of the counseling profession. CMHCs continued to expand their influence throughout the world, beginning with additional divisions and areas of specialty within ACA and other counseling organizations.

In 1992, the AACD (formerly the APGA) changed the name of the organization again to the American Counseling Association (ACA) in order to better reflect the identity of its members. In 1993, the National Academy merged with NBCC to combine their efforts toward a common certification for CMHCs, later known as the National Certified Counselor (NCC) credential (Smith & Robinson, 1995).

The U.S. government later passed the Health Insurance Portability and Accountability Act of 1996 (HIPAA, U.S. Government Printing Office, 2018) in an effort to preserve and protect the confidentiality of client information with health care professionals, including the records and information managed by CMHCs during times of service. This standard quickly became an essential law for all CMHCs to know intricately, especially in light of the highly personal content discussed within the counseling room. Many CMHCs are required to maintain HIPAA compliance with regular or annual training through their organizations or agencies.

2000s

Field (2017) highlighted some key areas of recognition with the federal agencies regarding mental health services throughout the early 2000s, and CMHCs continued to gain increased recognition by the federal government. Three main areas of recognition included TRICARE, Veterans Affairs, and Medicare. ACA and AMCHA have continued to promote the advancement of counseling expertise among the helping professions in relation to health care, as evidenced by finally achieving parity with social workers with the Department of Veterans Affairs in 2006. Field (2017) reported that, while AMHCA and CACREP have maintained a mutually respectful working relationship from the mid-1980s through 2009, AMHCA has continued urging CACREP to establish more rigorous standards for CMHCs.

ACA also began a professional advocacy effort known as 20/20 in 2005, which served to identify and communicate a common understanding of the goals and purpose of the counseling profession across the membership. This led to the formal definition determined at the 2010 ACA conference: "Counseling is a professional relationship that empowers diverse individuals, families, and groups to accomplish mental health, wellness, education, and career goals" (Guindon, 2011, p. 46).

2010s

As previously mentioned, the last state to institute counselor licensure was the state of California, which approved counseling licensure in 2010 (Field, 2017). After 34 years of advocating for licensure, with the state of Virginia passing the law in 1976, the counseling profession was officially recognized with the opportunity for professional licensure throughout all of the United States.

Political factors began making mental health counseling more available to the average consumer. CMHCs gained valuable recognition with the Patient Protection and Affordable Care Act (PPACA) in 2010, which made counseling available to everyone. Services from CMHC professionals soon became reimbursable by TRICARE in 2014, which was the insurance benefit for active and reserve military. Medicare reimbursement for CMHCs now has become one of the strongest focal points of legislative efforts for AMHCA and the counseling profession as a whole (Field, 2017).

International Counseling Development

The development and growth of counseling were not confined to the United States. The professional background remains different between countries as one might expect, even evident with a different English spelling of "counselling" that is commonly seen outside the United States. Many similarities also existed, as mental health counseling throughout the world became part of the movement to enhance human rights and necessary services after World War II (Perron, 2015). Never had there been such an overwhelming international response reflected with both military campaigns and humanitarian efforts than during this period (American Psychiatric Association, 2006). The importance of international counseling efforts and activity have continued to advance throughout the literature since that time (Gerstein, Heppner, Stockton, Leung, and Ægisdóttir, 2009; Hoskins & Thompson, 2009; Ng, Choudhuri, Noonan, & Ceballos, 2012; Ng & Noonan, 2012). The 1990s ushered in a time when nongovernmental organizations began recognizing the need for counseling services in response to disaster relief efforts around the world (Hinkle, 2014). Even though the United States had become internationally involved in health and relief issues since the 1940s, this period exhibited a greater focus on mental health support (Pape, 2012, Perron, 2015).

International Association for Counselling (IAC). A significant contribution to mental health counseling internationally could be attributed to the work of Hans Hoxter, known for his extraordinary contributions as a counselor, teacher, mentor, leader, and colleague (Borgen, 2003). In many respects, he rightly could be known most as the *father of international counselling* through his efforts in founding two professional organizations known as the International Association for Educational and Vocational Guidance and the International Round Table for the Advancement of Counselling (IRTAC, Borgen, 2003).

Initially working as a banker in Germany, Hoxter fled the Nazi regime and moved to England, where he quickly began serving the refugee groups affected by World War II (Borgen, 2003). In 1951, Hoxter founded the International Association for Educational and Vocational Guidance with the assistance of UNICEF in an effort to support individuals working to recover from the devastating impact of war. Recognizing that the needs of young people and adults extended far beyond vocational guidance, Hoxter soon recognized the importance of advancing his knowledge in counseling, and he studied concepts of psychology and counseling further, even under the well-known theorist, Jean Piaget (Borgen, 2003).

While counseling was continuing to develop in the United States, the growing interest in counseling concepts began advancing throughout the world in the 1960s. The International Round Table for the Advancement of Counselling (IRTAC) was initiated in 1966 with the first seminar held at the University of Neuchâtel, Switzerland. The purpose of this first seminar was to bring together the many people interested in counseling, guidance, and counselor education in one common place among countries. The annual conferences began taking the place of the seminars since 1966, and those attending continue to represent a variety of countries. Over 30 conferences have been held in more than 20 different countries. The Executive Committee of IRTAC decided to change its name to the International Association for Counselling (International Association for Counselling, 2018b) in 1997, because Hoxter decided the field had shifted significantly enough to change the name of IRTAC. IAC has reported the influence it continues to yield throughout the world (International Association for Counselling, 2018b), maintaining membership from over 94 different countries, and holding annual conferences with a conglomerate of helping professionals. Hoxter "worked to develop IRTAC into an International Non-governmental Organization that gained consultative status with the United Nations, ECOSOC [Economic and Social Council], UNICEF [United Nations International Children's Emergency Fund], UNESCO [The United Nations Educational, Scientific and Cultural Organization], ILO [International Labour Organization], and the Council of Europe" (Borgen, 2003, p. 86). If this was not enough, he continued advocating for the profession and also helped to establish the British Association for Counselling and Psychotherapy (BACP) and the European Association for Counselling (EAU, Borgen, 2003).

From the first conference in 1966, Borgen (2003) described the vision of the working groups that has continued to distinguish the collaborative nature at IAC conferences. Working groups became the central focus of the conferences, where counseling professionals would come to engage in greater depth of conversation to address life issues among the people they serve. At the IAC annual conference in Rome, Italy in September 2018, the CEO of IAC, Naoise Kelley, reported that representatives from counseling associations around the world participated in an annual "Associations Round Table" gathering, whose participants represented nearly 170,000 counseling professionals throughout the world. (N. Kelly, personal communication, September

23, 2018). Clearly the nature of this grassroots movement has continued to thrive, but still with much work to be accomplished.

WHO and NBCC-I. In the early 2000s, The World Health Organization (WHO) began collaborating with NBCC with an intention to address the concerns of mental illness across the globe as a human rights issue (Perron, 2015). This collaboration led to further development and resources for supporting the need that existed globally, and out of this effort the international division of NBCC was soon founded in November 2003 as NBCC-International (NBCC-I, Schweiger, 2005).

The WHO reported that one in four people around the globe will not only experience psychological distress, but also meet criteria for a diagnosable mental disorder at some point in their lives (Hinkle, 2014; WHO, 2005). The WHO estimated that more than 450 million people worldwide with mental health problems live without access to adequate services to address the needs (Hinkle, 2014; WHO, 2001). As a result of these startling numbers, the WHO (2005) produced the "Mental Health Atlas" to better understand the global shortage of mental health professionals, and it proved to be critical (Hinkle, 2014). The distribution of mental health resources was determined to be inequitably distributed throughout the world, with countries of lower socioeconomic status receiving far less mental health resources than wealthier countries (Hinkle, 2014; World Health Organization, 2005). The WHO soon created an action plan to address the concerns that became evident:

> The vision of the action plan is a world in which mental health is valued and promoted, mental disorders are prevented and persons affected by these disorders are able to exercise the full range of human rights and to access high-quality, culturally-appropriate health and social care in a timely way.
>
> (World Health Organization, 2013, pp. 5–6)

After NBCC created NBCC-I in 2003, the organization initiated the Mental Health Facilitator (MHF) program to offer adequate training to address mental health issues (Hinkle, 2014). This program was created to maintain the values of advocacy for mental health services, along with adequate training for lay providers of mental healthcare in local communities throughout the world where professional services were lacking. Hinkle (2014) explained:

> MHF training includes numerous topics such as basic helping skills, coping with stress, and community mental health services. The program consists of fundamental, integrated mental health knowledge and skills ranging from community advocacy and commitment, to specified interventions such as suicide mitigation.
>
> (p. 9)

The MHF program was taught for the first time in Lilongwe, Malawi in 2008, and NBCC-I has now proudly been able to report that more than 2750 MHFs, trainers, and master trainers throughout the world have taught the MHF program in 26 different countries.

There is little doubt that mental health counseling continues to make advances throughout the world, in ways that have not yet been recognized. Perron and Tollerud (2017) conducted a study of international counseling students studying in the United States, and observed that CMHC across the globe is beginning to make an impact as a result of ongoing origins in educational systems, a willingness to value collectivism (or cultural perspectives in general), and a willingness to remain open to counseling approaches (i.e., directiveness, harmony, psychoeducation). This willingness of the counseling profession must remain flexible and open to adaptation depending on cultural contexts and expectations.

Ongoing Efforts

Still much work needs to be done to strengthen the impact of clinical mental health counseling in an ever-changing world. In the United States, Bloom et al. (1990) emphasized the need to reconcile the whims of 50 state legislatures with creating the licensing laws that identify the mental health counseling profession. While maintaining the foundation of supporting individuals in life circumstances remains the same, the needs that CMHCs must be prepared to address continue to change.

Ongoing debate continues regarding the necessary standards for counseling online (Mallen & Vogel, 2005). This raises questions about how to regulate adequate training, the opportunities for underserved populations, and facility responsibilities (Mallen & Vogel, 2005). Other future trends that remain evident at conferences include portability of the counseling license throughout different states in the United States, neuroscience, technology (i.e., artificial intelligence), online and tele-mental health care, international advocacy, federal reimbursement for Medicare in the United States, multicultural competency, and advocacy for professional recognition across the world (American Counseling Association, 2018b). Trends around the globe include support for refugees and immigrants, school counseling, trauma counseling, serving disadvantaged populations, and many others (International Association for Counselling, 2018a).

Theories and Models in Clinical Mental Health Counseling

Clinical mental health counseling shares a valuable and historical relationship with the fields of psychology, education, and social advocacy. Many of the core theoretical models of approaching individuals, couples, and families are shared, and a commitment to evidence-based practice will necessitate a continued application of core theories from counseling and psychology in particular. While sharing a mutual commitment to improving the mental and psychological health of people that are served, CMHC maintains some distinct characteristics that set it apart with various areas of understanding the nature of support and interaction.

CMHC Identity

The importance of developing a counselor identity has continued to be reinforced since the Community Mental Health Centers Act of 1963 was passed, because this event initiated an influx of counseling practitioners that lacked professional licensure and professional representation. Another milestone in counselor identity might be considered the formation of AMHCA in 1978, which emerged from a grassroots effort to infuse mental health into the health care industry (Pistole, 2001). The establishment of CACREP in 1981 confirmed the importance of maintaining a standard that counselors be trained with an intentional professional identity in mind (Field, 2017). These milestones in forming the CMHC identity in the United States remain evident in the professional dialogue, and they play a major role in how theories and models are expressed within the profession.

CMHCs adopt a philosophy that is more focused on strengths and wellness as opposed to the clinical pathology or mental illness (Pistole, 2001). CMHCs have their origin in mental health community centers as a contributing member of a health care team (Pistole, 2001). This hallmark of collaboration has intrinsically established a sense of flexibility and openness to integrative care alongside the other helping professions. As a practitioner-oriented profession, CMHCs not only have established standards of practice identified through CACREP (Council for Accreditation of Counseling and Related Educational Programs, 2016; Pistole, 2001), but they also share common codes of ethics (American Counseling Association, 2014) by which they are expected to adhere.

Pistole (2001) defined the unique identities of CMHCs as professionals, offering care that is focused on individuals and families from a holistic, developmental, and contextual perspective. This means recognizing their ontological makeup as a physical, emotional, mental, social, and spiritual person. Individuals experience each of these holistic realities in different ways depending on their own developmental level. This will all be impacted by the contextual factors influenced by family of origin, community, government, race, ethnicity, religion, resources available, and socioeconomic status (Pistole, 2001).

Smith and Robinson (1995) emphasized that while many mental health services focus on illness or something that is "wrong" with them, CMHCs focus on the wellness an individual can achieve. Even if one is not experiencing difficulty, CMHCs adhere to the belief that counseling can generally improve the quality of life for anyone willing to engage the process. CMHCs emphasize the ability to provide care that is preventative, developmental, and educational, enhancing one's quality of health through the development of skills and awareness (Smith & Robinson, 1995). These traits are what distinguish CMHC from fields that adopt a more medical model approach and focus more heavily on diagnosis and treating mental illness (Spruill, 1999).

Training in Theories

When training CMHCs how to recognize and adopt theoretical foundations, counselor educators offer exposure to the same core theories that many other mental health professionals encounter. Fall, Holden, and Marquis (2010) describe how theoretical models of counseling help the developing CMHC address a number of different questions about the human condition. The core areas they advise students to determine is related to their views of human nature, the role (or influence) of the environment in personal development, the model of functionality, the view of personality changes.

Exposure to the core theories of counseling remains a matter of great importance in order to build the necessary skills and perspectives as a CMHC. Fall et al. (2010) identified 12 core theoretical categories that represent typical theoretical approaches to counseling, including: (a) Classical psychoanalysis, (b) Self psychology, (c) Adlerian counseling- Individual psychology, (d) Existential counseling, (e) Person-centered counseling, (f) Gestalt counseling, (g) Behavioral counseling, (h) Cognitive counseling, (i) Rational Emotive Behavioral theory (REBT), (j) Reality theory/Choice theory, (k) Constructivist approaches, and (l) Systems approaches. Corey (2013) similarly promoted nine categories of theories to consider within mental health counseling, which included: (a) Psychoanalytic therapy, (b) Adlerian therapy, (c) Existential therapy, (d) Person-centered therapy, (e) Gestalt therapy, (f) Reality therapy, (g) Behavior therapy, (h) Cognitive-behavior therapy, and (i) Family systems therapy.

Fall et al. (2010) were careful to note, "Identification of a guiding theory is not a single decision but, rather, is an ongoing process involving several steps or stages" (p. 11). Watts (1993) described a process upon which all developing counselors must embark in developing their theoretical focus. The stages progressed from the exploring stage, to the examination stage, to the integration phase, and finally to the personalization phase. Integration and personalization are not likely to occur in a counselor education program, but once CMHCs advance into professional practice and gain necessary experience of helping others (Watts, 1993).

Through the process of theory development among counselors, Corey (2013) reflected the general perspective that counseling professionals are most effective when they remain *authentic* and *therapeutic*. This means they are closely attuned to their own needs, style, and tendencies, and they work to support the needs of the client with openness, careful and thoughtful interactions, and mutual commitment.

Counseling Theory Research

While knowledge and application of theories remain highly important among CMHCs, it is important to note that theoretical language does not necessarily define the significance of what happens in the counseling room. Kaplan et al. (2014) researched the definition of counseling in order to establish clear principles for unifying and strengthening the profession. While the study did not target theories specifically, it provided a venue from which theoretical emphasis or identification could have emerged as a top priority of CMHC identity.

Kaplan et al. (2014) used the Delphi method to research the most commonly held definition of mental health counseling. The Delphi method was created in the 1940s to capture "expert opinions about complex issues or problems for which there are no verifiable, evidenced-based solutions" (Kaplan et al., 2014, p. 93). In the research process, *wellness*, *empower*, and *professional* were the top characteristics highlighted among the counseling professionals participating in the research study (Kaplan et al., 2014). *Lifespan* and *relationship* became included in the top five characteristics, and they were also used to develop a definition of counseling through multiple working groups. The final product accepted and adopted by the majority of participants resulted in the following definition: "Counseling is a professional relationship that empowers diverse individuals, families, and groups to accomplish mental health, wellness, education, and career goals" (Kaplan et al., 2014, p. 92). This definition was soon endorsed by 29 of the 31 professional organizations working on the project to identify the working definition.

Barth and Moody (2018) also conducted a study with 140 members of AMHCA to investigate the theoretical approaches that most influenced CMHCs current practice, and which skills were most often used. The study yielded a list of the most influential theories, which were ranked in the following order (from highest influence to lowest): (a) CBT, (b) Person-centered, (c) Strengths-based, and (d) Solution-focused. Because the study also found that CMHCs largely reported an integrative approach by using more than one theory in their practice, Barth and Moody recommended that further studies explore how counselors make decisions from shifting from one theory to another in practice.

Impact on the Individual, Family, and Community

CMHCs impact individuals, families, and communities by offering services in a variety of support settings. Much like other associations, ACA provides members with a list of available job opportunities through their website. There currently were 27 different categories listed for the types of job opportunities available for individuals seeking work as a CMHC (American Counseling Association, 2018a). Ten of the most common settings from this list of CMHC jobs included: (a) Advocacy/Non-profit, (b) College/University, (c) Community health center/Community clinic, (d) Government, (e) HMO, (f) Hospice, (g) Hospital (public or private), (h) Office of health care practitioners (group practice), (i) Pre-K-12 School, and (j) Private practice (American Counseling Association, 2018a).

Each of these settings represents areas that impact people at every level of service. NIMH (2018) reported that mental illness remains highly prevalent in the United States. Nearly one in five individuals experience a form of mental illness (44.7 million in 2016). The necessary care for providing for individuals related to the level of severity experienced by the individual or family. The WHO listed a variety of risk and protective factors that can affect the quality of life for individuals, and the quality of interaction with families (Ritchie & Roser, 2018). Ritchie and Roser (2018) reported for the WHO about how careful attention must go to: (a) individual attributes or behaviors, (b) social and economic circumstances, and (c) environmental factors that will influence mental health. CMHCs have the opportunity to engage individuals, families, and communities through a variety of the settings listed, and to foster the development of greater protective measures that will help people improve their mental health and quality of life.

Clinical Mental Health Counseling Practices

Counseling practices are not bound by theoretical assumptions as one might think, although theories certainly play an important role. Regardless of one's theory, the progression of skills outlined by Ivey, Ivey, and Zalaquett (2010) has become widely recognized as the premier description of basic counseling skills development. Ivey et al. utilized the terms *interviewing*, *counseling*, and *psychotherapy* to communicate similar concepts for counseling professionals to acquire. Ivey et al. believed that effective counseling interactions require accurate information (interviewing) and supportive therapeutic relationships (counseling), in order for psychological change to occur (psychotherapy).

Ivey et al. (2010) depicted counseling skill development through a pyramid model known as "the microskills hierarchy" (p. 15). This pyramid, conceptualized in Table 11.1, demonstrated a progression of skill development through which all counseling professionals must advance in order to provide competent and professional support to those receiving services. The foundation of the pyramid model highlighted *professional competence* at the base, including ethical and multicultural competence, with a focus on wellness. From there a basic focus on *attending behaviors* provided a counselor with the opportunity to engage the client with non-verbal actions and behaviors that emphasized the value of the individual or people. Such attending skills included eye contact, vocal qualities, verbal tracking, and body language.

Listening skills could be summarized as the next level to acquire in the microskills hierarchy. Listening included open and closed questions, client observation skills, encouraging, paraphrasing, summarizing, and reflecting feelings. Ivey et al. (2010) identified the next level in the hierarchy as *interviewing skills*, which were described with a five-step process for gathering information in a way that supports openness and an authentic relationship. The information from proper interviewing served as the basis for developing the interaction at a deeper level, and *action skills* made up the next level of interaction. This level built on the previous skills to essentially

Table 11.1 Ivey, Ivey, & Zalaquett's Microskills Hierarchy

Skill Level Progression	Description
Professional competence	Ethics, Multicultural competence, Wellness
Attending behaviors	Eye contact, Vocal qualities, Verbal tracking, Body language
Listening skills	Open and closed questions, Client observation skills, Encouraging, Paraphrasing, and Summarizing
Interviewing skills	Five stages: 1) Relationship, 2) Story and strengths, 3) Goals, 4) Restory, and 5) Action
Action skills	Confrontation, Focusing, Reflection of meaning and interpretation, and Reframing
Influencing skills	Self-disclosure, logical consequences, Information/ Psychoeducation, Directives
Skill integration	Integrating various skills, approaches, and perspectives based on different guiding theories of counseling, and based on different situations and experiences, and based on different cultural groups and contextual norms
Personal style and theory	Recognizing the influence of style, personality, experiences, beliefs, and perspectives that influence one's personal style of interaction; more extensive integration of theoretical concepts that combine with this style

Adapted form of the "microskills hierarchy" pyramid in Ivey, Ivey, & Zalaquett (2010), p. 15.

enhance client awareness of their situation through a collection of skills including confrontation, focusing, reflection of meaning, interpretation, and reframing.

The counselor builds further on this self-awareness by advancing to *influencing skills*, which include feedback, self-disclosure, logical consequences, information/psychoeducation, and directives. While each of the previous levels may be influenced by one's theoretical position on counseling approaches, the next level of *skill integration* is overtly focused on applying counseling theory based on the previous skilled approaches. The final area of development among counselors would be to determine one's *personal style and theory*.

The nature of the counseling skills exercised in any counseling interaction will build on more foundational skills that help support the professional relationship. While Sommers-Flannagan and Sommers-Flannagan (2015) promoted essentially the same sequence of skill development as Ivey et al. (2005), they also highlighted a number of different ways in which counseling and interviewing skills may be required to function. Some unique interactions included how one may be approaching someone with an intake interview, a mental status examination, a suicide assessment, diagnosis and treatment procedures, and with interviewing special populations in specific situations. This may include cross-cultural interactions, challenging clients, crisis situations, young clients, couples and families, and now even online or non-face-to-face settings (Sommers-Flannagan & Sommers-Flannagan, 2015).

SIDEBAR 11.1

In Practice: What Would You Do?

Juan is a licensed counselor who has managed his own private practice for the past five years. Juan specializes in depression and anxiety management, anger management, trauma recovery, and family issues, seeing adults, children and adolescents, and even couples. Juan does his own screening when setting up counseling appointments with new clients, as he wants to make sure he is a good fit for anyone coming for services.

> Mark is a 36-year-old Caucasian male who called and sets up an appointment with me, initially to deal with life transition difficulties. The initial screening convinced me this counseling relationship will be a good fit because Mark reported difficulty managing his anxiety with family conflict in general. In the first session, Mark revealed a bit more detail, making it clear he did not want to go to counseling, but it was required in order for him to leave an inpatient psychiatric unit. Mark reported that he had a suicide attempt because his wife wants to leave him. He is now tentatively back at home with his wife and two young kids since being discharged two days ago. Mark wants me to tell him how to approach his wife, and what decisions to make about his marriage. He admits to having a drinking problem, but that he loves his wife and kids a great deal.

Class Discussion

1. Based on the skills described by Ivey, Ivey, and Zalaquett (2010), how might Juan respond to Mark's request for direct answers?
2. What concerns might Juan want to address before moving forward in the relationship?
3. What skills may be necessary for supporting Mark with a therapeutic response?
4. What other resources may be necessary for supporting Mark beyond the session?

Theory and Practice

Within the study of a guiding theory, Barth and Moody (2018) also identified the most frequently used counseling practice skills. The skills identified among the 140 CMHC participants included: (a) demonstrating empathic understanding, (b) general encouraging, (c) encouraging self-care, (d) conveying genuineness, and (e) demonstrating unconditional positive regard. When reflecting on the developmental chart proposed by Ivey et al. (2005), these practices indicate a commitment to foundational concepts in order to support clients most effectively.

An international study by Perron, Tollerud, and Fischer (2016) further revealed the application of CMHC practices by evaluating how counseling professionals rank the most important traits of counseling professionals. Participants in the study, with expertise in counseling across the globe, expressed the highest value with counseling traits that could be summarized as: (a) the value of people, (b) personal character and development (of the counselor), and (c) multicultural intentionality. The highest trait counseling professionals identified overall was overwhelmingly identified by leaders in the field of international counseling as "Respect and preserve the dignity of all people" (Perron et al., 2016, p. 165). The top 12 out of 77 traits were able to be categorized overall as respect, self-awareness, people-focus, and culture.

While these practices are noteworthy for helping to formulate best practices, the nature of counseling practices change frequently depending on a variety of factors. The profession must remain active and vigilant with engaging the work reflective of the core values of the profession. These include a focus on wellness, holistic awareness, collaboration, and many other qualities that will help propel the CMHC profession into greater use throughout the world.

Appraisal and Diagnosis

Appraisal is a specific set of skills. Refer back to "Assessment and Testing" in Chapter 5 for more general information. Helping professionals must first and foremost identify mental health issues. Although not all clients have diagnosable disorders, all do have presenting concerns that the counselor must document. They can then select appropriate treatment goals and implement interventions that are most likely to be effective. When the counselor sets goals it is often called treatment planning, or action planning.

Human beings are not static. One issue may resolve and another may be presented to the counselor. Therefore, appraisal of the client's progress and current state is on ongoing activity and strategies are revised when needed.

CMHCs must be able to recognize mental conditions. In the United States, the *DSM* (American Psychiatric Association, 2013) is the categorical classification system used to make a diagnosis and identify different psychopathological disorders. Since the first version published in 1952, the *DSM* has undergone multiple iterations. The current 5th edition of the *DSM* is described as "a classification of mental disorders with associated criteria designed to facilitate more reliable diagnoses of these disorders" (American Psychiatric Association, 2013, p. xli). It recognizes "that mental disorders do not always fit completely within the boundaries of a single disorder" (p. xli). Cross-cutting symptom measures draw attention to symptoms that are important across diagnoses. Because of the possibility of mental disorder, counselors are trained in the use of the *DSM* even when their responsibility does not formally include diagnosis. Counselors must be able to identify disorders and recognize factors contributing to and maintaining problems. They must know when to refer to other mental health professionals if they are not qualified to diagnose or treat a disorder.

The *DSM-5* is organized on developmental and lifespan considerations and recognizes that diagnoses must also consider cultural issues. "Cultural meanings, habits, and traditions can also contribute to either stigma or support in the social and familial response to mental illness" (p. 14). Nevertheless, the *DSM* is not without controversy. Counselors must reconcile the difference in the philosophical stance of professional counseling with a need for assessment and diagnosis. Diagnosis and appraisal remain an important responsibility with which CMHCs must practice with competence.

Summary

This chapter offers a description of the development of Clinical Mental Health Counseling (CMHC) and the changes that have occurred over the course of its history. While some may be tempted to consider the origin of counseling as a by-product of psychology, history shows a much broader contribution from a variety of disciplines, including education, vocational guidance, and social reform. The development of CMHC professional identity was described with regard to key legislative progress over the past 50 years, societal needs that became satisfied through CMHC intervention, and the expansion of CMHC professional organizations.

CMHC practices continue to advance through developments in theory, skills, education, and practical intervention. CMHC values often are identified through approaches that are well-ness oriented, strengths based, holistic, developmental, preventative, and contextual. CMHCs receive extensive training in traditional counseling and psychology theories, which are crucial for supporting mental health, applying accurate concepts of appraisal and diagnosis, and supplementing the counselor identity promoted within the profession. CMHCs contribute to enhancing the quality of life among individuals, young people, couples, and families throughout the world in many settings, including educational settings, health care settings, private practices, and a variety of other settings that would require mental health expertise.

Many advances continue to offer a promising future for the CMHC profession. International counseling efforts reflect the expanse of the profession around the globe (International Association for Counselling, 2018b). New opportunities for integration and collaboration are becoming available to the CMHC profession regularly, and exciting new avenues of practice and research are emerging through specialties like neuroscience, technology, artificial intelligence, online and tele-mental health care, multicultural support and advocacy, and many others.

> *Without you, I might not have found me.*
>
> – outpatient client to his clinical mental health counselor

References

American Counseling Association. (2014). *ACA code of ethics*. Alexandria, VA: Author.

American Counseling Association. (2018a). *ACA career central*. Retrieved from https://careers.counselin g.org/jobs/browse

American Counseling Association. (2018b). *ACA conference and expo education sessions*. Retrieved from https://www.counseling.org/conference/past-conferences/atlanta-2018/sessions-events/education-sessions

American Psychiatric Association. (2013). *Diagnostic and statistical manual of mental disorders* (5th ed.). Washington, DC: Author.

American Psychological Association. (2006). APA's response to international and national disasters and crises: Addressing diverse needs. 2005 annual report of the APA Policy and Planning Board. *American Psychologist*, 61(5), 513–521. doi:10.1037/0003-066X.61.5.513

Barth, A.L, & Moody, S.J. (2018). Theory use in counseling practice: Current trends. *International Journal for the Advancement of Counselling*. doi:10.1007/s10447-018-9352-0

Bloom, J., Gerstein, L., Tarvydas, V., Conaster, J., Davis, E., Kater, D., Sherrard, P., & Esposito, R. (1990). Model legislation for licensed professional counselors. *Journal of Counseling and Development*, 68, 511–523.

Borgen, W.A. (2003). Remembering Hans: His ongoing legacy for guidance and counselling. *International Journal for the Advancement of Counselling*, 25(2/3), 83–89.

Brooks, D.K., & Weikel, W.J. (1986). Mental health counseling in an historical perspective. In W.J. Weikel & A.J. Palmo (Eds.), *Foundations of mental health counseling* (pp. 5–28). Springfield, IL: Charles C Thomas.

Corey, G. (2013). *Theory and practice of counseling and psychotherapy* (9th ed.). Pacific Grove, CA: Brooks/Cole.

Council for Accreditation of Counseling and Related Educational Programs. (2016). *2016 CACREP standards*. Alexandria, VA: Author.

Fall, K.A., Holden, J.M., & Marquis, A. (2010). *Theoretical models of counseling and psychotherapy* (2nd ed.). New York: Routledge.

Field, T.A. (2017). Clinical mental health counseling: A 40-year retrospective. *Journal of Mental Health Counseling*, 49(1), 1–11.

Gerstein, L.H., Heppner, P.P., Stockton, R., Leoung, F.T.L., and Ægisdóttir, S. (2009). The counseling profession in and outside the United States. L.H. Gerstein, P.P. Heppner, S. Ægisdóttir, S.A. Leung, and K.L. Norsworthy (Eds.). *International handbook of cross-cultural counseling: Cultural assumptions and practices worldwide* (pp. 53–61.). Thousand Oaks, CA: Sage.

Guindon, M.H. (2011). What? Answers about the definition of counseling, its past, and its present. In M.H. Guindon (Ed.). *A counseling primer: An introduction of the profession* (pp. 35–47). New York: Routledge.

Hinkle, J.S. (2014). Population-based mental health facilitation (MHF): A grassroots strategy that works. *The Professional Counselor*, 4(1), 1–18.

Hoskins, W.J., & Thompson, H.C. (2009, March). *Promoting international counseling identity: The role of collaboration, research, and training.* Paper based on a program presented at the American Counseling Association Annual Conference and Exposition, Charlotte, NC.

International Association for Counselling. (2018a). *IAC conference general program*. Retrieved from http://eventi.continuandoacrescere.com/index.php/en/program

International Association for Counselling. (2018b). *History of IAC*. Retrieved from https://www.iac-irtac.org/?q=history-of-iac

Ivey, A.E, Ivey, M.B., & Zalaquett, C.P. (2010). *Intentional interviewing and counseling* (7th ed.). Belmont, CA: Brooks/Cole.

Kaplan, D.M., Tarvydas, V.M., & Gladding, S.T. (2014). 20/20: A vision for the future of counseling: The new consensus definition of counseling. *Journal of Counseling & Development*, 92, 366–372.

Kline, W.B. (1999). The evolution of mental health counseling as a core mental health provider: Definition and identity. In S. Hinkle (Ed.). *Promoting optimum mental health through counseling: An overview* (pp. 15–18). Greensboro, NC: ERIC.

Mallen, M.J., & Vogel, D.L. (2005). Online counseling: A need for discovery. *The Counseling Psychologist*, 33(6). doi:10.1177/0011000005280182

Messina, J.J., & Seiler, G. (1981). *Ideal training standards for mental health counselors*. Tampa, FL: Advanced Development Systems.

National Institute of Mental Health. (2018). *Mental illness*. Retrieved from https://www.nimh.nih.gov/health/statistics/mental-illness.shtml

Ng, K.M., Choudhuri, D.D., Noonan, B.M., & Ceballos, P. (2012). An internationalization competency checklist for American counseling training programs. *International Journal for the Advancement of Counselling*, 34(1), 19–38.

Ng, K.M., & Noonan, B.M. (2012). Internationalization of the counseling profession: Meaning, scope and concerns. *International Journal for the Advancement of Counselling*, 34(1), 5–18.

Pape, R.A. (2012). When duty calls: A pragmatic standard of humanitarian intervention. *International Security*, 37(1), 41–80.

Perron, N.C.D. (2015). International counseling traits: Identifying counseling traits ranked most important by international counseling professionals through Q sort analysis (Doctoral dissertation). Retrieved from ProQuest. (12245).

Perron, N.C.D., & Tollerud, T.R. (2017). International counseling insights: A qualitative study exploring the perspectives of international counseling students. *Journal of Counseling in Illinois*, 4(1), 56–73.

Perron, N.C.D., Tollerud, T.R., & Fischer, T.A. (2016). International counseling traits: Identifying counseling traits ranked most important by international counseling professionals through Q sort analysis. *International Journal for the Advancement of Counselling*, 38(2): 159–176.

Pistole, M.C. (2001, December). Mental health counseling: Identity and distinctiveness. *ERIC Digest*, 1–6.

Ritchie, H., & Roser, M. (2018). *Mental health*. Published online at OurWorldInData.org. Retrieved from https://ourworldindata.org/mental-health

Schweiger, W. (2005). NBCC international. *The National Certified Counselor*, 21(2), 1–12.

Smith, H.B., & Robinson, G.P. (1995). Mental health counseling: Past, present, and future. *Journal of Counseling and Development*, 74. 158–162.

Sommers-Flannagan, J., & Sommers-Flannagan, R. (2015). *Clinical interviewing* (5th ed.). Hoboken, NJ: Wiley.

Spruill, D.A. (1999). Definition of mental health counseling: What is it? In J.S. Hinkle (Ed.), *Promoting optimum mental health through counseling: An overview* (pp. 9–13). Greensboro, NC: ERIC.

U.S. Government Printing Office. (2018). *H. Rept. 104–736 – Health Insurance Portability and Accountability Act of 1996*. Washington, DC: Author. Retrieved from https://www.gpo.gov/fdsys/search/pagedetails. action?granuleId=CRPT-104hrpt736&packageId=CRPT-104hrpt736

Watts, R.E. (1993). Developing a personal theory of counseling. *Texas Counseling Association Journal*, 21, 103–104.

Weikel, W.J. (1985). The American Mental Health Counselors Association. *Journal of Counseling and Development*, 63, 457–460.

Williamson, E.G. (1939). *How to counsel students*. New York: McGraw-Hill.

World Health Organization. (2001). *World health report*. Geneva: Author.

World Health Organization. (2005). *Mental health atlas*. Geneva: Author. Retrieved from http://www.who. int/mental_health/evidence/atlas/global_results.pdf

World Health Organization. (2013, January). *Draft comprehensive mental health action plan 2013–2020*. Geneva: Author. Retrieved from http://www.who.int/mental_health/mhgap/consultation_global_m h_action_plan_2013_2020/en/index.html

World Health Organization. (2017). *2017 Mental health atlas*. Geneva: World Health Organization. Retrieved from http://apps.who.int/iris/bitstream/handle/10665/272735/9789241514019-eng.pdf?ua=1

Chapter 12

Clinical Rehabilitation Counseling

Brandon Hunt

> *I dwell in possibility.*
>
> — Emily Dickinson

POINTS TO PONDER

- What is clinical rehabilitation counseling?
- How is clinical rehabilitation counseling different from other counseling specializations?
- What role did federal legislation have in providing counseling services to people with disabilities?
- What are the roles and functions and the scope of practice of certified rehabilitation counselors?

Clinical rehabilitation counselors are professional counselors with a specialization in counseling people with disabilities. The Rehabilitation Counseling Consortium (2005, as cited in Tarvydas & Maki, 2012a), defines a rehabilitation counselor as "a counselor who possesses the specialized knowledge, skills, and attitudes needed to collaborate in a professional relationship with persons with disabilities to achieve their personal, social, psychological, and vocational goals" (p. 4). While counselors with other specializations can and do work with clients with disabilities, clinical rehabilitation counselors are trained specifically to counsel clients living with disabilities with a focus on how the disability affects the person in terms of work, relationships, recreation, education, and socialization. Rehabilitation counselors also focus on the environmental context of disability by working to change and improve the social and physical environments within which people with disabilities live and work (Sales, 2012).

While rehabilitation counseling is a specialization within the profession of counseling, there are ways in which it is different from other kinds of counseling. First, rehabilitation counselors are trained specifically to counsel people with a wide range of disabilities, versus other counselors who focus on life adjustment issues for people without disabilities. Second, case management and care coordination services have historically played an important role in rehabilitation counseling. Third, rehabilitation counselors have traditionally worked in more diverse settings than other counselors (e.g., hospitals, group homes, independent living centers). Fourth, rehabilitation counseling was originally based on the medical model although it has become much more aligned with the strength-based, developmental model of other counseling specializations. Finally, rehabilitation counseling grew out of federal legislation, and the sub-specialties in rehabilitation counseling came about because of shifting priorities within that legislation (Leahy, Muenzen, Saunders, & Strauser, 2009; Sales, 2012).

Depending on how one defines disability the percentage of people living with disabilities can change but according to the Kraus, Lauer, Coleman, and Houtenville (2018), 12.8% of Americans had a disability in 2016, with 35% of people aged 65 and older having a disability, and as the U.S. population ages the number of people with disabilities will increase. According to the U.S. Census Bureau (as cited in Brault, 2012) in 2010 almost 57 million people (18.7%) not living in institutions had a disability and 38 million people (12.6%) had a severe disability. If people living with disabilities were recognized as a minority group they would be the largest minority group in the United States (Drum, McClain, Horner-Johnson, & Taitano, 2011).

Disabilities can be separated into five broad categories: physical (e.g., spinal cord injury, multiple sclerosis), sensory (e.g., visual impairment, hearing impairment), intellectual/developmental (e.g., autism, intellectual disability), mental (e.g., schizophrenia, bipolar disorder), and addiction (e.g., alcohol, methamphetamine). The term disability includes a wide range of illnesses and medical conditions that affect people's abilities to engage in typical activities of daily living, like reading, walking, or dressing, as well as their ability to perform activities that enhance their lives like work, recreation, and social activities (Koch & Rumrill, 2017).

Disabilities can be chronic or acute, congenital or acquired, intermittent or consistent, slow to emerge or acute, predictable or unpredictable with respect to symptoms and progression (Koch & Rumrill, 2017), and knowledge of these differences has an effect on how rehabilitation counselors work with clients. For example, the approach a clinical rehabilitation counselor might take working with a client who has recently acquired a spinal cord injury at the age of 42 is different from the approach she or he might use when working with a 42-year-old client with significant vision loss since birth. Regardless of the disability, it is important to remember the diagnosis describes the condition the person is experiencing, but not how the person is affected by the disability. While there is no universal definition of disability, there has been a shift to viewing disability "as a natural part of the human condition rather than as pathology, a deficit, or an abnormality" (Koch & Rumrill, 2017, p. 1).

History and Background of Rehabilitation Counseling

Rehabilitation counseling grew out of the medical model and clinical rehabilitation counselors typically need strong knowledge about the medical aspects of disabilities. There is disability-specific language clinical rehabilitation counselors use in their work. A *disability* is a physical or mental impairment or condition that limits an individual's functioning, meaning the person cannot do certain tasks as a result of their disability. People can have *functional limitations* (e.g., problems with mobility, seeing, speaking, reading), which are restrictions or the inability to engage in certain tasks or activities as a result of their disability. *Accommodations* are made to decrease barriers and work with people's functional limitations that allow them to engage in a wide range of life activities typically performed by people without disabilities. For example, a person may have impaired vision as a consequence of Type 1 diabetes that prevents the person from reading, which is a functional limitation. Using electronic books or readers on computers is an example of an accommodation. *Barriers*, sometimes called handicaps, can be physical or attitudinal blocks or challenges that prevent people with disabilities from engaging in everyday life activities. Barriers can arise in independent living, community integration, education, and employment settings.

Clinical rehabilitation counselors need to be aware of physical or social barriers and how to help clients work around those barriers. For example, before cell phones people with significant hearing loss could not talk directly to people on the phone (functional limitation) so they had to call a telecommunication relay system (accommodation) to place phone calls. The person with hearing loss would call the relay system using a special phone where they would type in information for the operator who would read that information to the person being called and then type the response back to the person with hearing loss. The development of cell phones where people could directly text to whomever they wanted to talk to provided people with hearing loss the independence to talk with anyone as long as that person has a cell phone, which became in effect an even more effective accommodation.

Clinical rehabilitation counseling was initially a separate profession developed to provide services specifically for people living with disabilities, typically through the state-federal vocational rehabilitation system, with a focus on case management and counseling. As a separate profession it had its own accrediting body (Council on Rehabilitation Education, CORE), professional organizations distinct from the American Counseling Association with their own code of ethics, and credential (Certified Rehabilitation Counselor [CRC]). Over time there has been a transition to make rehabilitation counseling a specialization within the counseling profession to more closely align with the essential counseling aspects of rehabilitation counseling as well as changes in the roles and functions of rehabilitation counselors (Tarvydas & Maki, 2012a). For example, as counselor licensure came into being some states did not include rehabilitation counselors in their licensure laws which prevented clinical rehabilitation counselors from being eligible for insurance reimbursement when working with clients with disabilities.

As Stebnicki (2009) noted, counseling is in the occupational title and clinical rehabilitation counselors should have "the same rights, privileges, and opportunities for becoming eligible for state licensure such as the Licensed Professional Counselor (LPC) credential" (p. 135). He advocates three career paths for rehabilitation counseling students: (a) vocational rehabilitation for people interested in working in state-federal rehabilitation programs, (b) general master's degree for people who want to focus on psychosocial adjustment and independence, and (c) addiction and mental health focus.

Rehabilitation Legislation

As noted above, rehabilitation counseling as a profession grew out of federal legislation and funding, particularly with a focus on helping people with disabilities to obtain or maintain employment. Entire books can be written on rehabilitation-related legislation, so only a summary of the more important legislation will be provided here. The first signification rehabilitation-related legislation was the Soldiers Rehabilitation Act of 1918, which provided funding for vocational rehabilitation services for veterans with disabilities to address the increasing need for services for military personnel who had acquired disabilities and were not able to return to their pre-military service employment. It was followed in 1920 by the Civilian Rehabilitation Act, which provided funding for services to help civilians with disabilities become employed or maintain employment. Both pieces of legislation focused on providing services for people with physical disabilities, but later Rehabilitation Act legislation and amendments expanded services to include sensory, developmental, and psychiatric disabilities. The Rehabilitation Act Amendments of 1992, for example, placed an emphasis on serving people with the most severe disabilities and increasing services to underrepresented minority groups who had traditionally been underserved or not served at all (Koch & Rumrill, 2017; Sales, 2012).

The Social Security Act of 1935 established the state-federal vocational rehabilitation system to provide services to people with disabilities and the focus remained on helping people with physical disabilities through counseling and work-related interventions. (Sales, 2012). The Rehabilitation Act of 1973 broadened the focus beyond vocational rehabilitation to include increased consumer involvement in their treatments plans (Sales, 2012). One of the most significant pieces of legislation to date is the 1990 Americans with Disabilities Act (ADA), often referred to at the Civil Rights Act for people with disabilities (National Council on Disability, 1993; Sales, 2012), which prohibits discrimination of people with disabilities in the areas of housing, employment, transportation, communication; and access to public accommodations; and required employers to provide reasonable accommodations to qualified candidates and employees with disabilities (Americans with Disabilities Act, 1990). The ADA defined a person with a disability as someone who: "(1) has a physical or mental impairment that substantially limits one or more of the major life activities of that person, (2) has a record of such an impairment, or (3) is regarded as having such an impairment" (Maki, 2012, p. 87). Major life activities include physically caring for oneself, performing manual tasks, walking, seeing, hearing, breathing, learning, and working.

The 1992 Amendments to the ADA emphasized "respect for individual dignity, personal responsibility, self-determination, and pursuit of meaningful careers, based on informed choice" (Rehabilitation Act Amendments, as cited in Sales, 2012, p. 46). And the 1998 Amendments noted the purpose of the ADA is to "empower individuals with disabilities to maximize employment, economic self-sufficiency, independence and inclusion, and integration into society" (Sales, 2012). The ADA continues to be amended to include a variety of chronic health conditions and emerging disabilities that were not initially included in the law (Koch & Rumrill, 2017). For example, the 2008 Americans with Disabilities Act Amendments Act (ADAAA) expanded how disabilities were defined to include emerging disabilities, revising the definition so people only needed to have one major life activity limited to qualify as having a disability to be protected under the ADA, as well as expanding access to state-federal vocational rehabilitation services and protections from discrimination (Koch & Rumrill, 2017; Maki, 2012). The Affordable Care Act also positively influenced services for people with disabilities, particularly with people with chronic health issues, with its focus on prevention and early intervention and the exclusion of preexisting conditions from health insurance coverage (Koch & Rumrill, 2017).

Clinical Rehabilitation Counseling Defined and Scope of Practice

As Tarvydas and Maki (2012a) noted, rehabilitation counseling includes "specialized knowledge of disabilities, the disability experience, and the socio-political-environmental factors that impact people with disabilities combined with counseling skills that help differentiate" (pp. 7–8) rehabilitation counselors from other counselors as well as other professionals who work directly with people with disabilities. Traditionally, rehabilitation counselors engaged in three main roles: counseling, coordination and case management of rehabilitation services, and consultation (with medical professionals, allied health professionals, employers, etc.). The amount of time spent in these roles has changed as rehabilitation counselors placed more and more emphasis on counseling, but clinical rehabilitation counselors still engage in these three roles with the amount of time spent in each role being dependent on the setting in which the counselors work.

According to the Commission on Rehabilitation Counselor Certification (CRCC), there are six underlying values for clinical rehabilitation counselors: (a) helping people with disabilities with integration, inclusion, and independence in the workplace and the community; (b) believing in worth and dignity of all people, including people with disabilities; (c) advocating for people with disabilities to have the same access to opportunities as all people; (d) viewing people from a holistic perspective; (e) focusing on people's strengths and assets; and (f) being committed to including clients in decisions about their treatment plans (Commission on Rehabilitation Counselor Certification, 2018b).

The Commission on Rehabilitation Counselor Certification (2016), which is the organization that created the Certified Rehabilitation Counselor (CRC) credential, also developed a Scope of Practice statement that reads as follows:

Rehabilitation counseling is a systematic process that assists persons with physical, mental, developmental, cognitive, and emotional disabilities to achieve their personal, career, and independent living goals in the most integrated setting possible through the application of the counseling process. The counseling process involves communication, goal setting, and beneficial growth or change through self-advocacy, psychological, vocational, social, and behavioral interventions. The specific techniques and modalities utilized within this rehabilitation counseling process may include, but are not limited to the following: assessment and appraisal; diagnosis and treatment planning; career (vocational) counseling; individual and group counseling treatment interventions focused on facilitating adjustments to the medical and psychosocial impact of disability; case management, referral, and service coordination; program evaluation and research; interventions to remove environmental, employment, and attitudinal barriers; consultation services among multiple parties and regulatory systems; job analysis, job development, and placement services, including assistance with employment and job accommodations; and provision of consultation about and access to rehabilitation technology.

(Scope of Practice Statement, para. 1)

Related to the Scope of Practice, for many years Leahy (2018) has conducted research on the roles and functions of rehabilitation counselors, helping to identify the required knowledge, skills, and work-related tasks. In general, the roles and functions of rehabilitation counselors include assessment, personal counseling, career or vocational counseling, case management, and job placement and retention (Leahy, 2018). With respect to core knowledge and skills required to be an effective clinical rehabilitation counselors Leahy (2018) identified the following:

(1) assessment, appraisal, and vocational evaluation; (2) job development, job placement, and career and lifestyle development; (3) vocational consultation and services for employers; (4) case management, professional roles and practices, and utilization of community resources; (5) foundations of counseling, professional orientation and ethical practice, theories, social and cultural issues, and human growth and development; (6) group and family counseling; (7) mental health counseling; (8) medical, functional, and psychosocial aspects of disabilities; (9) disability management; and (10) research, program evaluation, and evidence-based practices.

(p. 18)

Accreditation and Credentials

On July 1, 2017, CACREP (Council on Accreditation of Counseling and Related Educational Programs) and CORE (Council on Rehabilitation Education) merged and CACREP became the accreditation body for clinical rehabilitation counseling specializations within counselor education programs. Prior to this time master's level rehabilitation counseling programs were accredited by CORE beginning in 1972 (Leahy & Tansey, 2008). As a result of the merger the 2016 CACREP Standards (2015) define clinical rehabilitation counseling as a specialization:

focused on disability rights and empowering individuals with disabilities to achieve their own chosen goals. Instead of relying on a diagnose then treat approach to just change the individual, rehabilitation counselors seek ways to improve the accessibility of environments in which individuals with disabilities live and work.

(p. 50)

In the 2016 standards CACREP also committed to infusing knowledge and training about coun-seling people with disabilities across the core and specialty standards, since all counselors will work with clients with disabilities.

As with different counseling specializations, there are a number of different credentials clini-cal rehabilitation counselors can earn. Depending on state counselor licensure laws, students who graduate with a degree in rehabilitation counseling or a counselor education degree with a clini-cal rehabilitation counseling focus and pass the exam required for the CRC can become licensed in 16 states (Commission on Rehabilitation Counselor Certification, 2018a). This is similar to people graduating from a counselor education program and passing the National Counselor Exam (NCE), which is the exam connected with the National Certified Counselor (NCC) credential. Graduates of clinical rehabilitation counseling program are also eligible to become NCCs as long as they meet the eligibility criteria stated by the National Board for Certified Counselors. Students can get more information about both credentials at these websites: https://www.crccerti fication.com/about-crc-certification and https://www.nbcc.org/Certification/NCC.

In addition to creating the Scope of Practice for rehabilitation counselors, CRCC developed a code of ethics specifically for CRC that addresses disabilities and rehabilitation throughout the code (https://www.crccertification.com/code-of-ethics-4). While this code is specifically writ-ten for clinical rehabilitation counselors it can provide useful guidance for anyone working as a clinical rehabilitation counselor. Clinical rehabilitation counselors will also follow the code of ethics related to other counseling credentials they hold and the professional organizations to which they belong.

Work Settings and Clients Served

There are a number of reasons why it is important that counselors are trained to work with people with disabilities. People are living longer in the United States and as people age, they are more likely to acquire disabilities like heart conditions, arthritis, and hearing and vision loss. Continued advancements in medical treatments and technology mean people with disabili-ties are living longer and are being provided with additional opportunities to be integrated and engaged in their communities. For example, advances in psychiatric medications mean people living with mental illness can live and work in their home communities rather than having extended hospital stays. There is also a strong grassroots movement among people with disabili-ties that has led to more inclusion and decreased stigmatization of and discrimination against people with disabilities.

Clinical rehabilitation counselors initially worked in the state-federal vocational rehabilita-tion but over time that expanded to include a wide range of specialized rehabilitation settings including, but not limited to, psychiatric rehabilitation, physical rehabilitation, forensic reha-bilitation, addiction treatment, insurance rehabilitation, criminal justice, employee assistance programs, veterans programs, pre-K through 12 schools as well as colleges and universities, and transition services for school-aged youth (Tarvydas & Hartley 2018).

The number of people living with a wide range of disabilities is increasing as a result of advances in medicine and medical technology that allow people to live with more catastrophic disabilities, disabilities related to military service, an aging population in the United States, peo-ple experiencing increased violence and trauma, climate change and severe weather events that can cause or exacerbate existing medical conditions and disabilities (Koch & Rumrill, 2017), and increasing addiction, which means there is a greater need for trained clinical rehabilita-tion counselors. Changes in legislation have also created more opportunities for people with disabilities to be engaged in their communities by decreasing physical and attitudinal barriers in schools, work, and communities. Client self-advocacy and access to more information and resources through the Internet have also increased the number of people with disabilities who seek counseling and rehabilitation services.

With increases in accommodations and medical technology, more people with severe disabilities are seeking rehabilitation counseling, particularly vocational rehabilitation. Historically and even now people with disabilities are typically unemployed or underemployed compared with people without disabilities, or they may lose their employment as the result of acquiring a disability or if the symptoms of their disability increase leading to increased functional limitations. Clinical rehabilitation counselors can help people with disabilities find and maintain employment, help with adjustment to disability in the workplace, assist clients in finding accommodations to address work-related functional limitations, and eliminate physical and psychosocial barriers at work, and address workplace stigma and discrimination (Koch & Rumrill, 2017; Tarvydas & Maki, 2012b).

Emerging disabilities, as opposed to traditionally recognized disabilities, and an increase in the number of people with disabilities means a greater need for rehabilitation counselors or professional counselors trained to work with clients with a wide range of disabilities. Emerging disabilities (e.g., fibromyalgia, Lyme disease) include diseases and health conditions that are increasing in prevalence (e.g., diabetes, autism) and may be related to violence, environmental factors, or lifestyle changes (Koch & Rumrill, 2017). People with emerging disabilities

> are more likely to be women, economically disadvantaged, older, and members of racial/ethnic minority groups. These individual characteristics intersect with disability characteristics and social and environmental factors (e.g., stigma, discrimination, social injustice, inequities in health and health care, violence, climate change) to magnify the challenges presented by the disabling condition itself.
>
> (Koch & Rumrill, 2017, p. 22)

Clinical rehabilitation counseling is also different because it was traditionally more focused on interdisciplinary work with medical and allied health professionals. Certified rehabilitation counselors often work with a team of medical professionals who have different training, different orientations, and different ways of viewing disability, and they may have to help clients translate medical information and services so they can make informed and educated decisions about their health care.

While clinical rehabilitation counselors are trained to provide individual, group, and family counseling like other counselors, they are also trained in more specialized areas. For example, clinical rehabilitation counselors are trained to focus on maintaining or reducing the effects of disabilities and chronic health conditions as well how to evaluate and modify the environment to better accommodate people with disabilities, rather than trying to make the person adjust to the environment. Rehabilitation counseling can focus on personal concerns such as adjusting to and transcending living with a disability or career concerns such as finding a new career that accommodates the person's functional limitations. For example, a clinical rehabilitation counselor could work with a client and employer to make the workspace accessible for a person who has a newly acquired spinal cord injury.

Theories and Models for Rehabilitation Counseling

The core values of rehabilitation counseling include (a) awareness of interactions between the person and the environment, which includes physical and sociocultural influences; (b) a strengths-based approach; (c) a holistic approach, inclusive of all domains including work, social, education, recreation, disability and health-related, cognitive, sexual, and spiritual aspects of a person's life; (d) interdisciplinary approaches to services; and (e) focus on empowerment, dignity, and human rights (McCarthy, 2018). As part of the last element, McCarthy (2018) stresses the importance of clinical rehabilitation counselors being aware of their own views on disability as well as how to educate people about disability to fight ableism, (i.e., systemic bias against people living with disabilities), as well as serving as advocates for people with disabilities on individual, community, and policy levels. He also stresses the importance of accessibility and how to prevent or eliminate physical and attitudinal barriers that preclude people with disabilities from having equal access to all parts of society, as well as working to find accommodations that allow people to be better integrated into their environments and create opportunities for greater inclusion for people with disabilities. Finally, McCarthy (2018) stresses the importance of "asking before acting" (p. 80), which can happen on an individual level when a counselor, or anyone, asks the person with a disability if they need or want assistance before they intervene, all the way to a political level where we make sure to include people with disabilities in decision-making roles as stakeholders.

While clinical rehabilitation counseling developed out of the biomedical model, the theories and models for clinical rehabilitation counseling are similar to those used in clinical mental health counseling or addiction counseling. Since the range of possible models is large we will focus on two models: Biopsychosocial Model and Social Model.

The *Biopsychosocial Model* focuses on the interaction between people and their environments as they are influenced by biological, psychological, and social factors or dimensions in their lives (Smedema, Sharp, Thompson, & Friefeld, 2016). Biological factors include the level of impairment, pain levels, and functional limitations; psychological factors include mental health and wellbeing, coping skills, sense of self-worth, and level of hope; and social factors include social support, stigma, and social functioning. This was a shift from the biomedical model that focused on diagnosis and cure to a focus on health and wellbeing that includes people's physical bodies and functioning but also how people engage in activities and the context in which they function in their everyday lives. The focus is on adaptation and not pathology (Smedema et al., 2016). Working with clients with disabilities from a biopsychosocial perspective means being holistic and individualized in how one views the person, including understanding related causes and symptoms, possible diagnosis and treatments, pain management and treatment, functional limitations and related challenges due to environmental barriers, and knowing how all these elements have functional and psychosocial implications for clients (Koch & Rumrill, 2017). The Biopsychosocial Model uses a holistic, positive, and strengths-based approach to understanding the effect of disability on people's lives (Smedema et al., 2016).

The *Social Model* of disability, which developed out of the Disability Rights community, focuses not on the medical aspects of illness and cure but instead views disability as a political, cultural, social, and intellectual issue, with an awareness of the historical implications for understanding of disability (Hartley, 2018). Disability is viewed not as the sole defining quality or characteristic of a person but as one of a number of qualities that is part of that person's identity, like their gender or ethnicity. The disability is important and should not be ignored by counselors or society, but it is not the only important feature of the person (Smart & Smart, 2006). The focus is on understanding how the experience of having a disability is influenced by factors in the environment and how the environment can create functional limitations and barriers for people with disabilities. For example, a person's legs being paralyzed is not the problem using the Social Model. The problem is buildings with stairs and no elevators or sidewalks without curb cuts that are not accessible to people using wheelchairs (McCarthy, 2018). The problem is not the disability, it's the physical and social barriers that keep people living with disabilities from being fully integrated into society.

SIDEBAR 12.1

In Practice: What Would You Do?

Case 1: Lily is a 36-year-old, married African American woman, who was diagnosed with multiple sclerosis (MS) two years ago. She has been married for four years and has a two-year-old son. She has worked as an architect for the last ten years. Recent symptoms are numbness and leg spasms, and she has begun to use a cane. She states she has a positive relationship with her physician (a specialist in MS) but that it took five years for her to be diagnosed. She is referred to you, a rehabilitation counselor, to discuss possible job accommodations.

Discussion

- What are the rehabilitation counseling issues Lily is facing?
- What services might you, as a clinical rehabilitation counselor, provide for Lily? For her family?
- What employment-related services might you provide to help Lily maintain employment or find a new job?

More clinical rehabilitation counselors are being trained to view disability through the Social Model as a way to not only help clients but also as a way to eliminate bias and prejudice and place more emphasis on empowerment and client self-determination (Hartley, 2018). Awareness of the importance and power of language is central to the Social Model and goes beyond person-first language (e.g., a person with schizophrenia versus a schizophrenic) but using words and language that have meaning in the particular disability community and discussing the use of language with clients as a way to include the client as a self-determining person (Hartley, 2018). Within the Social Model clinical rehabilitation counselors also need to pay attention to how agency policies and practices might have a negative effect on clients receiving services and ensuring services are provided that view clients holistically and empowering clients to make their own decisions (Hartley, 2018). Finally, within the Social Model clinical rehabilitation counselors will continue to help people with disabilities become employed and maintain employment by addressing the stigma that often exists in the workplace and the barriers that exist that are not related to the disability or functional limitations (Hartley, 2018). The focus is on each person's response to disability, rather than focusing on adjustment and acceptance since those words imply an endpoint rather than addressing the experience of disability across a person's lifespan (Marini & Stebnicki, 2018).

Effects of Clinical Rehabilitation Counseling on the Individual, Family, and Community

Clinical rehabilitation counseling can empower people with disabilities to make choices that will enhance their lives. Each person's reaction to disability is influenced by a variety of complex factors, including the time of onset of the disability, the kind of disability, how the person perceives the disability, the person's cultural context, the person's psychosocial response to the disability, the person's coping skills and resilience (Marini & Stebnicki, 2018), support systems, personality and developmental stage in life, and previous experiences with challenging life events.

The effects of disability and the rehabilitation counseling process on people with disabilities are also noted throughout this chapter, including how to help people incorporate their disability into their sense of self and how to serve as advocates for themselves.

The rehabilitation profession, including rehabilitation counseling, has a long history of focusing only on the individual but in recent years has begun to focus more on the effects of disability on the family and how to incorporate family as allies into the rehabilitation process. As a partner in the counseling process clinical rehabilitation counselors can help clients and their families make decisions about their medical care, employment, and education, as well as social and recreation decisions. Clinical rehabilitation counselors can also educate families, with the client's permission, about the disability and the rehabilitation process, as well as helping family members work through their own biases and misperceptions about disability. Helping family members in their own adaptation to disability and how it affects the whole family, not just the person with a disability, can also be an important role for clinical rehabilitation counselors (Cottone, 2018).

SIDEBAR 12.2

In Practice: What Would You Do?

Bobby is a ten-year-old White male who was diagnosed with cerebral palsy (CP) when he was nine months old. He has hemiparesis (paralysis or weakness) on the right side of his body. He is able to walk with the use of a walker, and he uses a power wheelchair at school. His speech is affected by his CP to the point it is difficult for most people to understand him. He repeated the first grade and appears to be of average to slightly below average intelligence. He loves all kinds of sports, particularly college basketball and professional wrestling.

Maggie, Bobby's 16-year-old sister, is in the gifted program at her school and she takes a combination of regular and honors classes. Now that she has her driver's license she helps her mother with errands, and she is president of a service club at her high school. She also plays the drums in the school jazz band. Most of her friends do not know her brother has CP, and she rarely invites people to the house. Her boyfriend of one year spends a lot of time playing games and wrestling with Bobby.

Mack, Bobby's father, is 42 years old and he works as the head service clerk at an auto dealership. He was diagnosed with multiple sclerosis one year ago and although he takes medication, his symptoms (primarily dizziness and fatigue) are difficult for him to manage. He has seen a series of physicians to try to address his dizziness, which makes it hard from him to do his job on a daily basis.

Julia, Bobby's mother, is 40 years old and she is an elementary school teacher. She spends a lot of time taking Bobby to and from therapy appointments (physical therapy, occupational therapy, etc.), and enjoys going to yard sales every weekend. She is experiencing a lot of stress related to her son's disability and her husband's illness. She experienced a miscarriage two years before Bobby was born and worries the medication she was taking at the time may have caused the miscarriage as well as Bobby's disability. She is currently taking an antidepressant, prescribed by her family physician. The family's health insurance is provided through her employer.

Discussion

1. What needs do you think they have as an individual and as a family?

2. Thinking about each person, what clinical rehabilitation counseling and related services might be helpful and why?
3. Who should provide those services, and how would you make the appropriate referrals?
4. What additional information might you need to obtain to provide effective and appropriate services?

Clinical rehabilitation counselors can also use their advocacy skills and counseling skills to educate members of the community about people with disabilities, eliminating biases and discrimination through education. For example, counselors can help community members learn about disabling conditions and the role of all levels of government in providing services to people with disabilities. They can also teach people how to engage and interact with people with disabilities in ways that are affirming and inclusive and empowering to people living with disabilities. Examples of disability activism include the Deaf community working to have sign language recognized as a legitimate language, the grassroots efforts of people with physical disabilities in the 1960s that led to the recognition of independent living centers as a rehabilitation service, and people living with mental illness who founded the Recovery Movement that is now written into federal legislation (Tarvydas & Maki, 2012b). The need for disability activism continues today and clinical rehabilitation counselors can be part of that work.

Counseling Practices

Clinical rehabilitation counselors provide services throughout the rehabilitation process from outreach and determining eligibility for services to assessment and treatment planning to providing counseling and related services to follow-up (Koch & Rumrill, 2017). They use the same counseling techniques and practices as other professional counselors but they focus on counseling clients with disabilities. While there may be more emphasis on career counseling in some settings and more emphasis on personal counseling in others, the focus is still on counseling clients with disabilities from a holistic, wellness, strengths-based, developmental perspective. Clinical rehabilitation counselors focus on providing the core conditions of counseling, developing a counseling alliance, and using basic and advanced counseling skills, with awareness that those skills may need to be adjusted depending on the disability (Berven & Bezyak, 2015). For example, clinical rehabilitation counselors would place more emphasis on minimal encouragers and verbal responses for a client with a visual disability rather than relying on eye contact and nonverbal behaviors. Because some clinical rehabilitation counselors work with a range of medical and allied health professionals they need to understand the medical aspects of disability and case management, but their primary focus is on providing counseling services.

Motivational interviewing is a counseling approach that is being used more often in rehabilitation counseling since it has been found to be an effective and efficient treatment strategy for keeping clients engaged in the rehabilitation process. Motivational interviewing is a brief, directive, strengths-based, client-focused approach to counseling that can increase clients' motivation to change by working through their ambivalence toward change (Manthey, Brooks, Chan, Hedenblad, & Ditchman, 2015). There can be any number of disincentives to change for people with disabilities, including the length of time it can take to work through the state-federal vocational rehabilitation process, the possibility of losing eligibility benefits like Social Security Disability Income, and the challenges of finding workplace accommodations, and motivational interviewing can help clinical rehabilitation counselors and clients navigate these changes. The primary focus of motivational interviewing is using the counseling relationship to "reduce resistance and to promote client understanding, choices, and autonomy" (Manthey et al., 2015, p. 250), goals that are consistent with rehabilitation counseling philosophy.

Psychoeducation is also an important counseling strategy for helping clients learn more about their disabilities to increase their autonomy and self-efficacy. This can include health literacy and illness self-management so people can make informed choices about their medication and management of medication side effects, treatment options, nutrition, and navigating the health care system (Koch & Rumrill, 2017). Koch and Rumrill (2017) define health literacy as "the capacity of individuals to acquire, process, and understand basic health information and services so that they can make informed health decisions and take personal responsibility for their health" (p. 268) and clinical rehabilitation counselors can play an important role in helping clients develop and increase their health literacy skills. For example, clinical rehabilitation counselors can encourage clients to keep their own detailed records of their health care and review any electronic records for accuracy, and to bring someone with them to medical appointments to take notes and serve as support for the client (Koch & Rumrill, 2017). Clinical rehabilitation counselors should also be open to learning from their clients since many people living with disabilities have strong health literacy skills. Psychoeducation can be provided formally through workshops, discussion groups, or written/online materials or informally in an individual, group, or family counseling session (Koch & Rumrill, 2017).

Summary

All professional counselors work with clients with disabilities and/or clients affected by disability, whether they are aware of it or not. This chapter provided an overview of the roles and functions of clinical rehabilitation counselors as well as how this specialization is different from other counseling areas. Clinical rehabilitation counselors use all the same counseling skills, strategies, and interventions as other professional counselors with additional expertise in the psychosocial, medical, and vocation aspects of disabilities and their effects on clients.

> I didn't understand what "handicap accessible" meant until I became disabled. I could't maneuver my walker into the bathroom in city hall because the door opened in and it was too heavy to push. I felt helpless. And this was in the city hall! Thank you for noticing and making a difference!
>
> – client to her clinical rehabilitation counselor

References

Americans with Disabilities Act of 1990, 42 U.S.C. § 12101 et seq. (1990). Retrieved from https://www.law.cornell.edu/uscode/text/42/12101

Berven, N. L., & Bezyak, J. L. (2015). Basic counseling skills. In F. Chan, N. L. Berven & K. R. Thomas (Eds.), *Counseling theories and techniques for rehabilitation and mental health professionals* (2nd ed., pp. 227–246). New York: Spring Publishing Company.

Brault, M. W. (2012). Americans with disabilities: 2010. Current Population Reports, P70–131, U.S. Census Bureau, Washington, DC.

Commission on Rehabilitation Counselor Certification. (2016). *Code of professional ethics for rehabilitation counselors*. Retrieved from https://www.crccertification.com/code-of-ethics-4

Commission on Rehabilitation Counselor Certification. (2018a). *About CRCC*. Retrieved from https://www.crccertification.com/

Commission on Rehabilitation Counselor Certification. (2018b). *Rehabilitation counseling scope of practice*. Retrieved from https://www.crccertification.com/scope-of-practice

Cottone, R. R. (2018). Family and relationship issues. In V. M. Tarvydas & M. T. Hartley (Eds.), *The professional practice of rehabilitation counseling* (2nd ed., pp. 137–151). New York: Springer Publishing Company.

Council for Accreditation of Counseling and Related Educational Programs. (2015). *2016 CACREP standards*. Alexandria, VA: Author.

Drum, C., McClain, M. R., Horner-Johnson, W., & Taitano, G. (2011). *Health disparities chart book on disability and racial and ethnic status in the United States*. Durham, NH: UNH Institute on Disability.

Hartley, M. T. (2018). The disability rights community. In V. M. Tarvydas & D. R. Maki (Eds.), *The professional practice of rehabilitation counseling* (2nd ed., pp. 153–172). New York: Springer Publishing Company.

Kraus, L., Lauer, E., Coleman, R., & Houtenville, A. (2018). *2017 Disability statistics annual report*. Durham, NH: University of New Hampshire.

Koch, L. C., & Rumrill, P. D. (2017). *Rehabilitation counseling and emerging disabilities: Medical, psychosocial, and vocational aspects*. New York: Spring Publishing Company.

Leahy, M. J. (2018). Rehabilitation counseling professional competencies. In V. M. Tarvydas & D. R. Maki (Eds.), *The professional practice of rehabilitation counseling* (2nd ed., pp. 15–30). New York: Springer Publishing Company.

Leahy, M.J., Muenzen, P., Saunders, J.L., & Strauser, D. (2009). Essential knowledge domains underlying effective rehabilitation counseling practices. *Rehabilitation Counseling Bulletin, 52*, 95–106.

Leahy, M. J., & Tansey, T. N. (2008). The impact of CORE standards across the rehabilitation education continuum. *Rehabilitation Education, 22*, 217–226.

Maki, D. (2012). Concepts and paradigms in rehabilitation counseling. In V. M. Tarvydas & D. R. Maki (Eds.), *The professional practice of rehabilitation counseling* (pp. 83–110). New York: Springer Publishing Company.

Marini, I., & Stebicki, M.A (Eds.). (2018). *The psychological and social impact of illness and disability* (7th ed.). New York: Springer.

McCarthy, H. (2018). Concepts and models. In V. M. Tarvydas & D. R. Maki. (Eds.), *The professional practice of rehabilitation counseling* (2nd ed., 73–94). New York: Springer Publishing Company.

Manthey, T. J., Brooks, J., Chan, F., Hedenblad, L. E., & Ditchman, N. (2015). Motivational interviewing. In F. Chan, N. L. Berven, & K. R. Thomas (Eds.), *Counseling theories and techniques for rehabilitation and mental health professionals* (2nd ed., 247–278). New York: Spring Publishing Company.

National Council on Disability. (1993). *Americans with disabilities act watch – Year one: A report to the president and the congress on progress in implementing the Americans with disabilities act*. Retrieved from https://www.ncd.gov/publications/1993/April51993

Sales, A. P. (2012). History of rehabilitation counseling. In V. M. Tarvydas & D. R. Maki (Eds.), *The professional practice of rehabilitation counseling* (pp. 39–60). New York: Springer Publishing Company.

Smart, J. F., & Smart, D. W. (2006). Models of disability: Implications for the counseling profession. *Journal of Counseling & Development, 84*, 29–40.

Smedema, S. M., Sharp, S., Thompson, K., & Friefeld, R. (2016). Evaluation of a biopsychosocial model of life satisfaction in individuals with spinal cord injuries. *Journal of Rehabilitation, 82*, 38–47.

Stebnicki, M. A. (2009). A call for integral approaches in the professional identity of rehabilitation counseling. *Rehabilitation Counseling Bulletin, 52*, 133–137.

Tarvydas, V. M., & Hartley, M. T. (Eds.). (2018). *The professional practice of rehabilitation counseling* (2nd ed.). New York: Springer Publishing Company.

Tarvydas, V. M., & Maki, D. R. (Eds.). (2012a). *The professional practice of rehabilitation counseling*. New York: Spring Publishing Company.

Tarvydas, V. M., & Maki, D. R. (Eds.). (2012b). Rehabilitation counseling: A specialty practice. In V. M. Tarvydas & D. R. Maki (Eds.), *The professional practice of rehabilitation counseling* (pp. 3–16). New York: Spring Publishing Company.

Chapter 13

College Counseling and Student Affairs

Doris W. Carroll

Wisdom does not come overnight.

– Somali proverb

POINTS TO PONDER

- What is student affairs?
- How did college counseling develop on college campuses?
- Do all college campuses have college counseling?
- How is theory utilized within student affairs?

College student affairs have been an integral part of American colleges and universities for all of America's history. Over time, the scope and depth of student affairs services have changed and been altered as institutions developed new ways to best support students' academic success. Student affairs and its clinical specialty area, college counseling, collaborate and work together to promote essential holistic student development activities that support undergraduate and graduate student success. The purpose of this chapter is to describe the roles and functions of student affairs and college counseling within the framework of the Council for the Accreditation of Counseling and Related Educational Programs (CACREP) (2015) standards and practice guidelines. CACREP provides program practice standards as a context for directing student service programs and services on campuses. Standard five describes the work in college counseling and student affairs by noting that "[graduate] students who are preparing to specialize as college counselors and student affairs professionals will demonstrate the knowledge and skills necessary to promote the academic, career, personal, and social development of individuals in higher education settings" (p. 29).

We begin this conversation by traversing across the college campus to learn what are the essential student affairs functions that support a college student's personal/emotional wellbeing and academic success. Next, we describe what are the traditional functional areas within student affairs, including college counseling services, and describe them within a holistic framework of college student affairs. We close by summarizing the significance of college counseling and student affairs for colleges and universities.

Student Affairs

What are these diverse, complex set of campus services known as student affairs? Colleges, regardless of size, location, or core institutional mission, must have an organizational structure that provides resources and services to college students throughout their learning years on the campus. Over the decades, the organizational unit known as student affairs has been characterized as a stand-alone division on most U.S. college campuses with the senior student affairs administrator reporting directly to the college or university president, regardless of whether the organizational structure was centralized or de-centralized.

Whether the institution is a residential or commuter campus located within an urban, suburban or rural setting, colleges and universities are each charged to provide students with essential practical student services and program activities that teach, inform, and support their learning as they navigate their daily academic and social learning needs independent of parents and structured high school learning environments. In the discussion that follows, the historical beginnings of student affairs services on college campuses are described, and they highlight the relevance of recognizing and valuing these historical elements as central to the growth of college student affairs services and offices.

Historical Beginnings

History is an undervalued professional asset within student affairs, and yet, it is a useful tool for student affairs professionals for it promotes reflexive practice (Kimball & Ryder, 2014). Understanding the past can help make meaning of contemporary student affairs work; it allows for a complete, contextualized understanding of the present. The profession of student affairs has utilized the past as a way of thinking about those principles that undergird its present values.

The beginning of this historical self-reflection began with the 1937 publication entitled the *Student Personnel View* (American Council on Education, 1937), one of the earliest documents in the field to argue that a primary task of higher education was to "assist the student in developing to the limits of his [sic] potentialities and in making his contribution to the betterment of society…. This philosophy imposes upon educational institutions the obligation to consider the student as a whole…. It puts emphasis, in brief, upon the development of the student as a person rather than upon his intellectual training alone" (American Council on Education, 1937/1994, p. 68). This text was revised later in 1949, but its historical and practical significance to the student affairs is unmistakable. It established that student affairs was, and still is, responsible for promoting a holistic view of student development throughout their time on a college campus.

Today, this classic publication serves as a "historical touchstone" for the profession and sets the framework for establishing professional competencies and contemporary practice. In 2012, the profession celebrated this text's seventy-fifth anniversary (Worley & Wells-Dolan, 2012) and that occasion provided student affairs professionals the opportunity to examine current practices from this historical perspective. This re-examination resulted in an organizational reflection about how student affairs practices evolved over time and across institutional spaces. Furthermore, Worley and Wells-Dolan (2012) observed that looking at history yielded

> a "professional transformation" – moving from a workaday focus on what is provided to students in its most simplistic way to a broadened professionalized perspective that asked how we do, as student affairs professionals, go about the work of [promoting] student development in the services provided to students.

(p. 51)

Reflections about historical values connect directly to contemporary discussions about philosophies and competencies through such documents as the Professional Competency areas for student affairs practitioners (American College Personnel Association & National Association of Student Personnel Administrators, 2010), hereafter referred to as the *Joint Statement* and to

Learning Reconsidered (Keeling, 2006). Acknowledging the significance of these classic writings situates history as a practice-based skill and provides a context for defining a competent student affairs professional, establishing a philosophical basis for the profession, and articulating a foundation for an integrative model of theory-to-practice. Thus, history has a significant role in reflexive practice.

Student Affairs Organizational Structure

The organizational structure of student affairs has changed over the years as the institutional mission has either changed and/or been reorganized and students' academic and personal development needs have necessitated a structural shift. Dungy (2003) wrote that student affairs included four historical or traditional support units that were created in direct response to students' expressed identified student needs. Those units included admissions, records, financial aid, and counseling. Dungy observed that such student affairs services and campus resources supported the institution's academic mission by "helping students work through psychological and emotional issues that may affect their academic success and personal development" (Dungy, 2003, p. 345).

Depending upon the campus mission and institutional focus, student affairs units are utilized in support of academic success, and each office has numerous resources for addressing academic learning needs alongside adjustment, personal, emotional and developmental needs While the name and roles vary across institutional settings, Kuk and Banning (2009) discovered that in a survey of student affair administrators, respondents listed more than 50 units that fell under the large organizational umbrella known as student affairs. Those units ranged from academic advising, admissions, counseling, and housing to IT, bookstore, student union, child care, and Veterans services – just to note a few of these vast and expansive services, all of which are designed to address students' personal, emotional development and academic learning in both real time and virtually, online. Despite the specializations, student affairs offices share several organizational elements in common with regard to mission, assessment, and program evaluation.

Student affairs offices are concerned with personal, emotional development and wellbeing of students. They value personal growth of individual students and use developmental outcomes measures to assess student learning or student developmental progress. They assign student learning outcomes to the service delivery of each office across student affairs and collaborate with academic affairs to determine how academic success variables are met routinely. Additionally, many student affairs units or offices are charged to develop student-centered programs, services, and activities that fit, or are consistent with, the institution's mission. Their success in that endeavor is measured annually by state or local accrediting agencies and governing boards and informed by legislative funding support.

Today's student affairs' climate is changing for two distinct reasons. First, as colleges and universities face budgetary cuts, such cuts are felt across student affairs offices and units, and result in restricting student services or programs, or prevent the creation of new services to address new student developmental or academic support needs. Second, external constituents such as parents, legislatures, funding agencies, and community members have demanded increased centralization of decision making regarding students and student support services to allow for increased student engagement or for increased transparency, especially on large campuses.

Moreover, change is inevitable when student affairs units are combined with academic affairs to create one reporting unit headed by either a provost or an academic vice president. Such reorganization happens at the request of the university president or provost and is focused on streamlining either academic support services such as academic advising or providing improved academic service delivery for students. The outcome of such a reorganization is intended to enhance service delivery to a special cohort of students.

In summary, student affairs plays a central role in the lives of college students. Student affairs professionals are educated and trained to support the academic and personal development needs of college students across the entire campus. This large, encompassing administrative unit can be directed by either a student affairs or academic affairs vice president who reports to the university president, in most instances. CACREP and CAS standards inform student affairs professionals about best practices for student affairs professionals and the graduate faculty who teach and prepare such administrators. A significant and vital clinical specialty area within student affairs is college counseling, which is described in the discussion that follows.

College Counseling

College counseling is one of the four traditional student affairs units (Dungy, 2003) and, for this reason, it has a long and rich history on college campuses. Across institutions and college learning environments, college counseling and college counseling centers exist, and are described as specialized, direct clinical and outreach services. The purpose of these resources is to support students' academic success by helping them to resolve or manage personal adjustment, psychological, and developmental life issues that impact their daily lives as a student.

Counseling has been defined as "a professional relationship that empowers diverse individuals, families, and groups to accomplish mental health, wellness, educational, and career goals" (Kaplan, Tarvydas, & Gladding, 2014, p. 368). As a specialty field, college counseling involves an array of professional, direct clinical counseling services, and indirect consultative services that are designed to help college students to address a broad, robust list of mental health issues and concerns that occur with and among college students. College counseling involves the delivery of individual and group counseling direct interventions, consultation with campus faculty and staff, academic test and anxiety management, crisis/emergency services, and other mental health collaborations as requested by administrators or added due to emerging clinical need.

Similar to other areas of student affairs, college counseling remains concerned with and committed to the holistic development of college students. Toward this mission, college counseling centers perform several vital roles across the college campus. First, college counseling is designed to address the college student's personal and emotional development while supporting and assessing a student's specialized learning needs. Second, college counseling supports and promotes learning growth and helps students remove barriers to their academic success. Finally, college counseling supports traditional student adjustment issues and overall personal development and wellbeing.

College counseling involves a variety of clinical practice activities including, but not limited to, individual short- and long-term counseling, group counseling and psychotherapy groups, consultation with faculty and staff, crisis and emergency services, and preparing future counseling professionals through pre-doctoral internships and clinical services alongside psychological assessment and wellbeing and wellness activities (Fu & Cheng, 2017). These specialized clinical practice activities are carried out by college counseling professionals throughout the academic calendar year and summer sessions, in some instances.

College counseling helps students restore or return to a holistic equilibrium using a host of direct clinical services and applied learning resources whenever severe mental health issues, such as suicidal ideation or crippling anxieties, interfere with a student's capacity to engage with peers in social settings and participate in classroom activities (Association of University and College Counseling Center Directors, 2012). College counseling centers and their professional staff collaborate and provide leadership to other students affairs offices and to campus administrators. They examine systemic adverse or risky campus environmental issues that can, and do, interfere with a student's holistic development as well as academic progress.

Clinicians, college counseling administrators, and student affairs administrators agree universally that students are arriving on to college campuses with a significant increase in the severity of mental health presenting concerns. Researchers have reported that clients' presenting concerns have become increasingly complex and more severe than previous clients two decades ago (Benton, Robertson, Tseng, & Benton, 2003). Those same researchers reported increasing trends in several key areas, including developmental, depression, academic skills, grief, medication use, relationships, stress/anxiety, family issues, physical problems, personality disorders, suicidal thoughts, and sexual assault.

The American College Counseling Association (ACCA, 2014) reported that students on today's college campuses show an increasing complexity of presenting mental health needs. ACCA observed that there is increased utilization of college counseling centers among the college student population. That observation was confirmed by Francis and Horn (2016), who reported that while the majority of college students enroll, study, and graduate with no mental health concerns, an increasing number of students seek counseling for severe mental health issues, including difficulty concentrating and test-taking stresses to suicidal ideation (Beiter et al., 2015; Ioravoici, 2014; Lippincott, & Lippincott, 2007). Over the years, the percentage of college students seeking counseling services has remained constant, about 10–15% of the college student population, according to Rando et. al, as cited in Francis and Horn (2017).

When viewed together, college counseling services are more important than ever, and yet there appears to be no relief in this growing trend toward increased mental health service needs and increase the severity of presenting concerns. These realities have been well documented for a couple of decades with no evidence to imply that this trend will change in the immediate future.

SIDEBAR 13.1

In Practice: What Would You Do?

New small college president James C. Smith is facing some large institutional budget cuts by his trustees that will mean some significant cuts to student affairs and college counseling center services. The trustees have argued that students can receive counseling by the local mental health center and other student affairs services can be reassigned to teaching faculty to handle. President Smith is uncertain about the best way to respond to the trustees about the importance of student affairs and college counseling.

Class Discussion

1. What would you say to President Smith about the cuts to student affairs and counseling?
2. How would you explain to the college trustees just how vital student affairs is to the college?
3. Explain why it is important for a student to have counseling on campus.
4. How would you explain the importance of a holistic education to the trustees?

Student Development Theory

Theory is a necessary framework in order to do business in higher education. It allows student affairs and college counseling professionals to see interactions among and across students that would otherwise go unnoticed in higher education. Additionally, when theory is utilized in empirical research, it builds the argument for the study and provides a focus for the research. Theory provides a necessary framework for the development of research questions and supports the selection of relevant research variables, and guides data analysis and the interpretation of research findings. Theory's place and relevance in research and applied student affairs practices in well-established and documented precisely. Theory has equal significance and importance for student affairs and college counseling professionals today and sets the stage for future growth.

Student development theories are the foundation for student affairs practice. They provide a conceptual framework for student affairs and counseling work in so many ways. Theory defines how students grow, develop, and matriculate throughout the college years and articulates how student learn. Such theories help us understand how and what environmental influences shape students' learning and growth experiences. Student development theory provides a conceptual framework for assessing students' learning, evaluating their growth outcomes, and measuring their success outcomes.

Strayhorn (2016, 2006, 2013a) observed that theory refers to the plausible explanations of observed phenomena. It is a set of interrelated constructs, definition, and prepositions that present a systematic view of the phenomenon by specifying relations among variables with the purpose of explaining and predicting phenomena (Kerlinger, 1986, as cited in Strayhorn, 2016). Lastly, theory is necessary for sensemaking to occur across the campus.

The theoretical concept *Student Development* was first coined by Nevitt Sanford (1967) as an "organization of increasing complexity" (p. 47) and was embellished later by Rodgers (1991) to focus on students by defining student development as "the way that student grows, progresses, or increases his/her developmental capabilities as a result of enrollment in an institution of higher education (p. 27).

Four core organization concepts are critical to understanding and making sense of student developmental theories.

Challenge and support. This concept was introduced first by Nevitt Sanford (1967) in his *theory of challenge and support.* It noted that students need an optimal balance of life challenge and support in order for development to occur.

Dissonance. Most developmental theories suggest that, in order for development to occur, the individual must experience dissonance or "a crisis." This crisis is not a time of panic or disruption, but rather, it is a decision point – that moment when one reaches an intersection and must turn one way or the other (Widick, Parker, & Knelfelkamp, 1978, pp. 3–4). The individual's interest in resolving the dissonance or crisis creates the conditions around which development occurs. Dissonance may emerge from environmental forces, internal processes, or a combination of these elements.

Stages, phrases, statuses, and vectors. The language within student development theories is critical to their understanding. Most often, student development theory language describes an individual's placement or location along the developmental growth continuum or on a map. The specific terminology used determines their category in which family of theories or theorists and signals something important about the process of development and worldviews about how students and their experiences are best understood. Regardless of language, each is intended to capture some defining feature of an individual.

Epigenetic principle and developmental trajectory. The *epigenetic principle* is the idea that " anything that grows has a ground plan... and out of this ground plan, the parts arise, each part having its time of special ascendancy until all parts have arisen to form a functioning whole. (Erickson, 1980). Development occurs along a trajectory of simple to complex and in predictable stages or sequence. The content of development and the process of development will look different depending on the actual theory, but developmental movement is characterized by sequential movement along a trajectory.

Student development theories provide a conceptual roadmap upon which an individual can make sense of his/her own maturation and growth as defined or framed most often with the learning context of a college campus or similar learning environment. They have been extracted and advanced from sociology, psychology, education and the behavioral sciences. To the extent that student development theories talk about an individual's interaction with a learning environment, such theories have borrowed concepts and practical ideas from organizational and environmental climate research from business, communication sciences, and applied science specialty areas. The goal of all these theoretical and conceptual models is to articulate a student's pathway for growth, learning, and academic success as it takes place across student affairs offices, including college counseling services. What follows is a brief description of the student development theories and applied practice theories. Each is described briefly, and key elements are highlighted. Illustrations of theory applications are highlighted, also.

Psychosocial Theories

Such theories examine the content of development and view what individuals are most concerned about across periods of the life cycle. Psychosocial theories focus on persons throughout the life cycle, including adolescents, college students, and adults of all ages. Development takes place as a series of developmental tasks or stages which include qualitative and quantitative changes in thinking, feeling, behaving, valuing, and relating to others and to oneself. Psychosocial theorists include Arthur Chickering, Erik Erickson, and Ruth Ellen Josselson.

Cognitive Structural Theories

Such theories focus on the structure of thinking as applied to the content of the various psychosocial issues. Cognitive structural theories evolve from simple to complex and are focused on the interactions of the individual with his/her social world. Furthermore, they are hierarchical and sequential with each stage representing an increasingly complex way of making meaning.

Structure provides an information processing filter that enables the individual to make sense of experiences and new encounters in the world. The mind's structures arise one at a time, always in the same order, regardless of cultural conditions. The age and rate the person travels through each stage varies. Each stage builds upon the one before it. Early cognitive theorist Piaget (1965) saw development along two dimensions: from a concrete view of the world to an ability for abstract ideas; and from an egocentric action model to a reflective, internalized way of knowing.

Three fundamental principles are important to the cognitive approach: cognitive structures, developmental sequence, and interaction with the environment. Individuals are believed to form *cognitive structures* to help make sense of what it is they are experiencing. In *developmental sequence*, the cognitive structures evolve over time into more complex, differentiated, and integrated ones. Development proceeds through a predictable sequence, although at an uneven pace. In *interaction with the environment*, the resulting dissonance or disequilibrium comes from challenges or new information that existing cognitive structures cannot handle, and it forces a new accommodation or alteration of the cognitive structure.

Social Identity Theories

Social identity theorists emphasize the importance of looking at social identities in relation to one another rather than as discrete units of analysis. These theories attend to the roles or membership categories into which a person falls. Several social identity theories are gleaned from theoretical structures that incorporate the influences of such structures as power and oppression on development and the student experience while other structures are underexamined and

-researched. Included among these social identity theories are racial identity, cultural identity, sexual identity, gender identity, religion, disability, and social class identity development. These social identities intersect with one another, and a student's awareness of such intersections are important developmental markers for growth and change. Students attach personal meaning to their social identities in ways that can support their persistence toward degree completion. Colleges are encouraged to establish policies and best practices that support and protect students' rights to explore these intersecting identities in a safe learning environment. College and universities protect students' rights to declare and nurture these identities through their diversity and equity programs and services, activities that promote peer engagement and ensure students' entitlements and activities that best promote their personal and academic growth.

Typology Theories

Typology theories describe distinct but stable differences in learning style, type, temperament, or socioeconomic background. Scholars have argued that this model is not technically a developmental theory because typology theories do not describe the milestones of development. They shed light on personal characteristics or preferences and how they affect students in matching preferences to career plans or academic majors These theories provide valuable frameworks for thinking about how institutional challenges, environmental factors, and occupational settings influence various types of students. Among typology theorists are Carl Jung, Lawrence Kolb, and John Holland.

Theories of Organization and Campus Environment

Theories that focus on organization, organizational behavior, and campus environment emphasize the influence of these larger entities on student development and the student experience. These theories help to make sense of how the environment influences behavior through its interactions with individual characteristics (e.g., campus ecology theories). Student affairs researchers and practitioners have argued whether or not these models are technically considered a developmental theory since they do not describe the milestones of individual development. Instead, these theories work on the premise that individual students can experience the same environment differently, based upon their own level of development, and these theories seek to assign meaning to these environment interactions.

Holistic Development Theory

Baxter Magolda (2001, 2008) extended the work of Robert Kegan (1982, 1994) by creating a theory of self-authorship that is defined as a developmental capacity, one that is holistic because of the interrelated domains of interpersonal, identity, and cognitive development (Baxter Magolda, 2008). The task of creating or constructing a holistic theoretical perspective requires that individuals focus on the intersections of identities rather than on separate constructs. This holistic lens has been extended to examining diverse audiences (e.g., Abes, Jones, & McEwen, 2007; Torres & Hernandez, 2007) and highlights conceptualizing development as holistic in order to illuminate contextualized influences including privilege and oppression (Jones, 2009). Contemporary research seeks to verify that confronting racism is a developmental task and integral to holistic development.

Integrative Theories

Integrative theories examine the factors in development that simultaneously occur; they are useful in working with students to explore developmental environment through life histories.

Additionally, they are helpful with assessment techniques, student affairs programming, and developing ongoing college transition programs. Bronfenbrenner's theory (1979) is a popular integrative theory with four components: (a) process-interactions between organism and environment; (b) person-attributes of the person that shape the course of development; (c) context-critical location for interactions, and (d) time. Bronfenbrenner's theory has four levels of context, also. *Microsystems* are activities and roles in face-to-face settings either physical, social, or symbolic that invite, permit, or inhabit engagement for students. *Mesosystems* describe linkage and processes between two or more settings involving the developing student. *Exosystems* exert an influence on the campus environment, and *macrosystems* reflect an overarching pattern of systems.

Impact on Individual, Family, and Community

Student affairs professionals including college counselors are the center of the campus when it comes to supporting individuals and their families, and the communities that surround colleges and universities, in real time and online. Throughout a student's academic journey and throughout the college campus, student affairs offices are central to that individual's academic success and personal growth. Student affairs offices, especially admissions, student financial aid, housing, and professional academic advisors, are the first contact that prospective and transitioning students have with the campus. These professionals welcome students to the campus, embrace their learning, housing, and personal development needs, and engage their family members – all of them – in the transition process. Student affairs programs introduce students to the campus, educate and inform their families, and collaborate with community members to create a dynamic living/learning environment for students throughout their entire college experience.

Student affairs professionals welcome students to campus. They use their strengths and professional talents to engage new students and help them to feel part of the university campus through a myriad of welcoming activities and transition events that can begin as early as the junior year in school for the traditional age student coming right from high school to the campus.

Additionally, student affairs professionals support and welcome nontraditional students arriving on campus, including those in the military and veterans, adult learners, and distance learners. Student affairs offices collaborate with one another and engage academic affairs units to assure the academic success and personal growth of all college students, regardless of their unique learning needs or their college entry point.

Military veterans, their families, and dependents enroll on campus in nontraditional ways. Student affairs offices are usually the place where Veterans services or support centers are located on college campuses. For adult learners who arrive on campus just in time for evening courses or who request child care services in order for them to enroll in classes, student affairs services are their first stop for all the resources needed for the adult learner and his/her family, too. These students benefit from the array of learning (e.g. test-taking, stress management) and personal development resources offered through college counseling and are encouraged to use these resources from their first entry onto the campus.

Recently, colleges of all types have expanded to include distance learning opportunities for students at all academic levels from undergraduate through graduate and professional degree programs. These distance learners, while not physically on the campus, enroll with the same academic and personal development needs as residential students, albeit with added obligations such as work and family life responsibilities that complicate their learning opportunities and give context to their academic success and degree completion. Depending upon how or whether distance students pay fees for student service support, student affairs units can create specialized distance learning resources for these students. For example, distance students who require disability accommodation will connect and collaborate with those offices to request for distance learning accommodations and support from the disability office and content – specific academic advisors, to determine the exact online accommodation that is required to assure the distance student's success. Moreover, college counseling can offer online materials including apps about test anxiety or stress management, for example, that can be made available for both distance and on-campus learners alike.

Student affairs professionals recognize the importance of community in supporting students throughout their educational journey, and work collaboratively with community agency partners, including nonprofit, social justice and advocacy organizations, businesses, other educational entities, and legislative partners to create a learning environment that supports all students. Student affairs offices provide leadership to all those community partners that enhance the learning environment for college students, on and off campus.

Counseling Practices in Nonclinical Areas

Student affairs and college counseling become "first responders" for a wide range of counseling practices in nonclinical areas that support educational and personal developmental issues. Student affairs offices, including college counseling, are consulted by college administration about a wide range of nonclinical issues including, but not limited to, environment, safety prevention, technology security and safety, transportation, and policy development.

Campus environment issues are diverse and expansive. They can involve addressing homelessness and food-insecure students on some campuses. In these instances, student affairs offices provide the leadership to identify and support these students with food banks, financial resources, and temporary shelters, all done in collaboration with community partners. Similarly, environmental issues in the classroom speak to making certain the classroom, on campus or online, are safe and free of bias and open to all ideas. College counselors have an important role here through their partnerships with student advocacy groups and other student affairs offices to provide communication and anti-bias programs and workshops.

Technology, Security, and Safety Issues

Technology security and safety are unique environmental issues and student affairs offices collaborate with IT experts to develop a safe online learning environment for all college students. Their leadership informs and educates students, faculty and professional staff about the importance of developing technology security policies and practices that have a positive impact on residential and distance learning across a college campus. Student affairs professional staff provide leadership to the campus to best understand the adverse consequences of security breaches on students' wellbeing.

Structural issues such as transportation, walking paths, parking, building and road construction have a direct impact on the lives of college students. Student affairs assumes leadership in discussions about these issues. They collaborate with campus administrators in discussions about campus construction, transportation and walking paths, and access paths to campus and guide decisions that engage students in the change process. Student affairs are called upon as resources about such structural and environmental changes to guide such construction decisions that are educational and developmental.

Student affairs and college counseling professionals have assumed the leadership when colleges are challenged to develop weapons policies in response to state legislative and/or higher education governing board mandates regarding such matters as concealed carry and weapons in the classroom. In these instances, student affairs offices take leadership by advocating for institutional policies that promote students' learning and personal development best while protecting their civil rights. These professionals will conduct an educational workshop for students to educate them about weapons policies as they apply to housing and classroom settings.

In summary, student affairs and college counseling professionals engage in nonclinical area practices and decision making, involving transportation, safety, construction, and campus environmental issues that are educational and developmental. Their leadership, in collaboration with academic offices, student groups, and community partners, promotes educational and personal development for all college students, regardless of the institutional type and campus mission. The outcome of this leadership is a campus climate that is best designed and well suited for students' maximum learning and personal growth.

Summary

Student affairs and college counseling are essential college offices and administrative units that play a direct, and central, role in the academic success and development growth of all college students. These professionals are uniquely trained and educated with an emphasis on learning, development, and growth defined within the context of their professional specialty as articulated by CACREP and CAS Standards. Their campus services are broad, theory-driven, and outcome-based in ways that support students in their academic and personal learning journeys toward graduation and transition into the working world. Moreover, when needed, student affairs and college counseling professionals step away from their traditional assigned campus duties to advocate for students' issues and needs to central administration, trustees, higher education coordinating boards and external constituents in ways that enhance and improve students' educational and personal development. These professionals are an essential part of a student's academic success and provide essential leadership to the campus and community that enhance students' academic success and personal growth fully.

> I got letters emails, texts, and phone calls from student affairs professionals before and after I was admitted into college. Now I understand all the ways that student affairs supports me and my educational goals.
>
> – undergraduate student's posting about starting college

References

Abes, E. S., Jones, S. R., & McEwen, M. K. (2007). Using queer theory to explore lesbian college students' multiple dimensions of identity. *Journal of College Student Development, 48*, 619–636.

American College Counseling Association (2014) *Community College Survey*, Alexandria, VA: American College Counseling Association. Retrieved from www.collegecounseling.org

American College Personnel Association & National Association of Student Personnel Administrators. (2010). *ACPA/NASPA professional competency areas for student affairs practitioners*. Washington, DC: Authors.

American Council on Education. (1937). *The student personnel point of view: A report of a conference on the philosophy and development of student personnel work in colleges and universities*. Washington, DC: Author. Retrieved from http://www2.bgsu.edu/sahp/pages/1937STUDENTPERSONNELnew.pdf

Association of University and College Counseling Center Directors (AUCCD). (2012). *Survey of counseling center directors*. Retrieved from www.aucccd.org

Baxter Magolda, M. B, (2001). *Making their own way: Narratives for transforming higher education to promote self-development*. Sterling, VA: Stylus.

Baxter Magolda, M. B. (2008). Three elements of self-authorship. *Journal of College Student Development*, 49(4), 269–284.

Beiter, R., Nash, R., McCrady, M., Rhoades, D., Linscomb, M., Clarahan, M., & Sammut, S. (2015). The prevalence and correlates of depression, anxiety, and stress in a sample of college students. *Journal of Affective Disorders, 173*, 90–96.

Benton, S. A., Robertson, J. M., Tseng, W. C., Newton, F. B., & Benton, S. L. (2003). Changes in counseling center client problems across 13 years. *Professional Psychology: Research and Practice, 34*, 66–72.

Bronfenbrenner, U. (1979). *The ecology of human development*. Cambridge, MA: Harvard University Press.

Council for the Accreditation in Counseling and Related Educational Programs (CACREP) (2015). *2016 CACREP standards*. Retrieve, from https://www.cacrep.org/for-programs/2016-cacrep-standards/

Dungy, G. J. (2003). Organization and functions of student affairs. S. R. Komives, D. B. Woodard, Jr., & Associates (Eds.), *Student services: A handbook for the profession* (4th ed.), (339-357). San Francisco, CA: Jossey-Bass.

Erickson, E. (1980). *Identity and the life cycle*. New York: W.W. Norton & Company. (Original work published 1959).

Francis, P. C., & Horn, A. S. (2016). *Counseling services and student success. Research brief*. Minneapolis, MN: Midwestern Higher Education Compact.

Fu, M., & Cheng, A. W. (2017). College counseling services: Meeting today's demands. *Psychological Services, 14*, 403–406.

Iarovici, D. (2014) *Mental health issues and the university student*, Baltimore, MD: Johns Hopkins. University Press.

Jones, S. R. (2009). Constructing identities at the intersections: An autoethnographic exploration of multiple dimensions of identity. *Journal of College Student Development, 50*, 287–304.

Kaplan, D. M., Tarvydas, V. M., & Gladding, S. T. (2014). 20/20: A vision for the future of counseling: The new consensus definition of counseling. *Journal of Counseling & Development, 92*, 366–372.

Kegan, R. (1982). *The evolving self: Problem and process in human development*. Cambridge, MA: Harvard University Press.

Kegan, R. (1994). *In over our heads: The mental demands of modern life*. Cambridge, MA: Harvard University Press.

Keeling, R. (Ed.). (2006). *Learning reconsidered 2: Implementing a campus-wide focus on the student experience*. Washington, DC: American College Personnel Association; National Association of Student Personnel Administrators.

Kimball, E. W., & Ryder, A. J. (2014). Using history to promote reflection: A model for reframing student affairs practice. *Journal of Student Affairs Research and Practice, 51*, 298–310.

Kuk, L., & Banning, J. (2009). Designing student affairs organizational structures: Perceptions of senior student affairs officers. *NASPA Journal, 46*(1), 94–117.

Lippincott, J. A., & Lippincott, R. B. (2007). *Special populations in college counseling: A handbook for mental health professionals*. Alexandria, VA: American Counseling Association.

Perry, W. (1970). *Forms of intellectual and ethical development in the college years: A scheme*. New York: Holt, Rinehart & Winston.

Piaget, J. (1965). *The moral judgment of the child*. New York: The Free Press (Originally published in 1932).

Rodgers, R. E. (1991). Using theory in practice in student affairs. In T. K. Miller & R. B. Winston (Eds.), *Administration and leadership in student affairs: Actualizing student development in higher education* (pp. 203–251). Muncie, IN: Accelerated Press.

Sanford, N. (1967). *Where colleges fail; A study of the student as a person*. San Francisco, CA: Jossey-Bass.

Strayhorn, T. (2006). *Frameworks for assessing learning and development outcomes*. Washington, DC: Council for the Advancement of Standards in Higher Education (CAS).

Strayhorn, T. L. (2013). *Theoretical frameworks in college student research*. Lantham, MD: University Press of America, Rowman & Littlefield.

Strayhorn, T. (2016). *Student development theory in higher education. A social psychological approach*. New York: Routledge.

Torres, V., & Hernandez, E. (2007). The influence of ethnic identity on self-authorship: A longitudinal study of Latino/a college students. *Journal of College Student Development, 48*, 588–573.

Widick, C., Parker, C. A., & Knelfelkamp, L. L. (1978). Erik Erickson and psychosocial development. In L. L. Knelfelkamp, C. Widick & C. A. Parker (Eds.), *Applying developmental findings* (New Directions for Student Services, vol. 4, pp. 1–17). San Francisco, CA: Jossey-Bass.

Worley, D. L., & Wells-Dolan, A. (2012). Transport and telescope: Services for students, 1937–2012. In K. M. Boyle, J. W. Lowery & J. A. Mueller (Eds.), *Reflections on the 75th anniversary of the student personnel point of view* (pp. 46–52). Washington, DC: ACPA – College Student Educators International.

Chapter 14

Marriage, Couple, and Family Counseling and Therapy

Stephen Southern

Nobody, who has not been in the interior of a family, can say what the difficulties of any individual of that family may be.

– Jane Austen

POINTS TO PONDER

What are the characteristics of a Marriage, Couple, and Family Counselor?

- How did the MFC specialization develop?
- What are the major theories and models in MFC?
- What are the major professional associations?
- What are the major trends in MFC?

Marriage, Couple, and Family Counseling and Therapy (MFC) developed in response to the emphasis upon individual intrapsychic mechanisms in Freud's (1896/1962) original model of psychotherapy. Subsequently, there were developments in person-centered counseling (Rogers, 1957) and behavior therapy (e.g., Baucom, Epstein, Kirby, & LaTaillade, 2010), but the focus remained on changing the person (inside or out), rather than treating the family unit. Historically, some theorists or clinicians attempted to bridge the gap by attending to the individual in the family context (Bowen, 1978; Johnson, 1996). Recently, innovations in counseling afforded tremendous flexibility in perspective and opened many new approaches to facilitate change or growth in individuals and their families. The MFC viewpoint contributed substantially to the emerging models of counseling by emphasizing the properties of systems.

In family systems, members are viewed as *interdependent*, continuously influencing each other. One person's change in behavior affects the functioning of all the interconnected parts of the whole system. Family counseling and therapy have been most affected by the theory of systems. Systemic thinking is the foundation of the MFC specialization within professional counseling.

History and Background

Systems theory originated in modern approaches to planning and implementing regulatory systems, such as the self-correcting heuristics by which rockets reached their destinations. Wiener (1948) discussed cybernetics as "the scientific study of control and communication in the animal and machine." Cybernetics was applied to diverse fields including computers, robotics, neuroscience, and ecology. Complex systems, such as families, require multiple perspectives to understand the lived experiences of family members and to develop solutions that are meaningful and long-lasting. Family systems have properties or characteristics that are required in order to help individuals and family change in even broader contexts in which they exist, such as culture (Stanton & Welsh, 2012).

Family systems include the following properties. They interact in ways that lead to sameness or minimizing change (i.e., *homeostasis*), which could lead to symptoms or syndromes, or movement toward change (*morphogenesis*) and growth. Properties of family system are listed in Table 14.1.

The foundation of MFC upon systems thinking provided new ways to conceptualize clinical cases. A recent innovation in systemic treatment, *Integrative Systemic Therapy* (Pinsof et al., 2018) combined best practices from individual, couple, and family therapy into a single model, based on the importance of understanding systems and contents in formulating problems and solutions. MFC represents the most robust, integrative model in psychotherapy and professional counseling. The systemic model was a major departure from the intrapsychic (i.e., within the person's mind) view of the original therapy.

Psychoanalysis and Object Relations

Psychoanalysis was built upon the most individualistic intrapsychic model to describe causes of symptoms and methods for change. Freud (1915/1959) rejected the idea that couples or family

Table 14.1 Properties of Family Systems

Hierarchy	Human systems are nested in a hierarchy of subsystems which interact to influence decision making, distribution of resources, and rules and guidelines. Hierarchy includes society, community, family, relationships, individuals, and biological subsystems.
Boundaries	The boundaries of subsystems define membership and power, including who or what is included and excluded from influence and meaning. Boundaries may be missing, overly rigid or balanced, like the semi-permeable membrane of a healthy cell.
Ecology	Complex subsystems interact dynamically and members (elements) are influenced by multiple systems, including family, school, community, and culture. Operations of subsystems determine limits to sustainability and survival.
Synergy	Elements combine in such a way that the whole or total effect is greater than the sum of the parts.
Context	Individual behavior can be understood only in the context in which it occurs. Context requires understanding of the multiple systems of influence and flexibility in the perspective of the observer (counselor).
Function	Behavior generates consequences for social subsystems. Even not acting could influence the outcome of other members of the family.
Feedback	Information is exchanged among the subsystems such that operations change. Positive feedback leads to more of the behavior in question and negative information diminishes activity or behavior.
Cohesion	Individuals in family systems form and maintain bonds and alliances that contribute to boundary maintenance or change. Typical alliances are dyads and triads, which can be depicted graphically to show relatedness.
Change	A major characteristic of family systems is the balancing of change and remaining the same. In problem resolution, there are forces that facilitate growth through changing subsystems and constraints that limit how much change can occur at a given time.

Note: These properties are based upon descriptions of family systems included in the following classic and contemporary sources: Bowen (1978), Bronfenbrenner (2005), Minuchin (1974), Pinsof et al. (2018), and Watzlawick, Weakland, & Fisch (1974).

members could even be in therapy at the same time, claiming this could set off a potentially harmful "transference storm." However, students and colleagues revised the original psychoanalytic model to include *object relations*. Object relations represented parts of the developing ego in which early life experiences with caretakers established capacity for self-cohesion, self-soothing, and self-agency. Mastery of developmental milestones in the first three years of life, including a close, secure bond with the mother or caretaker (i.e., symbiosis) and readiness to venture forth into the world, was thought to influence significant relationships with others throughout life (Gomez, 1997, Horner, 1979).

An early form of couple's therapy (e.g., Dicks, 1967; Fairbairn, 1952), based on object relations, focused on the unconscious process by which opposite partners were attracted to one another, then attempted to control or change one another to resolve unfinished business in the family of origin. Neurotic couples, drawn together by *complementarity* (opposites attract), experience conflicts and move against or away from one another. Damaged object relations require concurrent treatment of the couple to understand and change processes that distort perception and communication in the troubled relationship. What cannot be resolved by the couple may be passed on or *delineated* to their children and the problem cycle continues. In recent years, objects relations evolved into the study and treatment of attachment problems in children and adults based upon pioneering work by Bowlby (1969) and Main and Solomon (1995). Counseling to promote secure attachment is a modern approach to improving capacity for intimacy in adults and closeness in committed relationships.

Psychoanalysis and object relations therapy evolved toward an interpersonal or family orientation based on the nature and quality of developmental experiences, starting in infancy and extending throughout the lifespan. Another major approach in the history of MFC emphasized attachment in terms of external attachment and other structures that could be observed in family interactions.

Structural Family Therapy

Salvador Minuchin (1974), a pioneer in the field of MFC, developed structural family therapy to describe the relationships among family members and intervene in dysfunctional interactions to facilitate healthy patterns and growth. He incorporated systemic concepts into the treatment model, addressing power dynamics, boundaries, and other structures. Structural family therapy shifted perspectives and influence strategies away from cause-and-effect efforts to change behaviors of individuals (first-order change) toward patterns or sequences of family interactions and alteration of family rules (second-order change). The structural family therapy model was integrated with medical intervention to treat such disorders as anorexia nervosa in *psychosomatic families* (Minuchin, Rosman, & Baker, 1978).

A major focus in structural family therapy is to conduct a structural assessment of the whole family system. The components of a structural assessment are included in Table 14.2.

The structural assessment reveals the status of the family coming for treatment and suggests some functions of the symptom in the *identified patient*, the troubled member who appears to be the "problem."

Internal Family Systems Therapy

Richard Schwartz (1995), a major contributor to understanding the metaframeworks of MFC, innovated a family therapy approach based in part on translating structural family therapy constructs to address internal or intrapsychic systems. His model affirmed that people have a healthy core Self that can restore wellbeing, a humanistic ideal. Each person has a Self that can lead parts

Table 14.2 Elements of a Structural Assessment

Role of the Symptom	Families may passively shape or actively encourage problem behavior in the identified patient, but the overall family system benefits in terms of organization and regulation.
Subsystems	There are nested subsystems that may be based on age, position, status, or social factors, including gender.
Cross-Generational Coalitions	Coalitions are typically covert or indirect and may involve an alliance of a parent and child against the other parent or caretaker.
Boundaries	Identity and closeness/distance are determined by boundaries. Classically, some troubled families are enmeshed, having diffuse boundaries, while others could be described as disengaged with overly rigid boundaries.
Hierarchy	The parental subsystem takes responsibility for setting boundaries and limits, making decisions, and assigning priorities while maintaining emotional connection with children.
Complementarity	Maintenance of polarized, opposite roles that contribute to conflict and constrain change including permissive/strict parents, good/bad children, and logical/emotional partners.
Family Development	Stages in the family life cycle in which members grow or change requiring renegotiation of boundaries
Strengths	Join with families in fair, culturally sensitive ways so labels are not used to pathologize or limit. Identify and apply strengths of family members to resolve problems.

Note: Elements were based on descriptions by Minuchin (1974).

of one's inner life through exercising compassion and leadership. The parts evolve over the lifespan assuming three basic roles: exiles, managers, and firefighters. Life trauma, family dysfunction, and polarized relationships contribute to parts taking on extreme roles in order to cope. The parts operate in an internal system to maintain homeostasis and handle crises by establishing boundaries and contexts and forming coalitions. Maintaining the status quo in the system contributes to symptoms and blocks opportunities for growth.

Similar to most family therapies, the self-of-the-therapist plays a central role in establishing contact with the inner Self of the client and accessing resources for change. The Internal Family Systems therapist helps a person identify parts, their functions, and facilitates guidance or direction from the Self, which is the capacity for curiosity, compassion, and acceptance. The therapist asks questions and makes suggestions to help the parts explore their functions and relationships: "How do you feel toward this part?" or "What is the relationship between these parts?" In trauma or crisis, parts perform overdeveloped functions in order to protect the system. Increasing Self leadership enables the person to achieve inner balance and harmony in interactions with others. Self increasingly steps in and organizes the internal system reducing rigidity and conflicts, encouraging collaboration, and facilitates parts working in harmony.

Internal Family Systems therapy, Structural Family Therapy, and Object Relations Family Therapy afforded a glimpse into the origin of MFC. The intrapsychic or psychodynamic approach expanded to work with couples and eventually families. Structural family therapy emerged from systems thinking to address presenting problems within the context of the whole family unit and its subsystems. Internal family systems applied structural family therapy and other systems constructs to the individual. The defining feature of the MFC specialization is the preference for looking at relationships from a systems perspective. This perspective has been expressed in the professional associations that represent marriage, couple, and family therapists and counselors.

Professional Associations

There are two major associations that guide professional practice in MFC: International Association of Marriage and Family Counselors (n.d.) and American Association for Marriage and Family Therapy (n.d.). Many MFCs are active members in both organizations by meeting standards for training and supervision, abiding by the codes of ethics, reading resources associated with the associations, and attending conferences or other continuing education opportunities. IAMFC is a division of the American Counseling Association, chartered in 1989 to represent the needs of professional counselors who specialize in work with couples and families. AAMFT is a national organization devoted to advancing practice for marriage and family therapists. Robert L. Smith has been a major contributor to the development of Marriage and Family Counseling, setting standards and recommending training (Smith, 1993; Smith, Carlson, Stevens-Smith, & Dennison, 1994).

Professional counselors in MFC may have graduated from a master's degree program in counseling accredited by the Council for Accreditation of Counseling and Related Educational Programs (CACREP). Accredited programs and standards for the area of specialization are published by CACREP (n.d.). The 2016 CACREP standards include requirements for foundations, contextual dimensions, and practice. The standards are introduced on the website.

> Students who are preparing to specialize as marriage, couple, and family counselors are expected to possess the knowledge and skills necessary to address a wide variety of issues in the context of relationships and families. Counselor education programs with a specialty area in marriage, couple, and family counseling must document where each of the lettered standards listed below is covered in the curriculum.
> (Council for Accreditation of Counseling & Related Educational Programs, n.d.)

Clinical members of AAMFT complete master's degree studies in departments of marriage and family therapy, accredited by the Commission on Accreditation for Marriage and Family Therapy Education (COAMFTE) (Commission on Accreditation for Marriage and Family Therapy Education, n.d.) or satisfying requirements for licensure as a Marriage and Family Therapy (MFT) in the state of practice. Professional counselors in MFC satisfy training and supervision requirements, which vary by state of residence or practice, to become licensed with the title Licensed Professional Counselor (LPC), Licensed Clinical Mental Health Counselor (LCMHC), or Licensed Clinical Counselor (LCC). Licensed professional counselors in other areas of specialization (e.g., clinical mental health counseling) usually have at least one course in marriage and family counseling/therapy. MFCs frequently complete at least one course in sexuality therapy and some states require coursework in sexuality for licensure.

IAMFC sponsors a quarterly peer-reviewed professional journal: *The Family Journal: Counseling and Therapy for Couples and Families.* The association sponsors sessions at the annual meeting of the American Counseling Association, conducts an annual conference, supports a certification, and offers international study opportunities. IAMFC offers award programs and mentoring for emerging leaders in the field.

AAMFT emerged from early efforts in couple's therapy and family life education to represent one of the newest professions: marriage and family therapy. Interestingly, AAMFT members frequently provide services to individuals, in addition to couples and families. Founded in 1942, AAMFT advocates for education, supervision, research, and practice of marriage and family therapy, as well as advocacy for policy and legislation affecting the family. In contrast, the American Counseling Association addresses a core counseling model, derived originally from school guidance, with specializations according to various populations or settings.

AAMFT provides tools and resources, annual conference and workshops, advocacy and career services, and a professional publication, the *Journal of Marital and Family Therapy*. The association offers a credential (Clinical Fellow) to members who meet the highest clinical, professional and ethical standards. The ethical standards of AAMFT can be accessed online (2015). IAMFC produced a Code of Ethics to complement the standards of the American Counseling Association (International Association of Marriage and Family Counselors, 2018).

Clinicians apply the marriage and family perspective in other professions, including social work, pastoral counseling, and psychology. Division 43 of the American Psychological Association is devoted to couple and family psychology. They publish a journal, *Counseling and Family Psychology*, and offer specialized training in conferences and workshop. MFC specialists who address sexuality issues should become familiar with the American Association of Sexuality Educators, Counselors, and Therapists (n.d.) which offers an annual conference, institutes, clinical credentialing (e.g., Certified Sex Therapist), and advocacy. The professional associations exist to promote standards of training and care, as well as best practices. Advances in MFC practice represent classic and contemporary advances in theory and models.

Both IAMFC (2018) and AAMFT (n.d.) promulgate codes of ethics which guide the practice of MFC specialists. The codes include ethics to which MFC specialists should aspire, as well as specific requirements for safe, effective practice. Typically, licensure laws in the states incorporate the ethical codes, but the legislatures may pass rules and regulations that typically are more stringent. Ethical guidelines are important in MFC practice because there are fundamental issues with such matters as informed consent to treatment and confidentiality of records. Significant ethical concerns for the MFC specialization are included in Table 14.3.

Ethical counselors are responsible for protecting consent, confidentiality, and wellbeing of clients. Since families are complex systems, MFC specialists are challenged to do no harm, protect

Table 14.3 Ethical Concerns in MFC Specialization

Who is the client?	When offering couple or family therapy, while there may be an "identified patient" or the case may be established in one name, the couple or the family is the actual client.
Who can consent to treatment?	Adults, parents, and guardians can sign informed consent for treatment. However, even children should assent. In some states, minor children are able to consent to treatment without adult consent.
Are records confidential?	Typically, those who are able to consent to treatment must authorize release of records. In couple counseling, both partners must sign the authorization.
What diagnosis should I use?	Some insurance companies or third-party payers may not pay for MFC services. This is likely in couple and sexuality counseling. It is unethical to use an individual diagnosis or billing code in these cases.
Can I keep secrets?	In meeting with an individual or subsystem of the family, information may be revealed that may be kept private based on treatment needs, but counselors should not hold secrets. The process of disclosure is an issue in working with couples and teenagers.
Can I do a custody evaluation?	When a counselor has been treating a child or a family, the counselor should avoid agreeing to conduct a custody evaluation, which could challenge objectivity and confound clinical and forensic roles.
Do I attend a child's graduation?	In the past, going to a client's graduation could be contraindicated due to concerns over multiple roles. However, attending such rituals could be therapeutic. The rationale for attending should be charted.
Must I report abuse?	In most states, counselors are mandated reporters of child, elder, and disabled abuse. Clients should be made aware of the limits to confidentiality.

Note: Ethical concerns in MFC were based on descriptions by Brendel & Nelson (1999); Lazarus (2002); Meara, Schmidt, & Day (1996); Southern (2012).

client rights, and respect autonomy in decision making. Counselors embrace aspirational ethics requiring multicultural sensitivity, examination of personal bias, and advocacy for social justice.

Theories and Models

The MFC specialization is based on several theoretical models and constructs emerging from the proliferation of psychotherapeutic approaches. Some of the theories represent applications of primarily an intrapsychic or individual tradition to the issues of couples and families. Other models grew from the systems perspective which defined the MFC field. Some contemporary approaches are *integrative* in that they combine individual and family perspectives, as well as intrapsychic, behavioral, and interpersonal constructs (e.g., Pinsof et al., 2018). This section will provide a brief overview of the major theories and models in the MFC specialization.

- Strategic Family Therapy
- Experiential Family Therapy
- Structural Family Therapy
- Cognitive-Behavioral Family Therapy
- Postmodern Family Therapy

Of all the family therapy theories and models, the constructs of strategic family therapy, experiential family therapy, and structural family therapy fit best the systemic perspective of MFC.

Strategic Family Therapy

Strategic family therapy was grounded in general systems and cybernetics theories, which came to be studied and applied in the Mental Research Institute (MRI). Several brief therapy approaches originated in attempts to innovate case conceptualizations based on systemic principles. Jay Haley(1987) in particular used enigmatic behavioral directives to interrupt problem sustaining sequences. Some of the strategic approaches used creative language, paradox, and even "prescribing the problem" to influence stuck family systems.

While an assumption is made that the family members' efforts to solve the problem actually maintain the problem, strategic family therapy was conducted respectfully by using warmth, humor, and social courtesy. Occasionally, the therapist would focus on the family member who had access to the most power, which could be a silent member or a more demanding person. There were no set techniques or goals since behavioral prescriptions were designed to be implemented with particular families. The therapist's role would be based upon the needs of the family unit and its resources. Haley (1987) observed, "The main goal of therapy is to get people to behave differently and so to have different subjective experiences." The strategic position is "What response from the therapist is most likely to produce change?" (p. 56).

Strategic family therapy was famous for two interventions intended to create conditions for new information and options to enter the family system: the *one-down position* and the *ordeal*. Bateson (1972) emphasized the cornerstone of strategic work: becoming "the difference that makes a difference." The one-down position of the therapist refocused the views and efforts of family members away from problem sequences toward helping the therapist be effective. The therapist could directly request support or express helplessness or hopelessness in order to engage family resources in a way that makes a difference. An ordeal could be constructed in which it is more difficult to maintain a problem sequence than to let go of the symptom and try something new. The therapist would help the family develop rituals or conditions that required extra time or effort before they returned to old "problem-solving" (i.e., problem maintaining) efforts.

Strategic family therapy required creativity, a willingness to experiment, and readiness for repositioning or changing the therapeutic stance to gain influence. Due to contemporary ethical norms for transparency, informed consent, and boundary limitations, strategic family therapy is less frequently encountered. However, the aesthetically oriented and creative model remains prominent in experiential family therapy.

Experiential Family Therapy

Virginia Satir (1972, 1983), a prominent woman in MFC, began her career at the Mental Research Institute (MRI). While she was interested in language, paradox, and strategy, Satir was committed to the use of metaphor, role playing, and experiential exercise. She identified five communication stances in family systems that were difficult to change: *congruent, placatory, blamer, super responsible,* and *irrelevant.* These stances enabled individuals to survive childhood within disqualifying, neglectful, or abusive family systems. Life learning contributes to the congruent stance in which needs of self and other are balanced across various contexts. The other survival stances tend to produce individual symptoms, family conflicts, and stuckness in the family.

The placator engages in people-pleasing: smoothing away difficulties and maintaining the appearance of normal functioning. The experiential therapist may help the placatory learn it is acceptable to disagree with others. The blamer in a dysfunctional family system may be critical or judgmental. There is a need to increase awareness of the thoughts and feelings of others and respect others. The super reasonable family member attempts to use logic and rules to block emotional expression and change. The therapist assists this member value internal, subjective realities and emerging feelings. The irrelevant stance involves lack of grounding in self, others, or context. This member challenges reason and subjective experience by functioning as a distraction. There is a need to recognize thoughts and feelings of oneself and others and share in the family valuing process.

The experiential therapist may help families see or experience their stances or other roadblocks to change through sculpting, choreography, and role play. These enactments afford immediate, moment-to-moment experience that tends to bypass typical cognitive and behavioral defenses. The family members do not talk about change, they become the change. Typically, these experiential exercises may be suggested by the therapist as coach and evolve through several scenes or sequences. Family members process their experiences gaining greater awareness of opportunities for change. Psychodrama may be used with a group of individuals from various family systems to address stuck points or gain insight into commonalities of survival in family systems.

Experiential family therapy involves humor, play, and creativity. Tools may be used such as a sand tray, art supplies, or music sources. Playfulness helps reframe problems that have been magnified. Engaging imagery and fantasy fosters new perspectives on problems and solutions. Satir (1972) recommended a *parts party* to explore individual attributes and relationships with other. In the parts party exercise, a person arranges chairs or draws them to include characters (real, historical, or imagined) one would invite to a party, such as a holiday gathering (Thanksgiving dinner). The client explores how the parts were selected and what would happen as they interacted at the party. This experiential activity embodies fantasy and spatial features such as proximity, boundary, and alignment.

Structural Family Therapy

The structural family therapist (like Internal Family Systems specialist) helps members become aware of their interaction sequences through manipulation of physical dimensions. The therapist directs family members and subsystems to represent a conflict or problem. This *reenactment* affords the opportunity to map, track, and modify family structures that maintain a problem sequence. The therapist acts as a stage director or coach in encouraging family members to depict roles, boundaries, hierarchies, alignments, coalitions, and other structural features. The family is encouraged to make changes to show alternative transactions. Chairs may be arranged to represent closeness or distance. Family members who do not talk are given the task to meet on the side and reach a decision about the next step in the exercise. Minuchin (1974) was highly creative in organizing reenactments that forced engagement in solutions such as dealing with an eating disordered family over lunch.

A variation of structural family therapy was developed by Murray Bowen. Bowen's *intergenerational therapy* applied structural constructs and visual aids to help families grow. His therapy model anticipated trends in cognitive therapy and integrative approaches to change. The therapy included insights from object relations and anticipated the contemporary focus on adult attachment. In Bowen's therapy, the family comes to understand a three-generational emotional process and its demands upon family members. Differentiation of family members from the family of origin enables an individual to act with mature autonomy and contribute resources to family togetherness. The therapy process helps members overcome emotional reactivity and regulate emotions by knowing where oneself ends and other begins without losing self or rational choice (Bowen, 1978).

A major contribution to family therapy was the construct of *triangulation*. This effort by a family, lacking sufficient differentiation to deal with emotional challenges, requires that two family members become closely aligned and draw in a third member. For example, a mother and child become overly close in order to enable, rescue, or punish an alcoholic father. Two parents who argue and feel like they are coming apart may focus on a child's asthma in order to stay together. All families have triangles. In extreme cases of parental anxiety, the unfinished business of a parent is "projected" upon a vulnerable child, who may be troubled or disabled, refocusing the attention of the family. Similarly, a family member may be "cut off" such that there is a loss of communication that reduces the emotional burden of the family. When emotional reactivity is great, triangulation is a problem-generating family dynamic that enables survival at the cost of growth.

The family moves toward healthy interdependence as a task of being fully human. It is viewed as an ongoing evolutionary process. Differentiation facilitates both tolerance of intimacy and healthy bonding. Families unable to differentiate may be fused in an "undifferentiated mass" that produces extreme symptoms. Other families are hampered by extremes of organization and hierarchy, get stuck in problem sequences, and cannot respond to opportunities for growth. The level of differentiation of the therapist sets the limits to how far the family may go. Therefore, training to become a Bowen family therapist involves careful attention to the differentiation of the therapist through family of origin work and reflection. The therapist helps other families increase differentiation by detriangulating and making rational choices about family business.

Cognitive-Behavioral Family Therapy

Behavioral approaches to family therapy typically included contracting and decision making to alter contingent consequences with a family unit (Stuart, 1980). Behavioral couple therapists helped partners establish contracts to increase positive and pleasurable interactions by exchanging rewards. Similarly, family members could meet and establish guidelines for chores and perhaps implement a point/token economy by which children earned rewards and privileges. These direct approaches teach skills needed to change interactional patterns but may not address underlying family issues. The cognitive revolution in behavior therapy encouraged family members to examine not only overt behaviors, but also self-talk and other thinking errors. Eventually, the cognitive-behavioral model identified patterns and sequences of problem behavior, as well as underlying cognitive structures that filtered experience (Baucom, Epstein, Kirby, & LaTaillade, 2010; Christensen, Jacobson, & Babcock, 1995). Acknowledgment of the influence of schemas or cognitive templates for organizing behavior change made cognitive-behavioral family therapy similar to other theories and models. Ongoing developments in cognitive-behavioral family therapy converge on two major trends in the evolution of field: psychotherapy integration and evidence-based practice. Two promising models for MFC specialists include emotionally focused therapy and functional family therapy.

Integrative couple and family therapy focuses on the patterns and sequences of behavior. Interventions address emotions, cognitions, and behaviors. Best practices from several models may be incorporated in a treatment package designed to address recurrent problems in family systems. When the best practices can be incorporated in a treatment manual, it is possible to train therapists to deliver empirically supported interventions to enhance the efficacy of behavior change. Some cognitive-behavioral approaches are designed to improve long-term outcomes. Gottman's (1999) *sound marital house* model was based on 30 years of laboratory and field research. It is intended to reduce emotional reactivity, reduce efforts in thinking, and increase communication and coping in unhappy couples. Other empirically supported methods include integrative behavioral couple's therapy in which traditional behavioral approaches are augmented by disrupting problem sequences and increasing choice in using new skills in difficult situations (Christensen, Jacobson, & Babcock, 1995). Therapists and family members collaborate in selecting targets for change and gain resilience or resources such that beneficial outcomes generalize and maintained.

Emotionally Focused Therapy (EFT) is one of the most thoroughly researched models in the MFC specialization. It is simultaneously integrative in that best practices from several approaches have been incorporated in the treatment package and evidence based through clinical research trials (Johnson, 1996, 2015). It integrates individual and systemic interventions, including intrapsychic and interpersonal processes. EFT addresses attachment theory and helps couples achieve stability, establishing a secure base for partners and a safe haven or container for changing the relationship.

EFT addresses the advancement of love in adult relationships by emphasizing the quality of attachment. There is a natural inclination toward establishing a pair bond with a partner. The relationship they form includes autonomy of each person, secure dependence in maintaining mutuality, emotional accessibility and responsivity, and tolerance for change and growth. Couple relationships are troubled by insecure attachment arising from childhood experiences and previous relationships. Disorders of attachment include anxious attachment, avoidance, and a combination of the two. Problems of attachment contribute to imbalance in the relationship and tendency to enact rigid, polarized roles. Insecure attachment contributes to a well-known pattern in troubled couples: approach-avoidance conflict.

Such conflicts translate into negative interaction cycles in which partners get trapped in roles such as pursuer or withdrawer (distancer). Pursuers experience anxious attachment and have difficulty tolerating separation or distance. Withdrawing partners create distance to avoid the demands of closeness or to protect the self from a perceived lack of safety. Pursuers feel hurt and alone; withdrawers feel judged or rejected. Patterns of pursuit and withdrawal establish limits for intimacy and set the stage for attachment injuries, which include betrayal, abandonment, and violations of boundaries and trust. An injury can occur when one partner is highly vulnerable and the other fails to offer nurturance and support. A relevant question for the therapist instigates investigation: "Is there any event in your relationship that was so painful or traumatic that it left you feeling unsafe or insecure?"

EFT is an integrative approach that involves a structured process. This enables replication and evaluation of the effectiveness of the approach. The steps of EFT integrate assessment and intervention. The approach examines individual and dyadic issues and combines psychoeducation, emotional containment, reenactments, and restructuring of interactions. The attunement of the therapist to each partner's inner world accesses primary emotions underlying secondary emotions of anger or withdrawal. The therapist models helpful approaches to receiving the emotional disclosures of one partner for the other. As partners gain experience in expressing emotions they gain strength in maintaining a secure bond and enjoying intimacy. Another evidence-based approach is also integrative, manualized (i.e., operations are explicit), and attentive to the needs of family members.

Functional Family Therapy (FFT) is an evidence-based treatment with over 40 years of empirical support (Sexton & Alexander, 2005). The model is especially appropriate for conduct-disordered and delinquent youth and their families. FFT integrates cognitive-behavioral and systemic interventions to understand the functions of problem behaviors within the family. Problem behaviors are adaptive in terms of the demands and stresses of daily life to in order to vary relational connection (the balance of closeness and independence) and hierarch, who has power and control. The FFT therapist identifies the problem functions and replaces old behaviors with new behaviors that fit the situation or meet needs. There is a multisystemic focus, characteristic of working with delinquents, involving school and community stakeholders including school staff, probation personnel, and extended family members. In order to reduce stigma and resistance, the therapist works with the whole family and subsystems in an ecological context. Participants focus on not only reducing problem behaviors, but also increasing protective factors associated with reduction of delinquent risk. It is imperative to shift from negativity, such as criticizing and blaming, to positive communication: active listening, empathy, and respect.

The FFT therapist directly intervenes in problem sequences to teach new coping mechanisms and effective behaviors. They assist family members in changing cognitions and behaviors, learning decision-making and problem-solving skills, and teaching parenting. All family members participate in sessions, which may include home visits. Cultural factors and preferences are incorporated in the intervention. Typically, therapists access resources and strengths by learning about the neighborhood and extended family system, inquiring about sports and hobbies, and developing healthy friendships. Problem-sustaining cognitive sets are replaced with new expectations and attributions, particularly thoughts associated with responsibility. Parents focus on clear rules and developmentally appropriate privileges; active monitoring and supervision of youths; and application of clear, consistent contingent reinforcement for positive behavior. FFT represents an effective means for addressing current problem behaviors and preventing future escalation.

There are several other evidence-based treatments that are noteworthy: *Dialectical Behavior Therapy* (DBT, Linehan, 1993), *Acceptance and Commitment Therapy* (ACT, Hayes, Strosahl, & Wilson, 1999) and *mindfulness based meditation/cognitive therapy* (Kabat-Zinn, 2003). These "third-wave" therapies continue the trends toward psychotherapy integration and evidence-based practice. DBT is especially helpful in dealing with emotion dysregulation and distress tolerance, which lead to symptoms and conflicts in efforts to reduce pain. ACT is helpful in dealing with values clarification in establishing a balanced lifestyle. The acronym corresponds to some basic principles of "third-wave" approaches.

- A=Accept and embrace difficult thoughts and feelings.
- C=Choose and commit to a life direction that reflects who one is and who the family is becoming.
- T=Take action steps toward this life direction, empowering purpose.

Both DBT and ACT incorporate mindfulness meditation and practices, intended to maintain or restore calm after upheaval.

Mindfulness Based Stress Reduction (MBSR) was developed by Jon Kabat-Zinn (2003). Similar to disciplines in Judeo-Christian and Islamic contemplative traditions, MBSR was derived from Buddhist meditation and integrated with cognitive-behavioral methods for improving physical and mental health. Variations on MBSR include breathing exercises, yoga or sitting postures, sensory focus, repetition of keywords, and calming the wandering mind and judgment. Mindfulness enables a person or couple to be present and maintain connection without fear or distress. Non-Western meditative practices anticipated "postmodern" models of understanding the lived experiences of family members. Postmodern theories and models are not based on a priori concepts. Rather, knowledge and wisdom emerge from interactions with clients who are the experts of their conditions.

Postmodern Family Therapy

Postmodern approaches arose in response to an overemphasis upon science and technology in behavior change. Instead of forcing clients into manualized, evidence-based therapies, postmodern approaches started with the lived experiences of the family members, who possess the resources and skills needed to change. Most of the postmodern methods involve immersion in a shared process and asking questions to better understand sequences in interactions. Creative techniques, such as metaphor and imagery, can be used to engage resources and refocus family members from problems to solutions.

Solution Focused Family Therapy (SFFT, de Shazer et al., 1986) helps clients generate spontaneous solutions to problems by identifying exceptions to habitual sequences or imagining miracles to disrupt a chain of events. It is possible to magnify and prescribe spontaneous solutions or engage clients in a series of questions to generate innovations. The SFFT specialist can ask *exception questions* to introduce novelty.

- Are there any times when the problem is less likely to occur or be less severe?
- Can you think of a time when you expected the problem to occur, but it didn't?
- Are there any people who seem to make things easier?
- Are there places or times when the problem is not as bad?

Otherwise, it is possible to innovate solutions by fast forwarding in time, using a magic wand, or another imaginary process. A frequent component of SFFT involves the *miracle question.*

> *If you awaken from sleep tomorrow and a miracle has occurred in this situation, how would (family member) know you changed?*

SFFT also uses *scaling* to assist family members in noticing what is possible and what change is needed. Clients are asked to scale their situation from zero to ten, with zero representing *when you decided to seek help* and ten *the best that things could be*. Each session the MFC specialist would ask one or more family members to scale the change process. If a father says, "We are only a 4," then the counselor might ask, "What would it take for your family to get a 6?" Answers to such questions evoke explanatory images and stories from families looking for new solutions to old problems.

Narrative Family Therapy is another postmodern approach that relies upon the generative quality of conversation to develop solutions and transform family systems (White & Epston, 1990). The MHC specialist holds expertise in facilitating a process, while the client(s) has expertise in generating the content. Clients construct meanings from the events in their lives. They explore inner dialogs, identify characters and plot lines, then start movement through a story. The client and counselor *co-construct* a new reality for family life by sharing the story. For many persons who face oppression or overcome adversity, they have heroic stories. Others express their sense of humor through family anecdotes that can be woven into new tapestries of meaning. Curiosity is a key feature in narrative approaches: the counselor and family members express curiosity and enthusiasm about learning and sharing more of the family story. Counselors must be willing to share parts of their own stories and demonstrate empathy through appropriate self-disclosure. Writing assignments (or recording in alternative media) facilitate the process of narrative therapy. Family members may be assigned the following homework exercises to share in session:

- Letters to themselves from aspects of themselves that represent emerging, future, or past selves.
- Letters to themselves from significant others from the present, past, or future.
- Letters to and from significant others (alive or dead) speaking in words kept private.
- Letters or journal entries to speak from parts of the self that are typically not acknowledged or expressed.

The letters and stories of family members who are co-constructing solutions are affected by *dominant discourses* that constrain change. Many problems arise when one's personal life does not conform to expectations or judgments from dominant others in society. Culture clashes may arise that need to be worked out in the restorying process. It is frequently necessary to remove bonds of oppression by overcoming "shoulds" and "oughts" and freeing the family from a "problem" imposed by a dominating view from society. Family therapy has a history of multicultural sensitivity, consciousness raising, and advocacy to help families understand the effects of dominant discourses (Foucault, 1982; Hare-Mustin, 1994).

SIDEBAR 14.1

In Practice: What Would You Do?

Alex is a couple counselor in a nonprofit MFC agency. In the course of an introductory session, it is clear that the partners are experiencing a lot of conflict even though they lived together for two years before deciding to get married six months ago. Each member of the couple feels misunderstood and judged. While they formerly enjoyed an active, satisfying sex life, they have not had sexual contact in three months. Sam and Blake are in their late 20s, college graduates, and starting careers in their fields. They argue about the decision to have a baby.

> Sam encouraged a reluctant Blake to attend this outpatient session. They have been arguing a lot about small matters and big decisions. Sam criticizes Blake for not doing chores and picking up personal items left around the house. Blake responded, "You are not my parent; don't tell me what to do." Sam continues, "I just want us to have a neat home; I never noticed you were so lazy when we were living together in the apartment. Sam and Blake recently moved into a townhouse and assumed additional financial responsibilities. Sam complained, "We never have sex anymore," to which Blake replied, "It is hard for me to feel close to you when

you are so critical." Blake began crying and said, "I always wanted to have a baby, but not if you are going to be mean all the time." The couple asks for help in improving communication, reducing arguments, and recovering their sex life.

Class Discussion

1. What does Alex need to know in order to understand the conflict of this newly married couple?
2. Do you think gender roles or expectations may have an effect?
3. If Alex found the couple to be *complementary* what are their opposite characteristics?
4. What might be the influence of the family of origin?
5. What might be the goals of couple counseling?
6. Could sexual orientation be an issue?

Impacts on the Individual, Family, and Community

Contemporary trends in society have dramatically affected MFT. Feminism and human rights advocacy influenced examination and revision of key family concepts including families of choice, gender identity and equity, sexual orientation, multiculturalism, and intersectionality (McCarthy & Edwards, 2011). Families are no longer defined exclusively by blood ties or kinship. Rather, family bonds may reflect choice to be identified as members or included in daily life. Families of choice arose to challenge patriarchy and heteronormativity by including friends and displaced persons in families as "affectional communities" (p. 57). Similarly, the cumulative effects of the feminist movement freed people of traditional genders as well as nonbinary or "fluid" individuals to participate in gender-free or gender-fair roles in committed partnerships, marriages, and families. Sexual orientation is increasingly nonbinary and may include normal asexuality as an expression of sexual health. Couples and families are becoming much more diverse in terms of race, ethnicity, religion, socioeconomic status, nationality, and other cultural criteria. The concept of intersectionality represents the needs, challenges, and strengths of individuals who simultaneously present two or more minority groups such as African American lesbians.

The construct of family is affected significantly by dominant discourses in society and narrative helps individuals and families tell their unique stories that may be otherwise subjugated (see Foucault, 1982). Feminist therapists promoted awareness of gender issues in family therapy (Brown, 2018; Papp, 1983). They raised issues of implicit power dynamics, harmful stereotypes, discriminatory practices, and patriarchal aggression. According to an informed professional perspective, family therapists free family members from the burdens of their gendered roles. Therapists are advocates and change agents in the multicultural context.

Sexual orientation issues affect case conceptualization, problem definition, and solution in family therapy. Parents and children of same-sex and heterosexual orientations must overcome traditional roles and expectations, avoid criticism or judgment, prevent internalized homophobia, and transcend social conventions to express their authentic selves with family and community support. There are unique forms of coming-out experiences for nonbinary, transgendered, and Queer persons. The lack of social support networks for LGBTQ individuals increases the importance of forming affectional communities and families of choice.

Multicultural issues affect the needs and preferences of families. Immigration status, acculturation issues, generational patterns, and cultural discrimination contribute to the ecology of problems. Language and cultural barriers among therapists and clients create professional, ethical, and hierarchal issues. Some members of ethnic groups prefer expert power in the therapist (e.g., Latino, Asian American, and recent immigrants), while others prefer relational power through social courtesy, respect, and collaboration. There is more variation in needs and preferences within one racial/ethnic group than between groups. Conflicting cultural messages and lack of cultural sensitivity in therapists contribute to the suffering of biracial family and intersectional persons who present several expressions of minority status. It is important for MFC specialists to understand their own biases, tolerate diverse viewpoints, and respect cultural healing traditions. MFC practices are among the most robust in psychotherapy for identifying tools and techniques that work without subjugating family members (Bernal & Domenech Rodriguez, 2012).

Counseling Practices

Counselors tend to specialize in practice according to their personal preferences and models of behavior change. Some counselors prefer to work with individuals, others believe change occurs in the relationship shared by a couple, while a few tolerate the complexities of joining with a whole family and its subsystems. MFC specialists are drawn to couples, parent and child, and other family units.

The way we look at people, based on personal and professional experiences, determines how clients present themselves for help. Individuals present their lived experiences through thoughts, feelings, and actions. Individual counselors focus attention on cognitions, emotions, or behaviors (or all three) in order to resolve a problem. Couple counselors prefer to examine interactions between partners, believing the problem will be found in the relationship. A family counselor looks for patterns of interactions, processes in relationships, and sequences that determine problem and solution.

Some counselors focus exclusively on observable behaviors, while others infer thought processes and emotions from overt behavior and speech. A few curious counselors imagine there are parts, structures, or relationships among subsystems that are revealed only by mining the depths of unconscious processes or scanning the vista of family interactions. MFC models converge on the assumption that the reality of human life is revealed by bonds or attachments among persons-in-environments, selves-in-contexts, and individuals-in-families.

MFC practice requires shifting through various lenses (perspectives) to discover a unique reality of a particular family's life, whether expressed by an individual, couple, or family unit. Each lens filters experience: admitting information consistent with a pre-existing model, rejecting contradictory or new information, and maintaining problems through confirmatory bias. In order to resolve problems MFC specialists try on various lenses to look at family subsystems.

Coming to understand a family system requires suspension of judgment. The counselor moves back and forth between immersion in family process and influencing members to view problems and solutions in new ways. Immersion in family process involves forming and sustaining a therapeutic alliance and joining with the members. The MFC specialist joins with all the members to sustain the treatment alliance. Joining is an important feature of MFC based on becoming like a member of the family: using their language and explanations, respecting their roles and values, and participating in their interactions Keeney & Ross, 1983; Minuchin, 1974). There are three helpful approaches for joining with a family system: radical not knowing, multidirectional partiality, and intersubjectivity.

Solution-focused therapy (de Shazer et al., 1986) introduced *radical not knowing* as a postmodern practice. Solution-focused therapists advised the counselor to empty one's mind of expectations and ask respectful questions of family members to understand their process. A similar approach is used by anthropologists and social scientists to understand members of a nondominant culture by reducing biased judgments and avoiding injurious actions.

Multidirectional partiality refers to each family member feeling so well understood and supported they conclude that the counselor is "on my side" (Boszormenyi-Nagy & Krasner, 1986). Feeling valued and supported, the family members open up to change by accepting the counselor and trusting the influence process. The sense of shared family loyalty facilitates a *centralizing engagement* in which member input and feedback can be channeled through the counselor (Minuchin, 1974). The MFC specialist is accountable to every family member, including those not present in the consulting room.

Intersubjectivity, a concept borrowed from contemporary psychoanalysis (see Southern, 2007), is a phenomenon in which one or more family members and a counselor engage in interactions that co-construct a vision of change. This creative approach blends intrapsychic and interpersonal contributions of all participants (counselor and family members) into a shared conceptualization of the problem and potential solutions. The process involves immersion in moment-to-moment experience and softening of habitual categories of information processing. The outcome of this nonhierarchical, egalitarian effort integrates conscious and unconscious elements, as well as individual and interpersonal, needs in an emerging version of the family story. In a sense, it means the family realizing, "This is us."

Selected Techniques

Strategic family therapy (Keeney & Ross, 1983; Haley, 1987) and narrative therapy (White & Epston, 1990) offer techniques for transforming family systems. Strategic techniques include the creative use of language to make old problem patterns solvable. Most families respond well to *reframing* problem statements into a new language based on strength. Instead of criticizing or pathologizing a family member (frequently the identified patient) the reframed feedback conveys acceptance or praise and mobilizes strengths. For example, the spouse of an alcoholic could be blamed for being controlling and punitive, obscuring resources for solutions. The counselor could reframe the confrontation by saying, "You are so resourceful in helping your family; I wish there were more time for you." Encouraging self-care facilitates a solution sequence.

Another helpful technique from narrative therapy is *externalizing the problem* (White & Epston, 1990). The intervention involves describing a family problem as external to the individual or system. No one is criticized or blamed. Involved family members brainstorm ways to neutralize or counteract the externalized opponent of family wellbeing. Consider a case in which parents argue in front of the children, unintentionally increasing their anxiety. If the problem of arguing were addressed directly, it could trigger blame (or more arguing) and engender shame and resistance. If the arguments were externalized as "Troublemaker," a character bothering the family, members could develop creative solutions: "The way we made friends with Troublemaker" or "when Troublemaker didn't need to visit." The problem sequence would then be *punctuated*, momentarily stopped or suspended, with a solution in which Troublemaker is appeased by family members sharing in chores or another joint effort.

Therapeutic Homework

MFC specialists use homework outside the scheduled sessions to catalyze change in daily family life. Homework takes the form of assessments, interventions, or both. The goal of an MFC session may be starting a process that extends beyond the consulting room. Two homework exercises are common in MFC: genogram and relational contracting. The genogram evolved from structural family therapy, Bowen family therapy, and family-of-origin therapy, and involves a graphic representation of family characteristics or patterns in relationships over several generations

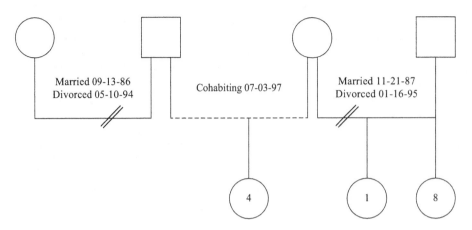

Figure 14.1 Sample Genogram.

(Framo, 1982; Kerr & Bowen, 1988; McGoldrick, Gersen, & Petry, 2008). Relational contracting emerged from both behavioral marital therapy (Stuart, 1980) and psychodynamically oriented couple therapy (Sager, 1976).

The *genogram* is a graphic representation of the family tree or genealogy. It can depict not only the genealogy of the family across three to five generations, but the qualities of their individual lives and relationships. Genograms can specifically address family patterns such as divorce, career, military service, religion, addiction, and other themes. Connections among family members are shown via lines and symbols. A sample of a simple genogram is offered in Figure 14.1.

In couple therapy, each partner could produce independently their multigenerational genogram in preparation for family-of-origin therapy. In this counseling practice, each member has the opportunity to understand the origins of themes and expectations and to empathize with the burden of unfinished family business. The MFC specialist helps the partners transcend pain or shame rooted in the past.

Relational contracting is another great technique for working with couples. Traditional behavioral contracts addressed exchanges of rewards, such as caring days or performing chores, on a quid pro quo basis (Stuart, 1980). Such contracts became more egalitarian and collaborative, integrating needs, wants, and preferences and using "change first" strategies for investing in the future of the relationship, rather than only striking short-term deals. The *relationship contracting* model of Sager (1976) translates well into therapeutic homework in which each partner completes independently the terms for an idealized agreement in which the most desired qualities were expressed. This "wish list" could include overt demands, which could have been expressed, but also needs that are vaguely felt or inferred from intrapsychic and interpersonal processes. The partners bring individual versions to the MFC specialist who initially compares and highlights areas of commonality. Over the course of several meetings, the counselor helps each partner understand the particular terms and collaborate in meeting as many needs or wants as possible. Then, the counselor helps the couple construct a shared relationship contract to which they can refer as issues arise or plans can be made. Therapeutic homework enables the MFC specialist to extend intervention beyond the session to the family home. Some homework assignments work well with particular families, but not others. Homework and in-session techniques should be adapted to be culturally appropriate and to meet the needs of the unique family.

Summary

Therapeutic homework and techniques derive from the traditions and theories in MFC. Postmodern approaches can be readily adapted to meet the needs of family members. Cognitive-behavioral and evidence-based approaches follow manualized protocols in order to maintain fidelity to the essential components needed for effectiveness. Strategic and structural family models are the most consistent with the origins of the specialization and the core focus on the family system. Experiential approaches help the counselor reach emotions and inner experiences that may not be volunteered in whole family therapy.

MFC interventions are conducted in the context of dominant culture. Counselors should receive specialized training and supervised experience needed for ethical and effective practice. Professional associations such as IAMFC and AAMFT define the standards and represent the interests of MFC practitioners. Trends toward psychotherapy integration and evidence-based practice suggest that the MFC model may be the best for addressing many individual and family problems. By carefully integrating the perspectives and methods of intrapsychic and interpersonal models, MFC specialists gain access to lived experiences in family systems and an array of creative, effective tools for helping.

> *I never realized there were so many approaches to counseling. Training in marriage and family counseling gives me tools for helping individuals and families by shifting my perspective. I feel better prepared to serve clients from many backgrounds.*
>
> – MFC graduate student

References

American Association for Marriage and Family Therapy. (2015). AAMFT code of ethics. Retrieved from https://www.aamft.org/Legal_Ethics/Code_of_Ethics.aspx

American Association of Sexuality Educators, Counselors, and Therapists. (n.d.). Retrieved from aasect.org

Baucom, D.H., Epstein, N.B., Kirby, J.S., & LaTaillade, J.J. (2010). Cognitive-behavioral couple therapy. In K.S. Dobson (Ed.), *Handbook of cognitive-behavioral therapies* (3rd ed., pp. 411–444). New York: Guilford.

Bateson, G. (1972). *Steps to an ecology of mind*. Northvale, NJ: Jason Aronson.

Bernal, G., & Domenech Rodriguez, M.M. (Eds.). (2012). *Cultural adaptations: Tools for evidence-based practice with diverse populations*. Washington, DC: American Psychological Association.

Brendel, J.M., & Nelson, K.W. (1999). The stream of family secrets: Navigating the islands of confidentiality and triangulation involving family therapists. *The Family Journal, 7*, 112–117.

Boszormenyi-Nagy, I., & Krasner, B. (1986). *Between give and take*. New York: Brunner.

Bowen, M. (1978). *Family Therapy in clinical practice*. New York: J. Aronson.

Bowlby, J. (1969). *Attachment and loss: Volume 1. Attachment*. New York: Basic.

Bronfenbrenner, U. (2005). *Making human beings human: Bioecological perspectives on human development*. Thousand Oaks, CA: Sage.

Brown, L.S. (2018). *Feminist therapy* (2nd ed.). Washington, DC: American Psychological Association.

Council for Accreditation of Counseling & Related Educational Programs. (n.d.). Section 5: Entry-level specialty areas-Marriage, couple, and family counseling. Retrieved from https://www.cacrep.org/section-5-entry-level-specialty-areas-marriage-couple-and-family-counseling/

Christensen, A., Jacobson, N.S., & Babcock, J.C. (1995). *Integrative behavioral couple therapy*. New York: Guilford.

Commission on Accreditation for Marriage and Family Therapy Education. (n.d.). Retrieved from coamfte.org

de Shazer, S., Berg, I., Kipchik, E., Nunnally, E., Moinar, A., Gingerich, W., & Weiner-Davis, M. (1986). Brief therapy: Focused solution development. *Family Process, 25*(2), 207–222.

Dicks, H.V. (1967). *Marital tensions: Clinical studies towards a psychoanalytic theory of interaction*. London: Routledge.

Fairbairn, W.R.D. (1952). *Psychoanalytic studies of the personality*. London: Routledge.

Foucault, M. (1982). *The archaeology of knowledge & the discourse on language*. New York: Vintage.

Framo, J. (1982). *Explorations in marital and family therapy: Selected papers of James L. Framo*. New York: Springer Pub. Co.

Freud, S. (1896/1962). The aetiology of hysteria. In A. Strachey (Trans.), *Standard edition of the works of Sigmund Freud* (vol. 3, pp. 214–215). London: Hogarth Press.

Freud, S. (1915/1959). Some character-types met with in psychoanalytic work. In E. Jones (Ed.), *Sigmund Freud, collected papers* (vol. IV). New York: Basic Books.

Gomez, L. (1997). *An introduction to object relations*. London: Free Association Books.

Gottman, J.M. (1999). *The marriage clinic: A scientifically-based marital therapy*. New York: Norton.

Haley, J. (1987). *Problem-solving therapy: New strategies for effective family therapy*. New York: Harper & Row.

Hare-Mustin, R.T. (1994). Discourses in the mirrored room: A postmodern analysis of therapy. *Family Process, 33*, 19–35.

Hayes, S.C., Strosahl, K., & Wilson, K.G. (1999). *Acceptance and commitment therapy: An experiential approach to behavior change*. New York: Guilford.

Horner, A. (1979). *Object relations and the developing ego in therapy*. New York: Jason Aronson.

International Association of Marriage and Family Counselors. (n.d.). Retrieved from iamfconline.org

International Association of Marriage and Family Counselors. (2018). International Association of Marriage and Family Counselors Ethics Code. *The Family Journal, 26*(1), 5–10.

Johnson, S. (1996). *The practice of emotionally focused marital therapy: Creating connection*. Philadelphia, PA: Brunner/Mazel.

Johnson, S. (2015). Emotionally focused couple therapy. In A.S. Gurman, J.L. Lebow, & D.K. In Snyder (Eds.), *Clinical handbook of couple therapy* (5th ed., pp. 97–128).

Kabat-Zinn, J. (2003). Mindfulness-based stress reduction. *Constructivism in the Human Sciences, 8*, 73–83.

Keeney, B., & Ross, J. (1983). Cybernetics of brief family therapy. *Journal of Marital & Family Therapy, 9*(4), 375–382.

Kerr, M.E., & Bowen, M. (1988). *Family evaluation: An approach based on bowen theory*. New York: Norton.

Lazarus, A.A. (2002). How certain boundaries and ethics diminish therapeutic effectiveness. In A.A. Lazarus (Ed.), *Dual relationships and psychotherapy*. New York: Springer.

Linehan, M. (1993). *Cognitive behavioral treatment of borderline personality disorder*. New York: Guilford Press.

Main, M., & Solomon, J. (1995). Discovery of an insecure, disorganized/disoriented attachment pattern: Procedures, findings, and implications for the classification of behavior. In M. Yogman & T. B. Brazelton (Eds.), *Affective development in infancy*. Norwood, NJ: Ablex.

McCarthy, J.R., & Edwards, R. (2011). *Key concepts in family studies*. London: Sage.

McGoldrick, M., Gerson, R., & Petry, S.S. (2008). *Genograms: Assessment and intervention*. New York: Norton.

Meara, N.M., Schmidt, L.D., & Day, J.D. (1996). Principles and virtues: A foundation for ethical decisions, policies, and character. *Counseling Psychologist, 24*, 4–77.

Minuchin, S. (1974). *Families & family therapy*. Cambridge, MA: Harvard University Press.

Minuchin, S., Rosman, B. L., & Baker, L. (1978). *Psychosomatic families: Anorexia nervosa in context*. Cambridge, MA: Harvard University Press.

Papp, P. (1983). *The process of change*. New York: Guilford Press.

Pinsof, W.M., Breunlin, D.C., Russell, W.P., Lebow, J.L., Rampage, C., & Chambers, A.L. (2018). *Integrative systemic therapy: Metaframeworks for problem solving with individuals, couples, and families*. Washington, DC: American Psychological Association.

Rogers, C.R. (1957). The necessary and sufficient conditions of therapeutic personality change. *Journal of Consulting and Clinical Psychology, 21*, 95–103.

Sager, C.J. (1976). *Marriage contracts and couple therapy: Hidden forces in intimate relationships*. Oxford: Brunner/Mazel.

Satir, V. (1972). *Peoplemaking*. Palo Alto, CA: Science and Behavior Books.

Satir, V. (1983). *Conjoint family therapy* (revised 3rd ed.). Palo Alto, CA: Science and Behavior Books.

Scharff, D., & Scharff, J. (1987). *Object relations family therapy*. Northvale, NJ: Jason Aronson.

Schwartz, R. (1995). *Internal family systems therapy*. New York: Guilford.

Sexton, T.L., Alexander, J.F. (2005). Functional family therapy for externalizing disorders in adolescents. In J.L. Lebow (Ed.), *Handbook of clinical family therapy* (pp. 164–191). Hoboken, NJ: Wiley.

Smith, R.L. (1993). Training marriage and family counselors: Current status and issues. *Counselor Education and Supervision, 33*, 89–101.

Smith, R.L., Carlson, J., Stevens-Smith, P., & Dennison, M. (1994). Marriage and family counseling. *Journal of Counseling and Development, 74*, 154–157.

Southern, S. (2007). Countertransference and intersubjectivity: Golden opportunities in clinical supervision. *Sexual Addiction & Compulsivity, 14*, 279–302.

Southern, S. (2012). Relational ethics: Ethics in couple, marriage, and family counseling and therapy. In J. Gregoire & C. Jungers (Eds.), *Counseling ethics: A journey of personal and professional discovery*. New York: Springer Publishers.

Stanton, M., & Welsh, R. (2012). Systemic thinking in couple and family psychology research and practice. *Couple and Family Psychology, 1*, 14–30.

Stuart, R. B. (1980). *Helping couples change*. New York: Guilford Press.

Watzlawick, P., Weakland, J., Fisch, R. (1974). *Change: Principles of problem formation and problem resolution*. New York: Norton.

White, M., & Epston, D. (1990). *Narrative means to therapeutic ends*. New York: Norton.

Wiener, N. (1948). *Cybernetics: Or control and communication in the animal and the machine*. Cambridge, MA: MIT Press.

Chapter 15

School Counseling

Jessica J. Lane, Täna Arnold, Lyndsey Brown and Samantha Holloway

It is easier to build strong children than to repair broken men.

– Frederick Douglass

POINTS TO PONDER

- How are the ASCA National Model and counseling theories utilized in professional school counseling?
- How can professional school counselors engage families and community members to better support the individual student?
- How are appropriate activities for school counselors different from inappropriate activities according to the American School Counselor Association?

Professional school counselors have adapted to the changing needs of the students they serve. Serving as a counselor in an educational setting brings diverse days and various facets to the role. This chapter will discuss the history and background of the school counseling profession; theories and models specific to school counseling; the impact of school counselors on the individual, families, and the communities; and finally current counseling practices.

History and Background

Evolution of School Counseling

Over the course of 100 years, the role of the school counselor has undergone many changes. As the needs of students and families continue to grow and change, the role of the school counselor has developed to better support the student. From position to program (Gysbers & Henderson, 2001; Kircher, 2007), school counseling has evolved from a focus on vocational guidance offered by the teacher, to a comprehensive school counseling program provided by counselors, to support students in the academic, career, and social-emotional domains.

   1800s and 1900s. School counseling programs first began to offer guidance toward a vocation. School guidance and counseling programs began in the late 1800s and early 1900s as a derivative of the Industrial Revolution, child labor issues, urbanization, immigration, and the need to match persons with jobs (Herr, 2002; Kircher, 2007). Through the Industrial Revolution, education changed in response to many economic, social, and educational concerns (Gysbers, 2017). According to Online Counseling Programs (2017), vocational teachers served a dual role, both as teacher and career leader, to orientate students to the workforce, assess their skills and abilities, and provide counsel and follow-up for job placement. Vocational teachers were impactful in making changes to better prepare workers for the workplace, having students find a purpose for their education, and changing school methods. Jessie B. Davis, a secondary principal considered to be the first school counselor, in 1907 (Gysbers, 2017) proposed a curriculum for guidance for grades 7–12 that included key ideas to develop character, avoid behavior problems, and consider lessons related to career interests.

1910s to 1930s. During this period, the progressive movement toward school counseling began. The role of vocational teacher or vocational counselor, a position with a list of duties provided by teachers and administrators (Gysbers, 2017), moved to a vocational guidance role where a subculture of child development, psychometrics, and mental hygiene were also incorporated (Gysbers, 2017). In the 1930s, separate positions for counselors emerged due to added work duties to meet the need of student mental health issues.

1930s to 1970s. The framework for school counseling continued to morph and expand to respond to the needs of the time. Guidance services provided assessment, information, counseling, job placement, and follow-up. Great gains were made over this time to expand the number of counselors and their role within schools. World War II, and the space race in particular, fortified school counseling demands. In the 1940s counselors and psychologists were used to recruit and train military personnel; military tests were used by schools and this helped to develop the school counseling movement. Funding for counseling within schools became available. Programs and training provided further development for vocational guidance in the schools. Emphasis was placed on teacher certification and experience required, and standardization of programming in colleges and universities. In 1954, the American School Counselor Association (ASCA) developed under the Personnel and Guidance Association, the forerunner of the American Counseling Association. This helped to enhance the role and function of school counselors. In 1958, the National Defense Education Act (NDEA), spurred by Sputnik and the space race, was intended to strengthen education and the nation's international leadership position in technology, defense, and security. It provided necessary funds to implement counselor education programs and strengthen the role of counseling by replacing many teacher-counselors with full-time counselors (Gladding, 2012). This nearly tripled the number of counselors in middle and high schools (Online Counseling, 2017).

The Elementary and Secondary Education Act (ESEA) of 1965 helped to provide professional development, supplemental programs, and elementary and secondary counselors. This act was the start of elementary school counseling programs, which continue to grow today, and supported the idea of a comprehensive school counseling program. Another developmental gain for school counseling during this time was the use of non-directive counseling skills. Specifically, the theory and work of Carl Rogers' (1951) non-directive counseling approaches helped to further develop the helping relationships between the counselor and student.

1980s to 1990s. As school counseling programs became more prominent, the role and function of the school counselor began to expand and vary widely; school counselors' work became further intertwined with the developmental, personal, and social issues of students. School counseling duties also encompassed academic success; state, national, and school initiatives; and the mental wellness of students. Educational reform and economic and social issues had an impact on schools as well. Thus, the needs and demands placed on school counselors created a myriad of counselor duties, which led to role confusion.

During this time, the field was looking for something more substantive that provided a clearer understanding of the direction, role, and function for school counselors. A need for structure and unification and for common language were deemed critical to the evolution of school counseling moving from a job position to a comprehensive program (Gysbers & Henderson, 2001; Kircher, 2007).

2000 and beyond. Recognizing a critical problem, national organizations and professional leaders such as Norm Gysbers (2017) worked to develop a comprehensive school counseling program to meet the multifaceted needs of today's students and schools. Comprehensive programming provides scope and sequence, and integral support to students' educational environment as they work toward achievement. Comprehensive programming has been strengthened and reinforced by the significant addition of the American School Counselor Association (ASCA) National Model (2012), which offers the framework for a comprehensive, data-driven school counseling program (American School Counselor Association, 2012). The use of a national model gives clarity and continuity to students, schools, and counselors alike. The ASCA National Model is critical to the work of today's school counselor. Further discussion of comprehensive programming and the ASCA National Model will be provided later in this chapter.

Theories and Models Specific to School Counseling

American School Counselor Association (ASCA) National Model

School counseling has had a varied background and has come a long way from the time of vocational guidance in the early 1900s (American School Counselor Association, 2012). The ASCA National Model was first published in 2003 and is continually being updated. Specifically, it shifted school counseling from responsive services for some students to a comprehensive school counseling program for everyone. The framework consists of four components: *foundation, management, delivery,* and *accountability.* Additionally, the ASCA National Model has four themes of leadership, advocacy, collaboration, and systemic change. It is important to note that the ASCA National Model brings school counselors together with one vision and one voice, which creates unity and focus toward improving student achievement (American School Counselor Association, 2012).

Foundation. Foundation refers to the solid ground upon which the rest of the comprehensive school counseling program is built. In particular, it is the "what" of the program and the "what" is defined as student knowledge, attitudes, and skills that are learned because of the school counseling program (American School Counselor Association, 2012). The main components of foundation are *program focus, student competencies,* and *professional competencies.*

Management. The management component refers to how one can deliver the school counseling curriculum and address developmental needs of every student. ASCA provides assessments and tools to effectively and efficiently manage a comprehensive school counseling program. These assessments and tools help the school counselor "develop, implement, and evaluate their school counseling program based on clearly defined priorities reflecting student needs" (American School Counselor Association, 2012, p. 41). Assessments and tools are detailed in the Counseling Practices section of this chapter.

Delivery. The delivery of the ASCA National Model refers to the method of implementing the school counseling program to students. Delivery is broken down into two parts: *direct student services* and *indirect student services.* In particular, direct student services are in-person interactions between the school counselor and students. Specifically, direct student services consist of school counseling core curriculum, individual student planning, and responsive services. Whereas indirect student services are services provided on behalf of the student as a result of the school counselor's interaction with others (American School Counselor Association, 2012), indirect student services consist of referrals, consultation, and collaboration. ASCA recommends that 80% or more of the school counselors' time be spent in direct and indirect student services.

Accountability. Accountability refers to the effectiveness of the school counseling program. To demonstrate accountability, school counselors analyze data from the school itself and the school counseling program to determine if positive change is occurring for students. School counselors share this data with teachers, administrators, and their school districts to show the impact of the comprehensive school counseling program on attendance, behavior, and achievement (American School Counselor Association, 2012).

SIDEBAR 15.1

In Practice: What Would You Do?

You are a school counselor in a middle school in the Midwest United States. Your school has 1,200 students in it and you are one of 3 licensed counselors in the building. There is a comprehensive school counseling program in place, complete with classroom guidance lessons, small group activities, and individual counseling as needed. Since you and your colleagues are able to go into the classroom regularly, you decide this would be a great opportunity to have the students complete a survey about the program. You have all 1,200 students complete the survey at the end of the fall semester with plans to tally the results before you all leave for the holiday break. Due to the busyness of the season, you end up putting the surveys in large boxes, labeled, in your counseling closet and promise to take care of it when you get back in January. January comes and goes, and you are unable to get to the surveys. You tell yourself you will take care of them before spring break, because you know you need to evaluate your program annually and it is important that you know if your program is being effective. Due to responsibilities and needs that continue to arise, you realize at the end of the school year that you never tallied the surveys and are at a loss as to what to do with them now.

Discussion Questions:

1. How does a professional school counselor operate when their student counselor ratio is over 1:250?
2. Why is it important to evaluate a school counseling program every year?
3. What should the counselors do with the surveys that they never evaluated?

Theories of School Counseling

In the same way that the American School Counselor Association Model has progressed for school counselors, so have counseling theories. To be an effective professional school counselor one must have sound knowledge of counseling theories and techniques (Corey, 2013). Theories provide a framework for conceptualizing student problems and determining a course of action (Halbur & Halbur, 2015). A technique will motivate a student to create movement or change (Erford, 2015). In particular, there are a variety of different realms of counseling theories. Some of the most notable approaches for professional school counselors are *psychodynamic, behavioral, humanistic, pragmatic, and constructivist.*

Psychodynamic. Psychodynamic theory states that childhood events have a great impact on adult lives. The most pertinent form of psychodynamic theory to school counseling is individual psychology. Individual psychology was developed by Alfred Adler (1963). He believed that humans are motivated primarily by social relatedness. Adler focused on early life development, the role one plays in their family, parenting styles, sibling rivalry, and birth order. The major points of individual psychology are that personality is developed in the early years of life and as creative individuals, people can change (Halbur & Halbur, 2015). The process of change is done through *private logic*. Private logic refers to personal cognitive and emotional abilities designed to help each person achieve life goals. Furthermore, when there is a disruption of private logic there needs to be a reconfiguration of private logic which will allow students to gain healthy goals and accomplish life tasks in socially useful ways (Halbur & Halbur, 2015). Common techniques that help accomplish reconfiguring private logic are: *I-Messages, acting "as if"*, and *spitting in the soup*.

Using the I-Message technique encourages individuals to substitute personal pronouns in any situation where they may be avoiding responsibility for their actions or feelings. Notably, these messages acknowledge the existence of a problem, feeling, or idea (Erford, 2015). The structure of an I-Message should follow I feel *(feeling)* when you *(behavior)* because *(consequence)*.

Acting "as if" refers to helping the student change not only perspective, but also behavior, which in turn leads to increased functioning (Erford, 2015). In particular, the counselor asks the student to act as if he has the skills to handle a difficult situation. It is common for the student to think of someone they know having these skills and then envision how that person would handle the situation (Erford, 2015).

"Spitting in the soup" is coined from an old German proverb (Erford, 2015). It is used to decrease student behavior and symptoms by first determining the underlying purpose, and then pointing out this purpose to the student (Erford, 2015). It should be noted that strong trust and a positive relationship between the student and counselor is critical for this technique to work.

Behavioral. The behavioral theory takes a different approach to students. Behaviorists believe that humans are a product of learning through conditioning and reinforcement (Halbur & Halbur, 2015). B. F. Skinner (1938) believed that people are the producers and the product of their environment. The major goals of behavioral theory are to address specific behaviors that help students learn to behave differently. It is important to note that for behavioral theory to work effectively data must be collected, goals must be set, and relevant interventions must be initiated (Halbur & Halbur, 2015). Some of these relevant interventions are a *behavior chart*, *token economy*, and *behavioral contracts*.

A behavior chart targets a specific behavior that needs to be changed. Behavior charts are created using three simple steps. First, the target behavior is defined. Second, the frequency and type of rating systems to be used are decided on. Next, the chart is created by clearly stating the behavior and when it will be monitored. Finally, the consequence of the behavior is decided on (Erford, 2015). Notably, behavior is reinforced throughout the day, week, month.

Token economy is a form of positive reinforcement in which students receive a token when they display the desired behavior (Erford, 2015). Specifically, students collect their tokens and then turn them in for a tangible reward. This is done by identifying the behaviors that need to be changed, creating and displaying the rules, and setting up the prices. Tokens should be safe, sturdy, easy to dispense, and hard to replicate (Erford, 2015).

Behavioral contracts are commonly used in the school setting. A behavioral contract is a written agreement between two or more individuals in which one or both persons agree to engage in a specific target behavior (Erford, 2015). Behavior contracts can be for an undesired behavior to decrease or a desired behavior to increase. There are multiple steps to a behavioral contract. They are: (a) identify the behavior to be modified; (b) introduce and discuss the idea of a behavioral contract; (c) develop the contract and present it to all involved; (d) outline the follow-up procedures; (e) initiate the program; (f) record progress; and (g) evaluate and modify as necessary (Erford, 2015).

Humanistic. In humanistic theory, counselors believe that humans have a basic inclination to become fully functioning, to develop and grow psychologically (Halbur & Halbur, 2015).

One of the most common humanistic therapies is person-centered. Person-centered therapy was developed by Carl Rogers (1951). Rogers viewed the world and human nature as positive, and that people strive to reach their potential and self-actualization. Self-actualization refers to moving toward one's greater potential. The major goal of person-centered is to help students continue on the path toward self-actualization. Indeed, counselors want to assist students in their growth process so they can better cope with problems as they identify them (Corey, 2013). Techniques used in helping to the road of self-actualization are *genuineness, unconditional positive regard*, and *empathy*.

Genuineness refers to the ability to be authentic. It can be difficult to be authentic, and authenticity requires self-knowledge and understanding as well as the ability to know and share one's self. Being genuine challenges the student in cognitive and emotional dimensions (Halbur & Halbur, 2015). Unconditional positive regard, or being accepting and nonjudgmental, is another common technique in the person-centered theory. Counselors must accept students at the core for being a human (Halbur & Halbur, 2015). Empathy is another common technique. Empathy refers to the ability to see the world through the eyes of another, and the ability to convey its insight. Empathy requires counselors to take a phenomenological approach and truly listen to the affective work of their students (Halbur & Halbur, 2015).

Pragmatic. The pragmatic theory focuses more on what people think and want, and how those thoughts are the root of their emotional and behavioral lives (Halbur & Halbur, 2015). Two common theories used in school counseling are *cognitive-behavioral* and *rational emotive behavioral therapy*.

Cognitive-behavioral therapy is a contemporary approach that is primarily attributed to Aaron Beck (1995). Cognitive-behavioral therapy (CBT) believes that people control how they feel by what they think. The main goal of cognitive-behavioral therapy is to teach and reduce emotional distress and corresponding maladaptive behavior patterns by altering or correcting errors in thought, perception, and beliefs (Bernard & Hackney, 2017). The premise behind CBT is to challenge faulty thinking and overgeneralizations. The school counselor helps the student to review and test those beliefs. Cognitive behavior therapy (CBT) is being used more frequently, particularly with students who are experiencing symptoms of anxiety and depression. *Cognitive restructuring, thought stopping*, and *reframing* are three common techniques used in cognitive therapy.

Cognitive restructuring is a common cognitive-behavioral technique in which the counselor helps the student identify and replace negative self-statements. This is done by exploring the student's typical thoughts when in a troublesome situation and the counselor using close-ended questions to help the student identify specific thoughts that occur before, during, and after the situation (Bernard & Hackney, 2017).

Thought stopping refers to helping the student develop ways of halting destructive or unproductive thoughts about self and others. Thought stopping can be the first line of response when working with a student who shifts toward negative or self-defeating thinking (Bernard & Hackney, 2017). Reframing is another common technique used in which the counselor helps the student recognize more constructive or realistic interpretations of events that were previously interpreted as negative. The main goal of reframing is for the counselor to take the definition of the problem and redefine it so that it opens the door to a more viable solution (Bernard & Hackney, 2017). Reframing can allow one to see the situation through another lens, which can offer an additional, perhaps more objective, perspective.

Rational emotive behavioral therapy (REBT) (Ellis, 2008) is another pragmatic theory and is similar to cognitive-behavioral therapy. REBT views humans as being born with a potential for both rational or straight thinking and irrational, or crooked thinking. The major goal of REBT is to change the way people think because thoughts, rather than events, cause emotional problems.

Primarily, the main goal is to reduce self-defeating, irrational thinking (Halbur & Halbur, 2015). Common techniques for REBT are *rational emotive imagery*, *humor*, and *role playing*.

The primary goal for rational emotive imagery is for the student to change emotions from unhealthy to healthy with the help of a counselor. This can be done in a seven-step process: (a) visualize an unpleasant activating event; (b) experience the unhealthy negative emotion; (c) change the emotion; (d) examine the process; (e) repeat and practice; (f) reinforce the goal; and (g) generalize the skills (Erford, 2015).

Humor is another technique used in rational emotive behavioral therapy. In particular, REBT fosters the development of a better sense of humor and helps put life into perspective (Corey, 2013). Humor has both cognitive and emotional benefits in bringing about change. It allows students to take themselves much less seriously by teaching them to laugh not only at themselves but at their self-defeating thinking (Corey, 2013).

Role playing is a technique used by counselors who believe their students need to develop a deeper understanding of, or change within, themselves (Erford, 2015). Role playing has emotive, cognitive, and behavioral components that allow students to figure out what they are telling themselves and how that is creating a disturbance in their lives (Corey, 2013).

Constructivist. Another counseling theory often used by school counselors is constructivist theory. One constructivist approach is *solution-focused brief therapy* (Berg, 1994; de Shazer, 1985). Solution-focused brief therapy is a future-focused, goal-oriented approach. Counselors who implement this theory believe that behaviors and emotions truly make sense only from that individual's unique perspective. The goal of solution-focused brief therapy is to assist students in finding their unique solutions. In particular, the goals of the student vary because each student is unique and so is their solution (Halbur & Halbur, 2015). *Scaling*, *exceptions*, and *miracle questions* are all common techniques used in solution-focused brief therapy.

Scaling is the technique that helps both the counselor and the student make complex problems seem more concrete and tangible. Scaling most commonly involves asking the student to give a number between one and ten that indicates where the student is at a specific point in time (Erford, 2015). Normally, ten is the most positive end and one is most negative on the scale. The scaling technique should be implemented when the goal is established and the scaling question can help the student move toward reaching the goal. Specifically, once the student has decided where they are at on the scale the counselor can ask questions to discover small steps the student could take to teach the next number (Erford, 2015).

Exceptions is another commonly used technique. Exceptions refers to how the counselor constantly listens for an instance of when the problem was improved. Indeed, this technique forces counselors to retrain their ears and listen for a potential solution, sources of strength, and personal resources (Erford, 2015). The miracle question refers to a technique that encourages students to imagine a future with no problems and then to identify how they can resolve the problems to create such a future. Notably, counseling usually entails a problem-focused direction but, using the miracle question, shifts that thought process to a generating solutions mindset (Erford, 2015). However, counselors must help assist students in making their proposed solution tangible, reasonable, and focused on themselves (Erford, 2015).

Effective professional school counselors must have sound knowledge of counseling theories and techniques (Corey, 2013). Theories and techniques help drive the school counseling profession by helping motivate change.

Impact on the Individual, Family, and Community

School counselors are in a unique position not only to serve students but to impact other important stakeholders. Through their work in the school community, counselors impact the individual as well as the family and community systems as a whole. Serving in leadership roles, collaborating with outside agencies, and teaming up with stakeholders in the students' lives are integral ways the school counselor can positively influence the systems that students are directly a part of. School counselors work to be an essential part of the social-emotional, academic, and career development of all students through their partnerships with the client, their families, and the community (Bryan & Holcomb-McCoy, 2007).

Impact on the Individual

School counselors impact the individual students they work with in a multitude of ways. Their ability to serve as an advocate for students within their educational process is second to none. Collaborating with other educational professionals such as administrators and teachers, having open communication with all stakeholders, and creating positive relationships within the school community are all ways that school counselors can work to support students within the school system. Promoting the social-emotional health of students can be achieved by assisting other members of the school community in the understanding of how classrooms will benefit academically if the overall wellness of their students is a focus. By promoting positive behaviors and removing barriers to achievement, school counselors boost the success of students at all age levels, both immediately and in the future.

Comprehensive school counseling programs are imperative to build a positive school climate as well as strengthen individual student achievement. These counseling programs are preventative in nature, especially in the area of academics. School counselors are in an ideal position to offer assistance to at-risk students and have been found effective in preventing students from dropping out of school (Kaufman, Alt, & Chapman, 2004). Students who are in schools with comprehensive school counseling programs have reported decreases in classroom and behavior disturbances (Mullins & Otwell, 1997). School counselors who provide academic group counseling services, as part of a comprehensive program, have been found to positively impact participating students' achievement by as much as 83% (Boutwell & Myrick, 1992).

Within the school organization, there is not any one person more qualified to reach all students than the school counselor. School counselors work with all students and advocate for their needs, so they can facilitate student success through school counseling core curriculum, individual student planning, and responsive services (American School Counselor Association, 2016). School counselors take a strengths-based approach to creating a culture and environment where students can be academically successful as well as emotionally strong. This method gives students autonomy in their career exploration and post-secondary planning from a young age, which boosts their self-efficacy and ability to be successful in the future (Sink & Edwards, 2008).

Impact on the Family

The school counselor is an integrated member of many systems. The school is a system as a whole, but counselors also become a part of each students' family system as well. Interactions within this system are a vast part of how successful school counselors' work can be. Forming positive relationships with students' families is critical in supporting student success. This can be a difficult terrain to navigate, as boundaries and confidentiality must be upheld while still working as a member of a collaborative team to support the student.

The school counselor is frequently the parents' first point of contact when they have concerns about their child. "School counselors are often in the position of sharing difficult information, resolving conflict, clarifying confusion, and providing resources to families when necessary" (Ebersole & Garner, 2014, p. 227). Establishing strong, working relationships with the family of students and working within the family system benefits not only the individual student but the family system as a whole. One vital role counselors play within the family system is helping to connect parents to the educational process. Often parents are not aware of the support that is offered within the school setting or ways that they can engage to better support their students themselves. School counselors can help to bring parents and other family members into the school process through educational opportunities such as parent information sessions or educational workshops. Topics can range from giving parents ideas of how to support the student emotionally to how to help students with homework and studying.

School counselors collaborate with families to ensure that student needs are met. Counselors have the responsibility of ensuring that the students are safe in their home environment and to work with families to help them to support their students. Parents and guardians play a vital role in the development and success of students, and because of this, partnerships between school counselors and the families of the students they serve are necessary for success (American School Counselor Association, 2016).

Families often see a different side of their student and can serve as valuable resources to the school counselor. What occurs at school and what occurs at home are not independent of each other; both impact the other. Having strong communication and positive relationships with families only serve to enhance the counseling relationship and the achievement of the student as a whole.

Impact on the Community

Communities benefit from productive members whose needs are met. Often, school counselors serve as a bridge between agencies, students, and their families. School counselors can provide valuable insight into the students' functioning, to the services students receive outside of the school, and in the school setting. Being an advocate for students in this way is an imperative part of serving the community as a whole (American School Counselor Association, 2016).

Part of working as a school counselor is facilitating the referral process to outside resources. School counselors have an ethical obligation to know local providers in the communities they serve and to know how to appropriately refer students and families when necessary (Hess, Magnuson, & Beeler, 2012). Lists of appropriate resources for outside agencies and resources should be available should a student or parent request them. Counselors not only collect the information from outside agencies but also take an active role in understanding the services they can provide, so they can more accurately refer students and families. Connecting families to outside support is vital to student success as well as the success of outside agencies. Professional school counselors are also involved in the networks that support students such as educational teams and wraparound services.

Education is a large predictor of future success, and attending post-secondary institutions can help propel students into a more rewarding future. High school counselors play a crucial role in this process as high school students who have had support in the area of college and career counseling are more likely to apply for college (Bryan, Moore-Thomas, Day-Vines, & Holcomb-McCoy, 2011). Students who receive school counseling services are more likely to thrive in post-secondary environments. Communities benefit tremendously by having citizens who are productive, contributing members.

Organizing activities to benefit the community by collaborating with local businesses and faction members impacts the community in a very powerful way. These connections with local partners not only benefit the businesses but can also potentially serve students' real-life learning opportunities. Relationships with these entities can open internship opportunities for students, provide financial means for the school counseling programs, and serve as opportunities to bring in businesses to educate students as well.

Counseling Practices

School counselors have large caseloads, often exceeding the recommended 250:1 student-to-counselor ratio. Comprehensive programming helps counselors address *all* students varied needs via classroom guidance, small group, and individualized counseling. As discussed, the ASCA National Model is broken down into four components: foundation, management, accountability, and delivery. It is recommended that school counselors spend 80% of their time on direct and indirect services to students in the delivery component. The other 20% of their time is set aside for the other three components – foundation, management, and accountability tasks. Within the school framework, there are activities that are classified as "fair-share responsibilities." These are tasks that are split among the entire staff to aid in the general running of the school. School counselors are included but they should only take up a small portion of the 20% (American School Counselor Association, 2012).

ASCA National Model Counseling Practices

Foundation practices. A comprehensive school counseling program is an intentional, data-driven, systemic, focused part of the school's overall academic mission. In the foundation component, school counselors write a mission and vision statement that aligns to the values and beliefs of students' future outcomes (American School Counselor Association, 2012). Then the school counselors align their program with the ASCA *Mindsets and Behaviors for Student Success: K-12 College- and Career- Readiness for Every Student* (2014), as well as with other state and federal standards and initiatives important to their program. The third piece of foundation practices is utilizing professional competencies. The ASCA School Counselor Competencies detail the knowledge, attitudes, and skills that ensure that school counselors are prepared for the rigors of this profession. Essentially, it is in this component that school counselors think about the big picture of their program, what they hope to see their students accomplish at the end of the program, and make sure that it is aligned to standards in much the same way as educators do in their classrooms. It is expected that all of this is tracked and written down. The mission and vision statement should be easily available to parents, teachers, and other stakeholders of the program. These statements can be printed in brochures, included in the school handbook, and posted on the school website.

Management practices. The management component is the use of organizational assessments and tools to maximize the effectiveness of comprehensive school counseling programs. Some of the tools that are encouraged and included in the ASCA National Model are (a) school counselor competency and school counseling program assessments; (b) use-of-time assessment; (c) annual agreements; (d) advisory councils; (e) use of data; (f) curriculum, small-group, and closing-the-gap action plans; (g) lesson plans; and (h) annual and weekly calendars (American School Counselor Association, 2012).

Competencies assessments refers to the achievement success in the domains of academic, career, and social-emotional development. Specifically, a counselor is looking to prepare students to lead fulfilling lives as responsible members of society. School counseling program assessments refers to assessments used to evaluate the school counseling program in comparison to the ASCA National Model. In particular, assessments help find strengths and weaknesses of the program and provide direction for program improvement. Use-of-time assessments help school counselors determine how much time is spent in each of the components of the ASCA National Model. Notably, this assessment should be done twice a year. An annual agreement outlines the organization and focus of the school counseling program and is made between the school counselor and the administrator. The advisory council is a specific group of stakeholders selected to review and advise on the implementation of the school counseling program. Use of data refers to the use of school data and how to use that data to drive the direction of the comprehensive school counseling program. In particular, this can be done through disaggregated data and then connecting it either as short- or long-term data as it reflects either achievement or behavioral data. Action plans are created to efficiently and effectively deliver the school counseling program and are conducted in either the school counseling curriculum, small groups, or closing-the-gap activities. Two other important areas of management are lesson plans and calendars. Lesson plans should include standards, objectives, materials, procedures, and a plan for evaluation. A well-developed annual and weekly calendar should have the what, when, and where school counseling activities will be held. These calendars should be available to parents, teachers, and other stakeholders and encourage active participation in the program.

Delivery practices. The delivery component is broken down into direct student services and indirect student services. Because school counselors should spend 80% of their time providing what school counselors call direct delivery services, evaluation can utilize the use-of-time assessment discussed in the management practices. A good way to remember the difference between the two services is, "direct services are provided *with* students, and indirect services are provided *for* students" (emphasis added) (American School Counselor Association, 2012, p. 83). Direct student services include classroom instruction and group activities of the core curriculum. The curriculum should provide knowledge, attitudes, and skills appropriate for the student developmental level in three content areas: academic achievement, career development, and personal/social growth. Using the School Counseling Action Plan from the management component is very useful here. This curriculum can be composed of manualized curriculums and counselor-created lesson plans, utilizing the ASCA *Mindsets and Behaviors*; it is most important that the curriculum is data-driven, and school counselors use evidence-based strategies whenever possible (American School Counselor Association, 2012). Individual student planning is also included in direct services. School counselors work with students to help them analyze and evaluate their abilities, interests, skills, and achievements to help them develop short-term and long-term goals. Students at the high school level will be making decisions on their future and will look to school counselors for advisement; using academic, career, and personal/social data, school counselors are able to have these important conversations (American School Counselor Association, 2012).

Responsive services are the third category of direct student services delineated by ASCA and include any activities that are done to meet the immediate academic, career, or personal/social issues of *any* student. These services may be initiated by students themselves, teachers, parents, or administrators. Within responsive services there are counseling activities and crisis response. Counseling activities are either individual or in small groups, are short-term, and are goal-focused to help students overcomes issues impeded achievement or success. During critical and emergency situations school counselors provide support and assistance. This can include interventions and prevention to help keep a situation from becoming even more severe.

Indirect student services are provided as a means to support students and their achievement, "promote equality and access for all students" (American School Counselor Association, 2012, p. 87). These services include referrals, consultation, and collaboration. Table 3.1 clarifies what is an appropriate activity and what is an inappropriate activity for school counselors and is included in the Executive Summary put out by ASCA.

Accountability practices. Accountability is the third component that is designed to be part of the school counselor's 20%. In this component school counselors analyze data that has been collected to make program decisions (American School Counselor Association, 2012). There are three sections of accountability: data analysis, program results, and evaluation and improvement. Data analysis allows school counselors to make decisions about their counseling program.

Table 15.1 ASCA Appropriate Activities vs. Inappropriate Activities

Appropriate Activities for School Counselors	Inappropriate activities for School Counselors
Individual student academic program planning	Coordinating paperwork and data entry of all new students
Interpreting cognitive, aptitude and achievement tests	Coordinating cognitive, aptitude and achievement testing programs
Providing counseling to students who are tardy or absent	Signing excuses for student who are tardy or absent
Providing counseling to students who have disciplinary problems	Performing disciplinary action or assigning discipline consequences
Providing counseling to students as to appropriate school dress	Sending students home who are not appropriately dressed
Collaborating with teachers to present school counseling core curriculum lessons	Teaching classes when teachers are absent
Analyzing grade-point averages in relation to achievement	Computing grade-point averages
Interpreting student records	Maintaining student records
Providing teachers with suggestions for effective classroom management	Supervising classroom or common areas
Ensuring student records are maintained as per state and federal regulations	Keeping clerical records
Helping the school principal identify and resolve student issues, needs and problems	Assisting with duties in the principal's office
Providing individual and small-group counseling services to students	Providing therapy or long-term counseling in schools to address psychological disorders
Advocating for students at individual education plan meetings, student study teams and school attendance review boards	Coordinating schoolwide individual education plans, student study teams and school attendance review boards
Analyzing disaggregated data	Serving as data entry clerk

From American School Counselor Association Executive Summary (2012). Alexandra, VA: Author. https://schoolcounse
lor.org/ascanationalmodel/media/anm-templates/anmexecsumm.pdf

Specifically, this can be broken down into two areas, data profile analysis and use-of-time assessment analysis. Data profile analysis refers to a summary of the school's achievement, attendance, behavior, and safety records over the years. Use-of-time assessment analysis refers to components of a comprehensive school counseling program such as the annual agreement, calendars, and curriculum. Program results look into the analysis of curriculum, small group, closing-the-gap activities. Analysis of curriculum looks at classroom activities while analysis of small group looks at effective interventions and how they help with the needs of the school. Finally, analysis of closing-the-gap refers to impact and overall effectiveness of program activities. Evaluation and improvement are done through analysis of school counselor competencies, school counseling program assessment, school counselor performance appraisal, and program goal analysis (American School Counselor Association, 2012).

Summary

This chapter presented the unique history of the school counseling profession, and how it evolved from a position to a profession that offers support in the areas of academic, career, and social-emotional support through a comprehensive program. School counselors utilize comprehensive programming and the ASCA National Model to meet the needs of all students, P-12, and provide intentional, data-driven, systemic approaches to support and enhance the school mission. This chapter outlined influential theories and techniques employed by professional school counselors to best meet the needs of students. Professional school counselors serve as a critical component in working with all stakeholders. Counselors often function as a liaison between student, school, family, and community.

> *School counselors help you figure out and work on what's going on inside of you – things like your feelings, worries, and goals.*
>
> – Luke, a first grader

References

Adler, A. (1963). *The practice and theory of individual psychology.* Patterson, NJ: Littlefield, Adams.

American School Counselor Association. (2012). *The ASCA national model: A framework for school counseling programs* (3rd ed.). Alexandria, VA: Author.

American School Counselor Association. (2014). *ASCA mindsets & behaviors for student success: K-12 college- and career-readiness standards for every student.* Retrieved January 19, 2019, from: https://www.sch oolcounselor.org/asca/media/asca/home/MindsetsBehaviors.pdf

American School Counselor Association. (2016a). *ASCA school counselor competencies.* Alexandria, VA: Author. Retrieved from: https://www.schoolcounselor.org/asca/media/asca/home/SCCompetencies.pdf

American School Counselor Association (2016b). *The school counselor and school-family-community partnerships.* Alexandria, VA: Author.

Beck, J. S. (1995). *Cognitive therapy: Basics and beyond.* New York: Guilford.

Berg, I. K. (1994). *Family based services: A solution-focused approach.* New York: Norton.

Bernard, J. N., & Hackney, H. L. (2017). *Professional counseling: A process guide to helping* (8th ed.). Syracuse University, Pearson Education.

Boutwell, D. A., & Myrick, R. D. (1992). The go for it club. *Elementary School Guidance & Counseling, 27,* 65–72.

Bryan, J., & Holcomb-McCoy, C. (2007). An examination of school counselor involvement in school-family-community partnerships. *Professional School Counseling, 10,* 441–454.

Bryan, J., Moore-Thomas, C., Day-Vines, N. L., & Holcomb-McCoy, C. (2011). School counselors as social capital: The effects of high school college counseling on college application rates. *Journal of Counseling & Development, 89,* 190–199.

Corey, G., (2013). *Theory and practice of counseling and psychotherapy* (9th ed.). Belmont, CA: Brooks/Cole.

de Shazer, S. (1985). *Keys to solutions in brief therapy.* New York: W. W. Norton.

Ebersole, D., & Garner, N. (2014). Working with families. In R. Byrd & B. T. Erford (Ed.), *In applying techniques to common encounters in school counseling* (pp. 226–233). Boston, MA: Pearson.

Ellis, A. E. (2008). Rational-emotive behavioral therapy. In R. J. Corsini & D. Wedding (Eds.), *Current psychotherapies* (8th ed., pp. 187–222). Belmont, CA: Thomson Brooks/Cole.

Erford, T. B. (2015). *40 Techniques every counselor should know* (2nd ed.). Hoboken, NJ: Pearson Education.

Gladding, S. T. (2012). *Counseling: A comprehensive profession* (7th ed.). Boston: Pearson.

Gysbers, N. (2017, October 27). *Norman gysbers: History of school counseling* [Video file]. Retrieved from https://videos.schoolcounselor.org/norman-gysbers-history-of-schoolcounseling

Gysbers, N. C., & Henderson, P. (2001). Comprehensive guidance and counseling programs: A rich history and a bright future. *Professional School Counseling, 4,* 246–256.

Halbur, D. A., & Halbur, K. V. (2015). *Developing your theoretical orientation in counseling and psychotherapy* (3rd ed.). Hoboken, NJ: Pearson Education.

Herr, E. L. (2002). School reform and perspectives on the role of school counselors: A century of proposals for change. *Professional school counseling, 5,* 220–234.

Hess, R., Magnuson, S., & Beeler, L. (2012). *Counseling children and adolescents in schools.* Thousand Oaks, CA: Sage Publications.

Kaufman, P., Alt, M. N., & Chapman, C. (2004). *Dropout rates in the United States: 2001* (Rep. No. NCES 2005-046). Washington, DC: U.S. Department of Education. National Center for Education Statistics, U.S. Government Printing Office.

Kircher, R. L. (2007). Counselor educators' perceptions of the preparation of school counselors for advocacy (Doctoral dissertation). Retrieved from K-State Research Exchange. http://hdl.handle.net/2097/270

Mullins, F., & Otwell, P. (1997). Counselor accountability: A study of counselor effects on academic achievement and student behaviors. *Georgia School Counselors Association Journal, 1*(4), 4–12.

Online Counseling Programs. (2017, February 7). Guidance to school counselor: The evolution of professional school counseling [online counseling programs blog]. Retrieved from https://onlinecounselingprograms.com/blog/history-of-school-counseling/

Rogers, C. (1951). *Client-centered therapy: Its current practice, implications, and theory.* Boston: Houghton Mifflin.

Sink, C., & Edwards, C. (2008). Supportive learning communities and the transformative role of professional school counselors. *Professional School Counseling, 12,* 108–114.

Skinner, B. F. (1938). *The behavior of organisms: An experimental analysis.* New York: Appleton-Century.

Part Three

How? Answers about Skills and Practices

The chapters in the section covers basic counseling skills. Because counselors must be aware of their own and others' thoughts, feelings and behaviors in order to do effective counseling, the emphasis is on self-growth and awareness through skills development. This is an integral part of professional identity. Techniques discussed include basic and advanced active listening, the counseling process, questioning, and the use of affective, cognitive and behavioral interventions.

Chapter 16

Basic Attending Skills

Mary H. Guindon

I am seeking, I am striving, I am in it with all my heart.

– Vincent van Gogh

POINTS TO PONDER

- What is the difference between content and process?
- What are the different types of self-awareness?
- What is the importance of good observational skills?
- How are nonverbal behaviors differentiated?
- What are the elements of a good therapeutic relationship?
- How do counselors physically attend to clients?
- How are counselors psychologically fully present to clients?

With this chapter you will begin the process of learning the specific behaviors that constitute basic counseling skills. Before you can learn what to say or how to respond to your clients, you must learn how to let your clients know that you are tracking and understanding them – that you are completely paying attention. We call this set of behaviors *basic attending skills*. Before you learn about these skills you must understand the difference between content and process in counseling.

Content versus Process

Reread the Craggy Mountain story in Chapter 1. The students presented there and in Chapter 8 serve as examples of content and process. Just as these students evaluated the characters in the Craggy Mountain story differently, they also had quite varied thoughts and feelings about what was going on during the class exercise. The story itself and students' statements about their evaluations are only part of what goes on in the classroom. Much more is happening than the surface discussions about these characters. Let's go back:

The students have been asked not only to rank the characters but also to defend their choices. They are handling the exercise differently. Since is it the first night of class, more is on their minds than the story itself. They are excited, energized, or concerned, even apprehensive, about being in this first class in their graduate program. They are acutely aware of each other and of the instructor's presence. They are concerned about how she might be evaluating their performance. These feelings stay with them throughout the exercise.

Clarence, the psychology aide, wants to do well and impress the instructor with the right answers. He takes the lead in opening up the discussions and hopes that others will see him as the "smart one" in class. Penny, the youngest member of the class and just out of her undergraduate days, believes this is a test and wants to make sure that she also has the right answers. This is driven by not wanting to make any mistakes. She feels anxious about her evaluations of the characters and prefers to keep them to herself. Tamika, the masseuse with a degree in sociology, doesn't much see the point of doing this exercise but will go through the motions rather than risk the embarrassment of not participating. She worries that she is coming across as aggressive although she does not feel it. Betsy, the bartender, feels quite a bit of anger at details presented in the story. She wants to champion her least offensive character and make sure everyone sees it as she does. She does not much like Tamika who finds that character the most offensive. Carlos, the Sergeant Major, doesn't care for the way Clarence has jumped right end, sees him as arrogant, and is just waiting for a chance to argue against his points. Jan, the divorced grandmother, doesn't like the fact that some of her classmates are arguing and wishes everyone would just calm down. She feels uncomfortable and worries about what the instructor thinks of her.

The students have been talking about the details of the story and their rankings – its content. *Content* is the concrete information exchanged between individuals. It is the overt ideas and material that people discuss. In counseling, clients and counselors discuss content when they talk about their issues about work or school, relationships, or an aspect of the client's behavior or self-perception.

Process is the manner in which people manage the information, ideas, and material they receive. What the students think about each other and the emotions they feel about whatever is going on throughout the discussions is called process. It is thoughts, feelings, and reactions to the discussion. It involves intentions, attitudes, beliefs, ways of speaking, body language, interpretations of content, and many other factors. It includes past experiences and personal values. Process also refers to the internal dialog that individuals engage in and it includes the nature of the relationship with others involved in an interchange. Johnson (1997) refers to these many factors as *noise*. "Noise is any element that interferes with the communication process," and "the success of communication is determined by the degree to which noise is overcome or controlled" (p. 107).

If you are to become a good counselor you must learn to be a good communicator. Counselors learn to minimize the interference of their own noise by first becoming aware of it. Communication is much more than talking. It is learning to listen and convey understanding that one has heard not only what was said but also what was meant. To become a counselor you must listen and that means to make no assumptions about what others are saying based on your own preconceived biases and expectations. In order to do this, you must first understand your own thoughts, feelings, and behaviors and how they influence your interactions and communications. All through this primer you have been tracking yours and others' thoughts, feelings, actions, and the context in which they life (TFAC). Here we will take a look at its importance in counseling content and process.

Awareness of Content and Process in the Self

We cannot overemphasize the importance of your honest and accurate awareness. As you interact with others, you must know what is happening within yourself. You must understand yourself well so that you can begin helping your clients to understand themselves. If you are self-aware, you are more likely to assist others with their self-awareness. If you are to help others, you must be able to see yourself fully. You must be able to pull back the curtain of your own perceptions and biases. You must work on clarifying your own wants, needs, and desires. You must come to understand who you are, what your stressors are, when you are at your best and when you are not, where your hot buttons came from and what to do about them, and why you interact with others as you do. Your self-knowledge will allow you to be more effectively engaged in a therapeutic relationship that is collaborative and without the hidden agendas that can block clients from achieving successful outcomes. For example, your beliefs about your professional competence and personal capability can affect your behavior as a counselor. Feelings of inadequacy may include either fear of failure or fear of success. Either way, you must come to terms with what these feelings are about so that they do not interfere with the work you must do with your client. You must consider things like your feelings about intimacy and closeness, desire for acceptance, need for power or control, perception of authority, fear of conflict, worry about appearing "impolite," and a myriad of other potential problem areas. As you identify your own possible issues, you must also be prepared to do something about them.

Do you have a good understanding of who you are, how you react, what drives you, what hinders you in your interactions with others? Where are you in the ability to match your behaviors to your thoughts and to your feelings? What can you do to not only become more self-aware but also to change those areas of yourself that need changing in order to become a more fully functioning person and a better counselor?

Johnson (2013) suggests six ways to increase your self-awareness. Through *introspection*, you gain self-awareness when you look inward at yourself and how you feel or think about aspects of yourself and your world. Through *self-perception*, you can become a good observer of yourself. As you go through your normal course of activities, you can monitor yourself to assess how you feel and what causes the feeling. In effect, you step outside of yourself in order to become aware of who you are and what you are like. *Verbal articulation* means expressing your introspection and self-perceptions. You do this when you write in your journal. You can also discuss and explain your feelings, thoughts, and actions to others. You may have the opportunity to do this in your class or you may want to find opportunities among your trusted friends and family. Through *social comparison*, you compare yourself to others, and in the process can come to know yourself better. This can assist you in discovering what you have in common with those in the counseling profession and discover your own distinctiveness. You should bear in mind that no objective standards exist to determine, for example, how kind, insightful, intelligent, or extroverted you are (Johnson, 2013). Perhaps one of the most powerful ways to increase your self-awareness is through *interrelationship* with a wide variety of people who are not like you. They can provide you with new perspectives and unique experiences and help you get in touch with who you are and what you have to offer the world. Last, through *feedback* from others, you can gain information about others' perceptions of you and your behaviors. You can ask those you know well and those you barely know. The concept of feedback is discussed later on in this text as it applies to giving feedback to clients. The same principles can be applied to asking others about how they see you or react to you.

Observing Content and Process in Others

Before you can convey empathy you must understand and experience as best you can what another may be experiencing. Each of us exists in a world that we see in a unique and personal way. No one else sees the world in exactly the same way. No one else can know another's world as she does or understand what exactly it means to her. In order to understand, you must observe behavior. Ivey and Ivey (2017) suggest that one of the most important skills in building rapport with a client is observation skill. You must hone your skill to be observant of others so that you can discern process as well as content. Observation allows the counselor to look beyond words for themes, patterns, and contradictions in expression.

Behavior is the overt manifestation of others' thoughts and emotions. You must see and attempt to understand what others' behaviors, however subtle, are actually telling you. Good observational skill includes attention to both verbal and nonverbal messages. Verbal messages interact with nonverbal messages to create a more complete portrait of communication. Try to catalog what you observe so that you can receive accurately what the person is trying to communicate to you. You will then begin to understand another's point of view.

Our perceptions of others create the ways in which we interact and relate to them. Bear in mind as you read the following types of nonverbal expression that the nature and meaning of nonverbal communication are influenced by culture (Lee, 2018; McAuliffe, 2013; Neukrug, 2016; Sue & Sue, 2016). It is tied to culturally specific ways of interacting and to cultural norms and expectations. Although nonverbal cues may be good indicators of underlying issues, and counselors use their observations to inform their hunches about their clients, counselors make no definitive assumptions without checking them out with their clients. Every client is a unique human being with his own distinct experiences to disclose and explore. The counselor needs to be able to understand the client's story in the broader context of his culture and history. For example, the context of factors such as gender and societal or family customs helps the counselor to make a more accurate tentative interpretation. In this chapter, we explore nonverbal expression, a significant factor in counseling. Clearly, understanding the nature and meaning of common nonverbal cues helps us understand others accurately, to convey empathy, and ultimately to set and achieve meaningful therapeutic goals and outcomes.

Types of Nonverbal Expression

Nonverbal behavior can be a more accurate indicator of feelings than words and is for the most part out of our conscious control (Corey & Corey, 2015; Johnson, 2013; Neukrug, 2016). Nonverbal expressions tend to be more uncensored than verbal ones, or more difficult to censor. Paying attention to nonverbal cues will give you important information about feelings, thoughts, and possible incongruencies with what is being said. A client's nonverbal behaviors can assist the counselor in detecting underlying meanings or hidden agendas. Attending to and interpreting nonverbal signals can uncover inner turmoil and unrecognized conflicts. Nonverbal parts of communication carry more than 65% of social meaning (Ambady & Rosenthal, 1992). They serve as the basis for how you communicate with your client, help you determine what to investigate, and inform the direction that counseling will take. The six basic types of nonverbal expression are physical appearance, body language, personal space, facial expression, voice, and change in behavior.

Physical Appearance

Physical appearance can be a sign of social adaptation or judgment, or level of self-care. Watch others' appearance, particularly their manner of dress and their level of grooming. They can indicate if the individual is feeling depressed or upbeat. Observe if individuals are appropriately dressed for the situation and their socio-economic circumstances. Try to understand what accounts for any inappropriateness. Be aware of a lack of interest in personal cleanliness. Be cognizant of others' general level of fitness. Also notice if there is anything different or unusual about appearance in general or from session to session. It can be an area of potential inquiry. For example, physical marks or injuries may indicate abuse, they may indicate self-mutilation, or they may simply mean a game of touch football with friends a few days earlier.

Body Language

Kinesthetics is that portion of nonverbal communication that concerns the use of the body. You must be observant of kinesthetic activity and its degree. Although not everyone uses the same kinesics to express the same nonverbal messages, they can be good markers of underlying emotions. You must pick up on what the client's body is signaling to you. You must pay attention to a sag in the shoulders or a straightening up. You must see rigidity in posture and tightening of fists or comfortable posture and relaxed hands. Nodding the head to indicate yes while saying no about something or shaking the head to indicate no while agreeing to something may be indicators of incongruence or confusion. However, also take cultural variations into consideration. Observe the level of energy. The closer the individual is to a topic of significance, the higher the level of energy, even in those who present with low energy.

Personal Space

Counselors must also observe how clients use their personal space. Most people have a proximity distance from others that is acceptable to them, a range within which they are most comfortable. Cultural differences can account for how physically close people comfortably interact. Some people prefer a wide personal distance. For others, distance is quite narrow. However, clients who sit as far away as they can and that shrink down to take up as little space as possible are conveying a different message than those who sit very close to their counselors, extend their bodies fully, and strew around their personal possessions prominently.

One element of personal space is touch. For some, human touch is comforting; for others, it can be unpleasant, even threatening. Consequently, the use of touch can be therapeutic or it can be problematic. Do not assume that touch is welcome.

Facial Expression

The face can indicate feelings that belie words. Tightening of facial muscles, biting lips, small flutters of the eyes, or a downturned mouth give clear signals of underlying emotions. Smiling or laughing while tears run down the cheeks is incongruent if the discussion is sad. In the U.S. dominant cultural terms, avoiding eye contact can indicate discomfort with the counselor, the topic, or the emotions felt. In other cultures, lowering of the eyes (i.e., lack of eye contact) can mean a sign of deference and respect of authority.

Voice

Paralinguistics is that portion of nonverbal communications that involves the use of the voice. Any fluctuations from an established pattern of speech should be attended to. It can form the basis of interpreting verbal expressions. Rate of speech and pitch of tone can indicate level of emotionality. Quickened speech may signify discomfort or embarrassment with a topic, or fear or anxiety. Speech that is noticeably slowed down from the individual's normal speaking pattern may indicate feelings of sadness or depression, or of simply thinking things through. Raising the volume of the voice may mean anger, of course, or it may mean joy and exuberance. Raising the pitch of the voice can point to the significance and importance of what is being said. Or, it can mean the topic of discussion is distressing. Deepening the pitch could indicate resentment or reticence. Inflections, silences, pauses, or spacing of words can give clues to mental states and significant therapeutic material.

Change in Behavior

You must not only be observant of physical appearance and body language; you must be aware of any changes that take place over time, either within a counseling session or between counseling sessions. They may be indicators of stress or resistance. During a session, a person may blush, develop temporary rashes around the neck or upper torso, or become pale. You need to make an assessment of what these involuntary manifestations might signify. Other changes to look for are dilation of the eyes, eyebrows shooting up, eyes closed or opened widely. Also significant is a quickening of the breath, or a chest that suddenly heaves up and down slowly. You need to consider what any of these might mean.

Between sessions, look for changes as well. Is there a deterioration of appearance over time? Is there an inexplicable change in the way the person habitually dresses? Is there a stronger interest or lack of interest altogether in topics that previously engaged them? Is there a change in weight? All of these and many other changes must be observed, noted, and possibly investigated.

Your Observational Skills

Just as you will continually take inventory of your own thoughts and feelings so that you are prepared to listen and react appropriately to the thoughts and feelings of others, you must continually take inventory of what others' behaviors may be telling you about their thoughts and feelings. You must attend to their words as indicators of what they are thinking and feeling. You must attend to their nonverbal actions as well. You began your observation of others at the beginning of this text through the TFAC exercises and through your journal entries. What have you learned about observing others so far? The chart at the end of the chapter (Table 16.2) presents a list of TFAC questions about others for you to consider. Answer them as completely as you can in your journal, even if you feel you do not know the answers. You may choose strangers, friends, or family members to observe. You may also be given exercises in your class that will give you the opportunity to observe your classmates and your instructor.

It is critical to make no assumptions without checking them out. Nevertheless, your own ability to observe details about verbal and nonverbal behaviors is a set of skills that will inform your opinion about others. When you hone your observational skills, you will better perceive what is going on in the phenomenological world of the client and thus better understand the client's frame of reference. You will use your hunches to lead you to investigate with your clients what their concerns are and how they affect them. While tentatively making inferences about observations, you must use your observations to describe your clients' behaviors accurately in written case notes and to your supervisor. "Any inferences made from observations must be viewed as hypotheses which need to be confirmed or denied over time" (Peterson & Nisenholz, 1999, p. 94).

SIDEBAR 16.1

In Practice: What Would You Do?

Maddie, 19, heard Stacey, who specializes in women's issues, speak on various kinds of abuse at the Women's Center and called for an appointment the next day. She said Stacey's talk made her realize that she may be experiencing abuse. Because of this possibility, Stacey squeezed in her between appointments but could only give her 30 minutes. Maddie appeared for her appointment wearing a pantsuit with a high-collared shirt and high-heeled sandals. She was quite animated when she talked. Stacey hopes Maddie will come back next week when she has more time but worries that she will not. She knows from her own personal as well as professional experience that Maddie should commit to counseling.

Turns out Maddie has a long history of emotional difficulties. She says she's had four episodes of what she calls "huge sadness and hopelessness" since she was 14. She's been married less than a year and knew Tom only two months before they eloped. Maddie has supported herself by cleaning homes since she quit school at 16. Her parents threw her out because she was "too wild." They haven't talked to her since. She says her work is all right and she couldn't do anything else anyway. She has spent most of her free time doing crafts. She lit up when she told me she used to put them in her client's houses to "pretty them up." Now Tom "doesn't want that crap" in their home. He calls her stupid and berates her by saying, "How can you clean houses when our apartment is such a pigsty?" I could hardly believe it! Maddie says he's never threatened to hit her and doesn't believe he will. She wants some tips on how to improve her behavior so that he won't get angry with her anymore. I think she should get out of there!

Class Discussion

1. How well did Stacey hear Maddie's story? What should Stacey check out with Maddie?
2. How aware do you think Stacey is of content and process in herself? In her client? Explain.
3. Which elements of a therapeutic relationship can you assume were present in this 30-minute session? Which elements might have been missing?
4. Is Stacey showing evidence of any of the four types of countertransference with this client? Why or why not?

The Therapeutic Relationship

Counseling is an active communication endeavor between two people (or more, in the case of a family or a group). Two people interact with each other with a specific goal in mind. This is a collaborative process in which each person takes on a prescribed role with specific responsibilities and behaviors. The counselor's role is to take the lead in providing a climate in which the client will be motivated to change. The counselor recognizes that she is in a position of social influence by virtue of her status. She is responsible for forming a relationship with the client. Without relationship, there is no influence. The job of the counselor is to connect with the client so that both counselor and client work together to resolve whatever concerns brought the client into counseling. This is the working alliance mentioned previously. The counselor is considered to be the more knowledgeable person in a helping relationship and thus has credibility just by the position she holds. Counselors are role models to their clients, whether intentional or unintentional. They are in a powerful position to model good human relationships. Yet modeling doesn't work without a good counseling relationship. As Doyle (1998) emphasized, "the burden is on you to employ appropriate verbal… and nonverbal communication skills to influence the direction, the duration, and the eventual effectiveness of the counseling process" (p. 147).

The relationship between the counselor and the client facilitates change in the client's behavior or cognition or affect or often a combination of all three. Although approaches between counselors vary depending upon theoretical orientation and not all stress the importance of relationship, for most professional counselors, a good therapeutic relationship helps people investigate their thoughts, feelings, and actions. It encourages self-disclosure that leads to the incentive for change, resulting in problem-solving ability, goal setting, and accomplishment.

Elements of the Therapeutic Relationship

An effective relationship encourages people to be open, honest and self-disclosing. How you build a relationship can determine whether or not a client will return. A good relationship provides a safe haven in which people can investigate and examine their issues. It can motivate them to make needed changes and sustain them as they implement those changes. The person-centered approach first introduced by Rogers (1951) focuses on the quality of the therapeutic relationship and emphasizes the optimal core conditions necessary for building a relationship in which effective counseling can take place. Among these conditions are empathy, respect, and genuineness.

You have learned in Part One about the importance of empathy. What is it, exactly, in the context of professional counseling? *Empathy* is the ability to track the client, where she is emotionally at the moment. It conveys the message, "I am hearing you." It is the counselor's ability to enter and experience the client's world and yet remain detached from it (Rogers, 1961). Without empathy, the process of understanding your clients well enough to assist them is limited. Yet empathy is a skill of the moment, not a skill over time. The level you convey varies. Empathy involves a good amount of insight and a complex set of communications skills.

Building a therapeutic relationship is not a one-time event. It must be maintained and nurtured. It can be fragile and easily lost. Empathy is both a personality attribute and a sophisticated skill. One can have the personal attribute of empathy without the ability to adequately convey it to another. No one can teach you empathy. You either feel empathy or you do not. However, your training program can teach you to approximate empathy through a specific set of behavioral skills. Without the ability to feel empathy for another, the skills would be empty indeed. Ultimately, a lack of empathy would hinder you from entering into a meaningful and productive relationship with a client. To be an effective counselor, you must have both the attribute and the skill.

Respect, or unconditional positive regard (Rogers, 1951), is the core of the therapeutic relationship. It conveys belief in the client's potential to cope with his life circumstances and to change what needs to be changed. The emphasis is on a belief that people possess an innate striving for self-actualization. The counselor creates a nonjudgmental, growth-promoting environment that helps the client examine his thoughts, feelings, behaviors, and his personal and social environment; encourages self-disclosure; and facilitates motivation for change and problem solving. The counselor conveys to the client that the counseling space is psychologically safe and that what he says will be held in confidence. She conveys that what he says will be accepted. Acceptance, however, does not necessarily mean approval of inappropriate or dangerous behaviors. It does mean that the counselor accepts the total person in his humanness and honors his right to feel what he feels and think what he thinks. The counselor communicates concern for the client without interjecting her own values. Respect also is something the client must feel for the counselor. The client does not automatically bestow it. Respect must be earned. It is bought over time.

To earn respect means the counselor must be genuine in the relationship. She is real, without pretension or false affect. Her responses are appropriate and sincere. *Genuineness* is not just a thought or an attitude. It is behavioral. The counselor openly expresses feelings and attitudes that are present in the relationship with the client. She is consistent. She learns along with the client. She is authentic in thought, word, and deed, thus serving as a model of a human being working toward congruence. At the same time, genuineness is not something the counselor says; it is something she is. To be genuine, a counselor is in touch with who she is, what her values are, and knows that her client has a right to be who he is and live by the values in his life.

More about the Role of Transference and Countertransference

As previously stated, counseling is not a customary social exchange. You have learned that one of the characteristics of counseling is transference. *Transference* is defined as feelings from past experiences and interactions with others that are out of conscious awareness and transferred into any current relationship. Gladding (2018) adds, "transference occurs when a person unconsciously reenacts a latter-day version of forgotten *childhood* memories and repressed unconscious fantasies" (p. 160). Transference is based on individual history, experience, and the current state of needs. A client may transfer to the counselor intense feelings from the past that emerge during counseling. She may come to believe that the counselor is thinking and behaving in ways that someone from her past behaved. She may have an unrealistic view of the counselor's role in the client's life. Consequently, she may react to the counselor in false or inappropriate ways. On the other hand, with skill, the counselor can use transference therapeutically to help the client come to terms with past relationships and experiences.

Countertransference occurs when the counselor experiences "positive or negative wishes, fantasies, and feelings that a *counselor* unconsciously directs or transfers to a *client*, stemming from his or her own unresolved conflicts" (Gladding, 2018, p. 40). At times, you simply may not like someone for nothing that they have particularly done. Or, you may have strong feelings of attraction for someone for no apparent reason. Therapeutic work and outcomes are negatively affected by the counselors' lack of awareness about the insertion into the relationship of personal beliefs, traits, attitudes, and needs.

Brems (2001) described four countertransference types: (a) *Issue-specific*: avoidance, negative reactions to, or heightened emotionality to specific topics; (b) *Stimulus specific*: avoidance, negative reactions to, or heightened emotionality to clients' external or personality features; (c) *Trait-specific*: counselor's habitual ways of relating to others in general such as encouraging dependency or seeking approval; and (d) *Client-specific*: reactions to specific client patterns of behavior or ways of relating. When any of the first three types arise, the counselor needs to be aware of possible countertransference, the impact it may have on the therapeutic relationship, and take steps to prevent it. When necessary, he should seek supervision or counseling to come to terms with any conflicts and issues that have emerged so that they do not interfere with the client's work. The fourth type, client-specific countertransference, however, can be appropriately used in the counseling session. The counselor's reactions to the client may provide important information on the ways in which the client behaves in other relationships. It can be the basis of therapeutic work with the client. "Client-specific countertransference… provides the self-aware clinician with added insight and empathy for the client" (Brems, 2001, p. 34). However, counselors must investigate thoroughly whether their reactions are actually aroused by the way in which the client is coming across to them and its similarity to how the client comes across to others, or by one of the other types of countertransference.

The Skills of Basic Attending

People seek counseling because they (a) want to make a change in some aspect of themselves or something in their lives, (b) they are faced with a choice they do not know how to make, (c) or they are confused about a conflict between individual (internal) and societal (external) values, or a combination. They want to tell you about their work or school, their relationships, their loneliness, their spiritual needs, or a combination of these. They want to convey content to you. In short, they need to tell you a story.

Your job is to listen to the story so that you understand it fully and accurately. Simple, attentive listening is powerful. How often have you had someone really listen to you with total interest and without comment or judgment? Counselors offer such focused attention. In itself it can be therapeutic. Counselors "attend in order to listen; they listen in order to understand. Understanding contributes to empathy and empathy engenders a readiness to respond" (Murphy & Dillon, 1998, p. 56). Attending to clients allows the counselor to be an effective discriminator of their needs. It communicates respect, of course, and it establishes a social influence base with the client from which productive work can come.

To attend to another is to give yourself entirely to being with that person without distraction either physically or psychologically. You must set up the conditions to hear both the content and the process of the story. You need to hear more than the words and sentences. You need to hear the underlying message and theme as well. You do so first by attending physically.

How to Attend Physically: Nonverbal Skill

The factors present in nonverbal expression discussed above in observation of others also apply to the counselor and how she comes across to the client. A skilled counselor uses nonverbal communications flawlessly. Young (1998) pointed out, "Perhaps nonverbals can be compared to the musical score in a movie. It can influence us tremendously, but we rarely notice that it is there" (p. 39).

There are several specific behaviors that can maximize the therapeutic relationship and encourage clients to tell their stories. Because you will focus your attention solely on your client, you must learn to keep your immediate reactions and impulses in check. You must minimize any internal noise you experience. You must use nonverbal skill to convey that you are listening, interested, and that you care about the client's story. Attending physically is the doorway to what can be done psychologically. It conveys empathy.

Egan (2019) describes the essential nonverbal behavior counselors can employ at the beginning of counseling using the acronym SOLER:

S Face your clients **SQUARELY.** This says you are available to work with them.
O Adopt an **OPEN** posture. This says that you are open to your clients and want to be nondefensive.
L **LEAN** toward your clients at times. This underscores your attentiveness and lets clients know that you are with them.
E Maintain good **EYE** contact without staring. This tells your clients of your interest in them and their concerns.
R Remain relatively **RELAXED** with clients as you interact with them. This indicates your confidence in what you are doing and also helps relax clients.

(pp. 16–17)

Egan's system is well known to professional helpers. When practicing these five behaviors, realize that they facilitate nonverbal behaviors; they are not rigid rules. Facing someone squarely (S) means turning your body toward your client. It tells the client that you are ready for and open to contact. It may be seen as both literal and metaphorical (Gladding, 2018). To be open (O) nonverbally means that your body should not be closed off to the client. You must ensure that your arms and legs are uncrossed. Crossed arms and legs can signify defensiveness or lack of interest. Taken together squaring yourself to another and being physically open convey interest and concern. They show that you value the person speaking enough to pay attention to what they say. For example, when I first learned Egan's system back in the late seventies, I practiced everywhere. One particular occasion, I remember a classmate joining me for lunch. I put down my fork and turned my body toward him. These two behaviors alone caused him to comment that I was a good listener.

When leaning (L) toward someone you should be careful to not lean too far forward or too close. Slight leaning indicates interest; leaning too close can invade your client's personal space. It can feel intimidating. When I was a doctoral student, I was supervising a master's student who was conscientious in applying the SOLER position. However, he was a 6'5" ex-football player and the counseling room was small. I watched in the two-way mirror as his client shrunk down and back from his very hulk! His intentions were the best, but he did not pick up on his client's nonverbals. When leaning toward a client, watch what he does and adjust yourself accordingly.

For eye contact (E) to be effective with most clients means looking with soft, gentle, and constant eyes. A hard stare does not convey warmth! Note that for some cultures staring directly is a sign of disrespect. Therefore, eye contact should be used judiciously and with sensitivity. I remember a Korean student who, because of his cultural upbringing, was so uncomfortable with eye contact that he would either overdo it entirely or not look at his client at all. This caused the client to wonder what was wrong with him, even suggesting that she come back another time when he felt better. You must do what is appropriate for your client and practice what works best for you.

Being relaxed (R) while practicing S-O-L-E can be difficult when these behaviors are new. Our students usually laugh when we suggest they relax as if to say that is impossible. It is possible and with time and practice you will find physically attending to be natural and comfortable. Being comfortable in your own body is essential. The more comfortable you are; the more comfortable your client will become.

SOLER is not the only way to attend physically. Your facial expression and your tone of voice are important. An interested, neutral-to-pleasant facial expression, and slight nodding of the head at important points while your client tells her story show that you are listening and trying to understand – that you are fully attending. Your voice should convey calmness and warmth. You should be sure that you do not talk too quickly or too slowly and watch volume and pitch as well.

Physically attending suggests minimizing any external distractions. Thus, you must monitor your own behavior. What you wear can speak volumes to your client. Your attire should be appropriate to the population with which you work. You would most likely choose to leave your expensive jewelry at home. You should neither dress too formally nor too casually for your work setting. If you are in a high school counseling setting, for example, you would not wear a corporate business suit, nor would you wear the jeans you might wear in a youth services community setting.

While you will be physically open to your client, you must take care not to use gestures that are distracting. If you talk with your hands using broad motions that punctuate the air, you will need to learn to tone them down. If you use no gestures at all sitting immobile, you may come across as closed even when you are being careful to sit physically open. You will need to learn to become somewhat more animated.

How to Attend Psychologically: Being Fully Present

To be fully present to another human being and to hear another's story one must not only attend physically, one must attend psychologically. Counselors learn to set aside their personal concerns before they ever enter the counseling session. Even when the counselor's own life may be in disarray, even if the counselor is experiencing emotional distress in his own life, he must put his own issues aside in order to attend to his client and her needs. This takes the ability to center oneself before entering the counseling interview room. You may find you will need to take a deep breath, let go of stress in your body, clear your mind of current extraneous matters, or prepare yourself in other ways to be fully attentive and present to your client.

To learn to attend psychologically, you must work on your ability to be respectful toward and genuine with everyone with whom you interact. You must be capable of feeling respect for others. This means prizing all others simply because they are human. You must prepare yourself to look at the world from the frame of reference of another no matter how different they may be from you. You must be able to convey that you understand another's perspective and their worldview. Thus, you must continually work on your own knowledge of diverse others. You must be sincerely genuine in your personal as well as your counseling relationships. In order to do so, you must develop the skill of genuineness in all segments of your life. To prepare yourself psychologically to be genuine means to learn to be nondefensive, spontaneous, and consistent in your interactions. You prepare yourself psychologically by being appropriately self-disclosing and self-sharing.

Just as those who come into a learning environment may not be ready to learn, those who come into counseling, may not be ready to work on their issues. Clients have the right to try you out and to test you. Are you ready to communicate genuineness and respect to others? Answer the questions in Table 16.1, "Communication Readiness Inventory," to get an idea of your current strengths and those areas in which you may need to improve.

You also prepare yourself psychologically when you cultivate a good memory. You must be able to remember and recall small details about the client and her circumstances. Detail facilitates relationship. Good memory is essential for good record keeping and just as essential to the therapeutic relationship itself. Active listening includes the ability to recall. There is perhaps nothing quite as disconcerting to a client as having a counselor who doesn't remember what she has disclosed. Names of significant people, places, and details of events are essential in gaining a better understanding of the individual's perception of the world. Listen for the who, what, where, when, why, and how of your client's story.

Table 16.1 Communication Readiness Inventory

Communicating Genuineness	**My Assessment**
When you communicate with others	
1. are you generally your usual, relaxed self?	
2. do you ever feel the need to take on a role (e.g., helper, organizer, leader, passive receiver)?	
3. are you consistent in your behavior with most or all people?	
4. do you self-disclose and share yourself openly and appropriately?	
5. is your use of language natural or is it stilted, or guarded?	
6. do you express your thoughts and feelings honestly?	
7. do you say what you mean and mean what you say?	
8. are you defensive when given less than positive feedback or do you hear it as constructively?	
Communicating Respect	**My Assessment**
When you communicate with others	
1. are you appropriately warm and approachable?	
2. do you avoid being judgmental?	
3. do you try to take over or control the direction of the discussion?	
4. do you see others as unique individuals, distinct from anyone else?	
5. can you be "for" another in a caring manner regardless of their life circumstances or situation?	
6. do you believe that others know what is best for themselves?	
7. do you assume their good will?	
8. are you frequently empathic without being overly sympathetic?	

Answer as honestly as you can. Assess yourself according to
N = Needs Improvement   A = Acceptable   G = Good   DN = Don't Know
If you are unsure, seek out a trusted friend, peer, or colleague and ask for their feedback.
After you have taken this Inventory, go back and circle those items by which you wrote "N." These are areas in which you need to seek out opportunities to develop new communications skills.

Counselors often prefer to attend fully by forgoing note taking during a session. Writing while the client is speaking can come across as not only inattentive but also as disrespectful. Unless you are doing an initial intake interview in which forms must be filled out, do not take notes during a counseling session. If you must fill out a form or write something down, let the client see it. Hand it to her. Writing about someone in their presence without allowing them to know what it is you write does not build trust. As much as possible and feasible, the place for note taking is directly after the interview. A good memory will aid you in remembering the essential elements of what transpired. At times, you may want to record your client. This facilitates your memory but can only be done with the client's full knowledge and consent. Some clients will not wish to be recorded. Therefore, your recall ability is essential. Good memory is critical.

Your Thoughts, Feelings, Actions, and Context Revisited

As you work with your clients, you will need to continually take inventory of your own thoughts and feelings so that you are prepared to listen and react appropriately to the thoughts and feelings of others. You began your self-awareness inventory at the beginning of this text through the TFAC exercises and through your journal entries. What have you learned about yourself and how you interact with others so far? In the TFAC chart for this chapter is a list of questions for you to consider. Answer them as honestly and clearly as you can in your journal. Realize that these categories are not mutually exclusive. We are whole human beings not easily compartmentalized. Nevertheless, strive to check off every box

Summary

This chapter is the first in the How of counseling. The difference between content and process in communication was presented with the aim of assisting students in understanding their own internal processes in interactions. Students were urged to work on understanding these inner processes through analysis of their own and others' thoughts, feelings, and actions. The chapter turned to a presentation of types of nonverbal expression and its significance in building students' observational skills. Next, the relationship between the counselor and client and the elements of empathy, respect, and genuineness in building the therapeutic relationship were presented. Included was a discussion of transference and countertransference. The chapter ended with the How of basic attending by presenting sections on nonverbal skill, or physical attending, and the importance of being fully present, or psychologically attending.

Why didn't anyone teach us this when we were kids?
— beginning student's comment after an in-class listening skills practice session

References

Ambady, N., & Rosenthal, R. (1992). The slices of expressive behavior as predictors of interpersonal consequences: A meta-analysis. *Psychological Bulletin, 111*, 256–274.

Brems, C. (2001). *Basic skills in psychotherapy and counseling.* Belmont, CA: Wadsworth, Brooks/Cole.

Corey, M. S., & Corey, G. (2015). *Becoming a helper* (7th ed.). Boston: Cengage.

Doyle, R. E. (1998). *Essential skills & strategies in the helping process* (2nd ed.). Pacific Grove, CA: Brooks/Cole.

Egan, G. (2019). *The skilled helper: A problem-management and opportunity-development approach to helping* (11th ed.). Boston: Cengage.

Gladding, S. T. (2018). *The counseling dictionary: Concise definitions of frequently used terms* (4th ed.). Alexandria, VA: The American Counseling Association.

Ivey, A. E., & Ivey, M. B. (2017). *Intentional interviewing and counseling: Facilitating client development in a multicultural society* (9th ed.). Boston: Cengage.

Johnson, D. W. (1997). *Reaching out: Interpersonal effectiveness and self-actualization*. Boston: Allyn & Bacon.

Johnson, D. W. (2013). *Reaching out: Interpersonal effectiveness and self-actualization* (11th ed.). Boston: Pearson.

Lee, C. C. (Ed.). (2018). *Multicultural issues in counseling: New approaches to diversity* (5th ed.). Alexandria, VA: American Counseling Association.

McAuliffe, G., & Associates (2013). *Culturally alert counseling: A comprehensive introduction* (2nd ed.). Thousand Oaks, CA: Sage Publications.

Murphy, B. C., & Dillon, C. (1998). *Interviewing in action: Process and practice*. Pacific Grove, CA: Brooks/Cole.

Neukrug, E. (2016). *The world of the counselor: An introduction to the counseling profession* (5th ed.). Boston: Cengage.

Peterson, J. V., & Nisenholz, B. (1999). *Orientation to counseling* (4th ed.). Boston: Allyn & Bacon.

Rogers, C. (1951). *Client-centered therapy: Its current practice, implications, and theory*. Boston: Houghton Mifflin.

Rogers, C. (1961) *On becoming a person: A therapist's view of psychotherapy*. Boston: Houghton Mifflin.

Sue, D. W., & Sue, D. (2016). *Counseling the culturally diverse: Theory and practice* (7th ed.). Hoboken, NJ: John Wiley & Sons.

Young, M. E. (1998). *Learning the art of helping: Building blocks and techniques*. Upper Saddle River, NJ: Merrill/Prentice Hall.

Table 16.2 *TFAC Chart – Thought, Feelings, Actions, and Context

Self	Thoughts	Feelings	Actions	Context	Other? (Specify)
What are my interpersonal needs and wants? Do I express them directly or indirectly?					
How do I interact with others? Am I assertive or nonassertive? Controlling or controlled?					
How do I express my emotions? Do others know how I feel? Do I hide my feelings or impose my feelings on others?					
What does intimacy mean to me? What forms of intimacy are most rewarding? Most intimidating?					
Do I allow for give and take with friends? Family? Acquaintances?					
Do I seek out ways to be with others? Are there too many or too few people in my life? How much time do I need alone? With others?					
What do my physical appearance, body language, facial expressions, voice, and personal space say about me?					
Others	**Others' Probable Thoughts**	**Others' Possible Feelings**	**Others' Observable Actions**	**Others' Apparent Context**	**Other? (Specify)**
How do others interact with me? With each other?					
How do others express their thoughts? What might their stated thoughts tell me about their emotions?					
What do I observe about physical appearance? What might it indicate?					
What do I observe about others' specific body language? What might it indicate?					
How do others use their personal space? What might it indicate?					
What do I observe about others' specific facial expressions? What might they indicate?					
What do I observe about others' use of their voice? What might it indicate?					

*For more information on TFAC, see Chapter 1.

Chapter 17

Basic Responding Skills

Mary H. Guindon

Wherever there is a human being, there is an opportunity for a kindness.

– Seneca

POINTS TO PONDER

- What are the four basic responding skills?
- When are counselors most likely to respond to content?
- What is primary accurate empathy?
- What are minimal encouragers and their purpose?
- How and in what circumstances do counselors use restatements or paraphrases?
- What is summarization and when is it used?
- Why do counselors refrain from interrupting and when are counselors justified in doing so?
- What is the significance of silence in counseling sessions?

Responding to Content and Process

In the last chapter, you learned that communication consists of content and process. You will respond to content when important information needs to be gathered or provided and when you want to convey understanding to the client. However, content alone is not enough. Process allows the counselor to interact more accurately with another human being. You will monitor your own internal processes as a way to be in touch with what your client might be experiencing. You will attend to both the verbal and nonverbal messages your client sends. You will also intentionally monitor and therapeutically use your own nonverbal messages to convey your empathic understanding.

This chapter concerns working with the client on content using basic responding skills. Later, you will learn more about working with process. In a real counseling session, skills are intertwined and not so readily deconstructed. For training purposes, however, we will begin with content and move to process once you have mastered the skills presented in this chapter and the next.

Primary empathy is the ability to tell the client "I hear you" and "I am tracking you accurately." Basic responding skills communicate primary empathic understanding. You will give minimal responses that encourage the client to continue talking and to tell her story. As the story unfolds, you will begin to respond by restating and paraphrasing what the client tells you, and you will pull together what the client have told you by summarizing. These skills allow you to show that you are staying with the client, not getting ahead of the story, or evaluating what you are told. These essential responding skills are necessary to build rapport and trust and are used throughout counseling stages. The way you listen and respond matters when building a relationship with another human being. You can either build a barrier or build a bridge to understanding. Human beings have a natural tendency to judge and evaluate statements others make (Johnson, 2013). Whether that evaluation is positive ("You are so right!") or negative ("You don't know what you are talking about"), the clear message is that you know more than the other person about his own story. By giving your point of view, you will miss really listening and risk creating a barrier to understanding. When you listen without evaluating, you build a bridge.

You have read that your job is to listen to your client's story. This means that you will resist the very human desire to evaluate the story with your thoughts and comments. You must listen therapeutically by allowing the client to speak without interruption even if she pauses between thoughts or words. The effective counselor not only refrains from evaluation; he is not judgmental. To be nonjudgmental means to put aside expectations or preconceived ideas of what the client might be saying based on one's own past associations. It means the counselor will listen to the entire story as a unique report of the client's reality. The counselor does not engage in selective listening because of stereotypical thinking about the client's socioeconomic class, race, gender, age, and so forth. To do any less is to not fully hear the story and risk the client believing that she is not heard, is misunderstood, or disrespected.

Earlier you learned that the way you present yourself physically and attend psychologically facilitates communication. You learned how to begin a conversation with a new client in the early stages of counseling. By mastering basic attending skills, you set the stage for open communication. You must now learn how to respond to the initial story. In my experience with students, I have found that questioning, appropriately or not, comes easily. Responding effectively takes much more effort and skill. From this point on, you will change the way you communicate. Let's begin by listening without asking questions.

Minimal Encouragers

Once you have invited your client to begin talking, how do you proceed? As you learned in Chapter 7, you will offer encouragement to speak. This encouragement is noninvasive, does not interrupt, and allows the client adequate space and time to tell her story. *Minimal encouragers* are those verbal and nonverbal behaviors that support the client's communication and encourage her to continue talking. They are the simplest interventions available to counselors. The counselor conveys that he is deeply interested and engaged in the story along with the client and wants to know more. By being heard, the client feels supported and understood in a safe environment. Minimal encourages allow clients the time and conditions to continue exploring the story and to delve into a topic more intensely or in greater detail. They allow the counselor to gain a better understanding of the client's point of view. Encouragers add nothing and suggest nothing. They do not lead the client in any particular direction. They can be therapeutically helpful just in themselves.

Three kinds of minimal encouragers are nonverbal, semiverbal, and the short phrase requesting more information. *Nonverbal encouragers* include the open body position described in the last chapter, slight head nodding, and an interested facial expression. *Semiverbal encouragers* include sounds or words that indicate understanding such as "uh-huh," "ahh", or "I see" and often accompany nonverbals. They also include simply repeating an important word or phrase used by the client, often with a slight questioning intonation at the end.

Example:

Client (Cl):   I don't care what they think!
Counselor (Co):   You don't care…? *(voice inflection)*

The third type of minimal encourager, *the short phrase*, goes beyond simple repetition to request additional information that does not lead or direct the client. Simple repetition of a phrase with a voice inflection indicating a question is one example. Other examples include phrases such as "Tell me more…," "And then what?," or "Talk more about that."

Example:

Bill is a 27-year-old waiter on a cruise ship.
Cl: I wish my mother would just leave me alone! I'm a grown man, after all!
Co: Tell me more about that.
Cl: She's on my case all the time about my job.
Co: Uh-huh…
Cl: She doesn't think it's good enough for me but it's my life, not hers.
Co: *(nodding)*
Cl: Just because I don't want to be a dentist like my dad doesn't mean I don't know what I'm doing.
Co: I see…
Cl: I want a different life.
Co: A different life…? *(voice inflection)*
Cl: Yes! One that makes me happier than he was.

The counselor uses minimal encouragers when he wants to give the client time to tell the story and when the client is willing to talk. They are interspersed with other techniques to keep the flow of conversation moving forward and when additional information is needed. Counselors do not use minimal encouragers when they want the client to discuss something else or when a client is unfocused, rambling, or ruminating.

A word of caution: Minimal encouragers can be misused if the counselor is not well trained or highly disciplined. Once learned, for example, minimal encouragers run the risk of being routinely applied or used by rote. Instead of genuinely tracking the client, the counselor is not really hearing at all. The point of minimal encouragers is to engage in the process of empathic understanding. The counselor must then convey that understanding back to the client. In the above example, the counselor is ready to communicate understanding. This is done through the next set of techniques.

Restatements and Paraphrases

Responding to content is a basic way to negotiate meaning with the client and convey empathy. You must restate in some form your understanding of what the client is saying to you. Restatement and paraphrasing are ways of conveying content. They are both concise reiterations of something the client has communicated. They are similar in purpose but vary slightly in structure. The purpose is to communicate understanding back to the client; to show the client that the counselor is tracking him accurately; to clarify that, indeed, she is accurate in understanding the content of the communication; or to emphasize something that the client has said because it seems either particularly significant or confusing.

Restatements and paraphrases are straightforward. They do not offer interpretations of the client's content or provide explanations of the story. Rather, both allow the client to hear the story from the counselor's mouth. In effect, the counselor holds up a mirror to the client so he can see for himself what might be occurring in his life. Therapeutic in themselves, restatements and paraphrases are strong tools in the counseling process. They are used routinely to further communication or judiciously to emphasize important material, refocus attention to significant aspects of the presenting issue, or allow the client to understand some previously not understood aspect of his story.

Restating

Restatements use the client's words to reflect content. They are like short-phrase minimal encouragers but move one step beyond them by repeating more of what the client has said. They are not only longer but more thorough. However, if you say exactly the same words in the same order that the client says them, you are not using the skill of restatement well. On the contrary, you are very likely to come across sounding like an insincere phony. You can be sure this "parroting" will stop the flow of communication and the advancement of the story.

Restatement uses the client's language and level of intensity to feed back an important aspect of what has been said. It repeats the basic idea using the same words but not necessarily in the same order. Restatements generally begin with an introductory sentence stem such as "What you are saying is…." or "You are saying that…." This is then followed with important or significant words used by the client.

Example:

Cl: I don't want to be a dentist like my dad. I want to work at something that makes me happier than he was.

Co: You are saying that you want to work at something that makes you happier than your dad was.

You can also simply repeat the client's statement without the stem.

Example:

Cl: I want a different life.

Co: You want a life that's different.

Restatements and phrase minimal encouragers can be interchangeable. The counselor decides which to use based on the recency of the comment or its proximity in time to the client's comment. In other words, if the phrase was the last thing said, the counselor might opt for a phrase minimal encourager. If the client has gone on to say a few more words or phrases and the counselor wants to return to important material and reflect that, she would opt for a restatement.

To use restatements, the counselor must take care not to interject new meaning or offer any kind of interpretation. This is perhaps one of the most difficult aspects of learning how to respond to content. Neophyte counselors can confuse interpretation of content with content itself This is a skill you will work on not only in the classroom but in your day-to-day interactions. It takes practice to master because you must sort out what it is you want to respond to without adding anything to what was communicated.

Paraphrasing

Paraphrasing is closely related to restatements and further removed from phrase minimal encouragers. The purposes are the same but paraphrases add content without adding an interpretation of content. Although restatements can clarify communication, paraphrases have the additional and main purpose of clarification and thus use different words from those used by the client. The counselor expresses her understanding of the client's story. The counselor attempts to reflect back content that was actually provided by the client, usually focusing on an important aspect or significant idea. Paraphrases challenge the client to hear what he has said as reflected in the counselor's words.

The counselor uses her own words to approximate what the client has said. Because the counselor is not using the client's exact words but must search for other words and phrases of her own, she must be sure to clarify that it is her own perception of the client's communication. A paraphrase expresses to the client what the counselor thinks he is saying by using a clarifying phrase as an introductory stem or at the end of the statement. The clarifier attempts to let the client know he is understood through the counselor's perception. Common examples of introductory stems are

"It sounds like you are saying…"
"It seems to me that you are saying…"
"I'm sensing that you…"
"What I hear you saying is…"
"What stood out for me is…"
"My take on what you've said is…"
"I see that you are saying…"
"In other words…"
"So…you are saying…"

At times, the counselor may choose to make a statement and add the clarifier at the end of the sentence instead. In this case, the counselor would make a statement to convey understanding of what the client has said and add one of these examples:

"Is that how it is?"
"Am I hearing you correctly?"
"Am I seeing this the way you mean it?"
"Is that about right?"
"Am I understanding you?"
"Have I got it?"

Although the above examples are grammatically a kind of questioning, they are considered clarifiers for the counselor's perceptions, not information-gathering questions per se. The discipline of asking questions will be presented in the next chapter.

Paraphrases, although still reflections of content, are powerfully therapeutic and have a major advantage over minimal encouragers and restatements. They minimize the chance of parroting and allow the counselor to pick up on what can be important areas for further investigation. The counselor can communicate clearly that what the client is attempting to say is actually heard even if the attempts are not particularly eloquent or articulate. By using other words, the counselor can convey that what the client says is important, that the counselor can clarify, even crystallize the client's meanings.

Example 1:

Cl: I don't want to be a dentist like my dad. I want to work at something that makes me happier than he was.

Co: So… you're telling me your dad is unhappy in his work and you want something more satisfying for your life.

Example 2:

Maria is an 11-year-old middle-school student who has been called into her counselor's office because her grades have fallen from As to Cs.

Cl: I don't like coming to school anymore. The girls make fun of me.

Co: You don't want to be here because the girls tease you.

Cl: Yeah. They whisper about me behind my back, but I can hear them. They laugh at me because I'm fat. I didn't use to be fat. It stinks!

C: It's not fair that the girls laugh at you and talk about you because you are heavier now than you used to be.

Cl: I'm not just heavy! I'm fatter and bigger than anybody else in my class. I'm a freak! I don't see why I have to come to school at all.

Co: You don't want to be in your class because you feel larger than everyone else. Is that how it is?

Cl: Yeah. Even my best friend won't hang out with me anymore. She wants to be in good with the other girls. She just stands there when they laugh at me and walks away with them.

Co: It seems to me that you are saying your best friend has turned her back on you and joined the girls who tease you. (*The counselor attempts to put herself in Maria's place. She believes that the rejection by the friend may be the key issue.*)

In paraphrasing, the counselor uses words that reflect the same level of emotional intensity and may use sensory words that seem to match the client's style of speech. That is, if the counselor believes the client to be more visual than aural, she might use "seeing" words over "hearing" words. The words the counselor chooses will help the client reflect on what he has actually said. The counselor holds up a bigger, higher magnification mirror. Clarification questions at the end of paraphrasing allow the client the opportunity to correct any misperceptions or distortions.

In using introductory stems or end-of-sentence clarifiers, be careful not to fall in the trap of overusing one or two repeatedly. Nothing will turn off a client quicker than cliché or canned comments. If you overuse them, you will put distance between yourself and your client, the exact opposite of your intent. Learn many of these and similar responses so well that they will come naturally to you and you can alternate them easily. Use terms that fit you best and those you are most comfortable with.

Paraphrasing also allows the counselor to let the client know whether or not she has, in fact, understood the client's story or point of view. When paraphrases are accurate, clients will say "Yes!" or "That's it!" or "Exactly!" or something similar. On the other hand, if the counselor has not understood or conveyed the correct understanding, the client has the opportunity to delve more deeply to make the meaning more clear. Counselors also welcome "No, it's not like that" comments because it causes the client to think through what he actually does think or feel and to clarify the story for himself as well as for the counselor. This is what negotiating for meaning is about. The counselor paraphrases until she truly "gets it" and the client communicates a point until he also understands it himself.

SIDEBAR 17.1

In Practice: What Would You Do?

Graham is a family practice counselor of many years' experience. He has been seeing working professionals, Joyce and Bill, for marriage counseling and anger issues for a couple of sessions. They ask if they can bring in Chad, their ten-year-old only child, after his fourth grade teacher urged them to.

> *Joyce says Chad never runs out of steam, that he's driving them both crazy. He won't ever stay in his seat. Bill says he doesn't see this except when Joyce is nagging him. He doesn't remember this kind of behavior when he was younger. Joyce says Bill just wasn't paying attention and the teacher wouldn't urge them to get help for Chad if it wasn't a problem. Bill just looked away when she said that. The first time I saw Chad, his parents stayed in my waiting room. He was a handful! He chattered nonstop and seemed to want constant attention. He interrupted me and jumped up on the chair laughing. He came right down, though, when I told him to. He's a likable kid. When I called his parents in, he sat quietly, didn't look at them, and seemed somewhat sullen. I'm going to refer him for testing. Meanwhile, I want to accomplish something with this family. I'm sure at the least he's reacting to his parents' problems. I don't think they are open to hearing that yet....*

Class Discussion

1. What can Graham do to build a bridge to Joyce and Bill? To Chad?
2. How effective do you think minimal encourages, restatements, and paraphrases would be with Joyce and Bill? With Chad?
3. What can Graham do to get a clearer idea of this family's story?
4. What can Graham do to get a better understanding of Chad's story, with regard to his behavior in school?

Summarization

Summarization is similar to restatement and paraphrasing in that it reflects content. Later, you will learn to use summarization to reflect emotions, although reflecting content is the most common usage. Summarization differs from paraphrasing in that it attempts to pull together the important parts of a conversation over more than one interaction. Counselors use it whenever they want to respond to more than one concept, idea, or message at a time. It can be used when a client brings up several issues at the same time and the counselor wants to feed back important areas mentioned. Summarizations are used periodically but judiciously and with less frequency than restatements or paraphrases. Counselors employ them during a session to review what has gone on so far and at the end of a counseling session to sum up or go over the main points of what has transpired. Summarizations are also used at the beginning of a session as a way of review. Sometimes, counselors use them when a client seems stuck and doesn't know what else to say or when there seems to be no direction to what the client is saying or when the client repeats the same material over and over.

Summarization is more than lengthy paraphrasing. The technique assures the client that he has been heard correctly. It helps the client hear what he has actually said and allows him to better understand his own story. He may gain clarity on a particular issue, problem, or achievement. It can provide the client with a new point of view on his own experiences.

Summarizations also provide clarity for the counselor. None of us is a mind reader. We use our empathy to put ourselves in another's shoes. We are our own best counseling instrument and play hunches based on our own past experiences. We can be right on target. However, we can be wrong or misunderstand. Summarization allows clients to correct our misperceptions. Summarization is a necessary skill and a powerful technique important in building trust, forging a relationship, and conveying caring.

Summarization is also a disciplined behavior. The counselor must be able to focus on many parts of the communication at the same time to pick up on significant elements. By definition, the counselor is selective. To summarize means to pick and choose what to attend to and reflect back to the client. It suggests that one of the client's statements or ideas is more important than others. By including a particular concept in a summary, the counselor in effect rewards the client by attending to and focusing on it.

Occasionally, the counselor will ask clients to provide a summary to learn what is most important to the client. This can also help clients decide what is most significant in the session, give focus to important issues, or provide clarity when they are stuck. It places responsibility for what to work on with the client. The counselor should be ready to assist the client, however, to pull a summary together; it should not be perceived to be a test (Egan, 2006).

Summarizations can begin with any of the introductory statements presented previously, although occasionally, a counselor may vary a summarization by beginning without an introduction. Other common introductory stems and sentences used in summarization include:

"From what I've heard so far…"
"As I see it, you are telling me…"
"Let's review what I think you've said so far."
"Let me see if I understand what you've told me."
"I want to make sure I've got this right."
"I'm not sure I understand. I think you've said…"
"As we begin today, I'd like to review my understanding of what went on last time."
"As we finish today, let me see if I understand what we've covered."

Example:

Jill is a 35-year-old widowed mother of 8-year-old twin boys. She wants to go back to school but is afraid she will not be able to work a full-time job, take care of her children, attend classes at night, and find time to study without negatively impacting on her children's needs. This is the beginning of the second session.

C: (*Summarizing first session*) Let's begin today with a review of what we've discussed so far. The way I understand it, you want to go back to school so that you'll be able to provide a better life for your children but you're afraid taking the time away from them will be harmful. You mentioned that you are not sure you can afford the tuition, babysitters, and the time it takes to finish your degree. You don't know how you can meet all the demands on your time. Is that about right?

Cl: Yes, I really want my kids to be okay with this. I try not to leave them with babysitters if I can help it. They lost their dad when they were just four. They shouldn't be without me, too. I don't like being gone…. I don't have to get this degree. I want it, mind you, but do I have the right to be so selfish? On the other hand, I guess I shouldn't feel selfish if it means we'll have more money for all the things they'll be needing in the long run. I wasn't left with much. But for now, I just don't know what to do.

Co: (*Summarizing*) If I'm understanding what you've told me, you want to go back to school so you can provide more for your kids but you think it's selfish. You're not sure it's the right thing to do. You don't like being away from them because they've lost one parent and you want to be there for them. Is that how it is?

Cl: Of course! I mean, it's bad enough I have to put them in day care after school until I can get them at six. Some nights I'd have to go right from work to class. I'd be gone such a long time. Past their bedtimes. I hate it when I can't be there!

Co: (Paraphrasing)You're saying you not only have to put them in day care after school but now you won't get home to see them before they go to bed.

In this example, the counselor summarizes the last session and continues with a summary when the client responds with several thoughts. She then responds with a paraphrase of the main gist of the client's primary concern. Summarizing allows the counselor to feed back a more succinct version of the client's main issue. The counselor wants to capture the essence of the client's point of view and attempts to do so in as few sentences as possible without losing important points. Summarization is not an excuse for the counselor to pontificate or make a speech. In general, the counselor uses two to four main sentences (beyond clarifiers) and then allows the client to respond.

Interrupting

Beginning counselors, in their desire to do a good job, may tend to talk more than necessary. In fact, some talk so much that the client doesn't have a chance! Generally, counselors do not interrupt when their clients are speaking. Remember that you are there to listen, not to give your opinion. If you find yourself interrupting or stepping on your client's words, stop and ask the client to go on. If you talk while the client is speaking, stop immediately and let the client finish. On the other hand, if the client interrupts you or steps in while you are speaking, stop what you are saying immediately and attend to your client.

Only on those occasions when clients are rambling without purpose or are incoherent will a counselor interrupt to help them focus and slow down. In these cases, counselors interrupt with intent. They don't talk over their clients or outtalk them in some sort of battle of wills. If the professional counselor judges that interrupting is more facilitative than for the client to continue talking, she stops the client in a forthright, open manner. She might use phrases like these or other similar ones:

"Stop for a minute. Let me see if I understand what you are trying to say."
"Slow down. I'm having trouble keeping up with you."
"Stop there. I'm not sure what this is all about"
"Let me interrupt you here. I'm unclear on what is most important to you."

When the counselor stops an overly talkative client, she may then go on to paraphrase or summarize or she may use questioning, which will be discussed in the next chapter. Or, she may wait to allow time for the client to refocus, slow down, or pick up on what is most important without further comment.

Therapeutic Use of Silence

Silence in counseling can be as powerful a therapeutic ally as what is actually said. Beginning counselors can be uncomfortable with silence. They may break a silence from their own sense of embarrassment or distress. It evokes awkward moments of social situations that all of us experience from time to time. Saying nothing can be as important as speaking in a counseling session, at times even more so. Silence lets individuals think through what they want to say and consider what they have just said. Counselors sit with the silence, allowing their client the time they need to process their thoughts, to work through an emotional moment, and to consider whether they are finished with a topic. If you jump in prematurely, you may stop the flow of significant work. Clients may need a pause before they continue. They are not looking for a response and you would do best to give them the space and time they need to move forward. When you remain quiet and attend nonverbally, a client can feel the support and caring communicated just by your presence. If you are not sure whether to respond or remain silent, opt for silence. If a silent episode goes on too long, you will respond with a question such as:

"What's going through your mind?"
"What's got you thinking?"
"What are you feeling right now?"

Putting It Together

Gathering the threads of a story until you really understand takes time. The best way to do so is to use basic responding skills. Begin practicing now with your fellow classmates, at home, and in your random conversations throughout your day. You will be surprised how people will open up to you and how much you will hear. Are you used to being told that you are a good listener? Or, have you been told that you give good advice? Remember that counselors are in the business of listening without preconceived notions, judgments, and evaluations. Counselors try not to form their responses while others are talking and certainly try not to come up with solutions as they listen.

Basic responding skills are not performed in a vacuum. They are part of a repertoire of rapport-building skills you will use from the beginning of the first encounter and whenever the client provides new information. The skills presented in this chapter are the simplest skills you will learn. Perhaps they are deceptively simple. They take practice and discipline. You will return to them again and again as counseling progresses from first session to termination. Use your TFAC chart at the end of this chapter to guide you as you practice and to observe others as they respond. Record your progress in your journal now and throughout the rest of this course.

The following example gives you an idea of how the four basic responding skills flow together in a session.

Julie is a 50-year-old middle manager in a financial planning company. She comes into counseling because she suspects some members of her staff go over her head to her boss. She wants to quit. This is the middle of the first session.

Cl: The buck stops with me. I make decisions for the office but no one respects my authority.
Co: (paraphrasing) Your staff doesn't seem to value your decisions. Am I understanding you correctly?
Cl. *That's right! I'm nothing more than an overpaid clerk anyway. I do all the grunt work! They have no idea how much I really do. If I weren't there, they'd have to do it.*
Co: (paraphrasing) You seem to be saying you do the bulk of the work and they don't even know it.
Cl: Yeah. When they go to the boss, they don't have all the facts. It's insulting!
Co: (restating). It's insulting when they go to the boss without all the facts.
Cl: You're damn right it is! Who do they think they are? I mean, I'm the one who got promoted into this job. I'm the one who worked hard, put in my time, took the extra training every chance I got. They have no idea how much expertise goes into my decisions!
Co: (nodding – minimal encourager) I see....

Cl: I have half a mind to quit just to stick them with the work. I wonder how good their deci-
      sions would be! The boss would kick them out the door at their first lame-brain scheme!
      But that's not me. I'm too professional to just walk out. I have too much integrity to do that
      to my boss. But I sure wish I could get out of there when they go behind my back!

Co: (*summarizing*) As I see it, you are telling me that your staff members don't understand how
      you come to your decisions or about how much expertise you really have. You'd like to quit
      when they go over your head but you are a professional and won't just leave your boss in
      the lurch.

Cl: That's it. I feel so stuck. (*Tears form and she lowers her head*)

Co: (*therapeutic use of silence*)

      Cl: (*Takes a deep breath and continues*) The thing is, I like my job. And some of my staff
      don't do that....

Co: (*minimal encourager*) Tell me more about that....

This example shows how therapeutic progress can occur when the counselor attends well and
responds to content alone. Questioning has not yet been necessary. You no doubt have picked up
on Julie's anger, frustration, and hurt. Because this is early in the first session and the counselor's
primary job is to build rapport and trust, she chooses to wait to address feelings. She is not yet
ready to help Julie work on solutions to the problem. She has not heard the entire story. When
the time is right, she will use questions appropriately, respond to feelings, and work with Julie's
thoughts and behaviors to help her make necessary changes. The next three chapters present
these basic skills.

Summary

This chapter presented the four basic responding skills of minimal encouragers, restatements,
paraphrases, and summarization. These skills allow us to learn from the client about his own
experiences and perceptions. They allow us to correct our misperceptions until we are as in tune
with the client's experience as we can possibly be. They help us guard against making assumptions and in themselves can be helpful to clients in understanding their own concerns. The
chapter included a section on interruptions and the importance of the therapeutic use of silence.

> *Stop repeating everything I say!*
> – practicum lab client to an earnest but inexperienced beginning internship counselor

References

Egan, G. (2006). *Essentials of skilled helping: Managing problems, developing opportunities.* Pacific Grove, CA:
      Thomson Brooks/Cole.
Johnson, D. W. (2013). *Reaching out: Interpersonal effectiveness and self-actualization* (11th ed.). Boston:
      Pearson.

Table 17.1 *TFAC Chart – Thought, Feelings, Actions, and Context

Self	My Thoughts	My Feelings	My Actions	My Context	Other? (Specify)
What happens when I use minimal encouragers?					
How am I doing at restatements and paraphrasing?					
How I am doing at summarizing?					
When am I most likely to interrupt others?					
How do I respond when others interrupt me?					
What is my past experience with silence in my interactions?					
What concerns do I have?					
Others	**Others' Probable Thoughts**	**Others' Possible Feelings**	**Others' Observable Actions**	**Others' Apparent Context**	**Other? (Specify)**
What have you observed about minimal encouragers in varying circumstances?					
What have you observed about restatements and paraphrases among your classmates? Your instructors? Others?					
What have you observed about summarization among your classmates? Your instructors? Others?					
How do others react when they are interrupted?					
How do others handle silence? In class? In social situations?					
What else can you learned about others' basic responding skills?					

*For more information on TFAC, see Chapter 1.

Chapter 18

Questioning Skills and Systematic Inquiry

Mary H. Guindon

"The time has come," the Walrus said, "to talk of many things."

– Lewis Carroll

POINTS TO PONDER

- What are some basic purposes of questioning?
- What is a closed question and when it is appropriately used?
- What are open-ended questions? When are they used?
- What makes "why" questions unacceptable?
- Under what circumstances are they appropriate?
- What are some other problematic questions and what makes them so?
- How are assumptive questions best used?
- What is systematic inquiry and when is it used?
- How do counselors respond to client questions?

Use of Questions

In the last chapter you learned that therapeutic progress can occur without asking questions. However, questioning is integral and indispensable to counseling. Questioning helps the counselor explore client concerns by eliciting relatively thorough and in-depth responses. Questions – also called probes – structure an intake session in a systematic way and acquire facts and information throughout counseling. They allow clients to communicate in more depth, can put them at greater ease, and can help them elaborate on their specific concerns. They can lead clients to consider aspects of their problems not evident to them but noticeable to the counselor. Questions also influence the direction of sessions by pointing out significant parts of the client's story. They are used to clarify confusing material, elicit specific examples of ambiguous or general statements, and introduce or review key points. Questions of any type indicate that the counselor thinks the client can profitably discuss a topic more fully (Johnson, 2013). They can have a strong impact on a client's growth and development.

To be a good counselor you must be comfortable with a not-knowing position, which can have distinct advantages: It reminds us not to make assumptions, makes it all right for us to not understand everything, and helps us realize that the expert in the room is the client. Saying "I don't understand" or implying it by asking questions is more useful in soliciting more information and gaining trust than implying "I know."

The appropriate use of questions is a counseling skill and a disciplined behavior. Counselors use questioning judiciously. They ask questions only when necessary to gain essential information or to further the therapeutic process. Before deciding to probe, you will ask yourself, "For whose benefit do I need this information?" If you are simply curious, the question is for your benefit, not the client's. It might be best to choose a basic response rather than ask a question. If the question takes the client off-topic, do not ask it unless you have a compelling reason to investigate a new area of inquiry.

Much of the discipline of asking questions involves choosing the kind of question most appropriate for the circumstances. Your question must add value. Gathering information is only one use of questioning and not necessarily the sole goal of the session (Egan, 2019). Questions can be used to gather new information, to clarify information about which the counselor is unsure, to encourage the client's self-disclosure, or to lead a client to an insight apparent to the counselor or to a conclusion reached by the counselor. Questions can be closed or open-ended. In order to understand open-ended questions more fully, we will begin with a discussion of closed questions.

Closed Questioning

Any question that can be answered by yes or no is a closed question, whether or not the client chooses to elaborate on his response. The form of the question, not the client's answer, makes a question closed. The counselor is responsible for structuring questions so they facilitate communication. Closed questions do not allow for this facilitation. They do not inherently encourage clients to share their feelings, thoughts, or behaviors.

Example:

Cl: I took off work to help out with our new baby. He's quite a handful.
Co: Is your new baby crying a lot?

Possible answers:
A1:   Yes.
A2:   No.
A3:   And how! We're not getting any sleep. I can't wait until he starts sleeping through the night.

A1 and A2 obviously do not provide much information or further communication. A3, although providing information, may not actually facilitate communication. It may not be on topic. By asking a closed question, the counselor has set the direction of the response. It may or may not be what the client wants to discuss. Most clients will respond to what the counselor asks. In the case of A3, the client might want to talk about his job, his relationship with his wife, or any number of other topics, not to discuss his baby's crying. By the counselor posing this closed question, the session may be off in a direction that is tangential to the client's concern.

Questions that can be answered by a quantity or a simple fact are also closed.

Example:

How many children do you have? (Three.)

Questions that refer to time or date or request a number are usually closed. Who, when, and where can be closed questions depending upon context. Examples include:

Who knew about it? (No one.)
When did you finish school? (Last year.)
Where did you live? (Here.)

These and other similar quantitative questions can be useful when soliciting information important to the progress of the session. Systematic inquiry and crisis situations rely on closed questions to solicit essential information. These uses are discussed later. With these exceptions, they should be used infrequently, with intent, and with caution. They should be on topic; they do not take the client away from his main point or cause him to lose his train of thought. Unless essential to the main point of the ongoing story, such questions can feel intrusive to the client. In the first example above, ask yourself: Is knowing how many children the client has germane to the discussion or is the counselor simply curious (i.e., for whose benefit is this knowledge)? If the number of children is important to the reason for counseling or therapeutic progress, it will either be discussed by the client or the counselor will ask when it becomes significant. The same applies to other similar closed questions.

Pay special attention to the use of words that begin with the letter D. Questions beginning with Do, Did, Does, Don't, Doesn't, or Didn't are likely to be closed. They can be answered by yes or no. Many "D" questions come across as judgmental or provide clients with an answer they may believe the counselor expects. They should be avoided unless there is a compelling reason to use them. Examples include:

Do you believe that'll work? (Maybe.)
Did you get your grades? (Not yet.)
Does it ever occur to you ...? (Sure.)
Don't you want to go along? (Yes.)
Didn't he come by after all? (No.)

Even though clients possibly may respond with lengthy discussions, they would do so in spite of closed questions. This is not an excuse to use them. Therefore, avoid closed questions when you are attempting to facilitate communication, help clients come to conclusions, solve problems, deal with issues, and most other activities that can occur during sessions. Closed questioning can be a waste of valuable time and lead to more short responses. In the last example above:

Didn't he come by after all? *No.*
Did you ask him? *Yes.*
Was he just late? *I don't know.*
Better to ask open questions in the first place!

Open-Ended Questioning

Effective questions not only gain information, but they also track clients and enhance their awareness and personal growth. Open-ended questions cannot be answered by yes or no. Most open-ended questions tend to facilitate more complete or detailed answers and give clients the freedom of direction to discuss their areas of concern. They increase the probability of detailed information and lengthy responses. They are more likely to elicit information that is in line with the client's rather than the counselor's agenda for discussion. Open questions focus a client who has disorganized thought processes, challenge perceptions, deal with resistance, and teach decision-making and goal-setting skills. To ask questions effectively is to facilitate clients' development and to assist them in resolving their issues. Correctly articulated questions open new areas never previously considered and end unproductive lines of communication. Most importantly, appropriately asked questions place the burden of work on the client, which is where it belongs. Open questioning may be the single most important basic skill you will learn. Well-placed questions can mean the difference between real therapeutic work and unproductive interviewing sessions.

How and What questions. The most powerful open-ended questions begin with How and What. Almost any closed question can be made open by recasting it using one of these two words. Let's use some examples from the last discussion on closed questions:

Closed: Do you believe that'll work?
Open: How might that work for you?
        What do you think will work?
Closed: Did you get your grades?
Open: How did you do in your classes?
        What were your grades?
Closed: Does it ever occur to you ...?
Open: What occurred to you about that?
        How might you solve that?
Closed: Don't you want to go with them?
Open: What are your thoughts (feelings) about going with them?
        How interested are you in going with them? (*This is an assumptive question discussed later*)
Closed: Didn't he come by after all?
Open: What happened when you asked him to come by?
        How did he respond when you asked him to come by?
Closed: Did you ask him?
Open: What did you ask him?
        How might you find out?
Closed: Was he just late?
Open: What happened then?
        How did it go?

In each of these cases, open questioning allows the client to respond more fully than closed questioning. By asking open questions, the counselor allows the client to decide not only how to respond but what exactly to respond to. When given the opportunity to respond to open questions, clients may very well answer in unexpected ways. Using the earlier example:

Cl: I took off work to help out with our new baby. He's quite a handful.
Co: How is that going?
A1: Great! I'd rather be home than at work. I just may become a house husband.
A2: Not so good. My boss says if I don't get back to work soon, he'll have to replace me.
A3: We're not getting any sleep. I'm overwhelmed and worried about how exhausted my wife is. We're not getting a chance to be alone either.

The same open question solicited different responses, all generated from the client's concern. Whenever you feel a closed question forming in your thoughts, take a moment to rephrase it into an open question. You will find that you gain more information more quickly when you allow your client to take the lead.

Questions beginning with When, although often closed, can be used to ask open questions.

Example:

Cl: I've definitely decided I'd like to learn to scuba dive.
Co: When might you want to pursue that?

Although the client might respond with a word or short phrase, this kind of question opens up the probability of elaboration. It could also be used to help focus the client on taking action. Who and Where questions can be used in the same way:

1.   Cl: I'd like to get to know some kids in the ski club.
      Co: Who especially interests you?
2.   Cl: I'm pretty sure I don't want to retire around here.
      Co: Where have you considered going?

Implied questions. Another type of open question is the implied question. It is a cross between encourager and question. It can take the form of a statement. The purpose is to encourage the client to talk. Statements include "I'm wondering what was going on," "I wonder how you responded to that," or "I'm not sure what led up to that" and others.

Could or Can questions are a special type of implied question. Although on the surface these are closed questions, in actuality they act more like minimal encouragers but tend to elicit more in-depth responses and request specific instances of general statements. They offer greater flexibility in response.

Examples:

1.   Cl: Tomorrow my daughter starts college. I don't know if I'm quite ready.
      Co: Could you tell me more about what you mean?
2.   Cl: I'm annoyed that Maurice went even when I asked him not to. He stood right there and agreed and then he turned around and did this!
      Co: Can you elaborate on what happened?
3.   Cl: People just don't seem to like me.
      Co: Could you give me an example of when that happens?

Could and Can questions used this way are clarifying questions. They ask clients to provide more information and at the same time allow them to process information they may not have considered previously. Could and Can are also used to ask clients to commit to a course of action. In these cases, the words "would" and "will" can be used as well, depending upon the strength of the request.

Examples:

1.   Cl: I'm ready to ask her why she left us.
      Co: Could (would) you be willing to ask her before our next meeting?
2.   Cl: I'm ready to quit smoking. I'm tired of it!
      Co: Can (will) you commit to doing that?

Effective questions are crucial to the therapeutic process. Many clients come into counseling expecting the counselor to give them answers. They often seek advice. Counselors help their clients learn that the answers are within themselves. They need our help in figuring out their own answers. The right questions do that. Counselors assist people in learning the process of problem resolution, decision making, and implementing choices.

Problematic Questioning

Some ways of questioning are not facilitative. In fact, they are counterproductive to the therapeutic process. Among them are Why questions, judgmental questions, and questions that require the client to pick among alternatives, or balloting questions.

Why Questions

As a general rule, questions beginning with Why should be avoided, especially by novice counselors. You must ask yourself "For whose benefit am I asking 'Why'?" Is it really necessary to know? Why questions can sound like evaluations. They require the client to justify her thoughts, feelings, or behaviors. Clients can feel defensive or uncomfortable to most Why questions. The most onerous Why questions are those that challenge clients to defend their actions.

Examples:

1. Cl: I studied hard but I copied from my friend's paper anyway.
    Co: Why did you do that?
2. Cl: I got to work late again. I overslept.
    Co: Why didn't you set the alarm?

Clearly, this kind of why questioning is going nowhere. Even worse are those that require people to defend their thoughts, feelings, or beliefs.

Examples:

1. Cl: I wish my dad would get off my back!
    Co: Why do you feel that way?
2. Cl: I think about her all the time.
    Co: Why?

These Why questions are unproductive and can lead to idle speculation. Many clients are unaware of why they think, feel, or behave as they do. Counselors are not in the business of providing long-term psychoanalysis. If a question about motivation is important to the therapeutic process, it will come to light over time. Your job as a counselor is to discern the Whys of your clients by looking for underlying themes.

Some Why questions are the counselor's way of offering advice and are inappropriate as well.

Examples:

1. Cl: I studied hard but I copied from my friend's paper anyway.
    Co: In future, why don't you try not copying?
2. Cl: I got to work late again. I overslept.
    Co: Why not set your alarm next time?
3. Cl: I think about her all the time.
    Co: Why don't you try thinking about other things?

Responses like these are not only unproductive; they are intrusive and judgmental. They suggest to the client that they are incapable of finding solutions to their problems. They can damage relationships and trust. Better alternatives for the above examples are 1) What do you think that's about? 2) What happened then? and 3) What's going on between you?

Disguised Why questions. Some questions that appear to be open-ended are actually Whys in disguise. "What caused you to do that?" may have the same effect as "Why did you do that?" "How is it you feel that way?" is similar to "Why do you feel that way?" Questions like these, although a step up from asking "Why?" directly, are generally unproductive in furthering the therapeutic process or assisting clients to make changes. This is especially true when the work takes place in a short number of sessions.

Although trained otherwise, some counselors want to give advice either because of their own unresolved issues or from their need to be in control. Disguised advice-giving Why questions include "What if you tried…?" and Have you tried…?" Unless a compelling reason prompts such questions, consider first not asking a question at all. Offer a response instead.

Example:

> Cl: I think about her all the time.
> Co: Uh-huh…
> or Co: (silence)
> or Co: She's on your mind a lot.

Appropriate use of why. Not all Why questions are problematic. They can serve a therapeutic purpose in the hands of a skilled counselor who has built trust and empathic understanding with the client. They are neither questions that are asking people to justify their thoughts, feelings, or actions nor questions that cause clients to feel uncomfortable. They are used in response to the client's needs or decisions and are used specifically to offer support.

Examples:

1. Cl: I think I'd like to try that sometime.
   Co: (at end of session) Why don't you consider trying it before our next session?
2. Cl: I'm ready to move out on my own. I'd like to figure out a way I can without upsetting everybody.
   Co: (near the beginning of a session) Why don't we work on that now?

As you can see, these are not really Why questions. In the first example, the counselor lets the client know that she believes he is able to move forward. In the second example, the client is indicating the direction he wants to pursue in session and the counselor is responding to that need. Until you are experienced, the word Why is best left out of your counseling vocabulary.

Judgmental Questions

Closely related to the Why questions are questions implying an evaluation or judgment of some aspect of the client. Counselors show their clients unconditional positive regard even when they may not approve of their actions. Thus, they must take care not to judge their clients in the way they ask questions even when the questions are open.

Example:

> Cl: I needed some money so I took it from my mom's purse but she caught me. She was furious!
> Q1: What were you thinking?
> Q2: How is that not stealing?
> Q3: Was that right?

These questions imply a negative judgment. They are not likely to solicit open communication from the client. More facilitative possible alternatives are:

What happened then?
How did you respond?
What might you have done differently?

Judgmental questions can embarrass or shame clients even when the intent is otherwise. They can cause clients to retreat from disclosing information. No one likes to feel judged. For many clients, the counseling office may be the only place they feel accepted. Even when clients are difficult or resistant, you must take care that your questions support, not hinder, their ability to be open and honest with you. Empathic understanding is key to every question you pose.

Shotgun and Balloting Questions

Counselors ask only one question at a time. They do not interrogate their clients or barrage them with questions. *Shotgun questions* are a series of usually closed questions asked one after the other with short client responses in between. Generally superficial, they add little to the course of counseling. Their usage indicates an inexperienced counselor. She may cover a lot of territory, but she does so at the expense of building a relationship or really finding out what is important to the client. In this example, the client wants to discuss a recent episode of memory loss after drinking:

Cl: I don't remember anything that happened after I got to the party.
Co: Where was the party? (*missing the point altogether*)
Cl: At my cousin's house.
Co: What was the occasion?
Cl: It was her birthday.
Co: How much did you drink?
Cl: I don't remember.
Co: Does that happen often?
Cl: I don't think so.
Co: Did you drive?
Cl: No, my boyfriend took me.
Co: Do you usually drink so much?
Cl: Only since I got to college.
Co: Where did you go to college?
Cl: Here in town.
Co: Did you graduate?
Cl: Not yet.
Co: How old are you now?
Cl: Twenty-three.

The counselor is way off target. He comes across as judgmental and attacking. He is not attending to his client, offering empathic understanding or much else in the way of therapeutic presence. Counselors ask questions that respond to what the client is telling them. First they listen, then they ask when it is relevant and necessary. Before asking an additional question, counselors make an empathic response either by responding to content, process, or feelings (discussed in the next chapter).

Counselors avoid asking multiple questions at the same time. *Balloting questions* are multiple questions that target slightly different aspects of the same issue or totally different issues. These questions cause the client to choose one of the questions to answer or attempt to respond to all of them. In either case, the client will be left feeling confused or will believe that the counselor is confused, not listening, or does not care. Let's take a look at the last client and the effect of balloting:

Cl: I don't remember anything that happened after I got to the party.
Co: What do you remember about the party? Were you there all evening? What's the last thing you remember?
Cl: We were there a couple of hours. I remember getting there and giving my present to my cousin. (*answers despite her counselor*)
Co: How much drinking did you do before you went? Or did you start drinking after you got there? Did you know you were drunk?
Cl: We had a beer beforehand.
Co: So you began drinking before you went to the party. Did you think you needed it? Is this what you usually do?

This is bad counseling on several levels. This kind of questioning indicates a lack of discipline on the counselor's part.

Balloting questions are especially common among beginning counselors who either are unsure what to ask or do not trust that their client understood their question or both. They rephrase the question over and over before allowing the client to answer. This is an example:

Co: Do you like your new job? What's it like? What's your favorite part? Are you glad you took it?

If you find yourself tempted to ballot, simply stop talking after you ask the first question, even if it is not exactly what you meant to ask. If your clients do not understand or if you are off-target, they will let you know.

SIDEBAR 18.1

In Practice: What Would You Do?

Rouyan is an outpatient counselor at a major Northeastern big-city hospital. She mainly works with addictions but also sees mental health patients referred from the emergency room. Although she is well versed in addictions and psychopathology, she sometimes worries about the labels and wonders if all her patients should have their diagnosable disorders follow them around forever. She has just begun counseling Eunice, a 64-year-old woman who was taken to the hospital emergency room by her adult children when she was found unconscious. After her release from the hospital, she was referred to Rouyan because of her long-term use of Valium.

> It seems the doctor who prescribed the medication refused to renew her prescription two years ago, so she kept changing doctors as often as necessary to get the Valium. Her children say that she has not been herself since her husband left her six years ago. They had encouraged

her to get some help earlier but she refused. She says she's not depressed or sad anymore and denies using Valium since she had the hospital "scare." I'm not so sure. Her kids tell me she's lied about it before. She won't talk to me about it or anything else for that matter. All she says is that she's fine and doesn't need a counselor and what she does is none of her children's business.

Class Discussion

1. What can Rouyan do to help Eunice open up to her?
2. What closed questions might Rouyan ask that would be appropriate?
3. Are non-judgmental questions the best course for counseling? Why or why not?
4. How important is it for Rouyan to find out what motivates Eunice in not talking with her children (i.e., the Why behind her behavior)?

Leading and Assumptive Questions

A way to influence people is to ask them questions that are deliberately designed to make them think in a particular way. Questions that guide the person in a desired direction or indicate the expected answer are called *leading questions*. They can include the answer, influence the client's answer, or point them to a desired answer. Leading questions are usually closed questions. They can be directional in that, although they may not indicate an answer, they minimize the possibility of other alternatives. Not only the words you use can be leading; your nonverbal body language and your voice tone can also lead. Leading questions are not really intended for client exploration and, thus, are not facilitative tools. In fact, many are not actually intended as questions at all. Examples are:

You aren't planning that, are you?
You don't really want to do that, do you?

These are directives disguised as questions ("Don't plan that" and "Don't do that"). They put the client in the position of either agreeing with the counselor or appearing argumentative. They may force the client toward the possibility of dishonesty. Counselors avoid leading questions and reframe them into nonleading questions such as "How do you plan to handle that?" and "What do you want to do about that (instead)?"

Assumptive questions are similar to leading questions but are generally open-ended. They make an assumption about something about the client or her concerns but do not provide an answer, although they do influence the direction of an answer. They can be on target and empathic or off target and counterproductive. They have the same pitfalls as leading questions but can be effectively used for therapeutic progress. When used well, the assumptive question can avoid a defensive first response often given by clients who are not yet wholly trusting of the counselor. For example, in this third session, this 40-year-old client continues a discussion about her inability to sleep at night. She is having nightmares the content of which indicate to the counselor that sexual abuse might have occurred in her childhood.

Cl: I just hate going to sleep. I wake up shaking in the middle of the night. I feel like a little kid.
Q1: *(leading question)* When you were a child, you remember the bad things that happened to you at night, don't you?

Q2:   (*inappropriate assumptive question*) What bad things happened to you when you woke up as a child? (*The question assumes the client woke up as a child and bad things happened.*)

Q2:   (*appropriate assumptive question*) What do you recall about waking up at night when you were a child? (*The question assumes only that the client woke up at night as a child.*)

The first question is likely to make the client uncomfortable and build a barrier to further disclosure. The second question will likely do the same because she is still being forced to think first and possibly exclusively about bad things that could have happened. The third question, on the other hand, allows the client to answer how she wishes and to reach any conclusion that she wants. At the same time it makes it safe to discuss waking up as a child without forcing her into a premature discussion about possible abuse. To use assumptive questions correctly takes experience. Until you gain more experience, you should only attempt them in the presence of a supervisor.

Systematic Inquiry

In the ordinary course of counseling sessions, the principles presented here on open questioning are in effect. In some circumstances, however, the use of closed, assumptive, and leading questions along with open questions is warranted. *Systematic inquiry* refers to a formalized procedure for gathering information. It uses a combination of questioning and basic responding. Although it can occur any time during counseling, it is most often implemented during intake sessions and in the cases of crisis.

Intakes

In the first session, a counselor must collect enough information to gain as complete an understanding as possible to formulate a treatment plan. As you learned previously, counselors must make an appraisal of their clients in order to plan effective counseling interventions. The counselor uses a formalized system of gathering information beginning with exploring the client's presenting concern and moving to collecting data about various aspects of the client's life. The counselor documents the client's history by using a combination of preset and idiosyncratic questions. Although intake interview questions can take many forms, typically they gather of demographic information; reasons for seeking counseling (i.e., the presenting concern); any previous emotional or psychological difficulties; the life circumstances such as significant relationships and work and leisure activities; cultural, religious and socioeconomic information; educational and work history; medical or health-related history; present or prior use of alcohol or drugs; and more (Seligman, 2004).

At the initial interview the counselor wants to establish the beginning of the counseling relationship and collect necessary information (Cormier & Hackney, 2016). She may also want to determine eligibility for services in a particular setting or she may decide to refer elsewhere. To meet any of these objectives, she will use all the skills presented so far and many more. She will structure the session, ask mainly open questions, and respond to content by using minimal encouragers, restatements, and paraphrases. She will use closed questions to elicit specific data, particularly demographic information. She will avoid Why questions, judgmental questions, balloting, and assumptive questions. Although she must cover a lot of ground in a short amount of time, she will not shotgun or ballot. Instead, she will respond after every question with a supportive statement before she asks another question. She will also respond to affect, which will be covered in the next chapter.

Crisis

Crises are time-sensitive events that come in many forms: suicide threats or actualities, disaster, life-altering accidents, rape, serious illness, violence, and many more. The counselor acts quickly to gather data and bring immediate assistance to the person in crisis. The counselor must gather the facts, determine the risk factors, decide if the person involved is in danger or if someone else may be in danger, review the relevant history that impacts on the situation, investigate resources, formulate a plan of action or treatment, and follow through. In these circumstances, he is likely to use a greater proportion of closed questions without sacrificing empathy and caring. Many crises such as suicide, disaster response, and rape have prescribed and formalized methods of systematic inquiry. Specialized training allows the counselor to combine his skills in effective questioning with needed interventions. Although beyond the scope of this discussion, interventions to respond to natural disasters and national emergencies are required areas of learning and are now infused throughout counseling program curricula.

Responding to Client Questions

Often clients pose questions to their counselors. They want the counselor to tell them what to do; to give them advice. You must learn how to handle questions directed to you. The traditional rule of thumb is that questions are deflected back to the client.

Examples:

1. Cl: I think my roommate stole my ring. I can't prove it but I'm pretty sure she did. Do you think I should tell her I know?
    Co: What would you like to do?
2. Cl: Whenever I get in class, I go blank. What should I do? Should I quit?
    Co: What would that mean for you?

In these examples, the counselor does not provide an answer but asks a question that allows the clients to consider their own perspective or course of action. However, deflecting questions can be taken to absurdity and may miss the point of the question altogether.

Some questions simply seek factual information. If this is the case, you will answer them directly. To do anything else would not make sense and would quite probably irritate your client!

Examples:

When does the new school year start?
Where do I find out about the job postings?
Who do I go to drop off these papers?
How high do I need to score on the SAT?

However, be aware that even information-seeking questions may actually be about an issue that needs your attention. You would answer the question and follow up with a response or question that encourages the client to discuss what concerns him. In the last example:

Cl: How high do I need to score on the SAT?
Co: It depends upon the school.
Cl: Do I really need to take it?
Co: Not for every school. You seem worried. Tell me what that's about.

Other questions might not be answered directly because they imply an area of concern that should be investigated more thoroughly. In this case, you should attend to the implied concern or help the client make an implicit concern explicit. Whatever the question, you need to be sensitive to the issue and focus on the real meaning behind the question.

Examples:

1. Cl: There's something I'm kind of curious about. Just hypothetical. Some of the kids were talking and I just wondered. What happens if someone gets caught smoking pot in the dorm?

    Co: It might end in a suspension. How comfortable are you sharing what's going on with me?

2. Cl: I'm worried about my mother. She's almost 80 and lives by herself and is getting forgetful. I do her shopping and check on her whenever I can but my job has to come first. I can't afford a live-in helper for her. Do you think I should get one?

    Co: I hear you saying that you think you aren't doing enough for your mother and worry that she needs more help than you can give her.

Some questions are best not answered for ethical reasons. Except in circumstances of harm to self or others and child abuse (the exceptions to confidentiality discussed earlier in this text), you may not reveal something that you have been told in confidence by one client to another client. You would not take sides in a conflict or dispute. In these cases, you would explain why you will not respond and then follow up with a question or response that addresses the underlying concern. In this example, Gerry and her husband, John, are receiving couples counseling and see the counselor individually as well.

Cl: What happened in your session with my husband? Did he tell you anything about what our son did?

Co: As I've explained, I can't discuss what goes on in our individual sessions. What's happened?

Cl: Well, he was really mad last night. Billy got home late and John walked out! What kind of father is he anyway? Don't you agree that he should stay home and deal with it?

Co: You're saying that you don't want John to leave when he's angry at Billy.

Client questions are quite normal and to be expected. Each question has significance and needs to be attended to carefully and responded to properly.

Putting It Together

Questioning is a powerful therapeutic tool during the beginning stages of counseling and you will rely on many kinds of questions throughout the middle and late stages as well. Add this set of skills to the basic responding skills as you practice with your classmates and with others in the ordinary course of your communications. Use your TFAC chart at the end of this chapter to guide you as you practice and to observe others in their use of these additional communication skills. As before, record your progress in your journal. The following example gives you an idea of how the appropriate use of questioning enhances the basic responding skills you have already learned. As you read this example, notice how the counselor uses a combination of responding to content and questioning to keep the flow of the session moving as she gathers essential information, supports the client, and begins building the therapeutic relationship.

Audrey is a 34-year-old female who was referred by her life partner. She was a biology teacher until three years ago when she completed a PhD in genetics. She now works for a textbook developer for a science corporation. She met with an intake worker before she arrived in the counselor's office.

Co: When you called for an appointment you mentioned to the intake counselor that you're dissatisfied with your work. (*encourager*) Could you tell me more about that?

Cl: Well...(*hesitates*) I'm not sure where to start. I guess I'm not exactly dissatisfied. I'm disappointed in my job. I'm not even sure what I want to do anymore.

Co: (*restating*) You're not sure what you want to do....

Cl: After all that training, I'm not at all sure I like the way I'm using what I learned in my doc work. Not only that, I'm not sure I want to use it!

Co: (*paraphrasing*) You're not using your training the way you wanted to and you're not certain it's what you want to do, is that how it is?

Cl: You got it! I like some of the things I do, though.

Co.   (*open question*) What parts do you like?

Cl: I get to do some events planning. We take our books to trade fairs and I like setting that up and going. That doesn't happen often, though, and isn't in my job description.

Co: (*paraphrasing*) You like going to trade fairs but it's not really a part of your job. (*clarifier*) Help me to understand what your job is like.

Cl.   Mostly I write curriculum for several textbooks, all the way from high school biology to advance genomics texts. I work alone. I'm the only one in my discipline there. There's no one to talk to; no one to discuss things with in the office.

Co: (*paraphrasing*) You sound to me like you are fairly isolated at work.

Cl: People are nice enough but we don't have much in common. When I need to talk over something, I usually get online or call my old professor. I wish he lived closer. He was my mentor.

Co: (*paraphrasing*)) You're saying you can turn to your mentor and his opinion means a lot to you. (*facilitative closed question*) How far away is he?

Cl: He's on the other side of the country. He's retired anyway. He thought I should take this job. He means so much to me. I wish I could be more like him. He's had a big impact on me.

Co: (*paraphrasing*) You took this job because your mentor, whom you admire, wanted you to, is that right?

Cl: Yeah. I think so much of him and he knows what I'm capable of. When I was in school, I liked the academic part but I had no idea what I should do. All I ever did before was teach. He helped me see that going back to teaching wouldn't be using my new skills or make me as much money as I make now.

Co: (*paraphrasing*) Your professor influenced the direction of your career. (*assumptive question*) How important was teaching to you?

Cl: I loved it! It was great seeing the kids learn and grow. It just didn't make enough money to support Tish and me. I taught at a private school. They don't pay well. She's a musician and doesn't make much. We want to have kids eventually so one of us had to get a higher paying job. So I got the doctorate but I miss teaching. Sitting in a room by myself writing curriculum isn't my idea of contributing.

Co: (*summarizing*) From what you've told me so far, although you used to love teaching, you decided to leave it and get a PhD. You took this job on your mentor's suggestion because it uses your new skills and pays you more. That's important since you and Tish want to start of family. But you don't like what you do a lot and it doesn't seem to be making a difference. Am I understanding you correctly?

Cl: Yeah. Sort of. When you put it that way, you make it sound like I should go back to teach-
       ing. Do you think I should?

Co: (responding to client's question) Only you can decide if that's what would be best for you. Is
       that something you'd like to work on with me?

Cl: Yes, I don't think what I'm doing now matters much but I like the money I make. I think
       I need to sort out what I want to do.

This example illustrates how a combination of basic responding skills and a few questions can
inform the counselor and help a client clarify her concern. Although the surface presenting concern is dissatisfaction with work, the real issue involves a clash in values: The client's conflict
between a career she loved and one that brings her a needed paycheck. The counselor will help
the client begin investigating her thoughts and feelings. Next you learn about advanced accurate
empathy and how to work with emotion.

Summary

This chapter presented the reasons for questioning in counseling. It discussed closed questioning,
open questioning, and how each is used, and reviewed the skill and discipline of questioning.
It continued with a discussion of problematic questions, assumptive questions, and systematic
inquiry. The chapter included a section on responding to client questions. Case examples illus-
trated questioning skills.

> *Stop it, mouth! You're going faster than I can think!*
> > – beginning counseling student trying to rephrase a closed question

References

Cormier, L. S., & Hackney, H. (2016). *Counseling strategies and interventions for professional helpers* (9th ed.).
    Boston: Pearson.
Egan, G. (2019). *The skilled helper: A problem-management and opportunity-development approach to helping*
    (11th ed.). Boston: Cengage.
Johnson, D. W. (2013). *Reaching out: Interpersonal effectiveness and self-actualization* (11th ed.). Boston:
    Pearson.
Seligman, L. (2004). *Technical and conceptual skills for mental health professionals*. Upper Saddle River, NJ:
    Merrill Prentice Hall.

Table 18.1 *TFAC Chart – Thought, Feelings, and Actions

Self	My Thoughts	My Feelings	My Actions	My Context	Other? (Specify)
How do I react when I am asked a closed question?					
How do I react when I am asked an open question?					
How comfortable am I asking open questions?					
How well do I do in rephrasing closed questions into open ones?					
How often do I say "Why"?					
How I am doing at avoiding problematic questions?					
How well do I use assumptive questions?					
How do I handle answering a question asking me for my opinion or advice?					
What concerns do I have?					
Others	**Others' Probable Thoughts**	**Others' Possible Feelings**	**Others' Observable Actions**	**Others' Apparent Context**	**Other? (Specify)**
How do others respond when asked a closed question?					
How do others respond when asked an open question?					
What have you observed about "Why?" questions?					
What have you observed about shotgunning and balloting?					
What have you observed about assumptive questions?					
What have you observed about how your instructors or other helping professionals respond to advice-seeking questions?					
What have you observed about systematic inquiry and crisis questions?					
What else can you learned and observed about the use of questions?					

*For more information on TFAC, see Chapter 1.

Chapter 19

Affect and Empathic Understanding Skills

Mary H. Guindon

Be yourself. Everyone else is already taken.

– Oscar Wilde

POINTS TO PONDER

- What is the difference between primary and advanced accurate empathy?
- What are the five major categories of feelings?
- Why is a wide vocabulary of feeling words essential to counseling?
- How and when are formulaic and nonformulaic feeling responses used?
- What is the role of congruence in counseling?
- How do counselors manage their own feelings?
- How is counselor self-disclosure used as a tool in counseling?
- What are some main affective interventions?

Empathic Understanding

Basic Empathy

You have learned that empathy is the counselor's ability to enter and experience the client's world and yet remain detached from it (Rogers, 1961). Basic empathy means counselors offer unconditional acceptance and understanding of feelings, behavior, and thoughts. So far, you have learned to express basic empathy through responding to content. The critical element of empathy is the ability to track the client's feelings in the moment. If a client is aware of a feeling and expresses it directly, the counselor responds to the feeling directly. This kind of response is in reality little different than responding to content:

Examples:

Cl: She accused me of always cheating on her. How could she say that? I'm offended!
Co: You sound angry.
Cl: I can't believe Andre dumped me. I cried all afternoon.
Co: You are feeling sad.

These responses, although conveying basic empathy by addressing an emotion, somehow miss the mark.

Primary Accurate Empathy

To convey empathy more accurately, the counselor must temporarily join with the client to explore the client's full experience. Primary accurate empathy is "a process in which the counselor listens for basic client messages and responds to them through paraphrasing and reflection of feelings so that the client begins to feel understood" (Gladding, 2018, p. 124). You will convey empathic understanding at every stage of counseling.

To respond to feelings, the counselor must first and foremost observe the client's nonverbal behaviors. As you recall, the six basic types of nonverbal expression are physical appearance, body language, personal space, facial expression, voice, and change in behavior. Review Chapter 16 for an explanation. To understand the client's affect, you must pay attention to all nonverbals. How the client expresses himself indicates a good deal about him and how he experiences his reality. You must attend to what the client says and put yourself in the client's position. You will ask yourself, "If I were in this person's place, expressed myself nonverbally this way, and said what he just said, how would I feel?"

To answer this question, you must recognize the basic emotion first. Then you must identify the level of intensity. Basic emotions are Sad, Angry, Happy, and Scared. Other feelings are combinations, levels, and nuances of these four. For example, irritated and furious are both Angry feelings. Startled and nervous are Scared feelings. Hurt can be a combination of Angry and Sad. Once you decide on the basic feeling or combination of feelings, you will try to identify the level of intensity. You must develop a rich feelings vocabulary so that you are able to approximate intensity. Table 19.1 lists some feeling words people use.

SIDEBAR 19.1

In Practice: What Would You Do?

Maddie, age nine, was referred to elementary school counselor Amy by her teacher because she frequently refused to come to school. So far her grades have not been affected. Amy met with Maddie's parents to find out what might be going on at home. They seemed somewhat worried but not overly concerned about her class work. They both work but have enough flexibility to stay home with Maddie when she doesn't want to go to school.

About four months ago, Maddie's grandfather died. Maddie had been close to both grandparents but now her grandmother rarely visits. Since the grandfather's death, Maddie cries at some point on the days she is in school. Her classmates have begun making fun of her. When I try to talk with her, she clams up. No matter what approach I take, she tears up. She says she is fine, except just mad at the kids for laughing at her. I tried to get her to talk about her grandparents. She tells me she doesn't know why her grandmother won't come over but she won't talk about her grandfather. I tried engaging her in some art work but she won't do that either. I'm not sure what else to do.

Class Discussion

1. What feeling words might Amy use with Maddie?
2. How can Amy use primary accurate empathy with Maddie?
3. Can Amy use advanced accurate empathy with Maddie at this point? Why or why not?
4. How congruent/incongruent is Maddie in her thoughts, feelings, and behaviors?
5. How appropriate would it be to address the parents' overt and/or covert feelings?

Once you have pinpointed a feeling, you must communicate your understanding at the level expressed by the client. Initially, you will make simple responses. The simplest are formula responses developed by Carkhuff (see Carkhuff & Anthony, 1979): "You feel _____ " and "You feel _____ because _____." At times, it might be appropriate to use the former alone. More often, the second formula is more appropriate. Let's use the previous examples:

1. *Cl:*   She accused me of always cheating on her. How could she say that? I'm offended!
    Co: (*How would I feel in this situation? I'd be angry. Level? I'd resent it.*)
    1. You feel resentful.
    2. You feel resentful because your girlfriend said you are always unfaithful.

2. *Cl:*   I can't believe Andre dumped me. I cried all afternoon.
    Co: (*How would I feel in this situation? I'd be sad. Level? I'd be in misery*)
    1. You feel miserable.
    2. You feel miserable because your boyfriend broke up with you.

The less formulaic way to respond to expressed feelings is through a flexible sentence structure. Feeling responses can contain a stem, a feeling, and a specific situation. They can end there or can also end with a clarifying phrase or sentence. Stems and clarifying phrases are similar to those used in responding to content presented in Chapter 17. Using the same examples:

1. *Cl:*   She accused me of always cheating on her. How could she say that? I'm offended!
    Co: (*stem:*) In other words, (*feeling:*) you feel resentful (*specific situation:*) when you are accused unjustly of being unfaithful. (*clarifier:*) Is that what how it is?
2. *Cl:*   I can't believe Andre dumped me. I cried all afternoon.
    Co: (*stem*) It sounds like you were (*feeling:*) miserable (*specific situation:*) this afternoon after your boyfriend broke up with you. (*no clarifier added*)

As you become more comfortable with the routine responses described here, you will begin to find your own way to use a natural communication style. Experienced counselors draw on their creativity in making empathic responses by using metaphors and analogies. At times, clients will use metaphor to describe how they feel and the counselor will try to accurately reflect the feelings behind the metaphor. For example, if the client says, "I could crawl under a rock for what I did," the counselor might respond, "You sound like you're embarrassed about it." At other times, the counselor will use metaphor to capture the essence of the feeling. If the client says, "I don't know when I've been so stressed out," the counselor might say, "You feel like you've been hit by a truck."

Of course, individuals can experience an array of emotions about a situation. They can also be confused or conflicted about how they feel. Another basic emotion is Confused. When people feel confused, the counselor identifies an underlying basic feeling and responds with an associated Confused feeling as a prelude to more advanced empathic understanding. The counselor cannot address every emotion all at once but will attend to them as they surface.

Responding to feeling is tentative and entails negotiating for meaning. As you respond with what you believe is the client's primary affective experience, you facilitate her ability to reflect on her experience and identify her emotions more accurately. When you respond accurately, your client will go on to share more about the feeling and the experience involved. When you have not pinpointed the exact feeling or its intensity, your response allows your client to consider what you have said and try it on for size. Your client will still respond with more about the feeling and the experience. As you strive for empathic understanding you assist your client in understanding herself.

Example:

Cl: I don't know what I should do. It's hard trying to keep up with my job and my own family, much less find the time to take care of my parents, too. I wish my parents weren't so dependent on me! I don't want anything awful to happen to them but they are driving me crazy!

Co: (*How would I feel in this situation? I'd be angry. Level? annoyed. I'd be sad. Level? sorrowful. I'd be confused. Level? unsure*) You sound annoyed that they need you so much and you're unsure about what to do about them.

Cl: Not really. I'm very sure that they should go into assisted living. They shouldn't be by themselves anymore. I can't handle them by myself but it's hard to do that to them. It feels terrible.

Co: So, I think you're saying you feel guilty about making this decision and are feeling quite down about how helpless they are now. Am I understanding you correctly?

Cl: I do feel guilty. I'm torn. I guess I didn't realize how sad I really am.

The counselor facilitates awareness by encouraging concreteness and specificity in the client's communications. The more specific the client's descriptions, the more accurate the counselor can be in joining with the client's experience and conveying empathic understanding.

Some clients will have the ability to express their experiences thoroughly and directly. Many others will express themselves indirectly through their nonverbal behaviors. The counselor's challenge is to explicitly convey the accurate understanding of the level and intensity of their client's precise feelings. When counselors convey understanding of feelings outside of clients' immediate awareness, we call this advanced accurate empathy.

Advanced Accurate Empathy

Advanced accurate empathy is a process by which the counselor uses herself as an instrument to (a) understand the client's hidden feelings that are outside of awareness, (b) make what is implied explicit, and (c) make connections between feelings and what they mean to themes in the client's life. Counselors use their own inner experience of the client by attending to their own intuitive feelings – their gut reactions or hunches. They share their hunches about their clients' overt and covert thoughts, feelings, and actions so that they may more clearly see their concerns. Hunches are not lost, random thoughts or feelings. They are based on natural empathy grounded in knowledge of human behavior plus training and past personal and professional experiences. Premature advanced accurate empathy, however, may intimidate the client or lose the therapeutic alliance. Before sharing their hunches, counselors take care to build a trusting, safe environment through appropriate questioning, basic responding to content, and primary accurate empathic responses.

Awareness of Affect

At the beginning of this text you were introduced to the importance of understanding thoughts, feelings, and actions. You have been asked to reflect on questions in the TFAC chart at the end of each chapter. Take a few moments now and look back over your journal entries for both your own self-awareness and your observations of others. How do you think you did at differentiating the differences between thoughts and feelings? Some people have a difficult time understanding the difference.

Affective experience consists of two parts: awareness and expression. Emotional awareness is an inner experience and indicates the individual's ability to recognize and accept feelings for what they are. Recognition consists of two parts: physical sensations and their correct interpretation.

Emotional awareness means the individual is sensitive to the physical changes that occur when a particular affect is present and is able to label it correctly according to an agreed-upon cultural meaning and situation. For example, a racing heart might mean excitement or fear depending upon circumstances. Awareness means the individual can differentiate between and among emotions. The individual is able to not only name a feeling but also identify its intensity and significance. The client's ability to understand the meaning of physical sensations indicates the level of awareness. In Table 19.1, you will notice that the word "hurt" appears under Sad and Angry. It might also appear under Scared or Confused. The physical sensations with each feeling are different depending upon context. Words to describe the feeling vary.

The affective experience also consists of the ability to express outwardly the inner experience of physical sensation. The client's ability to articulate the emotion with accuracy indicates acceptance of the emotion as real and legitimate. If a client says "hurt" when he means sad, he should be able to articulate that sadness through his verbal and nonverbal behaviors. If he means angry, his verbals and nonverbals will be different. If the inner experience and the articulation match, the client shows a good level of self-awareness. Some level of affective understanding has to be evident before feelings can be explored productively with the counselor. Although the two aspects of the affective experience – awareness and expression – are closely related, the counselor must be able to identify them separately because they have different implications for counseling.

Table 19.1 Common Feeling Words by Major Category

SAD	ANGRY	HAPPY	SCARED	CONFUSED
blue	aggravated	blissful	afraid	all at sea
crushed	annoyed	cheerful	alarmed	ambivalent
crying	cross	ecstatic	apprehensive	befuddled
degraded	displeased	delighted	anxious	bothered
dejected	enraged	content	concerned	dilemma
despairing	exasperated	elated	defenseless	disconcerted
despondent	frustrated	encouraged	distressed	disorientated
depressed	fuming	euphoric	disturbed	flummoxed
disappointed	furious	excited	dreading	flustered
disheartened	hateful	exhilarated	fearful	guilty
dismal	hurt	glad	frightened	hesitant
down	incensed	good	helpless	inadequate
downcast	indignant	gratified	hesitant	indecisive
empty	infuriated	great	horrified	puzzled
gloomy	irate	in rapture	in danger	perplexed
grieving	irritated	joyful	jumpy	baffled
heartbroken	livid	marvelous	nervous	mystified
hopeless	mad	optimistic	on edge	bewildered
hurt	miffed	overjoyed	panicked	stuck
lonely	offended	phenomenal	petrified	stumped
low	outraged	pleased	shocked	stupid
miserable	out of sorts	positive	startled	thrown dazed
melancholy	pissed off	satisfied	terrified	troubled
mournful	provoked	terrific	troubled	undecided
sorrowful	put off	thankful	uneasy	unsure
tearful	resentful	thrilled	unnerved	uncertain
unhappy	seething	tickled	upset	confounded
woeful	testy	upbeat	vulnerable	useless
wretched	upset	wonderful	worried	

When clients are aware that an emotion exists and that it is a valid one, they are then able to investigate the experience in the moment with the counselor. Without this awareness, healthy outer expression of the emotion will not take place. Some clients, of course, often react emotionally to what they discuss in counseling. They articulate their feelings openly. However, this expression may or may not be grounded in awareness of an actual internal emotional experience. Some clients may strongly deny that they are expressing a feeling at all whereas their affect (verbal and nonverbal behavior) indicates otherwise. This denial shows a lack of awareness of the actual internal experience of emotion.

When working with feelings, the counselor addresses unexpressed and unconscious emotional experiences. The counselor helps the client gain awareness of an underlying emotion, accept it, and openly explore its meaning and significance. Counselors help clients who cannot identify accurately their emotions describe their internal physical experiences and tie them to healthy and congruent outward expression of those experiences and the issues that generated them.

Treatment planning and specific interventions are based on the counselor's ability to work with affect and to help clients identify themes in their lives. Themes are habitual ways of experiencing the world. When clients are either unaware of their underlying and conflicting feelings or deny their existence and the effect on their thoughts and actions, incongruence exists.

Incongruence

Congruence is the accurate match between cognition and emotion, emotion and behavior, or cognition and behavior. Few people are congruent in all areas all the time. Conflicted feelings most often concern the experience or awareness of more than one contradictory emotion, or of an emotion incompatible with cognition or behavior. For example, one may feel joy at being promoted and fear about the ability to perform. Or, one could experience sadness at being rejected but identify the internal experience as anger. Incongruence between covert feelings and expression of overt feelings, or covert feelings and expression through overt thoughts and behaviors, are common presenting concerns. From childhood, people learn to deny their basic emotions and to dampen down their feelings. Through the process of normal socialization many children are taught that what they feel cannot be openly expressed or that they do not actually feel what they in reality do feel. To express legitimate anger at an adult who has been unfair or to cry when another child inflicts pain may not be acceptable or tolerated by a particular family or subculture or society, for example. Consequently, many people learn that their feelings are not real; some do not recognize the very normal and healthy physical sensations associate with affect for what they are. In other cases, people may not even know they are experiencing emotion at all.

If the counselor responds to only the overt, she makes an assumption that affect is either unimportant or not involved in the client's concern. Although some counseling theories do not address emotions, the beginning counselor in the process of learning basic skills must master the discipline of responding to affect. Often at the heart of counseling, affective interventions are some of the most meaningful and powerful tools the counselor can draw upon.

Managing Counselor Affect

Before you can address affect in others, you must manage your own. Throughout this text you have been asked to consider your own feelings. You learned earlier that counselors may not be able to assist their clients to a good level of emotional and mental wellbeing unless they themselves are emotionally healthy. You are not likely to become a good counselor unless you are willing to do the inner self-work necessary for personal growth. You must do what is necessary to be authentic and congruent in your thoughts, actions, and feelings. You must be aware of your own inner emotional experience and its outer expression. You must be willing to address any of your own unresolved personal conflicts.

In the following example, these two counselors-in-training are in the same group counseling class but are experiencing it differently. The group members are processing their decision to pursue a graduate degree in counseling. Thirty-two-year-old Jill was the first in her family to go to college. Twenty-four-year-old Tom comes from three generations of medical doctors.

Jill's inner experience: Jill describes the physical sensation as "butterflies in my stomach" with a sick, sinking sensation. Her awareness is that this means she is excited. She bites her lip, blinks profusely, and slumps down in her chair.

Jill: I'm excited. I had trouble when I was first in college. I struggled but got lots of help. I persevered and finally got my bachelor's degree. I asked myself, "If I can do that, why not graduate school?" I want to give back all the help that was given to me. I'm proud of myself.

Jill is able to describe her excitement but her nonverbals indicate something else. She is not attending to the sinking sensation that accompanies the butterflies. When she looks at the sensation, she is vaguely aware that she has felt this before when she is anxious or feels guilty. It could be her family does not emotionally support her desire for education. The theme might be "Who do you think you are?" Or it could be that she feels inadequate when she compares herself to her classmates, or she may be uncomfortable self-disclosing. It could indicate any other number of underlying feelings. She will need to investigate what these feelings are telling her. She will want to look at the theme that causes this incongruity of affect.

Tom's inner experience: Tom also describes a physical sensation as "butterflies in my stomach" and unusual tightness in his shoulders. The butterflies, he reports, are growing and churning. He clinches his hands into fists. His face is flushed.

Tom: I'm proud of myself, too. Mainly, I'm quite comfortable here. No offense but this course is a piece of cake. I suppose being a counselor is almost as good as being a doctor. My father and grandfather are doctors. I want to work in a hospital side-by-side with the psychiatrist and his staff.

Tom's description of butterflies is incongruent with being comfortable. His physical sensations may indicate some level of anger, frustration, or embarrassment. It could be that he feels embarrassed that he believes he has failed his family because he couldn't get into medical school. It could be that he is angry about it and perceives himself to be superior to his classmates. It could be that his theme is "I'm better than others." It could be that he is quite well suited in temperament to counseling and unsuited to the medical profession but wants his classmates to know of his family background. He will need to dig deeper to discover what his feelings are telling him about his goals and his authenticity. He will need to look closely at the possibility of denial of his true feelings.

Remember that counselors must be aware of the probability of countertransference when working with their clients. One way to minimize the possibility of countertransference interfering with your client's needs is to bring into awareness your own feelings about the important issues in your life. You need to make sure that your issues do not impede the work you must do with your clients, or confuse their affect with your own. While you use your hunches to help your clients recognize and come to terms with their own emotional responses, you must guard against mistaking your issues for theirs. Your hunches will help clients express directly what they have implied indirectly. You will help them draw conclusions about what their inner emotional experience means, and you will help them see the broader picture. You will help them understand what they may be overlooking. Your hunches are not wild guesses. They are based on your interactions with our clients. As counseling progresses, you will learn about their experiences, behaviors, their view of their world, their specific context, and much more. You will combine what you know about their thoughts, actions, and feelings along with your own emotional experiences to inform your hunches. To do any of this well, you must work on understanding your own emotional inner experience and its outward expression. Take a few moments to consider your own life and your emotional responses to it. The TFAC chart in this chapter is a place to begin. It is only a beginning. As you identify your own emotional climate, find ways to express yourself authentically, and identify important themes in your own life. Even if not required in your program of study, consider going for a few sessions of counseling.

Client Feelings Directed at the Counselor

At times, clients displace their feelings onto the counselor. They may rage against you or feel dependent on you. Beginning counselors often have a difficult time remaining objective yet empathic and accepting when they are the object of client's affective communications. It might be hard not to feel defensive when a client is angry with you or says you are making them cry. You must closely monitor your own feelings to determine if the affect directed at you is a legitimate area of concern or if it is a transference issue. In most cases, you must sit with your clients and let them express their feelings. You will come to understand that this is important therapeutic material to explore in session.

Example:

Cl: I don't want to do this anymore. You were supposed to be telling me what I should do, not go dredging up all these depressing feelings. I should never have come here. You're no help.
Co: It seems to me you're frustrated because I haven't given you solutions.
Cl: Yeah. What's up with that? All I wanted is an answer to get rid of my problems and all I get from you is heartache.
Co: So, you are saying that you're upset with me and unhappy because I don't have ready answers.
Cl: Yeah. I guess so…. I was unhappy when I came in here. Nothing seems to be going right. Why does it have to be this way? (*stares off into space*)
Cl: (*silence*)

Seek supervision if you are either unsure that the client's feelings are legitimately concerned with your own behavior toward the client or if you find yourself owning client feelings that should be rightly attributed elsewhere.

At other times, the client may be emotionally out of control. Later on in your studies, you will learn techniques to contain the emotion by helping clients learn that they are in control of their emotions and using self-disclosure to help the client understand the effect they have on others.

Counselor Self-Disclosure

Part of advanced accurate empathy is the counselor's willingness to be authentic, genuine, and transparent (Rogers, 1951). Counselors self-disclose how they experience their clients in the moment. When you are clear that your own issues are not getting in the way of experiencing your client, you will be able to monitor your own reactions and feed them back to your client. As you experience your client, so may the world outside of the counseling session. To give the client your authentic and genuine reaction can be enormously therapeutic when done in an atmosphere of warmth and Rogers' unconditional positive regard. You must ensure that you are nonjudgmental in the descriptions of your affective experience of the client. Giving feedback involves more than affect; it also includes offering reactions to client's thoughts and behaviors. We will discuss these aspects of client self-disclosure and guidelines for effective feedback in the next chapter. For now, our discussion targets the affective dimension only.

Counselor self-disclosure is a skill in the moment. It addresses the here and now, not the there and then of the client's experience or the counselor's experience of the client. In this example, the counselor and client have met for several sessions and have developed a therapeutic alliance. They are working on her feelings of devastation over having failed her first engineering courses in her freshman year.

Cl: (crying) I'm the only girl in class. It's not right. The fraternity guys get together and share old exams from their files. The professor curves the grades so I don't have a chance. I didn't have the guts to tell him what was going on.

Co: When I hear you say that, I'm feeling some of your anger.

Cl: I needed to get a good grade. It's not fair and it's not my fault. I can't tell my father I flunked. That's all there is to it. He's gonna just murder me!

Co: I'm also picking up on your anxiety. When I think about myself in a similar situation I was scared. I'm feeling how worried you are about what your father will do when he finds out.

Cl: He just can't find out.

Co: (picking up on nonverbals) As I look at you, I can feel how afraid you must be but also how indignant.

Co: I can't let him know I hate everything about engineering! I never wanted to be an engineer. He made me take this major. I can't argue with him.

Cl: (identifying a theme) It seems to me that with your professor and your father, you are outraged inside but apprehensive to speak up for yourself. I'm wondering if this is a common experience for you.

Co: I'm not supposed to make waves....

Immediacy

Counselors self-disclose how they experience their clients by responding to what has transpired between them. Immediacy is a technique in which the counselor discusses with the client the nature and quality of their relationship. Immediacy addresses the here-and-now interaction in session. Since transparency, genuineness, and authenticity create a therapeutic environment, immediacy is a tool that allows clients to experience an authentic connection with another human being. By disclosing how they experience their clients, counselors model genuine encounters in relationship. Immediacy sets the stage for the counselor and client to explore together any tensions in their relationship. It also provides the opportunity for the client to process with the counselor ways in which their relationship resembles the client's relationships outside the counseling office. When the counselor and client are of different racial, ethnic, gender, or socioeconomic backgrounds, the counseling relationship may be of some discomfort, especially to the client. If this is the case, immediacy allows the counselor to make the implicit issue of difference explicit, thus engaging clients in a significant aspect of their lives that may be the source of some of their concerns.

Whenever the counselor-client relationship seems to be an issue that impedes therapeutic progress, the counselor self-discloses this sense through immediacy. Immediacy, however, is not used to criticize either directly or subtly, nor is it used to reprimand clients for their openness, even if that openness includes criticism of the counselor. In this example, the counselor is a white, middle-aged woman and the client is a 16-year-old African American male from an economically depressed part of the inner city. They have met twice to discuss his transferring to a vocational education program with a paid work-study opportunity that would take him away from his honors classes.

Cl: I've got to go to work. My classes here don't mean a thing in the real world. You just don't get it.

Co: When I hear you say that, I think you mean I can't understand you because we are so different from each other. Is that it?

Cl: What could you possibly know about where I come from?

Co: I don't know unless you tell me. I guess I feel ineffective that I'm not helping you accomplish what you really want.

Cl: Well, what I want is to help my family. I've got to bring in some money now, not wait for some stupid college degree years away. What would some White lady from the 'burbs know about that? You have no idea!

Co: I have a sense of how loaded this race issue is between us, and how it's getting in the way of our work. I'm wondering if it would help to talk about it. How comfortable are you with that?

In this case, the counselor cannot help the client beyond a surface level until trust is built between them. Immediacy allows them to process a critical issue that interferes with their ability to work together.

Another purpose of immediacy is to explore with the client how the client's functioning in the counseling relationship might be indicative of how functioning in other relationships may be contributing to their problems, impeding their goals, or hindering progress in the session. In this example, the counselor and client, a 42-year-old twice-divorced woman, have been working together for several sessions. This is about 10 minutes into a 50-minute session.

Co: Georgia, when I hear you so often say no one ever likes you, I feel you are saying I don't like you either.

Cl: I wasn't talking about you! You have to like me – it's your job.

Co: I guess I'm feeling troubled that you aren't seeing this relationship as real to me.

Cl. *Well it isn't, is it?*

Co: I feel a deep connection with you and I care what happens to you. That feels real.

Cl: It does? Why didn't you ever tell me that?

Co: When you avoid telling me about how abandoned you must have felt when your two marriages ended, part of me wonders if exploring that further will lose the connection we've made so far. I don't want that to happen. I wonder if you may be feeling that, too.

Cl: Yeah. Well… I lose everybody I get close to….

Co: I'm thinking you're afraid that if you open up and get close to me, you'll lose me, too. I guess it would be less scary for both of us to keep our distance.

Cl: I want to open up to you but I do worry about what you think of me.

Co: How would you feel if we both open up about our relationship and what it means to each of us?

In this case, the client's experience of the counselor is directly related to her experiences with past relationships. Immediacy can help the client come to terms with her vulnerability in forming and maintaining relationships.

Affective Interventions

Using your hunches is a discipline that incorporates all the other skills you have learned so far and then adds your perspective. You will not attempt advanced accurate empathy until you have a solid relationship with your client. Recall that empathy is not a one-time event. It can be easily lost and must be reestablished with each new issue or aspect of the ongoing counseling process. Affective interventions begin with the ability to restate, paraphrase, summarize, and reflect feelings.

> *Example:*
>
> C: I told my mom about my problems with my boss, how he criticizes me for things other people did, and she just said, "Are you sure it's not your fault?" I got so angry! She didn't pay attention at all.

1. *Restatement:* You got angry.

A simple restatement to affect, although accurate, conveys no real sense of understanding. True understanding should be processed through the counselor who comes at the feeling from a slightly different place. Better to choose another level of responding:

1. *Paraphrase:* You became mad when your mom didn't listen and blamed you for the problems with your boss.
2. *Summarize:* Your mother didn't understand when you explained that your boss criticized you for things you didn't do. She seemed to blame you. You were mad. Is that how it was?
3. *Basic empathic reflection of feeling:* You are furious at your mother because she didn't listen and seems to think you're to blame.
4. *Advanced empathic reflection of feeling:* You felt devalued and misunderstood when she said that. It must hurt to not have your mother's support.

Affective interventions do not end there, however. Counselors must know how to handle their clients' feelings in session, whether they are angry, crying, or showing anxiety, or flat affect. Counselors identify a full range of emotions and use precise language to capture the emotions correctly. They help their clients become aware of their feelings by helping them investigate their physical sensations. They help them accept and explore their feelings and tie them to their presenting concerns and, later on, to their habitual ways of reacting. They help clients see the sources of their affect. The following are examples of some of the interventions that can be used to tap into feelings.

Examples of Affective Interventions

Having the ability to successfully use advanced accurate empathic reflection of feeling is often facilitative of change. Other times more is needed. Of the many examples of possible affective interventions, the following two are commonly used.

Sensation awareness. Some people are not aware of the physical sensations that accompany emotional arousal. Body awareness is an intervention that helps clients attend to physiological processes associated with affect. Clients are first taught to listen to the body in a natural state and then in an aroused state. They are taught to focus on normal breathing, their heartbeat, and various parts of the body by relaxing and then turning their awareness inward. They are asked to rank sensations as they tense and relax various muscles. They also learn to attend to body sensations as they express emotions and identify those sensations with various feeling states.

A behavioral technique associated with sensation awareness is progressive muscle relaxation. Each muscle group is tensed and the relaxed and clients attend to the differences. They learn to control tensions so that they can relax them when emotional arouse occurs.

Bringing past feelings into the present. Counselors use techniques associated with Gestalt therapy to become aware of feelings in the present that are grounded in past experience. In the Gestalt approach, the counselor facilitates awareness by assisting the client to look at feelings, behaviors, experiences, and unfinished situations from the past that interfere with healthy living in the present. Clients are encouraged to make their covert feelings overt. Techniques include identifying where in the body an emotion resides and experiencing it fully, noticing what other feelings emerge, imagining a feeling in an empty chair and giving it voice, exaggerating a feeling to get in touch with its meaning and significance, or staying with a feeling being expressed rather than running away from it.

Putting It Together

James is a 24-year-old graduate student who came to counseling to talk about his inability to concentrate on his studies. After three sessions, he begins to discuss his suspicion that his fiancée back at home is about to end their six-year relationship.

Cl: I've known Chrissy since she was the little kid next door. She was only 14 when we started dating. I'm the only guy she's ever dated. Now I think she might be having second thoughts.

Co: (*encouraging/clarifying*) Tell me more about what you mean by "second thoughts."

Cl: She doesn't say it but I think she wants to look around. When we're on the phone she tells me about going out with what she calls her "male friends." She says she's not dating but I wonder about what she's doing with these guys.

Co: (*paraphrasing*) When she tells you she goes out with other men, you worry that it's more than just innocent friendship, is that it?

Cl: I don't think Chrissy would mess around with anyone. She's kinda nervous that way, anyway.

Co: (*paraphrasing*) Am I hearing you say you don't think she'd cheat on you because she's anxious?

Cl: I hope she wouldn't. We waited until her seventeenth birthday to start umm… you know. I'm the only guy she's ever, well…. (*pauses*)

Co: (*silence*)

Cl: …. been with… that way.

Co: (*advanced accurate empathy*) I'm sensing you are embarrassed because you aren't used to openly talking about sex.

Cl: We were supposed to wait until we got married. We both come from very strict religious families. They would kill us if they knew! I've never talked about it before.

Co: (*advanced accurate empathy*) Talking with me is difficult for you.

Cl: Like I said, I never have.

Co: (*advanced accurate empathy*) You're afraid that if you open up to me, I'll judge you like your family would.

Cl: Well, wouldn't you? Don't you already?

Co: (*immediacy*) You believe I think poorly of you even though we've developed an honest relationship and I'm concerned about that.

Cl: We haven't talked about this before!

Co: (*immediacy*) It might be safer for us both if we didn't, yet it feels to me like a barrier between us if we don't. I wonder how much progress we can make together if we can't be comfortable with each other.

Cl: I guess I can try. I am comfortable with you. I like how you listen and don't judge me.

Co: (*immediacy*) I'm pleased to know that. Our relationship is important to me. (*open question*) What's troubling you the most about the situation with Chrissy?

Cl: She was underage! We both wanted it and we'd been together for almost three years. We knew we'd get married when I finish school. Still, I should have known better. Do you think it was wrong?

Co: (*deflecting direct answer/reflection of feeling*) I think you might be saying that you feel guilty about initiating sex with her even though you two were committed to each other.

Cl: I mean, we didn't wait like everyone thinks we have. I'm the reason she's not a virgin. Now who knows what she's doing and with how many... [*pauses*]

Co: (*advanced accurate empathy*) You're worried that she's having sex with other men because she had sex with you. You feel you're to blame if she's sleeping around.

Cl: I don't know what I think but it's driving me crazy! What if she breaks up with me? [*pauses*] Actually, I'm not sure I want to get married now.

Co: (*making a connection/summarizing*) Let me see if I understand. You aren't able to concentrate on your studies because you're distressed over the possibility that Chrissy is going to leave you. You know she's going out with other men and worry that she's having sex with them. If she is, you wonder if it's your fault. At the same time, you aren't sure what you feel about her anymore and that's causing you to feel even guiltier. It must be confusing.

This example illustrates how empathic understanding skills can substantially increase counseling effectiveness by addressing emotions underlying client's concerns. Although the presenting concern is about the client's ability to concentrate on his studies, the underlying issue is his feelings about the relationship with his fiancée. A significant problem is his belief that he is responsible for her behavior. While the counselor will continue to address the affect, he will move to helping the client explore his cognitions – his beliefs – about his responsibility, and when appropriate, will set behavioral goals to come to terms with his relationship as well as his ability to concentrate on his graduate work. In the next chapter, you learn about cognitive and behavioral responses and interventions.

Summary

This chapter discussed the basic elements of basic empathic understanding and advanced accurate empathy. It presented some fundamental ways to structure responses to overt and covert feelings. It discussed the inner experience and outward manifestation of feelings, their intensity and significance, conflicted feelings, and the role of incongruence of covert feelings with overt behavior and thoughts. It reviewed the importance of managing counselor affect and the therapeutic use of counselor self-disclosure. It continued with examples of affective interventions.

> *I didn't know I was supposed to feel. This is the hardest job I've ever had to do... and the best.*
> – successful 60-year-old attorney to his counselor

References

Carkhuff, R. R., & Anthony, W. A. (1979). *The skills of helping: An introduction to counseling.* Amherst, MA: Human Resource Development Press.

Gladding, S. T. (2018). *The counseling dictionary: Concise definitions of frequently used terms* (4th ed.). Alexandria, VA: The American Counseling Association.

Rogers, C. (1951). *Client-centered therapy: Its current practice, implications, and theory.* Boston: Houghton Mifflin.

Rogers, C. R. (1961). *On becoming a person.* Boston: Houghton Mifflin.

Table 19.2 *TFAC Chart – Thought, Feelings, Actions, and Context

Self	My Thoughts	My Feelings	My Actions	My Context	Other? (Specify)
How good am I at discerning my physical responses to affect?					
How good am I at differentiating my different emotions?					
How comfortable am I with expressing my emotion?					
What happens when I attempt authentic immediacy?					
How well do I pick up on my own incongruence?					
How am I doing at accurately picking up on affect?					
What concerns do I have about expressing my own feelings?					
What else concerns me?					
Others	Others' Probable Thoughts	Others' Possible Feelings	Others' Observable Actions	Other's Apparent Context	Other? (Specify)
How well do others express their feelings?					
How do others react when their feelings are heard?					
What have you observed about incongruence?					
What have you observed about advanced accurate empathy among your classmates? Your instructors? Others?					
What have you observed about authentic self-disclosure among classmates? Your instructors? Others?					
What else can you learn about others' affect?					

*For more information on TFAC, see Chapter 1.

Chapter 20

Responding to Thoughts and Behaviors

Mary H. Guindon

One's mind once stretched by a new idea, never regains its original dimension.
— Oliver Wendell Holmes

POINTS TO PONDER

- How are thoughts addressed in counseling?
- What are some common cognitive techniques and interventions?
- How do counselors give feedback?
- What is confrontation and how is it used?
- How do counselors work with client behaviors?
- What are some common behavioral techniques and interventions?

Throughout this book, you have learned the importance of building rapport and relationship. You have learned the interviewing skills of reflecting content and feelings and the use of questioning. You will use these skills throughout the entire counseling process from first encounter through termination. Alone they are not necessarily sufficient in helping clients make needed changes in their lives. At some point, most counselors offer more concrete assistance. In the early stages of counseling, the counselor comes to understand the client's story, identifies and clarifies problems, and pinpoints opportunities to help the client make changes. Using Egan's (2006) three-stage approach, in the second stage, the counselor helps the client set goals in order to find solutions to problems and encourages commitment once goals are agreed upon. At this point, the working alliance stage has begun and will continue until counseling ends.

The counselor's theoretical perspectives, the client's characteristics, and the nature of the problems to be resolved determine how the working alliance proceeds. It involves client action and counselor feedback. The most effective working alliances focus on client strengths rather than deficits. Although alliances might concentrate on changes in feelings, most counselors and other helping professionals target change in cognition or behavior or both. Cognitive approaches focus on perception, belief, attitude, and meaning. Behavioral approaches focus on observable actions and performance. Effective counseling interventions often include a combined cognitive/behavioral approach. In this discussion, they are presented separately although overlap between them is obvious.

Working with Thoughts

The cognitive approaches are grounded in the belief that individuals are responsible for what they think, feel, and say. Counselors help their clients recognize their thoughts and how they influence feelings and actions within their own unique context and culture. Once in awareness, clients are taught to assess the validity of their thoughts, dispute illogical thoughts and beliefs, and replace them with realistic and helpful ones. Cognitive-behavioral approaches go on to set goals for behavioral change based on new understanding.

The theories of Aaron Beck (1995) and Albert Ellis (see Ellis & Dryden, 1997) posit that emotional problems result from the way people think. Whether or not aligned with the work of Beck and Ellis, many counselors believe helping clients identify and modify thoughts is the key to positive change and successful coping (Seligman, 2004). That is, when thoughts are modified, feelings and behavior are also modified. Counselors help their clients recognize, articulate, and examine their thoughts to determine if they are valid, beneficial, effective, and useful. Through the process of cognitive restructuring, dysfunctional thinking is evaluated realistically and transformed into more functional thinking. This then is believed to produce an improvement in affect and behavior. Counselors elicit information about distressing situations in the client's life and identify their reactions to them. They then work with clients to bring into awareness self-defeating beliefs so that they can be disputed and ultimately changed. Most cognitive interventions begin during a counseling session and proceed to psychological homework outside the session. The client learns to recognize thought processes and their concomitant beliefs, then learns to change those beliefs that are irrational into rational beliefs based in reality rather than in faulty perception.

Level of Cognitive Functioning

Cognitive strategies are adapted to the client's level of thought processing. Cognitive developmental stages impact on the client's ability to understand and effectively use cognitive restructuring strategies. Very young children, people who are cognitively challenged or impaired, and those who are delusional or hallucinate are not likely to be good candidates. Counselors, therefore, should be aware of their client's capacity for unimpaired thought. They should also match their use of language to the client's abilities or educational level. Communication should be as concrete and specific as possible. Those with normal cognitive functioning but in whom command of English is limited are good candidates for cognitive restructuring if the counselor can communicate in their native language and is well versed in the nuances of the client's culture. Cultural awareness and sensitivity are critical: What is irrational in one culture may be quite rational in another.

Counselors differentiate between optimal cognitive functioning and temporary impairment. People in crisis or in heightened emotional states or those who are depressed but who, in normal circumstances, are not cognitively impaired are experiencing situational stress. Extreme stress takes its toll on the ability to think clearly. Consequently, during such times, cognitive restructuring may not be the treatment of choice.

Cognitive Interventions

Counselors use cognitive techniques throughout the counseling process. They can a) add clarity, b) reassure clients that what they experience is likely normal, c) provide needed information or instruction, d) assist clients in understanding their own thought processes, e) bring incongruities into awareness, and f) help clients reach important decisions.

Normalizing

Sometimes clients who experience normal reactions to stress or to abnormal situations fear that they are emotionally unhealthy, or in some way unstable. They may suffer common reactions such as extreme emotionality, nervousness, trembling, a pounding heart, inability to concentrate or sleep, or trouble breathing. Counselors use the strategy of normalizing to assure them that their reactions are universal, appropriate, even healthy. Through describing normal reactions common to their client's situation, the counselor explains that what they are experiencing is an expected response that can be addressed in counseling. For example, in the case of a traumatic event such as witnessing a shooting death, the counselor will impart information about stress reactions, responses to trauma, and feelings that commonly arise such as anger, depression, fear, or guilt. Helping the client understand that her reactions are within the norm of what other people in similar situations experience can be therapeutic in itself. Once the client recognizes her reactions as normal, the counselor and client can process various aspects of her specific experience in a nonjudgmental, safe environment. Although counselors take care to be objective and factual, they do not normalize reactions that are maladaptive or not healthy. For example, the counselor would not normalize a student's plan to beat up a fellow student who bullied him, although she would normalize the feeling of anger. "Normalization is used sparingly, never used dishonestly, and not used in isolation but only contextually" (Brems, 2001, p. 230).

Reframing and Relabeling

Two similar strategies, developed out of feminist and family therapy approaches, target restructuring of perceptions. Reframing changes perceptions by explaining an event or situation from a different and more positive perspective. For example, the counselor suggests to family members that they view their "bad child" and his acting out behavior from a new frame of reference. The hope is that they will come to see the child as trying the best he can to distract the parents from the acrimonious fighting he witnesses between them.

The strategy of relabeling attempts to give the client a different perspective on her negatively expressed behaviors or beliefs by describing them with more positive words. In the above example, the counselor would relabel the words "bad child" into "adapting child."

In cases where the client speaks negatively about herself, the counselor reframes or relabels her perceptions by reinterpreting what she says so that she can see herself in a new, more positive light. For example, if the client says, "I'm always stupid" when she is not able to make a choice, the counselor might relabel it as simply undecided or reframe it to perhaps "not yet having all the facts."

Reframing and relabeling can also be used to bring new perspectives to the behaviors of others in the client's environment. The counselor is factual and objective in reframing and relabeling. This is not an excuse for sympathizing, nor is it appropriate in cases where the client is early in the process of telling her story. The strategy is not used to argue with the client. If the client does not understand or accept the strategy, the counselor does not force the relabeling or reframing but goes on to another strategy. The client's needs come first over a particular technique.

Providing Information

You learned at the beginning of this text that giving advice is rarely helpful. Advice giving that places the counselor in the role of see-all, know-all sage takes control away from clients and disempowers them. Counselors do not provide information that is value laden or opinionated; they do not tell their clients what to do or think. However, to fully investigate and examine their issues, clients may need data and facts unknown to them but known to the counselor. Clients may also need additional facts when they have partial or incomplete information. Providing information is an educational intervention that can be therapeutic. It can change clients' reaction to a situation and help them set goals and make decisions. At times, counselor and client collaborate to share information with each other. The counselor may impart information germane to the client's concerns, then ask the client to research facts and return to discuss the findings.

Information giving is an integral part of the work of the guidance function of school counselors, student personnel counselors in higher education, and career counselors. Counselors in these and other settings routinely conduct workshops and training sessions on a multitude of topics such as life skills, stress management, conflict resolution strategies, communication skills, parenting skills, human developmental stages, job search strategies, college admissions requirements, career and life planning, assessment results, and the like.

In settings outside of schools these same topics may be presented through psychoeducation. Counselors provide information that addresses psychological or emotional needs of clients, often in family or group therapy or workshops. In addition to the topics discussed in the last paragraph, they may present additional topics such as anger management, death and dying, suicide prevention, addictions, alcohol and other substance use and abuse, and much more. Psychoeducational interventions offer objective information that does not judge or condemn clients for their thoughts, feelings, or behaviors, or contextual backgrounds but gives them facts. Psychoeducation does not stand alone as the only intervention of choice. It is one part of a treatment plan to address the client's presenting concerns, ongoing issues, or planning after termination.

Counselors take care to provide information only when it is relevant to the issues at hand. They try to avoid correcting clients just simply to do so, even when their statements are incomplete or incorrect, if their statements are not germane to the counseling goal and process. Giving information should be connected to the client's reason for being in counseling. It must be used only when appropriate. Counselors, as you have learned, do not make assumptions and this is particularly important to consider before giving details or concrete facts. At times, the client may already have the information and providing it may come across as patronizing. Better to check out what the client actually knows or has previously attempted in pursuit of a goal.

Giving Feedback

Although feedback generally addresses behavior, it is included here because one important way to change behavior is to bring into awareness through cognition. Feedback is used when the counselor wants to impart information to the client about himself so that he will consider changing behavior. The skill is not attempted until the quality of the relationship is positive and trusting. Feedback is a constructive, relationship-enhancing strategy. The client should feel better, not worse, as a result.

Five principles guide the use of feedback:

- Feedback is specific, descriptive, objective, and nonjudgmental.
- It provides information on what is right first, then gives information on what needs to be changed.
- It targets behavior that can be changed.
- It makes a request, not a demand.
- It is given directly or as close as possible after the problematic behavior occurs.

Counselors who, in the normal course of their work, interact with clients outside of the office are most likely to use feedback, although it does occur in individual and group settings as well.

Examples:

1. (*stopping eighth grader outside classroom*): Kelly, you seem to have a lot of good friends in school. Just now, you were so involved in talking with your friends that a student coming the other way couldn't get past you. You may not be aware that your book bag hit her. From now on, I'd like you to stand on just one side of the hall so others can get by. Would you do that?

2. (*to patient in addictions halfway house*): George, I've noticed that you do a good job keeping your room clean and performing your assigned duties promptly. This morning, however, I saw that you left your coffee cup and breakfast plate on the floor next to the TV. One of our rules is that all dishes go to the kitchen when we are finished so the person on KP can do them right away. In the future, we'd appreciate it if you would remember to do that.

3. (*to client at the beginning of the fifth session*): Ginger, I'm pleased by the way you have come prepared for each of our sessions. You do your homework and it's clear you are working on the changes you want to make. Nevertheless, you have arrived a few minutes later each week. Today, you were 15 minutes late and you seemed to be distracted by your lateness. When we don't start on time, we may not be able to accomplish what we need to. I'd like to ask you to be here in plenty of time to do our work together in here. Will you commit to that?

Identifying Patterns

In Chapter 17, you learned the skill of summarization to clarify a particular issue, problem, or achievement. To summarize means to pick and choose what to attend to and reflect back to the client. It ties together the client's feelings, behaviors, and thought patterns over a period of time. Counselors work with their clients to identify themes – habitual ways of experiencing the world. Interestingly enough, counselors find it relatively easy to discover client themes, whereas many clients find it difficult. They may fail to recognize that they act, feel, think, and relate to people in remarkably uniform and similar but at times maladaptive ways. For many, these habits are what bring them into counseling. When the counselor is able to identify and point out patterns of dysfunctional thoughts or less than optimal behavior or find themes across several areas, the client can discover a new point of view. Treatment planning and specific interventions can be based on the counselor's ability to help clients identify and understand these themes and patterns. Pointing out patterns through summarization and advanced accurate empathy can help the client recognize ingrained ways of thinking, core beliefs, or habitual behaviors that are dysfunctional or maladaptive. They can motivate clients for change. Pointing out patterns of thought involves identifying and tying together a common way of thinking across several events, situations, reactions, or content areas. Patterns in behavior or affect can also be identified along with thought to bring into awareness a unified system of the client's phenomenological experience.

When incongruence is not the issue the strategy is straightforward. Once the counselor brings the pattern to the client's attention, she works with the client to identify other instances of the pattern that manifest during session. The counselor encourages the client to identify the same patterns between sessions now that they are in awareness. Initially, this is a cognitive restructuring technique. Ultimately, when the client decreases problematic habitual patterns of thinking, he will work toward changing behaviors more aligned with new facilitative ways of thinking. If thought patterns and habitual behaviors indicate incongruence, the counselor uses the skill of confrontation, or challenge, to bring patterns of thought, feelings, or behavior into awareness.

Confronting and Challenging

When clients are either unaware of their underlying and conflicting feelings or deny their existence and their effect on their thoughts and actions, incongruence exists. Conflicted feelings most often concern the experience or awareness of more than one contradictory emotion, or of an emotion incompatible with cognition. Behaviors inconsistent with feeling and thinking are also incongruent. Counselors challenge clients by pointing out discrepancies and inconsistencies across the TFAC domains, as well as mixed communication messages. The intent is to help clients discover different ways of thinking that lead to new and healthier behaviors and feelings. Awareness of self-contradictions can promote change.

The word confrontation to describe the process of pointing out incongruity is unfortunate because of the connotation of argument or conflict associated with it. Perhaps challenging is more descriptive of the strategy. Counselors challenge their clients to look at their incongruities in a well-timed and calmly stated way. Tact and sensitivity are key.

When confronting, the counselor describes a discrepancy without evaluating it. The challenge is specific, not general. It points out differences between what the client states and what the counselor observes. The You/but format is commonly used.

Examples:

1. On the one hand, you say you are definitely over him but on the other hand you talk about how you go out of your way to be where he is. What's that about?
2. You are saying it doesn't matter to you when your classmates tease you but your fists are clinched, you have tears in your eyes, and you are trembling. What's going on?
3. You say you feel lonely and that you want to get out and renew old friendships, but at the same time, you play computer games and watch TV by yourself every night and all weekend. How does that work?

Interpreting

Usually counselors refrain from interpreting their clients' behaviors, feelings, thoughts, interactions, and attitudes. They do not see explaining meaning as particularly therapeutic. Sometimes, however, problematic client characteristics seem to manifest themselves so predictably and frequently that the counselor must address them. As the occasion dictates, counselors do inform their clients about their behaviors and interactions based on observation combined with professional expertise. In these cases, counselors operate from one or more of the existing models of counseling and psychotherapy that presuppose how people react in given situations. For example, when a client has been diagnosed with a disorder using the DSM-IV, the counselor would assume and might explain that ways she is behaving are part of the disorder's characteristics. If a client is diagnosed with one of the depressive disorders and reports not sleeping or eating, the counselor would interpret this as part of the disorder, or if the client is exhibiting signs of an anxiety disorder, the counselor would assume that she sees the world as frightening and unsafe, and would share this information in order to work on altering such cognitive beliefs. Interpretations help clients realize the meaning behind their attitudes and behaviors and can lead to therapeutic change, sometimes in profound ways.

Interpretation is a kind of challenge and as such, must be undertaken with care, and sensitivity. The strategy is used only for the benefit of progress toward goals. Interpretation is risky. It can portray the counselor as an expert, decrease the therapeutic relationship's realness, diminish its here-and-now quality, and increase intellectualizing (Neukrug, 2016).

Beginning counselors often want to interpret what others tell them in simulated sessions. For training purposes this skill is best left until you are toward the end of your training, or not at all, because it is so easy to misuse. Carl Rogers felt so strongly against using interpretation that he stated, "to me, an interpretation as to the cause of individual behavior can never be anything but a high-level guess.... I do not want to get involved in this kind of authoritativeness" (as cited in Kirschenbaum & Henderson, 1989, p. 352).

Decision Making

Sometimes clients are unsure what alternatives to take. The counselor can teach a process to make sound choices by using a decision-making model. Particularly prevalent in school, higher education, or career counseling settings, although useful any time a decision must be made, the counselor helps the client make a decision in a systematic way. Although several models exist, Gelatt (1962) developed a cyclical model still used today. Originating from business decision theory, it offered a conceptual framework for counseling. Gelatt stated that all decisions have essentially the same characteristics. They involve at least two alternatives. An individual first determines the purpose or objective of the decision and then gathers information (data) needed to make the decision. At this stage the information is objective. Having obtained relevant information, she then moves to a three-element strategies stage of a) prediction system, b) value system, and c) criterion. The *prediction system* allows the individual to consider possible alternative actions and their possible outcomes, and next their probable outcomes. The *value system* looks at the desirability of outcomes. This leads to the *criterion* strategy stage in which the individual evaluates and selects a decision. Gelatt distinguished between investigatory decisions that call for more information and final (terminal) decisions. An investigatory decision recycles back to a new purpose or objective and the process repeats until it results in a terminal decision. Counselors can teach clients this model, systematically processing with them each element of the model until they reach a satisfactory decision. Although this model continues to be widely used, Gelatt (1989) himself amended it. He proposed a new decision strategy called *positive uncertainty* that more appropriately presents a new framework to "help clients deal with change and ambiguity, accept uncertainty and inconsistency, and utilize the nonrational and intuitive side of thinking and choosing. The new strategy promotes positive attitudes and paradoxical methods in the presence of increasing uncertainty" (p. 252).

Over the years, other counseling-related decision-making approaches have been developed. Many are targeted toward specific areas of concern such as ethics, a particular culture or subculture, family, and career. The basic elements remain the same: At least more than one alternative exists, information is gathered, an alternative is chosen, and action is taken.

SIDEBAR 20.1

In Practice: What Would You Do?

John works in an employee assistance program in a manufacturing company in the Midwest. He has been seeing 24-year-old Linda for a few weeks. She came in distraught because her roommate never cleans up, contributes little to household chores, and rarely buys groceries. She often has different men overnight without letting Linda know. On a few occasions they've stayed for days. Linda does the cooking and cleaning for all of them even though they barely notice her. They don't offer to contribute to the groceries but do buy beer for themselves. She says she puts on her "happy face" but thinks most of them are "pretty scummy."

> *I feel stuck with Linda. In response to years of childhood verbal abuse, Linda has adopted a very compliant, nonconfrontational style of interacting with people, including me. Her concern about not getting along with her roommate has raised some unresolved issues from childhood about her inability to assert her rights and her admitted "learned helplessness." She clearly wants to please me. I set goals with her but I'm not sure they are the ones she wants. She says she does what I ask of her but nothing changes. I'm not sure if she really follows through.*

Class Discussion

1. What evidence is there for any cognitive distortions in Linda?
2. If you were Linda's counselor what approaches and interventions do you think would be appropriate?
3. What possible patterns of thinking and behavior might you want to check out with Linda?
4. To what possible goals might John be referring? How might he be more effective?

Working with Behavior

Traditional behaviorists believe that all behavior is learned. Thus, it can be unlearned and new behaviors relearned. Some behavior is healthy, appropriate, and beneficial; some is unhealthy, inappropriate, or undesirable. Most counselors use strategies to help their clients change maladaptive or ineffective behaviors and learn more adaptive or effective ones. Behavioral counseling focuses on client performance. It decreases an undesirable behavior or increases the likelihood of an effective behavior. It can change thoughts and feelings, too, although this is not the main purpose. Clients are actively involved in their own treatment through working with the counselor to analyze and define behavior; choose goals and develop plans for behavior change; practice new behaviors; monitor, evaluate, and modify their progress; and ultimately generalize new learned behaviors to other areas of their lives. The counselor plays an active role by teaching the client new ways of acting and reinforcing positive behavioral change through support and encouragement.

Behavioral Interventions

Behavioral interventions are specific and concrete. Counselors encourage clients to perform certain target behaviors so that their issues will be ameliorated or problems resolved. Activities can either take place in one session or can involve behavioral homework assignments between sessions. Common interventions included here are (a) goal setting and contracting,(b) modeling, (c) role play and rehearsal, (d) journal writing, (e) imagery and visualization, (f) therapeutic use of props, and (g) structured behavioral change techniques.

Goal Setting and Contracting

In setting goals, many counselors encourage clients to commit to action-based contracts. A behavioral contract is a mutual, explicit, verbal or written agreement between counselor and client. The client agrees to perform specific tasks or behaviors and the counselor agrees to offer expertise, support, and a place to process results. Contracts are concrete, time limited, and measured in terms of completion. In other words, the client agrees to certain actions in the immediate future, sometimes before the next counseling session, but always in a specified time period. People are more likely to complete a contract when they make an open commitment to put in the effort to reach their goals with the counselor and others (Seligman, 2004). Once the commitment is made in writing, the counselor will give homework assignments to help the client reach goals.

When a contract involves an ongoing change to a more desirable behavior such as quitting smoking, losing weight, or exercising, the counselor will first determine a baseline, or a measure of the current behavior. For example, the client will specify how many cigarettes she now smokes, or what she weighs, or her current exercise regime. The counselor and client then work together to determine what success will mean in terms of specific behaviors so that they know when the contract has been accomplished and by what date. They will also specify in the contract smaller, attainable steps that can be completed along the way to the main goal. For example, the smoker may commit to eliminating smoking only in certain situations and add a new situation each week. Or she may set a smaller goal of reducing the number of cigarettes each week. After the baseline is set, the client keeps a record of activities related to the goal each week so that she can track her progress. She may also keep a journal of her reactions along the way to meeting the contract.

Modeling

One important tenet of behavioral theory is the concept of observational and simulated learning. People can learn new behaviors by observing others and practicing new ways of acting in simulations. In this social learning process (Bandura, 1969), the actions of an individual or a group is a model that can change behavior in an observer. In other words, the observer learns from seeing others' performance without actually performing the behavior. The observer gains new knowledge, modifies behavior accordingly, and acquires a new way of behaving.

Counselors model behavior overtly, covertly, and symbolically. *Overt modeling* occurs when the counselor demonstrates through her own actions in the here and now, how to behave. Counselor self-disclosure is an example. The client as the observer identifies with the counselor's genuine behavior and learns authentic behaviors he wants to emulate. Another example is a career counselor who asks a client to job shadow an employee in a career of interest as a way of observing behavior in action. Counselors use *covert modeling* when they present imaginary scenarios to the client through role playing or role rehearsal or when they use visualization techniques. Each is described below. Counselors utilize *symbolic modeling* when they ask clients to observe behavior abstractly rather than face-to-face. Watching television, a video, or reading a book to observe target behaviors are examples of symbolic modeling. As part of your training, you will most likely see several psychotherapy legends, such as Rogers, Ellis, Perls, and others, actually counseling clients. You will learn by their example; i.e., they will model the use of specific techniques. When counselors assign videos to their clients they are providing opportunities for symbolic learning through observing models of target behaviors.

Role Play and Rehearsal

Role playing can be direct, indirect, or both. In *direct role playing*, clients play themselves in simulated scenarios. In *indirect role playing*, or role reversal, clients play someone else. At times, clients may alternate between the two. The counselor can also play a role, interacting with the client. Direct role playing allows clients to practice alternative behaviors. They rehearse how they will act in a real-life situation. An example is practicing a mock job interview. Indirect role playing allows clients to experience how another person may think, feel, or act in a particular simulated situation. The client acts as if he is another person whom he either wants to be like or wants to talk with. In the job interview example, the client may play the human resources person who will conduct the interview. Taking on both roles allows clients to dialog about the situation from both perspectives. A client is able to experience both sides of a situation. The client might play both interviewer and interviewee to gain perspective on the many possibilities that can arise in the real job interview and how he may come across.

Assertiveness training is another example in which role playing and rehearsal allow people to practice new behaviors before they actually attempt them in real situations. It is discussed later in this chapter.

Journal Writing

Counselors often assign journal writing as a method for self-discovery. This cognitive-, affective-, or insight-producing activity enhances the client's ability to get in touch with the authentic self. It is also a tool that is useful in tracking behavioral change. The focus of a journal can vary greatly. The journal you have been asked to keep throughout this text focuses on your place in professional counseling. It offers the potential of insight and action.

When the purpose is behaviorally focused, the client attends most to actions; however, thoughts and feelings are integral to the process. After setting a goal and delineating steps to reach the goal, the client is instructed to write regularly – but spontaneously – in a journal to describe activities, thoughts, and feelings that impact on the implementation of the goal. The approach includes instructions to describe rather than evaluate, analyze, or interpret whatever he wants to write about. Clients are also encouraged to write freely without concern for grammar and spelling. In the cognitive-behavioral approaches described earlier, the journal serves as a place to describe relevant events and behaviors, the irrational thoughts that emerge, and the resultant feelings evoked. Clients can then be taught to dispute the thoughts and reconstruct new, more functional thoughts and new feelings. Clients might then follow up with writing how behaviors will change as a result of the process and then act out the new behaviors, recording the entire process in the journal. Journals also provide a place to record target behaviors and steps toward reaching them over time. Clients will either bring the journal into a session where they review it with their counselor or, commonly, simply report on the results of journal writing.

Imagery and Visualization

Imagination can be a powerful ally in the therapeutic setting. The ability to visualize a desired outcome increases the likelihood of success in almost any area of human endeavor. Positive mental imagery can help clients see themselves coping with problems and performing successful actions. Visualization can promote relaxation, reduce stress, improve affect, and control pain and blood pressure. Clients, of course, can visualize spontaneously but generally the counselor guides the process. The client listens to the counselor who leads her through a relaxation and imagery exercise. Some therapists also use guided imagery in group settings. Guided imagery sessions are available for purchase. Many involve peaceful sounds such as gentle rain or a babbling brook, or music, usually classical or semi-classical in nature. One discipline specializes in guided imagery and music to evoke emotion and problem resolution through visualization. In visualization, the counselor first ensures that the client is in a relaxed state. Relaxation training is discussed later in this chapter. When the client achieves a good level of relaxation, the counselor introduces an imagery, or visualization, exercise.

Common guided imagery techniques include stress-reducing imagery, healing or pain control imagery, and mental rehearsal. In the latter approach, the client imagines a scenario and its ideal outcome. Individuals picture themselves going through each step of a situation and then successfully completing it. The resulting mental imagery can be solely a product of the individual's imagination or the counselor can suggest images to the client such as a calming place like a beach or a forest, or the counselor can guide the client through a specific situation. Guided imagery can be realistic with the client describing difficulties, visualizing the emotional reactions to problems, and their resolutions; or it can be fanciful and symbolic. Very real feelings of anger, sadness, or anxiety surface and can be resolved within the visualization. Although some people have difficulty imaging and may not experience actual images, they may experience vague feelings during the guided exercise. Even for these clients, the relaxation phase can still be useful and productive.

Another kind of imagery is used in Solution-Focused Brief Therapy (de Shazer, 1985). It asks the client to focus on a future point for success rather than the problem. Thus, counselors ask clients to envision what their circumstances would be like if the problem did not exist. The "miracle question" asks the client to respond by describing the world as if a miracle happened and the problem was gone. The counselor then helps the client make the "miracle" or its attainable equivalent a reality.

Therapeutic Use of Props

Some counselors use props to elicit imagery or to help clients consider their problems in new ways. For example, the counselor may wave a wand and suggest that the problem is gone and ask the client to visualize such a world; or he might use a crystal ball to imagine a different future. Once the client can visualize what her life might be like, the counselor assists in setting goals and supports her while carrying them out to reach in real life the imagined scenario. At times the visualization is unrealistic or unobtainable. In that case, the counselor uses the scenario as a springboard to create more reasonable and obtainable goals.

Props can also be used to describe and act out certain situations. A patient might be asked to choose and then manipulate items, such as dolls or puppets, that remind him of family members or difficult situations or feelings. Photographs or favorite objects can stimulate conversations and set the direction for further therapeutic work, especially useful with the elderly who suffer decreased cognitive functioning. Clients can also express themselves in nonverbal ways through creative arts. Creative arts therapy uses art, drama, dance, poetry, and music and can produce change in emotion and behavior. Play therapy is an example of the therapeutic use of props used with children and also effective with adults.

Structured Behavioral Change Techniques

Some behavioral interventions have been highly researched. Prescribed, structured steps in a specific order have been shown to be effective for behavioral management, stress, anxiety reactions and anxiety disorders. Common structured approaches include (a) token economies, (b) relaxation training, (c) systematic desensitization, (d) assertiveness training, and (e) paradoxical intent.

Token Economies. The use of token economies is a behavioral modification approach in which a client is given a valued object or token as an immediate and tangible reinforcer for appropriate behavior. Tokens are chips, stickers, points, or symbolic items given to individuals as rewards for desired behaviors. Clients periodically exchange the tokens for objects or activities attractive to them. Tokens are commonly used with school children to encourage appropriate behavior. They are also used in psychiatric hospitals, addictions clinics, prisons, and other settings with those with limited mental facility or with problems of behavioral control. For example, people in an inpatient addictions unit earn tokens by completing assigned duties, such as keeping their rooms clean or engaging in suitable interactions with others. They exchange tokens for privileges such as watching television, attending social events, or "buying" snacks or other items.

Relaxation Training. Relaxation training consists of a number of related approaches that allow the body to consciously relax. Most people carry stress and tension in their bodies and are unaware that they do so. Relaxation training brings into awareness the fact of bodily tension wherever it may be located and prepares clients to lessen the uneasiness often present when attempting new behaviors. Techniques include breathing exercises, meditation, yoga, biofeedback, nonstress-inducing exercise, progressive muscle relaxation, or a combination of two or more of these strategies.

In deep breathing, the client learns to bring air into the diaphragm, hold it, and then release it slowly while relaxing the body. In progressive muscle relaxation, the counselor teaches the client to first tense specific muscle groups through suggested motions and then relax them. The client tenses and relaxes different areas of the body, generally beginning with peripheral areas such as feet and hands and moving toward interior large muscles groups in the torso. The client tenses and relaxes each area while she uses deep breathing. The counselor uses a soft, soothing voice in directing the client's attention to work with each muscle group. Some counselors make tape recordings of their voices for homework assignments for daily practice. Many commercial products are also available. The client can be taught to make her own tape as well.

Systematic Desensitization. Systematic desensitization is widely used for a range of fears or anxieties such as school phobia; interpersonal anxiety; and fear of heights, animals or other objects, public speaking, flying, and the like. It is also useful for some physical complaints, or psychophysiological ailments like asthma, speech disorders, sexual dysfunction, and others. Based on the premise that an individual cannot feel anxious and relaxed at the same time, the process uses counterconditioning to eliminate negative feelings by pairing the emotional response with muscular or mental relaxation techniques.

The three parts of systematic desensitization consist of (a) teaching the client relaxation process described above, (b) developing a hierarchy of anxiety-causing situations, and (c) positioning relaxation and anxiety together in a specific situation. The counselor and client identify a target behavior and determine the specific situations that trigger the emotional response. The counselor helps the client construct an anxiety hierarchy by ranking the anxiety-provoking situations from those that evoke the least discomfort or intensity to those that evoke the greatest. The counselor introduces scenes from the anxiety hierarchy beginning with the least intense while the client maintains the relaxed state. They progress slowly as the client learns to relax and tolerate the anxiety-provoking situation and move over time through the hierarchy until feelings of anxiety or fear are diminished or neutralized. At first, the counselor uses visualization alone but as the client is able to let go of the anxiety, the counselor eventually introduces more realistic, simulated scenarios, and in time, the actual situation itself. The process is repeated until the situation that produces the anxiety is minimized. Homework assignments make up a portion of the work.

In *in vivo therapy*, counselors actually go with the client into the anxiety-provoking situation. For example, in the case of fear of flying, the client will initially visualize a plane in the therapy office, then move slowly through visualizing each step of a plane trip while feeling relaxed.

He may be assigned going to an airport and watching planes take off. He may board a plane but not take off. He will eventually take a plane trip while utilizing progressive relaxation either alone or with his therapist. The counselor acts as coach and reinforces positive behavior.

Assertiveness Training. Assertiveness training is a structured process that teaches clients how to appropriately act in their own best interests without infringing on the rights of others. The ability to be properly assertive is learned over a lifetime. Assertive individuals know they are worthy of respect, communicate their needs, and make reasonable demands of others. Unassertive people believe they have no rights and are not worthy of respect. They have difficulty expressing their needs, are anxious or fearful, do not act in their own self-interest, and are often taken advantage of. The process involves counterconditioning that replaces the anxiety and fear with new learned assertive behaviors. Clients learn a system of assertive behavior and practice it with the counselor and with other clients. Role playing, rehearsal, and modeling are used in a structured system over a period of time. Clients rank order situations in which they believe there is a low to high probability of being appropriately assertive and develop a plan to change behavior. They begin with the highest probable and thus least stressful situation and work toward acting appropriately assertive across more difficult situations. The counselor offers support and encouragement, and reinforces positive behavior throughout the process. Assertiveness training can be used with overly aggressive clients as well. They learn to change behaviors so that they do not infringe on the rights of others in a similarly structured process.

Paradoxical Intent. In paradoxical intent, the counselor tells the client to behave in a way that is the opposite of the targeted goal. The purpose of this technique is to decrease or eliminate problematic behavior by helping the client change his attitude about the behavior. Theoretically, people who are fearful of a particular circumstance actually create their fear through avoiding that which they fear. Used to reduce anxiety or stress, paradoxical intent prescribes the symptom and uses humor to help the client change his point of view about the behavior. The counselor helps the client identify the inappropriate behavior and then encourages him to enact the behavior in an extreme version. The client becomes aware that he has control over the behavior and thus can change it. Through this process, he learns he can detach from the problem itself. The counselor uses humor to help the client see the absurdity of the behavior. These steps are repeated until the behavior is minimized or eliminated. The counselor then teaches the client more appropriate behaviors. For example, a client is trying to lose weight but says she cannot stay on her diet because she must have ice cream. She says she cannot control herself. The counselor would tell her to eat nothing at all but ice cream as often as she possibly can for the next two weeks. The client will learn that she has control over what she eats. The behavior of eating ice cream will be reduced or eliminated, or possibly ice cream will be incorporated into the total calorie count in her balanced diet.

Putting It All Together

The strategies described in this chapter would not be used with all clients or in the same session. No matter what theoretical orientation or specific techniques you will find appealing, the first consideration will always be the humanity and individuality of your client. Consequently, the example given here can only touch on some of the information presented. The example combines basic skills of earlier chapters with a limited sampling of cognitive and behavioral approaches. As you read the example, try to identify the specific skills the counselor uses.

In the last chapter, James' presenting concern was the inability to concentrate on his studies. The underlying issue is his fear that his fiancée might be breaking up with him. He worries that she might be having sex with other men and believes he is responsible for her behavior. We pick up at the counselor's last summarization:

Co: (*making a connection/summarizing*) Let me see if I understand. You aren't able to concentrate on your studies because you're distressed over the possibility that Chrissy is going to leave you. You know she's going out with other men and worry that she might be having sex with them. If she is, you wonder if it's your fault. At the same time, you aren't sure what you feel about her anymore and that's causing you to feel even guiltier. It must be confusing.

Cl: It is, but I do know one thing for sure: Like I said, I'm the reason she's had sex. Who knows how many guys she's seeing and what she might be doing with them?

Co: Since you were Chrissy's first sex partner, you believe she's now having sex with lots of other men and it's your fault. Is that right?

Cl: It *is* my fault. I do wonder about it. I'm not there… so she might be sleeping around.

Co: And if she is, you're to blame? How is it that you are responsible for how she behaves now?

Cl: … I don't know…

Co: (*silence*)

Cl: I guess I'm not… really….

Co: (*silence*)

Cl: But I don't like to think she's cheating on me. I can't sleep or concentrate on anything.

Co: You're so upset that she might not be faithful to you that it's getting in the way of everything else.

Cl: Yeah. I bet she's not telling me the whole story about "dating" these "male friends."

Co: Earlier you said that you didn't think Chrissy would ever mess around with anyone but now you think she is. Which is it?

Cl: I'm no fool. I mean, I'm a guy. I know how it is.

Co: Tell me how it is for you.

Cl: Well… we've been going together a long time and I haven't seen her for months. I have my urges.

Co: Uh-huh…

Cl: I've been tempted by a woman in my program. We study together and go for coffee sometimes. I haven't made a move yet, but I don't know that I want to wait much longer. I have really strong sexual feelings for her and she's let me know she's interested. I find myself caring about her more all the time. It's driving me crazy!

Co: It sounds to me like you are attracted to a woman here more than you are to Chrissy. Which bothers you more – not starting an intimate relationship with a woman you care about here or Chrissy possibly having sex with men there?

Cl: (*hesitates*) I'm not at all sure…. I don't think Chrissy and I have much in common anymore. We are different people now. Still, she's my first love. But should she be my only love? What do you think?

Co: I think you're feeling all at sea because you know you've outgrown this relationship but at the same time you don't know what to do.

Cl: I don't know what's right…. (*looks into the distance, thinking*)

Co: (*silence*)

Cl: …. Actually… I think it's over. Maybe Chrissy feels the same way. Maybe she wants out, too.

Co: I think you're saying that you wonder if Chrissy wants to end your relationship as much as you seem to want to. How important is it for you to know?

Cl: I think it's essential. I can't go on like this!

Co: What can you do to find out?

Cl: I guess I'll have to ask her… .but not on the phone. I'm going home in a couple of weeks. Maybe I could talk with her then. I mean, I've got to!

Co: You want to talk to her in person about ending the relationship. How willing are you to commit to that with me?

Cl: You mean will I promise? I want to let her know how I feel but, honestly, I don't even know how to begin telling her that I want out of our relationship!

Co: Would you like to practice what you want to say with me?

Cl: That would help a lot.

James and the counselor will set a goal to talk with Chrissy while he is home. She will ask him to commit to a behavioral contract that lists the steps he will take to accomplish the goal. The counselor will go on to role playing and rehearsing with James over the next two sessions as they continue to investigate his feelings about his relationship with Chrissy and his readiness for a new relationship. He will learn relaxation techniques to help him with his ability to concentrate on his studies.

Summary

This chapter discussed the basic elements of working with thoughts and actions in counseling. It presented cognitive approaches that focus that on perception, belief, attitude, and meaning; and behavioral approaches that focus on observable actions and performance. It discussed the cognitive interventions of normalizing, reframing and relabeling, providing information and psychoeducation, feedback, identifying patterns and confrontation, interpretation, and decision making. The chapter continued by presenting information on the behavioral interventions of goals setting and contracting, modeling, role playing and rehearsal, journal writing, imagery and visualization, therapeutic use of props, token economies, relaxation training, systematic desensitization, assertiveness training, and paradoxical intent. It concluded with a sample transcript of a case study.

> *Those who bring sunshine to the lives of others cannot keep it from themselves.*
>
> – J.M. Barrie

References

Bandura, A. (1969). *Principles of behavior modification*. New York: Holt, Rinehart & Winston.

Beck, J. S. (1995). *Cognitive therapy: Basics and beyond*. New York: Guilford.

Brems, C. (2001). *Basic skills in psychotherapy and counseling*. Belmont, CA: Wadsworth, Brooks/Cole.

de Shazer, S (1985). *Keys to solutions in brief therapy*. New York: W. W. Norton.

Egan, G. (2006). *Essentials of skilled helping: Managing problems, developing opportunities*. Pacific Grove, CA: Thomson Brooks/Cole.

Ellis, A. E., & Dryden, W. (1997). *The practice of rational emotive behavior therapy* (2nd ed.). New York: Springer.

Gelatt, H. B. (1962). Decision-making: A conceptual frame of reference for counseling. *Journal of Counseling Psychology, 9*, 240–245.

Gelatt, H. B. (1989). Positive uncertainty: A new decision-making framework for counseling. *Journal of Counseling Psychology, 36*, 252–256.

Kirschenbaum, H., & Henderson, V. L. (Eds.). (1989). *The Carl Rogers reader*. New York: Houghton Mifflin.

Neukrug, E. (2016). *The world of the counselor: An introduction to the counseling profession* (5th ed.). Boston: Cengage.

Seligman, L. (2004). *Technical and conceptual skills for mental health professionals*. Upper Saddle River, NJ: Merrill Prentice Hall.

Table 20.1 *TFAC Chart – Thought, Feelings, and Actions

Self	My Thoughts	My Feelings	My Actions	My Context	Other? (Specify)
What irrational thoughts might I have and how do they influence me?					
When have I experienced the phenomenon of normalizing in my life?					
Have I experienced a time when I was aware of reframing or relabeling?					
How do I handle giving feedback to others?					
How do I react when I am challenged on my thoughts or actions?					
How good am I at setting and meeting goals?					
What is my past experience with role playing and rehearsal?					
What is my past experience with imagery or visualization?					
How assertive am I?					
What do I do take care of my stress and anxieties?					
What have I learned about myself from the TFAC journal exercise throughout this course?					
Others	**Others' Probable Thoughts**	**Others' Possible Feelings**	**Others' Observable Actions**	**Others' Apparent Context**	**Other? (Specify)**
What irrational thoughts have I observed in others? What is their influence?					
What happens when I or others use the skill of reframing or relabeling?					
What have I observed about feedback in class? In my family? Elsewhere?					
What inconsistencies do I notice in others?					

(Continued)

Table 20.1 (Continued)

Others	Others' Probable Thoughts	Others' Possible Feelings	Others' Observable Actions	Others' Apparent Context	Other? (Specify)
How do instructors and counselors use goal setting and contracting in their work?					
How do instructors and counselors use role playing and rehearsal in their work?					
How do instructors and counselors use imagery or visualization in their work?					
What other cognitive/behavioral techniques have I observed?					
What have I learned about others from the TFAC journal exercise throughout this course?					

*For more information on TFAC, see Chapter 1.

Final Comment

You have come to the end of your journal-writing journey. Take some time to go back over and carefully review all your entries. Answer these questions:

1. What patterns and themes have you discovered about yourself?
2. What have you learned about professional counseling and your place in it?
3. What do you see as the greatest strengths you bring to your program of study? To the profession?
4. What do you see as the greatest challenges you face in your program of study? In the profession?
5. Where will you go from here in your studies? In your life?

If we all did the things we are really capable of doing, we would literally astound ourselves.
— Thomas A. Edison

Appendices

APPENDIX A

Personal Journal

As you learn from each chapter in this book, consider your own thoughts, feelings, and actions and others' probable thoughts, possible feelings, and observable actions using the questions posed at the end of each chapter in the TFAC Tables. Describe your reactions in a journal. Do not evaluate, analyze, or interpret what you write. Attempt to express yourself freely without concern for grammar and spelling.

Practical Tips

- Instead of only using your computer, get a good-sized notebook devoted only to this exercise. Blank-page commercial journals are good but anything that expresses who you are is fine. You may use a handheld computer device or a laptop, although some research has shown that students who hand write out their notes on paper actually learn more.
- Take your journal with you wherever you go. If you wish, you may input your journal entries into your computer later.
- A journal is not a diary or for publication. Keep it in a safe place.
- Date every entry. Note which chapter you are addressing.
- Be specific! Use the TFAC tables.
- If you have writer's block or feel stuck, simply begin writing anything at all. If you can't think of anything else to write, write about being stuck.
- You may add clippings, artwork, letters, or anything else that helps you express yourself authentically.
- Write something every day.
- Experiment with different times of the day.
- Try out different places to write.
- As each week progresses you may find that you focus on one area over another. That's okay. Let what attracts you most guide you. You will want to write about what this might mean at the end of the semester but no analyzing now.
- BE WHO YOU ARE AND HAVE FUN!

Check off each cell as you address it in your journal. Make notes in the chart, if you aren't sure or don't know what to write. You may want to discuss these with your instructor for further clarification.

Example

Table A.1 Example TFAC Chart

Self	My Thoughts	My Feelings	My Actions	My Context	Other? (Specify)
Why am I considering a career in counseling?	X	X	? not sure	X	
What are my own motivators?	X	X	X	X	
How prepared am I to undertake this journey?	?? nothing comes to mind	??	X	X	
What are my concerns?	n/a	n/a	n/a	n/a	
What other questions do I have?				?? does this apply?	
How does my reality influence my reflections?	X	X	X	X	
Others	**Others' Probable Thoughts**	**Others' Possible Feelings**	**Others' Observable Actions**	**Others' Apparent Context**	**Other? (Specify)**
What have I learned about others in my class?	Use Jamie?		X	*How can I answer this?*	
What might be the point of view of my significant others as I undertake this journey?					Need to ask!
What might be the view of my instructor?	X	X	X	Don't know	
What else might I ask others?	n/a				
How does my reality influence my observations?	??				

APPENDIX B

Internet Resources for Professional Counselors

Ethical Codes of Selected Related Helping Professions

American Counseling Association
   www.counseling.org/Resources/CodeOfEthics/ TP/Home/CT2.aspx
American Psychological Association
   www.apa.org/ethics/code2002.html
American Mental Health Counselors Association
   http://www.amhca.org/assets/content/AMHCA_Code_of_Ethics_11_30_09b1.pdf
American School Counselors Association
   https://www.schoolcounselor.org/asca/media/asca/Ethics/EthicalStandards2016.pdf
National Career Development Association
   http://associationdatabase.com/aws/NCDA/asset_manager/get_file/3395
Clinical Rehabilitation Counselors
   https://www.crccertification.com/code-of-ethics-4
National Association of Social Workers
   https://www.socialworkers.org/About/Ethics/Code-of-Ethics/Code-of-Ethics-English

Professional Organizations

American Counseling Association
   www.counseling.org
   All Divisions, Regions and Branches can be accessed through
   https://www.counseling.org/about-us/divisions-regions-and-branches
   ACA listservs
   https://www.counseling.org/aca-community/listservs
   ACA Blogs
   https://www.counseling.org/news/aca-blogs
   ACA on Twitter
   http://twitter.com/CounselingViews
Council on the Accreditation of Counseling and Related Programs
   www.counseling.org.cacrep
National Board of Certified Counselors
   www.nbcc.org

Specialty Area Resources

ADDICTIONS COUNSELING.

American Society of Addiction Medicine (ASAM)
   https://www.asam.org/
International Association of Addictions and Offender Counseling (IAAOC)
   http://www.iaaoc.org/
NAADAC: The Association of Addiction Professionals
   https://www.naadac.org/
National Council on Alcoholism and Drug Dependence (NCADD)
   https://www.ncadd.org/

National Institute for Alcoholism and Alcohol Abuse (NIAAA)
    https://www.niaaa.nih.gov/
National Institute for Drug Abuse (NIDA)
    https://www.drugabuse.gov/
National Registry of Evidence Based Models
    https://www.samhsa.gov/ebp-resource-center
Substance Abuse and Mental Health Services Administration (SAMHSA)
    https://www.samhsa.gov/

CAREER COUNSELING.

National Career Development Association (NCDA) www.ncda.org
The Armed Services Vocational Aptitude Battery Test Battery (ASVAB)
    www.asvabprogram.com
University of Missouri Career Interests Game
    www.career.missouri.edu/career-interest-game
Publisher of the *Strong Interest Inventory, the Myers-Briggs Type Indicator*, others
    www.cpp.com
Clifton Strengths Finder 2.0 www.gallupstrengthscenter.com
Kuder www.kuder.com
Fee-based values assessment (Reile, first author of Chapter 10, developed and owns this site)
    www.lifecareervalues.com
Interest Profiler from O*Net www.mynextmove.org/explore/ip
USDL Occupational search engine www.onetcenter.org
Work Importance Locator www.onetcenter.org/WIL.html?p=2
Work Values and Occupations
    www.onetonline.org/find/descriptor/browse/Work_Values/
Psychological Assessment Resources (PAR) www.parinc.com
Self-directed Search SDS www.self-directed-search.com/
Skillscan www.skillscan.com
VIA Institute on Character (VIA Survey) www.viacharacter.org
Career Construction (Savickas) www.vocopher.com
Occupational Outlook Handbook www.bls.gov/OOH
O*NET www.onetonline.org

CLINICAL MENTAL HEALTH COUNSELING.

American Mental Health Counseling Association (AMHCA) www.amhca.org/
International Association for Counselling (IAC) www.iac-irtac.org/
National Board for Certified Counselors (NBCC) www.nbcc.org/
National Board for Certified Counselors-International (NBCC-I)
    www.nbccinternational.org/
World Health Organization (WHO) www.who.int/mental_health/en/
National Institute of Mental Health (NIMH) www.who.int/mental_health/en/
Substance Abuse and Mental Health Services Administration (SAMHSA)
    www.samhsa.gov/

CLINICAL REHABILITATION COUNSELING.

American Rehabilitation Counseling Association (ARCA)
    http://www.arcaweb.org/
Commission on Rehabilitation Counselor Certification (CRCC):
CRCC Code of Professional Ethics for Rehabilitation Counselors
    https://www.crccertification.com/code-of-ethics-4
Rehabilitation Counseling Scope of Practice
    https://www.crccertification.com/scope-of-practice
Commission on Rehabilitation Counselor Certification
    https://www.crccertification.com/about-crc-certification
National Council on Rehabilitation Education
    https://ncre.org/
Centers for Disease Control and Prevention – Disability and Health
    https://www.cdc.gov/ncbddd/disabilityandhealth/people.html
National Council on Disability
    https://www.ncd.gov/

COLLEGE COUNSELING AND STUDENT AFFAIRS.

American College Counseling Association (ACCA) www.collegecounseling.org/
AACRAO. The American Association of Collegiate Registrars and Admissions Officers
    https://www.aacrao.org/
ACPA. College Student Educators International
    http://www.myacpa.org/
American College Counseling Association
    https: www.collegecounseling.org/
ACUI. Advancing Campus Community
    https://www.acui.org/ ACUI.
Association for Collegiate College Counseling Center Directors
    https://www.aucccd.org/
Association for the Study of Higher Education
    https://www.ashe.ws/
ACUHO-I. Making Campus Home. Association of College and University Housing
    Officers-International
    https://www.acuho-i.org/
CAS. Council for the Advancement of Standards in Higher Education
    https://www.cas.edu/
NASPA. Student Affairs Administrators in Higher Education
    https://www.naspa.org/
NACADA. The Global Community for Academic Advising
    https://www.nacada.ksu.edu/
Resources Page for Task Force on Digital Technology. ACPA—College Student Educators
    International
    http://www.myacpa.org/tfdtsa/resources
The Center for Collegiate Mental Health (CCMH). Counseling and Psychological Association.
    Pennsylvania State University. University Park, PA/
    http:// www.ccmh.psu.edu
The Higher Learning Commission. HLC accredits
    https://www.hlcommission.org/

National Institute of Mental Health (NIMH)
    https://www.nimh.nih.gov/index.shtml

MARRIAGE, COUPLE, AND FAMILY COUNSELING AND THERAPY.

American Association of Marriage and Family Therapists www.aamft.org
American Association of Sexuality Educators Counselors & Therapists (AASECT)
    https://www.aasect.org/
International Association of Marriage and Family Counselors (IAMFC)
    www.iamfconline.org/
A tool for generating genograms: www.genopro.com/genogram/symbols/

TRAINING INSTITUTIONS AND ORGANIZATIONS

Family Therapy Training Network www.familytherapytrainingnetwork.org
Touro University www.tuw.edu
Adler University www.adler.edu
Brandman University www.brandman.edu
Drexel University www.drexel.edu
The Family Institute at Northwestern University www.family-institute.org
Ackerman Institute for the Family www.ackerman.org
Dr. Harry J. Aponte www.harryjaponte.com

SCHOOL COUNSELING

American School Counselor Association www.schoolcounselor.org
ASCA National Model
    www.schoolcounselor.org/school-counselors-members/asca-national-model
Collaborative for Academic, Social, and Emotional Learning www.casel.org
Elementary School Counseling www.elementaryschoolcounseling.org/
Framework for 21st Century Learning www.p21.org
The Six Pillars of Character www.chartercounts.org/

SELECTED OTHER COUNSELING-RELATED HELPING PROFESSIONS

American Art Therapy Association www.charactercounts.org
American Association of Pastoral Counselors www.aapc.org
American Music Therapy Association www.musictherapy.org
American Psychological Association www.apa.org
All Divisions of Interest can be accessed through: www.apa.org/about/division.html
American Psychiatric Association www.psych.org
American Psychiatric Nurses Association www.apna.org
Association for Play Therapy www.a4pt.org
National Association of Addiction Treatment Providers www.naatp.org
National Association of School Psychologists www.nasponline.org
National Association of Social Workers www.naswdc.org
National Rehabilitation Counseling Association www.nationalrehab.org
Rehabilitation Counselors and Educators Association
    https://rceapro.com/

Resources for Common Issues Presented in Counseling

The following resources concern some of the most common issues that occur in counseling settings of all types. They included websites about prevalent mental health and mental disorder in children and adults, crisis, stress, suicide, physical and sexual abuse, domestic violence, substance abuse, and more.

American Academy of Child & Adolescent Psychiatry www.aacap.org
American Association of Suicidology (AAS) www.suicidology.org
The American Institute of Stress www.stress.org
Anxiety Disorders Association www.adaa.org
Child Welfare Information Gateway (formerly National Clearinghouse on Child Abuse and Neglect Information) www.childwelfare.gov
Evidence-Based Practices Resource Center
    https://www.samhsa.gov/ebp-resource-center
National Alliance for Research on Schizophrenia and Depression www.narsad.org
National Alliance of the Mentally www.nami.org
National Center for Posttraumatic Stress Disorder www.ncptsd.va.gov
The National Foundation for Depressive Illnesses www.depression.org
National Institute of Child Health and Human Development www.nichd.nih.gov
National Institute of Mental Health www.nimh.nih.gov
The National Mental Health Association
    http://www.mentalhealthamerica.net
National Mental Health Information Center www.mentalhealth.samhsa.gov
PTSD: National Center for PTSD
    https://www.ptsd.va.gov/
Stop Bullying www.stopbullying.gov/

Index

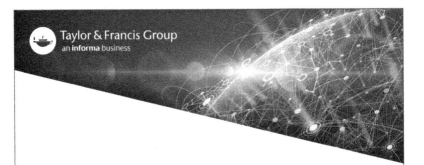